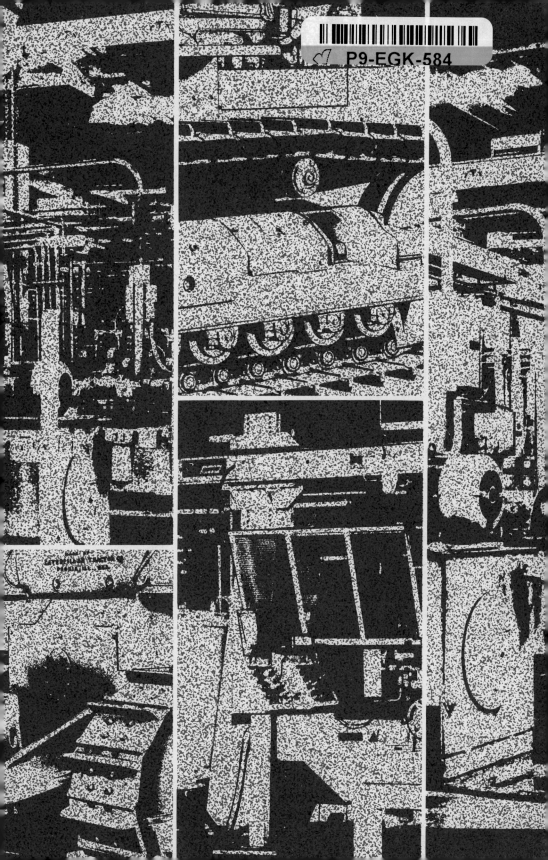

P9-EGK-584

# Industrial marketing

# Industrial marketing

**RICHARD M. HILL**
Professor of Business Administration
College of Commerce and Business Administration
University of Illinois

**RALPH S. ALEXANDER**
Philip Young Professor of Marketing (Emeritus)
Graduate School of Business
Columbia University

**JAMES S. CROSS**
Vice President
American Petroleum Institute

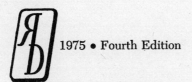 1975 • Fourth Edition

**RICHARD D. IRWIN, INC.**   Homewood, Illinois   60430
Irwin-Dorsey International   London, England   WC2H 9NJ
Irwin-Dorsey Limited   Georgetown, Ontario   L7G 4B3

© RICHARD D. IRWIN, INC., 1956, 1961, 1967, and 1975

Fourth Edition

*First Printing, January 1975*

ISBN 0-256-00010-7
Library of Congress Catalog Card No. 74–82925
*Printed in the United States of America*

*In memory of*
*RUTH  JACKSON  ALEXANDER*
*whose ready wit and infectious good humor*
*continues to inspire each of us*

# PREFACE TO THE FOURTH EDITION

THE FOURTH EDITION has been substantially reorganized, rewritten, and redirected. A number of new chapters have been added, those retained from earlier editions have been thoroughly revised, and all material is oriented toward marketing strategy. The new material places much greater emphasis on the marketing applications of such quantitative techniques as input-output analysis, PERT, time series analysis and decision trees than was present in earlier editions. The section on marketing intelligence includes a detailed discussion of the revised (1972) Industrial Classification System and its application to industrial marketing.

The arrangement of sections and chapters has been altered to reflect the evolution of marketing strategy from marketing intelligence to marketing control. A number of new cases also have been added which permit a better sampling of the contemporary issues in strategy and policy with which the industrial marketing manager presently is faced.

To those who regard decision making as the sum total of management and the mathematical model as the highest expression of managerial decision making, this edition will be something of a disappointment. In our judgment, the task of the manager includes such responsibilities as recognizing and defining problems, sensing opportunities, challenging and developing personnel, and shaping the structure of organizational relationships to match his firm's full potential. Such responsibilities necessitate the collection of relevant information, both numerical and nonnumerical, its analysis by appropriate techniques—only one of which is mathematics—the discovery and evaluation of alternatives, and the choice among alternatives.

Students in most collegiate schools of business are probably exposed to specialized courses in model building, business simulation, and computer programming. What they need in industrial marketing, in our opinion, is not more of the same, but some appreciation of the situations and conditions in which these techniques can be applied. The chief responsibility of the manager with regard to mathematical techniques lies in the formulation of concepts which underlie their use and the selection of factors to be incorporated in them. The construction of specific models and their subsequent programming can be left to the specialist, who is far more knowledgeable in these matters than the manager could hope to be, and who receives but a fraction of his annual pay.

An undertaking of this type owes much of its substance to persons other than those whose names appear on the title page. Foremost among them are the many businessmen who have discussed with candor the marketing problems they have confronted and their search for ways to resolve them. They not only supplied much of the material used in illustrations and cases, but afforded valuable insights regarding the practical difficulties which invariably arise in applying marketing principles to operational situations.

Another group to whom we are indebted is our colleagues and students who have been exposed to various parts of the revised manuscript. Their comments and suggestions have been most helpful in our efforts to present material in what we believe is a more concise, teachable format.

A project of this dimension places no small burden on the members of one's family, especially his wife, who invariably shares in the drudgery of typing and proofreading as well as endures the irritation of neglect. To the late Ruth Jackson Alexander, Dorothy Davis Cross, and Marilyn Fisher Hill we wish to acknowledge a debt of gratitude that is difficult to either measure or express.

*December 1974*                         R. S. ALEXANDER
                                        J. S. CROSS
                                        R. M. HILL

# CONTENTS

**PART I**
**Basic considerations**                                          1

1.  The industrial marketing system                              3

    Participants. Channels. The relationships: *Contracts of sale. Franchise agreements. Loyalty. Confidence. Reciprocity.*

2.  The industrial marketing concept                            14

    Marketing as a business philosophy. The functional dimension: *Mission definition. Market definition.* The organizational dimension: *Structural integration. Top management status. Customer-based organization structure.*


**PART II**
**The demand for industrial goods**                             35

3.  Demand and product characteristics                          37

    Market levels and product types: *Major equipment. Minor or accessory equipment. Fabricating or component parts. Process materials. Operating supplies. Raw materials.* Derived demand: *Influence of the ultimate buyer. Influence of business conditions. Influence of financial conditions. Influence of price.*

4.  The industrial customer                                     54

    Buyer motives: *The core variables: Quality, service, price. Savings. Assurance of supply. Buyer temperament. The special case of purchasing by public institutions.* Buyer characteristics: *Customer types. Buyer population. Size distribution. Geographical concentration.* Types of purchasing organization: *Business and institutional buyers. Governmental buyers.*

5.  Purchasing systems                                          78

    Recognition of need: *Documentation. Supporting investigation.* Sorting and appraising alternatives: *Competitive bids. Negotiation. Make or buy. Selecting the alternatives.* Order placement. Follow-up and expediting. Invoice handling. Receipt and inspection.

6. Value and vendor analysis                                              96

Value analysis: *Nature of the system. Operation of the system.* Vendor analysis: *Evaluating vendor capacity. Rating vendor performance. Vendor analysis and marketing.*


PART III
Marketing intelligence                                                  111


7. The marketing intelligence system                                    113

Defining informational needs: *Frequency of use. Urgency of response. Timeliness. Degree of detail. Accuracy. Life span. Form.* Elements of the system: *Hardware. Software. Programs. Personnel.* System design: *External information. Internal information. Developing the design.* Cost-benefit tradeoff.


8. Market identification: The search process                            131

The Standard Industrial Classification System: *Interpreting industry classifications.* Identifying market opportunities: *Finding new buyers in existing markets. Identifying untapped markets.* Comment on the 1972 S.I.C. revisions.


9. Market identification: The evaluation process                        147

The market profile. Trend outline. Demand potential: *Cumulative methods. Aggregate methods.* Problem profile.


10. Measuring marketing performance                                     167

Planning the marketing study: *Problem definition. Data collection and analysis. Recommendation.* Four basic measures of performance: *Sales analysis. Customer buying attitudes and practices. Cost analysis. Analysis of competition.*


PART IV
Marketing strategy: Product and service components                     183


11. The concept of strategy                                             185

The structure of plans: *Mission and strategy. Operating plans. Logistical plans. Organizational plans.* Formulating strategy: *Preliminary analysis. Choice of strategy components.*


12. Product definition                                                  198

Product development: *Generating new-product ideas. Preliminary appraisal. Product and market research. Process research. Prototype testing. Commercialization.* Determinants of the product mix: *Technology. Competition. Operating capacity. Market factors.* Company attributes.


13. Service definition                                                  216

The provision of parts: *Standardized parts. Unstandardized parts. The pirate parts problem.* Technical assistance: *Types of technical assistance.*

*Organization for technical assistance. Difficulties of rendering technical assistance.* Financial aid: *Terms of sale. Financing with warehouse receipts. Field warehousing. The use of factors. Commercial finance houses. Installment sales. Financial service policy.*

## PART V
## Marketing strategy: The channel component                               235

14. Channel strategy: The structural elements                               237

Industrial distributors: *Definition. Geographical distribution. Size characteristics. Operating characteristics. Why customers buy from distributors. Summary.* Manufacturer's and sales agents: *Definition and description. When manufacturer's or sales agents are useful. Agents have drawbacks. Summary.* Brokers. Manufacturer's branch houses: *Types of branch houses. Operating characteristics. Size of branches. What trades use branches? Objectives of branch distribution. Branch distribution can be costly.*

15. Formulating channel strategy                                            256

Conditions influencing channel structure. Relationships in the indirect channel: *Intensive versus selective strategy. Policy questions.*

16. Channel logistics                                                       274

The logistical plan: *The need for efficiency. The logistical system.* System operations: *Communication. Scheduling. Inventory control. Materials handling. Traffic management.*

## PART VI
## Marketing strategy: The price component                                 295

17. Conditions affecting price                                             297

Competition: *Firm size. Product type. Product life cycle. Price leadership.* The cost factor: *Direct and indirect (overhead) costs. Controllable and noncontrollable costs. Incremental and sunk costs. Opportunity cost. Joint and separable costs.* The nature of demand: *The behavior of derived demand.*

18. Pricing decisions                                                       312

New-product introduction: *The high-price strategy. The low-price strategy. Break-even analysis.* Competitive action: *New markets. Established markets. The choice of roles. The use of analogy and hunch.* Initiating a price change.

19. Pricing policies                                                        330

Net pricing. Discount pricing: *Trade discounts. Quantity discounts. Cash discounts. Legal considerations.* Geographic pricing: *Factory pricing. Freight allowance pricing.*

## PART VII
## Marketing strategy: The promotional component    341

20. Advertising    343

Advertising functions: *Disseminating information. Identifying new customers. Establishing recognition. Supporting salesmen. Motivating distributors. Stimulating primary demand.* Sales appeals. Message: *Formulation. Policy.* Media. Budgetary support. Measuring advertising effectiveness. Publicity: *Securing publicity. Measuring the effectiveness of publicity.* The use of advertising agencies.

21. Personal selling    363

Selecting salesmen: *Personnel profile. Sources of candidates. Selection aids.* Training: *Inexperienced trainees. Experienced salesmen.* Supervision: *Task assignment. Selling support. Day-to-day guidance.* Compensation: *Commissions. Bonuses.* Expense control: *Automatic allowance. Per diem allowance. Reimbursement.*

22. Sales promotion and public relations    381

Trade shows and exhibits: *Exhibitors' objectives. Exhibition scheduling and planning.* Catalogs: *Reasons for using catalogs. Catalog preparation. Catalog distribution.* Samples. Promotional letters. Promotional novelties. Entertainment. Public relations: *Planning the public relations program. Implementing the program. Tools and media.*

## PART VIII
## Marketing control    401

23. Strategic goals    403

Identifying market opportunity. Goals based on market share: *Projecting industry sales. Adjusting projections. Market share.* Goals based on sales forecasts: *Higher-degree polynomials. Asymptotic curves. Weighted moving average. Adjusting projections.* Goal definition.

24. Performance standards and instruments of control    429

Short-term goals: *Expense-based goals. Estimate of future expenses. Correlation-determined goals.* The marketing budget: *The sales budget. The expense budget. Practicing budgetary control.* The process of control: *The reporting system. Comparing standards and performance. Corrective action.*

Cases    445

Index of cases    695

Index    697

# PART I

## Basic considerations

A STUDENT beginning the study of any subject is wise at the outset to seek a general understanding of its nature, its dimensions, and its place in the scheme of things. So in Part I, we present a general concept of the kinds of things that are handled in the process of industrial marketing, its functions and importance in the economy, the kinds of agencies through which it is carried on, and the characteristic features of industrial and institutional demand that set the climate within which the industrial marketer must operate.

We have chosen to adopt the management approach in our study of the subject. In fact, the book might be more accurately titled, *The Management of Industrial Marketing*. We are aware that some who use the book may not have had introductory courses in management or the opportunity to read general books on that subject. Therefore, we have taken the liberty of including a brief discussion of management fundamentals whenever they are germane to the treatment of marketing operations.

# 1

# THE INDUSTRIAL
# MARKETING SYSTEM

IN ITS SIMPLEST TERMS a market is composed of buyers and sellers, exchanging goods and services and money. It is usually helpful, however, to also think of markets in terms of the channels through which buyers and sellers contact each other as well as of the relationships such contacts establish between buyers and sellers. A market system, therefore, includes at least three elements—participants, distribution channels, and relationships. The makeup and functions of this system are shaped by the demand for products and services it is intended to satisfy.

## PARTICIPANTS

One way to identify participants in the system of industrial marketing is to think of the national economy as composed of three broad divisions—extractive industries, manufacturing industries, and using or consuming units. The flow of products is predominantly from the extractive industries, through the manufacturing industries, to using and consuming units. While there is a backflow of products (equipment and operating supplies) from manufacturing industries to the extractive industries, its volume is small compared to the movement of products from manufacturers to ultimate consumers (individuals and households buying for personal satisfaction), government, business users, and exporters. The general nature of this flow is depicted in Figure 1–1.

You will notice in this illustration that manufacturing industries form a complex with both external and internal product flows. Externally, the complex faces in two directions: (1) procuring raw and semifinished materials from the extractive industries while supplying them with equipment and supplies; (2) selling capital goods, supplies, and consumer goods to households, government, business and institutional users, and exporters. Internally, it is engaged in the process of exchanging semi-

3

**FIGURE 1–1.  Product flow diagram**

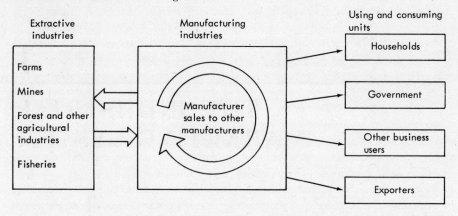

finished products, component parts, operating supplies, and equipment among the constituent manufacturing establishments.

Industrial marketing—as opposed, for example, to agricultural marketing, which we will not discuss—encompasses the movement of material from mines as well as the return flow of goods to mines, farms, fisheries, and other extractive enterprises. It includes the movement of goods to government, nonmanufacturing business users, and exporters, as well as between units within the manufacturing complex itself. The approximate dimensions of this flow as well as the relative importance of the broad classes of participants in it are shown below.

The most important group of business and industrial users is manufacturers, whose purchases amounted to approximately $332 billion in

| Producers | 1971 Income* | Purchasers | 1971 Outlay* |
|---|---|---|---|
| Manufacturers | 223.2 | Households | 664.9 |
| Service firms | 110.6 | Government | 232.8 |
| Financial firms | 98.7 | Business† | 152.0 |
| Mining and construction | | Exporters | 0.7 |
| companies | 54.2 | Gross Total | 1,050.4 |
| Transportation firms | 32.5 | Adjustment‡ | 194.7 |
| Communication firms | 18.2 | Total | 855.7 |
| Public utilities | 16.3 | | |
| Farms, forestries, | | | |
| fisheries | 26.5 | | |
| *Importers* | 6.9 | | |
| *Middlemen (wholesalers* | | | |
| *and retailers)* | 130.8 | | |
| *Government and its* | | | |
| *enterprises* | 137.9 | | |
| Total | 855.8 | | |

\* In billions of dollars.
† Investment and net addition to inventories.
‡ Less indirect business taxes, capital consumption allowances, and statistical discrepancy, plus subsidies minus surplus of governmental enterprises.
Source: *Survey of Current Business* (July 1972) pp. 7 and 8.

1970.[1] Included in this category are construction companies, transportation companies, commercial and financial enterprises, and institutions. Government includes state and local as well as federal government. In terms of dollar value, the major portion of exported merchandise is made up of goods for use in further production or provision of services.

Therefore, on the supply side of the industrial marketing complex the major participants are manufacturing and mining establishments. On the demand side of the system is a family of business and industrial users, government agencies and departments, and exporters.

Because of their importance as industrial customers, it is often meaningful to distinguish original equipment manufacturers (OEM's) from other manufacturers. The original equipment manufacturer is one who buys a material or component to incorporate into a product he makes and sells. For example, a diesel-engine maker who buys filters and gear boxes for use on his engines is classified as an OEM customer by suppliers of filters and gear boxes. For use in their businesses, other manufacturers buy products such as lathes, typewriters, and paper towels. The same manufacturer may, of course, be classified as an OEM account by some suppliers and as a user account by others.

Producers and users of industrial products are linked by a third group of participants, industrial middlemen. These may be identified as manufacturer's branches, merchant wholesalers or distributors, and agents. Manufacturer's branches, which are wholly-owned subsidiaries of manufacturing companies, usually perform a substantial array of marketing functions. The branch may stock products received in carload or truckload lots. This permits the manufacturer to combine the more expensive small-lot shipments from the branch to customers in its territory with lower carlot or trucklot rates over the longer distance from factory to branch. Such facilities are customarily referred to as branch *houses*. A branch *office*, on the other hand, does not carry stocks and serves primarily as headquarters for the field sales force. The branch office is usually intended to afford a convenient organizational unit through which to manage selling activity. Orders are forwarded for delivery by the home office or a franchised distributor or other cooperating middleman located in the territory covered by the office.

Merchant wholesalers or distributors are independently owned firms that buy products from manufacturers and resell them in the same, or almost the same, form to users and OEM's on their own account. They can usually be identified as *general* or *specialty* houses. The general merchants—or general-line or mill supply houses, as they are often called—handle a wide variety of industrial supplies and minor equip-

---

[1] *1971 Annual Survey of Manufactures, General Statistics for Industry Groups and Industries.* This exceeds outlay for business given in the preceding table, because the value there represents investment alone rather than gross expenditure for materials and supplies.

ment, which they sell to a diversified group of customers. The specialty houses may confine their stock to a particular category of products, such as office equipment, abrasives, or electrical supplies, or they may limit their market to a given trade or industry, such as hospitals and medical clinics, or hotels and restaurants.

Several types of agents participate in the marketing of industrial products. The most important of these in terms of both number of establishments and volume of sales are the *manufacturer's agents*. These firms represent only sellers, whom they serve on a commission basis. They typically represent a limited number of principals, and the relationship between principal and agent is usually a continuous one. Although manufacturer's agents do not take title to merchandise, many carry stocks on consignment. They ordinarily sell only a portion of the client-producer's output and limit their activities to specific geographic areas.

*Sales agents* operate in much the same manner as manufacturer's agents. They represent a limited number of sellers on a more or less continuous basis and charge a commission for their services. Unlike manufacturer's agents, however, sales agents usually sell to a given trade or industry group wherever its members can be found and do not limit their activity to any specific area. They are also likely to dispose of the entire output of the principal. By making an arrangement with a single sales agent, a producer can solve his entire problem of choosing marketing channels; if he markets through manufacturer's agents, he must make arrangements with a number of them if he expects to reach his entire market through this channel.

*Brokers* play no very significant part in industrial goods marketing, but they can provide some very useful services. While brokers negotiate and facilitate sales, they do not take title to the merchandise involved and ordinarily bear no responsibility for it or its condition. Often, they never even see the products they sell. In most circumstances, brokers possess no merchandise other than samples which they temporarily hold as a convenience to clients. They receive a commission for their services paid by the client on completion of the agreement and delivery of the merchandise. Their clients may be either buyers or sellers but not both in the same transaction. Brokers are most useful in marketing goods that are standardized or can be conveniently described by grade or trade designation. A variety of materials, some supplies, and a few small tools and items of equipment fall into this category.

While *commission merchants* play a highly significant role in the marketing of agricultural products, there is no reason why the average industrial products maker should want to consistently consign merchandise to an agent with whom he has no continuing contractual relationship and who may or may not be able to sell it. As a rule, commission merchants do not enter into long-term relationships with a producer, and may negotiate sales without the specific approval of their principals since they have physical custody and control of goods they sell.

Although *advertising agencies, consulting firms, transportation companies,* and *financial institutions* participate in the industrial marketing system on the demand side, they also make a unique contribution to the movement of goods between buyers and sellers and to the transactions which produce this movement. Practically all space advertising and perhaps the major portion of direct-mail promotion are developed by or in consultation with advertising agencies. Consulting firms have specialists—in design and applications engineering, market research, law, and management techniques—who can provide the expertise required to solve a wide variety of distribution problems. Transportation companies, including such specialized intermediaries as freight forwarders, supply all the services indispensable to the physical movement of merchandise. For purposes of simplification, these nonfinancial participants will be grouped together and identified as facilitating agencies.

## CHANNELS

The participants in the industrial marketing system are linked by both direct and indirect channels. The direct channel is traditionally defined as one in which the producer controls the distribution of his products from factory to user or OEM customer. Normally, this control is exercised through the manufacturer's branch house or office, although some manufacturers market direct from the home office without subsidiaries.

The indirect channel is identified by the presence of independent middlemen who limit the control a manufacturer can exercise over the marketing of his products. The extent to which control is diluted is determined by the type of independent middlemen employed, as well as by the relationships that prevail between manufacturers and middlemen and among the middlemen themselves.

At the risk of oversimplification, it may be useful to identify some of the more common channel arrangements through which industrial goods reach user and OEM customers.

*1. Manufacturer to branch house or branch office to customer.* This is the direct channel and is usually implemented through the manufacturer's own sales force. Typically, a system of branch houses is relied on for physical distribution of products sold.

*2. Manufacturer to distributor to customer.* Usually, manufacturers sell to wholesalers through a small sales force and ship goods to them in quantity lots, which are then sold in broken lots or individual items by the distributor's salesmen. There are, however, numerous variations of this general pattern. For example, some producers use agents to contact

**FIGURE 1–2.  The industrial channel network°**

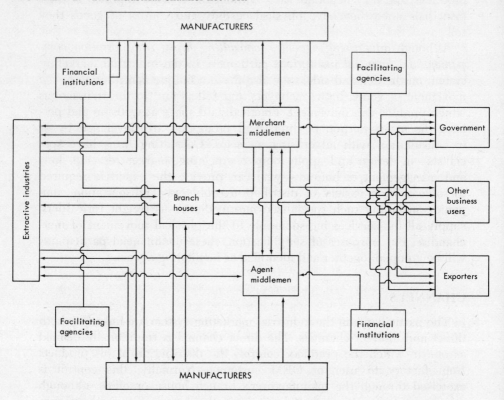

* Lines represent the flow of products and services. Arrows indicate the direction of flow.

distributors and some wholesalers drop ship, that is, order merchandise sent direct from the manufacturer to the customer. While the drop shipper is responsible for delivery and payment, and takes legal possession of merchandise, he does not physically handle it.

Other distributors depend heavily on manufacturer's detail men or missionary salesmen to sell products they stock, while they concentrate their own efforts primarily on physical distribution. In still other cases, the manufacturer's salesmen travel with the distributor's salesmen for the purpose of training and stimulating them to sell the manufacturer's products. As a rule, manufacturers who employ detail men—or whose salesmen instruct and assist distributor salesmen—are attempting to win some of the benefits of direct marketing without incurring all its costs.

3. *Manufacturer to agent to customer.*  The agent customarily makes initial contact with customers and performs a complete sales function, often supplying technical service where needed. Orders are usually referred to manufacturers who ship direct to the customer.

*4. Manufacturer to agent to distributor to customer.* This arrangement is sometimes used in markets composed of small and scattered customers not worth the manufacturer's individual attention but whose combined volume for a number of products is large enough to support marketing efforts. In a few industries, the agent is replaced by a super-jobber or warehouse distributor who sells only to other wholesalers.

5. *Mixed arrangement.* Each of the preceding channel arrangements, of course, represents a general type or class, and manufacturers create many variations within each of them as well as hybrid arrangements including two or more channel types. A manufacturer may use one channel for one product or group of products and another for a different product group, or reach one group of custmers through one channel and use a completely different channel for another customer group. He may sell direct to customers who are large, or potentially so, while using middlemen to serve smaller buyers. Manufacturers may even act as middlemen themselves, buying products from other manufacturers to fill out or supplement their own product lines, which they sell direct. In every instance, of course, the requirements of the market should dictate the makeup of the channel arrangement.

A simplified illustration of the channel network is shown in Figure 1–2. In later chapters, we will explore in much greater detail the operations of the units in these marketing channels and the problems the industrial goods manufacturer meets in selecting channels and units in them, as well as in managing his relations with them and their relations with one another.

## THE RELATIONSHIPS

The relations that exist among the participants who compose the various distribution channels for industrial products may be most easily identified as formal and informal. Among the formal relationships are the various contracts of sale and franchise agreements, which define the respective responsibilities and rights of buyers and sellers. The most significant of the informal relationships are loyalty, confidence, and reciprocity.

### Contracts of sale

Unlike the casual arrangements accompanying the sale of most consumer products, many exchanges of industrial goods involve a formal contract that stipulates the responsibilities and liabilities of each party. The complexity and detail of the sales contract naturally vary with the characteristics of the product or products, amount of the sale, nature of the services to be rendered, and number and character of the parties included.

Aside from the clarity and concreteness a formal statement lends to any agreement, a sales contract has certain benefits from a marketing standpoint. It enables salesmen to know precisely what the company is and is not prepared to do in behalf of its customers and products. The contract thus serves to minimize deliberate misrepresentation. Knowledge that the terms of an offer will appear in writing as part of a contract is an effective brake on ill-considered claims and empty promises.

Moreover, minimizing misunderstanding and argument about the exact terms of an agreement can save hours for salesmen and sales executive alike. As any businessman can testify, dealing with customer complaints can be a distasteful and time-consuming task, which often has its roots in misunderstanding or inadequate information.

When sales transactions involve products of a technical nature, as well as substantial sums of money and the ability to meet production schedules, the exact terms of an agreement written down for all parties to read can avoid much embarrassment and friction.

### Franchise agreements

Some form of continuing contractual arrangement is usually sought by manufacturers who market through independent middlemen. Such agreements are often in effect for an indefinite period, subject to cancellation by either party on proper notice. They generally summarize the services and prerogatives the manufacturer intends to give his outlets and what he expects of them in return. When some form of protection is offered or implied, the agreement is usually referred to as a *franchise*.

Franchises vary in the protection they afford the parties and in the obligations they impose on each. An *exclusive franchise* usually designates the distributor as the sole outlet for the manufacturer's products in the middleman's marketing area, and commits the producer to supply substantial aids—technical, financial, administrative, and promotional—to the distributor. Legally, the manufacturer cannot bind the distributor to reciprocate by handling no competitor's products; practically, he can bring powerful pressures to bear toward this end. He can also ask the distributor to commit himself to perform certain specific functions in promoting and marketing the products, such as carrying a standard stock, rendering certain designated services, and distributing sales promotion materials. This is a fairly typical arrangement in the heavy-equipment industry, in which the distributor's inventory commitment must be substantial, and technical service to the buyer-user is vitally important. It is not uncommon in other phases of the industrial goods business.

A far more common relationship is the *selective franchise,* in which the manufacturer limits the number of distributors who carry his products in a market area. While such selective distribution has definite advantages over so-called blanket distribution, under which a producer sells to every middleman who can be induced to buy, the manufacturer's control over the middleman is substantially less than in the case of an exclusive franchise.

## Loyalty

Industrial buyers may go to considerable lengths to help suppliers whose products and services they value. It is not unusual for buyers to permit valued suppliers to test new or redesigned products in their plants, to achieve greater flexibility and efficiency in planning production runs by placing orders well in advance of need, and to participate in joint research efforts. Buyers have also been known to assist trusted suppliers in financing machinery or inventory. Such actions cannot be attributed to charitable motives, but are based on the mutual advantage that both parties anticipate.

Suppliers who can be depended on to deliver what is ordered when it is needed, to render good service, and to cooperate with the buyer in meeting special requirements are not easy to find. The buyer tends to be loyal to such suppliers in order to hold their loyalty to him. Such loyalty is especially important to the buyer when the product to be bought is not a standard item but must be made to rigid specifications, when it is of small value but vital to the buyer's operations, and when the supplier's capacity cannot be easily or readily increased.

By the same token, a buyer who can be depended on to cooperate with a seller in product testing, market studies, advance placement of orders, inventory or equipment financing, and supplying timely information regarding design changes and price structure on his own products is a valued customer. Such customers can reduce a manufacturer's promotional and research costs, and can provide a reliable means of evaluating the effectiveness of his marketing effort versus that of competitors.

## Confidence

A powerful force in cementing relationships between suppliers and buyers of industrial goods is confidence. When asked what single factor has the most influence on their bestowal of patronage, a high percentage of purchasing officers will reply "confidence."

This confidence is a feeling of certainty that the supplier will do what he promises or will spare no effort or cost in trying to do it, that his claims with respect to his products and services can be accepted without serious question, and that he can be counted on to help execute special projects and to go all out to aid in emergencies. These are the chief elements in the buyer's confidence, but not the only ones; others are peculiar to individual cases.

Of course, the buyer enjoys an emotional satisfaction—mainly a sense of security—in dealing with suppliers in whom he has confidence. But, primarily, buying on the basis of the elements just outlined puts money in the bank for his company. The lack of any or all of these assurances may be costly enough to more than offset significant price concessions offered by less trustworthy suppliers.

Buyer confidence is not something a manufacturer gets as a natural right. He must earn it by performance over a period of time. No amount of advertising or salesmanship can equal a record of delivering the goods and services.

To be really solid, the buyer-seller relationship must be cemented by confidence on both sides. The seller must feel that the buyer will not abuse the seller's services or the terms on which he sells, that he will use the product for the purpose it is intended for and in the manner prescribed, and that he will not make exorbitant claims for adjustments.

Perhaps the importance of confidence in industrial marketing relationships arises from a mutual recognition of the weakness of the legal contract as an instrument of exchange in a business that is highly complex, often extremely technical, and fraught with intangible factors that are hard to measure but are very important in terms of use and cost. In a contract, it is usually possible to describe with some exactness the goods that are involved, but it is virtually impossible to put in writing the services that often constitute an almost equally important part of the transaction.

Neither party wants to sue to compel the other's compliance. The seller fears loss of the buyer's patronage and alienation of other buyers, and the buyer hesitates before the risk of incurring a bad reputation in the supplying trade. In the final analysis, the most potent sanction of an industrial purchase and sale contract is not legal action to enforce the letter of the agreement but the will of the two parties to carry out its intent.

### Reciprocity

A manufacturer of industrial goods often is both a seller to and a buyer from the same firm. He thus has the opportunity to use his purchases to generate sales by a threat, overt or implied, to withdraw patronage unless it is reciprocated. This practice has ethical, and perhaps legal, as well as broad, company-wide policy implications. For this reason, we will delay our discussion of reciprocity until a later chapter, when we have become a bit more familiar with the background of the issues it involves.

## SUMMARY

In this chapter, we have examined the nature of the industrial market. This involves a glance at (1) the participants—the extractive industries, the manufacturing industries, and the various types of establishments that use industrial goods; (2) the industrial marketing channels—branch houses and offices, distributors, and agents—and the most usual patterns in which the channel units are arrayed; and (3) the basic relationships that govern the behavior of industrial buyers and marketers—formal, such as contracts and franchises, and informal, such as loyalty, confidence and reciprocity.

# THE INDUSTRIAL
# MARKETING CONCEPT

MARKETING was presented in the first chapter as a collection of firms, each performing certain complementary functions, and all so inter-related as to form a goal-oriented system. The goal of the system is the satisfaction of customer needs. Since these customers are organizations—businesses, institutions, governments—their needs have unique characteristics. It is widely recognized, though, that marketing is more than a collection of functions or a process of matching product properties with the particular needs of individual customers. It is a way of conceiving of a business. This broader view of marketing is generally referred to as the marketing concept. As such, marketing has at least three dimensions which describe its character: the philosophical, the functional, and the organizational.

## MARKETING AS A BUSINESS PHILOSOPHY

Economists have traditionally viewed business as a resource-allocating device guided primarily by demand in the marketplace. This view largely ignores the efforts of business managers to create demand as well as search for novel ways to stimulate it. While many business decisions are concerned with the allocation of resources, these decisions are increasingly influenced by the search for new business opportunities. Modern businessmen not only are concerned with the allocation of resources to meet present demand but with the generation of new business ventures and the acquisition of new resources to exploit them. Consequently, there is good reason to view business as an input-output system. The input is composed of land, labor, money, and personal skills, while the output is not only goods and services to meet present demand but also new products and new product ideas for which no present demand exists. Such input-output systems are directed by man-

14

agers who must identify the opportunities (needs) to which the inputs of the system will be committed, decide on the extent to which these opportunities will be exploited (goals), acquire and/or develop the necessary resources (plans), commit these resources (direction), and evaluate the results of this activity (control).

The first and basic step is the identification of opportunity: the needs or family of needs the enterprise will be geared to satisfy. Since no business could possibly satisfy all types of needs, this decision is inescapable. The only options open to the management of a company are how the decision will be reached—systematically, haphazardly, or by default.

Peter Drucker's classic statement—that, being an organ of society, business enterprise must have a purpose which lies outside the business itself—has the ring of truth. He concludes that the only valid definition of business planning is not so much what management thinks the company is producing but what the customer thinks he is buying.[1] The moral is that management thinking must be adjusted not only to the language of the customer but also to his value system and to his logic. An era has arrived in which success demands that, instead of viewing the world exclusively through the eyes of the seller, management must view itself from the perspective of the buyer.

The multiplicity of choices generated by the expanding technology of the post–World War II era created real problems of understanding for the industrial buyer. This has been confounded by a multiplicity of appeals which more often than not project the historical attitudes of product developers rather than fulfilling the informational needs of buyers. The resulting credibility gap has fueled criticism of marketing and led industrial purchasers to greet sellers' claims with increased scrutiny and skepticism—a circumstance which raises the costs of both promotion and purchasing. The antidote for this malady is to conceive of customer satisfaction as an end rather than a means, and profit as a measure of the success with which this end is achieved rather than an end in itself. This is not a new idea, but it has only recently won wide recognition at top management levels.

The fact is that businessmen have admonished each other to keep the customer's interests in mind for decades. However, there was often a tendency to lump immediate buyers and end users together. "Customer orientation" typically meant adjusting prices and production to a level and volume the market would accept. Moreover, where a trade structure of dealers and middlemen existed, there was a tendency to regard end users as the responsibility of middlemen and to deal with these middlemen on a semi-exclusive basis. In essence, the agents,

---

[1] Peter F. Drucker, *The Practice of Management* (New York: Harper & Row, 1954), p. 37.

dealers, and wholesalers composing the trade structure were themselves regarded as the market. Such a focus precluded development of a marketing strategy based on superior value to the end user or utilization of the trade structure in a way which matched the needs of the end user.

The marketing concept not only envisages marketing as the focus of a business but advocates that all business thinking begin with the needs of the end user. This means that the properties with which industrial products and services are endowed, together with their distribution and promotion, should be derived from the businesses, government bodies, and institutions to be served rather than conceived for them. This suggests that the development of products and services should begin with the identification of needs that management desires to fulfill and the operational systems customers employ to fulfill them. This is the kind of intelligence from which the design of successful products and services evolves.

If every aspect of a firm's approach to its customers is to be determined by end-use requirements, those who direct the firm need to be intimately acquainted with the customer's business. A consciousness of the customer, the end-product customer, should permeate a business from top to bottom. This will not take place unless there is also acceptance from the top down that the only purpose of a business is to serve customers at a reasonable profit, that the beginning of all commercial activity is the determination of customer wants, and its end is their fulfillment. In essence, the marketing concept designates the welfare of the customer, the satisfaction of his needs, as the chief responsibility of business.

There are of course other concepts of business. There is the concept which affirms that the prime responsibility of business is to its owners and that management must place the highest priority on their interests. While those who espouse this concept might agree that focusing on the welfare of customers is in the best interests of stockholders, customer satisfaction is a means rather than an end. There is also the concept which holds that business exists for the welfare of its employees, that *their* welfare is its first responsibility. This point of view is one of the underpinnings of organized labor. The advocates of this position probably would not deny the importance of satisfying customers. However, they would probably reason that satisfied customers were necessary to assure a business the kind of stability which makes it a good employer.

This comparison is useful because it brings out the distinguishing characteristic of the marketing concept, viz., that the purpose business serves in society is that of satisfying customers' needs. Customer satisfaction is not a stepping-stone to some other condition or achievement. It is itself the end to which business managers should be directing their efforts. This implies no disparagement of stockholder or employee welfare. They are of vital importance because of the key role both play in providing the kind of financial and operational stability which makes a company a viable competitor for the patronage of customers.

## THE FUNCTIONAL DIMENSION

It is apparent that if business is to satisfy customer wants, they must be identified with a sufficient degree of specification to translate their characteristics into operational details and performance criteria. Otherwise, management would have little more than assumptions and surmises on which to base decisions concerning the design of products, services, and distribution networks. Merely asking purchasing agents, engineers, or plant foremen what they like or dislike about the products and services they are presently using may not produce the kind of meaningful information needed for such decisions.

The prime concern of the industrial marketer is how end users visualize their needs and the manner in which they endeavor to fulfill them. The most effective way of developing this kind of perception is through an examination of the tasks or functions which customers purchase products and services to perform. The principal thrust of such effort is identification of the operating systems businesses, governments, and institutions have evolved to meet their needs.

The nature of a task or function itself suggests the kind of products and services required to perform it. By the same token, analyzing an operating system (an interconnected series of tasks directed toward a specific goal) suggests opportunities for innovative products and services, i.e., those which span or eliminate tasks. These suggestions, both innovative and noninnovative, when matched against a company's existing and contemplated output capabilities indicate the nature and direction of future growth opportunities.

Obviously, no business could satisfy every industrial need. Not even a giant like the International Telephone and Telegraph Corporation attempts to do that. Functionally, then, marketing begins with the decision as to what general need (or needs) a firm will attempt to fulfill. This is the market mission. Businesses, government bodies, and institutions which have needs related to this mission can then be identified. This is the market. An analysis of the needs of this market in terms of the functions necessary to fulfill them reveals the various operating systems employed by the organizations in it. These different systems can then be related to desired product characteristics which in turn can be matched to the output capabilities of the marketer. From this matching process emerges the outline of future opportunity and the combination of product properties, pricing, promotion, and distribution services capable of exploiting it. This is the strategy.

## Mission definition

Formulating a statement of market mission which incorporates a reasonable balance between the desirable and the feasible involves at least three separate phases: (1) a situation audit, (2) the generation of alternative missions and strategies, and (3) the evaluation of alternatives.

*The situation audit.* An analysis of the company's situation is concerned not only with the strengths and weaknesses of the firm itself (self-audit) but with all the relevant measurable attributes of the environment in which its business will be conducted (environmental audit). The situation audit also is concerned with the competitive position of the firm with respect to other firms which may have similar or parallel missions (position audit).

Since few industrial enterprises at the present time start from scratch, with no connections to an existing operation, they have an ongoing status with certain capacities and incapacities. It is the purpose of the self-audit to discover these. This not only requires an objective appraisal of the firm's personnel, facilities, and financial status, but a coldly impartial assessment of the quality of its middle and top management as well as that of its principal suppliers. Formulating plans of any kind without a clear understanding of what an enterprise is capable of doing in the foreseeable future and what it is not capable of doing is inviting trouble.

The environmental audit would vary somewhat with the size of the enterprise (small firms are less subject to investigations than large ones) and the extent of the area over which it is prepared to operate. However, most environmental audits would contain at least the following items of information.

1. An inventory of known needs most compatible with the capacities of the company.
2. A profile of each of the anticipated major competitors.
3. An assessment of the state of technology and the extent of its variation within the given market area and among major competitors.
4. The economic outlook, short-term and long-term.
5. Existing or anticipated regulatory problems.

Since the position audit utilizes some of the information developed by the previous audits, its content will be shaped by their results. In general, though, the position audit is concerned with at least the following types of information.

1. Market share by territory and type of customer.
2. Profit contribution by product, customer, and territory.
3. Degree of control over channel members relative to that exercised by competition.

4. Level of the company's R & D expenditures relative to industry leaders.
5. Areas of the company's greatest relative technical competence.
6. Nature and strength of the company image relative to that of major competitors.

*Alternative missions and strategies.*   The information generated by audits should provide a number of ideas for realistic missions and suggest some alternative strategies for achieving them. Since the purpose of choosing a mission is to optimize the strengths of the company relative to those of competition, the objective is to identify needs which the company can fulfill with the greatest competitive advantage. Consequently, it is essential that alternative missions be clearly defined so that alternative strategies can be formulated and compared.

*Evaluation of alternatives.*   A common evaluation procedure is shown in Figure 2–1. Here the alternative strategies worked out for each prospective mission are evaluated on such bases as total cost, probability of success, and time required for accomplishment. As the diagram indicates, none of the suggested strategies may be acceptable, and management may be compelled to formulate additional strategies for consideration. In the event no practical alternative strategy can be worked out, the mission itself may have to be compromised or redefined so as to permit a strategy that is acceptable in terms of total cost and probability of success within the desired time limits.

Market missions have certain distinguishing characteristics. They incorporate a general statement of need which the company is prepared

**FIGURE 2–1.  A mission decision system**

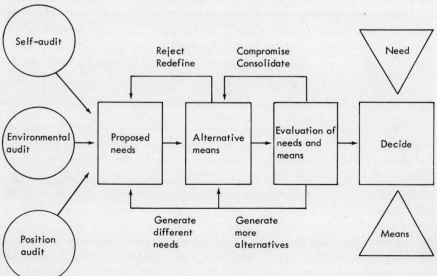

to fulfill such as the need for mobile power, for communication, or for transportation. Since identifying the generic need which an enterprise will seek to fulfill constitutes a statement of purpose, the mission defines the direction in which the business will endeavor to move. The mission also defines the theme or core idea which will characterize the efforts of an organization to meet the needs its management has selected. This theme might be technology, as in the case of Monsanto or Du Pont. It might be a raw material or a commodity, as in the case of ALCOA or the Owens-Corning Fiberglas Corporation. It might be a general type of product, as in the case of the Cummins Engine Company or the Caterpillar Tractor Company. It might also be a specific function like the transfer, storage, and retrieval of information, as in the case of IBM or Xerox.

## Market definition

Since the purpose of business is the satisfaction of customer needs, customers have to be identified in terms of their needs. This calls for some means of identifying organizations which have needs related to the company's mission and a system for classifying and segregating them into groups with similar operating systems. Since the characteristics of an operating system are shaped by the nature of the output it has been designed to produce, a logical way to classify, or segment, customers is by the nature of their output.

Once customers with needs related to the company's mission have been identified and grouped into appropriate segments, i.e., each segment containing firms with approximately similar operating systems, segments may then be examined for economic importance and significant trends. That is, an economic profile of each segment (number of establishments, average size, value added, value of shipments, etc.) can be developed and significant trends (declining numbers, increasing size, increased value of shipments, etc.) delineated. These measurements will enable the industrial marketer to determine those segments which represent the greatest demand for the products and services he is prepared to offer.

Segmentation of this type provides a rough definition of the market. What is missing is information concerning the specific kinds of tasks and functions which have to be performed in order to satisfy the needs identified in the various segments. Without this information, management does not know the kind of functional properties which will be required in products and services.

Industrial customers are decision-making units, controlling systems which transform raw materials, components, equipment, and effort into products and services, or items which will be further transformed by their own customers. Typically, an operating system represents a significant investment of resources and some emotional attachment on the part of its designers. Consequently, any marketer wishing to win the customer's patronage must provide a product or service which "fits" the system. To do this, the marketer must understand what the customer is doing technologically (functions) as well as teleologically (goals). This involves an understanding of supporting systems, such as purchasing and finance, as well as the production system.

*Supporting systems.* Since the customer's operating system is designed to fulfill the needs of his own customers or clients, understanding his system's goals almost always involves reaching into the customer's markets for information and insight. An understanding of the customer's marketing requirements is often the key to understanding the goals of his operating system and hence the kind of tasks his system needs to perform and the kind of technical flexibility it must have to function effectively.

An awareness of the different systems in use to meet customers needs alerts the industrial marketer to opportunities for product innovation. It also alerts him to how and where his own product and service can fit into these systems and what form of communication would most effectively influence the decision process in favor of their inclusion.

The various participants in the buying process and the relative influence of each is another indispensable piece of intelligence which only an understanding of the customer's purchasing system can reveal. Understanding the purchasing system is of particular importance because it can vary significantly within the same market segment. Depending on the size of the enterprise, the technical nature of the product or service required, the experience of the firm with the particular product as well as with the supplier of it, and the cost involved, a purchase might involve only one or two lower echelon managers or several key executives. An "intimate knowledge" of the customer's business implies an ability to predict the kind of decision process which will be set in motion by a given buying situation.

While the firm itself is but a subsystem of a larger system incorporating social groups, government, other businesses and institutions, it is nevertheless a basic unit of analysis for industrial marketers. Every firm usually includes a number of subsystems designed to achieve different ends, but these ends are related to management's overall objectives. The marketer who expects to relate his offering in a meaningful way to customers' needs must have a practical understanding of what goes on in the various systems which make up their businesses— businesses typical of those in each of the various segments of his total market.

Perhaps the most readily identifiable of the operating systems is the production system. A general description of the steps involved in the production system of a printing establishment, even if much abbreviated, may serve to illustrate the type of insight required to develop products or services which fit the needs of the system.

*The production system.*    The system involved in producing a book by a publisher who also does the printing is shown schematically in Figure 2–2 and includes a series of operations and decision points, each of which contributes in a unique way to the single purpose of making a book.

Although the process outlined here has been greatly simplified, it illustrates the manner in which a system can be divided into its constituent stages and those operations identified which are critical to the achievement of its purpose. The marketer then has a profile of properties which he can relate to his own existing and potential capabilities.

Any manufacturer who expects to sell products to the printing in-

FIGURE 2–2.    The Production system involved in printing a book

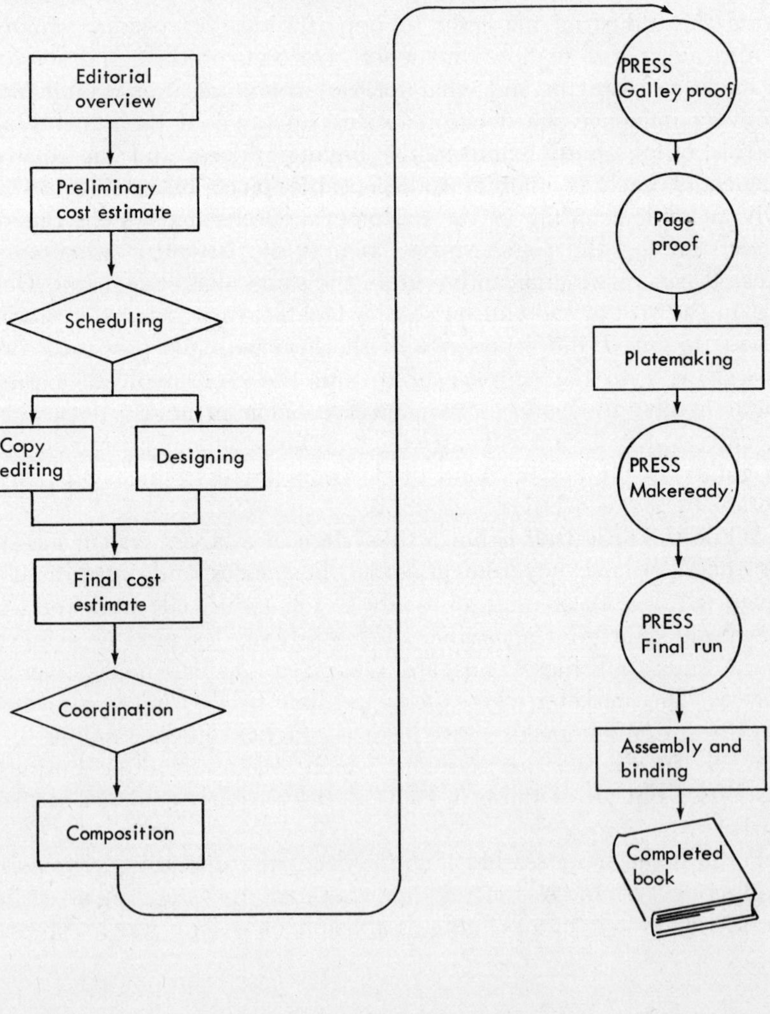

| *Stage* | *Operation* |
|---|---|
| Editorial Overview | Editorial staff identifies the publication's market, sets its price, and determines the proper format. |
| Preliminary Cost Estimate | An initial cost estimate is made based on the number and size of pages, number and types of illustrations, the method of printing (letterpress or offset), and the type of binding (soft or hard cover, stapled or spiral). |
| Scheduling | The plant superintendent's staff sets the date manuscript is to be submitted (in consultation with the author) and with the information assembled from the preceding two activities determines when the manuscript should be ready for printing. The superintendent also sets the date when the paper stock should be ordered, the plates made ready, the book jacket prepared, and binding completed. The final scheduling decision is publication date, i.e., the date when the completed book is delivered to the customer. |
| Copy Editing | When the manuscript is received it is scrutinized for grammatical inconsistencies, misspelling, and other errors. There may also be a certain amount of refinement of the material, such as the rephrasing and restructuring of sentences to render the text more comprehensible to its intended readers. |
| Designing | The design staff sets the tone of the publication through its choice of type, graphics, use of color, margins, texture of paper, placement of illustrations, binding and jacket specifications. |
| Final Cost Estimate | A price is attached to every element identified in the design phase and these are summed into a total cost-per-copy figure. |
| Coordination | The coordinator implements the schedule by ordering paper stock, inks and any special materials needed. He also assigns the proper equipment in the proper sequence. With the completion of this stage the manuscript goes to the printer. |
| Composition | The manuscript is converted into a form suitable for printing or for making printing plates. If letterpress, the so-called hot type, is used, characters (individual letters of the alphabet) must be assembled and the type set in metal. If the cold-type method is used, the manuscript is set by typewriter or photocomposition. These meth- |

| *Stage* | *Operation* |
|---------|-------------|
| | ods will produce camera-ready copy or film for offset printing (proofs pulled from hot metal type can also be used for offset printing). |
| Press—Galley Proof | The first impressions of the composed type are limited to the text material (no headings, captions, or illustrations). These impressions, called galleys, are reviewed for typographical errors, after which they are returned to the printer for corrections. |
| Page Proof | The printer makes up pages, and shows proof which is reviewed for page length and makeup. Corrected page proofs are returned to the printer where appropriate changes are made in the composed type or film. |
| Platemaking | All characters, images, and illustrations in the type or on the camera-ready copy are transferred to a metal or plastic graphic plate by which they can be mechanically or chemically reproduced on a page. |
| Press—Makeready | After a series of tests confirms that images will reproduce properly and that inks have been properly mixed, the plates are "locked in" the press for the final run. |
| Press—Final Run | All materials are assembled for feeding into the presses, and the press run is made. |
| Assembly or Binding | Printed sheets are cut and folded into pages which are glued, sewed, or stapled together, forming a "block" to which the book's cover is attached. |

dustry must build a product which either fits this system or makes it obsolete in some way. The progressive manufacturer usually will attempt the latter by designing a product, or products, which perform the operations at a given stage more efficiently than existing equipment, or which shortens the system's operating time by eliminating one or more stages, or which introduces an entirely new system to replace the old one.

Printing press manufacturers have introduced computer-controlled presses to reduce the time required in the press stage. Other manufacturers have endeavored to combine the platemaking and press stages by single machines which could perform both types of operations. Still more innovative are some copying-machine makers who have developed the quality of their machines' output to a level that copying can be substituted for printing. All that is needed is camera-ready copy for text as well as illustrations. This eliminates the composition, platemaking, and press stages, with considerable savings in both cost and time, particularly when a relatively small number of copies are involved.

A dramatic example of the envelopment of a whole system, and the obsolescence of all the equipment which composed it, by a single machine is given in Figures 2–3A and 2–3B. The earlier copying system required various items of equipment and material to produce legible copies of printed or typed pages. The Xerox copier not only does everything the old collection of equipment will do but does it many times faster and with higher quality results. Technologically, the machine is much more complex than an automobile.

Manufacturers of duplicating equipment saw an opportunity in the time and expense required in making metal plates for letterpress work.

FIGURE 2–3.  A comparison of copying systems

A. Circa 1945

B. Circa 1965

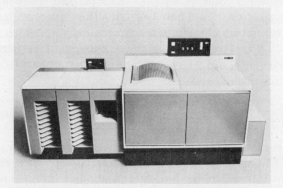

*Courtesy of Xerox Corporation. Agency: Needham, Harper & Steers, Inc.*

They developed machines capable of producing paper plates that make impressions so clear that only an expert can distinguish them from impressions made by metal plates. Although paper plates will not last as long as metal ones, they can be easily and inexpensively reproduced. For press runs of 1,000 copies or less, the use of paper plates means substantial savings in direct costs as well as in time.

The moral is that the manufacturer of printing, copying, and duplicating equipment must know not only the nature of his customer's end product (the kind of books printed and the number of copies involved) but also the details of the system employed to produce them. Only with this knowledge will he be able to help the customer with his operating problems or with visualizing design features that will improve the system itself.

The industrial marketer must understand how his customer's business functions well enough to identify the various systems which compose it. He must also determine which operations or stages within a particular system offer the most promising opportunities for his products and services. By focusing attention on functional systems rather than on competitive products his technical and applications people are better able to visualize a customer's operations as a whole and discover the common threads which connect its different parts or subsystems. Ability to help the customer solve his problems is enhanced because any common roots these problems possess are exposed. Therefore, the extent to which solutions to one problem provide a learning experience about others can be known with some degree of assurance. This knowledge when related to the marketers' technical and service capabilities give him a significant advantage in serving a customer over a competitor who does not have it.

## THE ORGANIZATIONAL DIMENSION

While accepted principles of organization hold true regardless of one's concept of a business, the marketing concept does involve certain organizational characteristics. These are: (1) the structural integration of all activities which directly influence customers or involve information about them, (2) the placement of these integrated activities under a single executive with top management status, and (3) sales structure based on customer characteristics.

### Structural integration

If the industrial marketer is to provide his customers with the products and services which match their needs, all activities which can influence the final sale must be so related and positioned in the organizational structure as to be mutually supporting. Advertising, personal selling, merchandising, public relations, and customer services must be actuated together as parts of the same functional system. In small organizations with narrow product lines this may be accomplished by the simple expedient of placing those in charge of advertising, personal selling, product development, sales promotion, public relations, or other related group on the same echelon.

In large organizations the problem is a little more complex, but essentially it is a matter of combining those personnel who influence customers into one team and those who handle information about customers into another. This can be accomplished by a number of different structural arrangements. The one shown in Figure 2–4 is a representative one. The responsibility of the marketing manager is to develop unity among the pricing, service, and promotional activities.

**FIGURE 2–4.  A bidivisional marketing structure**

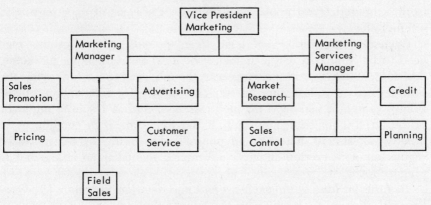

Unity means that the message carried by the company's advertising and the message presented by the company's salesmen are mutually reinforcing. All sales promotion and customer service efforts should amplify and reinforce the same message. It is unlikely that all marketing media will deliver a consistent message to the customer or that those in charge of each will follow a coordinated plan unless the organizational structure facilitates team effort and interaction among managers.

The marketing services manager heads what is sometimes called the "marketing intelligence group." Every business needs a nerve center which not only senses what is taking place in its environment, but translates this information into action plans. Some of the activities which are basic to such a group are continuous surveillance of the market, continuous review of legislative and legal developments, regular probing of buyer needs, and periodic analysis of pertinent economic data.

*Market surveillance.*  A condition about which one can be fairly dogmatic is that markets are constantly changing. Some changes are predictable—such as those associated with population growth, defense spending, and industrial expansion. Other changes are very difficult to anticipate. New discoveries like electrostatic copying and ultrasonic cleaning might generate whole new industries within a few years' time, or they might lie dormant for decades. Know-how for fast-freezing foods was perfected in the 1920s, but is was not until the 1950s that food processors showed much interest in freezing foods. Microwave heating, which can dry substances without loss of surface moisture or danger of fire, was developed during World War II but has only had limited use since that time.

On the other hand, it is foolhardy to dismiss any new technological development as inconsequential, particularly in an industry characterized by aggressive competition. A continuing large-scale "sweep" of the market is necessary to discover indications of impending change as well as clues to impending moves by competition. Without such information, management is limited to extrapolating wholly on the basis of experience and intuition.

*Review of legislative and legal developments.*  Few business men need to be reminded of the influence of legal restrictions on marketing decisions. What is worthy of emphasis, though, is the need for sufficiently comprehensive information about pending legislation and probable rulings to permit making a planned response. Such a response might be in the form of political opposition, if the stakes are high enough, or an orderly adjustment. There is an unmistakable trend toward increased regulation of marketing activity, and management has no choice but to prepare for it.

*Regular probing of buyer operations and decision systems.* . The time-honored dictum to know your customer's business as thoroughly as possible is as true today as it was a generation ago. However, what this knowledge should comprise and how it may be obtained are constantly changing. As a firm responds to new opportunities and adjusts to new threats its needs for both products and services are altered, as well as the way management perceives these needs. The timely acquisition and feedback of information concerning changes in buyers' needs and the priorities management has placed on their fulfillment require more than a good rapport with the purchasing department, although that is a very important condition and every effort should be made to preserve it.

The purchasing department is typically a service function, which responds to the requests of other departments. Consequently, some of the most important information for the industrial marketer is to be found in the operating areas which the professional buyer serves, as well as in the markets from which his company derives its revenue. It is not unusual to find industrial marketers researching consumer markets, because it is the consumer who ultimately must be satisfied. Any product weakness in the competition for consumer patronage will be reflected backward to the suppliers of materials and components included in the product or to the suppliers of machinery used to fashion it. Important insights into the needs and problems of a customer firm can often be found by studying the market performance of his products in comparison with that of other products of the same general class.

The marketer with a clear understanding of a customer's needs and problems can formulate a much more effective program for attacking them than would be possible without it. Industrial marketing is more than putting the right product in the right place at the right time and at the right price. It is helping the customer solve his problems, helping him save money, helping him to be a more viable competitor in the market place. The successful industrial marketer is not only a supplier of products for his customers, but an indispensible source of aid in resolving their problems.

*Periodic analysis of economic data.* Training, experience, and the demands of business make any marketing executive sensitive to data which presage shifts in the economic climate. The question is whether or not economic intelligence is readily available and in a form which permits its combination with market, legislative, and customer inputs. The prompt development of an environmental profile that is sufficiently comprehensive to support strategic decisions is an urgent need. Such a

**FIGURE 2–5.   Marketing structure of a large multiproduct company**

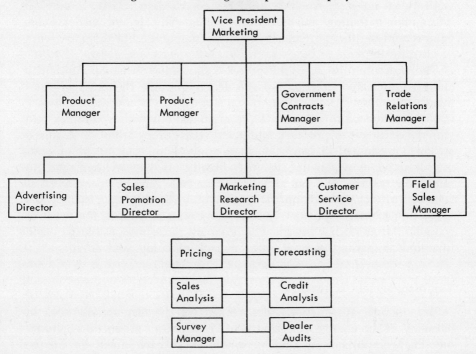

**FIGURE 2–6.  Organization chart of a medium-sized industrial enterprise**

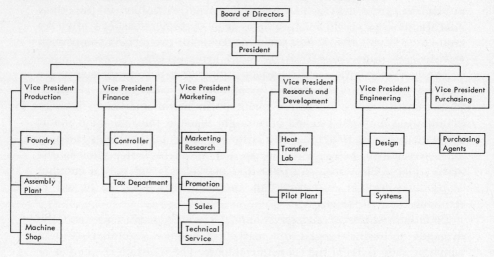

profile depends on the efficient integration of different informational inputs so that the total picture emerges. This is indispensible if management is to be capable of identifying the crucial environmental changes, anticipating their direction, and planning appropriate action. The achievement of useful informational integration requires workable organizational integration which produces coordinated activity among all information-gathering and processing units. This is not an easy organizational hurdle, particularly for large companies, but there are ways of clearing it.

The structure illustrated in Figure 2–5 shows the elementary authority and communicative relationships needed to provide the unity of command and consistency of direction which are basic to effective teamwork in the intelligence function. In large organizations with a complex and varied assortment of products additional staff groups are often required as shown in Figure 2–6. Nevertheless, the underlying principle of integrating all activities which directly or indirectly involve environmental information remains the same. Whether or not genuine team work is achieved in fact depends on the quality of leadership exercised by the Marketing Services Manager (and his superior) as well as the spirit of cooperation which has been engendered by those responsible for such functions as market research, sales control, planning, and credit.

### Top management status

In principle, all functional departments of the firm should work in harmony. If the company mission is to be achieved, production, marketing, finance, purchasing, and personnel must each make its unique contribution in a way which avoids conflict with other departments and avoids duplication of their efforts. In a well-managed business, these contributions are spelled out in a master plan or strategy. But if the strategy is to reflect a balance among the major functional elements of the business, those responsible for each must participate in the planning process as equals. This usually implies that the manager of each major function holds the rank of a top-echelon executive as illustrated in Figure 2–6.

The marketing concept does not imply that the only person qualified to be a company president is one with a marketing background, or that such people even make good presidents. It does imply that the business of business is the satisfaction of customers' needs and that the marketing department is the principle link between the firm and its customers. It follows that a customer-oriented marketing manager, as opposed to a product-oriented sales manager, should have an equal voice with those in charge of production, finance, and other departments, in shaping the company's mission as well as in formulating the strategy and policy to achieve it.

### Customer-based organization structure

It is a widely demonstrated principle of organization that the structure must fit the task to be performed. When this task is that of identifying the needs and problems of customers and helping them work out satisfactory solutions, the organization must be structured to "fit" the customers. If the needs and problems of customers are related to the products they produce or the type of service they render, and customers can be divided into fairly distinct groups, an organizational structure based on industries as shown in Figure 2–7 may provide the best fit. In this instance salesmen specialize by industry. Since they limit their attention to firms producing similar products and services, salesmen can assimilate a considerable amount of knowledge concerning customers' operations and problems. Often they can become very proficient in identifying ways their company can be of assistance.

The structure shown in Figure 2–7 would not be very appropriate for a company selling a product which had wide application in a number of different industries. A simple geographical basis might provide the best fit for customers in that instance. The same would be true of industrial marketers who reach their customers through independent middlemen. A company representative assigned to a particular group of dealers in the same general geographical area of a workable arrangement, particularly if the representative is supported by staff specialists whose expertise can be drawn upon whenever dealer problems tax his own knowledge.

On some occasions the best fit may be provided by organizing the

**FIGURE 2–7.  Marketing organization based on customer types**

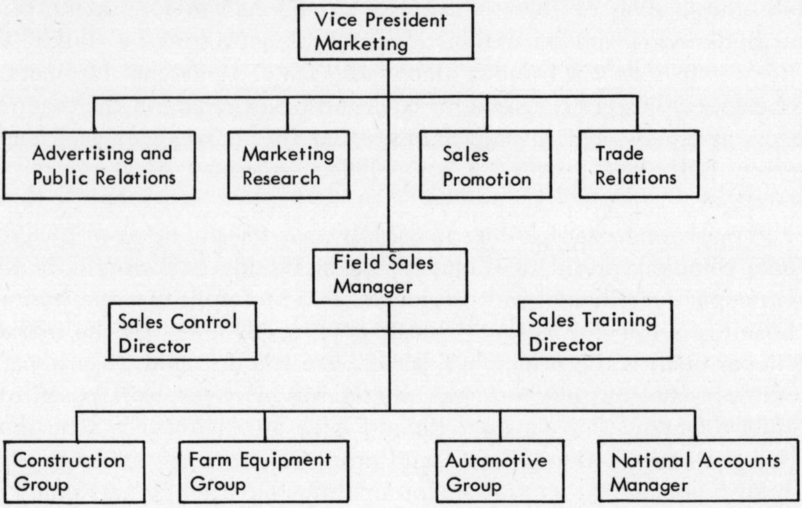

sales force along product lines rather than by territory or industry. This would tend to be true in companies marketing highly technical, sophisticated products, such as custom-made machinery, or with several distinctly different product lines. In such instances customers may well need the specialized product knowledge of the salesman who confines his efforts to a single type of product and has had the experience of adapting it to a variety of production, assembly, and engineering applications. The opportunity to effect significant reductions in cost, savings in time, or improved performance through the use of a given product may go unnoticed by the customer until discovered by the trained mind and experienced eye of a salesman who is thoroughly aware of a product's versatility and range of application. The use of product managers[2] represents a compromise of sorts between a product-based organization structure and one based on geographical areas. Although the salesman in the field would not be a product specialist, he would be supplied with product specifications, sales leads, and other information by the product manager and would probably have available to him the support of an applications engineer.

Some modification of these basic structural arrangements usually becomes necessary in the case of large customers, customers with special needs or requirements, and customers with whom special arrangements are in force. Large customers, merely because of the volume of business they represent or the complexity of their operations often warrant the assignment of a full-time salesman or representative. Such "house ac-

---

[2] Staff specialists who assume responsibility for planning and coordinating all aspects of marketing a particular line of products. (See Figure 2–5.)

counts" are carefully cultivated and frequently found in companies which move much of their output through independent middlemen.

A good example of customers with special needs and requirements are governmental bodies and public institutions. While the former may have professional buyers among their personnel, purchasing procedures may be prescribed by law. Coping successfully with formalized restrictions requires a familiarity with them and a negotiating skill which can only be developed by specializing in this type of account. This is also a characteristic of large public institutions. However, small government bodies, such as school districts and many private institutions such as small colleges and churches often make their decisions without the services of any professional buying personnel. Such accounts usually require a great deal of missionary and educational effort which can best be offered by representatives who devote their full attention to such requirements.

Industrial marketers may enter into special contractual arrangements with customers, thereby creating a different kind of relationship than that entered into with other customers. An agreement to purchase a certain quantity of merchandise from a customer in return for a given volume of sales would be such an arrangement. So would a contract to produce products to a customer's specifications under his trademark. Both arrangements call for interim contacts which do not fit neatly into the traditional structure of the marketing organization.

Reciprocal trading agreements may be determined more by the total relationship between two or more companies than anything a salesman can do. Consequently, such agreements are often negotiated at the highest level of authority, completely circumventing the marketing departments of the organizations involved. By the same token, private labeling agreements are frequently decided on the basis of competitive bids and may involve no marketing activity at all in the usual sense. In such instances, bid preparation becomes an important marketing activity, and the marketing organization of companies which actively compete for this business usually includes a contract department. In fact, so much industrial buying is done on the basis of competitive bids that a contracts department is a fairly common element of industrial marketing organization whether or not a company is in the private-label business.

# PART II

## The demand for industrial goods

THE CHARACTERISTICS of demand for industrial goods may perhaps be treated most effectively by separating these characteristics into three general groups: (1) those related to market levels and product types, (2) those related to the derived nature of demand, and (3) those related to the nature of the customer. In discussing the first and second groups, we will examine factors that influence the total volume of sales realized by all industrial sellers. Discussion of the third group will emphasize the conditions and qualities that induce customers to patronize one marketer rather than another.

# DEMAND AND
# PRODUCT CHARACTERISTICS

THE CHARACTERISTICS of industrial demand differ with the type of product involved as well as with the market level chosen by the seller. Both in turn are shaped by the derived nature of demand for the marketer's product offering.

## MARKET LEVELS AND PRODUCT TYPES

One of the unique characteristics of demand for industrial goods is that it may encompass any or all levels of the market from raw materials to finished products. It is useful to identify these different product-market levels not only because of the added insight about demand for industrial goods that can be gained, but also because of the advantage to the marketer of considering his products in the light of the conditions and manner in which they are most often bought. The proper choice of distribution channels and the most effective means of promotion often depend on the way in which buyers classify products.

It must be remembered, of course, that one cannot be very specific or precise in identifying these levels because of the tremendous variety of products involved—from complex, custom-made machinery costing many thousands of dollars per unit to mass-produced supply items of standard design and relatively little cost. In order to appreciate the differences in demand represented by different types of products it may be useful to identify at least the following general classifications: major equipment, accessory equipment, fabricating or component parts, process materials, operating supplies, and raw materials.

### Major equipment

This category includes large machines or other tools whose unit purchase prices are so great that expenditures for them are apt to be

FIGURE 3–1. A Multipurpose machine

Courtesy of Marion Power Shovel Company, Inc., Marion, Ohio.

This mammoth power shovel (note size of men standing at lower left base of the shovel) carries a 115-cub. yd. dipper at the end of a 300-ft. boom. It is used extensively in strip mining.

charged to a capital account. The cost of such items therefore becomes part of the buying firm's capital structure rather than a current expense. Some items of equipment, such as automatic measuring and control devices, should also be included in this cateogry even though they are not expensive and their cost is often charged to current expense. Since such items are vitally important to proper operation of the expensive machines that they are attached to, they are often bought in much the same manner as the machines themselves.

Major equipment is of two general types—multipurpose or standard machines and special or single-purpose machines. Multipurpose equipment can be used by a number of different industries or by many firms in the same industry. By minor adjustments or changes of parts, standard machines can often be adapted to several kinds of work within the general type of operation they are designed to perform. The substitution of dies or parts in a standard stamping machine, for example, enables it to stamp a variety of shapes and sizes.

Single-purpose machines, on the other hand, are designed to perform one particular operation and no other. A grinding machine, for example, may be designed to smooth a number of surfaces of varying hardness and have its abrasive elements set in an intricate and very exact planal relationship. Such a machine could become useless if the end product is changed so that the intricate grinding operation is no longer needed.

Typically, multipurpose machines tend to have a much longer life than single-purpose equipment, and the demand for them is likely to extend throughout several kindred industries. Since the original purchase price of such equipment can usually be amortized over a longer period than can the cost of single-purpose machines, annual fixed costs of its use are apt to be lower than those of more specialized equipment. The built-in versatility of standard equipment also makes unnecessary the detailed study of customers' production problems so characteristic of sales efforts in behalf of specialized machinery. As a result, the purchase of standard equipment is likely to involve much less preliminary planning and negotiation than the purchase of more specialized equipment.

Demand for special equipment is often confined to a single industry, even to one firm in the industry, because much of it is made to the buyer's specifications. Consequently, the negotiation of a purchase agreement often requires the closest kind of cooperation between the technical and sales staffs of buyer and seller. Since the value of the equipment may be destroyed not only by use but by relatively minor changes in design of the end product it is used to produce, the timing of purchases is usually determined by the incidence of model changes in the end product. The end product may not even be produced by the buying firm if it is a components or process materials house. The more limited application and life span of such machinery allows a relatively short period of time over which its purchase price may be amortized, and requires

**FIGURE 3–2.  Special purpose machine**

This Cross Transfer Machine drills, mills, taps, and bores compressor housings at the rate of 300 per hour. It is controlled by a single operator from a control panel (left photo). Design, construction, and installation of the machine required three years at a cost to the purchaser of $1,000,000.

that the dollar benefits of using it be considerably greater than for other more standardized equipment.

Since the unit price of major equipment is sometimes very high, its purchase may involve financial problems for the buyer. Therefore, firms that market such equipment must usually be prepared to arrange loans for their customers, to help them float issues of securities, to negotiate with investment concerns (such as insurance companies), to buy the equipment and lease it to the using firms, to make sales on an installment basis, or to lease their products instead of selling them.

### Minor or accessory equipment

Minor or accessory equipment is machinery used in an auxiliary capacity. Its unit price is usually much less than that of major equipment, and its cost is generally charged to current expenses, although small or poorly financed buyers sometimes place it in a capital account. For this reason and because of the relatively small amounts involved, such purchases are likely to be made in a more routine manner, to involve less negotiation, and to require the approval of fewer executives in the buying firm than is the case with major installation items.

Most minor equipment items are standardized and suited to the performance of a function involved in more than one of the operations of a business. For example, small lathes, fractional horsepower motors, and small tractors may be used in carrying on activities in several different departments or at several different stages in the production process. They are also likely to be useful in many different types of business. For these reasons, their demand is usually horizontal in nature in that it is not confined to one industry. As a result, the organization for marketing

**FIGURE 3–3.  Accessory equipment**

These products illustrate the extremes in accessory equipment from the small hand tool (top photos) used to remove metal burrs left by machining to the giant lift (lower photos) used in the installation and removal of jet aircraft engines as well as the loading and unloading of heavy cargo.

them must be much more widespread than is that for items of major equipment. Minor equipment must be sold through many more outlets, and the relations between the buyer and the maker can be less direct and immediate.

### Fabricating or component parts

It is characteristic of American industry that, except in rare instances, a single establishment does not carry out the entire production process from raw material to finished product. Typically, the work of production is carried on by a series of plants, often under diverse ownership, each performing a single operation or homogeneous group of operations on the material. As the process approaches the final, finished-product stage, the work of production becomes more and more a matter of assembling

FIGURE 3–4.  Typical
component part

*Courtesy of the York Division, Borg Warner*
*Corp., Decatur, Illinois.*

This compressor is the heart of an
automobile air-conditioning system.

finished parts, bought from different suppliers, into an article ready for
use and final sale. In some industries almost the entire production
process is one of assembly. Even large integrated manufacturers like the
major automobile producers, which have long sought to control their
supplies of component parts through ownership of subsidiaries, still find
it necessary to buy items from thousands of small suppliers.

Components are often bought on the basis of specifications prepared
by the purchaser, although many of them, such as batteries and tires in
the automotive industry, are standardized according to the specifications
of the parts manufacturer. In either case, the buying firm probably will
want to include commitments for an entire year's supply or a stated percentage of a year's supply in one contract. In order to assure uniformity
of quality, a buyer is under pressure to concentrate his purchases of
component parts with as few suppliers as possible, although to provide
continuity of supply, he may need more than one source.

In awarding purchase contracts for parts, the buyer is apt to place
heavy emphasis on uniformity and reliability of quality as well as on the
certainty and regularity of the seller's delivery service. This emphasis
arises because the buyer wishes to keep the stocks of component parts as
small as possible. Since their value is usually high in relation to the cost
of the materials in them, they are very expensive items to carry in inventory. If a buyer can rely on the quality and delivery service of his

supplier, he can reduce to a minimum his stocks of these highly expensive items. For these reasons, component parts are usually bought directly from the maker.

Some component parts retain their identity in the finished product. This offers buyers the opportunity of enhancing the sales appeal of their end products by incorporating in them a component of known market acceptance. On the other hand, if the replacement market offers a component maker a possible sales volume greater than the requirements for original installation, the manufacturer of the finished product may enjoy a decisive advantage in bargaining with the parts maker. In the tire business, for example, it has been shown that the car owner who needs a new tire exhibits a strong preference for the make that was on his car when he bought it. Tire manufacturers, therefore, have shown a willingness to make substantial concessions to the automobile-producing firms in order to get their tires installed as original equipment.

### Process materials

Process materials closely resemble component parts in that they usually enter into and form an indistinguishable part of the finished product. A pharmaceutical house may buy the acetate or acetyl of salicylic acid and an inert carrier or binding agent, mix them together, form them into tablets, put them into a container carrying its brand, and sell them as aspirin tablets. A food manufacturer may buy a variety of ingredients, mix them in proper proportions, and sell the resulting material on the market as a cake mix.

A few process materials either are broken up and dissipated in the production process without entering into the final product, or they act to bring about changes in the materials that enter into the product without themselves undergoing material change or forming a part of the finished article. A catalyst, for example, sets off certain chemical reactions without undergoing any change itself; it therefore can be used over and over again.

Process materials differ from component parts chiefly in that most of them cannot be identified so that they can be recognized in the finished product. For very few of them is there a replacement market. As a result, little is usually to be gained by advertising a process material over the head of its industrial user to the buyers of the final product. There are a few examples of such advertising, but they are not common.

Process materials tend to be bought on specifications prepared by the buyer or according to standards developed by the trade, often with the help of government agencies. For example, fine chemicals are usually bought and sold on the basis of U.S.P. standards, although one supplier may gain some advantage over another by building a reputation for exercising extreme care in making sure that the quality of every lot he sells conforms exactly to the standard, or exceeds the standard by a constant ratio, in purity or other desirable properties. However, this standardization is sufficient to throw considerable emphasis on price and service as competitive factors in the sale of process materials.

It is not unusual for a firm to buy certain types of process materials on requirements contracts or to purchase them speculatively, sometimes for future delivery. The negotiation of such contracts may be a matter of considerable importance to both the buyer and the seller and may be handled at high executive levels.

## Operating supplies

Operating supplies do not become a part of the finished product, but for the most part are continuously worn out or used up in the process of operating or facilitating the operation of an enterprise. Such items as paints, soaps and detergents, oils and greases, cleaning materials, pencils and ink, typewriter ribbons, and stationery belong in this category.

The typical operating supply is needed by many different firms in many different industries. The functions that such goods perform are likely to be common to many types of enterprise. This means that they must be marketed on a widespread basis. The methods by which they are marketed more nearly resemble those used in distributing consumers' goods than do those of any other type of industrial goods.

Supplies are generally bought in small quantities, although some purchasers are willing to enter into blanket or open-end contracts, whereby they commit themselves to buy their entire requirements of certain items from one, two, or three suppliers for a designated future period. When supplies are bought currently without benefit of such blanket contracts, they are usually purchased in a routine manner and according to a set pattern, which remains unchanged over considerable periods of time. When they are bought on blanket contracts, the contract may be the subject of much negotiation, but the work of placing delivery orders becomes a matter even more routine than in the absence of such contracts.

Operating supplies are usually standardized at least within the brand designations of the makers, although occasional buyers purchase on specifications they prepare for their own use. For this reason, there is little need for direct contact between the buyer and the seller. Because of the wide areas over which they must be sold and the smallness of the unit purchase, it is both difficult and uneconomical to establish and maintain such contact. They are likely to be marketed on an indirect basis through middlemen.

Purchasing agents and marketers of industrial goods often speak of MRO (maintenance, repair, and operating) items. In this category they usually lump operating supplies and at least the less expensive articles of accessory equipment. This is often a useful grouping, because these kinds of items tend to be bought in much the same manner and hence must be sold through the same kinds of channels and by the same methods.

## Raw materials

Raw materials are the basic materials of industry. They usually have undergone only such processing as is necessary for convenience in handling and transportation or for standardization to facilitate their use or purchase and sale.

Raw materials are supplied chiefly by agriculture and the lumbering, mining, and fishing industries. Those produced by agriculture are generally marketed in fairly small lots through elaborate marketing systems. Since their distribution is highly specialized and is in itself a separate subject of study, it will be given only incidental treatment here.

The industries, other than agriculture, that extract raw materials exhibit a strong tendency to integrate their extraction with the performance of at least the early processes of refinement and fabrication. In some industries, this integration is carried well along into the production process. For example, very few firms that use steel shapes or forms in their operations buy the raw iron ore or even the refined steel billets. The steel companies carry the production process from the ore in the ground through to the point where they are able to offer rods, beams, sheets, and other shapes to suit the purposes of their customers. The oil companies carry the process of integration through from the well to the industrial consumer, although there is a brisk trade among them to secure special kinds of crude, to dispose of excess supplies of it, and to offset shortages in their own crude production. Such transactions are generally negotiated at very high levels and involve large quantities. The mechanism for negotiating them is usually relatively simple and direct, though details of the bargaining process are often infinitely complex.

When raw materials are traded on the open market, they are usually bought and sold on the basis of recognized standards, expressed in terms of either grade designations or sets of specifications. Agricultural raw materials are usually vended on the basis of systems of grades sponsored and administered by the federal government. Chemicals may be marketed by grade or by specification; minerals may be sold by grade, by specification, or by the vein from which they were dug.

Various kinds of agents, especially brokers, are an important element in the system for marketing the part of the supply of raw materials that does not move in integrated channels. Much of the supply is usually controlled by integrated firms, and much of that part of the supply sold on the market consists of (a) an integrated firm's excess production over its own needs, (b) an integrated company's purchases to supply shortages in its own production of materials, and (c) an integrated company's purchases of materials with special characteristics that its own controlled sources of raw materials cannot supply. Thus, many of the buying and selling firms do not possess well-organized departmental units to make such purchases and sales. They do not do enough of this kind of business to justify maintaining such a unit. Therefore, this work is often done at irregular intervals by some executive as an addition to his usual duties. He does not have time to keep up with the market or to maintain adequate contacts with customers or sources. The agent offers both information and contacts when they are needed. Brokers, often operating almost entirely by telephone, are usually a feature of the unintegrated portion of the trade in a raw material.

## DERIVED DEMAND

Derived demand refers to the indirect way in which the need for industrial goods is generated, i.e., from the demand for the consumer goods or services they are used to make or provide. For example, the demand for sheet metal is derived from the demand for products made of sheet metal as is the demand for machines that cut and shape sheet metal. In general, the demand for industrial goods tends to depend on and fluctuate with the demand for the goods and services they are used to produce. Sometimes this characteristic results in spectacular changes. For example, *Sales Management,* June 20, 1967, estimated that the requirement of seat belts for all new cars would result in a demand for 352 million feet of webbing, costing about 320 millions of dollars.

Demand for an item used in maintenance and repair depends on general business activity and is usually determined by sales (expected as well as actual) of all the various articles produced by the manufacturing complex. By contrast, demand for a material or component at any particular time depends on the probable demand for articles to be made from it during the relatively near future (one or two production cycles) as estimated by the managers of firms that use the material in fabricating or processing operations. Demand for a piece of specialized machinery, on the other hand, is determined to a great extent by long-run forecasts of demand and profit possibilities for products the equipment is used to make. Such forecasts would normally cover a 3- to 10-year period, but are sometimes projected as many as 20 or 40 years into the future.

The maker of industrial products may have to look far afield to discover conditions which are likely to influence the demand for his output. The market for coal mining and processing machinery is likely to be affected by such varied circumstances as public concern with air pollution, the development of smoke abatement devices, the supply of fuel oil, and increased use of atomic power. The demand for food processing and packaging machinery is influenced by the ultimate consumer's desire for convenience both in buying and preparing food. A whole series of products, many of them now unknown, are certain to be affected by widespread sentiment to clean up our environment.

This characteristic of demand for industrial goods makes it necessary for their marketers to think in terms of end uses instead of products. The Owens-Corning Fiberglas Corporation, which produces much of the fibrous glass from which luggage, fishing rods, boat hulls, and numerous other consumer products are made, consistently advertises in consumer media, promoting products made of fiberglass reinforced plastic. The Caterpillar Tractor Company, a leading maker of earthmoving equipment, uses consumer media to stress the desirability of better roads, irrigation projects, and land reclamation. Both Monsanto and Du Pont heavily promote the virtues of carpeting made with their synthetic fibers. The present plight of the railroads is due in part to the preoccupation of their management with railroading instead of transportation.

### Influence of the ultimate buyer

The pivotal position of the ultimate buyer is particularly noticeable in the case of marketers who sell to manufacturers of original equipment (OEM's). Many OEM suppliers so identify their products that they can be recognized in the end product. Those who do often discover that they must select their customers with discretion. Otherwise, the prestige and reputation for quality that prompts this identification will be lost if the product is used in conjunction with supplementary materials of a shoddy nature or if the product it is incorporated into is of substandard quality or poor workmanship. It is known that several textile firms that emphasize the identity of their products in their promotion are rather selective in their choice of customers.

When the use of a manufacturer's product adds salability to the buyer's end product, derived demand can provide the manufacturer with a potent sales appeal. Some years ago, for example, the Reynolds Metals Company introduced an aluminum foil wrap to be used in packaging. One of the buyers of this material was a firm selling dried fruits. The firm advertised that its product was wrapped in aluminum foil, although the foil itself was concealed by an outer pasteboard container. A moderate increase in sales resulted. The metals company subsequently persuaded its customer to redesign its package so the foil would appear on the outside. When the new package was test marketed, it produced a dramatic increase in sales. The redesigned package, using foil on the outside, resulted in a more salable product for the fruit processor and a better customer for the metals company.

### Influence of business conditions

As a result of its derived nature, the demand for industrial goods may fluctuate violently because of changes in the tempo of business operations and subsequent shifts in inventory objectives. Typically, an industrial buyer's inventory objectives are expressed in terms of the quantity of an item necessary to satisfy operating needs for a stated number of days. Once the desired number of days of supply is determined, it is the purchasing officer's responsibility to adjust purchases and commitments to buy so that the stock of an item is always as close as possible to the amount necessary to sustain operations at the projected rate for the desired number of days. While this is an extremely difficult feat to achieve with accuracy, particularly with an inventory consisting of thousands of items, it nevertheless represents the objective toward which purchasing management works. For example, a purchasing agent is said to be buying on a 60- or 90-day basis.

When business conditions are bad, the number of days of stock established as the inventory goal is likely to be reduced due both to the easier availability of goods, accompanied by at least the prospect of lower prices, and to the uncertainty of future demand for the end product. When business is good and expectations are bright, the number of days supply is apt to be increased for the opposite reasons. These changes in inventory level have a multiplier effect when they are translated into purchase commitments. For example, if a firm operating on a three-month inventory experiences an increase in sales that steps up the use of material A by 100 units per month, its purchases of material A during the first month after the change are likely to be increased by 400 units. The firm would, of course, need an additional 100 units to support increased production during the current month and 300 additional units to build up a three-month inventory to back up the new rate of production.

This bulge in purchases may be diminished somewhat if the buyer decides to spread his inventory buildup over two or three months instead of concentrating it in one. This he may very well do, so that before making such a drastic inventory commitment he can assure himself that the sales increase is a continuing one and not a one-month flash in the pan. In either event, the increase in demand experienced by supplier firms is considerably greater than the increase in sales realized by the buying firm.

A drop in sales tends to make an even greater difference in purchases. Let us assume, for example, that a given firm sells 1 million units of its product per month and carries a 3-month supply of needed materials and parts in inventory. This means that the firm maintains an inventory of 3 million units of needed materials and parts and buys 1 million units each month to meet production requirements and maintain its 90-day stock. Suppose now that sales fall to 800,000 units per month and production declines proportionately. The company now needs only 2.4 million units of materials and parts in stock in order to achieve its 90-day inventory objective. It must reduce inventory by 600,000 units of materials and parts.

If management seeks to make the entire adjustment during the first month after the change in sales, the firm will place orders for only 200,000 units instead of the previous 1 million units. If management decides to spread the adjustment over the following 2 months, purchases will be reduced to 500,000 units per month. When many companies simultaneously follow such procedures, it tends to cause a drop in the demand for certain types of industrial goods entirely out of proportion to the decrease in demand for consumer end goods, which initiated the adjustment.

## Influence of financial conditions

The derived character of demand also gives financial considerations a great deal of leverage in determining how much of an item will be purchased. Such considerations are especially influential in the market for industrial equipment. This influence can be readily appreciated when it is understood that industrial purchasers must be influenced by the effect of their acquisitions on the net profits of their companies and, in some cases, even on the financial structure of their firms.

The purchase of materials influences profits chiefly through its effect on the cost of end products and on their attractiveness to buyers. Of course, the availability and speed with which materials can be procured influences the capital structure of a firm because of their effect on the working capital required for inventory. The more difficult it is to procure supplies of a given material, the greater the stock of the material that must be carried in inventory.

An equipment purchase affects profit as a result of both its initial cost and its effect on the cost and attractiveness of the end product. The obsolescence rate of equipment also affects capital structure through the size of reserve funds that must be established to replace it. The impact of such influences on the profit position and capital structure of buying firms is greatly multiplied by the forces of inflation and technological improvement.

The case of the Thompson Products Company is a classic example of the part financial considerations play in the demand for industrial equipment. Thompson Products bought a Warner Swasey 3A saddle lathe for $12,000. This was depreciated on the company's books on a 14-year basis, so that by the end of that period the Thompson Products Company had retained in its capital structure from cash inflow the sum of $12,000 as a depreciation reserve. In addition, it found that the lathe could be sold for $1,000 in the used machine market. But the price of a lathe of the same make and model was now $35,000, so it would be necessary to borrow or apply from retained earnings $22,000 in order to restore Thompson Products' production equipment to the original level of efficiency. The firm netted about 9 percent on sales before taxes. Income taxes took about 52 percent of this; to find the $22,000 Thompson Products had to commit earnings from almost $500,000 worth of sales.

But this was not all the bad news. When the machine was first bought, The Warner Swasey 3A saddle lathe was the best suited equipment for its purpose. But fourteen years later a new and improved model selling for $67,000 had been developed. So if Thompson Products wished to retain in the current technological environment the same position it had occupied when it had originally bought the lathe, it had to raise $54,000 of new capital or apply that sum from retained earnings, thereby reducing by that amount the funds available for new ventures. To earn this amount, Thompson Products had to sell $1.250 million worth of goods and services.

This saga illustrates the effect of financial considerations on the demand for industrial equipment; it also explains why many managements use the so-called cash flow method of analyzing the effect of equipment purchases on their financial situation. Without going into the intricacies of the method, it should be pointed out that net cash flow represents money that flows into a business but does not flow out again in the current course of operations—mainly charges for depreciation and reserves and net profit.

In addition to its general implications about the demand for certain types of industrial goods, this discussion suggests that industrial marketers should be prepared to analyze the effect the purchase of their products is likely to have on the profit position and financial structure of buying firms. They should also prepare their salesmen to talk in terms of the cash flow method in communicating the results of such an analysis to the prospective customer.

## Influence of price

Over short-run periods, the demand for many industrial products is likely to show a reverse elasticity.

*Materials, components, and supplies.* Ordinarily, when the price of an article declines, its demand tends to increase; when its price advances, the demand for it tends to fall. In the short run precisely the reverse is true of many industrial materials and some supplies. This is probably due largely to the training and experience of most buyers. When the price of a material declines, a purchasing agent is likely to withdraw from the market to the extent his inventory position and policy will permit, until he has an opportunity to study the situation and decide whether in his opinion the decline is merely a temporary fluctuation or represents the beginning of a continued downward trend. This means that even a small price decline sometimes has the effect of drying up demand for a time until the general market situation clarifies. If the market condition remains uncertain, buyers are likely to purchase from hand to mouth until it becomes more settled.

If the price of a material advances, however, the careful buyer is likely to wonder whether the increase portends the beginning of a general advance. If he concludes that this is the case, he is apt to make more than usually heavy commitments for his firm. The executive charged with the buying work of an industrial concern always looks good to his management when during a period of advancing prices the firm is able to use materials bought at lower price levels, and when during a period of falling prices the concern is able to use goods bought at current, or nearly current, prices. The resulting beneficial effect on the company cost structure lends flexibility to the firm's pricing practices for its end products.

These observations as to the reverse elasticity of industrial demand apply more accurately to the sum total of a given material sold than to the amount disposed of by an individual supplier, and to general price fluctuations more than to those of a single seller. For example, when the price of a standardized material declines slightly or one supplier lowers his price, purchasing agents who must buy to maintain stocks are likely to divert their purchases to those sources offering the lowest prices, and at the same time shrink the amount of their total commitments while studying the market. Therefore, a decline in the price of a single supplier may increase his sales while diminishing those of competing sellers by an amount in excess of that diverted to the price-cutting supplier.

It should also be understood that this observation applies almost entirely to the short-run behavior of demand. Over the long run, a decline in the price of a material whose purchase cost constitutes a primary factor in the expense structure of concerns using it is likely to increase the total sales of that article, since such a cost reduction is apt to make possible a decrease in the price of the goods made of the material and, in turn, increase the demand for them. This effect is limited in its scope, because comparatively few materials play such a large role in the cost structure of their end products that a reduction in their prices, in the proportions likely to occur, will make possible any significant decrease in the end product prices. In order to cause any appreciable effect on the price of an end product, moreover, the reduction in the price of its primary material must usually extend over a long period.

To repeat, the price change responsiveness of the overall demand for an industrial material depends to some degree on how important its price is as an element in the general cost structure of the using firm or of its end product. If the cost of a material represents a significant element in the cost structure of the average using firm or of its end product, a lowering of its price is apt to cause enough saving in the cost of the end product to make possible a reduction in its price, with a resulting increase in the demand for both the end product and its primary material. If, on the other hand, the cost of a material constitutes only a small fraction, say a few percent of the end product cost, a shift in its price may make a change in the end-product cost so small that no significant movement in the end-product price is justified, and there will be little or no shift in overall demand for the material.

If a product is of minor importance to the buyer, a shift in the price of a single supplier is likely to cause little change in the volume he sells. The small differential involved may easily be nullified by slight savings in inventory carrying charges made possible by the superior services of the regular supplier or by the added costs of buying such a product separately instead of as part of a large order from the regular supplier, whose price remains unchanged.

When quality or consistency of quality in materials and components is a matter of prime importance but not easily checked, demand responds very little to changes in the price of any individual supplier. For example, a customer who experiences good results in the use of a complex chemical or electronic part made by one supplier is not apt to shift readily to a new source simply because the new one offers a lower price. The buyer is likely to fear that imperceptibly slight or hidden differences in the essential properties of the two items will cause undesirable changes in the performance of his end product. A drastic price reduction may even rouse suspicions that the price-cutter has debased quality in some way that is not readily apparent. By contrast, demand for materials bought and sold on the basis of recognized standards tends to respond more actively to price changes by individual suppliers.

*Major and minor equipment.* On the whole, the demand for equipment is likely to be less responsive to shifts in price than that for materials, supplies, and components. Equipment price usually appears in the cost structure of the end product either as an element in factory overhead, which includes other items that cannot readily be identified with the product, or as a general depreciation figure. Both these figures usually include the capital charges on a number of machines, and are allocated on some basis that appears reasonable to the cost accounting executives. Therefore, it is a remote likelihood that a price reduction for a given piece of equipment will cause an end product cost reduction big enough to make possible a general price cut, with a resulting increase in demand for the end product and, eventually, for the equipment. Such a chain of causation may occur, but it is not common. It is more likely to happen with single-purpose, special machines than with multi-purpose machines whose capital charges are apt to be spread over the costs of many end products.

Even changes in an individual equipment marketer's price are not likely to bring about proportionate changes in the demand for his goods. Costs of operation, repair, and maintenance, precise suitability for the job, ease of adjustment, speed and productivity of operation, and other similar considerations are fully as important as, if not more important than, price in influencing patronage. Moreover, the buyer often prefers to use machines all of one make to perform one sequence of operations or to equip one unit of his shop. This preference may be due to the way their functions dovetail, because such an arrangement facilitates repairs and lessens downtime or because the stock of repair parts needed is reduced. Some equipment makers have capitalized on this tendency of buyers by selling packages of machines, each containing the units necessary to equip a certain type of shop or to perform a closely related group of operations. Undoubtedly, the machines in such a package are often made to function better when they are all used together than when tools of other makers are interspersed among them.

For these and other reasons, demand for industrial products—both on an industry-wide basis and on the basis of the individual maker—is usually sticky in its response to price change.

## SUMMARY

In this chapter we have discussed two sets of factors that shape the behavior of demand for industrial goods. One of these is the variation in the nature and uses of products themselves, whether they are items of major equipment, component parts, process materials, operating supplies, or raw materials. The other set of factors are those which affect the indirect way in which the need for industrial goods arises. Among the most important of these influences are business conditions, the nature of the ultimate buyer, financial conditions, and price. Together, these conditions describe the context in which buyer behavior takes place.

# 4

# THE INDUSTRIAL CUSTOMER

In ADDITION to its derived or indirect nature and the number of product-market levels at which it exists, demand for industrial goods is also characterized by a measure of economic objectivity stemming from the nature of the industrial customer. Of those who have anything to do with a business, the customer is the most important. All others are expendable. He is not. The business which offers him the goods he needs and wants, at prices he regards as reasonable, with services that facilitate his purchase and use of them, purveyed by methods that conform to the way he wants to buy has a good chance of success. The business which lacks any or all of these advantages suffers a very real competitive handicap.

## BUYER MOTIVES[1]

Unlike the ultimate consumer, the industrial buyer is motivated by budgetary considerations such as profit goals, expense quotas, and cost-benefit guidelines. He must be prepared to justify his purchases on the basis of measurable performance. Consequently, the considerations which influence the professional buyer's decision to patronize one supplier rather than another tend to be quality, service, and price—frequently in that order. These are not the only variables weighed by professional buyers, as later discussion will reveal, but they are undoubtedly the most common ones.

---

[1] For the reader who might wish to pursue this topic further the following references are suggested: Patrick J. Robinson and Charles W. Faris, *Industrial Buying and Creative Marketing* (Boston: Allyn & Bacon, Inc., 1967); Frederick E. Webster, Jr., and Yoram Wind, *Organizational Buying Behavior* (Englewood Cliffs, N.J.: Prentice-Hall, Inc., 1972); Theodore Levitt, *Industrial Purchasing Behavior* (Boston: Harvard Business School, 1965); Michiel R. Leenders, *Improving Purchasing Effectiveness Through Supplier Development* (Boston: Harvard Business School, 1965).

## The core variables: Quality, service, price

Although the seller's quality, service, and price—along with other considerations—are typically evaluated by the customer as a package, with the possibility of trade-offs among them, they will be treated separately here for the sake of simplicity.

*Quality.* The professional buyer tends to define product quality as that combination of properties which fits the product to its intended use. He probably wants these properties to be present in the product in precisely the degree needed to suit its purpose and no more. He is almost as reluctant to pay for extra quality (over and above a reasonable safety factor) that he does not need as he is to buy goods of inferior quality. And he is likely to feel that if unneeded quality is there, he pays for it regardless of the price. Obviously, any property of a product which enhances the life expectancy of another product with which it is used, or otherwise increases the value of that product to its ultimate buyer, is a significant quality factor.

A consideration inseparably related to product quality is the supplier's ability to deliver materials, components, and supplies of consistent quality. Assured consistency of quality can have important benefits for the buyer-user. It can reduce the need for meticulous and costly inspection and testing of incoming shipments. It does much to assure that the end product will be of uniform quality. For some materials, consistency of quality diminishes shutdown time and repair costs for delicate machines unable to handle materials of varying quality without adjustment, or machines that may be damaged by imperfections in the materials processed on them.

Consistency in product quality may also enable the customer to save on inventory, because if different shipments from the same source vary widely in quality, the buyer must carry enough stock to permit inspection, rejection, and replacement of a shipment without shutting down his operation. The degree of consistency in quality needed by a customer, as well as the range of tolerance permitted in quality standards, can usually be determined by a study of the customer's production system or other appropriate operating system.

*Service.* Businesses, governments, and institutions need a variety of services in addition to products and materials. The most common types of service requested are technical, replacement parts, delivery, information, and sales.

Problems of a technical nature are quite common wherever equipment, materials, and components are in use. Some vendors rely on their salesmen to provide the expert help users need to solve these problems. Other suppliers buttress their sales force with a cadre of trained specialists to whom salesmen or customers can refer difficult problems, or from whom they can get advice and consultation in handling them.

Still others supply their customers with written material they hope will enable the customer himself to handle all but the most complex and difficult technical use problems. For example, the Diamond Alkali Company distributed in one year some 8,000 copies of its *Chlorine Handbook,* 4,000 copies of its *Chromium Chemical Handbook,* and 8,000 copies of its *Silicates Handbook,* containing highly detailed technical information about the properties and uses of those types of chemicals.

The customer who has learned to rely on the technical advice and assistance of an industrial marketer in solving his materials-use problems may be hard to win away from that supplier by the appeals of a competitor. One such problem unsolved or improperly solved may cost the buyer much more than the savings resulting from a lower price offered by another source.

The availability of replacement parts for machinery and equipment is another vital concern to many businesses, government agencies, and institutions. Many equipment users prefer to make their own repairs, because by doing so they can save shutdown time of machines that affect the operation of an entire production complex, such as an assembly line or a processing group. Some of them maintain special shops within the plant for this purpose. Such plants generally carry stocks of parts from which they can draw to make repairs. Sometimes, such stocks include only the parts that must be replaced most frequently. Other firms carry standby machines to be used in case of breakdowns, and order parts as needed. The result is that no small fraction of the parts business is conducted in an emergency atmosphere. For these reasons, speed is a vital element in the service of supplying parts and replacements.

An added factor emphasizing the importance of speed is that even though the need for any part may occur very rarely, its timing is highly unpredictable and it is very urgent when it happens. The result is that a user who wants to be able to repair any breakdown that may occur must carry many parts he may not need for years and some he will never need. Thus, inventory is very high in relation to use. One firm found that in order to avoid shutdowns and stoppages of production it was forced to carry at all times about one and one half times the value of the parts it used annually.

An organization can reduce these uncertainties by preventive maintenance, but it cannot eliminate them. The size of the inventory the user must carry to supply his erratic needs will be materially reduced if his supplier offers a parts service which features:

1.  Adequate and representative warehouse stocks at points convenient to using centers backed by adequate factory stocks.
2.  Prompt handling and delivery of all orders.
3.  Reliable delivery information and promises.
4.  Willingness to give service out of the ordinary routine in emergencies.

The availability of replacement parts when needed, as well as that of any other needed material or product, is clearly dependent on the speed and certainty of a supplier's delivery service. The benefits accruing to the customer from speedy and reliable delivery are ones he can easily calculate in dollars and cents. The speedier and the more reliable the delivery service, the smaller the required investment in inventory. If a supplier's delivery service is erratic, the customer must base his inventory on the longest-experienced lead time between the ordering and the receipt of goods. While there is a trade-off between speed and reliability, a supplier whose delivery service is slower but more certain than that of his competitors is often preferred.

A service in almost universal demand by industrial customers is that of information about products and vendors' services as well as information about the trade or industry. In the course of visiting many firms in an industry, salesmen acquire facts about general trends, new developments, changes in personnel, and other trade information of interest to buyers. In many respects, salesmen serve as the eyes and ears of buyers on whom they call, and buyers usually appreciate the well-informed salesmen who can provide them with a variety of information of value to their firms.

*Price.* Professional buyers seldom rely solely on a vendor's quoted prices. They are much more concerned with what is often referred to as the *evaluated price.* This takes into consideration a variety of factors, such as the amount of scrap or waste resulting from the use of a material, the costs of processing the material, the amount of work a machine will do, the power it consumes, loss or damage liability, and a host of other variables that generate or minimize costs. For example, the price of a paint may be low, but it may be costly to apply. The coal with a low price per ton may be high in volatile material, ash, or fusable elements and low in Btu's. Steel is cheaper than aluminum; yet in many areas of the nation, particularly where rough terrain predominates, utility companies erect more aluminum high-voltage transmission towers than steel ones. The aluminum towers are not only cheaper to erect (by helicopter) but, being impervious to most elements of the weather, are cheaper to maintain.

The moral of the discussion is that the comparison of suppliers' price quotations is not the relatively simple matching process assumed in economic theory. It is a much more complicated process, involving factors peculiar to the operating systems of the customer. They are in large measure hidden from the supplier who makes no persistent investigative effort to discover them.

## Savings

Aside from the best combination of quality, service, and price, the industrial customer is also motivated to realize savings in the use of materials and equipment or in the methods by which they are procured. This motivation is especially pronounced in periods of accelerating costs.

The most obvious places professional buyers look for savings are in the substitution of materials and new types of equipment. Finding materials which possess the same properties as those in use but which are easier to process (higher output), safer to use (lower insurance rates), or cheaper to transport (less infreight) produce measurable savings. New types of equipment which will save labor through higher output per hour or per operator or will be cheaper to operate or maintain than present equipment is always attractive. The professional buyer is also sensitive to such intangibles as supplier-developed programs which can assist his company with perennial trouble spots like production scheduling, inventory control, and safety. The passage in 1970 of the Federal Occupational Safety and Health Act (OSHA) has elevated safety to an issue of major concern and made buyers sensitive to any purchase that might affect it.

Purchasing departments are under some internal pressure to produce measurable savings as a result of their activities. If they cannot, existence of the department is likely to be challenged by others who regard it as unnecessary. At best, a purchasing department which could not show significant savings over a reasonable period of time would be in danger of being downgraded to little more than a clerical function.

## Assurance of supply

Assurance of supply is vital to the purchasing officer. If the supply flow of an item is interrupted, probable resulting shortages may cause shutdowns of production operations. When a shortage threatens, the buyer may be able to avoid a shutdown by purchasing emergency orders from suppliers with whom he does not ordinarily deal, but such orders are apt to be expensive.

In spite of all that any supplier can do, his flow of goods to customers may be interrupted by strikes, accidents, fire, or natural catastrophies, such as floods, storms, or snow. Thus, no buyer can be even reasonably sure of continuity of supply so long as he purchases entirely from one supplier. Of course, if a material or component or machine is made to the buyer's individual specifications, and especially if its manufacture requires special machinery and has a long production cycle, he usually has little choice. He must rely on one supplier.

In the absence of such limiting factors, the purchasing officer is likely to buy an article from at least two suppliers, splitting his business between them. One probably will be preferred and will get the lion's share, but neither can get all of it. This is a matter of very great importance to the industrial goods marketer, since it limits not only the amount of business he can get from any one customer, but also the share of the total market he can hope to capture.

Usually, the purchasing officer administers this policy on the basis of individual items. Some buyers apply it across the board by establishing a maximum dollar amount they will purchase from any one supplier. This is not a particularly intelligent practice, since it limits the buyer's use of a good supplier who is highly diversified, and it discourages the vendor from improving his existing products and creating new ones.

It behooves the industrial marketing manager to try to learn the policies his most important customers follow in seeking continuity of supply and to plan his operations in conformity with them. Otherwise, he may waste time, money, and effort in reaching for volume that he simply cannot get.

## Buyer temperament

During recent years there has been much discussion of the part which nonrational factors play in industrial purchasing. Spectacular cases have been cited, such as the remark by a purchasing officer, "I wouldn't buy from that company because its salesman doesn't know when to end a call," and the case of the president of a firm who, fancying that he was snubbed at a convention by the president of his chief supplier, decreed that there would be no purchases from that firm. Some students have engaged in elaborate psychological transformations of economic into personal supplier selection motives, such as interpreting late delivery as a lack of supplier interest in the buyer's business and so an attack on the status and pride of the purchasing officer.

There can be no doubt that the purchasing officer is a human being before he is a purchasing officer; and the same is true of the other functional executives who influence buying. Each of them is interested in his own status, prestige, ambitions, and personal feelings, as well as in the welfare of the firm for which he works. Much of the time he may put his own interests ahead of those of the firm. But this does not necessarily mean that personal considerations dictate the majority of his buying decisions. In fact, the opposite may be true; his personal interests may point in the direction of his using economic motives in making such decisions.

One of the chief motives of a buying officer, or an executive with buying interest, is the preservation and enrichment of his own personal and functional status. Another is his ambition to be promoted. Another is his personal feelings towards the men with whom he works, such as his fellow executives and suppliers' salesmen. In the vast majority of buying situations the best way to serve the interest of status and ambition is to make the purchase that is the best economically for his firm. If he fails to do so consistently, he is liable in due course to have neither status nor promotion possibilities to worry about.

Since we tend to close our minds to people we do not like, it is undoubtedly true that the typical purchasing or buying influence executive finds it hard, if not impossible, to listen sympathetically or with understanding to the conversation of a salesman he does not like. Also it is true that when there is a clash of personalities within a buying firm, Executive A may oppose a course of action simply because B favors it. But this is a process that can readily prove self-defeating; for if the course of action involved is the right one economically, A may very well lose prestige and standing to B as a result of his behavior.

It is probably true that the personal feelings and emotions of purchasing officers and buying influence executives affect their business decisions. But their effect would seem to be not so much to subtract from the influence of economic considerations in the making of purchase decisions as to shift the relative emphasis that is placed on the different economic buying motives. It is probably true that the economic buying motives supply a rather rigid set of limitations within which personal or emotional motives act in influencing purchases rather than the reverse. After all, the safest thing to do in a buying situation is to make a purchase that can be justified on sound economic grounds.

## The special case of purchasing by public institutions

Purchasing by public institutions, such as state and local governments, school districts, and universities is influenced by legal constraints which can affect buying decisions in ways unrelated to the conditions discussed in the preceding paragraphs. One of the most common of these constraints is that regarding sealed bids. Many items purchased by public institutions must be selected on the basis of competitive bids. If a bid is not received by the indicated deadline, it must often be declared invalid and the bidder disqualified from competition regardless of his price, service, performance record, or the merits of his product. Another stipulation commonly associated with compulsory bidding is the requirement that each bid must be accompanied by a deposit. This is required for the purpose of discouraging bidding by financially weak or irresponsible firms and to assure that those which do bid will honor their quotations. A failure on the part of a bidder to include the required amount of deposit *with* his bid disqualifies him from consideration regardless of what he may be able to offer.

A number of states recently have added specific requirements concerning affirmative action programs in their legislation governing purchases by public institutions. Such legislation typically requires that any firm supplying a tax-supported institution in the state adopt a set of result-oriented affirmative action procedures in its hiring practices. These procedures are designed to bring (or maintain) the employment of minority groups in the firm to an acceptable level. Under most circumstances, it is not enough that the firm employs minority groups and women. The firm must have an acceptable Affirmative Action Program, i.e., one which conforms to the stipulations of the law. Without such a program a firm could be disqualified as a supplier even though it met all other stipulations of the law and was the lowest bidder.

## BUYER CHARACTERISTICS

The most meaningful way to characterize industrial customers is in terms of the different types of organization they represent, their size distribution, number, and geographical location. From the viewpoint of the marketer, an equally significant buyer characteristic is the way in which the procurement function is structured within the organization.

### Customer types

Industrial customers have already been broadly identified as businesses, institutions, and governmental units. Businesses include such diverse types of enterprises as manufacturers, construction firms, commercial establishments (retailers and wholesalers who buy equipment and supplies for use), transportation companies, service companies (hotels, laundries, and recreational enterprises), and certain professional groups (doctors and dentists). The most important of these various business customers are manufacturers. Probably next in importance in terms of volume of purchases are construction firms, followed by service companies, transportation companies, and commercial establishments, approximately in that order.

While manufacturing, construction, service, and transportation companies buy all kinds of industrial goods, commercial establishment purchases are confined largely to furniture and fixtures, cleaning and packaging materials, office supplies, and business machines and their accessories. Aside from office and other categories of supplies, purchases by the professional group are limited to specialized types of equipment. The same is true to a lesser extent of institutional buyers, although educational institutions are likely to have broader and more varied needs than other institutions.

Units of government may be divided into (1) departments of federal, state, and local governments and (2) administrative units, such as school districts and sanitary districts. Administrative units enjoy a substantial degree of independence in allocating purchases. Also included in the government category are the government-created, autonomous agencies, such as the Tennessee Valley Authority and the Port of New York Authority. As a result of rising expenditures for defense and the expansion of government into areas formerly reserved to private enterprise, the importance of governmental units in the market for industrial goods has increased at an accelerated pace over the past several decades.

## Buyer population

The basic unit for classifying nonmanufacturing businesses and institutions is the reporting unit. A reporting unit is generally a single establishment or a group of similar establishments under one control. It is an operating entity, which the Census Bureau counts once in each county in which it operates. Thus, all nonmanufacturing establishments that belong to a given firm are grouped into a single reporting unit if they are in the same county and engaged in the same kind of business.

Manufacturing businesses are classified on the basis of establishments, each representing an economic unit that produces goods or renders services, such as a mine, a factory, or a shop. An establishment is characterized by physical location, distinctive activity, and reportability. It is not identical with a business firm or legal entity, since either might consist of more than one establishment. In those cases the number of reporting units is smaller than the number of establishments and the average size of a reporting unit is larger. However, since the purpose here is not to compare one category with another but to present a general picture of the industrial market, lack of comparability between manufacturers and nonmanufacturers does not impair the usefulness of data on reporting units.

The number of reporting units in the industrial market and the general categories to which they belong are given below.

| Industry category | Number of reporting units |
|---|---|
| Agriculture, forestry, and fisheries | 31,418 |
| Contract construction | 296,094 |
| Finance, insurance, and real estate | 320,856 |
| Manufacturing | 290,966 |
| Mining | 23,100 |
| Retailing and wholesaling | 1,319,984 |
| Services | 989,523 |
| Transportation, communication and other public utilities | 127,751 |
| Unclassified establishments* | 111,475 |

* Includes reporting units that could not be classified in any major industry group because of insufficient information, as well as all institutions not included in other categories but covered by the Federal Insurance Contribution Act.

Source: *County Business Patterns*, United States Summary (1971).

Government buyers of industrial goods include not only procurement departments of the federal government but also about 4,500 agencies of states, counties, and cities of more than 10,000 population.[2] This omits many subsidiary governmental organizations, such as school districts, sanitary districts, and the like, which also buy industrial goods.

---

[2] *Census of Governments,* U.S. Department of Commerce (1967).

## Size distribution

Industrial buyers vary widely in size from the alley machine shops with no employees or a small municipality governed by a town board to such giant organizations as the General Motors Corporation or the Department of Defense. Although the industrial market is not one market but many, an important aspect of any market or market segment is the size distribution of buying units included in it. An awareness of the variations in size of at least the major categories of industrial buyers is basic to an understanding of the problems in serving them efficiently.

There are several ways of measuring size, but unfortunately the best way is not always a practical one because of the paucity of data. The most readily available measure and the one used here is number of employees. Where other more appropriate measures are available, such as value added in the case of manufacturers, these will also be used.

As indicated in Table 4–1, about 61 percent of all manufacturers have

**TABLE 4–1.  Size distribution of industrial buyers by industry**

| | Percent of total reporting units by employment-size class* | | | | |
|---|---|---|---|---|---|
| | Less than 20 | 20 to 49 | 50 to 99 | 100 to 499 | 500 or more |
| Agricultural services, forestry, and fisheries | 94 | 4 | 1 | 0 | 0 |
| Contract construction | 90 | 7 | 2 | 1 | 0 |
| Finance, insurance, and real estate | 91 | 6 | 2 | 1 | 0 |
| Manufacturing | 61 | 18 | 9 | 10 | 2 |
| Mining | 80 | 10 | 5 | 4 | 1 |
| Retail and wholesale trade | 90 | 7 | 2 | 1 | 0 |
| Services | 91 | 5 | 2 | 1 | 0 |
| Transportation and other public utilities | 80 | 12 | 4 | 3 | 1 |
| Unclassified establishments | 97 | 3 | 0 | 0 | 0 |

* Percentages computed by authors. Totals may not equal 100 due to rounding.
Source: *County Business Patterns*, United States Summary (1971).

fewer than 20 employees, while only about 12 percent have more than 100 employees. In contrast, 80 percent or more of the reporting units in all other industries have fewer than 20 employees, and with the exception of the mining and transportation categories, 90 percent of the nonmanufacturing reporting units are in this size class.

No equally comprehensive data such as sales volume or value of purchases is available for measuring the size distribution of all industrial buyers. However, considerable information is available on one of the most important categories of industrial buyers—manufacturers. For example, data are available for manufacturers on value added by manufacturing, a more meaningful index of size than either employment or value of sales. It is interesting to note that in 1970 35 percent (102,701 reporting units) of the total number of manufacturers had an annual value added of less than $500,000 per unit, on the average, while about 13 percent of the total (39,702 reporting units) had an average value added in excess of $2 million.[3] This means that most manufacturing establishments fall into a relatively narrow range of size from $500,000 to about $2 million in value added per establishment.

## Geographical concentration

The manufacturers' part of the industrial market is also concentrated geographically, as indicated by the fact that 14 states in the northeastern and north central part of the nation account for about 56 percent of the total value added by manufacturing and about 53 percent of the total value of shipments by manufacturers. No more than 18 states contributed 74 percent of the total value added by manufacturing in 1970 and 64 percent of the total value of manufacturers' shipments in 1970.[4]

From the marketing viewpoint the most meaningful measure of the degree of concentration is in terms of value of purchases. The total value of purchases by U.S. manufacturers in 1970 was slightly more than $332 billions. Over one half of this amount, $189 billions, was accounted for by manufacturing establishments in 12 states. Those in 6 other states accounted for an additional $16 billions in purchases.[5]

An even more striking indication of the concentration of industrial customers is given by county employment statistics. No more than 15 of the 3,000 odd counties in the nation have 23 percent of the total number of employees in the United States.[6]

Other classes of industrial buyers, such as state and local governments and institutions tend to follow the distribution of the populace they serve. Although data concerning the geographical distribution of these buyers is neither plentiful nor very specific, it is to be expected that the largest and most important of their number will be found in the population centers and the smallest in the more sparsely populated areas. Therefore, one would expect to find the largest of the nonmanufacturing buyers in New York, California, Pennsylvania, Illinois, Ohio, Texas, Michigan, New Jersey, Massachusetts, Florida, and Indiana—the 11 states in which over one half of our population resides.[7]

---

[3] *Annual Survey of Manufacturers* (1970). Percentages computed.

[4] *Annual Survey of Manufacturers* (1970).

[5] Ibid.

[6] *County Business Patterns* (1971).

[7] U.S. Census of Population, 1970.

**FIGURE 4-1.** Geographical concentration of industrial and commercial employment, 1972

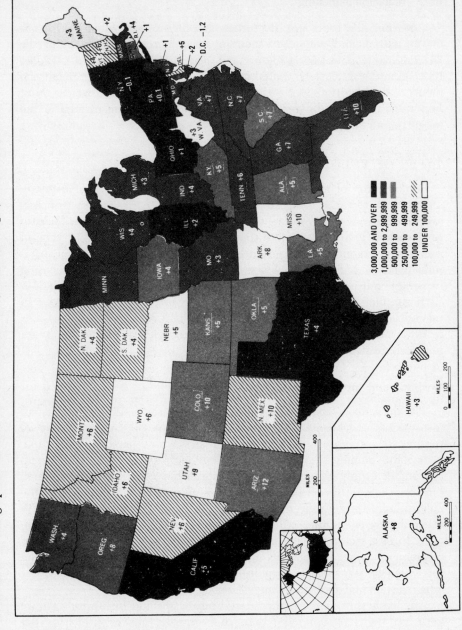

3,000,000 AND OVER
1,000,000 to 2,999,999
500,000 to 999,999
250,000 to 499,999
100,000 to 249,999
UNDER 100,000

Source: U.S. Department of Commerce, Social and Economic Statistics Administration, Bureau of the Census, 1973.

Governmental units and institutions are, of course, located in all parts of the nation, and with the exception of procurement agencies of the federal government their geographical distribution, at least on a volume basis, is probably closely related to that of the population. Since governments and institutions serve the populace, it is probable that the most important industrial buyers of this type tend to be concentrated in the major population centers.

## TYPES OF PURCHASING ORGANIZATION

Organization of the procurement function has striking similarities in all types of operations, regardless of the nature of the buyer's principal activity. However, government purchasing has certain unique features that warrant giving it separate treatment in this discussion. The type of purchasing organization required by business and institutional buyers is influenced by such factors as size of operation, the place of purchasing in the overall organizational structure, and policy concerning relations with suppliers. The type of purchasing organization used by governmental bodies is essentially determined by the level of government—i.e., federal, state, or local—and the size and complexity of the unit's administrative structure.

### Business and institutional buyers

*The influence of size.* The volume of purchases made by many small institutional and business buyers, i.e., those employing no more than 20 persons, is probably not great enough to warrant personnel who specialize in buying. Purchases by manufacturers in this size group amounted to only about $70,000 per establishment in 1967.[8] Such small buyers may well have a one-man purchasing operation conducted by the chief administrative officer or delegated in whole or in part, along with other duties, to another official such as a shop foreman or office manager. In either case, buying is likely to be a part-time activity relegated to moments when the officer's attention is not required by the function for which he is primarily responsible. As indicated by Table 4–1, most nongovernmental industrial buyers belong to this category.

It is likely that many medium-sized businesses and institutions (those with less than 100 but more than 20 employees) have purchasing departments but employ no more than two or three persons in each of them. Since buying is seldom confined to the purchasing department, even in many large firms, it is likely that a small unit could satisfy the needs of most medium-sized establishments.

Among larger establishments, i.e., those with 250 or more employees

---

[8] *Census of Manufactures,* Vol. 1, Summary and Subject Statistics, 1971. Purchases computed by subtracting value added from value of shipments.

each, probably all have some form of specialized purchasing staff. Although details of organization vary substantially from one enterprise to another, some generalization about departmental organization is possible. The most common pattern is that of specialized buyers under the general supervision of a chief purchasing officer who is concerned with policy making and other administrative matters as well as with buying. Generally speaking, a buyer is assigned to a specific commodity or group of commodities for which he is responsible. This responsibility usually includes selecting suppliers, placing orders, and expediting shipment, and may enbrace other activities related to the purchasing function, such as value analysis, inspection of incoming shipments, and control of inventory. (See Figure 4–2.)

**FIGURE 4–2.  Internal organization of a purchasing department**

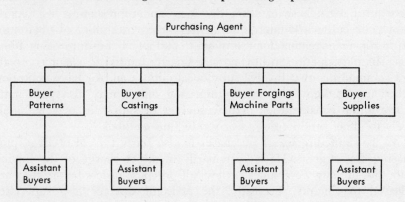

The allocation of commodities to different buyers is commonly made on the basis of similar physical characteristics (castings, machine parts, nonferrous metals) or of use characteristics (operating supplies and raw materials) or major source of supply. In the last instance, all items normally purchased through merchant wholesalers, for example, might be assigned to one buyer, while those bought through agents and brokers would be asgined to another, and anything purchased directly from manufacturers to a third.

Of course, numerous modifications of this general pattern are dictated by local conditions. A firm may use a single commodity in such volume that success or failure depends in large part on its proper purchase. In such a case, a major executive may assume responsibility for its purchase, while other items continue to be bought through the purchasing department. Examples of such commodities might be textiles for clothing, leather for shoes, or grain for breakfast cereals. Administrative policy may permit using departments to specify brands or trademarks on requisitions. This severely limits the freedom of the buyer in filling requisitions.

When the volume of purchases has grown beyond the capacity of the simple organizational pattern depicted in Figure 4–2, it is no longer feasible for each buyer to be personally responsible for all the detailed procedures involved in purchase transactions. As a rule, buyers are relieved of the clerical and routine tasks, to permit them to become specialists in evaluation of quality, selection of vendors, and negotiations. Similarly, departmental activities such as value analysis, economic research, traffic and routing, and other special services are usually segregated and assigned to staff positions, which support buying operations.

The chief executive of a large purchasing department, often titled Director of Purchasing, is more concerned with policy and other administrative duties than with the actual work of buying. He may be responsible for trade relations, coordinating purchasing policies and procedures with those of other divisions, and representing his department at executive and interdepartmental meetings, and may be responsible to top management for the overall conduct of the purchasing function. His participation in buying is ordinarily limited to major contracts and commodities that involve substantial outlays and/or have important policy implications. The chief purchasing officer may also participate in the initial consideration of new sources of supply or new materials likely to affect product design or production methods.

An assistant director of purchases is also fairly typical of large purchasing departments. He is customarily in direct charge of the buying staff, and in many companies reviews all purchase orders before they are released to vendors. Typically, the assistant director also supervises office services and any staff specialists who may have been appointed for traffic, value analyis, disposal and salvage of surplus and waste materials, follow-up, and expediting. (See Figure 4–3.) If inventory control is within the jurisdiction of the purchasing department, a stores manager also reports to the director of purchases, along with the assistant director. Generally speaking, such officers are line managers and are on the same organizational level.

For the most part, institutional purchasing departments are organized in a manner similar to those of industrial companies where the size of the operation makes it feasible to concentrate this activity within a single department. (See, for example, Figure 4–4.)

*Position in company organization.* Although substantial variations exist in individual cases, it is possible to identify several patterns of relationship between purchasing and other functional departments in businesses and institutions. In one pattern, the officer in charge of purchasing reports to the president or general manager, along with the heads of production, marketing, finance, personnel, and other functional departments. This pattern is commonly found in medium-sized firms and institutions. It is also found at the branch plants of companies in which

**FIGURE 4–3. Internal organization of a large purchasing department**

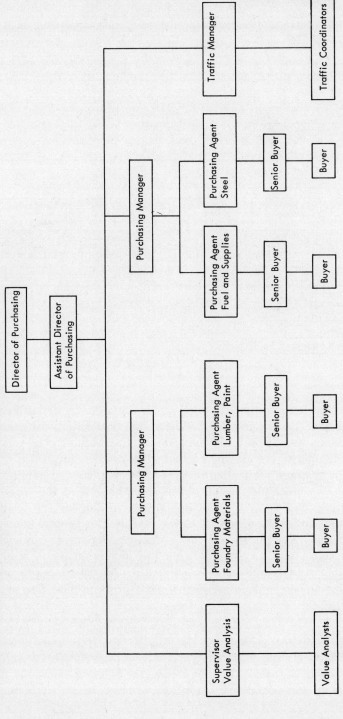

**FIGURE 4–4.** Internal organization of the purchasing department in a large educational institution

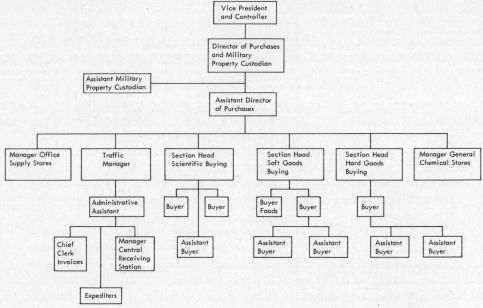

Courtesy of the Purchasing Diuision, University of Illinois.

purchasing is decentralized, with rather autonomous departments at the plant level. (See Figure 4–5.) Where this pattern prevails, the head of purchasing usually has sufficient status and authority to preclude the subordination of his activity to that of any other line function.

In large single-unit enterprises (or large plants of multiunit enterprises), the chief purchasing officer sometimes is in the second tier of executives, and reports to an operations, production, or financial vice president who, in turn, reports to the president or general manager. (See Figure 4–6.) The position of the purchasing department in such organizations tends to be a subordinate one in which emphasis is on service and support of a particular division rather than on materials procurement as an independent contributor to cost control or profits. This is less true

**FIGURE 4–5.** Company organization with purchasing department in first echelon

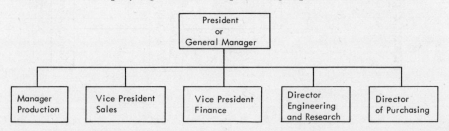

**FIGURE 4–6.** Company organization with purchasing department in second echelon

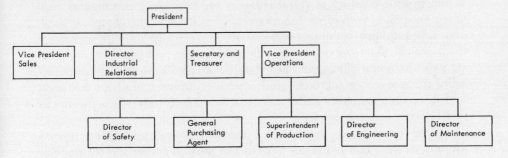

when the purchasing officer reports to a vice president of operations, along with the directors of manufacturing, engineering, and maintenance, for example, than when he reports to an executive responsible for production or finance.

As a rule, the purchasing department is placed under a financial executive, as in Figure 4–7, only in those companies in which top management places heavy emphasis on financial control. This may be done in a mistaken effort to avoid friction between operating divisions and purchasing or to concentrate financial responsibility as fully as possible in a single division of the company. Concentration of financial responsibility is sometimes sought by industrial firms that are primarily assemblers rather than manufacturers of the products they sell. In this instance, the cost of purchased materials is a very large share of the end cost of the finished product.

A third pattern characteristic of multiunit enterprises, particularly those whose various plants or divisions are in different industries, separates the operational and administrative phases of the purchasing function. Separate purchasing departments are established at the plant or division level, while a general purchasing department at company headquarters serves the entire organization in a staff capacity. (See Figure 4–8.) The headquarters purchasing staff ordinarily counsels top man-

**FIGURE 4–7.** Company organization with purchasing in second echelon

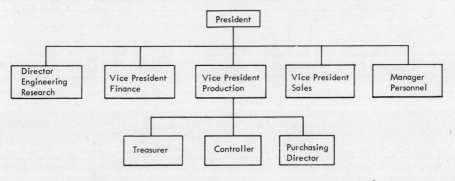

agement on procurement and materials policy, does research relevant to the overall conduct of purchasing in the company, coordinates procurement policy with other functional area policies at the company level, and may establish training programs for buyers and provide assistance to divisional departments on specific purchasing problems. In some instances, the home office purchasing staff may also have buying responsibility for major raw materials and capital equipment, and for items on which maximum quantity discounts can be earned only when the needs of all plants are consolidated.

At the plant level, the head of the purchasing unit often reports directly to the plant manager. Within the general framework of policies and procedures established by the home office, he usually has authority to procure all requirements of the plant in which he is located without approval from headquarters.

There are good reasons for branch plant autonomy with regard to the purchasing function in large multiplant companies. A substantial saving in inventory can often be achieved through a reduction in the time required to place and receive orders. Channeling orders through the home office in a large, diverse company usually consumes more time than placing them directly from the plant at which the requisition originates. A local purchasing official is usually more aware of local conditions that

**FIGURE 4–8.** **Multiplant company organization with divided purchasing responsibility**

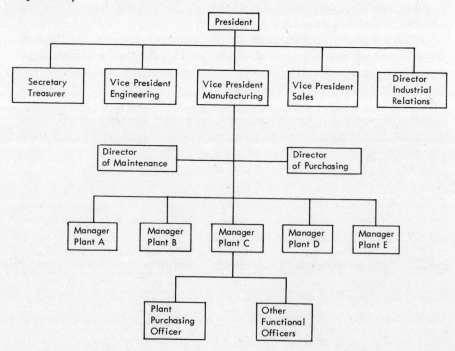

affect the speed and economy of procurement, such as transportation and storage facilities, climatic conditions, and local laws or customs, than are personnel at the home office. Then, too, if the branch plant manager is responsible for achieving a specific profit objective, he should logically have control over purchasing because of the effect of expenditures for material and equipment on plant operating costs.

*The influence of policy.* Since organization is a means, not an end, its characteristics reflect the nature of plans and policies to which management is committed. Plans for cooperative research with selected suppliers for improvement in cost and performance of purchased items requires personnel who know both the company's product needs and the technology of the products in question, and are free from the day-to-day routine of purchasing activity. This usually necessitates creation of a staff position to the head of the purchasing department, or a line position if product research (i.e., value analysis) is to be a continuing function of the purchasing department.

A policy of giving preference to local suppliers in a multiunit company often necessitates a certain amount of decentralization in the purchasing organization. The more widely dispersed are the plants and the more diverse the products they produce, the greater is the need for decentralization if local suppliers are to be favored without impairing the efficiency of procurement.

The policy with perhaps the most significant effect on organization of the purchasing function is that of reciprocity. This is particularly true of multiunit companies. The urge to select vendors on the basis of their value as present or potential customers is almost always present. It is greatly intensified during periods of depressed business activity, when every means of leverage may be exerted to make sales. The multiunit firm with a policy of encouraging reciprocity is usually obliged to center responsibility for selecting suppliers and placing orders at the home office. The home office purchasing staff is in the best position to determine how orders should be placed so as to derive the greatest sales benefit for the company as a whole. In a single unit firm, a policy of searching out reciprocal arrangements may reduce the purchasing department to a bookkeeping operation, since the sales department dictates placement of orders. As a result of frequent abuses of the practice, reciprocity is now frowned upon by the Federal Government. The Justice Department is proceeding against it and Congress may do so. Its influence on organization structure is likely to wane.

In multiunit companies, a policy of filling needs internally to the fullest extent possible also tends to centralize purchasing responsibility at the home office. Such a policy reduces the number of necessary plant-level purchasing decisions. Instead, a process of matching needs and resources internally is used. In this situation, purchasing becomes largely a clearinghouse operation. As a consequence, it can usually be carried out most expeditiously in the home office. A centralized purchasing staff is also often in the best position to place orders outside the company for needs that cannot be filled internally, since the final determination of which needs cannot be met internally must be made by central management.

A policy of meeting product needs internally also tends to de-emphasize the independence of the purchasing function in large single-unit companies. Depending on the extent to which make-or-buy decisions tend to favor making the needed product, the purchasing department will be placed under production or engineering rather than being made independent of these functions.

### Governmental buyers

Buyers for governmental departments and agencies belong either to federal or to state and local units. For the most part, governmental purchasing units are organized in a manner similar to those of businesses and institutions handling the same volume of orders. (See Figure 4–9.) There is, however, a greater emphasis on the clerical function in governmental purchases because of the more detailed procedures demanded by statutory requirements and a multiple authority relationship characteristic of government. The head of the purchasing department in a governmental unit frequently reports to a board of elected officials, who review and approve his decisions. Occasionally, however, the purchasing officer may be responsible to a city manager, a governor, or other official of comparable rank.

*Federal purchasing organization.* Purchases by the federal government are administered through four major types of offices: the General Services Administration, the purchasing offices of civilian departments and agencies, special purchasing agencies, and the Department of Defense. The General Services Administration was created in 1949 by the Federal Property and Administrative Services Act to direct and coordinate federal purchasing, as well as to centralize procurement of goods and services needed by the various branches of the federal government. The major procurement agency within the General Services Administration is the Bureau of Federal Supply.

While the various governmental departments may obtain their requirements by placing requisitions with Bureau of Federal Supply warehouses, they may also buy directly from suppliers by means of open-end contracts issued by the Bureau of Federal Supply. Departments with special requirements are also authorized to buy directly from suppliers on a bid basis. The departments of Agriculture and Commerce, the Veterans' Administration, the Federal Security Agency, the Federal Trade Commission, and the Tennessee Valley Authority are some of the units that buy directly from suppliers on a bid basis through their own

**FIGURE 4–9. Organization chart, department of purchasing contracts, and supplies, city of Chicago***

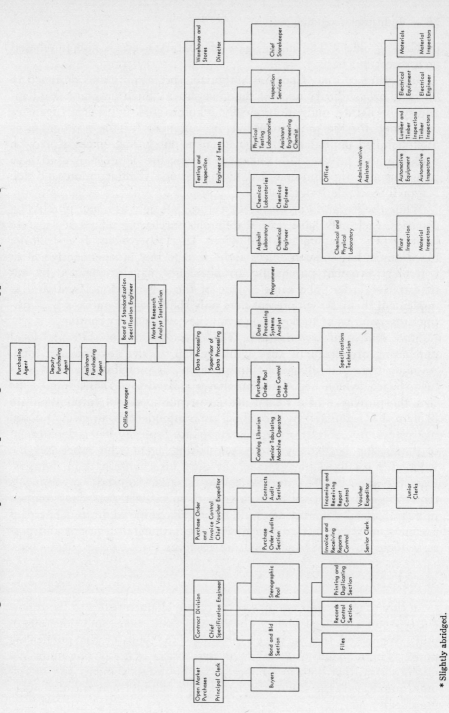

*Courtesy of John Ward, Purchasing Agent, City of Chicago.*

* Slightly abridged.

purchasing offices. The major share of military needs is also purchased on a direct bid basis.

From time to time, Congress authorizes special programs designed to fill some extraordinary need of the government. Such programs are temporary in nature and are typically administered by special agencies established for the purpose. While procurement for these programs is often handled through existing government purchasing offices, it may be made through private trade channels. Among the better known of these programs are the International Co-operation Administration and the National Stockpile Program.

While the *Federal Purchasing Directory* lists only 24 major purchasing agencies, each may have several different purchasing offices at separate locations, i.e., at regional or field offices. The Department of Agriculture, for example, has 18 such offices authorized to buy independently.[9] Most federal government purchasing arrangements may be changed by administrative order. The same is true of the organizational structure to implement them. So we present here only the broadest outlines with distinct reservations as to how long even they will remain constant.

*State and local organization.* The characteristics of state and local purchasing organizations vary with the size of the governmental unit. An unincorporated village of 500 inhabitants is probably governed by a town board, which negotiates purchases collectively. Depending on its size, the purchases of a school district or public school corporation are likely to be negotiated by the school superintendent or an elected board of trustees. By contrast, a large municipality typically has a department of purchasing headed by a city purchasing agent who supervises the work of specialized buyers much as does his counterpart in industry. (See Figure 4–9.) The purchasing organizations of state governments tend to resemble those of large cities, with specialized personnel grouped in a specialized department. Both are usually responsible to a board of accounts or city council, which reviews departmental decisions and possesses veto power over individual transactions.

## SUMMARY

In this chapter, we examined some of the characteristics of the different types of industrial buyers—businesses, institutions, and government units. We noted that in all classifications the bulk of the purchasing power is in the hands of a very small percentage of the buying units. We also observed that both in number of buying establishments and in volume purchased the industrial market is highly concentrated geographically.

We examined the organization of the purchasing function within the

---

[9] *Federal Purchasing, Specifications, and Sales Directory,* Small Business Administration, 1968.

using units. We found that in the typical small establishment the buying is done on a part-time, unspecialized basis. In the larger units, it is performed by a specialized department, with individual buyers handling special products or groups of products and staff men carrying on certain supporting activities, such as value analysis and expediting. In large multidivisional firms scattered geographically, we found various organizational arrangements designed to effect a working compromise between central control and the local autonomy of the operating branches, the most usual being a central policy-making and service group, with local units doing the actual buying. The buying organization of governmental units roughly parallels that of business concerns, with appropriate modifications to meet the legal requirements of government procurement work.

# 5

# PURCHASING SYSTEMS

Despite differences in the size and organization characteristics of industrial buying units, in the types of commodities purchased, or in the sources from which they are obtained, it is possible to identify elements common to the purchasing systems in use by many organizations. These elements can be divided into six general categories of activity: those pertaining to the recognition of need, those involved in the choice of means and sources to fill this need, the placement of the order, follow-up, invoice handling, and the receipt of items purchased. In one sense these activities are so obvious as to make any discussion of them appear pedantic. However, from the perspective of the marketer, the elements of the purchasing system are too important in the formulation of his strategy to treat them in a perfunctory manner.

## RECOGNITION OF NEED

Needs invariably emerge from using departments. However, their origin may not always be in the demands of manufacturing operations or the programmed replacement of worn and obsolete equipment. Needs may arise from the expansion of plant and facilities to capitalize on a favorable market position, from efforts to improve efficiency, from changes in existing products, and from new-product development. All these origins of need represent opportunities for creative marketing and are the kind of phenomena on which marketing intelligence should focus.

Since purchasing represents a service function, the purchasing system cannot be actuated until a need is recognized in some form of document authorizing buying action. The professional buyer commits his company's funds for items to be used by someone else in the firm. He must therefore insist upon an adequate and accurate description of what is needed as well as a clear identification of those requesting the purchase and authorizing the expenditure.

78

## Documentation

The actuating document may take several forms, such as a requisition, a bill of materials, an automatic reorder, or a budget. Familiarity with these documents is a small but significant constituent of the marketer's information base, because they affect the timing of purchases and indicate the manner in which they will be made. The nature of investigative efforts initiated in support of these documents also reveal to some degree the kind of services the buyer expects, the appeals likely to have the greatest influence, and the persons in the customer firm to whom appeals should be made.

***The requisition.*** This is probably the most common actuating form. It supplies a description of the items wanted by the using department along with specific directions concerning quality and quantity desired (see Figures 5–1 and 5–2). When signed by the appropriate official, the requisition empowers buying personnel to initiate action.

***The bill of materials.*** Establishments which manufacture products on order rather than for inventory probably recognize their needs in a

**FIGURE 5–1. General purchase requisition**

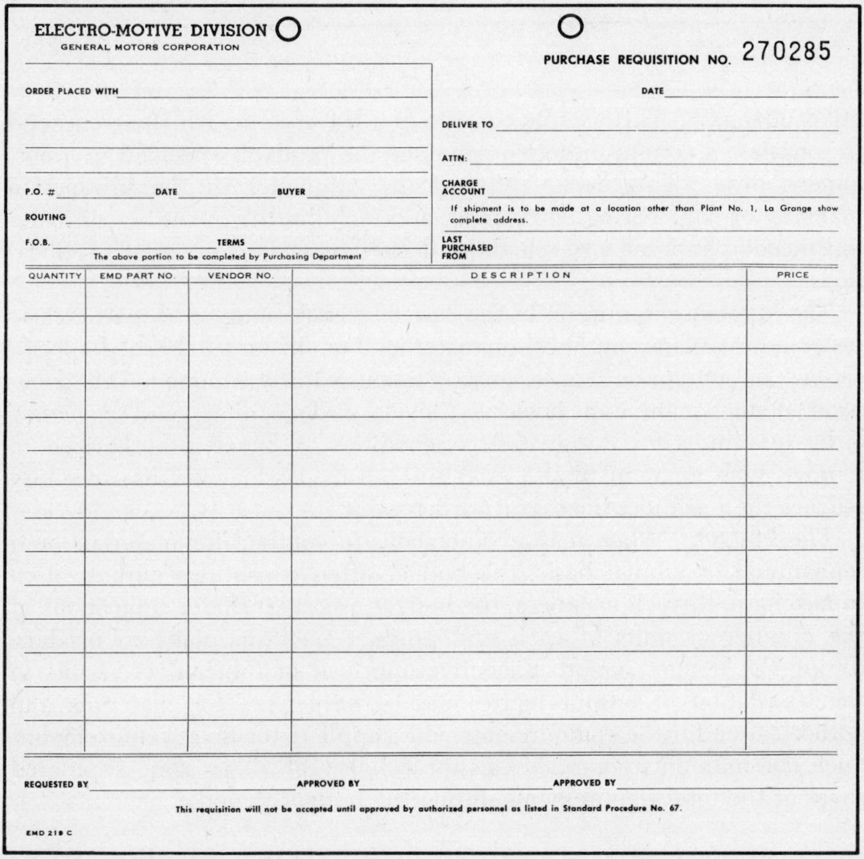

ELECTRO-MOTIVE DIVISION
GENERAL MOTORS CORPORATION

PURCHASE REQUISITION NO. 270285

ORDER PLACED WITH ____ DATE ____

DELIVER TO ____

ATTN: ____

P.O. # ____ DATE ____ BUYER ____ CHARGE ACCOUNT ____

If shipment is to be made at a location other than Plant No. 1, La Grange show complete address.

ROUTING ____

F.O.B. ____ TERMS ____ LAST PURCHASED FROM ____

The above portion to be completed by Purchasing Department

| QUANTITY | EMD PART NO. | VENDOR NO. | DESCRIPTION | PRICE |
|---|---|---|---|---|
| | | | | |

REQUESTED BY ____ APPROVED BY ____ APPROVED BY ____

This requisition will not be accepted until approved by authorized personnel as listed in Standard Procedure No. 67.

EMD 21• C

**FIGURE 5–2.   Production purchase requisition**

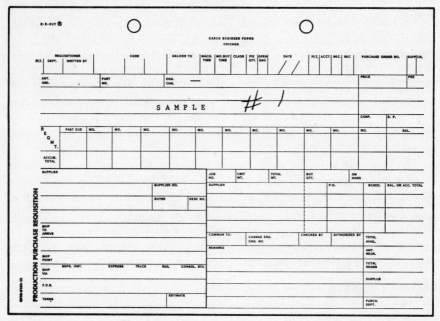

bill of materials. This usually consists of a list of items which are needed to complete a certain project or produce the products specified in a customer's order. This document typically originates in the production planning or engineering department and includes the quantities of materials needed and delivery schedules desired as well as material specifications.

*The automatic reorder.*   In the case of a continuing need, particularly for standard items, supplies, or materials bought on established specifications, an automatic reorder authorization is fairly common. This document defines minimum inventory levels, order points, and economic order quantities for designated commodities. A buyer is authorized to reorder such an item in the quantity specified whenever its inventory reaches the level identified as its order point.

*The budget.*   When it is advantageous to contract for materials on a semiannual or annual basis, the budget often constitutes authorization to purchase. In such instances, the budget usually includes projections of the number of units of each end product the firm plans to produce during the budget period. Executive approval of the budget results in the translation of output figures into requirements for materials and authorization for the commitments with suppliers for these requirements. Such commitments generally call for delivery of all or some stipulated share of the total requirements during the budget period.

## Supporting investigation

Translating need into formal documentation is more involved for major equipment than for most other purchases. Questions must be answered with respect to the best use of available capital funds, the desired rate of return on invested capital, alternative uses of available capital funds, operating costs, the effect on the company's tax liability, and technical service. Many of these questions can be answered only by top management, design or engineering specialists, or operating managers. Consequently, recognition of a need for capital equipment often involves an extended investigation of its urgency and of available ways in which it may be satisfied.

If it is decided to proceed to fill a need, the general type of installation and the operational requirements it will be expected to satisfy must be determined before any meaningful authorization to initiate procurement can be given to the purchasing department. These ends can often be served by conferences between design or engineering personnel and technicians of the using department, resulting in blueprints and specification sheets. With certain types of nonstandard machinery, however, it may be necessary to call on the assistance of potential suppliers to design prototypes of machines in order to arrive at the exact specifications desired.

In the purchase of a new item, the recognition and definition of need usually involve a number of the departments of a firm, such as engineering, finance, marketing, and production. A substantial amount of data verification and testing may also be required. Any modification of a routine purchase may involve much the same type of activity but to a lesser degree. In the case of a routine purchase, the supporting investigation is apt to be fairly simple. Expenses can be reduced by making it so.

## SORTING AND APPRAISING ALTERNATIVES

The alternatives available to most businesses, governmental agencies, and institutions in meeting their needs are to request bids from interested suppliers or to negotiate with them for the best combination of quality, service, and price. Most manufacturing concerns have a third alternative—to produce the needed items themselves.

### Competitive bids

A very substantial volume of both standard and special items is purchased on the basis of competitive bids. Government units and most public institutions are required to purchase on the bid system. Under the governmental system, a contemplated purchase is advertised well in advance so that any interested supplier may have time to submit a bid.

82    Industrial marketing

**FIGURE 5–3.  Request for quotation**

After a set date, no bids will be accepted, and all bids received by this time are opened, usually in the presence of the bidders themselves. The bids are made public, and the lowest responsible bidder is awarded the order. If no bids are acceptable, the purchasing officer ordinarily has no alternative but to reject them all and initiate the procedure again, calling for new bids.

The chief disadvantage of this alternative is that decision hinges solely on price. This can be alleviated, of course, by making the requirement of quality and service so definitive and unmistakable that price is the only real variable. This is easier said than done. To assure that quality and service will not be slighted in delivery, each bidder may be required to submit a performance bond along with his bid.

As a general rule, business buyers use the bid system primarily as a means of exploring or identifying the price factor. No market price exists for many nonstandard materials, complex fabricated products on which design and manufacturing methods vary, and items made to the buyer's specification. In these circumstances, asking for competitive bids is the simplest way of exploring price and evaluating the reasonableness of quoted prices. (See Figure 5–3.)

Having received competitive bids from a group of reliable suppliers, the buyer can select the lowest price offered or weigh it alongside other considerations. If there is a wide range of quotations, both excessively high and excessively low bids may be open to the question: Do the bidders understand the requirements? On the other hand, insignificant variation or identity in quotations is often ground for suspicion of collusion. Whether or not the low bid represents the best price must, in the end, be judged by comparison with other offers, with past experience, with the prices of similar products, and in light of the buyer's own knowledge of market conditions.

Selecting suppliers who will be invited to submit quotations often involves paring down a sizable list of sources to a relatively small one. If items are bought frequently, the purchasing department may have developed an approved list of firms invited to submit bids. While firms are periodically added to and dropped from this list, it usually remains intact for considerable periods of time.

In the case of nonroutine purchases, particularly items purchased for the first time, selecting suppliers to whom requests for quotations will be sent may involve more than a review of past experience with them. The appraisal effort may extend to on-site inspection of their facilities, extensive interviews with salesmen, and inquiries to purchasing officials in other firms who may have patronized these suppliers. The more important the purchase, the more exhaustive the appraisal.

## Negotiation

Most major purchases by businesses, private institutions, and numerous government agencies and departments are probably negotiated. The advantage of negotiation is that all pertinent factors can be brought under consideration and analysis. Requirements can often be adjusted to take advantage of the special strengths of particular suppliers, with the result that price, quality, or service advantages that would otherwise be missed can be gained.

Negotiation may begin with a bid or quotation that is later modified to reflect additional factors pertinent to the buying company's needs, which come to light during interviews between salesman and buyer. Negotiations may be carried on simultaneously with a number of competitive suppliers until enough information has been passed back and forth to enable the buyer to choose the supplier or suppliers he will patronize.

Negotiation is almost always employed in the purchase of new products, because with no experience in manufacturing such products bidders would have to inflate their quotations to allow for more than the normal contingencies. If a substantial margin should be paid, which in the light of subsequent manufacturing experience proves unwarranted, the business or institutional buyer, unlike the federal government, has no legal recourse by which to force renegotiation of the contract.

The successful negotiation of a purchase contract requires skill and experience. The buyer must be cognizant of the cost situation of his own firm as well as that of suppliers. He must be able to assemble facts meaningfully, to establish realistic price limits, and to appraise the effect of general economic conditions on the supply situation in industries from which the company fills its needs. It is clearly short-sighted to drive a bargain that will make the buyer's patronage unattractive or weaken the vendor as a reliable, continuing source of supply. On the other hand, the buyer must seek every advantage of price, service, and quality to which his company is legitimately entitled.

Negotiation between buyer and seller almost always involves some form of strategy, which is conditioned by the needs of the buyer relative to the eagerness of the vendor for his patronage. The supplier who urgently needs additional volume, who is uncertain that he will get the buyer's order, and who knows there is a limited amount of time to reach an agreement will negotiate in an entirely different manner than he would in the opposite situation. By the same token, the buyer who knows that the seller has little competition, who has little solid information on which to base a price analysis, who does not have much business to offer the supplier, or who is under some pressure to fill a need for a using department will also conduct negotiations in an entirely different manner than he would if the opposite situation existed.

It is also true that the supplier eager to get his foot in the door of a company, or to become established in an industry, is often willing to make special concessions. Similarly, the supplier without accurate records of cost is likely to have a rather wide range of acceptable prices to permit special arrangements. The fact that a given supplier has the lowest price does not always mean it is low enough; he may still be using his plant inefficiently. If this is true, and if other qualities of the vendor make him attractive as a source of supply, it is the responsibility of the purchasing officer to convince him of this and help his management to reduce its cost to a minimum without diluting quality. The professional buyer who has succeeded in developing alternative sources of supply is in a much stronger position to induce vendors to inaugurate cost-reduction programs than is the buyer without such alternatives.

Negotiations may take on a highly technical character, either because of the products involved, the amount of the purchase, or the implications for design, production, or other operations of the company. In these situations, a team of buyers may be used, including representatives from engineering, finance, marketing, production, and the legal staff, as well as the purchasing department itself. A similar team is often used by the interested supplier to make a comprehensive and detailed presentation to the customer. When such teams are involved, negotiation may be protracted and include a great deal of technical data.

Characteristically, alert purchasing departments have specific goals in view when negotiating with prospective suppliers. These objectives often incorporate a range of possibilities to permit flexibility. However, they are usually established on the basis of a careful examination of the company's needs and alternatives as well as the recognition that suppliers must make a profit, too.

## Make or buy

The alternative of extending a company's production system to include particular supplies, materials, or components involves far-reaching economic and social implications. Consequently, all that can be attempted here is a brief summary of the conditions that might lead a firm to produce rather than purchase needed products and the conditions that usually serve to restrict such action.

Occasionally, manufacturers are forced to make some of the products they might otherwise purchase because no suitable suppliers exist. This was true of some companies producing dry cereal for breakfast foods, for example, when they were unable to buy suitable roasting equipment. In other instances, companies may use such small quantities of some special item that vendors are not interested in producing it.

Firms that depend on materials or equipment of unusual properties or design sometimes manufacture them to preclude any interruption in supply or variation in quality, or to protect the design of their equipment —particularly, equipment of advanced technology. A company may also find it cheaper to manufacture a particular item than to buy it, although circumstances that generate such opportunities are rather unusual. It may happen that while the cost of manufacturing is no lower for the buyer than for suppliers, an exorbitant market price prevails as the result of a monopolistic supply situation, legal action, or collusion among sellers. Moreover, the company capable of manufacturing even a small part of its own requirements is in a stronger bargaining position in negotiating with vendors than is one that cannot produce any of its requirements.

In periods of depressed sales, a manufacturer may choose to make rather than buy certain items in order to utilize idle productive capacity. Even in periods of normal demand, management may decide to manufacture rather than buy certain items as a means of spreading overhead and reducing the share of overhead expense that must be charged against the company's end products.

While some circumstances argue in favor of manufacturing rather than purchasing a part or all of a company's requirements, several weighty considerations deter many firms from taking such action. One such deterrent is lack of administrative or technical experience in making the required articles. To manufacture an item may involve new equipment, new skills, and new supervisors. Moreover, every time another unrelated production unit is added to the original complex there is certain to be some loss of cohesion and unity in management, which is sure to produce a new set of technical and supervisory problems.

An equally serious possibility is that of losing market position in the company's own major products. This could happen as a result of the obsolescence or outdated design of components or fabricated parts used in the end products and manufactured by the company as a sideline. The price of a strong market position is usually constant research effort directed toward improved product performance and lower production costs. Companies that produce their own materials can rarely afford sufficient research to keep abreast, much less ahead of, firms for which such products are of major concern. As a consequence, it is likely to be only a matter of time until the company producing a needed component as a sideline falls behind major producers in quality and cost improvement. If the quality of its sideline component or material is a factor in the performance of the company's major products, the results of manufacturing instead of buying may well be disastrous.

The decision to make rather than buy can also result in a substantial loss of goodwill if the volume of discontinued purchases is sizable. Losing the goodwill of suppliers can have an adverse effect on the sales volume of a company in a number of ways. If reciprocity plays a part in marketing effort, the effect of curtailing purchases is readily apparent. If the displaced supplier is one through whom the manufacturer's end product is sold, the probable adverse effect on sales is equally apparent. The value of promotion received through the auspices of friendly suppliers is less obvious but nonetheless significant. The customer of any given vendor is very likely to be a supplier to other customers of this vendor. Good relations with suppliers, whose success will be enhanced by the success of their customers, can promote word-of-mouth advertising of a very effective kind. The opposite result can be expected from rebuffed and resentful suppliers.

A long-term consequence, which almost invariably plagues a firm that manufactures any substantial part of its own material requirements, is inflexibility in the use of materials, parts, and supplies. As a purchaser, a firm can buy from any source that offers the best combination of price, quality, and service. It is free to substitute items, shift from one source to another, or split orders among competing sources as terms and conditions warrant. This freedom is lost to a firm whose management is committed to procurement by manufacture.

## Selecting the alternatives

A decision to manufacture rather than purchase an item as well as a decision to call for firm competitive bids determines the means of procurement as well as the source. The process of selection is completed in the first and will be automatically determined in the second. If, on the other hand, it is decided to purchase rather than manufacture or to negotiate rather than to call for bids, the buyer must select a vendor to receive the order or a group of vendors among whom it will be divided. Although the complexity of the selection process varies with the nature of the purchase, it is determined in no small degree by the buyer's conception of what constitutes a good supplier and the usefulness of available information about suppliers.

*Characteristics of a good supplier.* All purchasing officers look for much the same qualities in the suppliers they patronize. Honesty, of course, is a prime consideration. Any evidence of a prospective vendor's dishonesty—to his customers or his employees, or in past dealings with the buyer—will generally result in his being given a low priority as a possible supplier. Equally basic is the capacity of a prospective supplier to meet the buyer's requirements with respect to quality, quantity, and delivery time. Any doubts about a supplier's ability to deliver commodities that consistently meet the buyer's specifications in the amounts and within the time period required will give the supplier a low priority, regardless of any other consideration.

Sound financial condition is another quality generally sought in a supplier as assurance that if given an order he will be able to maintain sufficient inventory, production facilities, and personnel to deliver it on the time schedule required. In addition, such qualities as a reputation for research, advances in technology, and alertness to new developments in the industry are usually desired in suppliers. Suppliers able to make suggestions and recommendations that effect cost reductions, product improvements, or better service to customers are especially valued.

Experience in manufacturing the products desired and location may be important considerations to buyers. Manufacturing experience weighs heavily in the case of a highly technical or very expensive product. Supplier location is an important consideration if the buyer wishes to avoid high freight costs, to lessen the risk of damage in transit, or if a policy of using local sources of supply is being pursued.

*Information sources.*   Numerous sources of information are typically used by purchasing agents to determine the extent to which prospective suppliers possess desired qualities. The most reliable and accessible source is usually the buying company's own records. If these have been properly kept, they should reveal such information as suppliers' promptness in response to requests for quotations or other data, promptness in handling rejections, acknowledging orders, and settling complaints, certainty of delivery, and the extent of suppliers' cooperation with engineering, research and development, production, or other departments trying to solve some problem.

Salesmen are, of course, an important source of information, particularly for suppliers with whom the buyer has had no previous experience. Salesmen serve as a source of information not only about their own companies but also about developments in the industry to which they belong. Catalogs are another common source of information, as are trade journals, advertising, and trade directories. Various analytical methods for treating this information are discussed in the following chapter.

## ORDER PLACEMENT

Placing an order usually involves the use of a purchase order form (see Figure 5–4), even in emergency situations when usual procedures are set aside. It is also true that all conditions of the purchase agreement may not be stipulated in the purchase order. Some suppliers may insist that the purchaser sign a sales agreement that affords them a degree of protection not specifically assured by the buyer's purchase order. An example of this would be a clause in the sales agreement binding both parties to submit any dispute arising between them to commercial arbitration. How unyielding a supplier is in such matters usually depends on the extent to which a strong seller's market exists in the commodity being purchased, the complexity of the transaction, and the relative bargaining strength of the two parties.

Firms that sell products used in volume and purchased repetitively over a period of time, such as maintenance and repair items and production line requirements, usually suggest *blanket* or *open-end* orders to buyers. Such orders include all terms and stipulations needed for the purchase of a given product or products over a considerable period of time. For example, an engine manufacturer may purchase his predicted requirement of hose connectors for the coming year in a single order. Subsequently, releases of specific quantities may be made against the order as required by his production schedule. (See Figure 5–5.) In some instances, it may be possible to tie the preparation of purchase order

**FIGURE 5–4.**  Purchase order form

**INTERNATIONAL HARVESTER COMPANY**

CENTRAL PURCHASING DEPARTMENT     **PURCHASE ORDER**

401 NORTH MICHIGAN AVENUE, CHICAGO, ILLINOIS  60611

TELEPHONE  AREA CODE 312  527-0200

SHIP AND INVOICE TO
OR
SHIP TO

INVOICE TO

PURCHASE ORDER NUMBER

THIS PURCHASE ORDER NUMBER AND OUR PART NUMBER OR CODE, MUST APPEAR ON EACH INVOICE, PACKING LIST, SHIPPING CONTAINER AND CORRESPONDENCE.

G.O. BUYER | REQUISITION NO.

THIS ORDER IS GIVEN AND ACCEPTED SUBJECT TO ALL CONDITIONS HEREIN AND PRINTED ON THE REVERSE SIDE HEREOF.
SEND ACCEPTANCE OF THIS PURCHASE ORDER DIRECT TO LOCATION TO WHICH INVOICE IS TO BE SENT.

TERMS          F.O.B.          V.I.A.          DATE

ACCOUNT NUMBER          DELIVER TO   P.O. COPIES REQUIRED FOR

FEDERAL EXCISE TAX ▶   ☐ FOR FURTHER MANUFACTURE - SEE EXEMPTION CERTIFICATE ON REVERSE SIDE   ☐ FOR RESALE - SERVICE (EXEMPTION CERTIFICATE NOT APPLICABLE.)

DELIVERY SCHEDULE:  MATERIAL MUST BE SHIPPED TO ARRIVE AT OUR LOCATION ON DAY INDICATED.

| JAN. | FEB. | MAR. | APRIL | MAY | JUNE | JULY | AUG. | SEPT. | OCT. | NOV. | DEC. |
|------|------|------|-------|-----|------|------|------|-------|------|------|------|
|      |      |      |       |     |      |      |      |       |      |      |      |

STATE SALES AND USE TAX ▶   ☐ FOR USE   ☐ FOR USE NONTAXABLE   ☐ FOR RESALE-REGISTRATION NO.

| QUANTITY | OUR PART NUMBER OR CODE | SUPPLIER NUMBER AND/OR DESCRIPTION | PRICE |
|----------|-------------------------|-------------------------------------|-------|
|          |                         |                                     |       |

**INSTRUCTIONS: Invoice in DUPLICATE**

Mail all invoices and bills of lading same day goods are shipped. Render a separate invoice for each shipment against this purchase order if partial shipments are made. Provide packing list in each shipment.

GFX-50
E.A.G.O. MAT

**INTERNATIONAL HARVESTER COMPANY**

BY _____

releases into the production scheduling procedure and forward them to the purchasing department for transmission to the vendor. It is not unusual for such open-end orders to remain in effect until changes in design, material specifications, or conditions affecting price or delivery make new negotiations desirable or necessary.

The formal purchase order may be eliminated altogether in the case of automatic reorder systems. It has already been observed that such systems involve agreement on minimum inventory levels, reorder points,

**FIGURE 5–5.** Form used for releasing quantities of an item under an open-end order

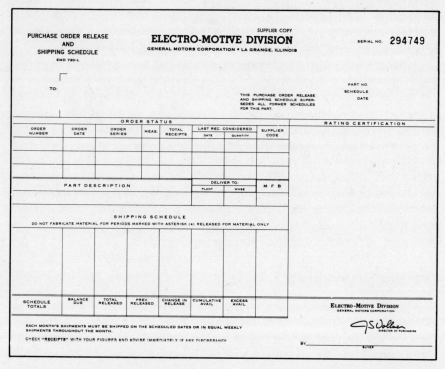

and reorder quantities. When the inventory of an item falls to the established reorder point, this information is automatically relayed to the supplier by memorandum, telephone, or teletype. He then delivers the standard order quantity usually accompanied by a sales slip. The slips are accumulated by the buyer and paid at regular intervals. This is a particularly useful system when buying items subject to routine purchasing, such as supplies. Since it eliminates a considerable amount of paper work by both buyer and supplier, the system has been extended to numerous other purchases not of a routine nature.

## FOLLOW-UP AND EXPEDITING

Ideally, it should not be necessary to follow up an order. But purchase orders are not always prepared so that suppliers can interpret them accurately, and the suppliers themselves are not always fully cooperative. They do not always honor the delivery dates to which their salesmen have committed them, and when running short of material they may shift production facilities to other orders without notifying either their sales departments or their customers. Suppliers have also been known to give priority to the more profitable orders on their books, and to view such contingencies as labor difficulties and mechanical break-downs with more optimism than conditions warrant. Consequently, there is almost invariably a need for some kind of follow-up.

Although follow-up procedures in current use are too varied to permit much generalization, responsibility for initiating them usually rests with the buyer who places the order. His more intimate knowledge of who should be contacted in the vendor firm and the greater likelihood that he can get prompt action without jeopardizing friendly relations with the seller usually account for his key role in follow-up action. Follow-up procedure itself may involve no more than a telephone call, a series of letters, or a questionnaire. On the other hand, it may include a group of specialists, expediters, who spend virtually full time keeping suppliers on schedule. Expediters are often vested with considerable responsibility and spend much of their time visiting suppliers' plants to investigate deliveries and to keep shipments moving.

## INVOICE HANDLING

The receipt of an invoice is not only notification of shipment, it is notification of what has been shipped and the exact nature of the supplier's claim against the buyer. Since no transaction is complete until the invoice has been verified and the claim against the buyer paid, the way invoices are handled is a matter of some consequence. A common practice is to attach to the invoice a list of items to be verified as soon as it is received. If any information called for by this checklist does not appear on the invoice or if any information appearing there does not agree with the purchase order, the invoice is ordinarily returned to the vendor for correction. In many cases, a special form is used for this purpose.

Even though the return of an incorrect invoice is a routine operation for both buyer and seller, it represents much lost motion and adds nothing to the efficiency of the buyer or to his estimate of the seller. Many marketers do not include invoicing in the marketing function. Nevertheless, careless invoicing by a vendor, which requires the customer to spend a disproportionate amount of time in checking and returning his invoices for correction, can have a deleterious effect on repeat business. While buyers are not apt to be very reticent about such annoyances in their interviews with salesmen, it is not unusual for salesmen to be indifferent about following up such complaints.

There appears to be considerable difference of opinion as to whether invoice verification and approval is a function of purchasing or accounting. In practice, every conceivable arrangement involving both

**FIGURE 5–6.  Expediting form**

UNIVERSAL BLEACHER CO.
1303 N. McKINLEY AVE. -- P.O. BOX 640
CHAMPAIGN, ILLINOIS 61823

*Purchase Expediter*

PLEASE REPLY IMMEDIATELY

☐ BY PHONE

☐ BY WIRE

☐ ON THIS FORM

USE WINDOW
ENVELOPE
FOR RETURN.
FOLD HERE  *To*

PLEASE SAVE YOUR TIME AND OURS, BY COMPLETING THIS
FORM RATHER THAN WRITING A LETTER. FORM MAY BE
RETURNED IN A #10 WINDOW ENVELOPE. FOLD AS
INDICATED AT UPPER LEFT.

DATE

| OUR PURCHASE ORDER NO. | YOUR INVOICE NO. | YOUR ORDER NO. | INVOICE DATE | INVOICE AMOUNT | REFERENCE |
|---|---|---|---|---|---|

ORDER INFORMATION
1. ( ) Please rush PRICES.
2. ( ) Acknowledge our order and give SHIPPING DATE.
3. ( ) Please mail us ACCEPTANCE COPY of our Purchase Order.
4. ( ) Is this order considered COMPLETE?
5. ( ) Please inform us about items BACK ORDERED.
6. ( ) CHANGE made on above order. Please acknowledge.

ACCOUNTING INFORMATION
15. ( ) We require_____INVOICE COPIES.
16. ( ) INVOICE enclosed RECEIVED IN ERROR.
17. ( ) We are RETURNING attached invoice.
18. ( ) PURCHASE ORDER NO. incorrect or missing.
19. ( ) PRICE ☐ TERMS ☐ DISCOUNT ☐ do not agree with quotation.
20. ( ) Please forward CORRECTED INVOICE or CREDIT MEMO for following reason:

  ( ) Quantity incorrect.          ( ) Extension incorrect.
  ( ) Should be F. O. B. destination. ( ) Unit price incorrect.
  ( ) Material wrong or defective.
21. ( ) SALES TAX not applicable. Exemption No. is_____.
22. ( ) We have no record of RECEIVING INVOICE NO_____ shown on your statement. Please send duplicate invoice.

REMARKS

SHIPPING INFORMATION
7. ( ) RUSH shipment. ADVISE earliest shipping date.
8. ( ) Will you SHIP on date requested?
9. ( ) WHY did you not ship as promised? WHEN will you ship?
10. ( ) IF SHIPPED advise method.
11. ( ) What PARTIAL shipment can you make and WHEN?
12. ( ) When can BALANCE of order be shipped?
13. ( ) Please make certain order is SHIPPED VIA_____.
14. ( ) Please make SHIPMENT RELEASES as shown under Remarks.

SERVICE AND OTHER INFORMATION
23. ( ) If order has been shipped, MAIL INVOICE today.
24. ( ) Please forward CERTIFIED WEIGHT slip.
25. ( ) Please forward SHIPPING NOTICE.
26. ( ) Please show PURCHASE ORDER NUMBER on papers referred to or attached.
27. ( ) Material not received. TRACE AND ADVISE.
28. ( ) Please forward receipted FREIGHT BILL.
29. ( ) We have NO RECORD of transaction covered by your invoice. Advise date of shipment, name of person placing order and furnish signed delivery receipt.
30. ( ) Please complete and return our REQUEST FOR QUOTATION

  dated_____.

SIGNED

*Reply*

DATE                    SIGNED

PLEASE RETURN THIS COPY TO SENDER WITH REPLY
PINK COPY IS FOR YOUR RECORDS

departments can be found. As a general rule, however, it is the purchasing department that authorizes payment and must be satisfied that the terms of the purchase agreement have been met.

## RECEIPT AND INSPECTION

With the exception of large, multiunit companies, the receipt and inspection of incoming merchandise is usually centralized in a single unit, either directly or indirectly responsible to the purchasing depart-

FIGURE 5–7.   Form used for reporting receipt of purchased merchandise

| YORK | DIVISION OF BORG-WARNER CORPORATION | | | | | | | | |
|---|---|---|---|---|---|---|---|---|---|
| | D E C A T U R   W O R K S | | | | | | | NO. | |
| | RECEIVING REPORT | | | | | | | | |

| RECEIVED FROM | | | ADDRESS | | | | DATE | | |
|---|---|---|---|---|---|---|---|---|---|
| SHIP VIA | | | COLLECT | PREPAID | PRO. NO | PACKING SLIP NO. | CHECKED BY | | |
| REQUISITION NO. | PURCHASE ORDER NO. | ACCOUNT NO. | DEPT. NO | DELIVERED TO | | C TONS | BOXES | KEGS | LOOSE |
| PART NO. | DESCRIPTION | | | | | AMOUNT REC D | REJECTED | | ACCEPTED |
| REASON FOR REJECTION | | | | | | INSPECTED BY | | | DATE |

M.S. 1011

**REC. DEPT.**

ment. The receiving unit commonly reports incoming shipments on some form of "materials received" memorandum. (See Figure 5–7.) Typically, copies of the memorandum are forwarded to the purchasing department to be checked against the invoice, to the stores department for entry in inventory records, and to the using department as notification of fulfillment of its requisition. In some companies, a copy is also sent to the traffic division.

In addition to the verification of quantities received, it may be necessary to verify quality as well. In many firms, inspection of quality is limited to a representative sample of each shipment. Some receiving departments have a specialized inspection division whose personnel determine how and when inspection of incoming shipments will be made.

## SUMMARY

This chapter is based on the proposition that the industrial marketer must know the way his customer buys. To this end it has been organized around the six common elements of most purchasing systems. The various ways in which the need for a product or service may arise and is given formal recognition and the alternative ways in which this need

FIGURE 5–8. A general purchasing system

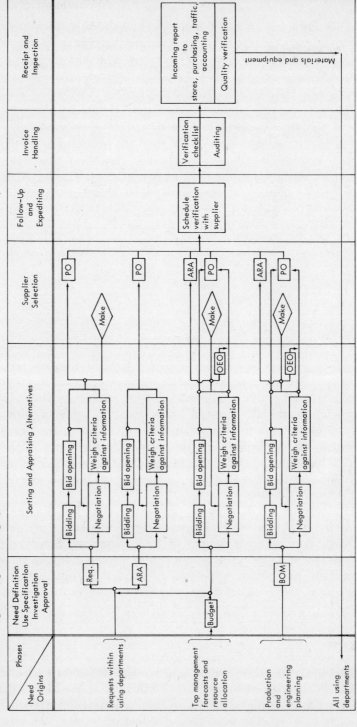

Key: o—decision node either/or
Req—Requisition
ARA—Automatic Reorder Agreement

BOM—Bill of Materials
OEO—Open-end order
PO—Purchase order

may be satisfied have been noted. The more important factors involved in selecting a supplier and the sources of information about them were briefly discussed. Order placement, follow-up, and receiving were also covered with a view to disclosing how they mesh with the other activities to form a system to procure materials and services efficiently, economically, and within the time frame desired by using departments.

Much of the discussion of industrial marketing problems in later chapters is based on the assumption that the reader has at least a rudimentary knowledge of the purchasing function. The successful marketer of industrial goods must of course have much more than this.

# 6

# VALUE AND
# VENDOR ANALYSIS

THE TECHNICAL NATURE of both the manufacture and use of many industrial products as well as the persistent upward trend in costs have placed a high priority on the proper identification of needs and alternative means of supplying them. To these ends, purchasing managers have developed two kinds of supporting systems with important marketing implications because of their bearing on the choice of both products and suppliers. These are value analysis, sometimes called value engineering or cost improvement, and vendor analysis.

## VALUE ANALYSIS

Most value analysis systems probably have their conceptual roots in the ideas of work simplification developed by Allan Mogenson in the early 1930s. The purchasing officer begins the buying transaction with the definition of desired quality submitted by the using department and endeavors to procure this quality at minimum cost. The essence of quality is suitability. To the extent that an item incorporates costly features or properties that do not contribute in some significant way to either the efficiency of the production process or the salability of the buyer's end product, its value is impaired. Value improvement, therefore, begins with an analysis of the purpose or function an item is purchased to fulfill. The objective, of course, is to effect a revision of the specification or quality definition of the item that will permit a reduction in its cost without impairing its suitability.

It is apparent that value analysis cuts across lines that customarily divide functional responsibility. Although the determination and definition of quality requirements are the responsibility of using departments rather than purchasing, purchasing clearly has responsibility for value. Consequently, the systematic search for the most economical means of satisfying the requirements of using departments has been widely accepted as a legitimate extension of purchasing activity. This involves the effort to recast the technical description of purchased parts, materials, components, and equipment so that their specifications will more accurately reflect their purpose or function.

## Nature of the system

The search for improved value generally proceeds in two stages: (1) a review of existing product specifications in the light of use requirements and (2) the identification and elimination of unnecessary cost factors.

*Review of product specifications.* The need for value analysis arises from several situations that may result in product specifications that do not completely match use requirements. Products are often developed and marketed on tight schedules that allow the maker little time for investigation of all possible avenues of low-cost manufacturing methods and processes. Later reviews of these products may be chiefly concerned with making minor improvments rather than with scrutinizing specifications with regard to both manufacturing and customer requirements. Moreover, it is not unusual for manufacturing technology to advance so rapidly that a product in production only a few years may contain significant excess cost elements unless it is periodically reviewed in the light of new methods and technology. Antiquated make-or-buy policies may limit the consideration of offers by outside specialty suppliers. Such situations can result in thousands of dollars of excess cost, not as a result of something that is done wrong, but as a result of something that is not done at all, viz., periodic scrutiny of the parts, components, subassemblies, and materials that enter into the end product.

While such reviews of specifications do not imply distrust or disparagement of the engineering skill and judgment represented in the original statement of need, they do recognize the ever present possibility of improvement in specification and design. These reviews also recognize that in mass production no unit saving is too small to be worthwhile. A difference of one cent per unit, where thousands of units are being produced annually, can result in substantial savings or losses. For example, a leading automobile manufacturer realized savings of $64,000 per year simply by changing one small component from a forging to an equally serviceable screw-machine product. While the new product was only $\frac{1}{10}$ of 1 cent cheaper per unit than the forging, 16 were used in every car.

1. What the material or part under consideration contributes to the end product?
2. What is the minimal function it must perform to give the end product the desired performance capabilities?
3. How much this minimal function or contribution is worth?

Depending on the nature of the product, these questions will raise such detailed inquiries as:

1. Does the part or material used need all its features?
2. What else would perform the same function?
3. Can it be made at lower cost?
4. Can it be obtained from another dependable supplier for less?

The purpose of such questions is to determine how equivalent performance can be achieved at lower cost and how the combined knowledge of engineering, manufacturing, and purchasing personnel can best utilize alternative materials, newer processes, and abilities of specialized suppliers to speed this achievement.

*Identifying and eliminating unnecessary costs.* Establishing that the cost of a particular part or material is unnecessary or unreasonable involves the analysis of its price as well as of its function or contribution. Although many cost factors may be subsumed in a supplier's price quotation, price analysis ordinarily begins with the cost of production. The supplier's basic production cost may be relatively fixed by the design, materials, and methods specified by the buyer. If it can be assumed that buyers select suppliers whose production methods are efficient and whose costs are competitive, price analysis must focus on design, materials, and production methods. This is almost always the case, even though there is some variation among suppliers on other factors that influence price, such as overhead charges, distribution and promotion costs, quantity differentials, profit margins, and pricing policies.

Careful appraisal and analysis of design, materials, and production methods often points the way to elimination or modification of unnecessary features of design and the cost of the manufacturing operations they entail. The result is usually a part or material with properties that more economically satisfy the use requirement intended for it. An example of this identification and elimination of unnecessary cost is provided by a manufacturer of timing devices who purchased the motor that activated the timing mechanism from a leading supplier of electrical appliances. Since the motor represented the most expensive part of the end product, it was selected first for investigation when a value analysis section was established in the company's purchasing department. Disassembly of the motor revealed that most of the structural components were made of brass. Since the primary function of the structural members was to provide support and rigidity to the motor housing, substitution of a cheaper metal or alloy of adequate strength seemed possible. A conference was arranged with members of the supplier's design and engineering staff and representatives of several primary metal suppliers to study the design and materials of the housing. As a result, aluminum alloy was substituted for brass in all supporting members of the motor housing, with a reduction in price that saved the buyer $15,000 annually.

## Operation of the system

A value analysis system is an organized sequence of investigation aimed at challenging existing product specifications, design, and production methods. Such systems are usually controlled by a value analysis group consisting of representatives from purchasing, engineering, manufacturing, accounting, and other departments with a functional interest in the product under study. The purchasing representative is generally called on for information regarding supplier capabilities and to provide liaison with suppliers to solicit their suggestions and draw on their store of knowledge and technical capacity. Engineers typically supply technical evaluation of suggestions, while the manufacturing representative appraises them in the light of his knowledge of production methods and processes. The role of the accountant is usually that of cost analysis and verification of cost-price data. Other specialists, such as marketing officers, may be called on for their ideas and evaluations of suggestions as to end-product customers' preferences, attitudes, and problems.

Since few products are so well designed and manufactured as to discourage any thought of significant improvement, deciding what to analyze seldom presents a problem. The issue is usually which parts, materials, and components have a value analysis priority, and this is often decided by the importance of their contributions to the total cost of the buyer's end product or service. However, the sales department of a company may occasionally quote prices below cost in order to get the company's foot in the door of an important account. If such quotations have the approval of top management, the value analysis group may be called on to try to salvage some profit out of the order. But it is generally agreed that such activities do not represent the best use of value analysis and should be confined to rare occasions.

Given criteria for identifying products to be analyzed, value analysis systems incorporate at least four types of activities: (1) the determination of the product's (part, material, or component) function, (2) the identification of alternative means of performing its function, (3) the testing of each alternative, and (4) the formulation of a recommendation. Determining the function of a part, material, or component is perhaps the most important of these activities, because it requires a clear, succinct statement of what the product does and it leads to the identification of other means of doing it. For example, a shovel moves dirt, but what else could be used to move dirt—a broom, a blast of air, a stream of water? Gasoline provides energy through combustion, but what else provides energy—light, chemical action, fermentation? What else could be used to write with instead of a pencil or to preserve food instead of a can or a refrigerator?

Ideas generated by the identification of function are then tested and appraised, often with the cooperation of prospective suppliers. After a cost analysis of the most promising ideas has been completed, proposals are typically submitted to the appropriate engineering, design, or production official for approval.

The implications of this type of activity for the industrial marketer are significant. Normally, a new product is developed and produced for a limited, exploratory market in order to determine its need and acceptance. If accepted, it increases rapidly in sales during its growth period and ultimately levels off. To get this device into production and up to projected sales volume often requires the expenditure of considerable engineering effort. Once this volume is reached, however, engineering, design, and other creative talent tends to be directed toward the development and manufacture of other new products. Unfortunately, this is the juncture at which imitative competitors tend to enter the market and endeavor to take business away from the originator. Such invasion of the originator's market is usually successful if he ceases to make continued improvements in the performance or cost of his product. It is at this point that value analysis can be a most effective tool in weeding out unnecessary cost and maintaining the competitive vitality of the original product. This is also the point where suppliers (sellers) with an appreciation of value analysis and a positive program for contributing to it can strengthen their position with customers who may have considered them as marginal.

The need for this kind of work persists throughout the life of an industrial product. Value analysis may even be worthwhile in making deletion decisions. When a product is sick or suffering the infirmities of age, value analysis may suggest production changes or product modifications that reduce cost or increase marketability to prolong its profitable life. On the other hand, such a study may confirm the conclusion that the product has outlived its usefulness and should be deleted.

The industrial marketer can use value analysis of his own and competing products to supply his salesmen with information about the competitive strengths and weaknesses of his product in use, which the salesman can translate into selling appeals. The salesman gains strength from a knowledge of his products and those against which he must compete.

## VENDOR ANALYSIS

In reality, a supplier represents an extension of the buyer's manufacturing or operating capacity without the attendant implications of ownership and control. Not only must the quality of a supplier's product match the specifications of the buyer, but his delivery performance also must conform to the buyer's manufacturing schedule or other operational timetable. The vendor's price is an indivisible part of the total cost of getting materials to the point of usage in the buyer's plant, office, or other facility. Any delay in delivery or deviation in quality adds to the buyer's procurement costs.

In consequence, buyers must be certain that their suppliers meet the standards of performance and quality for which their own operations have been planned. Rapid advances in product technology and the spiraling demand for goods and services characteristic of many industries have given an air of urgency to ways of accurately assessing vendor capabilities. Most of these methods are concerned with the identification, definition, and measurement of vendor capacity to satisfy the buyer's particular requirements.

To the extent that buyer requirements can be satisfied by materials that are traded in the open market on official or generally accepted specifications or standards, a buyer requires commodities rather than capabilities. However, when requirements are unique, calling for special design, performance, or reliability features, or when they entail expensive tooling, extended periods of preparation, high setup costs, and involve large quantities of material over extended periods of time, the purchasing department's job is to buy capabilities as well as products.

### Evaluating vendor capacity

To the extent that the buyer recognizes vendors as extensions of his own resources and operational capacity, he must appraise them in terms of their technological, productive, financial, and management capability.

*Technical and production capability.*   A vendor's capability in technology refers to the excellence and extensiveness of his design and development engineering, production engineering, test engineering, and tool engineering. Adequate know-how and sophistication in these various phases of engineering is necessary to assure consistency in the quality of products before, during, and after production. Vendor production capability refers to the efficiency and completeness of his manufacturing facilities and practical know-how, as well as the means to extend or supplement them through both subcontracting and procurement.

Analysis of a vendor's technical and production capability usually involves on-site inspection of his facilities and visits with his key officials in production, purchasing, engineering, and sales. The trained mind and the experienced eye can quickly appraise conditions in the vendor's plant, observe the variety of standard and special equipment used, the adequacy of inventories to support production schedules, and the orderly conduct of manufacturing operations. Such visits can also afford the opportunity to observe testing and quality control procedures, as well as the assortment of products and components manufactured.

*Financial capability.*   A vendor's financial capability is usually measured by his credit standing, cash flow, equity, and working capital. Of equal importance is the ease with which the vendor can augment capital funds through borrowing or additional investment. Financial ratios, particularly those that indicate liquidity, are important tests of financial capacity. A good profit record over a period of years is a reliable indication that the vendor will be able to raise more funds, if necessary, from creditors or investors.[1] By the same token, vendors with a large net worth are usually able to raise funds readily because the owner's investment provides a cushion of safety for creditors. Similarly, a large net worth to debt ratio provides a basis for more credit.

The volume of sales the vendor has predicted and plans to make is also an indication of financial soundness. A company with annual sales typically within a range of $500,000 to $1 million, for example, would probably find itself in difficulty if it attempted to increase sales to $5 million a year, even if it had previously been in a strong financial position. On the other hand, a firm with a sound financial position should be able to support a modest increase in sales without difficulty.

Financial analysis often brings to light weaknesses that make a vendor undesirable as a supplier. The types of firms likely to fail financial tests are new firms of limited net worth and experience, rapidly expanding firms, firms that refuse to divulge information about their financial condition—secrecy often hides weaknesses—and small firms, because there is generally greater uncertainty about their ability to command additional funds if they are needed.

*Management capabilities.*    The ability of a vendor firm's management to plan, organize, integrate, and control its facilities, manpower and materials, time, and cost is a critical but elusive quality. In evaluating it, buyers usually seek to identify the vendor's key management people— their titles, responsibilities, experience, and extent of formal education. The nature of a vendor's planning, scheduling, and inventory control systems also indicates management's caliber. Equally revealing is information about machine and manpower loading, how requirements are released—by job, by lot, or by forecast—and whether the company requires certifications and tests of quality from its own suppliers.

Once the buyer's system of evaluation has eliminated those vendors who do not quality for patronage, it is common practice to rate those who remain in the light of experience with them.

## Rating vendor performance

The objective rating of vendor performance is a matter that eluded any form of measurement criteria for years. But significant progress has been made in this direction, particularly among large buyers, through the development of and experimentation with vendor-rating systems.

A vendor-rating system entails the establishment of performance rating standards so that the buyer can validly distinguish between good

---

[1] The net profit record itself may not show the full success of the company, particularly a small company, because the drawing account of the owner may include more than reasonable salaries and expenses.

and marginal suppliers. The purpose of the rating system is to supply tangible guidelines that will improve judgment in all areas of resource selection. Past experience with a vendor's quality and delivery is important for this purpose as is past experience with his services—technical, financial, and managerial. Past prices, however, are usually not significant, and quoted prices are significant only to the extent that they can be expressed in terms of the value of the product quality, delivery, and service package offered by the supplier.

As a rule, rating systems reflect the cost buyers must incur, supplier by supplier, in satisfying their requirements. For example, suppliers may be rated on product quality in terms of three categories of cost—defect prevention, defect detection, and defect correction. The sum of these quality costs for each supplier is then expressed as a percent of the total value of materials purchased from him.

Delivery performance is similarly rated in terms of acquisition and availability costs. These costs represent such expenditures as follow-up and expediting time, telegraph and telephone expense, field expediting and surveillance costs, and premium transportation charges, as well as manufacturing losses due to supplier's delivery failures and resulting shortages. These, too, are usually expressed as a percentage of the value of materials purchased from each source.

Suppliers are also rated in terms of the value they contribute to the buyer in addition to product quality and delivery performance. Such added values are loosely classified as service and given a variety of cost equivalents. When price, quality, and delivery considerations produce equal or nearly equal ratings, it is evident that service ratings could have a decisive influence in the choice of a preferred supplier.

*A vendor rating system.*[2] The Development Project Committee on Standards for Vendor Evaluation of the National Association of Purchasing Management recently published several different plans for vendor performance evaluation. Although these plans represent a considerable variation in method and approach, all rely on the four major procurement variables as bases for measurement, viz., price, product quality, delivery, and service. In the interest of brevity, we will limit our discussion to the plan that has probably elicited the widest interest. The *cost ratio plan* incorporates a vendor performance evaluation formula that enables a buyer to factor a vendor's price on the basis of performance criteria. The formula incorporates a quality rating, a delivery rating, and a service rating in such a way that a minus ( − ) weight favors the vendor and a plus ( + ) weight detracts from him. The individual factor ratings are compiled separately and then combined into the final composite rating. Let us examine the nature of these ratings.

---

[2] Much of the material presented in this section was provided by William D. Kellner, Manager, Purchasing Support, the General Electric Company.

*The quality rating.* The quality rating is a composite of the percent of the total number of defective items purchased by the buyer from a given supplier, multiplied by a disposition factor. The number of defective items purchased is determined by sampling, whereas the disposition factor is a weight based on the standard cost of disposing of defective material and expressed as a decimal fraction. The various ways in which defective items are disposed of and the relative costs of each are given under disposition factor in Table 6–1. In a fairly representative company experimenting with the cost ratio plan, the cost of using a defective item involves writing a quality data report and having a conference that includes the quality control engineer, the project engineer, the incoming-material inspector, and, occasionally, the customer. To scrap and reorder a defective item in this company requires a written quality data report, a letter to the vendor requesting corrective action, disposition of the inventory of defective items, issuance of a second purchase order, and a second incoming inspection. If a defective item is returned to the vendor and reordered, the cost elements are a written quality data report, a letter requesting corrective action, a shipping notice, packaging of material, issuance of a replacement purchase order, and a second incoming inspection. As a last resort, the company may rework defective items and use them. If this alternative is chosen, the costs incurred include a quality data report, the scheduling of manufacturing operations necessary to rework the material, direct labor, and attendant overhead cost. If the vendor accepts the cost of reworking, then the only cost incurred by the buyer is that of billing the vendor. This rating system does not include cost of original inspection which may vary as a result of difference in packaging and other factors.

The example shown in Table 6–1 assumes a sample lot of 100 pieces

**TABLE 6–1.  Quality rating**

*Formula*

1.00 + % defective (disposition factor)

*Percent defective*

Number of defective units in a sample lot divided by the number of units in the sample

*Disposition factor*

| | |
|---|---|
| Use as is | .05 |
| Scrap and reorder | .14 |
| Return and reorder | .15 |
| Rework: | |
|     *a*. Billed to vendor | .03 |
|     *b*. Absorbed | .43 |

*Example*

| Units inspected | Units rejected | Disposition |
|---|---|---|
| 100 | 50 | Use as is |

$$\text{Quality rating} = 1.00 + \left(\frac{50}{100} \times .05\right) = 1.025$$

drawn at random from the vendor's shipment, of which 50 were found to be defective. If the decision was to use the defective pieces, the vendor's quality rating would be 1.00 plus ($^{50}\!/_{100} \times .05$), giving a value of 1.025.

***The delivery rating.*** In developing the rating system for delivery performance, company management established standard costs resulting from improper delivery. A weighted cost factor was then assigned to the different delivery possibilities, from two weeks or more ahead of schedule to more than six weeks late. Costs that entered into the standard cost base from which the weights were derived were the expense of idle factory time and replanning created by delinquent shipments, as well as travel, telephone calls, and living expenses created by the necessity of expediting delivery. Application of the delivery rating is shown in Table 6–2.

**TABLE 6–2.   Delivery rating**

*Formula*

   Delivery rating factor and expediting factor to be added to or subtracted from quality rating

*Delivery rating factor*

   a. 2 weeks or more ahead of schedule............................ +.01
   b. 1 to 2 weeks ahead of schedule.............................. −.01
   c. 0 to 1 week ahead of schedule.............................. .00
   d. 1 week late............................................. +.01
   e. 2 to 3 weeks late........................................ +.05
   f. 4 to 6 weeks late........................................ +.10
   g. More than 6 weeks late................................... +.20

*Expediting factor to be added to delivery rating*

   a. 1 vendor contact........................................ .00
   b. 2 to 3 contacts.......................................... +.01
   c. 4 to 5 contacts.......................................... +.02
   d. More than 5 contacts..................................... +.03
   e. Delivery information supplied voluntarily.................. −.01

It will be noted that delivery two weeks or more ahead of schedule is given a penalty rating( + ), as is delivery more than one week late. An early shipment (in excess of two weeks ahead of schedule) in this company causes a premature expenditure of planned inventory funds, while a shipment one to two weeks ahead of schedule eliminates expediting and affords some flexibility in processing material through the inspection routine. Delivery on or no more than one week ahead of schedule is typical. Penalties understandably go higher with progressively delinquent shipments.

The delivery factor is supplemented by an expediting factor shown in the lower half of Table 6–2. The weighting used here is also a standard cost, computed from the history of telephone and telegraph expense incurred to expedite shipments. A contact is defined as a prepaid telephone or telegraph toll. Although vendors are expected to voluntarily provide shipping information, one expediting contact per purchase order is usually considered routine.

*The service rating.* Vendor performance of the various business functions normally associated with his product is given a service rating, and the weights used are based for the most part on judgment (see Table 6–3). Vendors are expected to promptly handle rejected material and requests for quotations, as well as to acknowledge purchase orders by return mail. Cooperation and assistance given by the vendor in resolving purchasing problems are greatly appreciated by most buyers and,

**TABLE 6–3.  Service rating**

*Formula*
Service factor to be added to or subtracted from quality rating

*Promptness in replying to RFQ*

| | |
|---|---|
| On time. | 0.00 |
| Late. | +0.005 |

*Promptness in handling rejection*

| | |
|---|---|
| Within 1 week. | 0.00 |
| More than 1 week. | +0.005 |

*Promptness in acknowledging order*

| | |
|---|---|
| Within 1 week. | 0.00 |
| More than 1 week. | +0.005 |

*Cooperation*

| | |
|---|---|
| Solve engineering, QC, manufacturing problems. | −0.005 |

*Vendor trip required*. +0.01

*Supplied all special documents with order*

| | |
|---|---|
| Yes. | 0.00 |
| No. | +0.005 |

*Financial status\**

| | |
|---|---|
| Satisfactory. | 0.00 |
| Needs special attention. | +0.01 |

*Facility survey*

| | |
|---|---|
| Adequate. | 0.00 |
| Outstanding. | −0.005 |

*Salesman calls*

| | |
|---|---|
| Regularly. | 0.00 |
| Infrequently. | +0.005 |
| Helpful. | −0.005 |

*Vendor has participated in seminar, value engineering workshop, or engineering conference in past 6 months*

| | |
|---|---|
| Yes. | −0.01 |
| No. | 0.00 |

\* Need not be reported if last report is less than two months old.
RFQ—request for quotation.
QC—quality control.

under this system, earn an extra credit. On the other hand, if the buyer must travel to the vendor for any reason other than a goodwill or routine visitation, a demerit ( + ) weight is given. Frequently, special documents, certifications, or catalogs are required with shipment, and these are identified in the purchase order. If a vendor fails to supply them with the shipment, and as a result the work of processing it through the inspection and receiving routine is delayed, the vendor is also given a demerit ( + ) weight. The importance of a vendor's sound financial condition is also recognized in this system, and if a buyer is obliged to give a special attention to the vendor's financial status the latter receives a demerit ( + ) weight.

The company used in this illustration conducts a survey of vendor facilities before awarding contracts to new and untried vendors. This is to verify the supplier's ability to maintain a consistent level of product quality and production volume. A vendor with above-average facilities commands greater confidence in his ability to perform as agreed than one whose plant and equipment are considered to be just average for the industry. Consequently, vendors in the above-average facility category are given a higher service rating than the average.

**TABLE 6–4. Vendor rating**

| Commodity code | Vendor code | Quality control rating | Delivery rating | Service rating | Composite rating |
|---|---|---|---|---|---|
| HA | 0971 | 1.025 | +.05 | +0.005 | 1.08 |
| HA | 1121 | 1.15 | −.01 | .00 | 1.14 |
| HA | 1340 | 1.075 | +.12 | .00 | 1.195 |
| HA | 1590 | 1.43 | .00 | − .02 | 1.41 |
| HA | 2697 | 1.03 | .00 | + .01 | 1.04 |

*Example:*

| Vendor code | Price quoted | Vendor rating | Cost to stock | | |
|---|---|---|---|---|---|
| 0971 | $30.00 | 1.08 | $32.40 | | |
| 1590 | 24.00 | 1.41 | 33.84 | | |
| 2697 | 28.00 | 1.04 | 29.12 | | |
| 1121 | 26.00 | 1.14 | 29.64 | | |

This company also expects vendors to maintain good communications with the company's purchasing agents. Salesmen who familiarize themselves with the company's problems and provide assistance in solving them are of real value, and this is reflected in the weighting factor. Vendor participation in educational activities is also a factor in the rating system, because both vendor and customer usually share their benefits.

*The composite rating.* In Table 6–4, the quality, delivery, and service ratings are combined for five vendors of the same commodity. The top half of the table shows the quality, delivery, service, and composite ratings. Use of the composite rating in factoring the prices of four vendors who bid competitively is illustrated in the bottom half of the table.

The decision on which vendor to select becomes less difficult when it can be demonstrated that vendor 1590, whose price is lowest, is not the vendor with the most economical offer. A purchasing agent could readily justify a decision to buy from vendor 2697. However, if delivery is an important factor in the contemplated purchase, he would be justified in paying a few cents more to buy from vendor 1121, who has the best delivery rating.

Most of the data used in such systems are programmed into a computer. The only manual collection of information is ordinarily represented by a checklist that buyers execute for each purchase to supply ratings for service and expediting. This data is also added to the captive data of the computer, and cost elements and weighting factors are periodically reevaluated.

### Vendor analysis and marketing

The importance to the industrial marketer of knowing how he is or may be rated by the purchasing departments of his customers can scarcely be overstated. In many companies, the purchasing department controls more funds than all other departments combined, and represents the seller's chief contact with using departments. While the precise nature of vendor-rating systems used by purchasing departments vary substantially from one company to another, all are aimed at enabling the purchasing agent to reap the greatest possible benefits for his company per dollar expended. The successful marketer must therefore formulate his plans with full recognition of the type of analysis his performance will be subjected to and the standards it must satisfy. If an awareness of customer needs is the point where market planning begins, the criteria by which customers appraise marketing performance suggest the goals toward which marketing plans should be directed.

### SUMMARY

In this chapter, we have examined two types of analysis used by buyers to appraise a supplier's effectiveness: value analysis, which applies to products, and vendor analysis, which deals with the character and capacity of the supplier and the operating relationships between him and the buyer.

Value analysis involves the review of product specifications in relation to requirements, the identification of unnecessary cost elements, and suggestions for their elimination. This is a cooperative activity requiring participation by several groups of specialists, such as engineering, manufacturing, and accounting, usually under the leadership and coordination of purchasing.

Vendor analysis is usually a purchasing department activity, with incidental contributions from other areas. It seeks to appraise the capability and actual or probable performance of the vendor in the areas of technology, production, financial strength, and management. Several mathematical systems have been developed for rating vendors; all rely on four main variables—price, product quality, delivery, and services surrounding the buying transaction. We have described one of these systems in some detail.

This chapter brings to a close our study of the industrial buyer. We are now ready to tackle some of the problems to be solved in trying to market goods and services to him.

# PART III
# Marketing intelligence

## RAW MATERIAL FOR MARKET IDENTIFICATION
## AND THE FORMULATION OF STRATEGY

INTELLIGENCE is information in a form, degree of detail, and timeliness which renders it useful to decision makers. He who plans and acts without it is courting failure. This is especially true of marketing, because the forces which affect success in the market place are varied and often nebulous. This characteristic tends to make marketing information hard to get and difficult to analyze.

During recent years the gathering and analysis of marketing information has received considerable attention. This has been due to an increased understanding of its importance to effective marketing as well as to the widespread use of the computer. The computer can store information in a volume impossible before its advent and can perform sophisticated analyses that were impossible before.

In the next four chapters is a discussion of the general nature of marketing intelligence, how it is used, and the techniques employed in its development. Chapter 7 describes the elements of an ongoing system of data collection, storage, analysis, and delivery to managers. Chapters 8, 9, and 10 treat the development of informational inputs into the system with particular reference to those which are required for market identification and the formulation of strategy.

# 7

# THE MARKETING INTELLIGENCE SYSTEM

IT IS DOUBTFUL if there is a marketing executive who has not at one time or another known the frustration of wanting information he was certain was in the possession of someone in his company—if he only knew who it was. It is also doubtful that anyone trying to design an information system has escaped the equally frustrating experience of asking what information marketing executives wanted only to receive answers that were inane or impossible. The problem of adequate marketing intelligence is not only that of defining what information is needed to reach sound decisions, but of designing a system of collection, storage, and retrieval that is capable of producing it on demand. The cost of data processing alone dictates that both problems be attacked with care and patience. The situation in many industrial companies is not unlike that depicted in Figure 7–1.

## DEFINING INFORMATIONAL NEEDS

It would seem that the type and nature of information needed by managers in the performance of the marketing function could be determined simply by asking them. Unfortunately, human nature and semantics combine to assure that despite the unequivocal directness of such an approach, it may not yield useful results. Like consumers in the market place, managers may find it impossible to decide specifically what they want until given a choice. While one manager may request every category of information he has ever had occasion to use, however infrequently, another may suggest no more than he is presently receiving but request it a month earlier and free of errors.[1]

---

[1] The story is frequently told of the sales manager who requested a complete printout of the performance of his product line by customer, by territory, price, model, and order size. His request produced a stack of paper which had to be wheeled into his office on a dolly.

113

**FIGURE 7-1**

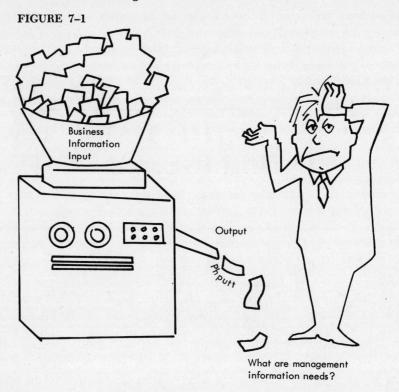

Business
Information
Input

Output

Ph-putt

What are management
information needs?

The system designer may receive some reasonable suggestions through the direct approach, particularly if he presents the manager with an assortment of prototype reports, asking which he would use if they were available. Eventually, though, he will have to probe deeper to unearth those needs which the manager, with his mind tuned to the demands of the present, may not recognize. The shifting nature of buyer needs and the changing environmental context require that some means be found to discover types of information which will be required for future marketing decisions. Otherwise the information system which evolves may be ideally suited to satisfy yesterday's decision needs rather than those of today and tomorrow.

Since a manager needs information because he has to make decisions, information needs are determined by the type of decisions managers must make. This usually entails a listing of the various officers involved (Director of Marketing, Product Managers, Sales Manager, Sales Training Director, Advertising Manager, and Market Planning Director, for example), followed by a study of their job descriptions and any reports they regularly prepare. Where voids or inconsistencies appear, interviews with the people holding these jobs may fill in the missing pieces. At least it should be possible to assemble a tentative list of decisions from such an investigation, which can be circulated among marketing managers for editing. These managers should also be asked to indicate the relative importance of each decision, how frequently it arises, what sources of information are typically consulted, and how satisfactory these sources have been in the past.

Beginning with the decisions which have been designated as most important but for which existing information sources are considered inadequate, the systems designer must determine what kind of information is needed to reach important decisions soundly. This will probably require more interviews and more refinement. In pursuit of this end one is usually well-advised to engage in the widest possible consultation with personnel in the marketing function. This provides an opportunity to become informed about the full spectrum of marketing activity and about its unique contribution to the success of the company as those involved perceive it. Of equal importance is the fact that the process of discussion and consultation often elicits many valuable ideas. Since organizations, particularly large organizations, appear to be cold and formalistic, there is almost always a need to place deliberate emphasis upon the human element in data communication. This cannot be done unless numerous human ties are created and the isolation of individuals and groups from each other is reduced to a minimum.

Inevitably, some types of information considered necessary may

**FIGURE 7–2.  Information flow in a multidivision corporation**

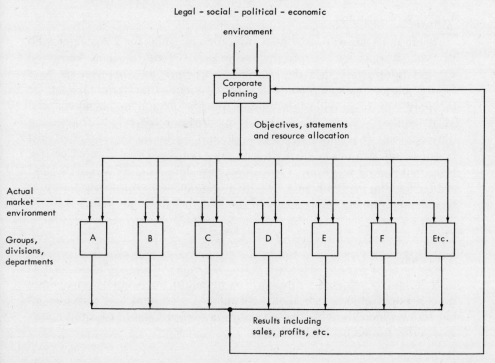

have to be provided by special studies. This might be the case with information concerning profitability at various levels of sales volume and price. Other types of information, such as price elasticity or the probability of retaliatory action by competitors, may have to be supplied by market research. However, with patience and persistence the categories of information which are needed, and which can be handled by the system which exists or is contemplated, is certain to emerge.

To provide the systems designer with sufficient guidelines, each category of information needs specific definition. The manner in which particular types of information are assembled and coded for storage as well as the responsiveness of the retrieval system are influenced by the frequency with which information will be called for, how quickly a response will be expected, how current the information must be, how much detail is required, how accurate it must be, how long it should be retained in storage, and the form in which it should be transmitted to the user.

### Frequency of use

Information which is used daily or weekly requires different handling than information that is needed only monthly or quarterly. A manual system may be adequate for the latter whereas the former may be impossible without computer assistance.

### Urgency of response

There is no need to provide a computer terminal for a manager who can wait a week for the information he uses. Of course, if he knows he can get information in a day, he may wait four, five, or even six days before requesting it. On the other hand, a computer terminal may be the only way to provide information quickly enough to managers who must counter surprise moves by competitors or react to fast-breaking developments in a labor dispute. It should be borne in mind that just because data can be handled rapidly, does not mean that a rapid system is a good one. If a system is able to accept data, analyze it rapidly and return it to the decision maker who is in no position to properly interpret its meaning, the operating speed of the system will create more problems that it solves.

### Timeliness

It is clearly a needless expense to maintain information on a daily basis if information a month old will suffice. For forecasting purposes an old series which contains revised data may be preferable to a more current series subject to later revision.

## Degree of detail

It is also a needless expense to break down daily sales of a product by salesman, territory, and customer (or break down monthly sales into daily sales) if an aggregate figure is all that is needed. This is the virtue of beginning with decisions and working backward to information. It is one way of circumventing man's squirrel-like tendencies.

## Accuracy

It is doubtful that many decisions hinge on an accuracy of plus or minus 1%, yet information people sometimes strain to supply this kind of data. Accuracy has a time dimension, too. Approximate data on a current basis may be satisfactory, although data with a sampling error of, say, no more than 5% may be needed within a month or by the end of the quarter.

## Life span

Information has a tendency to accumulate and the more it does, the more information is needed to keep track of the accumulation. As C. West Churchman has observed, information, in effect, is a reproductive organism that has no morals and goes around generating offspring without any consideration of the effect of its own "population explosion."[2]

An information system is not a library and material should be deleted as soon as its useful life has expired. While legal considerations may dictate how long some categories of information should be retained, the age of information used in the decision process is probably the most reliable guide with regard to the retention of most other types of data.

## Form

Wherever feasible, information should obviously be made available to the manager in a form which best serves his needs. This might be something as ordinary as a file card or typed memorandum. On the other hand, his needs might call for an elaborate computer printout, the appearance of data on a television screen, or telephone communication with a data bank. It should go without saying that the urgency of the decision and the rank of the manager have an important bearing on what form of information communication is feasible.

## ELEMENTS OF THE SYSTEMS

A system is a set of components (including people) that works together in some disciplined form of regular interaction to achieve a

---

[2] C. West Churchman, *The Systems Approach* (New York: Dell Publishing Co., 1969), p. 127 f.

specific end. It is a goal-oriented device. As such, management must specify what the information system is supposed to do for whom before the systems people can begin to design it. The former is somewhat simpler than the latter.

It is fairly evident that the goal of a marketing information system is to supply marketing managers at all levels of the organization with the data needed for decision making and in a form that is most convenient for them to use. Who should have access to what information is another question. At least two safeguards need to be built into the information system; one that will preserve privacy, and another that will prevent illegitimate use. A great deal of confusion and ruffled feelings can be avoided if criteria governing access to the data can be decided upon at an early stage in system design.

With specific definition of what information is to be fed into the system and criteria established to govern access to it, the system designer is ready to begin his work. The basic elements with which he works are hardware, software, programs, and people.

## Hardware

The physical equipment and facilities which perform the necessary electrical, mechanical, and optical functions required to assemble, store and retrieve information are generally referred to as hardware. Some of the more imaginative technocrats predict that as computer-based information systems begin to mature, they will increasingly take over the decision-making responsibilities of supervisory and middle management. There can be little doubt of the computer's ability to generate increasing quantities of information for decision making at all levels of management. There can be little doubt, too, that computer technology will continue to penetrate deeper into the organization structure and significantly improve the quality (and quantity) of information available to lower echelon managers. The resultant of these two forces, however, would seem to be better decisions rather than fewer decisions.

For a number of years computer manufacturers have placed primary emphasis on creating a balance between input, computation, and output. While the availability of terminal devices to be attached to the computer has presented a bottleneck, significant progress has been made in the development of terminals, as for example in the design of desk-top devices for executive use. By means of a small boxlike device an ordinary telephone can be used to communicate directly with a computer that may be thousands of miles away. With the advent of "touch-tone" or push-button telephones, it is possible to use the keyboard as an adding machine, a calculator, or in principle, as a small computer. Another acoustically coupled device enables the manager to transmit documents through the telephone.

**FIGURE 7–3.  Equipment layout for management information system**

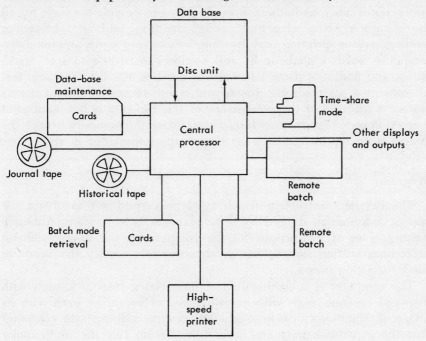

The capability of an information system will differ with such characteristics as the operating speed of the computer, the size of its memory, the repertoire of operating instructions, availability of peripheral equipment, and connections to remote terminals. For  illustrative purposes, a possible arrangement of hardware is given in Figure 7–3. There could be numerous other arrangements. In addition to the central processor there might be one or more disc units for an extended memory, high-speed printer for output presentation, a satellite computer for remote batch operation, teletype equipment to provide time-share capability—to mention some of the more obvious modifications which could be incorporated.

### Software

Software represents the set of instructions which tells the computer how to operate. It translates the demands of the system designer into machine-readable form, providing the general logic which enables the hardware to do its work. While it is possible for those who design an information system to develop their own software, the process is very involved and time consuming. As a rule, an existing computer language, such as FORTRAN (FORmula TRANslator), COBOL (Common Business Oriented Language), BASIC (Beginners All-purpose Symbolic Instruction Code), and others, is used. They can provide the logic for all the computer skills, viz., multiplying, dividing, adding, subtracting; reading, writing, printing, and drawing; memorizing words and numbers; arranging words alphabetically and numbers according to size; translating; and finding a particular word or number in a list. The acid test of software is its facility in identifying where requested information is stored. A measure of its performance of this function is the number of correct pieces of information transmitted minus the number of times the system is unable to respond even though the information exists.

## Programs

The detailed instruction which must be carried out to obtain the specific information desired by some manager is a program. Although writing a set of instructions for the computer is not a very difficult procedure, writing instructions which accurately convey the needs of the information user is.

The computer is a combination of interrelated machines, each with a special function, each with its own speed of operation, each with its own cost. The objective is to so schedule programs through the computer that the expensive units are never idle. To do this the programmer must have exceptional rapport with those requesting information. Otherwise, he will not be able to properly instruct and schedule this expensive, electronic servant. The situation is eased somewhat by the fact that while information needs vary in detail from one echelon to another and from one functional area to another, there are many types of information desired by all managers. If these areas of common need are carefully identified, the task of the programmer can be considerably eased.

## Personnel

While most of the obstacles encountered in the design and operation of an effective marketing information system yield to patience and intelligence, such systems are not the essence of simplicity . . . and they are subject to change. Consequently, it is necessary to have the various tasks connected with the design, installation, and operation of these systems performed by personnel who are thoroughly competent. Moreover, the skills required to keep the hardware functioning properly differ from those necessary for programming and for the organization of software. Since the marketing information system would not be the only use of a firm's computer facility, the personnel problem is shared with other using departments.

Another aspect of the personnel problem is the impact of the computer on an organization. Potentially, at least, the ramifications of this subject could fill several books.[3] However, an example may be sufficient to illustrate its implications. A rather common occurrence is the assignment of responsibility for a computer facility to the accounting department, where it is likely to be regarded as a replacement for their old bookkeeping machines. This can cause resentment and conflict between accountants and other departments having uses for the machines' capabilities, particularly if the accountants claim first priority.

One of the more obvious solutions to this problem is to assign the computer facility to a separate administrative unit with no line relationship to any of the big using departments such as marketing, production, accounting, purchasing, or finance. Although a number of companies have an independent computer service department included in their organizational plans, implementation sometimes proves difficult. But the longer it is delayed, the more the effectiveness of the marketing information system is likely to be impaired.

## SYSTEM DESIGN

Management is concerned with two broad types of information: that which is generated outside the firm, and that which is generated, within it. The task of the system designer is to determine what kind of system can best assemble, store and retrieve such information.

### External information

Information generated outside the firm may be directly related to its activities, such as selling, advertising, servicing, or related environmental characteristics independent of the firm. The latter is information about conditions that affect the company's opportunities and performance. Examples of such information are the presence of new industry in a given territory, a decreasing share of a customer's business, a new competitive product, the authorization of a new roadbuilding program by local government. Each has potential decision implications for one or more marketing executives of the firm.

Such information, of course, varies in the extent of its availability. The number, size, and location of potential buyers, for example, is usually available in, or can be readily derived from published sources. The results of vendor evaluation studies by customers and their basis for splitting orders is a little more difficult to acquire. Since this type of information must be gathered from some form of survey or sleuthing by salesmen, its value must be carefully related to its cost. The most difficult information to collect is that regarding the intentions of competitors. To get this may necessitate becoming involved in commercial espionage.

---

[3] Cf. Thomas L. Whisler, *The Impact of Computers on Organization* (New York: Frederick A. Praeger, Inc., 1970).

Judging from the recent spate of literature on the topic, the possibility of espionage is receiving increased attention.[4]

## Internal information

Internally generated information relates to the firm's operating performance (such as customer orders, inventory condition, cash flow, personnel changes, and costs) and also to the direction in which the firm is supposed to be moving (corporate goals, sales forecast, performance quotas, budget guidelines), and what is taking place in the various operating units (status of new product ideas, proposals for new product introductions, internal financial statements). For the most part, information concerning the firm's operating performance moves upward through the organization from bottom to top, while information regarding the firm's objectives move down from top to bottom. Information relating to the activities of various operating units moves horizontally. Much of this information enters the formal and informal communication system of a company as a by-product of operations rather than in response to any formal requests. See Figure 7–4.

The crucial considerations are that information of immediate importance to decision makers reaches them in time to be useful, that its flow be expedited to those who need it most urgently, and that only information of significance beyond the present be captured for storage. It is not reasonable to assume that decision makers know the sources of needed internal information or that because some of them do, it can be permitted to go unmanaged.

Simulation techniques can be very useful in demonstrating to anyone

---

[4] Richard M. Green, Jr., *Business Intelligence and Espionage* (Homewood, Ill.: Dow Jones–Irwin, Inc., 1966); "I Spy," *Columbia Journal of World Business* (May 1969), p. 47; "If You Quit, I'll Sue," *Forbes* (December 15, 1968), p. 40; "Trade Secret and the Mobile Executive," *Dun's Review and Modern Industry* (October 1968), p. 60; "Trade Secrets—What Price Loyalty?" *Harvard Business Review* (November–December, 1968), p. 66; "Real-Life Private Eye," *Electronic News* (May 19, 1969), p. 18; "Two Sides of Spying," *Chemical Week* (October 28, 1967), p. 108; "Hunting Industry Spies," *Business Week* (October 1, 1966), p. 42; "Carrying Information Across State Lines," *American Druggist* (September 12, 1966).

In a recent decision by the Fifth Circuit Court of Appeals, the Du Pont Company was awarded damages in a case dealing with industrial espionage. Du Pont had developed a new but unpatented process for producing methanol and had taken what the court regarded as reasonable precautions to safeguard it. Nevertheless, an aerial photograph taken directly above the site of the company's new methanol plant during construction revealed parts of the secret process. Photographers who took the pictures were found liable for disclosure of trade secrets.

While the court recognized that industrial espionage is a popular sport, the opinion included the comment that "our devotion to free-wheeling industrial competition must not force us into accepting the law of the jungle as the standard of morality expected in our commercial relations. Our tolerance of the espionage game must cease when the protections required to prevent another's spying cost so much that the spirit of inventiveness is dampened." *Marketing News* (October 1970), p. 5.

**FIGURE 7–4.** Information flow beginning with the receipt of a customer's order and ending with delivery of ordered merchandise to customer

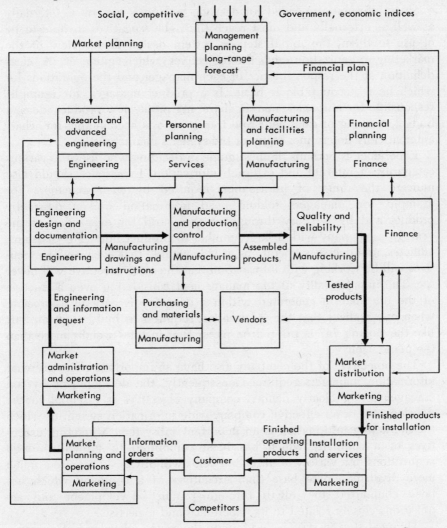

*Courtesy of General Electric Company*

who might doubt it the effect of information delays on marketing efficiency. As early as 1959, Jay Forrester was able to demonstrate the impact of delays in the transmission of information on marketing decisions. He developed a technique that enables one to make a cost-benefit analysis of the effects of changes in the speed of information transmison within an organization.[5]

---

[5] Jay W. Forrester, "Advertising—A Problem in Industrial Dynamics" *Harvard Business Review* (March–April, 1959), pp. 100–110.

**Developing the design**

Since information needed for decision making is generated internally as well as externally and must reach the right executives in time to be of use to them, the initial step in system design is a review of the marketing organization and the objectives which guide it. A clear definition of the responsibilities of each manager and the operations for which he is accountable is basic. Is a product manager, for example, responsible for unit sales, market share, net profit, new product ideas, a budget, training of salesmen? Specifying "who is accountable for what" automatically determines many of the system's characteristics.

Experience is perhaps the best guide in deciding who uses the various categories of internal and external information. Experience should also indicate the range of information required by each manager. For example, top managers seldom need information broken down by product and by territory throughout the world for every day of the year. In a company with a large number of product lines plus divisions, affiliates, and overseas operations, it is inevitable that even senior executives will be working with information that the chief executive will never see. The impracticality of top management considering even a fraction of the information generated within a company is easy to appreciate when one realizes that the information required to build a jet aircraft like the Boeing 747 is printed on paper that in total weighs more than the plane itself!

The objectives of the company also have an important effect on what information managers require. Consequently, the development by top management of clearly defined company objectives is essential to the development of an effective company-wide information system of which the marketing information is an important subsystem. Marketing executives of a company which has been committed to growth through acquisitions in a variety of unrelated fields will obviously require a much more diversified data base than executives of a company which has been committed to growth through product development and acquisitions closely related to its experience and expertise.

The next step in system design is to determine what kind of a system is best suited to the information needs required to discharge managers' responsibilities. To what extent should the system be automated? Should it include simulation models or simply an exception-reporting routine? Even an exception-reporting system requires a well-defined set of decision rules as to what constitutes an "exception." For example, a product manager might specify that he wants to know when sales, profit, sales expense, and market share deviate from planned values by 5% or more in any territory. Furthermore, when such a deviation occurs, he will want information on competitors' prices, competing products, competitive advertising, distribution channels used by competitors, a synopsis of information contained in the salesmen's call reports, and customers' sales. With explicit decision rules, an automated exception-reporting system could be devised without great difficulty.

It is important, of course, that the system designer resist the temptation to make the system more sophisticated than the managers who will be using it. The quality of information can be upgraded much more easily than the quality of managers, but little can be gained by doing so. For best results the two should be kept as well balanced as possible.

It is also pertinent to observe that companies which have enjoyed substantial success in developing a smoothly functioning information system usually began their development in piecemeal fashion, perfecting an exception-reporting system first before moving on to anything else.

An extensive research study conducted by Diebold Associates concluded that many companies spend sizeable sums to develop technically impressive marketing data bases, information systems, and corporate models of all descriptions, which marketing men find of little use. The study recommends that instead of printing huge quantities of data, only the exceptions should be compiled, such as salesmen failing to achieve quotas, sales activities exceeding budgeted expenses, markets in which the company is losing its competitive position, customers with declining purchases, product lines having slow sales movement, declining profit margins.[6]

The installation of a well-designed exception-reporting system may reveal a surprising number of problems. The ability of such a system to monitor sizeable quantities of detailed information is likely to confront managers with many more weaknesses and misfires than they anticipated. It is not unusual that the need to know what produced the deviations from plans prompts managers to request the incorporation of some diagnostic procedure into the system, which of course substantially extends its scope and sophistication.

At this juncture, the system designer is ready to consider such questions as the nature of the data file or bank, the form and method of data display, and the selection of a computer.

*The data bank.* The file, bank, or other storage unit of information collected for future use is the heart of the information system. Since it is so difficult to foresee all of the important information needs of management, and since systems initially developed tend to evolve into more complex designs, the central information file or bank should contain only data in disaggregated form. Admittedly, it is almost always more economical to aggregate data. Combining all package sizes of a product, lumping all price variations into a few broad classifications, reporting only standard time periods (e.g., months or quarters), and identifying no geographical area smaller than a sales territory or a

---

[6] *Marketing News* (August 1970), p. 6.

region saves time and simplifies procedures. However, data in aggregated form precludes many types of analysis because of its inflexibility. The aggregate or disaggregate nature of information required has an important bearing on information collection, processing, and storage—three collateral functions of the data bank.

*1. Data Collection.* The effort to develop or find information requested by managers or regarded by them as necessary to discharge their responsibilities can involve anything from a quick reference to an industrial directory to an expensive field survey. Marketing research departments typically spend a substantial amount of time in this activity.

In addition to specific searches, data collection should include regular scanning of newspapers, magazines, trade journals, and special reports, and even interviewing of individuals with good outside contacts, such as company salesmen and purchasing agents. Such regular scanning of a variety of sources can reveal a host of significant information such as changes in buyer attitudes, new tactics by competitors, price changes, new product entries, and new market opportunities was well as legal and political developments of significance to marketing executives. This not only relieves marketing managers of the onus of keeping abreast of an increasing flood of literature, but takes advantage of the overlapping informational needs of different managers.

*2. Data Processing.* Quality information requires care in validating, abstracting, and indexing as well as storage. All information is not equally valid, and users should be alerted to its errors and degree of inaccuracy. A market-share estimate based on a consumer panel, for example, may vary as much as 20 percent from the true value (at the 95 percent confidence limit), and a readership estimate may have a sampling error as high as 50 percent.

While data aggregation is not recommended, the abstraction of other forms of information can be very helpful. The reading of lengthy reports merely to discover whether or not they contain useful nuggets of information or to find some elusive statistic is wasteful of executive time. While the editing and condensation of incoming materials runs the risk of omitting something of value, this risk must be balanced against the advantages of supplying a manager with a succinct statement of contents.

A set of concise descriptions which will permit efficient classification for purposes of storage and retrieval is an obvious necessity. Indexing must also offer ready identification of what information users are interested in. For example, information relating to a new chlorinated solvent to be introduced by Dow Chemical Company might be filed under "solvents," "Dow Chemical Co.," and "new products," so that managers interested in solvents, new products, or Dow Chemical Co. would be able to find this information readily. A good indexing system is an important key in both rapid information retrieval and rapid dissemination of information to executives who can use it.

*3. Data Storage.* At the risk of being repetitious, it should be emphasized that marketing managers probably will not have a dominant voice in the design and management of the company information system of which the marketing information system is a part. Requirements for data storage will depend upon the use specifications of all departments. Although technical help is necessary for discussions on equipment and storage techniques, management has the responsibility of assuring that the hardware chosen will meet information system specifications at the time of installation, which may be some years beyond the planning stage, with which this discussion is concerned.

*Data presentation.* Implicit in information system design is the question of how information should be presented. One important aspect of this question is the degree of man-system interaction to be expected. At one extreme a manager would receive printed information in the form of regular reports; at the other he would obtain almost instantaneous response from a time-sharing or on-line computer. In between these extremes of "distance" a manager might make special requests for information from the storage files or data bank.

On-line computer systems have a great advantage in speed of access to information. Critics of these systems argue that managers do not need to know what happened as of the close of business yesterday.[7] This may be true. But there are benefits in being able to receive split-second responses. A manager's willingness to formulate questions and get data on which to base decisions may depend on the ease and speed with which he can retrieve answers from the data bank.

## COST-BENEFIT TRADEOFF

Generalizations about how much an effective marketing information system will cost, or how valuable it is, are difficult to make. Since many companies already have available much of the raw data required, particularly that of an internal nature, collection costs should not be large. It is the storage of the data and its transformation into useful information which account for the big cost increases. Unless a company has accounting procedures, such as interdepartmental billing, which track the cost of manpower assigned to a program, it would be virtually impossible to determine the cost of developing an information system.

A relatively simple, noncomputer system could probably be designed and put in operation for only a few thousand dollars. At the other extreme, highly complex computer-based systems might cost several million dollars.[8] A large company with sales at the $500-million level should expect to invest several hundred thousand dollars (plus equipment

---

[7] John Dearden, "Myth of Real-Time Management Information" *Harvard Business Review* (May–June, 1966), p. 123.

[8] Donald F. Cox and Robert E. Good, "How to Build a Marketing Information System" *Harvard Business Review* (May–June, 1967), p. 153.

**FIGURE 7–5. Detailed marketing information flow diagram generated by customer orders**

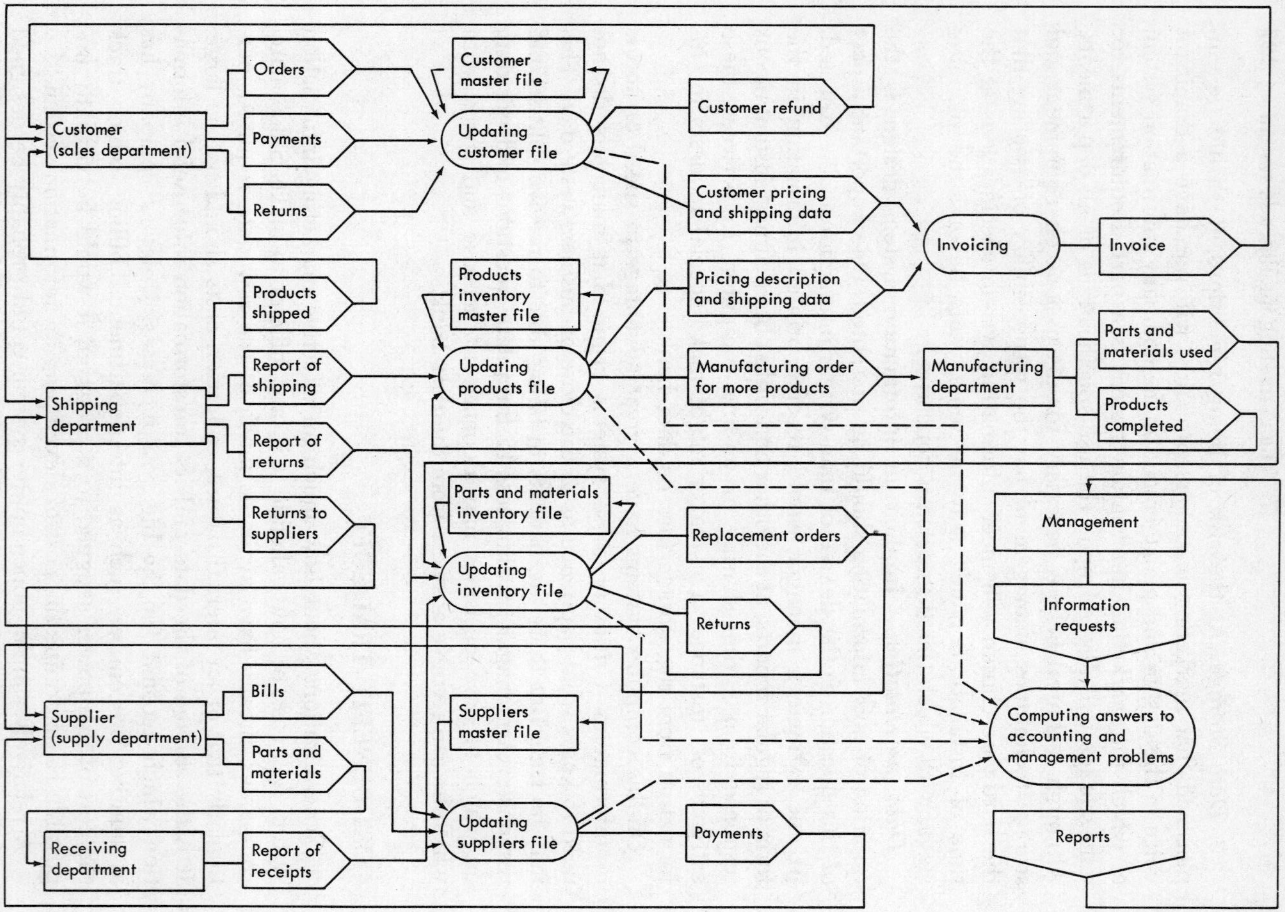


*Courtesy of General Electric Company*

charges) to design and implement a comprehensive computer-based information system.[9] Moreover, development costs will continue, as it is probable that management will periodically want to upgrade the system.

If top management is asked to authorize expenditures of this magnitude, they will surely demand justification of the value of the system. Computer-based systems, such as those used for accounting purposes, have usually been justified on the basis of the reduction in personnel and other administrative costs they achieved. Few advanced marketing information systems could be justified on that basis.

However, the cost reduction test is neither sufficient nor appropriate for marketing information systems. Their chief purpose is to help the marketing manager make better decisions, not to reduce clerical and administrative costs. The only legitimate way to justify such systems is in terms of the improvement they make possible in marketing efficiency. Unfortunately, this is not any easy estimate to make. On the other hand, if management is involved, as it should be, in working out the specifications of the system, it should be possible to formulate a meaningful estimate, however imprecise, of the system's benefits. Moreover, an information system need not be undertaken and justified in a single giant step. As stated earlier in this chapter, the recommended procedure is to develop the system one piece at a time. This involves smaller budget requests and simpler cost/benefit evaluations.

All talk about "total" information systems is nonsense. In the first place, it is impossible. And in the second place, it is liable to be uneconomic. Much information that might be desired is so costly and time-consuming to get that the greater soundness of decision or more exact precision of control that might result from it is not worth the cost. The manager of the marketing information service must at all times maintain an economic balance between the probable benefits of added information and the costs of getting and processing it. He needs to keep an eye on the effect of his operations on the profit-and-loss statement.

## SUMMARY

Many marketing executives suffer painful distress from at least two maladies that will not be found described in any medical dictionary— information anemia and information indigestion. The former is simply a lack of sufficient information to make rational decisions or an inability to absorb the information presented. One of the most distinguished sufferers from this ailment was none other than Henry Ford. Charles E. Sorensen gives us an interesting insight into Mr. Ford's affliction in his book, *My Forty Years with Ford*. As Mr. Sorensen described it, production of the Model T was climbing toward 10,000 cars a day in 1926, but sales were declining and Ford salesmen were clamoring for a new

---

[9] Ibid.

product to compete with the better looking and better performing Chevrolet. Although Ford was still outselling Chevrolet by two to one, the ratio two years earlier had been six to one.

Mr. Sorensen observed that despite the evidence of need for a change, Mr. Ford ignored it. "The only trouble with this car," he said, "is that we can't make it fast enough."

Information indigestion results from a steady diet of information, some of which is useful to decision making, but much of which is worthless. It has been said that if placed end to end, the information available in most industrial companies would reach half way to the moon.[10] Unfortunately, this doesn't help the marketing manager, unless he happens to be employed by an aerospace company.

A high corporate official of RCA summed it up like this, "The chief executive knows that the problems of the business are hidden somewhere in this mass of information, but he can't find them."[11]

An equally indigestible situation is that in which marketers are getting plenty of information in easy-to-read form, but it is not the information they need to make marketing decisions. The cure for this and most other informational maladies is an information system whose designer started with the kind of decisions marketing managers were called upon to make and worked backward to the type of system which would provide the information suggested by the nature of these decisions. Since information flows upward, downward, and horizontally through the organization, it is especially important that the collection and retrieval apparatus be tuned to those multidirectional flows as well as to the information sources related to marketing decisions.

The initial step in the formulation of such a system is a definition of the informational needs of decision makers. Beginning with the types of decisions which they regard as most important, the systems designer identifies the types of informational input needed and the frequency of the need and the degree of urgency involved. He must also determine the timeliness, degree of detail, accuracy, and form which these inputs should possess. When the dimensions of these inputs are clearly specified, the functions of collecting, storing, processing, and retrieving the appropriate data can be planned. The hardware, software, programs, and people necessary to perform these functions must then be combined into a system capable of producing the required informational outputs on demand. However, each element of the system, as well as the design of the system itself, must be considered in light of the inevitable trade-off between what executives think they need and what the company can afford.

---

[10] John F. Hayes, "Meeting the Information Needs of Top Management" (*5th Annual Conference,* Pittsburgh Chapter, American Marketing Association, February 29, 1968).

[11] Ibid.

# MARKET IDENTIFICATION: THE SEARCH PROCESS

FOR MANY BUSINESSES, the development of new markets is the only means of survival and growth. Finding untapped markets for existing products and evolving new ventures to meet new needs are often more important in the long run than the activity of existing business. Consequently, identifying and screening market opportunities is a continuing process for many manufacturers. Almost all methods employed in this process make extensive use of the Standard Industrial Classification System (S.I.C.). Information gleaned from the search for new markets is a basic input for the marketing intelligence system.

## THE STANDARD INDUSTRIAL CLASSIFICATION SYSTEM

The need for comparability of statistics describing the national economy prompted the development of a classification system to encompass all industrial, commercial, financial, and service activities. Initially developed by the Office of Statistical Standards (Bureau of the Budget),[1] the Standard Industrial Classification System provides a sound definitional basis for the collection of statistics by government agencies as well as the collection and analysis of data by marketers.

All economic activity is defined in the S.I.C. system, separated into classes, and each class is assigned a code number. The general classes are Agriculture, Mining, Construction, Manufacturing, Transportation, Wholesale Trade, Retail Trade, Finance, Services, Public Administration, and Nonclassifiables. Each of these general classes is divided into *major groups* (two-digit code), each major group is divided into *subgroups* (three-digit code), and each subgroup is further divided into *detailed industry categories* (four-digit code). The classifications are based

---

[1] Now the Statistical Policy Division of the Office of Management and Budget.

primarily on product manufactured or handled and/or services rendered. They are listed, each with a complete description, in the Standard Industrial Classification Manual. See Figure 8–1.

The S.I.C. manual is published by the Office of Management and Budget, Executive Office of the President, and is distributed through the United States Government Printing Office. The 1972 edition contains 84 major (2-digit) groups, 596 (3-digit) subgroups, and 976 detailed industry categories (4-digit groups) in the 11 general divisions mentioned in the preceding paragraph.

The basic unit of classification is the establishment rather than legal entities of companies. An establishment is an economic unit which produces goods or renders services, e.g., a mine, a factory, a branch house. It is characterized by physical location, distinctive activity, and reportability. It is not identical with a business concern or firm, since the latter may consist of a number of establishments.

The controlling factor in classifying an establishment is its major activity. This is generally determined by the product or group of products the establishment produces or handles or the services it renders. In the

**FIGURE 8–1.  Standard Industrial Classification Manual (partial table of contents)**

# Contents

| | Page |
|---|---|
| Introduction | 9 |
| Part I.  Titles and Descriptions of Industries | 15 |
| Division A.  Agriculture, forestry, and fishing | 17 |
| Major Group 01.  Agricultural production—crops | 18 |
| Major Group 02.  Agricultural production—livestock | 22 |
| Major Group 07.  Agricultural services | 25 |
| Major Group 08.  Forestry | 29 |
| Major Group 09.  Fishing, hunting, and trapping | 30 |
| Division B.  Mining | 31 |
| Major Group 10.  Metal mining | 32 |
| Major Group 11.  Anthracite mining | 35 |
| Major Group 12.  Bituminous coal and lignite mining | 36 |
| Major Group 13.  Oil and gas extraction | 37 |
| Major Group 14.  Mining and quarrying of nonmetallic minerals, except fuels | 39 |
| Division C.  Construction | 45 |
| Major Group 15.  Building construction—general contractors and operative builders | 47 |
| Major Group 16.  Construction other than building construction—general contractors | 49 |
| Major Group 17.  Construction—special trade contractors | 52 |
| Division D.  Manufacturing | 57 |
| Major Group 20.  Food and kindred products | 59 |
| Major Group 21.  Tobacco manufactures | 70 |
| Major Group 22.  Textile mill products | 71 |
| Major Group 23.  Apparel and other finished products made from fabrics and similar materials | 82 |
| Major Group 24.  Lumber and wood products, except furniture | 90 |
| Major Group 25.  Furniture and fixtures | 96 |
| Major Group 26.  Paper and allied products | 100 |
| Major Group 27.  Printing, publishing, and allied industries | 106 |
| Major Group 28.  Chemicals and allied products | 111 |
| Major Group 29.  Petroleum refining and related industries | 127 |
| Major Group 30.  Rubber and miscellaneous plastics products | 129 |
| Major Group 31.  Leather and leather products | 133 |
| Major Group 32.  Stone, clay, glass, and concrete products | 136 |
| Major Group 33.  Primary metal industries | 145 |
| Major Group 34.  Fabricated metal products, except machinery and transportation equipment | 153 |
| Major Group 35.  Machinery, except electrical | 167 |
| Major Group 36.  Electrical and electronic machinery, equipment, and supplies | 184 |
| Major Group 37.  Transportation equipment | 196 |
| Major Group 38.  Measuring, analyzing, and controlling instruments; photographic, medical and optical goods; watches and clocks | 202 |
| Major Group 39.  Miscellaneous manufacturing industries | 211 |

**FIGURE 8–1.**  *Concluded*

6                    STANDARD INDUSTRIAL CLASSIFICATION

Part I. Titles and Descriptions of Industries—Continued                                    Page
    Division E.  Transportation, communications, electric, gas, and sanitary services.... 219
        Major Group 40.  Railroad transportation----------------------------- 220
        Major Group 41.  Local and suburban transit and interurban highway
                         passenger transportation---------------------- 221
        Major Group 42.  Motor freight transportation and warehousing----- 224
        Major Group 43.  U.S. Postal Service----------------------------- 227
        Major Group 44.  Water transportation--------------------------- 228
        Major Group 45.  Transportation by air-------------------------- 231
        Major Group 46.  Pipe lines, except natural gas------------------ 232
        Major Group 47.  Transportation services------------------------ 233
        Major Group 48.  Communication-------------------------------- 235
        Major Group 49.  Electric, gas, and sanitary services------------- 237
    Division F.  Wholesale trade------------------------------------------ 241
        Major Group 50.  Wholesale trade—durable goods----------------- 242
        Major Group 51.  Wholesale trade—nondurable goods------------- 251
    Division G.  Retail trade--------------------------------------------- 259
        Major Group 52.  Building materials, hardware, garden supply, and
                         mobile home dealers--------------------------- 260
        Major Group 53.  General merchandise stores-------------------- 262
        Major Group 54.  Food stores---------------------------------- 263
        Major Group 55.  Automotive dealers and gasoline service stations... 265
        Major Group 56.  Apparel and accessory stores------------------- 267
        Major Group 57.  Furniture, home furnishings, and equipment stores.. 269
        Major Group 58.  Eating and drinking places-------------------- 271
        Major Group 59.  Miscellaneous retail-------------------------- 272
    Division H.  Finance, insurance, and real estate---------------------- 277
        Major Group 60.  Banking------------------------------------- 278
        Major Group 61.  Credit agencies other than banks-------------- 282
        Major Group 62.  Security and commodity brokers, dealers, exchanges,
                         and services--------------------------------- 285
        Major Group 63.  Insurance----------------------------------- 286
        Major Group 64.  Insurance agents, brokers, and service--------- 288
        Major Group 65.  Real estate--------------------------------- 289
        Major Group 66.  Combinations of real estate, insurance, loans, law
                         offices-------------------------------------- 291
        Major Group 67.  Holding and other investment offices----------- 292
    Division I.  Services----------------------------------------------- 295
        Major Group 70.  Hotels, rooming houses, camps, and other lodging
                         places-------------------------------------- 296
        Major Group 72.  Personal services---------------------------- 298
        Major Group 73.  Business services---------------------------- 301
        Major Group 75.  Automotive repair, services, and garages-------- 309
        Major Group 76.  Miscellaneous repair services----------------- 312
        Major Group 78.  Motion pictures----------------------------- 315
        Major Group 79.  Amusement and recreation services, except motion
                         pictures------------------------------------ 317
        Major Group 80.  Health services------------------------------ 321
        Major Group 81.  Legal services------------------------------- 324
        Major Group 82.  Educational services------------------------- 325
        Major Group 83.  Social services------------------------------ 327
        Major Group 84.  Museums, art galleries, botanical and zoological
                         gardens------------------------------------- 329

case of manufacturing establishments, value of production is the measure used to determine the major line of activity or primary product. Some classifications in the manufacturing division are also defined in terms of operating characteristics or stage of production in which an establishment is engaged. For example, in Major Group 20, "Food and Kindred Products," establishments belonging to the *Blended and Prepared Flour* industry (S.I.C. 2045) produce self-rising and blended flour from purchased flour, while establishments belonging to the *Flour and Other Grain Mill Products* industry (S.I.C. 2041) mill flour from grain and blend it all at the same location. See Figure 8–2.

In the distributive trades, retail establishments are distinguished from wholesale establishments on the basis of their customers. A retail establishment is one selling primarily to individual consumers or households. Within this general category, retail establishments are classified on the basis of merchandise handled and type of selling, e.g., over the

**FIGURE 8–2.  Sample page of S.I.C. Manual (showing a part of Subgroup 204, "Grain Mill Products")**

**204      GRAIN MILL PRODUCTS**

**2041  Flour and Other Grain Mill Products**

Establishments primarily engaged in milling flour or meal from grain, except rice. The products of flour mills may be sold plain or in the form of prepared mixes or doughs for specific purposes. Establishments primarily engaged in manufacturing prepared flour mixes or doughs from purchased ingredients are classified in Industry 2045, and rice milling in Industry 2044.

Bran and middlings, except rice
Bread and bread-type roll mixes, *mitsc*
Buckwheat flour
Cake flour, *mitsc*
Cereals, cracked grain : *mitsc*
Corn grits and flakes, for brewers' use
Dough, biscuit : canned-  *itsc*
Durum flour
Farina, *mitsc*
Flour : blended, prepared, or self-ris-
ing—*mitsc*
Flour : buckwheat, corn, rye, and wheat

Flour mills
Flour mixes, *mitsc*
Graham flour
Granular wheat flour
Grits and flakes, corn : for brewers' use
Hominy grits, except breakfast food
Meal, corn
Milling of grains, except rice
Pizza mixes and prepared dough, *mitsc*
Semolina (flour)
Sorghum grain flour
Wheat germ
Wheat mill feed

**2043  Cereal Breakfast Foods**

Establishments primarily engaged in manufacturing cereal breakfast foods and related preparations.

Breakfast foods, cereal
Coffee substitutes, made from grain
Corn flakes
Corn, hulled (cereal breakfast food)
Farina (cereal breakfast food)
Hominy grits, prepared as cereal break-
fast food

Infants' foods, cereal type
Oatmeal (cereal breakfast food)
Oats, rolled (cereal breakfast food)
Rice breakfast foods
Wheat flakes

**2044  Rice Milling**

Establishments primarily engaged in cleaning and polishing rice, and in manufacturing rice flour or meal. Other important products of this industry include brown rice, milled rice (including polished rice), rice polish, and rice bran.

Flour, rice
Milling of rice
Polishing of rice
Rice bran, flour, and meal
Rice, brewers'

Rice, brown
Rice cleaning and polishing
Rice polish
Rice, vitamin and mineral enriched

**2045  Blended and Prepared Flour**

Establishments primarily engaged in the preparation of blended flours and flour mixes or doughs from purchased flour. Establishments primarily engaged in milling flour from grain are classified in Industry 2041.

Biscuit flour, prepared : *mfpm*
Bread and bread-type roll mixes, *mfpm*
Cake flour, *mfpm*
Cake mixes, prepared :  *mfpm*
Dough, biscuit : canned—*mfpm*
Doughnut flour, prepared : *mfpm*
Doughs, refrigerated : *mfpm*
Farina, except cereal breakfast food :
*mfpm*

Flour : blended, prepared, or self-ris-
ing—*mfpm*
Gingerbread mix, prepared : *mfpm*
Pancake flour, prepared : *mfpm*
Phosphated flour, *mfpm*
Pizza mixes and prepared doughs,
*mfpm*

counter, mail order, or vending machine. Establishments which sell to retailers or to nonhousehold users are classified as wholesale and are differentiated within the wholesale trade division by type of merchandise sold.

Establishments not included in the manufacturing or distributive trades divisions are classified by the kind of service performed, such as transportation and other public utilities, finance, and real estate. Establishments which perform a variety of other services for individuals, businesses, government, and other organizations are included in a separate services division. Specialized services are in the same general divisions as their customers. For example, establishments serving agricultural enterprises are included in the agricultural, forestry, and fishing division, while establishments serving transportation enterprises and mining companies are included in those respective divisions.

### Interpreting industry classifications

While an industry class represents a grouping of establishments engaged in the same or similar lines of activity, this does not imply that such establishments possess similar physical characteristics. A "grocery store," for example, may vary from a small "mom and pop" business with no paid employees to a giant supermarket. Similarly, two manufacturing establishments producing the same end product may differ substantially in their use of materials, manpower, and machinery. One establishment may produce the product from basic raw materials, employing a lengthy manufacturing process, while the other may merely assemble the product from purchased materials and parts. The difference in the purchasing requirements of two such establishments is rather striking, yet both would be included in the same S.I.C. class. This is an important fact for the market analyst to bear in mind.

It is also important to recognize that the classification of establishments on the basis of their major activity involves at least two assumptions. The first is that all establishments in the same category engage in similar activities. It would seem reasonable to suppose, for example, that most of the output of establishments in the *Household Refrigerators and Home and Farm Freezers* industry (S.I.C. 3632) would consist of household refrigerators and freezers. (See Figure 8–3.)

**FIGURE 8–3. Sample page of S.I.C. Manual (showing Subgroup 363, "Household Appliances")**

186                    STANDARD INDUSTRIAL CLASSIFICATION

Group  Industry
No.    No.
362            ELECTRICAL INDUSTRIAL APPARATUS—Continued

3624   **Carbon and Graphite Products**

Establishments primarily engaged in manufacturing lighting carbons; carbon, graphite, and metal-graphite brushes and brush stock; carbon or graphite electrodes for thermal and electrolytic uses; and other carbon, graphite, and metal-graphite products.

Brush blocks, carbon or molded graphite
Brushes and brush stock contacts: carbon, graphite, etc.—electric
Carbon specialties for electrical use

Carbons, electric
Electrodes, for thermal and electrolytic uses: carbon and graphite
Lighting carbons

3629   **Electrical Industrial Apparatus, Not Elsewhere Classified**

Establishments primarily engaged in manufacturing industrial and commercial electric apparatus and equipment, not elsewhere classified, such as blasting machines, and fixed and variable capacitors, condensers, and rectifiers for industrial applications. Establishments primarily engaged in manufacturing condensers, capacitors, and rectifiers for electronic end products are classified in Group 367.

Battery chargers, rectifying or non-rotating
Blasting machines, electrical
Capacitors, a.c.: for motors and fluorescent lamp ballasts
Capacitors, except electronic: fixed and variable
Condensers, except electronic: fixed and variable
Condensers for motors and generators
Current collector wheels, for trolley rigging

Electrochemical generators (fuel cells)
Inverters, nonrotating: electrical
Mercury arc rectifiers (electrical apparatus)
Power conversion units, a.c. to d.c.: static-electric
Rectifiers (electrical apparatus)
Series capacitors, except electronic
Static elimination equipment, industrial
Thermo-electric generators

363    **HOUSEHOLD APPLIANCES**

3631   **Household Cooking Equipment**

Establishments primarily engaged in manufacturing household cooking equipment, such as stoves, ranges, and ovens, including both electric and nonelectric types. Establishments primarily engaged in manufacturing household cooking appliances, such as hot plates, grills, percolators, and toasters are classified in Industry 3634. Establishments primarily engaged in manufacturing commercial cooking equipment are classified in Industry 3589.

Barbecues, grills, and braziers for outdoor cooking
Cooking equipment, household
Gas ranges, domestic

Microwave ovens, household
Ovens, household: except portable
Ranges: electric, gas, etc.—household
Stoves, disk

3632   **Household Refrigerators and Home and Farm Freezers**

Establishments primarily engaged in manufacturing household refrigerators and home and farm freezers. Establishments primarily engaged in manufacturing commercial and industrial refrigeration equipment, packaged room coolers, and all refrigeration compressor and condenser units are classified in Industry 3585, and room dehumidifiers are classified in Industry 3634.

Freezers, home and farm
Ice boxes, household: metal or wood
Refrigerator cabinets, household: metal and wood

Refrigerators, mechanical and absorption: household

In 1967, however, only 59% of the output of establishments in this classification consisted of household refrigerators and freezers. The remaining 41% consisted of refrigeration machinery, household washers and dryers, and parts for household appliances—in that order of importance.[2] Only 71% of the output of establishments in the *Measuring and Dispensing Pump* industry (S.I.C. 3586)—which makes metering pumps used in gasoline service stations for gasoline, diesel fuel, and air—consisted of pumps. The remaining 29% of the industry's output consisted of compressors, elevators, and moving stairways, and valve and pipe fittings— in that order of importance.[3]

The proportion of an industry's output that is accounted for by the product or products described in the industry's definition is known as the *specialization ratio*. This was 59% in the case of the household refrigerator and freezer industry and 71% for the measuring and dispensing pump industry referred to in the preceding paragraph. The higher this ratio the more homogeneous the output of an industry and the closer this output conforms to its S.I.C. definition. For the manufacturing industries as a whole, the degree of product homogeneity within industry classes appears to be high. Specialization ratios less than 85% are rather scarce.

The second assumption inherent in the major-activity basis of classification is that establishments belonging to a given category account for a large proportion of the total activity included in that category. There is clearly some variation in the validity of this assumption. While almost the entire output (96%) of wooden household furniture in 1967 was produced by establishments in the Wooden Household Furniture industry (S.I.C. 2511),[4] only about 38% of the total output of steel pipe and tubes was accounted for by establishments in that industry (S.I.C. 3317).[5] The largest share of total production of steel pipe and tubes, 62%, was produced as a secondary product by steel mills (S.I.C. 3312).[6] Similarly, almost all (97%) of the drugs for human and veterinary use were produced by establishments in the Pharmaceutical Preparations industry (S.I.C. 2834),[7] but only 67% of the total output of animal fats and oils was accounted for by establishments in that industry in 1967.[8] Most of the remaining 33% of animal fats and oils was produced as a by-product by establishments in the Meat Packing industry (S.I.C. 2011).[9]

---

[2] *U.S. Census of Manufacturers,* 1967, Vol. II (Industry Statistics), Part 3, pp. 36B–15 f.

[3] Ibid., p. 35G–17.

[4] Ibid., Part 2, p. 25A–13.

[5] Ibid., p. 33A–17.

[6] Ibid.

[7] Ibid., p. 28C–10.

[8] Ibid., Part I, p. 20H–13.

[9] Ibid., p. 20A–12.

The share of total national output of a product which is produced by establishments in the industry for which it is the primary product is known as the *coverage ratio*. In 1967 this ratio was 97% for the Pharmaceutical Preparations industry, 96% for the Wooden Household Furniture industry, 67% for the Animal and Marine Fats and Oils industry, and 38% for the Steel Pipe and Tube industry.

The coverage ratio will generally be low when the primary product of an industry is included in the definition of another industry. This is the case for industry categories which are distinguished on the basis of stage of production or type of operation. Establishments in the Blended and Prepared Flour industry (S.I.C. 2045), for example, accounted for only 63% of the total output of blended and prepared flour in the nation in 1967.[10] It will be recalled that these are establishments using purchased flour. Most of the remaining output of this product was produced by establishments in the Flour and Other Grain Mill Products industry (S.I.C. 2041), establishments which mill flour from grain.[11] These examples of the varying degree to which production of a class of products can be attributed to a particular industry identified with the product illustrate the need for careful prior analysis in using the S.I.C. for market measurement. Both the specialization ratio and the coverage ratio are important indicators of reliability.

It must also be borne in mind when using industry statistics that many establishments are owned by other establishments, which take their entire output for the production of other products. These captive establishments are classified in the industry of their principal product or products just as if they were independent enterprises. Accurate interpretation of industry statistics requires that one be alert to the possibility of interplant transfers. Appropriate allowances must be made if the latter appears to be significant relative to the volume of commercial sales.

An additional question of interpretation frequently arises because the range of products included in industry classifications varies considerably. Some industries are limited to a single product. The Beet Sugar industry (S.I.C. 2063), for example, includes only establishments engaged in the manufacture of sugar from sugar beets. The Storage Battery industry (S.I.C. 3691) includes only establishments manufacturing alkaline and lead acid batteries. Other industries, however, like Farm Equipment (S.I.C. 3522) or Machine Tools (S.I.C. 3541 and 3542) include a broad range of products. The latter quality is characteristic of many so-called Not Elsewhere Classified categories. These generally represent combinations of products whose makers or handlers are too small in terms of sales volume, number of employees, or other economic factor to warrant a separate classification for them.

An additional analytical tool is available for use in measurements in-

---

[10] Ibid., p. 20D–15.
[11] Ibid., p. 20D–15.

## FIGURE 8–4.  Product classes in the farm machines and equipment industry

**35A-22**                                    ENGINES AND TURBINES AND FARM MACHINERY AND EQUIPMENT

TABLE 6A-8.  **Farm Machines and Equipment: 1967 and 1963**

| 1967 Census product code | Type of farm equipment | Number of companies | Total Quantity (number) | Total Value ($1,000) | Domestic Quantity (number) | Domestic Value ($1,000) | Export Quantity (number) | Export Value ($1,000) |
|---|---|---|---|---|---|---|---|---|
| | | | | **1967 — Shipments** | | | | |
| | WHEEL TRACTORS AND PARTS AND ATTACHMENTS, TOTAL...................... | | (X) | 1,198,529 | (X) | 1,051,141 | (X) | 147,388 |
| | Complete tractors (except garden), total¹........................ | (NA) | 241,096 | 986,168 | 213,284 | 864,106 | 27,812 | 122,062 |
| 35221 04 | 9 to 34 P.T.O. hp.............................. | (NA) | 15,878 | 38,186 | 48,760 | 125,125 | 3,943 | 9,537 |
| 35221 05 | 35 to 39 P.T.O. hp.............................. | (NA) | 36,825 | 96,476 | | | | |
| 35221 06 | 40 to 49 P.T.P. hp.............................. | (NA) | 25,939 | 77,252 | 23,548 | 70,147 | 2,391 | 7,105 |
| 35221 09 | 50 to 59 P.T.O. hp.............................. | (NA) | 32,378 | 114,499 | 28,181 | 99,758 | 4,197 | 14,741 |
| 35221 11 | 60 to 69 P.T.O. hp.............................. | (NA) | 26,978 | 110,174 | 23,802 | 96,622 | 3,176 | 13,552 |
| 35221 12 | 70 to 79 P.T.O. hp.............................. | (NA) | 31,461 | 146,039 | 26,947 | 124,209 | 4,514 | 21,830 |
| 35221 13 | 80 to 89 P.T.O. hp.............................. | (NA) | | | | | | |
| 35221 14 | 90 to 99 P.T.O. hp.............................. | (NA) | 51,495 | 266,802 | | | | |
| 35221 16 | 100 to 119 P.T.O. hp.............................. | (NA) | 13,117 | 83,100 | 62,046 | 348,245 | 9,591 | 55,297 |
| 35221 17 | 120 P.T.O. hp and over.............................. | (NA) | 7,025 | 53,640 | | | | |
| | Attachments and parts, total²........................ | (NA) | (X) | 212,361 | (X) | 187,035 | (X) | 25,326 |
| 35221 21 | Attachments²........................................ | (NA) | (X) | 33,424 | (X) | 27,484 | (X) | 5,940 |
| 35221 23 | Parts²............................................. | (NA) | (X) | 178,937 | (X) | 159,551 | (X) | 19,386 |
| 35223 -- | PLANTING, SEEDING, AND FERTILIZING MACHINERY, TOTAL........................................ | (NA) | (X) | 169,001 | (X) | 156,258 | (X) | 12,743 |
| | Corn planters: | | | | | | | |
| 35223 11 13, 15 | Drawn 2-, 4-, 6-row, and larger................. | | | | | | | |
| 35223 17 | Mounted......................................... | 12 | 55,054 | 27,987 | (D) | (D) | (D) | (D) |
| 35223 20 | Corn and cotton planters (drawn and mounted)...... | | | | | | | |
| 35223 30 | Listers and lister planting attachment units...... | 6 | 2,707 | 2,054 | (D) | (D) | (D) | (D) |
| 35223 35 | Potato planters, drawn or mounted................. | | | | | | | |
| 35223 41 | Transplanters, drawn or mounted................... | 9 | 11,382 | 2,124 | (D) | (D) | (D) | (D) |
| 35223 44 | Grain drills, including legume planters........... | 8 | (D) | (D) | (D) | (D) | (D) | (D) |
| 35223 49 | Broadcast seeders (end-gate, mounted and drawn)... | 7 | 22,762 | 1,039 | (D) | (D) | (D) | (D) |
| | Fertilizer distributors, drawn or mounted: Dry (including lime spreaders): Gravity distribution: | | | | | | | |
| 35223 50 | Drawn (5 feet and over)..................... | 21 | 7,936 | 3,787 | 7,329 | 3,625 | 607 | 162 |
| 35223 53 | Mounted (5 feet and over)................... | 7 | 1,631 | 446 | (D) | (D) | (D) | (D) |
| 35223 51 | Centrifugal distribution....................... | 18 | 10,418 | 9,113 | 10,134 | 8,974 | 284 | 139 |
| 35223 52 | Liquid......................................... | 9 | 3,311 | 2,373 | 3,119 | 2,269 | 192 | 104 |
| 35223 54 | Anhydrous ammonia.............................. | 8 | (D) | (D) | (D) | (D) | (D) | (D) |
| | Manure spreaders, conveyor type (ASAE rating): Power-take-off (single beater): | | | | | | | |
| 35223 55 | Under 130 bushel capacity.................. | 9 | 6,479 | 2,890 | 6,288 | 2,783 | 191 | 107 |
| 35223 56 | 130 and under 200 bushel capacity.............. | 18 | 16,468 | 10,573 | 14,310 | 8,992 | 2,158 | 1,581 |
| 35223 59 | 200 and over bushel capacity................ | | | | | | | |
| | Power-take-off (multiple beater): | | | | | | | |
| 35223 64 | Under 130 bushel capacity.................. | 7 | 4,419 | 3,951 | 3,259 | 3,138 | 1,160 | 813 |
| 35223 65 | 130 and under 200 bushel capacity.............. | | | | | | | |
| 35233 66 | 200 and over bushel capacity............... | 7 | 1,074 | 1,303 | (D) | (D) | (D) | (D) |
| 35223 63 | Ground drive................................... | 3 | 2,641 | 1,179 | 2,402 | 1,071 | 239 | 106 |
| | Manure spreaders, tank-type: | | | | | | | |
| 35223 67 | Open tank (flail unloading)..................... | 9 | 7,991 | 11,326 | 7,811 | 11,151 | 180 | 175 |
| 35223 68 | Closed tank (for liquids only).................. | | | | | | | |
| 35223 70 | Front and rear mounted loaders (farm type), manure and general utility (except beet and sugar cane loaders)....................................... | 24 | 35,078 | 16,240 | 30,050 | 13,918 | 5,028 | 2,322 |
| 35223 77 | Row crop unit planter attachments (quantity in number of rows)................................ | 7 | 37,803 | 4,722 | 35,397 | 4,452 | 2,406 | 270 |
| 35223 81 | Other planting, seeding, and fertilizing machinery | 37 | (X) | 8,385 | (X) | 8,048 | (X) | 337 |
| 35223 84 | Attachments.................................... | 29 | (X) | 21,978 | (X) | 20,169 | (X) | 1,809 |
| 35229 30 | Parts (replacement units only)................. | 47 | (X) | 17,827 | (X) | 17,011 | (X) | 816 |
| 35224 pt. | HARROWS, ROLLERS, PULVERIZERS, STALK CUTTERS, AND SIMILAR EQUIPMENT, TOTAL................ | (NA) | (X) | 179,625 | (X) | 168,585 | (X) | 11,040 |
| | Harrows: | | | | | | | |
| 35224 01 | Spike-tooth harrow sections..................... | 24 | 147,767 | 4,930 | 145,194 | 4,843 | 2,573 | 87 |
| 35224 02 | Spring-tooth harrow sections.................... | 21 | 64,253 | 5,491 | 62,077 | 5,346 | 2,176 | 145 |
| 35224 03 | Tine-tooth harrow sections...................... | 7 | 27,219 | 957 | (D) | (D) | (D) | (D) |

See footnotes at end of table.

Source: *U.S. Census of Manufacturers,* 1967, Volume II (Industry Statistics), Part 3, pp 35A-22.

volving industry categories like farm equipment and machine tools which include a variety of different products. This is the *product classification system* developed by the Census Bureau from the S.I.C. manufacturing industry classifications. These product classes are relatively homogeneous groupings of individual product types within an industry category. They are assigned a seven-digit code, the first four digits of which identify the industry and are the same as the S.I.C. code. The fifth digit identifies the product class and the remaining two identify the individual product. The added refinement which this provides is shown in Figure 8–4. Corn and cotton planters, for example, are identified by the number 3522320. The first four digits (3522) indicate that the product belongs to the Farm Machines and Equipment industry, the fifth digit (3) indicates that it is a type of planting, seeding, and fertilizing equipment, and the remaining two digits (20) identify it as a piece of equipment designed to plant corn and cotton.[12]

For many purposes, the establishment of product classes has the effect of dividing the four-digit S.I.C. categories into smaller classifications. This is particularly true for industries such as Farm Machines and Equipment in which establishments do not ordinarily produce the full range of products of the industry but tend to specialize in a few selected products. The 1967 Census of Manufacturers includes about 10,500 7-digit categories, while 12,000 to 13,000 such classes are included in the Annual Survey of Manufacturers. The latter is available during intercensal periods and is, in effect, a miniature census of manufacturers.

The allowances and adjustments which must be made in using the S.I.C. reflect the inherent complexity of American industry. Collection of data for the great variety of individual establishments and its presentation in a manageable number of significant classifications represents a Herculean task. On the one hand lies the danger of classifications which are too broad to have genuine usefulness. Equally undesirable, though, are classifications so narrowly defined that establishments included in them either account for a small part of the type of production implied by the title or are also engaged to a significant degree in activities included in other classifications. Although much remains to be done in the development of meaningful industry classifications, the 1972 revision represents notable progress.

## IDENTIFYING MARKET OPPORTUNITIES

The firm with a comparatively small market share but a good product may find its greatest opportunity among organizations which have a need for its products and services but are not presently customers. For many companies the most fruitful search effort is that for needs they are

---

[12] Ibid., Part 3, 35A–22.

not presently meeting but have the requisite technical capacity to satisfy. This is the type of search required by a strategy for growth based on new-product development and expansion into previously untapped markets.

### Finding new buyers in existing markets

Identifying new customers for current applications of a company's existing product line usually proceeds in two phases. The first is classifying present customers by S.I.C. This provides a list of market segments for which a considerable amount of secondary data is available. The second phase consists of developing an enumeration of the firms in each segment and comparing this list with the company's customer list. This provides a positive identification of the noncustomer firms in each market segment.

*Classifying customers.* Customers can be readily segregated on the basis of four-digit S.I.C. classes by ascertaining the primary product or type of operation of each and matching this characteristic with the appropriate industry definition. A partial list of customers segregated by S.I.C. is shown in Figure 8–5.

*Identifying noncustomers.* Every state has an industrial directory of some description published privately or by a department of the state government. These directories provide a complete census of commercial and industrial firms doing business in the state, identifying them by name

**FIGURE 8–5. Classified customer list (Midstates Steel and Wire Company, Crawfordsville, Indiana)**

General Building Contractors (152)
    Allenby Brothers
    Allied Construction Company
    Barber & DeAtley, Inc.
    Barker Builders, Inc.

Roofing and Sheet Metal Contractors (1761)
    Bash Roofing Company
    Butler Roofing
    Clear Construction Co.
    Econ-O-Way Roofing & Siding
    Fox Bridge Co.

Concrete Contractors (1771)
    Byrd Construction Company
    C B M Concrete Company
    Custom Concrete Corp.
    Falls Stone and Masonry Co.
    Grant Concrete Service
    H & M Concrete Construction

Structural Steel Erectors (1791)
    A-K & L Inc.
    Bulk-Tel Construction, Inc.
    Pelco Structures, Inc.

and location. A number of directories list firms by four-digit S.I.C. industries. Many which do not follow S.I.C. definitions list each firm twice: by product produced or handled—usually in a "Buyers Guide" section; and again under city of location.

The manufacturer whose customers are classified by S.I.C. or by product categories—if the appropriate state directories are not based on S.I.C.—can match his customer list against the list of firms in the appropriate state directories, category by category. Firms included in an industrial directory in every category in which a manufacturer has customers, but are not included in his list of customers represent potential new customers.

Suppose, for example, that an East Coast manufacturer of paints and varnishes wishes to know how many furniture manufacturers in the state of North Carolina are not among his customers. If the firm's customers are already classified by S.I.C., reference to *County Business Patterns* (Figure 8–6) would disclose 579 manufacturers of furniture and fixtures (S.I.C. 25) in the state in 1971. In order for this manufacturer to determine how many furniture accounts in North Carolina he has been failing to sell, he simply needs to compare the number of present customers in S.I.C. 25 in North Carolina with the number of "reporting units" in this classification in the state. There may or may not be good reasons for a discrepancy between the two lists; but any substantial discrepancy may well represent untapped market opportunity.

The names and addresses of manufacturers missing from the firm's customer list in North Carolina can be obtained from the *North Carolina Directory of Manufacturing Firms*. Like a number of other state directories, entries in this directory are listed alphabetically, by four-digit S.I.C. number, and alphabetically by county. In addition to state industrial directories, the *Dun and Bradstreet Reference Book*, which gives a nearly complete listing of all businesses and is based on the S.I.C., is compiled for every community in the nation. Current editions of the Reference Books, however, are available only to subscribers of the Dun and Bradstreet rating service.

Listings of a particular kind of business in a given area sometimes may also be secured from mailing-list houses, the research departments of newspapers serving the area, local chambers of commerce, or business associations. These sources are often able to supply specialized and detailed directories for their immediate locality. Membership lists of national trade associations—when they can be obtained—and telephone directories can be useful in pinpointing prospects.

## Identifying untapped markets

An untapped market might be one of two types: an industry in which a manufacturer discovers new applications for his existing products, or

# FIGURE 8–6.   A sample page of *County Business Patterns*

## NORTH CAROLINA                                                                121

### TABLE 2B. **States, by Major Industry Group: 1971** —Continued

(Excludes government employees, railroad employees, self-employed persons, etc.—see "General Explanation." Size class 1 to 3 includes reporting units having payroll during 1st quarter but no employees during mid-March pay period.   "D" denotes figures withheld to avoid disclosure of operations of individual reporting units)

| SIC code | Industry | Number of employees, mid-March pay period | Taxable payrolls, Jan.-Mar. ($1,000) | Total reporting units | Number of reporting units, by employment-size class | | | | | | | |
|---|---|---|---|---|---|---|---|---|---|---|---|---|
| | | | | | 1 to 3 | 4 to 7 | 8 to 19 | 20 to 49 | 50 to 99 | 100 to 249 | 250 to 499 | 500 or more |
| | TOTAL . . . . . . . . . . . . | 1 492 035 | 2 058 284 | 84 951 | 40 734 | 17 858 | 15 055 | 6 578 | 2 241 | 1 521 | 621 | 343 |
| ... | AGRICULTURAL SERVICES,FORESTRY,FISHERIES. | 5 955 | 5 606 | 831 | 458 | 188 | 139 | 37 | 4 | 3 | 2 | – |
| 07 | AGRICULTURE SERVICES AND HUNTING. . . | 5 558 | 5 207 | 739 | 398 | 169 | 130 | 33 | 4 | 3 | 2 | – |
| 08 | FORESTRY. . . . . . . . . . . . . . | 110 | 77 | 15 | 6 | 3 | 4 | 2 | – | – | – | – |
| 09 | FISHERIES . . . . . . . . . . . . . | 287 | 322 | 77 | 54 | 16 | 5 | 2 | – | – | – | – |
| ... | MINING. . . . . . . . . . . . . . . | 4 518 | 8 009 | 142 | 34 | 18 | 20 | 45 | 17 | 7 | – | 1 |
| 10 | METAL MINING. . . . . . . . . . . . | (D) | (D) | 3 | | 1 | 1 | | – | 1 | – | |
| 14 | NONMETALLIC MINERALS, EXCEPT FUELS. . | 3 804 | 6 307 | 125 | 29 | 15 | 19 | 41 | 16 | 4 | – | 1 |
| -- | ADMINISTRATIVE AND AUXILIARY. . . . . | (D) | (D) | 10 | 1 | 2 | – | 4 | 1 | 2 | – | |
| ... | CONTRACT CONSTRUCTION . . . . . . . . | 98 283 | 141 747 | 9 194 | 4 232 | 2 287 | 1 709 | 647 | 211 | 78 | 23 | 7 |
| 15 | GENERAL BUILDING CONTRACTORS. . . . . | 34 047 | 49 785 | 2 338 | 941 | 626 | 450 | 201 | 71 | 33 | 11 | 5 |
| 16 | HEAVY CONSTRUCTION CONTRACTORS. . . . | 17 082 | 25 871 | 885 | 329 | 189 | 200 | 89 | 48 | 20 | 9 | 1 |
| 17 | SPECIAL TRADE CONTRACTORS . . . . . . | 46 791 | 65 159 | 5 957 | 2 959 | 1 470 | 1 055 | 354 | 91 | 24 | 3 | 1 |
| -- | ADMINISTRATIVE AND AUXILIARY. . . . . | 333 | 897 | 13 | 3 | 2 | 4 | 2 | 1 | 1 | – | |
| ... | MANUFACTURING . . . . . . . . . . . . | 690 804 | 973 272 | 8 129 | 1 644 | 1 129 | 1 583 | 1 381 | 784 | 895 | 449 | 264 |
| 20 | FOOD AND KINDRED PRODUCTS . . . . . . | 34 871 | 48 751 | 691 | 129 | 86 | 136 | 171 | 77 | 67 | 19 | 6 |
| 21 | TOBACCO MANUFACTURES. . . . . . . . . | 19 505 | 33 140 | 53 | 3 | 1 | 9 | 16 | 6 | 8 | 4 | 6 |
| 22 | TEXTILE MILL PRODUCTS . . . . . . . . | 267 007 | 336 650 | 1 412 | 105 | 75 | 150 | 271 | 184 | 310 | 184 | 133 |
| 23 | APPAREL AND OTHER TEXTILE PRODUCTS. . | 70 425 | 68 941 | 509 | 44 | 27 | 38 | 61 | 104 | 142 | 75 | 18 |
| 24 | LUMBER AND WOOD PRODUCTS. . . . . . . | 25 821 | 28 342 | 1 696 | 595 | 398 | 408 | 177 | 77 | 37 | 4 | – |
| 25 | FURNITURE AND FIXTURES. . . . . . . . | 64 373 | 85 144 | 579 | 84 | 45 | 96 | 126 | 63 | 84 | 58 | 23 |
| 26 | PAPER AND ALLIED PRODUCTS . . . . . . | 18 075 | 33 788 | 141 | 9 | 8 | 17 | 35 | 32 | 27 | 8 | 5 |
| 27 | PRINTING AND PUBLISHING . . . . . . . | 14 809 | 23 277 | 632 | 196 | 118 | 171 | 89 | 32 | 18 | 5 | 3 |
| 28 | CHEMICALS AND ALLIED PRODUCTS . . . . | 23 615 | 44 306 | 234 | 34 | 37 | 55 | 44 | 33 | 16 | 6 | 9 |
| 29 | PETROLEUM AND COAL PRODUCTS . . . . . | (D) | (D) | 9 | 4 | 1 | 3 | – | 1 | – | | |
| 30 | RUBBER AND PLASTICS PRODUCTS, N.E.C.. | 12 630 | 16 609 | 118 | 13 | 16 | 25 | 25 | 11 | 17 | 6 | 5 |
| 31 | LEATHER AND LEATHER PRODUCTS. . . . . | 3 092 | 3 968 | 34 | 10 | 6 | 5 | 5 | – | 3 | 3 | 2 |
| 32 | STONE, CLAY, AND GLASS PRODUCTS . . . | 13 393 | 20 116 | 344 | 56 | 53 | 100 | 82 | 24 | 20 | 6 | 3 |
| 33 | PRIMARY METAL INDUSTRIES. . . . . . . | 5 676 | 10 327 | 67 | 8 | 6 | 19 | 13 | 7 | 8 | 3 | 3 |
| 34 | FABRICATED METAL PRODUCTS . . . . . . | 14 311 | 23 642 | 312 | 62 | 43 | 67 | 67 | 35 | 25 | 11 | 2 |
| 35 | MACHINERY, EXCEPT ELECTRICAL. . . . . | 26 949 | 51 636 | 574 | 145 | 106 | 143 | 94 | 31 | 30 | 17 | 8 |
| 36 | ELECTRICAL EQUIPMENT AND SUPPLIES . . | 33 376 | 56 421 | 132 | 12 | 9 | 25 | 13 | 13 | 24 | 15 | 21 |
| 37 | TRANSPORTATION EQUIPMENT. . . . . . . | 9 136 | 13 462 | 138 | 34 | 19 | 28 | 14 | 21 | 13 | 6 | 3 |
| 38 | INSTRUMENTS AND RELATED PRODUCTS. . . | 4 899 | 8 309 | 41 | 7 | 6 | 6 | 7 | 2 | 5 | 6 | 2 |
| 39 | MISCELLANEOUS MANUFACTURING INDUSTRIES. | 4 460 | 5 828 | 145 | 46 | 24 | 34 | 22 | 6 | 11 | 1 | 1 |
| -- | ADMINISTRATIVE AND AUXILIARY. . . . . | 24 160 | 60 272 | 265 | 48 | 44 | 48 | 48 | 24 | 30 | 12 | 11 |
| ... | TRANSPORTATION AND OTHER PUBLIC UTILITIES | 82 147 | 155 053 | 2 900 | 1 095 | 484 | 679 | 367 | 133 | 92 | 26 | 24 |
| 41 | LOCAL AND INTERURBAN PASSENGER TRANSIT. | 4 382 | 5 297 | 348 | 155 | 71 | 74 | 32 | 8 | 7 | 1 | – |
| 42 | TRUCKING AND WAREHOUSING. . . . . . . | 35 933 | 69 276 | 1 629 | 700 | 267 | 342 | 204 | 66 | 30 | 9 | 11 |
| 44 | WATER TRANSPORTATION. . . . . . . . . | 1 597 | 1 640 | 48 | 17 | 11 | 8 | 7 | 1 | 2 | 2 | – |
| 45 | TRANSPORTATION BY AIR . . . . . . . . | 3 802 | 8 915 | 99 | 19 | 16 | 18 | 9 | 4 | 4 | – | 2 |
| 47 | TRANSPORTATION SERVICES . . . . . . . | 1 275 | 1 566 | 99 | 40 | 25 | 20 | 10 | – | 4 | – | – |
| 48 | COMMUNICATION . . . . . . . . . . . . | 21 799 | 38 251 | 425 | 66 | 69 | 167 | 49 | 29 | 30 | 7 | 8 |
| 49 | ELECTRIC, GAS AND SANITARY SERVICE. . | 12 359 | 28 138 | 240 | 77 | 21 | 43 | 52 | 24 | 14 | 6 | 3 |
| -- | ADMINISTRATIVE AND AUXILIARY. . . . . | 921 | 1 758 | 16 | – | 2 | 7 | 2 | 1 | 3 | 1 | – |
| ... | WHOLESALE TRADE . . . . . . . . . . . | 90 535 | 167 254 | 7 022 | 2 374 | 1 645 | 1 860 | 842 | 220 | 66 | 13 | 2 |
| -- | ADMINISTRATIVE AND AUXILIARY. . . . . | 2 228 | 4 444 | 468 | 26 | 11 | 15 | 8 | 5 | 2 | – | 1 |
| ... | RETAIL TRADE. . . . . . . . . . . . . | 243 165 | 260 324 | 25 953 | 12 474 | 5 910 | 5 118 | 1 821 | 428 | 155 | 34 | 13 |
| 52 | BUILDING MATERIALS & FARM EQUIPMENT . | 13 359 | 17 298 | 1 419 | 510 | 355 | 404 | 129 | 17 | 2 | 2 | – |
| 53 | GENERAL MERCHANDISE . . . . . . . . . | 46 909 | 48 731 | 2 169 | 976 | 382 | 371 | 232 | 118 | 66 | 17 | 7 |
| 54 | FOOD STORES . . . . . . . . . . . . . | 35 544 | 37 139 | 3 389 | 1 929 | 587 | 512 | 233 | 79 | 38 | 8 | 3 |
| 55 | AUTOMOTIVE DEALERS & SERVICE STATIONS | 42 951 | 59 466 | 6 270 | 3 718 | 1 199 | 876 | 378 | 82 | 15 | 1 | 1 |
| 56 | APPAREL AND ACCESSORY STORES. . . . . | 18 605 | 16 993 | 2 324 | 944 | 695 | 513 | 135 | 29 | 8 | – | – |
| 57 | FURNITURE AND HOME FURNISHINGS STORES | 11 944 | 15 491 | 1 935 | 887 | 565 | 403 | 70 | 10 | – | | 1 |
| 58 | EATING AND DRINKING PLACES. . . . . . | 42 574 | 28 312 | 4 005 | 1 446 | 928 | 1 091 | 446 | 73 | 18 | 3 | – |
| 59 | MISCELLANEOUS RETAIL STORES . . . . . | 27 086 | 29 677 | 4 355 | 2 038 | 1 182 | 928 | 190 | 15 | 2 | – | 1 |
| -- | ADMINISTRATIVE AND AUXILIARY. . . . . | 4 193 | 7 217 | 87 | 26 | 17 | 20 | 8 | 5 | 6 | 3 | 2 |
| ... | FINANCE, INSURANCE, AND REAL ESTATE . | 69 175 | 116 968 | 6 183 | 3 308 | 1 307 | 899 | 437 | 145 | 56 | 23 | 8 |
| 60 | BANKING . . . . . . . . . . . . . . . | 18 539 | 30 655 | 296 | 3 | 17 | 84 | 100 | 54 | 25 | 11 | 2 |
| 61 | CREDIT AGENCIES OTHER THAN BANKS. . . | 9 551 | 15 743 | 1 045 | 333 | 400 | 230 | 59 | 17 | 4 | 2 | – |
| 62 | SECURITY, COMMODITY BROKERS & SERVICES. | 1 355 | 3 941 | 89 | 32 | 16 | 24 | 12 | 2 | 3 | – | – |
| 63 | INSURANCE CARRIERS. . . . . . . . . . | 20 332 | 38 742 | 796 | 230 | 115 | 187 | 185 | 48 | 19 | – | 4 |
| 64 | INSURANCE AGENTS, BROKERS, & SERVICE. | 5 447 | 8 590 | 1 486 | 1 031 | 309 | 122 | 19 | 5 | – | – | – |
| 65 | REAL ESTATE . . . . . . . . . . . . . | 11 243 | 14 094 | 2 170 | 1 503 | 374 | 216 | 53 | 18 | 4 | 1 | 1 |
| 66 | COMBINED REAL ESTATE, INSURANCE, ETC. | 776 | 1 207 | 201 | 118 | 58 | 24 | 1 | – | – | | |
| 67 | HOLDING AND OTHER INVESTMENT COMPANIES. | 624 | 1 207 | 94 | 56 | 17 | 12 | 8 | 1 | – | | |
| -- | ADMINISTRATIVE AND AUXILIARY. . . . . | 1 308 | 2 789 | 2 | | 1 | | | | | | |
| ... | SERVICES. . . . . . . . . . . . . . . | 196 951 | 220 218 | 22 086 | 13 468 | 4 376 | 2 774 | 925 | 299 | 169 | 51 | 24 |
| 70 | HOTELS AND OTHER LODGING PLACES . . . | 15 081 | 11 131 | 1 274 | 637 | 200 | 229 | 149 | 42 | 15 | 2 | – |
| 72 | PERSONAL SERVICES . . . . . . . . . . | 27 724 | 25 972 | 4 984 | 3 179 | 991 | 592 | 162 | 41 | 17 | 2 | – |
| 73 | MISCELLANEOUS BUSINESS SERVICES . . . | 21 490 | 23 162 | 1 547 | 695 | 334 | 295 | 146 | 51 | 16 | 7 | 3 |
| 75 | AUTO REPAIR, SERVICES & GARAGES . . . | 9 358 | 11 377 | 2 024 | 1 379 | 378 | 202 | 54 | 5 | 5 | 1 | – |
| 76 | MISCELLANEOUS REPAIR SERVICES . . . . | 4 772 | 6 483 | 1 064 | 714 | 207 | 120 | 16 | 6 | – | 1 | – |
| 78 | MOTION PICTURES . . . . . . . . . . . | 3 035 | 2 137 | 263 | 56 | 52 | 125 | 24 | 6 | – | – | – |
| 79 | AMUSEMENT AND RECREATION SERVICES, NEC. | 6 529 | 6 081 | 840 | 449 | 173 | 151 | 51 | 13 | 2 | 1 | – |
| 80 | MEDICAL AND OTHER HEALTH SERVICES . . | 50 083 | 58 951 | 4 127 | 2 823 | 784 | 284 | 93 | 49 | 51 | 25 | 18 |
| 81 | LEGAL SERVICES. . . . . . . . . . . . | 3 254 | 4 072 | 1 243 | 1 000 | 183 | 55 | 5 | – | – | | |
| 82 | EDUCATIONAL SERVICES. . . . . . . . . | 23 909 | 33 856 | 855 | 405 | 179 | 147 | 62 | 25 | 29 | 5 | 3 |
| 84 | MUSEUMS, BOTANICAL, ZOOLOGICAL GARDENS. | 77 | 67 | 15 | 9 | 3 | 3 | – | – | – | | |
| 86 | NONPROFIT MEMBERSHIP ORGANIZATIONS. . | 21 874 | 19 014 | 2 542 | 1 362 | 624 | 375 | 104 | 46 | 26 | 5 | – |
| 89 | MISCELLANEOUS SERVICES. . . . . . . . | 9 397 | 17 533 | 1 274 | 748 | 256 | 187 | 59 | 15 | 7 | 2 | – |
| -- | ADMINISTRATIVE AND AUXILIARY. . . . . | 368 | 382 | 34 | 12 | 12 | 9 | – | 1 | – | | |
| ... | UNCLASSIFIED ESTABLISHMENTS . . . . . | 10 502 | 9 833 | 2 511 | 1 647 | 514 | 274 | 76 | – | – | – | – |

an industry in which needs are found which require products of novel design and function which he is capable of developing. Both types of opportunity can be identified in much the same way—with an investigation of all S.I.C. categories for clues to needs the company might be able to satisfy. If such an investigation is to be performed effectively, a great deal of technical knowledge and a broad understanding of manufacturing processes is usually required. Even large firms often draw upon the services of outside consultants for such work.

Essentially, each four-digit classification is studied with two questions in mind.

1.  Could establishments making that kind of product or performing that kind of operation make use of any product or service this company could supply?
2.  Could this company perform any operation or function which establishments in this classification are performing better than they are doing it?

While the answer to either question is rarely self-evident, it is often possible to eliminate industries in which a manufacturer is reasonably confident that the answer to both questions would be negative. Obviously, if the answer to both questions is negative with respect to any given industry, that industry does not represent a prospective market and can be eliminated from further consideration. Those industries for which the answer to one or both questions is affirmative, or even a qualified affirmative, warrant further investigation, because they represent possible new markets.

This type of investigation results in a list of industries (four-digit S.I.C.'s) which, because of the products each produces or the type of operation in which each is involved, need what the marketer can supply. The next step is an evaluation of each industry to determine which ones represent the greatest potential markets. This aspect of market identification is discussed in the following chapter.

Although the logical first step in market identification is the specification of need, companies often find themselves with products which they must decide to market, license, or abandon. Research and development efforts almost invariably produce unintended spin-off products, and by-products are an inevitable consequence of many manufacturing processes. As a consequence, management must frequently find ways of making a quick assessment of the market for embryo products.

Attempting to identify specific industries which have a need for such products is often premature because there may be considerable uncertainty regarding what the product can do. When Dow Chemical Company faced the question of what to do with 1,1,1 trichlorethane, a chemical co-product in the manufacture of Saran Wrap, it was decided to market it initially to Dow's own customers. The chemical had the properties of a cold cleaning solvent with low toxicity and a high flash-point. Since it was not known what additional uses the chemical might have, management wisely decided to let users of the chemical discover new applications for it. As a result of customer ingenuity, and R & D success in developing inhibitors to lower the chemical's volatility and reduce its corrosiveness, 1,1,1 trichlorethane inhibited soon became the "product with a thousand uses." Applications were found in such widely differing industries as missile manufacturing, appliance making, chemical specialties, public utilities, pharmaceuticals, and printing. As suggestions from users led to the development by Dow of additional inhibitors, the use of 1,1,1 trichlorethane inhibited expanded from cold cleaning (a small market) to vapor degreasing (a relatively large market) and finally to chemical processing (a sizeable market)—far beyond anything initially envisaged by its developers.

William H. Reynolds tells the story of the relatively sophisticated West Coast electronics firm which developed an electronic recording device with a visual output, something like an oscillograph. The product differed only in degree from other, similar, products on the market but was more accurate, possessed certain other advantages, and was more expensive.

Through its research the firm identified virtually every establishment in the nation which would have any conceivable use for the product. There was little reason to believe that many of them would find its increased accuracy or other advantages of much value. Serious consideration was given to dropping the product, but management finally decided to attempt to recover at least a part of its development cost. The product was advertised in media reaching the companies identified as the best prospects and salesmen made regular calls on these firms. As expected, sales were slow, but no one was particularly disappointed.

But gradually inquiries began to drift in from companies not identified as having a need for the product. The tenor of the inquiries was, "We understand you have a thing that is accurate to four nines in measuring fluctuations of this particular type. We have used mechanical measuring instruments before because nothing electronic was stable enough. Could you send us specs?"

Sales rose steadily. Customers suggested applications and the most unlikely industries found ways to use the product. The company began by seeking to win a small share of an existing market, but found itself dominating a new market larger than the one in which it had hoped to find a minor niche.

The advertising this company now uses employs a variety of trade media and the principal message of its copy is almost, "To whom it may concern: we have this thing with these characteristics. Can you use it?" It eventually became a standing joke in the company to try to think of an industry with no conceivable use for this product and then attempt to sell it to them. Some outrageously facetious suggestions proved to be sound in practice.[13]

The moral of these two examples is that procedures and techniques should never be substituted for thinking. If the application of a product is clouded with uncertainty, or if one suspects that it might have hidden versatility, field testing is a logical first step in market identification. Even a fairly informal and unstructured field test should provide insights regarding application that will make subsequent analysis of S.I.C.'s much more meaningful.

## COMMENT ON THE 1972 S.I.C. REVISIONS

The S.I.C. system was designed to permit the orderly classification of economic activity at a time when the structure of the national economy was much simpler and changes in it were much more gradual than at present. Since 1950 the economy has been in an almost constant state of flux. New industries have emerged, new technology has wiped out old industries, the service sector has ballooned into an unprecedented prominence, government at all levels has become a potent economic force, and many industries have so expanded in scope that they can only be fitted into existing classifications on very tenuous grounds.

Unfortunately, the S.I.C. system has not been able to keep up with these changes and is still relatively static compared to the economy it is supposed to mirror. Some industries still have no apparent S.I.C. definition. The packaging industry, for example, has no S.I.C. home, but is divided among 5 different classifications: S.I.C. 26 (Paper and Allied Products), S.I.C. 28 (Chemicals and Allied Products), S.I.C. 32 (Stone, Clay, and Glass Products), S.I.C. 33 (Primary Metal Products), and S.I.C. 34 (Fabricated Metal Products). Moreover, such current events as the institution of wage and price controls, high unemployment in specific industries such as aerospace, freight rate setting by the I.C.C., and the advent of the Occupational Safety and Health Act emphasize the need for more precise definition of economic activity.

It has been suggested that an expansion of the present four-digit classifications to a five-digit system would help to alleviate some of the weaknesses of the present system. It would also provide for a computer sort out that would bring together parts of present S.I.C. industries which form a distinct industry not now included in the classification system. However, until the next revision, new industries will have to be placed into one of the existing classifications, and those who use the system must make the appropriate adjustments.

---

[13] William H. Reynolds, *Products and Markets* (New York: Appleton-Century-Crofts, 1969), pp. 150 f.

## SUMMARY

When the use properties of a product are well known, market identification can be greatly facilitated by use of the Standard Industrial Classification system. It is not a universal panacea, but it is a valuable tool for many industrial marketers.

The system provides a catalog of all economic activity in the nation classified by product produced, service rendered, or type of operation. The confidence with which these classifications can be used to identify industries with a need for a given type of product is indicated by a specialization ratio and a coverage ratio. The former indicates the extent to which establishments in a given industry specialize in the primary product of that industry. The coverage ratio indicates the proportion of total national production of a product which is accounted for by establishments in a given industry.

The S.I.C. is useful in identifying both new customers for old products as well as new customers for new products. The former can be done by classifying present customers by two-, three-, or four-digit S.I.C.'s and comparing the firms in this list with the total number of firms in the same S.I.C.'s for each state in which the marketer does business.

New customers for new products can be identified by examining each four-digit S.I.C. for establishments which because of the product they make, services they render, or operations they perform, need what the marketer is prepared to sell. If the range of performance characteristics of a new product is uncertain, the examination of S.I.C.'s should be preceded by sufficient field testing to establish the nature of its versatility.

# MARKET IDENTIFICATION: THE EVALUATION PROCESS

ALL PROSPECTIVE new markets are not equally attractive. One industry can differ substantially from another in terms of the potential for growth in sales and profits it represents to the marketer. Appraising the relative value of alternative market opportunities is an important part of market identification. Whether there is but a single identifiable market opportunity under consideration or one which can be divided into a number of distinguishable segments, the development of a market profile is a useful approach. For a comprehensive evaluation, a market profile usually needs to be supplemented with an outline of trends in the market or market segment, a measure of the demand potential it represents, and a definition of the problems which are likely to be encountered in developing its potential.

## THE MARKET PROFILE

A market profile consists of those endogenous characteristics which have a significant bearing on demand or the way in which it can be developed. Not all such characteristics may be measurable—such as the extent to which buying authority is diffused—and the cost of developing some measures may be prohibitive. Nevertheless, it is usually possible to develop useful profiles with available data.

The basic ingredients of a profile of a market or market segment are:

> Number of establishments
> Geographical location of establishments
> Number of employees
> Value of shipments
> Value added by manufacturing
> Capital expenditures by establishments
> Degree to which establishments are specialized
> Importance of their output in the national total

If markets are defined in terms of S.I.C.'s, data pertaining to each of these characteristics are available in the U.S. Census. A manufacturer of fibrous glass, for example, identified manufacturers of tire cord, manufacturers of wooden household furniture and metal household furniture, and makers of steel pipe and tube as potential users of fibrous glass. The profile of these industries provides some revealing comparisons. The Tire Cord and Fabric industry is the smallest of the four in terms of number of establishments, but the establishments in this industry are substantially larger than establishments in the other three, both in terms of average value of shipments and average number of employees. Tire cord and fabric manufacturers also do more manufacturing than establishments in the furniture industries and have the highest investment per employee in the four industries. The high specialization and coverage ratios indicate a high degree of product homogeneity among these establishments and their dominance in the manufacture of this product. (See Figure 9–1.)

FIGURE 9–1.    Profile of four market segments, 1967

|  | Tire cord & fabric S.I.C. 2296 | Wooden household furniture S.I.C. 2511 | Metal household furniture S.I.C. 2514 | Steel pipe & tube S.I.C. 3317 |
|---|---|---|---|---|
| Number of establishments......... | 27 | 2002 | 338 | 96 |
| Location of establishments | | | | |
| California.................... | | 479 | | 19 |
| Florida...................... | | 143 | 41 | |
| Georgia..................... | 7 | | | |
| Illinois...................... | | 138 | 52 | 13 |
| Indiana..................... | | 111 | | |
| Massachusetts................ | | 123 | | |
| Michigan.................... | | 113 | | 13 |
| New Jersey.................. | | 137 | | |
| New York................... | | 412 | 116 | |
| North Carolina............... | | 159 | | |
| Ohio........................ | | | 18 | 17 |
| Pennsylvania................. | | 187 | 35 | 27 |
| Southern states.............. | 14 | | | |
| Texas....................... | | | | 7 |
| Western states............... | | | 76 | |
| All other states.............. | 6 | | | |
| Value of shipments............. | 504,724.00 | 1,857,002.00 | 595,285.00 | 1,071,346.00 |
| Per establishment............. | 18,693.50 | 928.07 | 1,761.20 | 11,159.85 |
| Value added ($1,000)........... | 107,156.00 | 993,200.00 | 289,425.00 | 416,544.00 |
| Per establishment............. | 3,968.74 | 496.10 | 856.29 | 4,339.00 |
| Production employees........... | 9,786 | 124,699 | 25,733 | 20,893 |
| Per establishment............. | 362 | 62 | 76 | 218 |
| Capital expenditures ($1,000)...... | 11,180.00 | 11,171.00 | 6,840.00 | 17,988.00 |
| Per establishment............. | 414.07 | 5.58 | 20.24 | 187.37 |
| Per employee................. | 1.14 | 0.09 | 0.26 | 0.86 |
| Specialization ratio (%).......... | 87 | 94 | 88 | 91 |
| Coverage ratio (%)............. | 91 | 96 | 89 | 37 |

Source: *U.S. Census of Manufacturers*, 1967, Volume II, Parts 1 and 2.

It can be inferred from this comparison that of the four industries, Tire Cord and Fabric is made up of the largest units, with greater automation, and with the most extensive manufacturing operation. With a relatively small number of large establishments, it would be a less costly market to reach than either of the furniture industries, which have a large number of small establishments. The trend in each of these elements of the profile, together with measures of demand potential and a definition of the anticipated problems associated with each, add important dimensions to the identification of markets.

## TREND OUTLINE

The direction and degree of change in each of the profile elements are indicated in Figure 9–2. A comparison of the changes can reveal

FIGURE 9–2.   Direction of change in profile of four market segments, 1958–67

|  | Tire cord & fabric S.I.C. 2296 (%) | Wooden household furniture S.I.C. 2511 (%) | Metal household furniture S.I.C. 2514 (%) | Steel pipe & tube S.I.C. 3317 (%) |
|---|---|---|---|---|
| Number of establishments | − 13 | 9 | −16 | 4 |
| Value of shipments | 105 | 28 | 20 | 37 |
| Value added | 54 | 40 | 32 | 50 |
| Production employees | − 14 | 14 | 5 | 7 |
| Capital expenditures | 82 | 85 | 9 | 85 |

Source: *U.S. Census of Manufactures*, 1967, Volume II, Parts 1 and 2.

significant characteristics of an industry or market segment. A decrease in the number of establishments accompanied by an increase in employment and value added would signify an increase in the size of the average establishment. A decrease in the number of establishments and employment accompanied by an increase in the other elements of the profile spells increased automation. An increase in the value of shipments unaccompanied by increases in value added and capital expenditure signifies rising prices. A decline in the coverage ratio indicates an erosion of an industry's position in the sense that other industries are producing an increasing proportion of its primary product or service. A much larger increase in value added than in either employment or value of shipments indicates rising labor productivity and is usually accompanied by sizeable increases in capital expenditures, as in the case of the wooden household furniture and steel pipe and tube industries.

## DEMAND POTENTIAL

How much total business an industry or market segment represents, i.e., how much of a given class of product an industry can absorb, is a central question in evaluating markets. There are several ways of developing such estimates. While there is no attempt here to treat the many variations in estimating techniques, the major procedural elements of several widely used methods are discussed in some detail. These can be divided into cumulative methods and aggregative methods.

## Cumulative methods

Most cumulative methods are based either on statistical measurements or on market surveys. Statistical measures require a link between the product or service in question and published data. They rely only partially on the collection of original information from a cross section of prospects. The survey method, by contrast, depends primarily on information collected in the field through interviews, questionnaires, or observation. It is a method of demand measurement based on original rather than secondary information.

*Statistical measurements.*   The development of a link between product purchases and published data can be rather simple or very involved, depending on the circumstances. Nevertheless, the following steps have general application.

1. Determine the total requirement for the type of product in question by present customers in each S.I.C. under study. The total requirements of one's customers for certain types of products over a given period of time can frequently be learned by the simple expedient of asking them. Where such inquiries are refused or ignored, salesmen may be familiar enough with customers' operations to estimate their total demand for products of a given type. If not, comparisons may sometimes be made with other customers of the same size and class whose total requirements are known.

A manufacturer's present customers in an industry class make up a sample, of sorts, of the class as a whole. If there is doubt that they are representative of their S.I.C., this method should not be used unless a sample can be completed with noncustomer establishments willing to disclose the desired information on product usage. It is important to recognize in this respect the distinction between product requirements or needs and product purchases. It is the former which is required for measurements of potential rather than the latter.

A cannery, for example, will require a specific number of "cans" during the course of a packing season, but it may purchase tin cans, aluminum cans, or glass jars. A building contractor will require a certain quantity of subflooring material over a given period of time. But he may purchase hardwood, softwood, plywood, or composition board. The important marketing question is not how much of what particular products an establishment is buying, but how much of the firm's material requirements could be fulfilled by a particular product or line of products.

Measuring market potential is a matter of determining the extent of need for the properties and qualities possessed by a type of product. Since needs for such properties and qualities are reflected in purchases, demand measurement should include purchases of all products capable of fulfilling given functions or uses.

2. Correlate product requirements of customer establishments with a variable related to output for which accurate published data are available. The variable which probably satisfies these two criteria for the largest number of establishments is employment. In each S.I.C. in which present customers are considered to be a representative sample of the industry, customers' total requirement for a given type of product may be correlated with their total employment. If the degree of correlation is high, the marketer has a link between product needs and published data in those S.I.C.'s in which customer establishments are typical of other establishments in the class.

A little practice in the use of correlation usually makes it possible to judge the relationship between two variables from a scatter disgram with reasonable accuracy. An example of a scatter diagram used in this way is given in Figure 9–3. This is one of the easiest ways of identifying the *evidence* of relationship.

FIGURE 9–3.  Evidence of relationship, using a scatter diagram (*Monarch Valve Company, customers in S.I.C. 3561, 1972*)

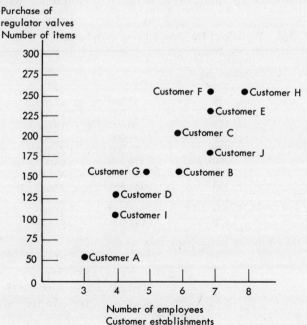

The degree of relationship may be calculated mathematically using the formula

$$\frac{N\Sigma(XY) - (\Sigma X)(\Sigma Y)}{\sqrt{N\Sigma X^2 - (\Sigma X)^2}\;\sqrt{N\Sigma Y^2 - (\Sigma Y)^2}}$$

in which $X$ is the number of employees, $Y$ is the number of regulator valves purchased, and $N$ is the number of comparisons, i.e., 10 in this example. The nearer the correlation coefficient is to $+1.0$ or $-1.0$, the closer the relationship of the two variables under study. Between these two extremes, it is a matter of judgment as to whether or not the degree of association is great enough to justify estimates of demand on the basis of the number of persons employed. The significance of the relationship can also be determined mathematically. The appropriate procedures are discussed in most texts on business and economic statistics. (See Figure 9–4.)

3. Apply the purchase-employment relationship. If the degree of correlation between purchases of a given product by present customers and their employment size is considered significant, one of two procedures may be followed. The average number of items purchased per employee may be computed and this ratio applied to total employment in the appropriate market area or areas. Or, total demand for the product may be estimated by applying the coefficient of correlation to total employment in the appropriate market area or areas.

The first alternative may be illustrated by reference to Figure 9–3.

FIGURE 9–4.   Worksheet for simple linear correlation

| Number of employees X | Purchases of regulator valves Y | XY | Y² | X² |
|---|---|---|---|---|
| 300 | 50 | 15,000 | 2,500 | 90,000 |
| 400 | 100 | 40,000 | 10,000 | 160,000 |
| 400 | 125 | 50,000 | 15,625 | 160,000 |
| 500 | 150 | 75,000 | 22,500 | 250,000 |
| 600 | 150 | 90,000 | 22,500 | 360,000 |
| 600 | 200 | 120,000 | 40,000 | 360,000 |
| 700 | 175 | 122,500 | 30,625 | 490,000 |
| 700 | 225 | 157,500 | 50,625 | 490,000 |
| 700 | 250 | 175,000 | 62,500 | 490,000 |
| 800 | 250 | 200,000 | 62,500 | 640,000 |
| 5,700 | 1,675 | 1,045,000 | 319,375 | 3,490,000 |

Let $N$ = the number of comparisons, then

$$\text{The Coefficient of Correlation} = \frac{N\Sigma(XY) - (\Sigma X)(\Sigma Y)}{\sqrt{N\Sigma X^2 - (\Sigma X)^2}\;\sqrt{N\Sigma Y^2 - (\Sigma Y)^2}}$$

$$= \frac{10(1,045,000) - (5,700)(1,675)}{\sqrt{10(3,490,000) - (5,700)^2}\;\sqrt{10(319.375) - (1675)^2}}$$

$$= \frac{902,500}{965,902.99} = .93$$

The present customers of this firm in S.I.C. 3561 purchased 1,675 regulator valves in 1972. Since these firms had a total employment in 1972 of 5,700 production workers, their purchases of regulator valves were approximately 3 valves for every 10 employees. With this estimate of the ratio of valve purchases to production employees for a sample of establishments in S.I.C. 3561, one can refer to total employment in this industry given in the most recent edition of the *Annual Survey of Manufacturers*. Total employment in the Pump and Pump Equipment industry in 1970 was 80,500.[1] On the basis of the ratio of valve purchases to employees in the sample of customers, total purchases in this industry for the nation as a whole would be estimated at 24,150 items (80,500 ÷ 10 × 3).

The second alternative requires the formulation of an estimating equation which describes the relationship between an independent variable, in this instance, employment, and a dependent variable, purchases of regulator valves. When the relationship between two such variables is linear, as it appears to be in Figure 9–3, it can be described by the equation $Yc = a + bX$. In this equation $Yc$ equals the estimated number of products purchased, $a$ equals the number of products purchased when employment is zero (a theoretical value which lies outside the range of observation), and $b$ represents the amount of change in the number of products purchased with every change in total employment.

Values for $a$ and $b$ can be solved in the following manner:

$$\Sigma Y = Na + b\Sigma X \text{ or } 1,675 = 10a + 5700b$$
$$X\Sigma Y = a\Sigma X + b\Sigma X^2 \text{ or } 1,045,000 = 5700a + 3,490,000b$$

Solving for $b$:

$$(1,675 = 10a \quad + \quad 5700b)\ 5700$$
$$(1,045,000 = 5700a + \quad 3,490,000b)\ 10$$

$$\overline{\phantom{xxxxxxxxxxxxxxxxxxxxxxxxxxxxxxxxxxxxxx}}$$

$$9,547,500 = 5700a + 32,490,000b$$
$$10,450,000 = 5700a + 34,900,000b)$$

$$\overline{\phantom{xxxxxxxxxxxxxxxxxxxxxxxxxxxxxxxxxxxxxx}}$$

$$902,000 = \qquad\qquad 2,410,000b$$
$$b = .37427$$

Solving for $a$:

$$1,675 = 10a + 5700(0.37427)$$
$$-10a = 2133.3390 - 1,675$$
$$a = -45.8339$$
$$\text{Therefore } Yc = -45.8339 + 0.3743X$$

With this equation an estimate of regulator valve purchases, $Yc$, can be obtained for any given value of employment, $X$. Establishments in the Pump and Pump Equipment industry, with a total employment of 80,500, could be expected to purchase approximately 30,085 regulator valves annually.

---

[1] *Annual Survey of Manufacturers*, 1970, General Statistics for Industry Groups and Industries, p. 18.

The latter is the more accurate of the two estimates of market potential, because it is more sensitive to the influence of employment size on product purchases. If a seller's customers in a given industry are genuinely representative of other establishments in that industry, a correlation of .93 between customer employment and product among these customers provides a more reliable estimate of industry purchases than a simple average.

This method of measuring the market potential of an industry is applicable for any product for which the marketer can link its purchases (or the purchases of a product for which it could be substituted) and a measureable independent variable (such as employment) which is related to the product's use. In the event that an S.I.C. represents a potential market in which the marketer either has no customers, or those he has are not representative of other establishments in the industry, it would be necessary to conduct a survey. In this instance, the population of establishments in the industry could be assembled from state industrial directories and a random sample of appropriate size selected. Depending on how much was already known about the industry, information could be collected by mail, questionnaire, telephone, or personal interview. Due to the necessity of establishing a rapport with the respondents and of determining the nature of the manufacturing process, the personal interview is usually the most effective.

*Assembling information from sample establishments.* Direct inquiry by means of questionnaires or interviews is usually the simplest and the most successful means of gathering information about product purchases or usage. Purchasing managers and buyers are frequently very candid with regard to the product requirements of their companies, particularly when the interrogator is a salesman. There is generally little reason for a purchasing manager to withhold information regarding product needs from salesmen. A salesman representing a possible new supplier may be, and often is, in a position to help the buyer meet his company's needs on better terms than he now enjoys. Although there is probably a tendency to be more revealing with representatives of present suppliers than with "outsiders," it is in the purchasing manager's best interest to keep opportunity alive for new sources of supply. This end could scarcely be achieved through a policy of concealing information concerning company product needs.

In the case of establishments which do not respond to direct inquiries, it is sometimes possible to get assistance from sympathetic noncompeting firms which are suppliers of these establishments. Also, buyers are willing at times to reveal the percentage of their total requirement a given product line represents, although they are not at liberty to disclose the absolute amount of the product they customarily use or purchase. In this instance, it becomes necessary to estimate the sales volume of the establishment.

Persons experienced in an industry are usually able to develop indicators which, while crude, make possible fairly reliable estimates of an establishment's total sales. Such indicators vary with different industries and with different establishments within an industry. In the service industries the type and number of machines in use is sometimes a meaningful indicator of business volume. The output of printing establishments is frequently estimated on the basis of the size and number of presses in operation. A scatter diagram is often all that is needed to determine which of several indicators is the most reliable, by comparing each with the output of establishments in a selected category whose operating results are known.

*Market area surveys.* Two types of surveys have been widely used by industrial marketers: surveys of buyers and surveys of facilities. Since there is an extensive literature on the subject of surveys, only a summary treatment will be given here.

*1. Survey of buyers.* The initial step in surveying buyers is to establish clearly the boundaries of the area to be studied. Usually, a special map is needed for this purpose, one which shows the main arteries of transportation and the more important political boundaries. A tabular listing of individual communities within the area also should be prepared and keyed to the map. Depending on whether or not the area is regional or national in scope the appropriate subdivisions within it might be counties, cities, metropolitan areas, or states.

A list of buyers can be compiled from state industrial directories after the appropriate types of buyers have been identified from the S.I.C. system. Care should be taken to identify captive establishments when compiling the buyer list. The parent organization of captives may not be included in directories or other sources as users of a product or service. A college or university, for example, might operate a sizeable print shop in connection with its physical plant. But it is not likely that the college itself would be listed in any of the sources where other users of printing paper would be found. If such captive establishments are a significant factor in the market, their omission from the enumeration of buyers could result in a substantial underestimate of the market potential.

It is not always possible to identify probable users of a product from published sources. Sometimes prospects must be identified by observation. This is apt to be true of products which have a variety of applications. It may be necessary to see or physically inspect a place of business before deciding whether or not a product of a given type would be needed.

Before selecting a group of firms representative of those on the buyer list, the list itself should be stratified by size and kind of business. The indicator of size which is perhaps most widely accepted is the number of paid employees. However, any common denominator of size, such as sales volume or the amount of a given type of equipment in operation, could serve as a basis for stratification. It is important, though, to choose a characteristic for which adequate information is available.

What steps should be taken to assure that samples drawn will be representative depends on the size of the sample and the knowledge of those doing the sampling. Essentially, the proper size of a sample is a matter of judgment; judgment concerning the accuracy that is required, the degree of risk that is permissible, and the cost that is reasonable. The subject of sampling and sample design will be discussed further in the next chapter.

Multiplying the average product requirements determined from each sample by the total number of establishments in each stratum from which samples were drawn and summing the estimates for each of the strata in which a market segment or industry was divided supplies an estimate of its demand potential. Such an estimate must be related to the level of operation which is normal for the period under consideration. A printing press, for example, will use a certain amount of paper per hour. The number of houses a building contractor erects in a year will determine his need for lumber, concrete, siding, and other building material.

2. *Survey of facilities.*   The survey method of estimating demand potential does not always require the enumeration and sampling of buyers. It may require instead the enumeration and examination of facilities or equipment related to the use of a given type of product. Since the survey technique has already been discussed, this type of application of it will be explained with an illustration.

When glass-lined steel smokestacks were introduced, their manufacturer wanted to estimate demand for them in several high-density industrial areas. Since the glass lining was virtually impervious to corrosion, the major cause of smokestack deterioration, these stacks had a much longer than average life span. Moreover, installation of the stacks required no special skills and no welding was necessary. Stack sections were completely formed, requiring only the fitting of gaskets and bolting together, so that any local contractor with hoisting equipment could put them in place. Since sections were also lined on the outside with glass, no painting was required. Although the initial price of the glass-lined stack was somewhat higher than its conventional counterpart, there was virtually no maintenance cost involved. Maintenance costs of conventional stacks, on the other hand, increase with the age of the installation.

In view of the impressive advantages of the new product, it was concluded that every establishment erecting a new smokestack was a potential customer. On the basis of installation and maintenance costs, it was also concluded that under cost conditions a material saving could be realized by replacing a conventional smokestack which had been in use more than ten years with a glass-lined unit. The market potential of the new product, therefore, equaled the number of smokestacks in use more than ten years plus the number of new stacks scheduled for erection. Since the need for a smokestack, compared to the need for a chimney of the residential sort, is influenced by a number of factors, there was no available published material from which the number of smokestacks in any given area could be derived. It was necessary, therefore, to conduct an area survey of smokestacks and the establishments owning them.

The survey was conducted in three phases. The first was a tour of the designated industrial areas by automobile and helicopter to physically count the smokestacks, classify them by size, and identify the structures on which they were erected. The second phase consisted of interviewing a sample of establishments with an investment in smokestacks to determine the age of the stacks and depreciation practices concerning them. Finally, building permits issued for industrial construction were examined to determine the probable number and size of new smokestacks to be erected.

### Aggregate methods

Due to lack of sufficient data on an establishment basis or the costliness of a survey, aggregate methods may represent the only practical approach to measurement of demand potential. The aggregate approach links demand to economic factors which reflect the capacity of an industry or market segment to consume or use a product. There are a number of estimating methods of this type used by industrial marketers. They vary from simple benchmark techniques employing but a single factor, such as expenditure on plant and equipment, to very complex calculations requiring higher mathematics. Fundamentally, these methods differ chiefly in the economic indicators which are used or in the manner in which these indicators are related. Since anything resembling an exhaustive treatment of research methods is beyond the scope of this book, attention here will be limited to the input/output technique. This is regarded by many as the most accurate method of estimating demand potential on an industry basis.

*The input-output system.* The basic conception of input-output analysis is the existence of a fundamental relationship between the volume of an industry's output, or sales, and the amount of its purchases, or input. In principle, the output of any industry can be traced to the markets in which it is sold. But in a highly diversified economy characterized by industrial specialization, direct consumer sales represent only a portion of the sales of many industries and are completely absent in the sales of others. Consequently, that portion of the output of an industry which is sold to another industry for further processing is called *intermediate* product, for it is used by its purchasers for current input in their production processes. The output of an industry not sold to another industry represents *final demand.*

Final demand is defined as the spending of consumers, government, investors (capital formation and net inventory accumulation), and sales to export markets. Since this is the definition of Gross National Product, the input-output data can be related directly to the GNP accounting framework. Since the net output of any industry is equal to the sum of its sales to other industries and to final users (consumers, government, investors, and exporters), the flow of goods and services among and between industries and ultimate users can be notationally described as follows:

$$X_i = x_{i1} + x_{i2} + \cdots \cdots \cdots x_{in} + Y_i$$

In which

$X_i$ = sales of any industry
$i = 1 \ldots$ n industries
$x_{ij}$ = sales of the $i^{th}$ industry to the $j^{th}$ industrial user
$j = 1 \ldots$ n industries
$Y_i$ = sales to ultimate users

If an equation is written for each industry, a system of equations results which is called a *transactions matrix*. The transactions matrix incorporates three sectors: an output sector, an intermediate demand sector, and a final demand sector.

| *Output sector* | *Intermediate demand* | *Final demand* |
|---|---|---|
| $X_1$ | $= x_{11} + x_{12} + \cdots x_{1n} +$ | $Y_1$ |
| $X_2$ | $= x_{21} + x_{22} + \cdots x_{2n} +$ | $Y_2$ |
| . | . . . | . |
| . | . . . | . |
| $X_n$ | $= x_{n1} + x_{n2} + \cdots x_{nn} +$ | $Y_n$ |

Each row to the right of the output sector describes the distribution of $i^{th}$ industry's output among the different $j^{th}$ industry customers and final customers with the exception of the $x_{11}$ and $x_{22}$ variables. These describe that part of the output of an industry which is retained within the industry, i.e., the sales of establishments in that industry to other establishments in the industry. Since each sale is also a purchase, the columns of the intermediate sector describe the purchases of each $j^{th}$ industry from each of the different $i^{th}$ industry suppliers. The transactions matrix describes the sales-purchase relationship in a selected period and is therefore an "input-output" table.

The sales-purchase, or input-output, relationship among industries, government, and households is illustrated in Figure 9–5. This abbreviated input-output table gives the output, or sales, of each of six industries in the vertical columns while the distribution of each industry's sales to the other industries is shown in the horizontal rows. Since a sale or unit of output of one industry is a purchase or unit of input of another industry, each figure in a row is also a figure in a column. Each column shows from what other industries a given industry obtains its needed input of goods and services.

**FIGURE 9–5.   A simple input-output table (billions of dollars)**

| Inputs \ Outputs | | Agriculture | Chemicals | Electrical equipment | Machinery | Lumber | Furniture | Inventory change (+) | Exports | Government purchases | Gross private capital inventory | Households | Total gross output |
|---|---|---|---|---|---|---|---|---|---|---|---|---|---|
| | | | | | Processing Sector | | | | | Final Demand | | | |
| Agriculture | | 10 | 15 | 1 | 2 | 5 | 6 | 2 | 5 | 1 | 3 | 14 | 64 |
| Chemicals | Processing sector | 5 | 4 | 7 | 1 | 3 | 8 | 1 | 6 | 3 | 4 | 17 | 59 |
| Electrical equipment | | 7 | 2 | 8 | 1 | 5 | 3 | 2 | 3 | 1 | 3 | 5 | 40 |
| Machinery | | 11 | 1 | 2 | 8 | 6 | 4 | 0 | 0 | 1 | 2 | 4 | 39 |
| Lumber | | 4 | 0 | 1 | 14 | 3 | 2 | 1 | 2 | 1 | 3 | 9 | 40 |
| Furniture | | 2 | 6 | 7 | 6 | 2 | 6 | 2 | 4 | 2 | 1 | 8 | 46 |
| Inventory change (−) | | 1 | 2 | 1 | 0 | 2 | 1 | 0 | 1 | 0 | 0 | 0 | 8 |
| Imports | Payments sector | 2 | 1 | 3 | 0 | 3 | 2 | 0 | 0 | 0 | 0 | 2 | 13 |
| Payments to government | | 2 | 3 | 2 | 2 | 1 | 2 | 3 | 2 | 1 | 2 | 12 | 32 |
| Depreciation allowances | | 1 | 2 | 1 | 0 | 1 | 0 | 0 | 0 | 0 | 0 | 0 | 5 |
| Households | | 19 | 23 | 7 | 5 | 9 | 12 | 1 | 0 | 8 | 0 | 1 | 85 |
| Total gross outlays | | 64 | 59 | 40 | 39 | 40 | 46 | 12 | 23 | 18 | 18 | 72 | 431 |

When a column is read vertically, the numbers indicate what the industry identified with the column consumes from other industries. When a row is read horizontally, the numbers indicate what the industry identified with the row ships to other industries. The double-entry pattern of the table reveals how the flow of trade links each industry to all the others as well as to government and household sectors. Such a table can be developed in as much detail as available data permit and the purpose requires.

It will be observed that the table is divided into a processing sector, a payments sector, and a final demand sector. The *processing sector* contains the industries producing goods and services. In an authentic input-output table, this sector would be greatly expanded. The 1963 tables published by the U.S. Department of Commerce contain over 80 industries.

The *payments sector* occupies the last five rows across the bottom of the table and includes: (1) negative inventory changes, i.e., the depletion of previously accumulated stocks of finished goods, (2) imports, (3) payments to government in the form of taxes for the "purchase" of police and fire protection, national defense, and other public services, (4) depreciation allowances representing the value of plant and equipment used up in the production of goods and service, and (5) households which supply the personal services and labor to industries, government, and other households listed across the top of the table.

The *final demand* sector consists of the last five columns on the right-hand side of the table. This is the independent sector in which changes occur which are transmitted throughout the remainder of the table. It includes: (1) positive inventory changes, the addition to inventory accumulated by the industries along the left-hand side of the table, (2) exports, (3) government purchases by all levels of government, (4) gross private domestic investment which indicates spending by industries for new plant and equipment, and (5) household purchases from industries, importers, government, and other households in the left-hand side of the table.

The Gross Output column shows the total sales of each industry in the left-hand side of the table to other industries in the processing sector for current production, exporters, government, and households as well as sales of capital goods. Its total equals the total of the *gross outlay* row, which is the sum of total purchases by each industry in the processing sector. Since each purchase is also a sale, the totals of each of the first six rows is exactly equal to the totals of each of the first six columns. This is not true of the remaining columns and rows, because inventory depletion would not necessarily equal inventory accumulation, imports seldom balance exports, and depreciation allowances would not match new capital investment. But the sum of each row's totals must equal the sum of all the column totals because total purchases of all goods and services (including government and personal services) must equal the total receipt of all goods and services.

It can be observed in Figure 9–5, for example, that establishments in the Electrical Equipment industry sold $7 billion worth of goods to establishments in the Agriculture, Forestries, and Fishing industry, $2 billion worth of goods to establishments in the Chemical industry, and $8 billion worth of goods to other establishments in the Electrical Equipment industry; sales to the Machinery, Lumber, and Furniture industries were $1, $5, and $3 billion, respectively.

Figure 9–5 also indicates that sales of establishments in the Electrical Equipment industry were not limited to other industrial establishments. They sold $3 billion worth of goods to foreign countries, $1 billion in goods to various government agencies (local, state, and federal), and $5 billion in goods to individual consumers (households). At the same time these establishments produced $2 billion worth of goods which were not sold, but were added to inventories, and invested $3 billion in new plant and equipment. The total gross output of the industry, output which went to the six different industries in the processing sector, exporters, government, households, into inventory, and into capital equipment amounted to $40 billion.

During the same period (reading down the 3rd column from the left) one can see that establishments in the Electrical Equipment industry purchased $1 billion worth of goods and services from establishments in Agriculture, $7 billion in goods and services from establishments in the Chemical industry, and, as observed in an earlier paragraph, $8 billion worth of goods and services from other establishments in the Electrical Equipment industry. These establishments also purchased $2 billion worth of goods and services from the Machinery industry, $1 billion from the Lumber industry, and $7 billion from the Furniture industry. Establishments in this industry also depleted their inventories by $1 billion, purchased $3 billion worth of goods and services from foreign sources, paid $2 billion in taxes (purchased services from government), used up $1 billion in capital equipment, and purchased $7 billion worth of labor from households.

***Estimating market potential.*** The determination of how much demand would be generated as the result of a given increase in the output of an industry requires the use of *input-output coefficients.* A coefficient measures the inputs required from each industry to produce one dollar's worth of output in any given industry. The underlying assumption is that larger outputs require more inputs, i.e., using the previous notation, $x_{ij} = F(X_j)$, and that the relationship between inputs and outputs is linear. This linearity is indicated by adding a constant $a_{ij}$ to the equation so that it becomes:

$$X_{ij} = a_{ij}X_j$$

At least in the short run, this appears to be a valid assumption. The relationship between input and output in any given industry is a function of technology, and there is impressive empirical evidence that the level of technology in any given industry changes slowly.[2] Consequently, the following equation has general validity:

$$X_i = a_{il}X_1 + a_{12}X_2 \ldots \ldots \ldots a_{in}X_n + Y_i$$

Each $a_{ij}$ value is estimated from past ratios of $X_{ij}/X_j$. In terms of the transaction matrix in Figure 9–5, $a_{ij}$ is calculated by dividing each entry

[2] W. Duane Evans and Marvin Hoffenberg, "The Nature and Uses of Interindustry Data and Methods," *Input-Output: An Appraisal, Studies in Income and Wealth,* Vol. 18 (Princeton, N.J.: Princeton University Press, 1955); Anne P. Carter, "Changes in the Structure of the American Economy, 1947 to 1958 and 1962," *The Review of Economics and Statistics,* Vol. XLIX, No. 2 (May 1967); Beatrice H. Vaccara, "Changes Over Time in Input-Output Coefficients for the United States," *Applications of Input-Output Analysis,* Vol. 2 (Amsterdam, The Netherlands: North Holland Publishing Co., 1970).

in each column of the processing sector by the column total less the value of inventory depletion. This expresses the net input of each industry that goes to a given industry (including intra-industry transactions) as a percent of the total output of that industry. The values in Figure 9–6

FIGURE 9–6.   Input-output coefficients

| Producing | Agri-culture | Chemi-cal | Electrical equip-ment | Machin-ery | Lum-bering | Furni-ture |
|---|---|---|---|---|---|---|
| | | | *Direct purchases per dollar of output (cents)* | | | |
| Agriculture............ | 16 | 26 | 3 | 5 | 13 | 13 |
| Chemical.............. | 8 | 7 | 18 | 3 | 8 | 18 |
| Electrical equipment............ | 11 | 4 | 20 | 3 | 13 | 7 |
| Machinery............. | 17 | 2 | 5 | 20 | 15 | 9 |
| Lumber............... | 6 | 0 | 3 | 36 | 8 | 4 |
| Furniture.............. | 3 | 10 | 18 | 15 | 5 | 13 |
| Total direct purchases..... | 61 | 49 | 67 | 82 | 62 | 64 |

show how much each industry listed across the top of the table would have to purchase from each source industry on the left hand side of the table for each one dollar of output. For each dollar's worth of production, establishments in the Chemical industry would require 26¢ in purchases from the Agriculture industry, 7¢ in purchases from other establishments in the Chemical industry, 4¢ worth of purchases from the Electrical Equipment industry, 2¢ worth of purchases from the Machinery industry, and 10¢ worth of purchases from the Furniture industry.

In the same manner, if the output of the Chemical industry were increased by $100, assuming relatively stable technology throughout the industry and its suppliers, the direct inputs, i.e., demand for the products of other industries, will be increased by the following amounts.

| Demand for products from: | Will be increased by: |
|---|---|
| Agriculture................................. | $26.00 |
| Other chemical establishments................... | 7.00 |
| Electrical equipment manufacturers.............. | 4.00 |
| Machinery manufacturers....................... | 2.00 |
| Furniture makers............................ | 10.00 |
| Increase in direct demand...................... | $49.00 |

This example is limited to direct purchases from industries in the processing sector. It is evident, however, that any increased output by the Chemical industry will not only lead to an increased demand for electrical equipment, for example, but the Electrical Equipment industry will also require more inputs from Agriculture, the Chemical industry, Machinery, and others.

The conceptual and empirical problems of quantifying the impact of a given increase in demand throughout the processing sector are very involved. However, benchmark input-output tables for the United States are available for the years 1947, 1958, and 1963. Portions of the 1963 tables are reproduced from the *Survey of Current Business* (November 1969) in Figures 9–7 and 9–8.

The table in Figure 9–7 corresponds to the processing sector of Figure 9–5. It shows the dollar value of the input from each industry to each user. Reading across the table shows the markets in which the output of the industry named at the left is sold. Reading down a column gives the inputs purchased by an industry from each of the industries listed at the left.

**FIGURE 9–7.   Interindustry transactions, 1963**

[In millions of dollars at producers' prices]

| Industry No. | For the distribution of output of an industry, read the row for that industry. For the composition of inputs to an industry, read the column for that industry. | Livestock and live-stock products | Other agricultural products | Forestry and fishery products | Agricultural, forestry and fishery services | Iron and ferroalloy ores mining | Nonferrous metal ores mining | Coal mining | Crude petroleum and natural gas | Stone and clay mining and quarrying | Chemical and fertilizer mineral mining | New construction | Maintenance and repair construction | Ordnance and accessories |
|---|---|---|---|---|---|---|---|---|---|---|---|---|---|---|
| | | 1 | 2 | 3 | 4 | 5 | 6 | 7 | 8 | 9 | 10 | 11 | 12 | 13 |
| 1 | Livestock & Livestock Products | 4,750 | 1,819 | 117 | 192 | | | | | | | | | |
| 2 | Other Agricultural Products | 7,897 | 769 | 117 | 550 | | | | | | | | 328 | (*) |
| 3 | Forestry & Fishery Products | | | 35 | | | | | | | | | | |
| 4 | Agricultural, Forestry & Fishery Services | 445 | 1,053 | 74 | | | | | | | | | 3 | (*) |
| 5 | Iron & Ferroalloy Ores Mining | | | | | 55 | 7 | | | (*) | 1 | | | |
| 6 | Nonferrous Metal Ores Mining | | | | | 25 | 263 | (*) | | (*) | | | | |
| 7 | Coal Mining | 6 | 1 | | | 5 | 1 | 410 | | (*) | 5 | 1 | | 1 |
| 8 | Crude Petroleum & Natural Gas | | | | | | | | 297 | | | | | |
| 9 | Stone & Clay Mining and Quarrying | 1 | 85 | | (*) | 5 | (*) | 1 | | 17 | 5 | 478 | 289 | |
| 10 | Chemical & Fertilizer Mineral Mining | | 35 | | | | 6 | (*) | | 1 | 31 | | | |
| 11 | New Construction | | | | | | | | | | | | | |
| 12 | Maintenance & Repair Construction | 200 | 367 | | | 1 | 7 | 14 | 379 | 11 | 3 | 17 | 7 | 6 |
| 13 | Ordnance & Accessories | | | | | | | | | | | 5 | | 161 |
| 14 | Food & Kindred Products | 3,554 | 2 | 44 | 34 | | | | | | (*) | 26 | 3 | |
| 15 | Tobacco Manufactures | | | | | | | | | (*) | | | | |
| 16 | Broad & Narrow Fabrics, Yarn & Thread Mills | | 9 | | | (*) | (*) | | | | (*) | 31 | (*) | |
| 17 | Miscellaneous Textile Goods & Floor Coverings | 9 | 29 | 62 | 41 | (*) | (*) | (*) | 2 | (*) | | 124 | 3 | (*) |
| 18 | Apparel | | | | | | (*) | | | | | 29 | 13 | 4 |
| 19 | Miscellaneous Fabricated Textile Products | 17 | 43 | 1 | | | | | | | | 7 | (*) | |
| 20 | Lumber & Wood Products, Except Containers | 2 | 2 | | | 2 | 10 | 17 | (*) | (*) | (*) | 3,553 | 723 | 16 |
| 21 | Wooden Containers | | 97 | | 14 | | | | | | | | | 5 |
| 22 | Household Furniture | | | | | | | | | | | 342 | | (*) |
| 23 | Other Furniture & Fixtures | | | | | | | | | | | 184 | 4 | 2 |
| 24 | Paper & Allied Products, Except Containers | 12 | 1 | (*) | (*) | (*) | (*) | 1 | 2 | 6 | 2 | 208 | 71 | 3 |
| 25 | Paperboard Containers & Boxes | 2 | 3 | | 86 | | | | | | | 4 | | 7 |
| 26 | Printing & Publishing | 5 | 9 | (*) | (*) | (*) | (*) | (*) | (*) | (*) | | 2 | 1 | 1 |
| 27 | Chemicals & Selected Chemical Products | 57 | 1,424 | (*) | 1 | 21 | 56 | 38 | 101 | 34 | 20 | 201 | 84 | 16 |
| 28 | Plastics & Synthetic Materials | | | | | | (*) | | | (*) | | 1 | (*) | 1 |
| 58 | Miscellaneous Electrical Machinery, Equipment & Supplies | 6 | 25 | 2 | (*) | (*) | (*) | 1 | 1 | 1 | (*) | 37 | 10 | 18 |
| 59 | Motor Vehicles & Equipment | 7 | 14 | | (*) | 2 | 2 | 8 | 3 | 15 | (*) | 36 | 14 | 1 |
| 60 | Aircraft & Parts | | | | (*) | | | | | | | | | 1,868 |
| 61 | Other Transportation Equipment | (*) | 4 | 21 | | (*) | 2 | 9 | | (*) | (*) | 4 | (*) | 17 |
| 62 | Scientific & Controlling Instruments | | | 1 | | (*) | 1 | | 4 | | | 206 | 70 | 40 |
| 63 | Optical, Ophthalmic & Photographic Equipment | | | | | | | | | | | 4 | 77 | 53 |
| 64 | Miscellaneous Manufacturing | 2 | 2 | (*) | (*) | (*) | 1 | (*) | (*) | (*) | 1 | 86 | | 1 |
| 65 | Transportation & Warehousing | 606 | 308 | 44 | 26 | 126 | 30 | 46 | 281 | 34 | 39 | 2,143 | 490 | 28 |
| 66 | Communications; Except Radio & TV Broadcasting | 52 | 83 | | | 1 | 2 | 4 | 9 | 1 | 3 | 180 | 79 | 52 |
| 67 | Radio & TV Broadcasting | | | | | | | | | | | | | |
| 68 | Electric, Gas, Water & Sanitary Services | 96 | 204 | (*) | 1 | 27 | 41 | 65 | 141 | 62 | 36 | 205 | 90 | 26 |
| 69 | Wholesale & Retail Trade | 870 | 843 | 56 | 42 | 21 | 28 | 58 | 145 | 54 | 14 | 5,453 | 1,702 | 93 |
| 70 | Finance & Insurance | 156 | 315 | 3 | 6 | 7 | 25 | 28 | 94 | 29 | 6 | 401 | 161 | 27 |
| 71 | Real Estate & Rental | 289 | 2,020 | | 41 | 111 | 42 | 73 | 2,246 | 45 | 11 | 307 | 134 | 30 |
| 72 | Hotels; Personal & Repair Services exc. Auto | | | | | | | | | | | | | 10 |
| 73 | Business Services | 139 | 836 | 1 | (*) | 33 | 14 | 26 | 106 | 22 | 6 | 2,959 | 281 | 110 |
| 75 | Automobile Repair & Services | 76 | 161 | 7 | 1 | 4 | 2 | 8 | 42 | 19 | 1 | 235 | 101 | 9 |
| 76 | Amusements | | | | | | | | | | | | | |
| 77 | Medical, Educational Services & Nonprofit Organizations | 181 | 13 | | | 1 | 1 | 2 | 5 | (*) | 2 | 57 | 24 | 8 |
| 78 | Federal Government Enterprises | 4 | 4 | (*) | (*) | 1 | 1 | 2 | 5 | 1 | 2 | 18 | 8 | 10 |
| 79 | State & Local Government Enterprises | (*) | 1 | (*) | (*) | 1 | | 1 | 3 | 2 | 1 | 28 | 10 | (*) |
| 80A | Directly Allocated Imports | 2 | 214 | | | | | | | | | | | |
| 80D | Transferred Imports | 174 | 221 | 428 | | 423 | 213 | 2 | 1,046 | 106 | 88 | | | 18 |
| 81 | Business Travel, Entertainment & Gifts | 18 | 32 | 18 | 16 | 3 | 7 | 11 | 67 | 11 | 2 | 359 | 154 | 49 |
| 82 | Office Supplies | 1 | 1 | (*) | (*) | (*) | | 5 | | 1 | (*) | 17 | 7 | 10 |
| 83 | Scrap, Used & Secondhand Goods | | | 5 | | 1 | 5 | | 1 | 5 | | 38 | | |
| 84 | Government Industry | | | | | | | | | | | | | |
| 85 | Rest of the World Industry | | | | | | | | | | | | | |
| 86 | Household Industry | | | | | | | | | | | | | |
| 87 | Inventory Valuation Adjustment | | | | | | | | | | | | | |
| I. | Intermediate Inputs, Total | 19,992 | 12,437 | 1,153 | 1,190 | 984 | 893 | 1,097 | 5,338 | 901 | 336 | 39,629 | 8,663 | 3,777 |
| VA. | Value Added | 6,692 | 14,830 | 598 | 582 | 475 | 625 | 1,540 | 6,926 | 1,123 | 360 | 25,890 | 11,132 | 2,525 |
| T. | Total | 26,684 | 27,266 | 1,751 | 1,772 | 1,429 | 1,519 | 2,637 | 12,265 | 2,024 | 696 | 65,519 | 19,794 | 6,302 |
| TR. | Transfers[1] | 810 | 961 | 709 | 650 | 555 | 337 | 3 | 1,365 | 358 | 116 | | | 1,589 |

Reading down column 10, for example, it can be observed that in 1963, establishments in the Chemical and Fertilizer industry purchased $31 million worth of material from other chemical and fertilizer mineral mining establishments, $20 million from establishments making selected chemical products, $39 million in services from transportation and warehousing establishments, $36 million in services from electric, gas and water utilities—to mention a few.

The table in Figure 9–8 corresponds to the input-output coefficients table of Figure 9–6. The columns in this table show the cents worth of input required by each industry at the top of the table from each industry along the left side of the table for each dollar of output. For example, for each dollar of output the Chemical and Fertilizer Mineral Mining industry requires $0.06 worth of services from the transportation and warehouse industry. Consequently, by reading across the appropriate row, i.e., the industry to which his own firm belongs, the marketer can quickly determine the relative importance of different markets for his primary

FIGURE 9–8.    Direct requirements per dollar of gross output, 1963

[Producers' prices]

| Industry No. | For the composition of inputs to an industry, read the column for that industry. | Livestock and livestock products | Other agricultural products | Forestry and fishery products | Agricultural, forestry and fishery services | Iron and ferroalloy ores mining | Nonferrous metal ores mining | Coal mining | Crude petroleum and natural gas | Stone and clay mining and quarrying | Chemical and fertilizer mineral mining | New construction |
|---|---|---|---|---|---|---|---|---|---|---|---|---|
| | | 1 | 2 | 3 | 4 | 5 | 6 | 7 | 8 | 9 | 10 | 11 |
| 1 | Livestock & Livestock Products | 0.17800 | .06673 | .06687 | 0.10823 | | | | | | | |
| 2 | Other Agricultural Products | .29596 | .02819 | .06665 | .31040 | | | | | | | 0.00493 |
| 3 | Forestry & Fishery Products | | | .01992 | | | | | | | | |
| 4 | Agricultural, Forestry & Fishery Services | .01667 | .03863 | .04243 | | | | | | | | .00005 |
| 5 | Iron & Ferroalloy Ores Mining | | | | | 0.03846 | 0.00089 | 0.00004 | | 0.00002 | 0.00215 | |
| 6 | Nonferrous Metal Ores Mining | | | | | .01782 | .17332 | .00010 | 0.00002 | .00225 | .00013 | |
| 7 | Coal Mining | .00021 | .00002 | | | .00361 | .00090 | .15561 | (*) | .00227 | .00087 | |
| 8 | Crude Petroleum & Natural Gas | | | | | | | | .02418 | | | |
| 9 | Stone and Clay Mining and Quarrying | .00006 | .00311 | | (*) | .00339 | .00029 | .00026 | | .00860 | .00772 | .00729 |
| 10 | Chemical & Fertilizer Mineral Mining | | .00129 | | | | .00408 | .00001 | | .00072 | .04442 | |
| 11 | New Construction | | | | | | | | | | | |
| 12 | Maintenance & Repair Construction | .00750 | .01344 | | | .00060 | .00491 | .00549 | .03093 | .00543 | .00394 | .00027 |
| 13 | Ordnance & Accessories | | | | | | | | | | | .00008 |
| 14 | Food & Kindred Products | .13319 | .00008 | .02529 | .01933 | | | | | | .00010 | .00040 |
| 15 | Tobacco Manufactures | | | | | | | | | .00007 | | |
| 16 | Broad & Narrow Fabrics, Yarn & Thread Mills | | .00034 | | | .00001 | .00019 | | | | .00043 | .00047 |
| 17 | Miscellaneous Textile Goods & Floor Coverings | .00035 | .00106 | .03536 | .02296 | (*) | .00010 | (*) | .00017 | | .00006 | .00189 |
| 18 | Apparel | | | | | | .00001 | | | | | .00044 |
| 19 | Miscellaneous Fabricated Textile Products | .00065 | .00158 | .00072 | | | | | | | | .00011 |
| 20 | Lumber & Wood Products, Except Containers | .00008 | .00008 | | | .00169 | .00651 | .00636 | .00001 | .00002 | .00043 | .05424 |
| 21 | Wooden Containers | | .00355 | | .00798 | | | | | | | .00823 |
| 22 | Household Furniture | | | | | | | | | | | .00281 |
| 23 | Other Furniture & Fixtures | | | | | | | | | | | .00317 |
| 24 | Paper & Allied Products, Except Containers | .00044 | .00004 | .00022 | .00003 | .00015 | .00026 | .00038 | .00014 | .00287 | .00289 | .00317 |
| 25 | Paperboard Containers & Boxes | .00006 | .00011 | | .04877 | | | | | | | .00007 |
| 61 | Other Transportation Equipment | (*) | .00016 | .01184 | | .00006 | .00122 | .00337 | | .00006 | .00044 | .00007 |
| 62 | Scientific & Controlling Instruments | | | | .00040 | | .00025 | .00033 | | | | .00317 |
| 63 | Optical, Ophthalmic & Photographic Equipment | | | | | | | | .00036 | | | .00007 |
| 64 | Miscellaneous Manufacturing | .00006 | .00007 | .00012 | (*) | .00001 | .00067 | (*) | | .00002 | .00003 | .00136 |
| 65 | Transportation & Warehousing | .02272 | .01131 | .02517 | .01445 | .08811 | .01947 | .01760 | .02293 | .01661 | .05592 | .03271 |
| 66 | Communications; Except Radio & TV Broadcasting | .00196 | .00303 | | | .00091 | .00115 | .00134 | .00070 | .00030 | .00402 | .00275 |
| 67 | Radio & TV Broadcasting | | | | | | | | | | | |
| 68 | Electric, Gas, Water & Sanitary Services | .00360 | .00749 | .00009 | .00045 | .01868 | .02667 | .02469 | .01148 | .03054 | .05155 | .00313 |
| 69 | Wholesale & Retail Trade | .03260 | .03090 | .03215 | .02380 | .01502 | .01827 | .02199 | .01180 | .02669 | .03059 | .06323 |
| 70 | Finance & Insurance | .00583 | .01155 | .00188 | .00322 | .00476 | .11637 | .01076 | .00763 | .01423 | .00832 | .00612 |
| 71 | Real Estate & Rental | .01082 | .07407 | | .02324 | .07753 | .02748 | .02769 | .18312 | .02212 | .01622 | .00469 |
| 72 | Hotels; Personal & Repair Services exc. Auto | | | | | | | | | | | |
| 73 | Business Services | .00519 | .03068 | .00038 | .00002 | .02282 | .00923 | .01080 | .00881 | .01076 | .00882 | .04516 |
| 75 | Automobile Repair & Services | .00285 | .00589 | .00387 | .00051 | .00073 | .00151 | .00293 | .00343 | .00932 | .00137 | .00358 |
| 76 | Amusements | | | | | | | | | | | |
| 77 | Medical, Educational Services & Nonprofit Organizations | .00677 | .00047 | .00018 | .00017 | .00054 | .00068 | .00077 | .00039 | .00019 | .00262 | .00087 |
| 78 | Federal Government Enterprises | .00015 | .00015 | .00018 | | .00080 | .00082 | .00068 | .00043 | .00050 | .00230 | .00028 |
| 79 | State & Local Government Enterprises | .00002 | .00003 | .00017 | .00003 | .00040 | .00057 | .00024 | .00025 | .00112 | .00043 | |
| 80 | Gross Imports of Goods & Services | .00659 | .01594 | .24437 | .00006 | .29580 | .14007 | .00083 | .08531 | .05336 | .12564 | |
| 81 | Business Travel, Entertainment & Gifts | .00066 | .00117 | .01002 | .00094 | .00231 | .00453 | .00409 | .00544 | .00274 | .00547 | |
| 82 | Office Supplies | .00003 | .00003 | | .00025 | .00023 | .00023 | .00030 | .00041 | .00041 | .00032 | .00026 |
| 83 | Scrap, Used & Secondhand Goods | | | .00309 | | .00037 | .00344 | .00033 | | .00233 | .00145 | .00059 |
| V.A. | Value Added | .25080 | .54388 | .34163 | .32835 | .33257 | .41171 | .58412 | .56475 | .55470 | .51735 | .39516 |
| T. | Total | 1.00000 | 1.00000 | 1.00000 | 1.00000 | 1.00000 | 1.00000 | 1.00000 | 1.00000 | 1.00000 | 1.00000 | 1.00000 |

products and services. When the most important markets have been identified, the coefficients for each of them can be multiplied by their current dollar output from the most recent Census of Manufacturers or Annual Survey of Manufacturers to produce dollar estimates of potential by market segment or industry.

## PROBLEM PROFILE

The attractiveness of an industry or market segment not only depends upon the nature and trends of its economic characteristics and its demand potential but the kind of problems which are apt to be encountered in developing the market. Unless the company has had some experience in the industry, which is unlikely if it is a new market, management will probably require some type of survey or field testing. In the case of an existing product, the operating characteristics and application techniques of which are well known, a survey of production facilities which would include interviews with engineering and production personnel would probably unearth the most serious obstacles which might be encountered in penetrating a market.

If the product is one which the company has not previously marketed, a field test is probably the quickest way to identify problems. Both the survey and the field test would involve prototypes or product samples. However, the objective of the survey is the collection of information rather than the sale of the product. In a field test, an effort is made to sell and/or service the product, i.e., to duplicate every marketing activity that would be undertaken in the event of full-scale marketing effort.

Properly conducted surveys and field tests can reveal serious applications problems which would be difficult to foresee on the basis of laboratory or in-house tests. Olin Industries developed bonded metal and successfully marketed it to the U.S. Treasury for use in coinage. The chief virtue of bonded metal is economy. By using a relatively low cost metal like steel or copper for the core of a sheet metal and bonding a more precious metal to its surface, the strip can be given the appearance of the precious metal and the strength of the cheaper metal. The silvery appearance of dimes, nickels, and quarters in current use is the result of a thin strip of cupro nickel bonded to both sides of a strip of copper. This saves both silver and nickel while investing coins with the appearance, weight, and electrical properties of the old coins which were 60% silver.

Dwindling supplies of many metals prompted Olin's interest in the commercial possibilities of bonded metal. On the basis of its economic advantages there appeared to be many promising applications for bonded metal in both industrial and household products. Systematic field tests, however, disclosed two unanticipated obstacles to the marketing of this product: inability to control rusting at the exposed edges of the metal and inability to recover scrap. The rust problem rendered bonded metal undesirable for many uses in which its other qualities would have given it a competitive advantage. The loss of scrap (once bonded, metals cannot be separated) placed the product at a cost disadvantage in competition with more expensive metals whose scrap could be easily recovered.

## SUMMARY

Evaluating various industries or market segments which have a need for the products and services a manufacturer can offer involves at least four measures of suitability: market profile, trends in the characteristics which make up the profile, demand potential, and a problem profile. The market profile includes those endogenous variables which have a direct effect on demand for the manufacturer's product offering or the way in which it can be developed. The analysis of trends in the variables reveals the nature and direction of change taking place in the industry or market segment, while the demand potential indicates the total amount of business which the industry or segment represents. The problem profile indicates the obstacles which the company can expect to encounter in its marketing efforts.

In many respects the most difficult measure to apply is that of demand potential. Both cumulative and noncumulative methods are at best approximations. Nevertheless, measurements based on either correlation or input-output analysis are not guesswork. Either technique when properly applied can provide the marketer with a far better index of market opportunity than he is likely to develop without them.

The development of a market profile, a trend analysis, a measure of demand potential, and a problem profile for each segment or industry provide an effective filter for separating genuinely promising market opportunities from those which are superficially attractive. It should enable the marketer to identify with some confidence his target segments— those which offer the most rewarding opportunities and in which he can expect to have the greatest competitive advantage.

# 10

## MEASURING MARKETING PERFORMANCE

DATA PERTAINING to the quality of marketing performance are another important input to the marketing intelligence system. They are useful in both planning and control of marketing effort as well as the identification of market opportunity. Virtually all firms have the option of developing their present markets more intensively or penetrating new ones. Measures of market opportunity may indicate significant untapped potential in existing markets. However, these may have to be matched against measure of marketing performance to determine whether a more intensive effort in existing markets represents a better strategic choice than committing the same resources to the penetration of new markets. The measures which are most frequently employed for this purpose are analyses of sales, costs, buyer behavior, and competition. Although the exact procedures to be followed would vary from one type of study to another, such investigations possess enough in common that all would employ the same general methods of investigation and analysis.

### PLANNING THE MARKETING STUDY

Investigative efforts generally include at least three broad phases: problem definition, analysis, and recommendation. While some analysts might suggest additional phases and others might prefer to give them different names, any attempt to generate information systematically requires direction, appraisal, and response.

#### Problem definition

The first step in any investigation is to formulate an accurate statement of purpose. In some instances the purpose may be perfectly obvious, as in the case of measuring demand potential of an industry or market segment. But even there a clear statement of purpose can be useful in identifying the type of information and the kind of analysis that is required. A careful formulation of ends to be achieved can head off much muddled thinking and much wasted effort at later stages.

In the case of a relatively complex investigation, such as that involving buyer attitudes, a preliminary investigation may be needed to gather key information from a range of informed sources. Data concerning major aspects of a problem from a few carefully selected sources can be very helpful in revealing its true dimensions. It may even be helpful to formulate key hypotheses or statements of assumed relationships between two or more variables. These hypotheses are then either verified or disproved by the ensuing analysis.

The final result is not only a clear statement of purpose but a clear indication of the most fruitful methods of analysis. This makes it possible to identify the types of information needed, the sources from which it should be collected, and the appropriate methods of collecting it.

## Data collection and analysis

When information has to be collected from the field, as opposed to published sources or company records, a sample usually must be designed. It is rarely feasible to attempt a complete census of any industry.

*Sample design.* Since there is an extensive literature on the subject of sampling, the treatment of it here will be limited to some of the unique aspects of industrial surveys which affect sample design.

*1. Variability in the number of users.* Some industrial markets have relatively few buying and using units. Manufacturers of railroad equipment, for example, have only about 355 possible nongovernmental buyers of their equipment—the 355 companies operating line-haul railroads.[1] Airplane manufacturers have only about 33 nongovernmental customers —the 33 domestic air carriers.[2] By contrast, a chemical company marketing chlorinated solvents would have literally thousands of possible buyers.

*2. Variability in types of users.* There are wide differences among industries as to the manufacturing processes employed, and wide differences within even any one industry in the way any one product is used. These variations may be due to differences in technical experience as well as in the age and design of the production machinery.

*3. Importance of a relatively few buyers.* It is very common for a few firms to account for a major share of the purchases of a given product. A market situation in which as few as a half dozen companies buy

---

[1] U.S. Interstate Commerce Commission, *Annual Report and Transport Statistics of the United States,* Part 1, p. 10.

[2] U.S. Federal Aviation Administration, *F.A.A. Statistical Handbook of Aviation,* p. 2.

70 to 90 percent of the materials or specialized equipment sold in an industry is not uncommon.

4. *Multiple buying.* The policy of splitting orders among several suppliers is probably widespread. This can substantially limit the market potential for any given supplier and seriously bias a sample if it is unrecognized.

5. *Checking for faulty sample.* In view of these characteristics, it is usually advisable to stratify industrial buyers by size and to have a complete coverage of the largest establishments. It is also advisable to examine the initial results of a survey for indications of faulty sample design. For example, it may be discovered that some industries or market segments believed to have an important need for a product in fact have little or no use for it and can be eliminated from the survey.

Furthermore, it may be discovered that establishments in an industry or market segment that was thought to be reasonably homogeneous show substantial variation in their use of a product. In this instance, more interviews should be conducted within this industry to be sure that the usage picture which emerges is reasonably complete. The reverse of this situation occurs when initial interviews within an industry or market segment disclose an unexpectedly uniform pattern of product usage. In this instance consideration may be given to reducing the size of the sample. The cardinal principle is to seek enough and only enough information to help solve the problems at hand.

*Sample size.* Whenever a seller seeks information about a number of prospective customers by examining only a few of them, there is sure to be some error involved regardless of how the sample is selected, unless all establishments in a given stratum are very similar. The less similarity among the establishments in a given stratum, the greater the deviation is likely to be between the characteristics of the sample drawn from that group and the true characteristics of the group itself. Stratification serves to reduce variation, but in many market situations, cannot eliminate it.

The greater the probable variation in product needs among a group of establishments, the larger the sample must be in order to reduce to a given limit the sampling error, i.e., the deviation between demand indicated by the sample establishments and the true demand of the group from which the sample was drawn. For example, if it is decided that the sampling error should not exceed 5 percent, the sample drawn must be considerably larger than if an error of 20 percent is acceptable. Furthermore, the less risk management is willing to accept that the sampling error might exceed the desired limits, the larger the sample must be, and vice versa.

When management has assigned a value to the limits of accuracy it desires and the degree of risk it is willing to accept, the proper size of the sample may be computed mathematically. It may be discovered, however, that a sample large enough to reduce sampling error to the desired limit would involve an intolerable expense. In this event, some compromise would have to be reached between accuracy and cost. Unfortunately, accuracy, cost, and sample size all tend to rise and fall together. As a result, the amount of money the marketer regards as commensurate with the importance of market measurement may in the end be the chief determinant of sample size.

Information may be collected from sample establishments by questionnaire or interview. Aside from questions of cost and feasibility, personal interviewing is generally the better alternative. If it is suspected that substantial differences exist among buyers and prospective buyers for a given type of product, an interviewer is in a position to qualify or interpret information which might otherwise be misleading. The interpretive capabilities of an interviewer are often needed when information of a technical nature is involved, such as engineering specifications or accounting practices. The opportunity of the interviewer to probe and clarify reported information is also important in the case of industries in which use or "consumption" of a product varies sharply with the type and size of equipment employed or in which a significant number of establishments are operating at something less than their normal capacity.

**Gathering field information.** Information from the field may be gathered by personal interviews, telephone interviews, and/or mail questionnaires.

*1. Personal interviews.* Interviews may be conducted by members of the company's marketing research department, by part-time interviewers hired and supervised by department personnel, by research firms that specialize in marketing surveys, or by salesmen or other types of company employees. Typically, industrial interviewing requires a high order of knowledge, intelligence, and tact, because it is often impossible to develop a questionnaire form which can be used uniformly throughout a given survey.

Differences in manufacturing systems and purchasing practices, even within the same industry, usually require a questionnaire guide or outline which allows the interviewer a considerable amount of discretion in seeking information. For this reason interviewers must have sufficient knowledge of operating practices in an industry to permit effective discussion with respondents.

The demands of effective interviewing have led a number of industrial marketers to use salesmen for this purpose. A well-trained salesman regularly gathers and enters in his call reports information of great value to decision makers, especially with regard to competitors' activities. Companies with experience in the use of salesmen as field interviewers have found that the best results are generally obtained when the information requested is limited to that which the salesman recognizes as being important to himself as well as to his company, and information which can be secured during his regular sales calls. But as in the use of other interviewers, it is essential that salesmen understand the objectives of the survey and be instructed in ways to obtain the needed information and in how it should be recorded.

Despite the success with which some companies have used salesmen as interviewers, there are good reasons why their usefulness in this function is limited. The major limitations lie in the temperament and personal characteristics of the average salesman. He tends by nature to be an extrovert and not inclined to analyze situations objectively or in detail. He is apt to resent paper work and resist additional demands for it. Moreover, a salesman's relations with his customers are crucial to his success. He may be unwilling to jeopardize them by seeking information he suspects the customer may not wish to give or may consider him as impertinent in requesting.

From management's viewpoint, the most serious objection to the use of salesmen as interviewers is probably the expense it represents. Good salesmen are costly, in terms of both salaries and expenses. They have special skills which should be used to increase company sales and build customer goodwill. From a cost standpoint it is difficult to justify the diversion of their time to survey work unless they have idle time which otherwise would be wasted. This may be true in the case of highly seasonal products.

2. *Telephone interviewing.* The telephone is so much a part of the business executive's life that there appears to be little resistance on their part to telephone interviews. Moreover, telephone interviewing eliminates travel for the interviewer, and requires less time of both the interviewer and the respondent than does a personal call. However, it is difficult to hold long or detailed discussions by telephone and questioning a respondent by telephone becomes awkward if he must consult company records to provide meaningful answers. Sometimes writing to a respondent in advance of a telephone call, asking for his or her cooperation in assembling the needed information, is helpful. But it should be realized that the high degree of persuasive skill needed by the interviewer is often difficult to exercise even during a personal call. It may be well nigh impossible over the telephone.

3. *Mail questionnaire.* The chief drawback in collecting information by mail is the nonrespondent. Since replies to a mail questionnaire may come mainly from individuals or companies with a particular interest in the subject of the inquiry, returns as high as 75 percent cannot be assumed to be representative of the industry or market segment being surveyed. Since many surveys are concerned with the conditions under which products are used as well as the amount of use, it is very important that the proportion of users to nonusers among the nonrespondent group be known. Consequently, the results of a mail survey cannot be used as a basis for marketing decisions until some attempt has been made to determine the product-use pattern of the nonrespondents.

In some instances recirculating the questionnaire with a different letter and a stronger appeal for cooperation is sufficient to recover most of the nonrespondents. Since returns from additional mailings are subject to the same type of bias as were the original returns, personal or telephone interviews with nonrespondents are often more successful than additional mailings.

The sample of nonrespondents should include a suitable range of business sizes and other pertinent characteristics. It is often advisable to design two such samples of identical composition and analyze the results of each separately. Small differences in the results of the two surveys would suggest low variability and indicate that the sample was adequate. Substantial variation between the two samples would suggest the need for additional sampling to ascertain the true characteristics of nonrespondent companies.

Measurement of the bias introduced by the inevitable partial return of a mail questionnaire may seem sufficiently complicated and troublesome to discourage its use. While there are some grounds for this attitude, the total cost of a mail survey is likely to be much less than the cost of data collected by personal interview. Moreover, industrial marketers have made extensive and ingenious use of mail surveys in probing fringe markets for untapped opportunities, testing the effectiveness of advertising, detecting customer dissatisfaction, and sensing the nature of the company's image.

*Analytical methods.*    The weighing and interpretation of data involves more than a simple tallying of answers to questions. While a wide range of statistical and graphic techniques is available to the analyst, particular attention must be given to variation in product application and purchasing practices among different industries or market segments. An industry or market segment which may initially appear homogeneous may in fact consist of several segments, each of different importance and each with somewhat different requirements. Whatever method of analysis is employed, it needs to incorporate a system of weights which adequately reflect the relative importance of various product users and nonusers whose replies are being evaluated.

## Recommendation

To the executive who must make decisions, the researcher owes not only a complete statement of the facts he has assembled and his analysis of them, but also his opinion as to what they mean in terms of action and the reasons which support that opinion. The latter is particularly significant if the recommendations affect the work of a number of units in the organization. Personnel in these units are apt to be much more effective in implementing a decision if they understand the facts and the analysis which gave rise to it.

In most instances a follow-up study is advisable—to determine how recommended action is progressing and to test the validity of the original analysis. Such a review may bring to light unsuspected factors, either not recognized at the time of the original study or given inadequate attention. Since changes in industrial markets can at times be very rapid, a situation existing at the time the field data were collected may have changed substantially by the time recommendations based on them were proposed. A follow-up study may also bring to light errors in planning which should be avoided in subsequent surveys.

## FOUR BASIC MEASURES OF PERFORMANCE

Although there are a variety of measures which can be employed to assess marketing performance, the analysis of sales, costs, buyer attitudes, and competition provide indispensable insight in determining the direction of future marketing efforts.

### Sales analysis

Sales volume is one of the most important variables affecting profits. Other important determinants are the dollars of gross margin yielded by the sales of various products to different customer groups and the expenditures incurred in making these sales. The source of sales information is the sale of a specific product to a specific customer. This is recorded on an invoice which may contain several lines, each giving the number of units of a product ordered, a description of each product, the price of each, and the extended amount, which is obtained by multiplying unit price by quantity. These, with other items of information on the invoice, may be analyzed to give any desired arrangement of sales data in any degree of detail. Information regarding such detail as size, color, material, model—and other characteristics of individual products ordered —are necessary for production planning and inventory control but are seldom required for measures of marketing performance.

*Data sources.* Sales information is ordinarily derived from invoices prepared when shipments are made to customers. The total value of all invoices sent to customers within an accounting period, such as a month or a year, represents total gross sales. Returns and allowances are deducted from this figure to yield net sales.

When purchasing specifications require special designs or features or when a plant is oversold and must schedule production ahead, there may be a time lag of weeks or months between the placement of orders and the preparation of invoices. If this time lag is substantial, unfilled orders must be included with sales information, because invoices would not reflect current sales. This practice requires careful surveillance, because unfilled orders do not always equal shipments. Orders may be cancelled or changed. Cancellations are likely to be substantial with any shift from a seller's to a buyer's market, with any softening of prices (unless buyers are protected by price guarantees), or with any decline in the level of business activity.

*Performance by geographical area.* Depending on how the marketer has organized his marketing effort, performance by geographical area is a basic item of marketing intelligence. Any subdivision of a total market area that is meaningful from the standpoint of the marketer and feasible from the standpoint of data collection would be suitable. This type of classification is usually easy to make and supplies an indication of the company's strengths and weaknesses geographically. The indication of relative strength and weakness is much sharper, of course, if an estimate of total industry sales is also developed on a geographical basis, particularly for the marketer's key product lines.

*Performance by product.* The fact that products which carry the highest margins or possess the greatest sales potential are not always the ones which fire the imagination of salesmen is an old and familiar story. Unless management takes steps to assure that the distribution of selling effort matches the profit and sales potential of various products, sales performance is apt to be unbalanced. That is, sales volume is likely to be less on new and unestablished products than the market possibilities of these products suggest it should be. At the same time, volume on well-entrenched or low-margin lines is likely to indicate that much more attention and effort is being given to them than their profit possibilities justify.

The basic question, of course, is what sales volume *should be* realized, line by line. While a conclusive answer can seldom be formulated to a question of this nature, a useful index of sales performance can be developed by using the best selling product as a standard and expressing the sale of other products as a percent of that standard.

*Performance by salesmen.* Unless salesmen's territories correspond exactly to geographical subdivisions, classifying product sales by salesman is also a useful indication of realized and unrealized opportunity. The amount of business each salesman generates can be determined by summing sales made to all customers in each salesman's territory. This alone does not reveal how much profit he generates or what success he has had in developing his market. An estimate of market potential is needed for each salesman's, or sales representative's, territory to provide a benchmark against which actual sales can be compared. In order to determine whether a salesman is putting forth the amount of effort the potential of his territory warrants requires such information as calls per day, calls per order, and average order size.

The profit earned by a salesman is a function of margin as well as volume. Consequently, the ratio of gross margin to sales is another important index of a salesman's performance. Since gross margin varies with different products, the ratio of gross margin to sales can be helpful in determining whether a salesman is devoting sufficient time to high-margin items.

*Performance by customer.* Studying variation in sales performance by class of customer helps to bring into sharper focus weaknesses disclosed by geographical, product, and salesmen's performance. Since different types of customers often involve individual problems and special consideration, it is useful to measure performance by kind of business and by account. Grouping sales data by kind of business, e.g., steel companies, railroads, chemical plants, automobile manufacturers, and others, provides a measure of their relative importance in terms of the amount of business each represents. At times it may also be useful to divide each individual customer's purchases by size of order, frequency of orders, and gross profit on orders. This enables the marketer to identify those customers which buy a large proportion of high-margin items and those which do not, but it also identifies those which are costly to serve because they place small orders frequently. The latter may nevertheless represent genuine sales opportunities.

## Customer buying attitudes and practices

Although buying attitudes and practices are likely to vary not only from one industry or market segment to another but also within the same industry or segment, it is usually possible to discover some general patterns. The manufacturer of a material or component part often finds it profitable to study the buying behavior of customers for the end products his material or parts are used in.

Either the marketing research department or the sales force of a manufacturer should investigate the buying practices and procedures of the important customers in each industry and market segment the company serves. Among the more important questions to be answered are:

1. What functional activities are sufficiently affected by a given purchase that the men responsible for them have something to say about the purchase?
2. What part in the purchasing procedure does each of these men play?
3. To what type of product information are they most receptive?
4. What buying appeals are most likely to influence them favorably?
5. What are the most effective and economical ways of transmitting the selling message to these men?
    a. If through salesmen, what should be their qualifications?
    b. If through advertising, what media should be employed?
6. What kinds of buying appeals would be most effective?
7. What are the delivery requirements?

8. What are the other service needs?
    a. At the time of sale.
    b. After the sale.
9. What are the customary discount structures and credit terms?
10. How important is reciprocity?

The addition of new products, even when sold in existing markets, raises questions about buying procedures and practices that past experience with other products does not answer. When strategy calls for penetrating new markets with either new products or existing ones, information regarding buyer behavior must be developed to guide sales and advertising.

Such data must usually be developed through field investigation. This may involve calls on a sample of companies representative of an industry or market segment. If so, special attention should be given to those buying in large quantities. If a small fraction of the establishments in an industry account for a large proportion of the industry's total sales, it may be advisable to include all these establishments in the sample because their buying practices may differ considerably. Another source of intelligence which should not be overlooked is sellers of noncompeting products which are used in the industry.

## Cost analysis

The costs of serving customers, filling orders, supporting salesmen in the field, and promoting products also are important items of intelligence, particularly when making a choice between penetrating new markets or developing existing markets more intensively. Two of the most useful forms of analysis, and perhaps the most common, are the analysis of expense categories and the analysis of functions.

*Expense category analysis.* One of the most useful ways of analyzing various categories of expense is the identification of broad trends in their behavior. When compared with sales, such trends can reveal weaknesses before they become problems and in a general way explain the underlying causes of profit performance.

The simplest way to identify the trend of a given category of expense is to plot its values over a period of time and draw a free-hand line which best describes the path of the series. A freehand trend line is usually accurate enough for most purposes, but if greater accuracy is desired mathematical techniques may be used.

A useful way to identify trends that is somewhat more precise than the freehand method, and less mathematical than most objective methods, is to express values as a percent of some base—usually the first year of a series. The cumulative change as well as the rate of change in each item of expense, and in the total, can be determined for any desired period. Knowing, for example, that the salaries of warehouse personnel have increased an average of 5 percent each year, that promotional costs have gone up at the rate of 5.6 percent each year, and that insurance costs have increased at an annual rate of 0.9 percent provides management with an important guide in formulating expense projections.

Since some expenses vary with sales volume, it is also meaningful to express each significant item of expense as a percent of sales and examine their behavior over time. Such a comparison reveals the changes which have occurred in the importance of various expenses and which items are most sensitive to changes in sales volume.

Expense categories which are relatively fixed decline as sales volume increases, while those which are variable tend to increase with increases in sales. Obviously, one would expect some categories of expense to vary with sales. Such costs as salaries, sales commissions, traveling, supplies, and communications would surely occasion no surprise if they increased along with sales. By the same token, such items as donations, dues and subscriptions, and equipment depreciation would seldom be expected to vary substantially with changes in the volume of business.

Insofar as expense items vary as expected, one need not be concerned about them so long as their absolute amounts can be justified. But expenses that do not vary as expected or whose absolute amount appears unreasonable should receive management's attention. One of the most effective ways of identifying expenses which are "out of line" is by plotting them on a scatter diagram. Any item which rises or falls with the volume of business will produce an identifiable path or line (depending on the number of pairings) when plotted against sales on a scatter diagram. While a fixed-cost item would also result in a path or line if paired with sales on a scatter diagram, the path or line would be horizontal or nearly so.

The path traced by an expense which varies with sales, on the other hand, would have a definite slope. The question, though, of distinguishing between the pairings of fixed and variable costs is rather academic. Since fixed costs, by definition, do not vary substantially from one year to the next, they can be easily identified without plotting them on a diagram.

Expenses, then, which are closely related to the volume of sales should produce an identifiable sloping path when paired with sales on a scatter diagram. Any marked deviation in the behavior of a variable expense from its general pattern will stand out conspicuously when that expense is paired with sales. An illustration of the usefulness of the scatter diagram is given in Figure 10–1. Traveling expenses for salesmen of a building hardware manufacturer show only a slight correlation with sales volume, although this is a cost which one would ordinarily expect to change in direct relation to sales. It is difficult to draw a freehand line which best describes the path of these pairings because no one path is

FIGURE 10-1. Relationship of salesmen's salaries, commissions, and traveling expenses for a manufacturer of building hardware, 1960-71

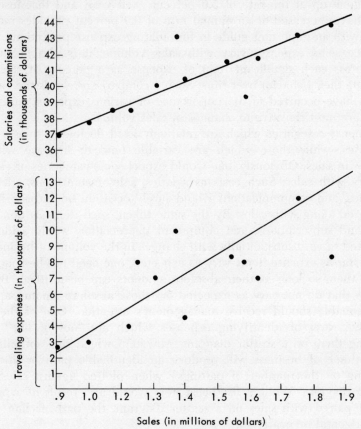

very evident. Salesmen's salaries and commissions, as could be expected, show a close correlation with sales volume. One can draw a freehand line describing the relationship of these pairings with some confidence. The departure of salary and commission costs from the general pattern in two of the twelve years is clearly shown here.

A substantial number of expense categories may not fall neatly into either a fixed or variable classification. They may contain elements of both, and their absolute amount may be more determined by company policy than by sales volume. While such expenses may tend to change with increases and decreases in sales, the amount of the change may not be proportionate to changes in sales. For this reason it is often enlightening to compute the coefficient of correlation for all significant categories of expense. Those categories which change in direct proportion to changes in sales would have very high correlation coefficients, e.g., .85 to 1.0; whereas those with less sensitivity to sales volume would have correspondingly lower coefficients.

The same sort of diagnosis could be made, of course, by plotting expenses and sales on the same graph so that the gradients of the various cost curves could be compared with that of the sales curve. Such a comparison would enable one to readily identify an expense which was "out of line," because it would increase at a faster rate than sales, or because it should be changing at the same rate as sales and does not.

*Functional analysis.* The segregation of marketing functions for purposes of measuring their costs is dependent on the existence of an accounting system which reflects the marketing functions or at least permits the regrouping of existing accounts under appropriate functional headings. When the accounting system makes this possible, the two general alternatives in the allocation of functional costs are complete allocation and partial allocation.

The purpose of complete allocation is the determination of a net profit figure. To this end, the given product, customer, or other element must be charged with its direct as well as its fair share of indirect costs. The latter involves some difficult procedures. To make a full allocation of costs to products, for example, the analyst must decide whether some products are more difficult to sell than others, and if so, what degree of variation in sales resistance exists. An even more perplexing situation exists when a sales force is not being used to capacity, as might be indicated by an ability to handle additional lines or serve additional customers without additional manpower. On what basis should selling costs be allocated to the new products and customers? Comparatively few analysts have an answer to such questions in which they expresss much confidence.

The alternative of partial allocation permits one to escape such perplexities by charging a given function only with costs directly related to it. Only those costs would be considered which would be affected by an addition or diminution in the performance of a given function. This provides a measure of relative profitability in the form of a contribution to the costs of indirect and partially utilized functions. When the direct, fully utilized functional costs related to given products, customers, or territories are subtracted from the net sales attributed to those customers, products, or territories, the excess—a dollar amount—represents that element's contribution toward the remaining expenses of the enterprise. Products, customers, and territories which show the smallest excess of net sales over direct and fully utilized functional costs are relatively unprofitable. In the event substitution was feasible, management would attempt to find new products, customers, or territories (new markets) which promised to provide a greater contribution to indirect costs.

## Analysis of competition

The effectiveness and strength of competition in all its aspects has an important bearing on the attractiveness of various market opportunities. The ability of a manufacturer to penetrate a new market with a high demand potential, or further develop an existing market, is largely dependent upon his ability to compete with other manufacturers with an interest in the same customers. A thorough analysis of competition ordinarily proceeds in two phases: identification and appraisal. It is necessary to know who the competitors are or are likely to be before one can assess their capability and effectiveness.

*Identifying competitors.* Perhaps the most obvious way to identify competitors is through salesmen's call reports. When a sale is lost or the size of an anticipated order reduced, the salesman can usually be relied upon to discover whether or not it was due to a competitor's action, and if so, the competitor's identity.

If a substantial proportion of a manufacturer's sales are made through independent middlemen, this kind of information may not be reported with much regularity. A manufacturer seldom has the control over a distributor's salesmen that he has over his own. In this event, some other source of information must be found. One alternative is to make use of district or regional sales managers, each of whom is responsible for the sales performance of a group of independent distributors. Through regular visits to help distributors sell and merchandise the company's product line, a district sales manager is sure to acquire a substantial amount of data concerning competitors. This information is of limited usefulness, though, unless reporting procedures have been developed which assure its regular entry into the marketing intelligence system.

A useful adjunct to salesmen's call reports and the reports of district or regional sales managers in identifying competitors is the S.I.C. It will be recalled from Chapter 8 that each four-digit classification describes the types of products made and services rendered by establishments included in that class and that many state industrial directories list firms by four-digit S.I.C. code. Consequently, an examination of S.I.C. categories by a manufacturer should reveal those classifications in which products are capable of performing the same functions and meeting the same needs as his own. Reference to industrial directories for states in which the firm is actively seeking customers, or considering doing so, should disclose the names and locations of most firms with competing products and services.

*Appraising competitors' strengths.* The share of market held by a competitor is a basic indicator of his strength and should be estimated by the marketer at the time an industry or market segment is being evaluated. Market shares can seldom be determined with accuracy, but as in most marketing measurements, accuracy is a relative matter. It is more important to know the approximate position of different competitors in a given industry or market (i.e., which seller has the largest share, which has the next largest share, etc.) than to know, for example, whether a particular firm has 24 percent of the market or 19 percent of it. The importance of market share measurements is that they enable management to separate those firms which should be watched very closely from those which warrant only occasional surveillance.

The strength of a competitor, like that of any marketer, is a function of the quality of his product line, the ingenuity and appeal of his promotional efforts, the effectiveness of his pricing, and the efficiency of his distribution system. An indication of product quality can frequently be determined through examination by engineering personnel or through customers or personnel in noncompeting firms who have had experience with the products. Another indicator of product quality and engineering sophistication is the amount of money a firm invests in R & D effort. Although this information is not readily available—there is no obligation to enter it in annual reports—even rough approximations can be useful in separating those competitors which are systematically pursuing product improvement and product innovation programs from those which are not.

Unfortunately, not all companies are willing to provide detailed financial information to reporting organizations such as Moody's or Dun & Bradstreet. This is particularly true of firms in which the ownership interest is closely held. However, careful search of government publications and transcripts of hearings before various regulatory agencies, as well as court cases, can provide significant insights, particularly when combined with information from other sources such as trade journals, call reports, and public information releases.

The effectiveness of a competitor's promotional effort can often be ascertained by scrutinizing the company's advertisements and promotional literature. While these sources will not provide much insight into the quality and force of personal selling efforts, call reports should contain a considerable amount of detailed observations regarding this aspect of a competitor's promotional activity.

The nature of a competitor's pricing tactics and strategy must usually come from observation and from call reports as well as buyer studies. The rationale behind a competitor's pricing may have to be surmised from financial results. It is often difficult or impossible to trace the contributions of different products to a rival's total financial picture. However, by piecing together bits of information, it is sometimes possible to develop estimates of production costs and margins for different product lines which are accurate enough to predict what a competitor's pricing response might be in a given situation.

The customers of a competitor are probably the most reliable source of information about the efficiency of his distribution system. Slow deliveries, back orders, damaged merchandise, and inaccurate invoices are ordinarily indicative of a malfunctioning channel—unless these are characteristic of the industry at a particular time. This type of information is somewhat more difficult to obtain in an industry or market segment which is new to the marketer. Even in this instance, however, a carefully planned survey can unearth enough clues to enable an experienced analyst to construct a fairly reliable picture of the strengths and weaknesses of a competitor's channel network.

## SUMMARY

We have observed that virtually all industrial marketers have the option of developing their existing markets more intensively or undertaking a penetration of new markets. Which of these general choices represents the best strategic alternative depends in part on the strengths and weaknesses of a company's marketing efforts as indicated by measures of marketing performance.

Planning an investigation of performance usually incorporates three broad phases: problem definition, analysis, and recommendation. Problem definition involves the formulation of a clear statement of purpose which may include two or more hypotheses to be verified or disproved by the analysis. Since it is seldom feasible to attempt a complete census of any industry, the analysis phase usually includes sample design and the collection of data as well as methods of analysis. For the sake of executives who must reach decisions, the conclusion of an investigation should be formalized in a statement of recommendations along with the rationale which supports them.

Although there are a variety of performance measures which may be employed, analyses of sales, costs, buyer behavior, and competition should supply indispensable insight in determining the direction of future marketing effort. Evaluating sales performance by geographical area, product, salesman, and customer often provides a particularly useful outline of marketing strengths and weaknesses. When this information is supplemented with data regarding purchasing practices of customers (and prospective customers) as well as an analysis of marketing costs by category and function, a revealing picture of a firm's marketing capabilities and incapabilities should emerge. In many instances this picture can be brought into sharp focus with the identification of competitors and an evaluation of their capabilities.

# PART IV

# Marketing strategy: Product and service components

STRATEGY is the link between the firm and its environment. While the mission of a firm describes what kind of business it is, the strategy describes how its management proposes to implement the mission over the long run. Since the environment includes investors, suppliers, government, and other businesses as well as customers, the strategic planning of a manufacturer must encompass finance, procurement, research, and industrial relations as well as marketing.

In this section we treat marketing strategy as an element of the overall strategy of an enterprise. Similarly, marketing strategy is viewed as having five components, two of which—product and service—are discussed in this section. The remaining components—channels, price, and promotion—are discussed in the following three sections.

Since marketing intelligence is the raw material of the planner, we also seek to show how the data-gathering and analysis discussed in Part III influences and, to some extent, shapes strategy in marketing.

# 11

# THE CONCEPT OF STRATEGY

THE MARKETING ACTIVITIES conducted by a manufacturer of industrial products are an integral part of the company's total operating system. In a well-managed firm, marketing is carefully meshed with production, finance, research, purchasing, and other functions of the business so as to make the maximum contribution to company objectives. For this reason it is useful to identify the major types of plans by which the operations of a manufacturing enterprise are directed. These may be designated as strategic, operational, logistical, and organizational. Since concern here is with the strategic plan, the unique features of marketing strategy and its major supporting elements are treated in the first part of the chapter. In order to place marketing strategy in its proper perspective, it is helpful to consider the planning structure to which it belongs and the relationship it bears to other parts of the structure. The development of strategic plans is treated in the latter part of the chapter.

## THE STRUCTURE OF PLANS

A plan is a goal-directed system of action. It specifies the actions which must be taken and the sequence in which they must occur in order to achieve some future objective. Basic to all planning is the generic need which the company will seek to satisfy, i.e., its mission. This is clearly a top-management decision and one which cannot easily be altered once management has decided to commit the resources at their command to that end. A strategic plan is one which describes the allocation of a firm's resources which the management believes will achieve the corporate mission with the greatest efficiency over the long run. Supporting the strategy and contributing to its implementation are plans for the operations, logistics, and organization called for by the

185

strategy. Together, these constitute a hierarchy of objectives, and plans to achieve them, which make up the guidance system of an enterprise.

## Mission and strategy

As it is used in an everyday sense, the word strategy carries the connotation of a particularly adroit or skillful plan. Some writers have been more precise and defined a strategy as a *complete* plan, so complete that it is unlikely to be upset by any recognizable outside force. It is a set of directions which specifies which choices a firm will make in every conceivable situation which available information enables management to identify.[1]

The term strategy is derived from *strategikos,* a word which the Greeks used to describe what the commanding officer did in a military campaign. The military commander is charged with a mission and must allocate and position the forces under him in a way which offers the greatest probability of achieving it. Since the enemy is not likely to accommodate him by revealing what they plan to do, the commander must base his strategic decisions on assembled intelligence about the enemy, the terrain over which military operations will be conducted, and any other factors which have a bearing on the ability of his forces to function as well as those of the enemy.

In view of the seriousness of such matters, the time frame in which they take place is generally long enough to permit the systematic collection and analysis of information. It follows that strategic decisions can be no better than the quality of intelligence on which they are based. This accounts for the high position of the intelligence function in military organizations and the extreme lengths (U-2 planes, electronic bugging, spy networks, and other cloak-and-dagger operations) to which governments go in implementing it.

But business is not warfare. The mission of a military commander is decided by his government. While he may have an input, his role is that of an actuator rather than a formulator. The mission of a military operation is generally to defeat the enemy. This is of such paramount importance that the statement of mission is apt to be clear and unencumbered by qualifications. The mission of a business enterprise, on the other hand, can seldom be stated with such singleness of purpose. It might be to move materials, or to supply mobile power, or to transmit, process, store, and retrieve information. However, these aims have to be refined and qualified in order to bring about a sensible match between the capabilities of an enterprise and the opportunities it seeks to exploit.

In essence, the mission identifies those aspects of a company which

---

[1] John Von Newmann and Oskar Morgenstern, *Theory of Games and Economic Behavior* (Princeton: Princeton University Press, 1953), p. 79; and J. D. Williams, *The Compleat Strategist* (New York: McGraw-Hill, 1966), p. 16.

are to be enduring and unchanging over a relatively long period of time. It defines the central character of an enterprise and the individuality it has for its members and its various publics. The "personality" of firms like Xerox, IBM, Monsanto, and Caterpillar reflects aspects of company direction and intent which are likely to persist through substantial changes in the allocation of their resources. Intent and direction tend to persist because the basic determinants of an organization's characteristics serve to perpetuate continuity. The basic character of an enterprise and the core of its special competence are separate from the manifestations of these characteristics which appear in its products, policies, and communications. The latter is the domain of business strategy.

In a business sense, strategy defines products, but it defines them in terms of what they should do rather than what they should look like or be made of. It identifies the markets and market segments for which products are now or will be designed, the means by which operations will be financed, and the emphasis which will be placed on the safety of capital as opposed to income. These are decisions which would change over time as environmental conditions, company resources, and the erosion or expansion of opportunities suggested new approaches and priorities.

To invest a strategic plan with the responsiveness and flexibility it must have to provide reliable long-range direction under changing circumstances, it may be subdivided into sectors or components with particular attention to such functions as finance, industrial relations, research and development, and marketing. Our main concern here, of course, is with the marketing component.

*Marketing strategy.* That part of the company's strategic plan which deals with the development of its products and services, the stimulation of demand for them, the determination of their prices, and the makeup of channels through which they reach customers represents marketing strategy. Its major elements are product and service definition, promotion, pricing, and distribution.

*1. Product definition.* Since a product is simply a bundle of properties, it should possess those properties which fit the needs of target markets in a way which will give the marketer the greatest competitive advantage. Due to the diversity of needs, few manufacturers produce but a single product or even a single line of products, i.e., products which serve the same general purpose or are so closely associated that customers buy them together (e.g., grinding wheels, power transmission equipment, crawler tractors). In order to penetrate and hold their markets, many industrial firms find it necessary to produce a number of product lines, i.e., a *product mix.*

What the product mix should include is of course a basic question. Corollary questions are the range of items or models to be offered within each product line as well as the level or levels of quality and versatility each line should possess. Since quality and versatility involve engineering design, it must also be decided whether the company should be a leader in design or a follower of others who carry on the pioneering work.

Another strategic consideration is whether the principal source of new products should be internal or external. Without a substantial commitment to research and development effort, few new products can be generated internally. For this reason many companies elect such alternatives as copying the unpatented products of other firms, negotiating royalty arrangements with them, purchasing outright the manufacturing and sales rights to products, or acquiring the companies which make them.

*2. Service definition.* Depending on the nature of the product offering and the needs of firms composing the target markets, service may be indispensable in winning and holding customers. In a strategic sense, service can be defined as any activity undertaken for the express purpose of aiding customers. While this is a rather nebulous statement, it does exclude such activities as frequent sales calls, local availability of inventories, and warranties which of course aid customers but are seldom undertaken expressly for that purpose. What does fit into this concept are such activities as pre-sale engineering studies, technical consultation, and performance testing, as well as such conventional post-sale aids as financing, operator training, installation and maintenance. Despite the high cost and the abuse which so often accompany it, customer service is a core element in the strategic plan.

*3. Promotion.* Advertising, personal selling, and sales promotion are all ways in which a marketer can stimulate demand for his products. The central problem of marketing is that of bringing about buying action. In its essence, promotion is the function of inducing customers and prospective customers to buy the company's products in quantities and at prices which yield satisfactory profits. Utilizing promotion involves decisions on at least three key issues: how to use advertising, to what extent personal selling should be employed, and the most effective way to supplement both with such supporting efforts as displays, trade shows, exhibitions, and demonstrations.

*4. Pricing.* The prices at which products should be sold represent a complex interaction of ingredients which includes legal considerations as well as considerations of cost and demand. These considerations must be weighed against a background of competition and industry practice. Since price may seldom be the dominant factor in making a sale, long-range decisions regarding it need to be carefully integrated with decisions concerning the other four elements of strategic planning for marketing.

*5. Channels.* There are a number of alternatives a manufacturer may employ in reaching nonhousehold buyers. In many market situations, some are strikingly superior to others. Since the marketing channel is an extension of the manufacturing enterprise itself, channel strategy should embrace both the internal marketing units of a firm and the external intermediaries. Consequently, it not only involves the choice of intermediaries, but also the relationships which should prevail among them and between them and the manufacturer. It is particularly important that channel strategy recognize the emergence of new customer groups, impending changes in existing groups, and the impact of these on customer needs; although these factors are an issue in all elements of the strategic plan.

## Operating plans

While mission and strategy define the direction in which management intends to move an enterprise and the general means which will be employed to achieve progress in that direction, day-to-day implementation of strategy requires more detailed guidelines. This is the function of operating plans. The most important of the operating plans are tactics, policies, and programs.

*Tactical plans.* The word "tactics" is derived from the Greek word "deploy," which referred to what a military commander in the field did when he arranged his forces on a battlefield in the presence of the enemy. In this situation speed, secrecy, and flexibility are essential to success. However, the commander can deploy only those forces which have been allocated to him. His tactical plans must be carried out within the scope of the strategy which defined the distribution and commitment of forces. Tactics must fulfill the strategy.

Turning to business, one can identify a similar relationship. Although "long" and "short" are relative terms, tactical planning is shorter range than strategic planning because its purpose is to fulfill the strategy in a specific situation under a particular set of circumstances. It follows that tactical plans are also more narrow in scope than strategic plans. Although "broad" and "narrow" also are relative terms, an implementing effort is more limited in both its time and operational dimensions than the general effort of which it is a part.

Since the time and operational dimensions of a plan are a function of the organizational level at which they are formulated, tactical plans can be distinguished from strategic plans on the basis of where they originate in an organization. Strategic planning is a corporate level, top-management activity. Depending on the size and complexity of the organization, strategic decision making may extend to division level management, but this would be at the discretion of top management.

On the other hand, tactical planning is an activity of operating management at the department and district levels. For example, the decision to recover development costs on all new products as quickly as possible by selling them at premium prices is a strategic decision and one which originates with top management. Approving the request of a district manager to sell a new product to a particular buyer below prevailing prices in order to penetrate a new market is a tactical decision which originates in the field. The decision by Xerox to lease its copying machines instead of selling them and to make the same machine available under a number of different fee structures based on usage was a strategic decision. However, the specific fee arrangements which are available to any given customer are decided at district and regional levels. These are tactical decisions.

*Policies.* A policy represents a guide or decision rule to be applied in a given area. Policies deliberately sacrifice the flexibility of tactical planning in order to prevent lower-level managers from making decisions which are too sensitive or too difficult to be left to them. Policies also force consistency in operations of a recurring nature that take place under similar circumstances. For example, decisions not to deal in used equipment, not to quote prices over the telephone, to advertise only in medical and pharmaceutical journals, or not to sell on consignment are policy decisions.

Unlike strategy, which must take outside environmental forces into account, policy concerns matters which are largely under the control of management. It must therefore be consistent with the mission and strategy of an enterprise as well as flexible enough to permit change when the conditions which prompted the policy no longer exist.

*Programs.* Courses of action designed to achieve particular and (often) limited objectives are programs. Although some programs may be recurring, such as sales training programs, the training objectives and budget allocation are apt to change with each new entering "class." The types of programs which are rather typical of industrial marketers are incentive programs in support of new products or attempts to penetrate new markets, promotional programs to bolster sales in a period of sagging demand, cost reduction programs to permit price adjustments on products under severe price pressure, and product development programs to bring promising new product ideas to commercialization in the shortest possible time.

Depending on the difficulties encountered in pursuit of an objective, a program might be either of short or long duration. When the program objective has been achieved, the program comes to an end and the resources committed to it may be reallocated to other activities in the organization. A marketing program can be developed to meet any situation in which a specific end can be identified and systematic effort is needed to attain it.

Programs can be distinguished from policies in that they are action oriented rather than control oriented and usually require budget support. They differ from tactical plans in that their duration may be either short or long term; the need for speed, secrecy, and flexibility in their formulation is less urgent; and, by consequence, the planning process itself can be more deliberate and thorough than is often possible with tactical plans.

*Supporting plans.* Since policies require enforcement, management must usually make some provision for it. The exact detail and order of such provisions is generally referred to as *procedure*. A procedure defines a chronological sequence of action. It stipulates the precise nature and order of activity to be followed in putting a policy into effect. If a procedure requires one or more steps or actions which in turn involve a sequence of steps, such as verifying the credit rating of a prospective customer, the procedure itself may have to be supported by *methods*. A method specifies how a particular step in a procedure is to be performed so as to assure comparability of results.

Programs may also require supporting plans if they involve special skills or special knowledge for their execution. In such instances it is often advisable to institute specific *projects* within a program. Typically, a project is confined to techniques and methodology—the how-to detail that is so often needed to execute the phases of a program. A project is a very flexible type of plan. It can be adapted to any undertaking which can be separated into phases with reasonably predictable termination dates.

Some phases of a program may require the exact sequencing and timing of physical operations to assure satisfactory results. Testing a chemical for toxicity in a program designed to eliminate unsafe products from the company's product line would be an example of a phase requiring precise sequencing. Such plans are commonly referred to as *schedules*. They identify in advance every movement or step in a series necessary to properly perform a given task with efficiency.

### Logistical plans

Strategic and operational plans require resources for their implementation. Manpower, money, equipment, and facilities called for by strategic and operational planning must be acquired, assembled in the proper relationships, and assigned to the appropriate line and staff units. The systems of action for accomplishing these ends are logistical plans. It is their function to provide the material and personnel support for business operations.

### Organizational plans

Contrary to the impression one may draw from observing a great bureaucracy (either public or private) at work, organization is a means rather than an end. When other plans spell out the what, when, and how of future action and the manner in which required human and physical resources will be acquired, organizational plans define the machinery which will perform the operations. They identify the relationships between personnel and resources as well as the authority and communications networks that will produce desired actions.

## Summary

Each of these five general types of plans plays a part in a well-developed marketing effort. Together, they complement each other like the fingers of one's hand and form an integrated structure resembling that shown in Figure 11–1. Although some reference will be made to each of these planning categories in subsequent chapters, the main concern will be with strategy. The purpose here was to explain the function of strategy and place marketing strategy in its proper perspective.

## FORMULATING STRATEGY

For purposes of discussion, it is convenient to divide the planning process into several steps or stages. The divisions used here are not

FIGURE 11–1.  The planning structure

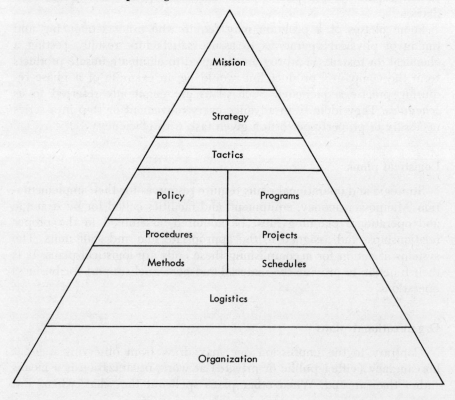

necessarily standard or universal. Other writers and practitioners may prefer other breakdowns perhaps as good or better than this one. It should also be recognized that the chronological implication of this sequence of steps found here is largely false. In a typical planning operation, a number of them may be going on simultaneously and at least one of them—the collection of marketing information—must go on all the time if it is to be done properly.

Nor is the planning process itself so distinct from operation in either timing or nature as its treatment here would imply. While carrying out the current plan, management must be preparing others for the future and, at the same time, making such amendments to current ones as may be demanded by changing conditions and newly discovered information.

## Preliminary analysis

Before one can do intelligent planning about anything, he must know about it. This is true even of the simplest situation. The more complex the situation the more detailed the knowledge concerning it must be in order to plan for it realistically. The technical nature of most industrial goods complicates market planning for them. For example, the demand for a material, component, supply item, or piece of equipment may be changed profoundly and abruptly by changes in technology. An improvement in the technique of making castings may increase the demand for castings and reduce that for machined parts and the equipment that machines them; technical developments in making and using plastics may take business away from metals; electronic transistors largely destroyed the market for tubes; the development of synthetic fibers has eroded the market for natural fibers, and on and on.

This uncertainty of total demand for the individual firm is aggravated by the small number of large users which characterize many industries. A shift in patronage by any one buyer can subtract heavily from the sales volume of one supplier and add substantially to that of another. Moreover, the derived demand for industrial goods subjects the industrial marketer to all the uncertainties that beset the marketer of consumer goods whom he supplies.

Consequently, the analysis which precedes the formulation of marketing strategy includes both the situation analysis discussed in Chapter 2 and the analysis of potential markets discussed in Chapters 7 through 10.

*Situation analysis.* The situation audit, together with the evaluation of alternative missions and ways (strategies) of pursuing them, is indispensable because this identifies the needs which a marketer is capable of fulfilling with the greatest competitive advantage. Since this determines the direction of strategic planning, the data generated by a situation audit are basic inputs to marketing strategy.

*Market identification.* Various market identification techniques can be employed to identify broad categories of customers with needs that match the marketer's capabilities, and to subdivide them into measurable subgroups or segments. The selection of target markets by weighing the profile, trends, demand potential, and problems of each segment provides the subjects on which strategic planning must focus if it is to be effective.

*Analysis of target markets.* In order to decide which elements of the marketing strategy should be employed, the relative emphasis each should receive, and how they should be linked with each other, more specific intelligence about each target market is usually desirable. It is especially important to know as thoroughly as possible the production system in which one's products will be used. The marketer needs to know how his products are used, the techniques employed in their application, the difficulties users have encountered with them, and how they have overcome or adjusted to these difficulties. It is also important for him to keep abreast of changes in the technology of his target markets that may affect the application or performance of his products or they will soon be out of date.

In addition to intelligence related to product adaptability, application, and performance in his target markets, the strategy planner needs information about customer and prospective-customer firms themselves. He needs to know what individuals within a firm exercise buying authority, or influence those who do, as well as the selling appeals most likely to motivate them. The planner also needs to investigate the internal politics of important or potentially important buyers to discover shifts in power and influence that are taking place or likely to occur. An especially important category of customer intelligence is that concerning new end-products in the planning or development stage which may result in a demand for new materials or equipment.

Another important strategy input is intelligence concerning available channels through which products can be moved to customers. Changes constantly occur in the marketing services rendered by individual outlets or types of outlets, and in the struggle for power and influence that incessantly goes on among them. General trends do not supply enough insight on which to base strategy decisions. The planner needs to know the behavior and performance of individual outlets.

By the same token, knowledge about individual competitors is another valuable strategy input, particularly that concerning product quality, uses, and appeals. Equally significant, though, is intelligence about a competitor's delivery and service performance and his reputation for being helpful to customers and keeping his promises. This knowledge and that generated by other measures of marketing performance, notably sales and cost analysis and the relevant economic indicators, round out the intelligence needs of the planner.

## Choice of strategy components

The central problem in choosing the components of a marketing strategy is to find that combination of components which will produce the maximum net revenue. In principle, the solution of such a problem is relatively simple. It involves the application of marginal analysis; that is, the use of each component should be pushed to the point where the return from an additional dollar spent on it exactly equals the return from an additional dollar spent on any one of the others. A top limit is placed by the maximum amount of money the management of a firm feels it can afford to spend, or by the point at which an additional dollar spent on any one or all of the components will not bring in a cash flow of more than a dollar; usually, it is the former. While this principle is simple, any attempt to apply it is bound to be infinitely complex. This complexity arises not so much from the mathematical problems involved as from the difficulty of forecasting results of the use of the different components. If the results of applying each element of strategy could be accurately foreseen, a mathematical formula can be developed that would make the principle readily workable.

But it is very difficult to forecast the results of taking any given marketing action unless these results can be measured. This is possible with only such strategy components as direct mail advertising or promotional material designed to bring in orders or inquiries. With most of them, though, the measurement of results is at the present time largely a process of more or less intelligent guessing and the exercise of seat-of-the-pants judgment. In spite of the lack of adequate means to forecast the results of marketing action, or even to measure them, the marketing manager cannot avoid trying to do so. Unless he does, he cannot plan. During recent years, much study has been devoted to attempts to improve both measurement and forecasting in this area. One may expect that during the coming years, these efforts will be continued and probably intensified.

At this point, what appears to be the most promising approach to the problem is that of measuring the preliminary or intermediate, rather than the end, results of marketing effort.

For example, most attempts to measure the effectiveness of magazine and trade journal advertising have sought to discover whether a given advertisement was noticed, read, or remembered. Radio and TV rating services report the number of people who listened to or viewed a program. This is only the beginning of the story. In order to be effective, advertising copy must call attention to itself so that prospective customers or persons who influence buying will read it or listen to it. It must get its message across to the buying or influencing group in a way which motivates them to adopt a pattern of thought or action desired by the advertiser. The objective of an advertisement is conviction or action. But none of the usual tests of effectiveness even approach this point.

Part of the reason for this state of affairs is that the objectives of many advertising pieces and campaigns are not clearly stated or even envisaged by those who prepare them. When they are, the objective of each advertisement tends to differ from that of every other one, with the result that it is impossible to measure all of them with a single standard. This suggests that the task of measuring the effectiveness of any marketing action should begin when its use is planned. For example, when an advertising or sales promotion effort is planned, its objectives should be stated in the most specific terms possible. If this is done, there is some chance that a method of verifying its results can be devised.

Suppose the objective of an advertising effort is to generate inquiries. One might ask how many inquiries could be expected and how much business they should produce. The planner must have some figures in mind in order to decide whether the advertising will be worth its cost. It should not be too difficult to establish a system of records and analysis that would indicate how near the campaign came to achieving its goal.

Consider a less tangible objective, such as creating or changing customer attitudes or company image. If it is decided to do this by advertising, the marketing manager must believe that the change in attitude, once achieved, will be worth more than the cost of the advertising. Once the decision has been made as to what the change is really worth, attitude surveys can be used to determine the degree to which change was actually effected and the return which was realized on money spent. It is true that all such dollar appraisals are made on nebulous grounds, but if estimated with care they are apt to be accurate enough to provide a reasonable measure of results. Once management has accumulated some experience with estimates of this type, it is often possible to predict outcomes with sufficient confidence to formulate strategies effectively.

The stage should now be set for a meaningful discussion of the different components of marketing strategy and the factors which influence the nature of their contribution to the strategy.

## SUMMARY

Corporate or business strategy is part of a pyramidal structure of plans which is directed toward the pursuit of a company's mission. Strategy supplies the long-range conceptual blueprint which describes how the company will move to fulfill its mission. Depending on the size and complexity of an enterprise, strategy may incorporate financial, procurement, industrial relations and research sectors of components as well as marketing. These different strategic sectors or components are in turn supported by operational, logistic, and organizational plans.

Since the survival of any business is a function of its ability to find buyers for its products and services, marketing is a core element of business strategy. Marketing strategy is in turn composed of sectors or components relating to product definition, service definition, promotional effort, pricing, and distribution channels. The question of how these should be combined into a marketing strategy can be approached in two general phases: preliminary analysis and choice of components. The former is an extension of the situation analysis and market identification studies discussed in earlier chapters, while the latter represents an application of marginal analysis.

# 12

## PRODUCT DEFINITION

THE SPECIFIC COMBINATION of properties which should be designed into a manufacturer's product line and the assortment of models and items which will give the firm the greatest competitive advantage are shaped by a multitude of forces. The statement of mission and the identification of target markets provide the general focus. Design engineering, however, needs more specific direction. Since many of the forces which influence this direction are not within management's control, a considerable amount of adjustment to shifting market opportunities and competitive action is required. For this reason it is important to have long-range guidelines for products in mind, rather than to drift with the tide.

A well-conceived definition of the kinds of products which mesh with the company's capabilities and will move it in the direction of its mission facilitates planning throughout a company. It imparts direction and focus both to research and operating efforts. It represents perhaps the best assurance that opportunities which will enhance the firm's future earning power and growth are not overlooked because middle management does not know what top management wants.

The various forces affecting product definition are discussed in three sections. The first is concerned with new-product development, while the second deals with the issue of product mix. The third section treats company strengths and weaknesses germane both to diversification and simplification of the product line.

### PRODUCT DEVELOPMENT

The entire product development process is characterized by a number of factors which complicate its conduct. The first is that all functional units of the enterprise are involved at various points, and many of them throughout the entire process. They must be carefully mobilized and their natural resistance to cooperative action overcome.

Second, many different types of activity must be carried on con-

198

currently. Practically all of these are necessary prerequisites to later activities. Thus, there is an acute problem of timing, requiring the establishment of target dates and follow-up to determine progress. For products that require a substantial amount of technical research and development work, the period from the original concept of the idea until commercialization is typically five to ten years.

Third, is the need for several check points at which the project is considered in all of its aspects, and decisions are reached—whether it should be abandoned, put on the shelf, or continued at a given rate of work. There is no magic number of such points, although the most obvious occur at:

1. Preliminary screening of new-product ideas.
2. The time substantial amounts of expenditures are authorized for research and development.
3. Authorization for prototype manufacture and market or use testing.
4. The decision regarding full-scale manufacture and marketing.

The process of reviewing the project in its manifold technical and economic aspects at each of these check points becomes increasingly more detailed and thorough as larger and larger amounts of company resources must be committed by decisions to continue it.

Fourth, new products that are quite similar to the present line in production and selling characteristics will not require a process of development so elaborate or as long as those that are more alien to the established knowledge and know-how of the company organization.

The nature of these complicating factors indicates the desirability of systematizing the search for new products. While the appropriate elements of a product development system would vary from one firm to another, certain activities are basic to the process itself. These include at least the following phases:

1. Generating new-product ideas.
2. Preliminary appraisal of new product ideas and selection of projects.
3. Product and market research.
4. Process research.
5. Prototype testing in production and marketing.
6. Commercialization.

With the exception of the second step, the appraisals that are likely to be made near the end of one phase and the beginning of the next have been omitted.

## Generating new-product ideas

It is almost a truism that new product ideas should match the capabilities of the enterprise and be generated in sufficient number to present a real choice of opportunities. Both internal and external sources should be consulted.

*Internal sources.* Stimulating a flow of ideas internally is largely a matter of gaining and holding the interest of groups in the organization. One means of doing this is to provide adequate machinery for prompt acknowledgement, review, and decision regarding new-product ideas submitted by insiders. Delay in acting on such ideas is apt to be interpreted as lack of interest on the part of management and can dampen creative effort. Financial rewards can also be effective in generating ideas, particularly if they are offered promptly. Some of the more obvious internal sources of new-product ideas are Research and Development departments, technical service staffs, salesmen, executive personnel, company sales records, and patent departments.

*1. Research and development departments.* For companies large enough to support them, R & D departments are usually fruitful sources of new-product ideas. As a rule, research personnel are very imaginative and accustomed to working with new concepts. Although they are not always fully aware of the commercial requirements of new products, this limitation can be met in part through the efforts of the research director to create in his staff an understanding of cost and profit problems. An important characteristic of research personnel as a source is that they are typically thinking ahead to future technology and are not likely to be influenced by current industrial practices.

In addition to ideas that may spring from an R & D department, an active program of research inevitably produces many "spin-off" products not included in the primary research objectives. When research directed to a certain end turns up new-product ideas not contemplated in its original purpose, they are usually shelved for reexamination at a future time. Too often, they are forgotten. These by-products of research frequently represent promising opportunities, either for development by the company or for sale or license to other firms. One chemical company found it very worthwhile to review the new-product projects it had placed on the shelf (because they did not fit company needs closely enough), and through license arrangements or sale, to exploit these properties and derive some income from them.

*2. Technical service staffs.* Technical service personnel are usually a good source of product ideas due to their close contact with the problems of applying company products to customer needs. Service personnel frequently specialize by customer industry and thus have an intimate knowledge of their changing needs. Dealing with complaints about the technical characteristics or performance of products often suggests new-product ideas. Without proper encouragement, though, technical service men are likely to be interested only in improvements to present products rather than in new products. While the former are important, it is the latter which offers the greatest new business potential.

3. *Company salesmen.* A salesman often displays the same tendency to relate ideas primarily to present products as do technical service personnel. However, a salesman is in a particularly good position to discover opportunities for new products because of his day-to-day contact with customers and his familiarity with competitive products. If he is alert and has the right kind of contacts with influential managers inside the customer firm, he may be able to identify the direction of customer research and development. This provides important clues to the types of materials and equipment they are likely to need in the future.

The value of the industrial sales force as a source of new-product ideas depends in part on the marketing channels used by the company. If sales flow mainly through distributor channels, these provide a sort of insulation between user and company with regard to detailed knowledge of the user's needs and desires. Even in this case, however, an alert sales force will maintain close contact with the most important customers of distributors and will attempt to keep in close touch with distributors and their salesmen about the problems and conditions of product use.

4. *Executive personnel.* Executives in sales, production, research, and general management have an intimate view of the needs and probable future course of the company. They represent a source of ideas that should be consistent with company capabilities and potential. Some of them are likely to possess an intuitive sense of profit opportunities and of the proper timing for maximum exploitation of them. In addition, they are apt to have access to the high-level trade grapevines that often carry surprisingly accurate news about the product planning and development activities of customers and competitors.

5. *Company sales records.* Analyses of company sales results by product lines and by items is useful in indicating the need for redesign of some products and the approaching obsolescence of others, as well as the types of products that have won strong buyer acceptance.

6. *Company patent departments.* Personnel staffing patent departments should not be overlooked as sources of new-product ideas. They are trained to think in terms of new products. For the alert, motivated employee, patent searches as well as the writing of patent descriptions can generate new-product ideas.

*External sources.* A variety of sources of new-product ideas may be found outside the company. The most common are probably competitors, free-lance inventors, and trade literature.

1. *Competitors.* Successful competitors can often be a source of valuable clues concerning the number of items or models which should be included in the product line. The concept of a full line is somewhat difficult to define. While it is often desirable to sell more than a single product or a single product line, the point of diminishing returns is difficult to identify. The number of product lines and the breadth of these

lines that competitors are selling successfully may serve as a crude yard-stick in determining the product mix that is best for one's own company. If new products are called for, the general nature of these products is already outlined by competitors.

2. *Free-lance inventors.* Although not the important source of new-product opportunities they once were, free-lance inventors are still credited with some important product innovations. Business men will not soon forget C. F. Carlson's copying machine or Edwin Land's camera. Both men were turned down by blue-chip companies and forced to form their own enterprises—Xerox and Polaroid.

3. *Trade literature.* Literature searches, both in United States pub-lications and those of foreign countries, have proved fruitful for some companies. In a number of instances, equipment developed in foreign countries has later appeared in the United States through import chan-nels. The practice of following foreign technical literature enabled one domestic company to develop similar equipment and have it on sale in this country before imports appeared.

4. *Other outside sources.* These include professional society meetings, trade shows, exhibits, government research programs, university research programs, and consulting organizations. The problem in using such sources is how to tap them without an excessive expenditure of time and energy.

### Preliminary appraisal

This phase has two major purposes. The first is to eliminate ideas that are clearly unworthy of further consideration. The second is to select from among the remainder those with enough promise to warrant ex-ploratory work by technical research. Great reliance is usually placed on the experience and judgment of executives in conducting the screening process. Because of the multiplicity of issues which affect the desirability of pursuing any specific new-product idea, it is often useful to develop a checklist of questions to be answered, such as that shown in Figure 12–1.

Checklists are no substitute for analysis, but they have the merit of preventing the omission of vital questions in the heat of pursuing what initially appears to be an exciting idea. If the company product mix is fairly homogeneous, one such list may serve the purpose; if not, it may be necessary to have more than one. Although it is essential that the entire range of conditions influencing the success of an idea be con-sidered, it is not necessary that detailed information about each be available at this time. The emphasis, rather, is on detecting negative issues that might suggest abandonment of the idea.

Major considerations in the appraisal of a new-product idea usually include expected profit potential, the competitive situation, the general adaptability of the company to the new product, and the scale of in-

FIGURE 12–1.  New-product evaluation checklist

Research and Development
   Extent of Research Know-How
   Patent Status
   Chance of Technical Solution
   Manpower Availability
   Extent of Technical Service Required
Market Research
   Estimated Size of Market
   Market Trend
   Price and Demand Stability
   Product Competition
Market Development
   Chance of Commercial Success
   Market Development Requirements
   Time Required to Commercialize
   Value Added to Customer's Product
   Similarity to Present Product Lines
Sales
   Effect on Present Products
   Requirement for Technical Service
   Suitability of Present Sales Force
   Sales Costs
   New Customers—Type and Quality
   Estimated Annual Sales
   Captive Use
Manufacturing
   Required Corporate Size
   Facility Availability
   Process Familiarity
   Availability of Raw Materials
Finance and Control
   Anticipated Return on Investment (Before Taxes)
   New Fixed Capital Payout Time
   Ratio of Production Cost to Selling Price
   Research and Development Cost Payout Time
   Ratio of Research Cost to Market Potential
Corporate
   Contribution to Company Goals
   Contribution to Corporate Image
   Possible Government Reaction

vestment that would be necessary in relation to the funds the company has available. Marketing considerations include the approximate size of the market, the trends operating within it, marketing methods that would be necessary for successful sale, price structures, and so forth.

Many new-product ideas involve problems of technical design. Thus, it becomes necessary to judge the technical feasibility of the idea and estimate the likelihood of success in solving technical problems. Production considerations also enter in the form of the nature of production facilities required, approximate costs of production, availability of materials, and continuity of their supply. At times, legal considerations also enter, both as to the patent situation and as to hazards that may accompany customer use of the product.

### FIGURE 12–2.  Formula for selecting new products

|  | *Total possible score* |
|---|---|
| *Estimated volume of sales (annual)*\* ..................... | 10 |
| under $250,000.................................... Not considered |  |
| $250,000–1 million............................... 2 |  |
| 1–5 million...................................... 5 |  |
| 5–15 million.................................... 10 |  |
| 15 million and up............................... 7 |  |
| *Market protection*† ...................................... | 20 |
| Product patentable............................... 20 |  |
| Chemistry highly complex (nonpatentable)............. 15 |  |
| Much production know-how needed (nonpatentable)...... 15 |  |
| High investment needed (nonpatentable)............... 10 |  |
| *Marketing factors*‡ ..................................... | 10 |
| Technical service needed......................... 4 |  |
| Sold to present customers........................... 6 |  |
| Sold to a new trade.............................. 4 |  |
| Sold to both..................................... 6 |  |
| *Bulk*§ .................................................. | 10 |
| Made and sold in carload or trainload quantity......... 2 |  |
| Made and sold in truckload quantity.................. 5 |  |
| Made and sold in drum quantity..................... 10 |  |
| Made and sold in smaller quantities (unless value very high)............................ 2 |  |
| *Estimated net profit on investment*‖ ..................... | 20 |
| Less than 6% after taxes................... Not considered |  |
| 6–7%.......................................... 6 |  |
| 7–9............................................ 10 |  |
| 9–10........................................... 15 |  |
| 10 plus........................................ 20 |  |
| *Nature*# ............................................ | 15 |
| Involves human health............................ 15 |  |
| Involves animal health............................ 10 |  |
| Involves nutrition (human or animal)................. 10 |  |
| Other.......................................... 7 |  |
| *Kind of research needed*\*\* .............................. | 10 |
| Biological and organic............................. 10 |  |
| Other.......................................... 5 |  |
| *Special factors*†† ....................................... | 5 |
| Government clearance needed....................... 5 |  |
| Other........................................... ? |  |
|  | 100 |

\* A product with less than $250,000 annual sales is apt to get lost in the shuffle and not receive proper managerial attention. The larger its sales volume above about 10 to 12 million, the more likely the product is to be worth the attention of giant competitors, such as Du Pont or Monsanto.

† This company is very good at highly complex chemistry and has a lot of production know-how in dealing with it. Relatively high investment keeps out the quonset hut and reconverted garage competitors.

‡ This company is strong in its technical service. Products sold to present customers can be handled by the present sales force and marketing channels. Those sold to a new trade are harder to introduce but not subject to volume limitations imposed by customer purchasing officers.

§ This company is not good at handling carload business but in applying large-scale techniques to relatively small batches or production runs.

‖ This company's average earnings on investment are about 7.5 percent after taxes. To carry on the necessary research and build retained earnings to finance new projects, it must net that or more.

# The company has a traditional position in the field of public health and nutrition, and its people are oriented in that direction.

\*\* Management has found it difficult to organize and conduct research outside the field of special competence and interest of its scientific personnel. A laboratory is more than a lot of apparatus and the scientists to man it.

†† Management has developed great skill in presenting products to government regulatory bodies so as to secure their prompt action and, generally, their approval. Nothing crooked is involved here, but merely a thorough understanding of the regulatory standards used and the tests and facts and the manner of their preparation and presentation that these bodies demand. Confidence engendered by careful testing and honest reporting is also heavily involved.

Several firms have attempted to develop formulas to use as tools in making new-product decisions. Such a formula worked out for use by a fine chemical house is shown in Figure 12–2, with some changes to protect confidential information. A critical total score was worked out by applying the formula in retrospect to a number of products the company had introduced and comparing scores with actual performance.

Such a formula assures that all the factors generally significant in a new-product decision are considered in a systematic, uniform manner. But its use has dangers. When men have a formula, they tend to quit thinking. Any new-product idea may have one feature that outweighs all others and that is not general in the sense that few other ideas, or none, have it. A formula is apt to be disastrous if used by a committee or staff group composed entirely of conformists. It may work well for a group that contains one or more highly vocal people who always look for the unusual in every situation.

### Product and market research

This phase includes the technical, economic, and market research carried on after an idea has been selected as a project after the preliminary appraisal. The amount of technical research necessary will vary greatly, depending on the difficulties involved in achieving a satisfactory product. The more similar the new product is to those currently being manufactured, the less likely is the need for significant amounts of technical work. During this phase, the physical properties of the new product are determined, small quantities are prepared in the laboratory, research on possible uses is initiated, preliminary work on patents starts, and preliminary estimates of production costs are made. Some industrial products, especially materials and supplies, lend themselves to limited field distribution of sample quantities, and thus permit preliminary evaluation of their suitability to the needs of selected customers.

It is usually advisable to prepare a study of the economic possibilities of the new product at this time which would seek answers to such questions as:[1]

a. What is the precise market or segment of the market in which the new product promises the greatest benefit to users?

b. How much effort will be needed to generate an acceptable revenue, and how much will it cost?

c. How much new investment must customers make in order to use the new product?

d. How much change must customer firms make in their present production techniques and routines to use it?

---

[1] F. E. Webster, Jr., "New Product Adoption in Industrial Markets," *Journal of Marketing* (July 1969).

*e*. Have customers got the technical and application skills needed to use the new product?

*f*. How many people in the typical customer firm must be convinced before a sale can be made and how hard are they to reach?

*g*. How solid are relations between the typical customer and his present supplier?

*h*. What buying motivation can we offer the customer, such as reduction in cost, an increase in attractiveness and volume of the end product, or possible increase in its price?

*i*. What risks will the user of the new product incur?

*j*. How fast will any information we may supply permeate the typical customer firm?

*k*. Are there any built-in customer roadblocks to trying or adopting the new product?

### Process research

In point of time, this phase may overlap the preceding one as the technical group begins to investigate the most feasible way of producing the new product and developing information needed for patent application. The best way to test various manufacturing techniques may be to build a pilot plant and produce the product in small quantities. Quality control problems are also investigated during this phase.

### Prototype testing

With modest amounts of the product available, market development personnel can begin field testing with a selected group of customers who agree to cooperate, often in return for assurances of preferential treatment if the product proves satisfactory. All information gathered from field evaluations is relayed back to the technical group who review it for clues to possible flaws in product design.

During this phase there is often a review by an appropriate executive committee which makes recommendations concerning the future disposition of the project. These are based on the results of research completed in earlier phases together with relevant marketing and economic data. Further research might be recommended if information seems inadequate, further technical work might be authorized if serious product defects have been discovered, or the project might be abandoned.

If continuance of the project is recommended, larger field tests would be undertaken that would more nearly approximate conditions of actual marketing. The regular sales organization would begin familiarizing its members with the product, and promotional strategy would be worked out along with decisions concerning selling methods. It also would be necessary about this time to choose a brand name for the product and determine package design.

The makers of certain kinds of industrial materials and equipment face legal hurdles in introducing new products. For example, before the producer of a chemical used in medicines can market it, he must gain approval of the Food and Drug Administration by supplying evidence that it will do what he says it will do, and will have no more than allowable toxic side effects. In order to gain clearance, he must submit the results of approved independent clinical tests to satisfy the Administration.

This requirement has both good and bad effects on the manufacturer's marketing activities.

1. It delays the introduction of the product. Not only does it take a long time to complete clinical tests, but after they are submitted the manufacturer must await completion of any supplementary tests the Administration decides to make and the slow unwinding of its bureaucratic red tape, which is further delayed by chronic undermanning due to the niggardly policy of Congress in dealing with its budget.

2. The conduct of such clinical tests and presentation of their results in a form that suits the needs of the Administration is an art in itself.

3. The timing of the Administration's release may bear no relation to the ebb and flow of demand. Many diseases are seasonal, and the release of a product at the end of the season may lose the maker a whole year in its introduction to the market. Nor can the time of release be forecast with any accuracy. So marketing plans must be prepared in detail and then held in abeyance, often to become outdated before they can be put into effect.

4. On the other hand, once the Administration issues a release, this in itself goes far to assure users that the product will do what is claimed for it, and thus materially eases the marketing task.

The maker of a food additive must have a release from the Administration, showing that its use will have no dangerous toxic effects on the people who consume the end products containing it. The manufacturer of a plant protective material, or one designed to cure or prevent diseases of animals or fowl, or to stimulate the growth of animals, poultry, or plants must obtain such a release, assuring that no toxic residue remains in the meat, milk, eggs, fruits, or vegetables when prepared for human consumption. This requirement adds all the handicaps mentioned above in connection with medicinal materials, but does not establish that the product will do what it is designed to do. It constitutes merely a manufacturer's hunting license to try to capture sales, and affords no particular help in doing so.

Aside from the benefits of the Administration's work in protecting the public health, most manufacturers of such materials welcome these

FIGURE 12–3.   Product development procedure

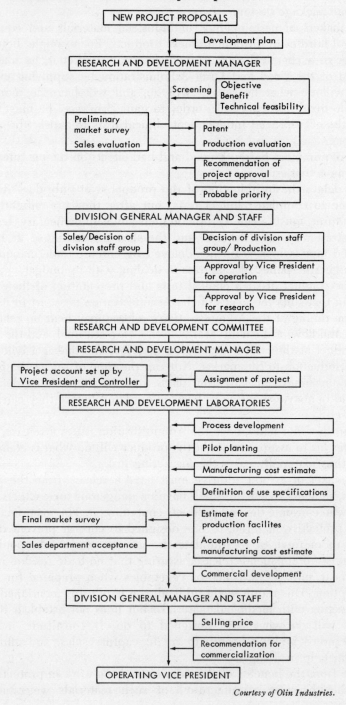

NEW PROJECT PROPOSALS

Development plan

RESEARCH AND DEVELOPMENT MANAGER

Screening → Objective / Benefit / Technical feasibility

Preliminary market survey / Sales evaluation

Patent / Production evaluation

Recommendation of project approval

Probable priority

DIVISION GENERAL MANAGER AND STAFF

Sales/Decision of division staff group

Decision of division staff group/ Production

Approval by Vice President for operation

Approval by Vice President for research

RESEARCH AND DEVELOPMENT COMMITTEE

RESEARCH AND DEVELOPMENT MANAGER

Project account set up by Vice President and Controller

Assignment of project

RESEARCH AND DEVELOPMENT LABORATORIES

Process development

Pilot planting

Manufacturing cost estimate

Definition of use specifications

Final market survey

Estimate for production facilites

Sales department acceptance

Acceptance of manufacturing cost estimate

Commercial development

DIVISION GENERAL MANAGER AND STAFF

Selling price

Recommendation for commercialization

OPERATING VICE PRESIDENT

*Courtesy of Olin Industries.*

restrictions because they tend to preclude irresponsible producers from plaguing them with a type of competition very difficult to combat.

The makers of many kinds of building materials and equipment must see to it that the safety and fire-resisting properties of their products meet the requirements of the Board of Fire Underwriters and the local building codes. Since the codes differ from city to city, meeting their standards may be very cumbersome, time-consuming, and expensive.

A considerable amount of information is available regarding the new product as a result of prototype testing. Firm estimates of full-scale production costs, probable product uses, buyer reaction to prices, market potential, and other results of market evaluation tests are at hand. With this data one can predict the time required to recover development costs and the rate of return the product can be expected to earn on the funds invested in it. If the results look impressive when compared to alternative investment opportunities, a recommendation for approval will probably be forwarded to top management for final action. This is the point at which large sums of money are committed to the manufacturing and marketing of the product.

### Commercialization

New products approved for commercialization enter the final phase of the development process. During the period required to get into full-scale production various activities started in earlier phases, such as package design, promotional literature, and advertising copy can be completed. Depending on the similarity of the new product to present products and its estimated market potential, it might be assigned to an existing division, to a new division specifically established for it, or to a new enterprise owned wholly or partially by the developing company.

The organizational process is illustrated in Figure 12–3.

## DETERMINANTS OF THE PRODUCT MIX

Conditions which appear to exert a major influence on the product-mix decision are technology, competition, operating capacity, and market factors.

### Technology

Comparatively little industrial research is basic in the sense that it is directed to the discovery of new principles or knowledge. By far the greatest industrial use of research and development is in the application of existing knowledge to the development of new products and processes or the improvement of existing ones. The rate of technological change is accelerating, and technical research is unquestionably the most basic force affecting the product mix of the individual company.

## Competition

A second important determinant of a firm's product mix is changes in competitors' product offerings. Closely related is the introduction of competitive products by companies not now considered to be competitors. This has happened increasingly in recent years, with the growing tendency of industrial firms to enlarge their product mixes to include product lines in fields and markets not previously served.

Changes in competitive products represent a direct challenge to a company, and if the change is a truly significant improvement, it may prove disastrous unless it can be matched or surpassed within a reasonable length of time. This matter of the time element explains why firms seemingly in a solid product position spend large sums on research to discover new products that render their present ones obsolete. When asked why his firm was doing this, one chief executive replied, "If we don't, some one else will."

In addition to changes in their product designs, competitors may make changes in their overall product mix and put a rival at a competitive disadvantage. As will be pointed out later, there are important forces favoring a product mix of considerable breadth. Broadening product lines may be a real advantage in distributor relations and in lowering selling costs.

The number of competitors may change. An increase in numbers is likely to result in keener competition and lowered profit margins. Significant increases in numbers of competitors is especially likely in industries where the capital investment necessary for entry is modest. In such situations, a product that enjoys a rapid increase in sales is likely to attract many new entrants into the field, some of whom will not survive the period of consolidation, or "shakeout," as it is sometimes called. In industries that require large investment, increases in the number of competitors are less dramatic. When they occur, the new competitors tend to reach for volume by cutting price, which reduces both the dollar sales and the gross profit rate of the original innovator. The result is that as soon as a firm introduces a new product on the market, it starts research to improve it and to find other new products to replace it when competition develops.

## Operating capacity

Another important factor influencing a marketer's product mix is underutilized capacity. Since production facilities are usually composed of complexes of interrelated machines, changes in production capacity can rarely be made in small increments. When demand outruns existing facilities and a new equipment complex is brought on line, there may be a period in which it is not totally utilized in satisfying existing demand.

In such situations it is very common for management to be under pressure to find new products which the equipment can make. Similarly, when a marketing organization is established to serve a particular territory for a given product line, it often becomes apparent that salesmen could handle other lines as well, and pressure is generated to find other products they can sell profitably.

It is well known that many profitable firms do not pay out all their profits in dividends. Retained earnings become part of the firm's capital structure and must be invested. New products are one of the investment opportunities into which underutilized funds are often channeled.

Many manufacturing processes involve by-products which must either be used internally, marketed, or disposed of as waste. Growing concern with industrial wastes may be expected to stimulate greater efforts than in the past to turn them into products which can either be used internally or marketed. The latter instance, of course, leads to an expansion of the product mix.

### Market factors

Although declines in demand are disturbing to management and may result in an expansion of the product mix in an effort to replace lost business, upward changes are also of significance. Management's responsibility is to capitalize as fully as possible on expanding product fields just as much as it is to meet the challenge of declining markets. These changes in demand are of various types.

*Shifts in customer's product mix.*  Goods which enter into customers' products such as parts and components are vulnerable to changes in the product lines manufactured by customers. If the customer is himself an industrial goods producer selling to other industries, his shift may be triggered by changes *his* customers have found necessary. Depending on the direction of change, pressure for an expansion or contraction of his own product mix is apt to result.

In addition to the product demand shifts brought about by customers' changes in product line design to meet their own customer needs, some regular customers may engage in diversification programs that expand their product mix. This offers opportunities for the sale of additional quantities or for modification of the seller's product mix to capitalize on additional business available from them. Since diversification programs often grow out of a decline in business or the fear of a future decline, there may well be concurrent drops in normal demand.

*Changes in availability or cost.*  A material or part used in making an end product may become scarce or its price may go up so as to distort the competitive relationships in either the component or the end product market. This necessitates product modification by the firm supplying the components and by consequence alters its mix of products.

*Changes in manufacturing processes.*  Manufacturers of special purpose machines are particularly vulnerable to changes in the manufacturing processes of their customers. A change in process can render their
machines obsolete, forcing a constriction in the product mix.

*Shifts in location of customers.*  Transportation costs are important for
many types of industrial goods. These costs limit the geographical extent
of the market that can be profitably served by an industrial marketer,
and any shift of customers out of this market area can result in major
declines in sales and the necessity for replacing this lost business with
other products. Sometimes migration of industry into the area economically served by a producer helps offset losses from outward migration.
Some manufacturers, however, have been so closely tied to particular
industries—for example, textiles—that large-scale migration becomes a
death sentence unless the supplier also moves.

*Changes in levels of business activity.*  Nearly every producer faces
some type of seasonal pattern of sales, and also is vulnerable in greater
or less extent to major shifts in the level of general business. Some companies have extended their product mix by adding lines whose seasonal
patterns offset those of their present lines, and thus have obtained a
reasonably even rate of total production and sales activity throughout the
year. This consideration also applies to distributors who may feel the
need for a product mix that evens out seasonal fluctuations.

In somewhat similar fashion, some companies have sought to add
product lines less sensitive to business-cycle fluctuations than are their
existing ones. Many manufacturers of machinery, particularly in the
major equipment groups, are concerned about their sensitivity to cyclical
drops in demand and would like to meet this drop through diversification.
Cyclical fluctuations are often of the rolling type in that demand does
not decline in all industries at the same time. When this happens, a supplier who diversifies to sell to a number of industries may diminish the
sharpness and extent of the decline in his sales volume.

In addition to changes in general business activity, there may be
variations in local or regional markets or in individual industries.

*Government controls.*  The last several decades have been a period of
war and general tension in international relations. It seems certain that
for many years in the future there will be a high level of government
spending for national defense, coupled with the possibility of limited-
scale military action. Under such conditions, certain materials are of great
strategic importance, and the government may take steps to limit their
use for civilian purposes in order to manufacture military material or to
build stockpiles. Such government controls have widespread ramifications through industry, and tend to cause major changes in sales volume
for particular product lines. When there is no possibility of substituting
materials, little product action can be taken. Frequently, however, such
a tight material situation may encourage experimentation and research

on substitute materials to perform the function. This leads to changes in product mix.

## COMPANY ATTRIBUTES

The types and variety of products which are appropriate for a company are also a function of the firm's inherent strengths and weaknesses. The general method of appraising a firm's capabilities is to take an inventory of its present position and trace the route by which it has arrived there. An important part of this procedure is to make continuous comparisons with competitors. Such comparisons should not be limited to industrial marketers who make comparable product lines, but should be extended to those who make goods that can serve as satisfactory substitutes for the firm's products. It should also include the likelihood of customers going into the business of making goods the firm now supplies them. Although the yardstick of competitive practice is reasonably adequate for most situations, in some cases competition may be so weak that other yardsticks must be found in order to make sound appraisals of the company. Such yardsticks may have to be adapted from analogous situations and, while necessarily crude, are nonetheless useful.

Company attributes with the most direct bearing on product definition are its marketing performance, production capabilities, R & D strength, financial slack, and the abilities of the executive group.

*Marketing performance.*  The ability of an enterprise to market a certain type of product to certain types of customers at a profit, as revealed by sales analysis, is an important indicator of the kind of products which fits the firm's marketing expertise. The costs of serving various types of customers in different locations, filling orders, supporting salesmen in the field, and promoting products (as revealed by cost analysis), is one way of separating products which present attractive opportunities from those which do not. Regularly conducted sales and cost analyses also reveal the capacities and incapacities of the distribution channel. This intelligence supplies an important insight into the types of products a company can market efficiently and those which it cannot.

*Production capabilities.*  The historical development of a firm and the human skills which have been accumulated in its labor force largely determine what it can produce, at least in the short run. How readily its production system can be adapted to the requirements of different products affects the time required for full commercialization of a new product and by consequence the payout period. As a rule, the longer the payout period, the riskier the venture.

*Research and development strength.*  It is very difficult to find satisfactory yardsticks to measure the accomplishments of research. A firm may get some idea of the strength of its research effort by comparing its expenditure per dollar of sales with the average for its industry. Battelle

Memorial Institute released a study of R & D funding for 1973 in which estimates were developed for a number of industries on the basis of expenditures per dollar of sales. Some representative ratios reported in the study were: Chemicals and Allied Products, 4.13; Fabricated Metal Products, 1.60; Machinery, 0.95; Electrical Equipment and Communication, 0.32; Professional and Scientific Instruments, 1.14.[2]

The record of actual accomplishments in developing new products, improving existing products, and uncovering new applications for old products is a good indicator of whether a firm should venture into a high technology field or avoid it.

*Financial slack.*  The successful introduction of new products may require a substantial investment in R & D, in various types of technical and marketing studies, in new plant and equipment, as well as in market development work itself. The availability of funds for this purpose is of course a limiting factor, but so is management's willingness to spend them. In closely held companies, the latter is a particularly important consideration. But even in firms which are not closely held, management must consider alternative investment opportunities and choose those which promise the most attractive return. The less financial slack available to management the narrower the range of choice.

A corollary issue is ease of entry into a particular market. Production of some types of products demands large-scale investment, and companies with limited financial resources cannot enter the markets for such products. In contrast, entry is relatively easy in industries where capital requirements are low. Such industries tend to be characterized by keen competition and low rates of overhead expense. Companies accustomed to operating in high-investment industries are justifiably cautious about entering low-investment fields because experience has shown that they may have difficulty competing on price.

*Interest and abilities of the executive group.*  Diversification of a firm's product line may lead it into fields in which executives have little experience, only a superficial knowledge, and no real interest. While the limitations of experience and knowledge usually can be offset by recruiting new talent, the interest factor is difficult to assess because it can wax and wane with circumstances. It may surface only when unforeseen difficulties cause a lengthening of the expected payout period. If a product development period of three or four years has been predicted, but it begins to appear that six or seven will have elapsed before the product passes its break-even point, management may become pessimistic and pull out when the payoff is just around the corner. Disappointing initial performance can easily result in the abandonment of promising new product ventures unless the chief executives thoroughly understand the nature of the venture and are emotionally committed to it.

---

[2] Battelle Memorial Institute, *Probable Levels of R & D Expenditures in 1973* (Columbus, Ohio: January 1973), p. 6.

# SUMMARY

Product definition concerns the various properties which are designed into the manufacturer's product line and the assortment of models and items, i.e., the product mix, which makes up his total product offering. The conditions and circumstances which need to be considered in formulating this definition can be divided into those which influence the development of new products, those which relate to the product mix, and those which stem from the attributes of the company itself.

New-product development involves several stages, beginning with the generation of new-product ideas and their appraisal to eliminate those unworthy of further consideration. Products which warrant additional investigation are identified and technical work is begun on them along with appropriate economic and market research. During this stage the physical properties of the new product are determined, small quantities are produced in the laboratory or pilot plant, preliminary investigation of patent rights is begun, and initial estimates of production costs are made. If initial expectations are fulfilled, development of the product proceeds through process research, prototype testing, and commercialization.

The major determinants of the product mix are technology, competition, operating capacity, and market factors. Accelerating technology is undoubtedly the basic force affecting the product mix of the individual company, with competitive pressures running a close second. In some companies, underutilized capacity is an important influence along with such market factors as shifts in the product mix of customers, changes in the availability and/or cost of materials, new developments in manufacturing processes, changes in the level of business activity, and government controls.

The type and variety of products which are appropriate for a company are also a function of the firm's inherent strengths and weaknesses. Those attributes of a company with the most direct bearing on product definition are the strength of its marketing performance, the extent of its production capacity, the quality of its R & D effort, and the abilities of its executive group. The amount of financial slack available may also be an important influence on product definition.

# SERVICE DEFINITION

PRODUCT AND SERVICE are closely related elements of marketing strategy but have sufficiently distinctive features to warrant separate treatment. Those services most common to industrial marketers are the provision of parts, technical assistance, and financial aid.

## THE PROVISION OF PARTS

The manufacturer of machinery and equipment must determine in what way the handling of parts can contribute most to the long-term thrust of the enterprise. All machines have parts that wear out or break. When this happens, the machine is generally useless until the part is replaced. The availability of parts to the equipment users is, therefore, a vital factor in the manufacturer's effort to give satisfaction to the user. Some equipment manufacturers buy practically all their parts from firms that specialize in producing them; others make many of them in their own plants. Some parts, such as ball or roller bearings, are mainly standardized; others are made to specification to suit the needs of the machine maker who orders them. Both the manufacturer of standardized parts and the builder of the machines of which they are a component have an interest in seeing to it that replacement parts are supplied to machine users.

### Standardized parts

The manufacturer of standardized parts to be used for replacements must determine the channels through which he will seek to sell them to machine users. He may sell only to manufacturers of the machines, relying on the machine makers to distribute to users. Or he may also sell to the users, either direct or through distributors. If his chief market is for

216

replacements, and his product is used in making many types of equipment so that for replacement use it has a horizontal market, he will find it desirable to sell through distributors. If he relies heavily on the distributors to cultivate and serve the replacement market, he must determine whether to sell direct to all manufacturers for original installation or to service some or all of them through his distributors. The distributor will undoubtedly bring pressure to get all the original installation business. Unless the distributor is able to handle original installation contracts at about the same price the manufacturer can supply the same buyers, the parts manufacturer must expect to lose a certain amount of the original installation business if he succumbs to this pressure.

*The machine manufacturer as a channel.* As a distribution channel for standard replacement parts included in his machine, the machine manufacturer suffers from the disadvantages: (1) that his markup is usually higher, since it is likely to be tied to the markup he enjoys on the machines themselves; (2) his points of distribution, where he carries stocks from which to service users, are apt to be fewer than those of the distributors; and (3) his marketing organization is likely to be heavily preoccupied with the sale of machines, with the result that the sale of parts does not receive the attention it should. On the other hand, the machine manufacturer is under considerable pressure to furnish a good replacement parts service, since the reputation of his machines depends heavily on it. In addition, he may find that in the process of giving good replacement parts service he is able to maintain contact with the user between purchases of equipment. Usually, this works out with something less than complete satisfaction, because parts are generally a matter of routine procurement, handled entirely by the purchasing department, while the engineering and other departments usually have a great deal to say about equipment buying. The replacement parts contact, however, is often close enough to enable the salesman who makes it to get advance notice of projected purchases of equipment, which enables the machine manufacturer to get in on the ground floor in the negotiations for them.

## Unstandardized parts

When the machine manufacturer makes his own parts, or has them made to his own specifications, he may sell them for replacement use either direct through his own organization or to distributors for resale to users. If he renders the repair and maintenance service himself and most of his customers depend on him for it, he may find it best to handle this business himself. If his customers are equipped to do their own repair work, he may find it desirable to service replacement parts demand through distributors. In this manner, he is likely to gain wider distribution through warehouses more conveniently located to his customers than are his own branch warehouses. Moreover, if he refuses to make his own parts available for sale by distributors, they are liable to turn to the pirate parts manufacturers as a source of supply. He may be able to head off this tendency or hold it to a minimum by making his own parts available to them.

## The pirate parts problem

If an equipment manufacturer's parts replacement demand is active and the business of supplying it is profitable, those parts are likely to be made and sold by producers who specialize in them. These are known as pirate parts manufacturers. Some of these firms make parts that are just as good as those of the machine maker; others use shoddy material and poor workmanship.

Purchasing agents patronize pirate parts manufacturers for two main reasons. First, such a producer is often a local firm on whom the buyer may rely to furnish other items, or to supply emergency needs. In order to keep him in business, the buyer gives him some of his parts business so that the local supplier can enjoy the advantages of mass production and sale. Second, the pirate can often supply parts at lower prices than can the machine manufacturer. Since he usually copies the machine manufacturer's parts, the pirate has little or no developmental and engineering costs; if he is a local operator, his shipping costs are generally low; and he is likely to have little sales cost and little or no service expense. In addition, as indicated above, the machine manufacturer often gears his gross profit margin on parts to his margin on the completed machines. The second is generally much higher than the first when handled alone.

The chief drawbacks to buying parts from the pirate manufacturer are the following.

1. The buyer may make himself liable to legal action by the machine manufacturer if the part is covered by a patent giving the manufacturer the sole right to "make, use, and vend" it. This is usually not too serious, as the machine maker is unlikely to jeopardize future sales of an expensive machine by alienating a customer through legal action over a relatively inexpensive part.

2. The source of supply is insecure. Most pirate producers are small and highly flexible, so that any one of them may at any time turn to the production of some other more profitable article. This also is not too serious, since the buyer can almost invariably call on the machine maker for the service. Some embarrassment may be involved, but usually little real loss.

3. The pirate producer often has little or no quality control. The parts are no more reliable than their maker.

4. The pirate maker gives little or no service, so that the user must carry larger inventories of parts than would be necessary if he bought from the machine manufacturer or one of his distributors. But this expense may be more than offset by price advantages.

5. The parts produced by the pirate are often not closely standardized and, hence, sometimes do not fit. This requires greater inventories, and the expense of returns and making claims. Also, they sometimes lack finishing. This requires a certain amount of machining by the user, which may offset any price saving enjoyed.

6. Buying parts from the pirate tends to weaken the machine manufacturer as a source of the much more important item—the machine itself—and may in the long run cost the buyer much more than the small saving he may enjoy in procuring the parts.

There are several steps by which the machine builder may attempt to diminish the inroads of pirate parts makers on his business.

1. He may offer users of his machines price concessions for an annual contract to supply parts. The contract will be effective only if the volume of parts bought by the average user is great enough to justify a concession that will be attractive to the buyer.

2. He may keep his prices down to a point where parts making offers no real inducement to the prospective pirate. This is probably the most effective method.

3. He may make stocks of parts readily available to users of his machines. If his own branch warehouses are not sufficiently numerous or conveniently located to the users, he may be able to achieve this end by marketing through distributors.

4. He may make his parts catalog complete and detailed. Since the parts business is an offshoot of the main machine business, it is often regarded as the stepchild and fails to receive the attention needed to assure its retention. The parts catalog is sometimes incomplete and inconveniently arranged for the buyer's use.

5. He may constantly improve the machine and keep down the prices of the new models. This forces the pirate to constantly shift his production processes, and reduces the profit he can make from the business. But it also increases the development and engineering costs of the machine maker.

## TECHNICAL ASSISTANCE

The provision of engineering and other forms of technical assistance is an important strategic element for equipment makers. This is especially true for manufacturers of specialty and custom-made equipment. For standard types of machinery technical assistance often consists of helping the customer choose a machine or combination of machines that will best perform the job he wants done; it may also involve making minor modifications of standard machines, or making and affixing attachments to them so that their operations more exactly fit the needs of the buyer. Rendering technical service also constitutes a problem to the sellers of some kinds of supplies, such as belting, abrasives, and lubricants, and many materials, such as metals, plastics, and chemicals.

Most firms that sell these types of industrial products are compelled to make available to their customers and prospective customers some sort of engineering or technical service. If such a concern fails to do so, its sales are likely to suffer because of customer resentment at the lack of a service expected, or because of gratitude to service-rendering competitors for their help in solving difficult problems. Such a firm may also find that its products are giving something less than satisfactory performance in use because they are not handled in precisely the proper manner.

### Types of technical assistance

Engineering or technical assistance may assume any or all of the following forms.

1. It may include no more than provision of technical information about a product and its uses, generally on request of the customer or prospective buyer. Such information usually includes suggestions about the way in which the product may be applied to the specific operating needs of the buyer. Most firms that make industrial products probably do some of this kind of work.

2. Through his engineers or technicians, the seller may make a thorough study of a buyer's needs to determine exactly the kinds of machinery, supplies, or materials he should use, and precisely how they should be used. For example, a rubber-belting manufacturer offers the services of a force of power transmission engineers who are prepared and equipped to study the power transmission needs of the customer and recommend a complete program for satisfying them.

3. Engineers or technical men employed by the industrial goods marketer may work with a prospective buyer's technical staff in developing equipment to meet his needs or in developing a process by which he may most effectively use a material or supply. This work may involve designing a special machine or making changes in standard machinery. It may also involve the development or modification of a process employed, for example, by a chemical product user. The marketer who renders this sort of service must expect that some prospective buyers will accept it gratis and then, when plans are drawn, invite other suppliers to bid on the job.

4. The seller may maintain a force of technical experts to install his equipment in the buyer's plant after sale, or he may work with the buyer's technical staff in doing this job. The same kind of help may be supplied in getting a process or a service under way—for example, a chemical process or a mechanical record-keeping system.

5. The seller may supply technicians to train the buyer's employees in the proper methods of using and caring for the equipment he sells. Probably the most widely known example of this sort of service is that supplied by manufacturers of mechanical record-keeping and computing equipment, who are prepared both to train routine operators of such

machinery and to teach executives in charge of the work how to use the equipment to get out of it the maximum service. Such technicians are constantly on call to give advice and help in working out difficult problems, even after the training period is over.

### Organization for technical assistance

When an industrial goods manufacturer needs to render considerable technical or engineering assistance in the course of his marketing work, a special unit of the company is usually set up to take charge of it. There is no substantial agreement on where such a technical service unit should be placed in the organization. In some firms, it is an arm of the engineering department; in others, it is a part of the development department; in still others, it is lodged in the marketing area.

There are logical reasons for each of these locations. The marketing manager may feel that he should be in control so that the men in the unit will constantly be kept aware that its primary purpose is to make sales by creating satisfied customers. He feels that unless the men who do this work are under his control, they will not be sales-oriented. On the other hand, the men must be technicians. What they work out in the field, the plant technical men must implement. The engineering executives usually fear that if the men who do the field work are under marketing department control they will, in their anxiety to promote sales, promise technical features that cannot be delivered.

All technical assistance requires a detailed knowledge of the specifications and properties of the product. Some of it necessitates at least minor modifications in its characteristics. These matters are within the province of the engineering function, so engineering executives often feel that since their people and facilities are very likely to be called in to solve a technical service problem they should be in on it from the beginning and have charge of it. All this seems reasonable, although there is little doubt that such service administered by the engineers will emphasize its purely technical aspects and minimize its customer relations objective.

Location of technical assistance work in the development department probably represents a compromise of the issues between marketing and engineering. Its interests cross-section those of the other two; it is generally charged with the task of overseeing the commercial development of new products and new uses of existing products.

There seems to be no spot in the organization into which this unit ideally fits and should always be placed. Its location should probably be determined in each company on the basis of the nature and extent of technical assistance work to be done, and the executive personalities involved.

When technical assistance needed is not too complicated and does not require too much time, it is usually performed by the salesmen, who in such a case probably have some training as technicians. They may be supported by a technical assistance unit in the branch, or at the home office, to which they can refer problems and requests for information beyond their own ability to handle.

### Difficulties of rendering technical assistance

*Administration.*   The administration of a technical assistance program is usually a difficult task. It is apt to be costly and, unless watched constantly, tends to grow to such proportions that it is prohibitively expensive. The men who render the service must be thoroughly trained technicians of considerable ability. If the service cannot be made thoroughly reliable and of outstanding quality, it is probably better not to try to render it.

*Possible abuse.*   The most painful managerial headache associated with rendering technical service, however, is its susceptibility to abuse. Firms that give such service are often called on to render it to companies or persons who have no intention of becoming customers. Many manufacturers can probably duplicate the experience of a chemicals maker whose technical service unit was called on by a small customer for help in working out the proper way to use imported competing materials of inferior quality. Small buyers demand services entirely out of proportion to any purchases they may possibly make. A buyer with a contract to place may ask for technical help from several suppliers in planning and preparing specifications for the article he proposes to buy, synthesize their proposals, and ask each of them to bid on the synthesis, perhaps in competition with other firms that do not offer such assistance.

It is difficult, if not impossible, to avoid a certain amount of abuse in technical assistance. Some firms have tried with varying success to charge for all or for certain parts of the engineering assistance they render. This is apt to work satisfactorily when business is good and demand is heavy; but few suppliers have the courage to stick to it when business is bad and orders are scarce. Perhaps to stick to it under such conditions would exemplify poor judgment more than courage. It might not be a bad idea for firms heavily committed to the supply of technical service to use the techniques of motivation research to try to find out just how influential it actually is in gaining patronage.

## FINANCIAL AID

The industrial goods maker, like his counterpart in the consumer goods field, must usually provide some financial aid in the form of credit extensions or credit arrangements for his customers. The help the manufacturer is prepared to give the customer in financing the purchase of his product is very definitely a part of the product-service benefit package his marketing organization has to sell. So it is a matter of primary importance to the marketing manager. Of all executives in his company, he is in the best position to know how much of such help is needed and in what form it will be most useful and acceptable to the customer.

The stock-carrying service of the industrial goods manufacturer also creates a need for financial management decision and action. Stock-outs do not usually create or facilitate sales. The marketing manager is in the best position to know how much stock-outs cost the firm in lost sales volume and how much finished goods inventory is needed to prevent or to hold them to a planned percentage of orders received. He is not always equipped to balance the costs of stock-outs against the expense of carrying the inventory necessary to avoid or hold them to an economical minimum.

Both of these matters belong in the domain of either an executive in charge of physical distribution or the chief financial officer who manages the working capital of the firm. Some understanding of the costs and the mechanism for providing these customer services can enable the marketing manager to be much more helpful in making and administering working capital policy. He can hardly avoid having something to say about the formulation of such policy, nor would he be wise to avoid it if he could, for through his salesmen and his subordinate executives he must play a part in carrying it out.

## Terms of sale

When a sale is negotiated, the buyer and seller usually agree on certain conditions under which payment is to be made. These are commonly referred to as terms of sale or credit terms. They indicate the extent to which the seller is willing to use the credit service as a means of capturing the buyer's patronage. These terms tend to be uniform throughout a trade, with such minor modifications as individual firms may see fit to make. Table 13–1 shows the credit terms commonly used in a number of trades engaged in manufacturing and selling industrial goods.

Perhaps some explanation of the meaning of the terms most commonly used will aid us in seeking to understand their implications.

Net cash generally means that the buyer is expected to pay the full amount of the bill within 10 days after the date of the invoice.

Net 30 or net 60 means that the buyer obligates himself to pay the face of the bill within 30 or 60 days after the date of the invoice.

Two percent, 10 days, net 30 days, often written 2–10–30 or 2, 10, net 30, means that if the buyer pays within 10 days after the date of the invoice he is privileged to deduct 2 percent from the face of the bill, and that he is obligated to pay the full amount of the bill within 30 days after its date. One percent (or ½ percent), 10 days, net 30 has the same meaning, except that he is privileged to deduct only 1 percent or ½ percent as the case may be.

Net, 10 proximo means that the buyer is expected to pay the face of

**Table 13–1. Terms of sale of industrial firms**

| Type of Manufacturer | Terms |
|---|---|
| Chemicals | Net 30 days, most frequent |
| | 1%, 10, net 30, also |
| | Net 10 proximo |
| Concentrates, extracts, syrups | 1%, 10, net 30 |
| Cotton cloth | Net 10, on duck 2%, 10, net 30 |
| Cotton goods converters | 70 days, usually |
| | 2%, 10, 60 extra, sometimes |
| Foundries, gray iron | Net 30 |
| | ½ or 1%, 10, net 30, sometimes |
| Malleable iron | ½%, 10, net 30 |
| Brass and bronze | ½ or 1%, 10, net 30, or |
| | Net 30 |
| Machine shops | Net Cash or net 30 |
| | 1 or 2%, 10, net 30 |
| Industrial machinery | Net 30 after completion and delivery of smaller machines |
| | Agreed down payment, balance on delivery or on installments for large machines |
| | On special work for new customers one third down with order, payments monthly as work progresses, full payment on delivery |
| Metal stampings | Net 30, sometimes 1%, 10 |
| | New accounts, ⅓ to ½ on order, balance 10 days after delivery |
| Paper boxes: | |
| Setups | 2%, 10, E.O.M. |
| Fiber boxes | 1%, 10, E.O.M. |
| Structural steel: | |
| Fabricated | Net 10 proximo and net 30 |
| Erection materials | Payment 10th of each month of 90% of value of all materials shipped, stored, or ready to ship, balance net 30 days after completion of contract |
| Airplane parts | 1%, 10, net 30 |
| Rayon, silk, acetate piece goods | Net 60 or 70 |

SOURCE: Abstracted from Roy A. Foulke, *Terms of Sale* (New York: Dun & Bradstreet, Inc., various years).

the bill on or before the 10th day of the month following that in which the invoice is dated. For example, if a firm buys materials on these terms and receives a bill dated January 15, it is obligated to pay the full amount mentioned therein on or before February 10.

Two percent, 10, E.O.M. means that if the buyer pays within 10 days of the date of the bill, he may deduct 2 percent from its face; otherwise he is obligated to pay the entire amount by the end of the month.

Two percent, 10, net 30, 60 extra means that if the buyer pays within 10 days of the date of the bill, he may deduct 2 percent from the face of it, but if he takes his full credit period, he has 90 days to pay the total amount of the bill. Such terms are generally used by firms that sell to customers who, in turn, either resell the merchandise or process it and sell the resulting product to buyers whose demand is seasonal. It is a way of helping the customer to meet heavy requirements for working capital caused by the seasonal nature of his business.

In general, the credit terms used by industrial goods firms are somewhat simpler than those offered by consumer goods makers. This is probably due, at least in part, to the fact that the channels of distribution commonly employed in the industrial goods business are more direct, and that such goods flow to market through a more limited variety of outlets. For example, the consumer goods manufacturer may have to sell direct to some large retailers, such as department stores, chain systems, or mail-order houses, while at the same time distributing through wholesalers. Each of these types of buyer may demand a different set of credit terms. On the other hand, the industrial goods maker is not likely to find it necessary to sell through more than the direct channel and the industrial distributor.

On the whole, the terms used by industrial marketers seem to be somewhat less liberal than those offered by firms selling consumer goods. For example, cash discounts for payment within 10 days are somewhat less generally allowed, and net terms without discount seem to be rather more commonly required. Extra datings are less generally offered, although their place has been taken to a large extent by longer net terms, such as 60 days net. It is probably true that by and large the problem of administering credit terms is less complicated in the industrial goods business than in the consumer goods field. Of course, individual trades provide exceptions.

## Financing with warehouse receipts

The warehouse receipt offers a means by which the industrial goods manufacturer can finance at least part of his inventory-carrying operations.

There are two types of wareohuse receipts—negotiable and nonnegotiable. When goods are stored on a negotiable receipt, ownership of them can be transferred by an endorsement on the receipt by the person to whom it is drawn. In order to remove the goods or any part of them from storage, the holder of the receipt must present it and endorse an acknowledgment that he has received the goods removed. The merchandise covered by such a receipt belongs to the holder of the receipt properly endorsed.

When goods are stored on a nonnegotiable receipt, they belong to the person whose name appears on the receipt. He can transfer them to another only by assignment or by turning in the receipt and requesting the issue of a new one, drawn to the buyer. They can be withdrawn from the warehouse on presentation of a warehouse release order signed by the person to whom the receipt is drawn.

The industrial goods marketer can borrow on a warehouse receipt by signing a note to a financial institution, such as a bank, and depositing the receipt in proper form as collateral. If the receipt is a negotiable one, he must endorse it to the lending establishment. If it is nonnegotiable, he must have the receipt drawn to the lender and deposit it as collateral. Banks generally prefer the nonnegotiable document, since then the receipt need not be taken from the bank when partial withdrawals are made.

When merchandise is withdrawn from the warehouse for delivery to customers, the owner may either pay the portion of his loan representing the value of the amount withdrawn, or may execute a trust receipt for it. Such a receipt usually contemplates repayment of the value of the goods covered within a limited period of time; it is also apt to limit the uses that may be made of the goods while covered by the receipt.

The usefulness of warehouse receipts issued by a regular commercial warehouse to an industrial goods marketer is usually limited to the financing of reserve stocks of finished goods or stocks earmarked to service the needs of customers buying in substantial quantities. For example, a cabinet manufacturer is reported to use such receipts to finance supplies of cabinets held in the major radio and television manufacturing centers. From these, he can quickly supply the needs of customer firms. Can manufacturers customarily maintain large stocks at strategic points in canning areas during the packing season. Thus they are able to make quick deliveries to the packing plants, whose needs may vary considerably according to weather conditions. A manufacturer of copper wire and electrical parts stores products at points convenient to producers of electrical equipment and appliances. The same plan is employed by a maker of industrial cleaning compounds. All these firms make some use of warehouse receipts to finance these stocks, thereby making it possible to obtain the maximum use of their working capital while at the same time maintaining adequate stocks conveniently located to service their customers.

The manufacturer who wants to use warehouse receipts to finance the holding of materials in his own storeroom or of finished stocks in his own warehouse or distributive branch can obviously make little use of the traditional type of public warehouse receipt. To meet his needs, a practice known as field warehousing has been developed.

### Field warehousing

When this plan is used, the industrial marketer stores materials or finished goods in his own plant or distributive branch warehouse. He leases the warehouse or the part of it in which the merchandise is stored to a field warehousing firm, which takes legal possession of the premises. Usually, the warehousing concern hires one or more of the employees of the marketer as warehouse custodians: they are transferred by mutual consent from the payroll of the marketer to that of the warehouseman. The field warehousing firm issues warehouse receipts covering the merchandise held by its custodians. The marketer can then deposit these receipts with a financial institution as collateral for a loan on the merchandise. Advances ranging from 60 to 85 percent of the value of the goods may be obtained on such loans. The legal nature of these receipts and their acceptability as collateral differs little, if any, from the traditional type of warehouse receipt.

The field warehouse may also be located on the premises of a customer of the industrial marketer. For example, a can manufacturer customarily sells cans to a packer whose storage space is apt to be vacant, or nearly so, for several months immediately prior to the opening of the canning season. The packer stores the cans; the can manufacturer arranges for a field warehousing firm to lease the packer's storeroom and officially take custody of the cans until they are needed during the packing season. The warehousing firm issues receipts, which the can manufacturer is able to use as collateral for loans at his bank. The cans are where the packer can quickly get them when needed; the manufacturer frees working capital with which to make more cans.

## The use of factors

For a long time, the factor has been an important element in financing marketing operations in the textile industry. His services have been used most extensively in the parts of the industry that make semifinished materials.

There is a strong tendency for the use of factors to spread to many other industries, some engaged in industrial goods production and marketing. No intrinsic feature of the factor's activities would prevent his use by the maker of almost any sort of industrial goods, except perhaps the manufacturer of very heavy and expensive specialized equipment, which must be financed on long-term commitments.

A manufacturer can effectively use a factor for two types of financing service connected with the marketing operation. The factor can be of material aid in financing the carrying of inventories. He can also be used to finance the extension of credit to customers through his accounts receivable service. The second service is his most typical and the one in which he is most skilled and proficient.

*Accounts receivable.* When the manufacturer extends open-book credit to his customers on a 30- or 60-day basis, the funds he has tied up in the goods delivered are to all intents and purposes dead for the period of the credit extension. During this time, he cannot use them to earn additional profits. The factor offers two kinds of service to help the manufacturer avoid this loss.

The factor is prepared to buy his client's accounts receivable outright.

Then, he usually collects the accounts from the customers and assumes all credit risks. Obviously, when this is done the manufacturer must maintain credit extension standards satisfactory to the factor or even allow the factor to check the credits when extended. In some cases, the arrangement provides that the client will make collections and remit to the factor, although this is not the usual practice.

The manufacturer may also pledge his receivables to the factor as collateral for a loan. When this is done, the work of collecting the accounts is carried on entirely by the borrower, and the factor assumes no risk of their uncollectibility. The manufacturer's customers have no knowledge that their accounts have been pledged.

Which of these two arrangements the manufacturer chooses to adopt depends largely on four considerations. If he needs or wants some form of credit insurance on his accounts, their outright sale without recourse provides a means of getting it. Once the sale is made, he no longer stands to lose by reason of a customer's default. It the manufacturer wants to avoid the tedious and expensive record-keeping work involved in maintaining accounts receivable and collecting them, outright sale offers the best method. Neither of these considerations are apt to be of prime importance to the industrial goods marketer, because his customers are usually relatively few in number, their credit standing is better than average, and their routines of payment are generally more or less standardized.

On the other hand, the manufacturer must consider the effect of his financial operations on the goodwill of his customers. Some may be disturbed by or resent the sale of their accounts. This is especially important to the industrial goods marketer. In appraising the reliability and financial strength of suppliers, the purchasing officer often examines their credit standings. The sale of accounts receivable accompanied by their collection by the factor may be interpreted as a dead giveaway of the lack of adequate working capital, and may lead to the withholding of orders when reliability and certainty of delivery are of the essence in the transaction. In some trades, also, there is a prejudice against the sale of accounts receivable. It is regarded as a confession of weakness on the part of the firm that sells them. This consideration also has special significance to the industrial goods vendor for the reasons just outlined.

The factor's charges for the accounts receivable service include two elements. He collects a commission ranging usually from 0.5 to 1.5 percent of the net amount of the receivables taken over. To this, he adds an interest charge on the funds turned over to the client. Cash discounts taken by the client's cutomers are offset against the first of these charges. The charges themselves may vary with business conditions.

*Financing inventory holdings.* The factor is also usually prepared to lend funds on materials held in warehouse pending sale. Such accommodations range from 50 to 80 percent of the market value of the goods, depending on the client's financial condition, the character of the goods, market conditions, and the reasons for the borrowing. When the factor makes such a loan, he takes a lien on the merchandise, which he registers with the appropriate official, thereby giving notice to other creditors of the client firm that the goods covered by the lien are not to be relied on to meet its general obligations. When such goods are sold, the factor is prepared to cancel the lien and substitute an accounts receivable transaction for it.

*General services.* The factor sometimes extends loans on a client's general credit and, on rare occasions, lends funds to finance his clients' equipment purchases. In general, however, his services are designed to supply their working capital requirements rather than to augment their fixed capital funds.

## Commercial finance houses

The commercial finance house is usually considered an institution that confines its operations to financing installment purchases of high-unit-value durable consumer goods—and many do. But numerous large houses of this type also carry on a considerable business in financing industrial goods marketing. They are especially well equipped to provide funds for the purchase and sale of equipment and somewhat less interested in or adapted to financing inventories or ordinary accounts receivable.[1] In 1968, one such house carried about $881 million of industrial financing.

Some of these firms are prepared to give the industrial marketer financial service for accounts receivable much the same as that provided by the factor. They tend more to make loans on such accounts as collateral rather than to purchase them. Their basic charge for this service is a rate of a fraction of 1 percent per day of the gross amount of receivables pledged. For the ordinary marketer of industrial goods, the commercial finance company probably offers a more readily accessible source of accounts receivable service than does the factor, because most factors specialize largely in the textile business. Therefore, their understanding of the problems peculiar to other industries is not so great.

Because of its wide experience in the medium- and long-term credit field, gained in its business of financing installment purchases of consumer goods, the commercial finance house is well qualified to render the same kind of service in the industrial goods field. Several firms of this type have developed very flexible arrangements for industrial installment financing. They are prepared to investigate a client borrower's operations and to work out a financial program that will enable him to pay off an

---

[1] Much of the information used here was obtained from publications of the CIT corporation, and in conversations with its executives.

equipment loan in a manner that will not handicap his operations or dangerously commit his future income or working capital.

These arrangements usually take the form of notes, which fall due at strategic intervals best suited to fit in with the borrower's expected receipts of income and other commitments of working capital, or a program of installment payments whereby he can pay for the equipment out of current income, which he is using the machine to produce. Sometimes, these arrangements become highly complicated. One case reported involved a four-way deal participated in by a printing machinery manufacturer, a printer who bought the equipment, a large customer of the printer for whose work the machine was needed, and the finance company.

Can manufacturers make and sell to packers machines for sealing filled cans. Two large can makers arranged with a commercial finance company to handle the installment selling programs by which they distributed these machines to the food packers. The same finance company operates an installment system by which an electronic and sonic device manufacturer sells to fishing vessel operators a sonic depth sounder for locating schools of fish. This firm also offers to dentists an installment arrangement to finance needed equipment purchases. This and other commercial finance companies have sought to adapt their services to fit into the distribution needs of industrial marketers.

Manufacturers of expensive industrial equipment, materials, or components, the inventories of which absorb a large part of the capital of the typical customer, often find it desirable to arrange with finance houses to make credit available to customers of good standing. Many buyers are likely to look on such ready-made financial arrangements as a distinctly worthwhile part of the service offered by the supplier. They may represent the difference between making and losing a sale.

### Installment sales

A considerable amount of industrial equipment is sold on an installment basis. There are no figures from which to make any reliable estimate of the extent to which this device is used. It is certain that in total dollar volume it falls far short of the volume of consumer goods installment sales. It is also probably true that the percentage of total sales of industrial equipment made on this basis is much smaller than that in durable consumer goods.

There is probably less real need for the installment sales contract in industrial goods marketing. Comparatively few machines are so high in unit price that their purchase constitutes a significant drain on the capital structure of the buying firm. The business house also has available sources of capital, such as sales of securities, bank loans, and loans from finance companies, which are denied to many consumers or available to them only on terms they do not want to accept.

On the other hand, an installment purchase contract for a piece of industrial equipment usually constitutes a sounder extension of credit than does such an arrangement applied to the sale of a consumers' goods item. First, the industrial buyer probably has planned his purchase somewhat more carefully and on a more businesslike basis than the consumer usually bothers to do. He is apt to match future income against future outgo a little more realistically. Second, more detailed and reliable credit information about the industrial buyer is usually available. Third, if the industrial purchaser's estimates of his future business are sound, he will generally be able to apply money earned by using the equipment to pay off the debt he incurred in buying it. To some degree, the equipment pays for itself. Installment credit seems a sound method of financing the sale of industrial equipment.

Some industrial marketers offer a sort of hybrid lease-installment arrangement. This works somewhat as follows.

The manufacturer of a machine selling at $48,000 leases the machine to a user under contract providing for a monthly payment of, say, $2,000. At the end of 12 months, the user has the option of buying the machine by applying, say, $12,000 out of the $24,000 he has paid during the year to a purchase price, which has been scaled down at a fixed depreciation rate. If the depreciation period were set at 8 years, for example, the scaled-down price would be about $42,000. The remaining $6,000 of the monthly payments received by the seller applies to financing charges, maintenance charges, and profit on the financial operation as such. Similar adjusted options are offered at various stages during the period of the lease. These figures are very rough approximations and probably are not entirely realistic; but they should convey an idea of the general nature of the transaction.

This arrangement has the advantage of enabling the user to have the benefit of the machine without initially committing any large block of capital to its purchase. At any of the stated option periods, he may acquire ownership of the machine if that benefits him financially. Seemingly, it may also enable him to charge off the lease payments as a current expense in his income tax computations. This may be a snare and a delusion, however, because the Bureau of Internal Revenue generally tends to take a dim view of such arrangements. Therefore, the marketer who is tempted to use this sort of contract should submit it to the careful scrutiny of his attorney and tax adviser, so that the arrangement he offers allows the user the maximum legitimate income tax benefits possible. He should also be very careful to see that his advertising and sales promotion materials and his salesmen give no false impressions of the tax benefits safely available to the user under the contract. The irritation generated in the user in the course of a losing encounter with the Bureau of Internal Revenue is very liable to rub off on the marketer who proposed the deal in the first place.

### Financial service policy

The industrial goods marketer may adopt any one of three policies in his approach to the problems involved in the relations between marketing and finance.

1. He may completely ignore the sales possibilities of the credit service, aside from financing the necessary inventory, and devote his attention to stimulating sales by other methods, relying on the prospective buyer to provide his own purchase financing. This policy is apt to seriously limit sales, especially during periods when he must sell in a buyers' market. On the other hand, it means that he gets cash for all the sales he makes, and his rate of capital turnover is not reduced by the impounding of large sums in accounts receivable.

2. The industrial marketer may finance the stocking and sale of his goods entirely out of his own capital through open-book account, installment sale, or some other credit arrangement. The execution of this policy requires large working capital; it results in a slow rate of turnover of working capital; it involves, in many cases, a high cost of record-keeping and correspondence with customers; and it is apt to bring about losses of customer goodwill because of the sometimes drastic steps that must be taken in making collections. On the other hand, this policy enables the marketer to keep all his financial strings in his own hands, and to regulate his relations with customers unhampered by the ideas and interference of third parties whose primary interest lies in money management.

3. The industrial goods manufacturer may avoid the detailed activities involved in providing financial service to his customers but arrange with some sort of financial institution to supply such services. He usually cannot work through a bank to do this, but must turn to a factor, a commercial finance house, or some other type of concern specializing in industrial financing operations.

### SUMMARY

The provision of parts is often looked on as a stepchild. The results are that poor parts service handicaps the original sale of new equipment or that the pirate parts makers get the business. Both of these difficulties can be minimized or eliminated by a sound system for marketing parts.

Engineering and technical assistance is necessary. Whether it should be rendered by the engineering department, the marketing department, the development unit, or some combination of them depends on the nature and importance of the service and the conditions under which it must be rendered. This assistance often is subject to grave abuses.

The chief financial problems in marketing industrial goods cluster around the costs of carrying inventory and of carrying accounts receivable. Both may be financed out of invested capital at the cost of slow turnover of capital funds. Borrowing on warehouse receipts may be used to finance inventory. Factors may be used to finance both inventory and credit extensions, as may commercial finance houses. Industrial equipment is well suited to financing by installment sales.

# PART V

## Marketing strategy: The channel component

THE DISTRIBUTION CHANNEL is an extension of the manufacturer into the markets he plans to supply. The manner in which products and services are made available through it is a function of its structure as well as the relationship which prevails among its different elements or intermediaries. The basic choice is whether this structure will be composed of captive (owned) or independent units. The nature of this choice and the different types of intermediaries available are discussed in chapter 14. The various issues to be resolved in determining how the selected structure will be used and the relationships which should prevail within it are discussed in chapter 15.

Since a distribution channel exists for the purpose of moving merchandise and making services available, channel strategy also involves planning of a logistical nature. How efficiently the channel structure functions as a delivery system depends in large part on the quality of logistical planning and its execution. This element of channel strategy is treated in chapter 16.

# 14

## CHANNEL STRATEGY: THE STRUCTURAL ELEMENTS

A MARKETING CHANNEL is composed of outlets through which a manufacturer's goods may flow to market. However, channel strategy is not simply a question of choosing one system of outlets rather than another. It involves the way these outlets are related to each other and to the manufacturer as well as the kind of direction and control the manufacturer exerts. The various types of distribution outlets available to industrial goods manufacturers are discussed in this chapter, while the issues of channel relationships, direction, and control are treated in the following chapter.

The types of outlets available and the functions they perform represent the structural elements of channel strategy. They have an important part in actuating the strategic plan and form the principal constraints within which it must operate. Some distribution outlets, such as manufacturer's branch houses and branch offices, are part of the internal organization structure of the manufacturing firms. Others, such as distributors or wholesalers, manufacturer's agents, sales agents, and other types of agents, are usually independently owned and operated enterprises, although some "tame cat" distributors are owned and controlled by the manufacturer.

Some of these outlets buy, own, and carry stocks of the goods they sell. Others act as agents and merely arrange contracts of purchase and sale. Let us first consider the most important group, the distributors.

### INDUSTRIAL DISTRIBUTORS

#### Definition

The term "industrial distributor" is used with various meanings. For purposes of analysis here, they are identified as middlemen who buy and sell products for industrial uses. All offer manufacturers the services of taking title to and stocking products, assuming some of the risks of marketing, and maintaining reasonably close contact with buyers.

Some distributors stock a wide variety of supplies and small equipment, and sell to a diversified group of customers. These are known in many industries as general-line distributors or mill supply houses. Others specialize—either in the products they handle or in the customers they serve. Firms in the former category may limit their inventories to such narrowly defined product categories as office equipment and supplies, abrasives, or electrical equipment and supplies used by a broad spectrum of industry. Other distributors which confine their marketing efforts, for example, to dentists, hotels and restaurants, or beauty and barber shops, specialize by customer.

Table 14-1 presents information about some of the more important groups of industrial distributors. A study of this table discloses several significant characteristics about these middlemen as a group. The most obvious feature is that all have increased in number, some categories rather dramatically. Sales per establishment have also increased in every category. Employment increased in most categories. By any of these measures industrial distribution is a growth industry.

**TABLE 14–1.  Statistics of selected groups of industrial distributors**

|  | Number of establishments | | | | Sales per establishment (000) dollars | | | |
|---|---|---|---|---|---|---|---|---|
|  | 1948 | 1958 | 1963 | 1967 | 1948 | 1958 | 1963 | 1967 |
| Industrial chemicals............ | 1,075 | 2,805 | 3,163 | 3,380 | 637 | 533 | 641 | 750 |
| Electric wiring materials, equipment*.................. | 2,159 | 3,106 | 7,644 | 8,625 | 395 | 675 | 549 | 872 |
| Construction materials......... | 2,467 | 4,467 | 5,687 | 5,715 | 460 | 459 | 534 | 574 |
| Commercial machinery......... | 1,640 | 4,255 | 5,639 | 5,931 | 196 | 237 | 256 | 325 |
| Industrial machinery (general).. | 239 | 2,366 | 2,391 | 1,682 | 1,386 | 369 | 432 | 622 |
| Oil well supplies.............. | 1,005 | 1,444 | 1,555 | 1,746 | 714 | 679 | 540 | 846 |
| Industrial supplies (general and specialties)............. |  | 6,180 | 7,247 | 7,658 |  | 415 | 502 | 679 |
| Industrial supplies (general).... |  |  | 1,172 | 1,555 |  |  | 821 | 822 |
| Mechanical power transmission equipment................. |  | 596 | 815 | 1,046 |  | 409 | 424 | 689 |
| Professional equipment and supplies.................... | 2,353 | 3,663 | 4,467 | 4,633 | 239 | 366 | 463 | 624 |
| Surgical, medical, hospital supplies.................... | 643 | 1,387 | 1,243 | 1,252 | 334 | 467 | 647 | 890 |
| Service establishment supplies... | 3,520 | 4,014 | 5,158 | 5,679 | 211 | 259 | 274 | 332 |
| Transportation equipment...... | 609 | 1,387 | 1,660 | 1,670 | 416 | 444 | 518 | 817 |
| Iron and steel products†........ | 1,466 | 3,247 | 1,880† | 2,178 | 988 | 985 | 1,949 | 2,869 |
| Nonferrous metals†............ | 240 | 849 | 278† | 481 | 2,069 | 1,677 | 2,166 | 3,382 |
| Construction equipment........ | 906 | 2,143 | 2,358 | 3,022 | 861 | 936 | 1,108 | 1,209 |

* Includes electrical supplies and electronic parts and equipment houses in 1963 and 1967.
† Drop shippers omitted in 1963 and 1967.
Source: Reports of the Wholesale Census, 1948, 1958, 1963, 1967.

Although it is difficult to draw any conclusions from the behavior of expenses over the two decades prior to 1967 (half the categories experienced increases while the remainder experienced decreases), it is clear that industrial distributors as a group maintained a remarkably stable relationship between sales and expenses during a difficult period. It is equally evident from Table 14–1 that, as a group, industrial distributors have amplified their role as storehouses for industry. The number of days' stock on hand has increased in nearly every category since 1948. In some industries this figure has more than doubled.

## Geographical distribution

Industrial distributors are highly concentrated geographically. They are found mainly in areas that have a heavy concentration of manufacturing establishments, for that is where the industrial market is. As one would expect, a large percentage of the total number of distributors with the lion's share of distributor sales is found in large cities (i.e., those with 500,000 or more population) or in the industrial and trading satellites of these cities. See Table 14–2. Indeed, only 6 to 9 states account for 42 to 62 percent of the total number of distributors

| Employees per establishment | | | | Expenses as percent of sales | | | | Number of days' stock on hand | | | |
|---|---|---|---|---|---|---|---|---|---|---|---|
| *1948* | *1958* | *1963* | *1967* | *1948* | *1958* | *1963* | *1967* | *1948* | *1958* | *1963* | *1967* |
| 10 | 7 | 8 | 9.4 | 13.4 | 14.8 | 15.2 | 16.0 | 22 | 17 | 21 | 58 |
| 11 | 11 | 9 | 12 | 16.2 | 14.6 | 17.5 | 17.2 | 39 | 25 | 39 | 46 |
| 16 | 10 | 10 | 10 | 22.1 | 19.1 | 18.2 | 20.1 | 23 | 26 | 27 | 44 |
| 8 | 7 | 7 | 8 | 24.4 | 25.1 | 24.9 | 25.6 | 36 | 39 | 38 | 50 |
| 41 | 8 | 9 | 11 | 17.3 | 21.5 | 20.9 | N. A. | 44 | 39 | 34 | 55 |
| 9 | 7 | 6 | 8 | 9.2 | 12.0 | 14.4 | 11.8 | 41 | 32 | 37 | 41 |
| | 9 | 10 | 12 | | 20.3 | 20.2 | 20.2 | | 40 | 39 | 49 |
| | | 15 | 14 | | | 19.3 | 19.2 | | | 46 | 58 |
| | 9 | 9 | 11 | | 21.1 | 21.7 | 20.8 | | 47 | 54 | 64 |
| 12 | 11 | 11 | 13 | 25.7 | 24.3 | 23.8 | 22.7 | 55 | 42 | 45 | 54 |
| 13 | 11 | 12 | 14 | 22.8 | 21.2 | 20.0 | 19.8 | 46 | 36 | 39 | 46 |
| 7 | 7 | 7 | 8 | 19.1 | 24.7 | 26.3 | 26.2 | 46 | 35 | 40 | 41 |
| 10 | 9 | 10 | 12 | 18.6 | 21.7 | 21.2 | 18.3 | 38 | 37 | 44 | 75 |
| 19 | 17 | 27 | 32 | 14.9 | 18.4 | 16.7 | 15.6 | 36 | 49 | 52 | 64 |
| 21 | 14 | 23 | 22 | 7.3 | 8.1 | 13.6 | 10.4 | 20 | 23 | 35 | 34 |
| 20 | 13 | 17 | 18 | 16.5 | 18.8 | 18.2 | 18.6 | 52 | 62 | 68 | 94 |

TABLE 14–2.     Wholesaling in the seven largest metropolitan
areas,* 1967

| Trade group | Percent of establishments | Percent of total distributor sales |
|---|---|---|
| Electrical supplies and equipment† | 26 | 26 |
| Electronic parts | 30 | 45 |
| Chemicals | 33 | 45 |
| Commercial equipment | 22 | 31 |
| Construction machinery | 14 | 15 |
| Industrial machinery | 27 | 28 |
| Industrial supplies | 26 | 28 |
| Professional equipment and supplies | 34 | 35 |
| Service establishment equipment and supplies | 28 | 37 |
| Metal service centers | 19 | 35 |
| Construction materials | 22 | 31 |

* Boston, New York City, Philadelphia, Los Angeles, San Francisco, Detroit, Chicago.
† These firms handle some consumer's goods.
SOURCE: U.S. Bureau of the Census, *1967 Census of Business, Wholesale Trade.*

and from 43 to 66 percent of their total sales. The heavy concentration
of industry in such states as New York, Pennsylvania, California, Illinois,
and Texas is readily apparent in Table 14–3.

## Size characteristics

The typical industrial distributor is a small firm. Annual sales of less
than $500,000 is not uncommon. On the other hand, large firms capture
most of the business. This characteristic has considerable significance
for the industrial goods manufacturer. By aggressively selling to a
relatively small number of distributors in his industry, the manufacturer
frequently has an entree to a large share of the potential business in his
market. A collateral benefit of this strategy is often a reduction in the
expenses of selling and physical distribution. As a rule, the larger distributors have a lower ratio of total expense to sales than do small ones.
Consequently, by being selective in his choice of distributors, the margin
of gross profit a manufacturer must allow is often significantly less than
that which would be required if he chose to sell through every distributor
who was willing to handle his products.

Manufacturers who pursue a policy of selective distribution often
sell to other distributors at the same prices charged industrial users.
However, some manufacturers refuse to sell to nonselected distributors.
In such instances these firms must buy from the larger, selected distributors if they wish to stock the manufacturer's product. This is most likely
to occur in the case of highly regarded manufacturers and popular trade
markets.

**TABLE 14–3.    States of greatest concentration of selected groups of distributors, 1967**

| | Chemicals | Commercial machines and equipment | Construction mining machinery | Construction materials | Electrical Apparatus Equipment Supplies | Electronic parts equipment | Industrial machinery equipment | Industrial supplies | Metal service center | Professional equipment service | Service establishments equipment supplies | Transportation equipment |
|---|---|---|---|---|---|---|---|---|---|---|---|---|
| California | X | X | X | X | X | X | X | X | X | X | X | X |
| Florida | | X | X | | | | | | | | X | X |
| Illinois | X | X | X | X | X | X | X | X | X | X | X | X |
| Michigan | | X | X | X | X | | X | X | | | X | |
| New Jersey | X | X | | X | X | X | | | | X | X | X |
| New York | X | X | X | X | X | X | X | X | X | X | X | X |
| Ohio | | X | X | X | X | X | X | X | X | X | | |
| Pennsylvania | X | X | X | X | X | X | X | X | X | X | X | |
| Texas | X | X | X | X | X | X | X | X | X | X | X | X |
| Number of states checked | 6 | 9 | 8 | 8 | 8 | 7 | 7 | 7 | 6 | 7 | 8 | 6 |
| Percent of total number of distributors in nation in states checked | 51 | 53 | 42 | 52 | 52 | 53 | 53 | 51 | 48 | 53 | 53 | 62 |
| States checked had distributors making following percentage of total national trade sales | 51 | 57 | 43 | 53 | 51 | 64 | 50 | 54 | 66 | 54 | 57 | 63 |

SOURCE: U.S. Bureau of the Census, *1967 Census of Business, Wholesale Trade.*

## Operating characteristics

Industrial distributors generally perform a number of functions which make them a viable marketing channel for many types of industrial goods. Typically, these can be classified as selling, warehousing, financing, and service.

*Selling.* According to trade sources the average industrial distributor has 6 or 7 outside salesmen, each of whom costs a minimum of $5,000 to train. Typically, an outside salesman requires from $15,000 to $20,000 a year in the form of direct compensation, fringe benefits, travel and entertainment expenses.[1] These figures have risen substantially over the past two decades because salesmen have become increasingly regarded as territorial marketing managers for whom selling the company's full line of products and developing new accounts through missionary work are only one area of responsibility. Salesmen are increasingly expected to service accounts, feed back marketing intelligence to superiors, and cooperate with other company personnel in controlling expenses, pre-

---

[1] *Industrial Distribution* (September 1970), pp. 52 f.

paring records and reports, retraining old salesmen as well as training new ones.

In addition to their sales forces, many distributors maintain showrooms and at least the larger ones publish catalogs. Showroom displays can be a potent selling tool, particularly when combined with facilities for small-order handling. Indeed, many manufacturers look upon the distributor as a form of retail store for businessmen where fill-in and emergency orders can be conveniently placed.

The value of showroom displays to the distributor probably depends on several conditions. If his warehouse is located near the factories he serves, he is likely to have many buyers who examine his displays while waiting for their orders to be filled. Specialty distributors would tend to derive more benefit from such traffic than the general-line distributor since they are likely to have more novel items to show. All wholesalers of course have many items which do not lend themselves to interesting displays. On the other hand, management must be willing to invest the time and effort which are indispensable prerequisites to effective showroom displays.

A well-prepared catalog with adequate descriptive material and up-to-date price information is also an effective selling tool. Such catalogs may contain as many as 1,000 pages and list over 15,000 items. Needless to say, they are expensive to compile and customers must be properly guided in their use.

*Warehousing.* Carrying inventory is a basic feature of wholesaling, and industrial distributors are well known for this function. General-line distributors often carry as many as 20,000 items in 600 to 700 product lines. Even a specialty wholesaler, such as an electrical supply firm, may carry some 60,000 items from as many as 300 different suppliers. Although a large steel warehouse may carry no more than 10,000 items, such firms are usually prepared to shear and cut steel stock into almost any size and shape desired by steel users.

As a rule only general-line distributors stock competing lines of merchandise. Specialty firms are apt to follow this policy only in the case of highly standardized items. This of course reflects the more intensive market coverage provided by a specialized distributor.

Differences in the scope of the warehousing function between general-line and specialty distributors is reflected in the average size of their facilities. A survey of warehouse facilities conducted by *Industrial Distribution* magazine revealed that general-line distributors average about 28,000 square feet of warehouse space per establishment, whereas the comparable figure for specialty firms is 20,000 square feet.[2]

*Financing.* Virtually all distributors do some financing beyond the proverbial ten-day, open-book terms. The survey of distributor opera-

---

[2] *Industrial Distribution* (March 1970), p. 58.

tions conducted annually by *Industrial Distribution* magazine has almost always indicated some accounts receivable in the 90-days-or-more category. While some of these accounts are "slow" and others eventually become bad debts, all such accounts in the 90-days-or-more classification are not unintentional, at least not at the time of the survey.

The most recent annual survey indicated that accounts receivable did not represent more than 1 percent to 19 percent of average gross sales of distributors in 1969, and that accounts outstanding 90 days or more were less than 10 percent of average accounts receivable. Nevertheless, it is interesting to note that the Wholesale Census for 1967 showed that distributors' outstandings ranged from 9.5 percent of sales for transportation equipment and supplies to 15.6 percent for professional equipment and supplies. This represented between 35 and 57 days' credit.[3]

More significant than the modest financial aid distributors provide their customers is the financial assistance they provide manufacturers in the very act of buying and storing merchandise. By providing a volume cash market through which their suppliers can recover capital that would otherwise be invested in inventories, distributors perform an important financial service.

***Supplier and customer service.*** The service that is perhaps most commonly available through industrial distributors is delivery. Many distributors maintain their own trucks and are able to give prompt delivery in their territories—often in a matter of hours on emergency orders. The manufacturer's transportation costs are also minimized whenever he can ship in large quantities and pass off to a distributor responsibility for broken-lot shipments. Since distributors can generally combine products of different makers in making deliveries, they are usually in a better position to spread the high costs of handling broken lots than are most manufacturers.

Many distributors are also equipped to provide manufacturers of mechanical or technical products with installation, maintenance, and repair service on a local basis. Distributor sales and service personnel are often able to render assistance in the solution of production problems involving their supplier's products, which benefits both the supplier and the customer. In many instances, distributors are also able to keep customers informed about new applications of their products, new engineering or performance data related to their use, and improved methods of maintenance or repair.

## Why customers buy from distributors

The distributor's usefulness as an outlet for the manufacturer of industrial goods depends to a great extent on his usefulness to the buyers

---

[3] Ibid.

of the manufacturer's products. The manufacturer can market success-fully through distributors only if the users of his products find it desirable to buy through distributors. In appraising the distributor as a marketing channel for industrial goods, it is useful to examine more carefully the services he is equipped to render to the firms which use him as an outlet, the advantages users may enjoy as a result of purchasing from him, and the conditions likely to influence industrial buyers to patronize him.

*Fast, economical delivery.* Speed and certainty of delivery offer several important benefits. The most obvious, of course, is a reduction in inventory, which in turn reduces inventory carrying costs (estimated by various trade sources at 10 to 15 percent of its value, annually) and lessens the likelihood of losses due to obsolescence and price declines. By reducing the time between the placing of an order and its delivery by the vendor, production planning can be more flexible than if the lead time were quite long.

In some cases the distributor may be able to deliver goods at lower prices than those the buyer would have to pay if he purchased direct from the manufacturer. Distributors who own their own trucks often make no specific charge for delivery while manufacturers may ship f.o.b. factory, which means that the buyer must pay the freight. If we add to this the inconvenience of goods damaged in shipment and the time in-volved in negotiation (sometimes through a third party) for their replacement, local delivery by a local distributor is often unbeatable.

Similarly, the distributor is able to purchase many of the products he handles in carload or truckload lots. The small manufacturer-user often cannot purchase in such lots. Consequently, the distributor can usually offer savings in such instances which result from a combined car-lot rate and a less-than-carlot rate, which is less than the less-than-carlot rate the buyer would have to pay on orders delivered from the manufacturer.

If the buyer does not have his own siding, the distributor can some-times offer a significant saving on incoming merchandise delivered by rail. If such a buyer purchases such merchandise direct, he will have to pick up each shipment at the freight depot and transport it by truck to his plant. Dealing with a local distributor can eliminate this extra haul and the more trips between freight depot and plant that can be elimi-nated the more significant are the savings in transportation costs offered by the distributor.

*Product information.* Distributors' catalogs are usually compendiums of quality, price, and availability information about the products of many manufacturers. Through their visits, the distributors' salesmen keep this information up-to-date. As a result of their wide contacts with the trade, these men can often supply their customers with general information about many products which the more highly specialized salesmen of the manufacturer-supplier do not have. Of course, when the buyer wishes highly detailed technical information about specific materials, supplies, or equipment, he cannot always expect to get it from the distributor's salesman, but must contact the manufacturer.

*Credit.* To the small buyer, the industrial distributor usually offers a convenient and reasonably liberal source of credit. Since the distributor is generally a local concern, he should be more familiar with the business, character, and financial needs of the small local buyer than the manufacturer-supplier can be. As a result, he ought to be able to extend credit in situations when the manufacturer, operating at long range, would not be justified in taking a chance. However, census data indicate that in general, manufacturer's stock-carrying branches sell a slightly larger percentage of their total volume on credit than do the industrial distributors serving the same industries.

*Technical service.* The proximity of the industrial distributor to his customers enables his salesmen to have a detailed knowledge of their operations. If these salesmen visit their customers frequently, they are often able to give them a type of service that cannot be duplicated by the manufacturer-supplier. For example, a steel warehouse offers to cut metal stock to the specifications of the small buyer—a service the steel mill cannot afford to render, except to the large purchaser.

## Summary

The viability of the independent distributor as an outlet for industrial goods is assured by a number of circumstances. Obviously, buyers are compelled to purchase from distributors those items which they use in quantities too small to purchase direct, or which makers sell exclusively through distributors. It is a common practice of manufacturers to refuse to handle orders below a given quantity or to allow no discounts on them. The latter practice usually renders an indirect purchase more economical than a direct one, particularly when the distributor can lump together a number of small orders for diverse items. In these circumstances, the savings in acquisition costs can be significant.

Even large industrial buyers must depend on distributors to meet emergency and fill-in orders. Since the wise purchasing agent will be well aware that no business can exist on emergency and fill-in orders alone, even large industrial buyers are likely to divert enough of their regular purchases to local distributors to make their accounts profitable ones for these middlemen to serve. A consideration which gives strong support to such a policy is that enough may be saved on inventory investment alone, through fast delivery, to more than offset the quantity discounts sacrificed by not buying everything direct.

During recent years, purchasing officers have laid great emphasis on reducing inventories through automatic reordering systems for many items. Such a system can usually be negotiated more readily with a distributor than with a series of manufacturers. The business of only the larger user customers of the average manufacturer justifies such an arrangement. By purchasing a number of items from one distributor, the smaller firm can make the arrangement worthwhile to him. This has been a strong factor in inducing the use of distributors as suppliers.

## MANUFACTURER'S AND SALES AGENTS

### Definition and description

The manufacturer's agent and the sales agent operate in much the same manner. Each represents sellers only. Each operates on a commission basis. Each represents a limited number of principals with more or less continuity rather than playing the field as does the broker or the commission merchant. Neither takes title to the goods he handles, although many manufacturer's agents carry stocks on consignment.

The two agents differ in that the manufacturer's agent sells only a portion of the producer's output and limits his activities to a certain geographical area, while the sales agent usually sells to a given trade group wherever its members may be found and usually contracts to dispose of the entire output of his client-producer. By making an arrangement with a single sales agent, the producer can solve his entire problem of choosing marketing channels; if he markets through manufacturer's agents, he must make contracts with several of them in order to cover the entire market. Manufacturer's agents are much more important in the industrial goods business than in consumer goods marketing.

### When manufacturer's or sales agents are useful

The maker of a single industrial goods item, or a narrow line of them, with limited sales volume in the average market area, faces a difficult problem in marketing his output. In most territories, he cannot hope to capture enough volume to support his own sales force and distribution machinery unless he is willing to wholesale the products of other manufacturers; then he takes over all the managerial headaches that go with being an industrial distributor. On the other hand, since his line is limited he can hardly expect that the industrial distributor, if he decides to market through this outlet, will devote much effort to promoting his goods. His handicap is much more pronounced if his product requires special sales promotional effort.

The manufacturer may try to escape this dilemma by using the manufacturer's agent or the selling agent, who handles a narrow line of products—usually not over 30—and so may be expected to devote much more attention to each one and to know much more about each one than the distributor could possibly know. These agents may even prove useful to the full-line manufacturer who wants to market direct to users but finds demand so thin in certain portions of the country that such sales would be prohibitively expensive, or who discovers that a certain market for his products, although not yielding large sales volume, requires specialized technical knowledge and close customer contact. In either case, the large manufacturer is likely to employ manufacturer's or selling agents as part of his marketing system.

Both types of agents offer certain advantages as distributive outlets for a manufacturer's goods in the industrial market.

*Low marketing cost.* Available expense data for the various types of industrial middlemen are not fully comparable. For example, net profit must be added to the cost percentages of distributors and agents when comparing their total contribution to the delivered cost of a given product to that of a manufacturer's branch. Similarly, when comparing the cost of marketing through agents with that of marketing through distributors, the expense of physical distribution must be added to the agent's fees. All types of agents, even the stock-carrying manufacturer's agent, typically sell for delivery from the manufacturer's plant. Consequently, the manufacturer must perform all the functions involved in moving ordered merchandise from his factory or warehouse to that of the buyer.

In spite of these adjustments, it is very likely that the cost of marketing through manufacturer's agents and sales agents is less than that of going through industrial distributors or manufacturers' branches, unless the manufacturer's products enjoy a heavy demand. When using agents, selling costs are not incurred unless sales are made. Obviously, the cost of marketing through them remains unchanged in relation to sales regardless of business conditions, unless the commission rate is changed, which occurs very infrequently.

*Established contacts.* As going concerns, both types of agents offer the benefits of buyer contacts and good will built up over the past. This can prove valuable to the manufacturer introducing a new product or attempting to penetrate a new market with an existing product. Both situations are likely to involve markets in which the manufacturer has not sold before. In the case of a manufacturer's agent, a new product may benefit significantly from being sold alongside complementary products already being marketed by the agent.

The sales agent can be particularly helpful to the manufacturer lacking marketing experience. Firms heavily oriented to the defense and aerospace industries were desperately in need of marketing experience when spending on these programs was severely cut back in the late 1960s. Such firms often manage to obtain access to the entire market for their products through one sales agent. Such an agent can frequently perform the entire marketing function for a company that is ill-equipped to do it.

*Competent selling.* Either type of agent is likely to offer a better quality of sales effort than does the industrial distributor. By virtue of the smaller number of products handled, agent salesmen can devote to each of them an amount of promotional attention and study that the distributor salesman cannot match. Even the manufacturer of an extensive line of products may discover that an agent can support a specialty item with an imaginative and comprehensive sales program that he finds difficult to duplicate through his own sales force. However, this strength of agents is somewhat offset by the fact that the sales agent may also be selling products which compete directly with the manufacturer's product. And the manufacturer's agent, while not selling competing products, is selling other products which compete for the attention of his salesmen. Therefore, no one manufacturer's product gets the full attention of any salesman. It is generally known that a salesman can seldom make a real pitch for more than four or five products on any given sales call.

## Agents have drawbacks

Against the advantages of low marketing cost, established contacts, and competent selling, the use of agents as marketing channels must be balanced against the drawbacks of loose control, lack of flexibility, and divided loyalty.

*Loose control.* Because agents are not on the payroll of the manufacturer who uses them, nor are they solely dependent upon him for their income, they are far less susceptible to control than the manufacturer's own sales force. It is especially difficult to induce agents to do any kind of missionary or development work which does not immediately result in sales on which they can collect commissions. On the other hand, it is probably true that the manufacturer can maintain a greater measure of control over the process of marketing his products if he uses agents than if he uses industrial distributors. The latter, of course, own his products; and while they can only make a profit if they sell them, with hundreds of suppliers and thousands of items, they have many more sales alternatives than do agents.

*Lack of flexibility.* Since the manufacturer's agent typically sells at a price fixed by his principal, he is usually uninitiated in the subtleties of competitive bidding. The sales agent is much more likely to have a greater measure of discretion with respect to price, and can vary price in response to situations calling for flexibility. In either event, the manufacturer-principal is usually obliged to enter the situation because of the agent's lack of familiarity with basic cost and output information.

It should be noted that the industrial distributor suffers the same disadvantage, and even to a more pronounced degree, since his natural reluctance to vary price is augmented by the knowledge that in so doing he may reduce his own margin.

*Divided loyalty.* This disadvantage is especially true of the sales agent due to the fact that he probably handles competing products. It is often argued by these agents that because they do carry competing products they can obtain a larger share of the potential business than would otherwise be possible. They then divide the total business among their clients in such proportions and in such a manner as to afford the greatest amount of profit to each of them. This is probably true of an agent that sells a semifabricated material, such as a fabric, made in several grades or varieties, the costs of which are likely to vary among his manufacturer clients. But the fact that the sales agent's clients must compete with one another for his services, even after the bargain of representation has been agreed upon, remains a serious disadvantage to the manufacturer.

### Summary

Both the manufacturer's agent and the sales agent offer to the manufacturer without market contacts, the producer of a narrow line, the maker of a specialty item sold to a highly specialized trade, or the producer of high-volume products seeking to penetrate areas where volume is small a selling service that is generally superior to that of the industrial distributor, and sometimes superior to that which the manufacturer himself can provide. Agents can often do this at a cost that compares favorably with that of the distributor as well as that of the manufacturer who sells through his own branches. If an article is bulky so that users generally buy in carload or truckload lots, or is of high value in relation to its bulk so that transportation and handling costs are no large element in its final delivered cost, the agent may be a valuable part of the manufacturer's distribution system.

## BROKERS

While brokers play no very significant part in industrial marketing, they can provide very useful distribution services under some circumstances. If goods are standardized or can be conveniently described by grade or trade designation, the broker may offer a convenient method of selling them. Many materials, some supplies, and a few types of small tools and equipment fall into this category.

Brokers can be useful to the manufacturer who finds himself with an excess supply of a commodity on hand—more than he can sell to his usual customers within an economical storage period. As a consequence of his wide, up-to-the minute, and detailed knowledge of a trade and its members, a broker is likely to know of some firm or firms willing to buy the excess. Such information and subsequent contact is well worth the broker's commission.

Chemical manufacturers sometimes find themselves with a supply of a by-product which they are not prepared to market but which is known to be commercially useful. Rather than dump such products as waste, they often employ brokers who successfully dispose of them at prices which make a positive contribution to company overhead. However, in order to have brokers available and willing to take such products, manufacturers should regularly offer at least a small portion of their primary output for sale through this channel.

## MANUFACTURER'S BRANCH HOUSES

Makers of industrial goods probably make less use of the manufacturer's branch house as a channel of marketing than do consumer goods producers. The firm that makes equipment to specification has little, if any, need for stock-carrying branches, except perhaps to maintain inventories of parts at points convenient to users; practically all its shipments must be made direct to the customer. The limited area within which an article that has a vertical demand can usually be sold, because of the tendency of firms in any one buying industry to locate near one another, restricts the need another fairly large group of industrial goods manufacturers has for branch houses. The large quantities in which the biggest volume of many industrial goods is bought tend to favor shipments direct from factory to user as against distribution through branch houses. These factors tend to limit the number of industrial goods firms that use branch houses, and to reduce the number operated by firms that do market through them. In spite of these limiting forces, however, the branch house occupies a significant position in the marketing system for industrial goods.

### Types of branch houses

The two types of manufacturer's branch houses are stock-carrying and nonstock-carrying. As a general rule, goods are shipped to the stock-carrying branch in carload or truckload lots, thus permitting lower carlot or trucklot freight rates over the longer portion of the trip to market. They are then fanned out from the branch in smaller shipping lots to users or, in some cases, to distributors. This arrangement allows the manufacturer to enjoy a favorable combination of freight rates and to render a speedy and reasonably sure delivery service to his customers.

The nonstock-carrying branch house is primarily a sales headquarters. It usually consists merely of an office from which operate the salesmen who travel the branch territory. Its chief function is usually to afford a convenient organizational unit through which to manage the sales activities of the company.

## Operating characteristics

Table 14–4 shows certain statistical facts about branch houses that handle selected types of industrial goods. From the material presented in it, a number of conclusions about the nature and functions of the two types of establishments can be drawn.

The typical stock-carrying branch is a good-sized concern, having a manager, and perhaps an assistant manager, a force of salesmen, a warehouse staff to handle the stock, and a clerical staff to carry on the order routine, and, in many cases, to prepare and send out the invoices and maintain a fairly complete set of accounts. The salesmen in such an establishment are usually of two types. The inside salesmen remain in the office or showroom, and serve customers who visit the branch to seek information and advice, to place their orders in person, or to ask immediate service to satisfy emergency needs. The outside, or field, salesmen usually work out of the branch as a headquarters, calling on customers and seeking to make sales. The branch usually keeps its own

**TABLE 14–4.**  Statistics of selected groups of manufacturer's branches, 1967

| | With stocks | | | | | Without stocks | | | |
|---|---|---|---|---|---|---|---|---|---|
| | *Number* | *Sales per branch ($000)* | *Employees per branch* | *Expenses as percent of sales* | *Number days' stock* | *Number* | *Sales per branch ($000)* | *Employees per branch* | *Expenses as percent of sales* |
| Industrial chemicals............... | 563 | 6,438 | 36 | 11.1 | 143 | 793 | 8066 | 17 | 3.6 |
| Electrical supplies and apparatus..... | 705 | 60,567 | 39 | 8.8 | 23 | 1075 | 2681 | 9 | 5.1 |
| Electronic parts and equipment...... | 121 | 3,236 | 21 | 10.6 | 12 | 334 | 2390 | 7 | 4.7 |
| Air conditioning, refrigeration equipment, supplies.............. | 48 | 2,431 | 21 | 12.3 | 38 | 170 | 1890 | 8 | 6.3 |
| Commercial machines and equipment...................... | 2,345 | 1,383 | 36 | 27.4 | 25 | 290 | 1356 | 23 | 23.2 |
| Construction and mining machinery, equipment..................... | 96 | 2,999 | 18 | 9.2 | 45 | 53 | 4572 | 12 | 4.6 |
| Industrial machinery, equipment..... | 1,100 | 1,495 | 18 | 14.7 | 31 | 1086 | 1449 | 8 | 8.4 |
| Industrial supplies................. | 677 | 1,834 | 16 | 12.1 | 27 | 617 | 3051 | 7 | 3.9 |
| Professional equipment and supplies........................ | 654 | 524 | 12 | 22.2 | 30 | 124 | 1438 | 13 | 10.0 |
| Service equipment and supplies...... | 161 | 693 | 12 | 22.5 | 55 | 26 | 799 | 9 | 17.6 |
| Transportation equipment and supplies........................ | 35 | 5,555 | 57 | 17.0 | 69 | 75 | 5391 | 13 | 4.2 |
| Construction materials.............. | 476 | 1,421 | 22 | 16.1 | 29 | 583 | 3778 | 13 | 5.8 |

inventory records; it may or may not perform its own accounting work and bill customers for the orders it fills. The varying extent to which these and other functions are performed explains, in part, the wide differences in the average number of persons employed by branch houses in the different trade groups.

The nonstock-carrying branch is usually a much smaller establishment in terms of employees, although not in sales volume. Its personnel may be composed primarily of salesmen and a small supervisory and clerical staff, usually confined to one or two persons. Its primary function is to sell; the orders it receives are transmitted to the factory or home office to be filled from there. It is thus able to handle a given volume of business with a much smaller staff than can the branch that maintains inventory. The difference in functions performed by the two types is also indicated by the difference in expenses as percentages of sales. In all the trade groups listed in Table 14–4, the expenses of the stock-carrying type are much greater than those of the branches that do not carry stocks—in some cases, several times as great.

### Size of branches

As in most of the trade groups, a high percentage of the total volume of business is done by a small percentage of the establishments. In most of them, well over half of the sales volume is transacted by branches that sell more than $1 million annually; these usually constitute less than 30 percent of the total number of establishments in the group.

The advantages of the large branch in the matter of cost are very apparent. The manufacturer of industrial goods whose potential volume in an area is small will find it very expensive to distribute there through a branch house. For this reason, it is not uncommon for a firm to sell direct through branches in concentrated industrial areas and through distributors or manufacturer's agents in territories where demand is thinner.

Analysis shows an even greater concentration of manufacturer's branches in the big metropolitan centers than was found to exist among distributors. For example, over half of the manufacturer's branches that handle primary metal products, with about 80 percent of the sales, are in cities with a population of 500,000 or more; about 56 percent of the fabricated metal products branches, making slightly more than half the total sales, are in such cities; and over one third of the branches that market machinery, with slightly more than half the sales, are in such places. This tendency is emphasized by the fact that many producers of small-bulk items maintain branch warehouses in one or two cities such as Chicago, New York, San Francisco, or Los Angeles, out of which they make deliveries to large users and to distributors. Many distributors cannot order such items in carload or truckload quantities of a single article or of several products in the same freight classification. By using a few branch houses, producers are able to obtain a lower combined freight rate to many markets than they could get if they made all deliveries from the factory. For example, almost half of the sales of stock-carrying branches of fabricated metal products manufacturers are made to distributors. Slightly under one third of the sales of construction- and mining-machinery branches is made to such buyers.

## What trades use branches?

Manufacturer's branch houses and distributors are the two chief channels through which industrial goods flow to market. Their relative importance in different trades varies considerably. For example, of the total 1967 volume of industrial chemicals sold to industrial users by distributors, manufacturer's branches, and agents, 15 percent was handled by distributors, 80 percent by branches, and about 5 percent by agents. On the other hand, 80 percent of the construction machinery volume was handled by distributors, 16 percent by branches, and about 4 percent by agents. For construction materials, the figures were: distributors 48 percent; branches 45 percent; agents 7 percent.

In general, supplies manufacturers seem to lean heavily on distributors to move their goods to market. Highly technical products, such as bulk chemicals and electrical apparatus, and bulky materials, such as metals, are marketed largely through manufacturer's sales branches. Logically, all machinery might be expected to be sold direct or through branches, but construction machinery and metalworking machinery are exceptions. The casebooks are replete with examples of relatively small firms making specialized types of equipment that market either through distributors or agents. In no small percentage of the cases, the reason is probably an engineering or production-minded management that prefers to settle the troublesome marketing problems by turning them over to specialists. Financial considerations may also be influential in this decision.

## Objectives of branch distribution

Through branch house distribution, the manufacturer of industrial goods accomplishes several things. By means of the direct contact with customers that results from the efforts of the sales force, which usually constitutes a part of the branch staff, he is able to apply heavier and more highly skilled promotional pressure on users of his product than would be possible otherwise. This is true of both types of branches; in fact, it is usually the chief reason for the existence of the nonstock-carrying house. The distributors' salesmen, handling the products of many manufacturers, cannot be expected to devote much effort to selling any one of them, or to be especially skilled in doing so. The branch house salesman has nothing to sell except the products of the firm that employs him, and he may be expected to know a lot about them.

By operating well-trained technical specialists out of the branch, the technical goods maker can offer his customers expert information, help, and advice, that his competitor, selling through distributors, will find difficult to match.

In his branch house, the equipment maker can maintain strategically located stocks of parts, as well as repair facilities and mechanics equipped to keep his machines in working order in his customers' plants. In some trades where it is customary to depend on the supplier for repair work, this is a factor of very great importance.

Through his branch houses located in industrial centers, the manufacturer of supplies, small tools, and materials is able to render a delivery service to his large customers that he might find difficult or impossible through distributors.

The direct contact with the trade that results from branch house operations serves a multitude of minor purposes. Through its salesmen, the branch can be a fruitful source of information about the market and developments that are taking place in it. One branch house in a system can be used as a guinea pig in which to try out new products, new methods of selling, new techniques of servicing customers, and other changes that may be very profitable if they prove sound, but which—if applied generally throughout the company before testing in a small area—might seriously disrupt the entire operations of the firm and prove extremely costly and wasteful.

### Branch distribution can be costly

The chief drawback of the branch-house system of distribution lies in its expense. Such an operation has a habit of developing costs of its own, often not anticipated before it is actually put into effect. It creates its own overhead costs, loads the company with an entirely new set of personnel obligations that may be difficult to diminish when costs must be cut, engenders a need for plant and equipment not otherwise required, and adds tremendously to the work of supervision and management, and to the staff required to carry it on. Establishing a branch-house system is a major enterprise for a company of any size. For a company whose sales potential is limited, and whose market is thin, the cake may not be worth the candle.

### SUMMARY

Let us summarize. Distributors are the most numerous and most important group of middlemen handling industrial goods. Some of them are general houses trading in a wide variety of products; others specialize in handling one or a narrow line of products or in serving one group of customers. As a group, their number has tended to increase, their average sales to increase slightly, their costs to remain fairly constant, their average number of employees to increase, and their stocks to increase in relation to sales.

They are highly concentrated geographically, and most of their volume is in the hands of relatively few large houses. We observed several of the operating features that affect their usefulness as outlets for the manufacturer's goods. Industrial users find it desirable to buy from the distributor because he usually can give quick delivery, his use saves paper work in buying, he can sometimes offer lower prices, adjustments are easier to negotiate, he may enable the buyer to save freight costs, and he is a good source of trade information. The patronage of the distributor thus comes mainly from (1) the firm too small to buy direct, (2) the large firm for emergency needs and items bought in small amounts, or as a means of reducing inventory.

Manufacturer's and sales agents are useful outlets to producers of a single item or a narrow line of articles, to the manufacturer with limited finances, and to all kinds of manufacturers in areas where demand is thin or trade contracts are lacking. Advantages in using agents are that their costs are often relatively low and the producer incurs no costs unless sales are made, they offer contacts to the firm entering a new market, and their sales service is more specialized and intense than that of the distributor. But the manufacturer who markets through agents loses control over his marketing operations, lacks flexibility in bidding, incurs excessive costs when volume is large, loses speed of delivery, quality of technical service, and selling drive in comparison with his own sales force. Brokers and commission merchants are useful mainly in special situations.

Manufacturer's branch houses are of two types—those that carry stocks and those that do not. Through the branch house, the manufacturer gets better sales service, more adequate and representative stocks, and control of technical and maintenance service. But branch houses are often so costly as to be prohibitive.

# 15

# FORMULATING
# CHANNEL STRATEGY

A VIABLE channel strategy embraces both the internal marketing units of a firm and its external intermediaries. Consequently, formulating the channel component of marketing strategy involves an analysis of conditions which have a bearing on the best choice among structural alternatives as well as on the relationship between them and the manufacturer which will be most productive.

In general, the industrial marketer has a choice of three types of structural arrangements.

1. Direct to users through the manufacturers own sales force, with or without a network of branch warehouses.

2. Indirect to users through agents or wholesale distributors. In most instances manufacturers sell to distributors to industrial users; in others, manufacturers might sell through agents who resell to distributors as well as to end users. The choice of an indirect channel system also involves the choice of a selective (only one or a few outlets in each market area) or intensive (a number of outlets in each market area) relationship.

3. Mixed structure, in which the nature of the structural network differs with the segmentation of the market. One segment may buy the manufacturer's product in standard grades, while another may want special quality variations or demand very rigid tolerances with much technical service. While indirect distribution may be suitable for the former, direct distribution may be required for the latter.

## CONDITIONS INFLUENCING CHANNEL STRUCTURE

Some conditions which influence the choice of channel structure arise from the nature of the market; others are related to the peculiarities of the product; still others are linked to the character and situation of the firm itself. Those treated here are in no sense exhaustive, but they do have wide applicability.

*Is the market horizontal or vertical?* If a manufacturer's product can be sold only to the members of one or a few industries, and the number of firms in each industry is small, direct distribution probably is the most profitable method. Relatively few salesmen will be needed to make direct contact with all probable users. If branch warehouses are needed, the number necessary is likely to be small. Closer contact can be maintained with customers and prospective customers, and the opportunities to make sales are usually improved by this marketing method.

If, on the other hand, the market is horizontal and the product must be sold to buyers in many industries, the number of buyers probably is large, and the chances of economically reaching all or a large portion of them usually are enhanced by selling through distributors. The costs of setting up and operating a sales force large enough to contact all or a substantial portion of the users are liable to be excessive, and the expense of providing and maintaining branch warehouses to supply them may prove to be unbearable. For example, most industrial supplies producers make use of distributors in their marketing systems, as do the makers of small tools widely used by many industries.

*Is the market potential large or small?* If the nature of a product is such that a substantial volume of sales is available in the average area served by a single salesman or branch warehouse, direct marketing may prove profitable. If, on the contrary, the probable volume of sales in a market area is small, the direct method may be too expensive.

The volume of sales necessary to support a direct selling organization can be illustrated with a simple example. Suppose a manufacturer makes industrial products that can be sold to 30,000 firms, which must be called on about once every two weeks. The average salesman of such industrial goods can make about 8 calls a day, or 40 a week. He can thus handle about 80 accounts. To maintain proper sales contact with 30,000 customers, the manufacturer would need about 375 salesmen. A conservative figure for the cost of such salesmen, including compensation and expenses, would be $15,000 a year for each one, or a total of $5.625 million a year for the force.

In addition, such a sales force would need one field supervisor for about every ten salesmen. Again this is a conservative estimate; about one for eight would be a more realistic ratio. The operating cost of each man would probably be about $20,000 a year, and if the company used 37 of them, the total cost of field supervision would be about $740,000 annually. The cost of the sales force involved in direct marketing would thus aggregate about $6.365 million, and this does not include the expenses of division managers and the supporting staff needed to administer such a force.

Add the cost of providing adequate warehouse space, which would vary widely in different parts of the country, the expense of office space for the administrative staff, and the costs generated by a staff of order-handling clerks, order pickers, packers, and shippers needed to service the large volume of relatively small orders, which are likely to characterize direct distribution, and we probably have another $3 or $4 million. If a firm with this sort of a distributive organization realizes a gross profit of 40 percent, it must have total sales of over $25 million just to meet its costs of distribution alone. If it is to get its distributive costs down to the general average of industrial concerns—somewhere between 5 and 15 percent—it must be a big business. Direct marketing, a simple answer to the problem of choosing channels, is often a very costly one unless there is a volume of sales sufficient to support the expense.

*To what extent are the possible purchasers concentrated geographically?* The tendency toward localization of industry makes it possible to market direct to the user many industrial products whose small sales volume would preclude the possibility of selling direct, even to retailers, if they were consumer goods. If 70 or 80 percent of the total possible sales volume of a product is concentrated in one or two limited market areas—not unusual with industrial goods—the makers of such a product are likely to find that there is enough volume available in those areas to support direct marketing. By marketing direct, a manufacturer may cut himself off from the remaining 20 or 30 percent of the total volume, although he may be able to capture part or all of his share of it through distributors located in the areas of thin demand.

*What are the purchasing policies of the user?* If the typical user of an industrial good purchases in small orders and for quick delivery, its marketer probably will find it least costly and most satisfactory to sell through distributors. By combining the user's needs for several kinds of items, the distributor may be able to turn previously small orders for any one manufacturer whose goods he handles into economically sized orders composed of products from several makers. By combining the sale of one manufacturer's goods, on which the gross profit is small, with those of other manufacturers, who make items that enjoy higher margins and are sold to the same users, although sometimes in small quantities, the distributor may assemble a line that has possibilities of satisfactory profit, even though it would not be profitable for any one of the manufacturers to try to sell his product direct through his own facilities. For example, dental supply houses sell dentists the supplies and materials they use, on which the margin of gross profit is modest, together with equipment, which carries a wider margin. This is true of many laboratory equipment and chemicals distributors, hotel and restaurant supply houses, and distributors of bottling extracts, equipment, and supplies.

If the user purchases supplies or materials on a volume or requirements contract, the goods to be delivered in increments throughout a year or half-year period, direct contact is more apt to be necessary, and direct factory shipments may be feasible. If, however, the user buys on a hand-to-mouth basis, or attempts to control inventories by ordering when stock falls to a fixed point, the marketer must usually either maintain branch houses from which quick and reliable deliveries can be made— an expensive operation—or sell through distributors who, if properly selected, can be expected to carry stocks at points convenient to the users.

An ongoing change in buying habits may be expected to exercise a pronounced effect on the choice of channel structure for supplies, standardized components, and materials bought in relatively small bulk. In the past, it was common for purchasing officers in large firms to insist on buying direct in order to avoid paying the distributor's margin, and in the hope of getting quantity discounts. The rising costs of placing orders as well as holding inventory have raised doubts about such policies.

Many firms have streamlined purchasing by setting up continuing relations with selected suppliers with whom orders are placed by telephone, unpriced simplified purchase order, or even a tub-file inventory punched card. Orders are totaled and paid every ten days or at the end of the month instead of on an invoice created for each order. While each item may be bought in smaller quantities, many items are bought from one source and often on one order.

For this system to work, the purchasing officer must select one or two distributors and place all his orders with them. This vastly increases the importance of the distributor as an outlet for the makers of many supplies, materials, and component parts. It also may be expected to decrease the effectiveness of the limited franchise arrangement, whereby the manufacturer markets through only one or two distributors in a market area. For example, if a firm that uses abrasives concentrates all its purchases of supplies, materials, and minor equipment with one or two distributors, an abrasives manufacturer whose products are franchised to another distributor in the area has no chance to get the business.

This method of buying has been growing rapidly, and new refinements are constantly being added. How far it will go and how long it will last are unanswered questions. It seems likely that some streamlining of expensive order procedures and closer control of inventory are here to stay.

***What is the gross profit margin?*** If a manufacturer's product or products carry a wide margin between production cost and the price the user will pay, he may find it profitable to sell through his own sales force and make delivery himself. In this way he may increase revenue from added volume more than he adds to marketing costs. If the market situation is such that the spread between cost and selling price to user is narrow, the marketer is denied the necessary margin area within which to pursue such a strategy. He must make his channel decisions primarily in the interest of low marketing cost rather than high sales volume.

The choice is usually not nearly so clear-cut as we have stated it here. The nature of the market for some narrow-spread items is such that while the use of the direct channel may increase the total dollar outflow for marketing activities the greater volume of sales it brings results in a smaller marketing cost per dollar of sales.

*How volatile is the price?* The price of many industrial materials and some supplies is highly volatile. The maker of such an item who markets through distributors has a constant problem in adjusting the margins to compensate for shifts in price. If he does not make such adjustments, he finds that part of the time distributors are overcompensated in dollar receipts for the services they render, while part of the time they do not receive enough for handling his product to make satisfactory selling, stocking, and handling services worthwhile. As a result, the pressure is in the direction of marketing channels involving less complicated price-margin relationships, such as direct sale or the use of agents paid on a commission or per-unit fee basis.

*Must the product be installed?* Many industrial products must be installed in the users' plants or establishments. In some cases, such as of heavy, complicated machinery, the nature of the product and the market is such that the work of installation must be done by the maker, or he must advise or aid the buyer in doing it. This tends to induce the use of direct channels of marketing. In other cases, such as of communication equipment for use in apartment buildings, office buildings, institutions, and factories, specialized contractors have been developed to do the work of installation. In such a situation, it is often desirable that the product be sold to the user by a local firm that can also make on-the-spot arrangements for installation and follow-through. This points toward the use of distributors. Sometimes, the local situation is such that the user who wants to buy direct and make his own installation, or have the manufacturer make it, cannot do so without the danger of a strike or boycott by unions or contractors' associations.

*How much technical service does the product require in use?* Many materials, such as chemicals, and some types of highly technical equipment, such as accounting, recording, and statistical analysis machines, demand the services of carefully trained technical experts if the user is to enjoy the maximum benefit from them. The buyer of a chemical may want to mix it with a carrier not previously used or in proportions he has no experience with. He expects advice and help from the seller to obtain the desired result. If the user of electronic recording and computing equipment wants an analysis or a control result not contemplated when it was installed, he expects the equipment maker to tell him how to get it. Such service is usually more satisfactory when relations between maker and user are direct.

*How important is quality?* The quality specifications for some materials must be very exact and the quality tolerances very narrow. This is especially so with materials that go into food or drug end products and with electronic or mechanical control components, although it is true of other items as well. Even the most meticulous inspection procedure will not prevent an off-quality lot from occasionally getting into the hands of customers whose use of it in their end products may have, at worst, lethal and, at best, unsatisfactory effects. When this happens and is discovered, a recall operation must often be conducted to recover all the off-quality lot and replace it with satisfactory goods. The recall operations of the automobile companies are cases in point. When the article has moved to market through indirect channels so that the maker has no record of the users who finally bought it, this may be a highly expensive process and one of dubious success. Therefore, this condition points toward the use of direct channels of marketing.

It also sometimes happens that different users of a material or component want a variety of quality gradations so numerous that it is not practical to reduce them to a system of standard classes. In such cases, each batch or lot for each customer's order must be produced to specification. If such goods are marketed through indirect channels, it is difficult to be sure that specification requirements are accurately communicated and that the proper lots are delivered to customers in the distribution process. In such a situation, the direct channel is much more effective and satisfactory to both maker and user.

In general, when an industrial product is made to specifications set by the user, direct distribution is indicated. When it is made to standard specifications or in only a few variations or quality gradations, it may be marketed through indirect channels.

*How bulky is the item?*  If a product is so bulky that most of its users buy in carload or truckload lots, the tendency toward direct-to-user distribution is very strong. Unless speed of delivery is of prime importance to the buyer, or his rate of use of the commodity is subject to more than ordinary fluctuations, there is no reason for the manufacturer to maintain branch houses; he can sell direct through his own salesmen for factory shipment.

This is also true if he makes an article so small in bulk that it is generally shipped by express or parcel post. Transportation expense usually constitutes so small a percentage of the total cost of such a product that the savings to be made by carload or truckload transportation would probably be much more than offset by the expenses of maintaining a branch house system. If his customers require speedy delivery, or the nature of their operations gives rise to emergency needs for a product, its maker may be justified in maintaining branch houses.

The same considerations apply to the marketing of such products through distributors. In handling them, the distributor lacks one of his big advantages—the saving in transportation cost he makes possible by buying in bulk lots and selling in less-than-carload or less-than-truckload lots—thus causing the goods to move at the lower bulk freight rate throughout the greater part of their journey to market. These difficulties do not apply to an agent in handling such articles, since he usually sells for factory shipment.

*What kind of repair and maintenance service does the user need and how much?* If the product is so complex that it must be serviced by highly skilled specialists, the manufacturer must maintain some sort of service stations from which they can operate and in which stocks of parts may be carried. Such stations can just as well be used for branch houses. If the article is one the average mechanic can repair, customers will rely very little on the manufacturer for repair service. Then, the marketer may need to see to it that supplies of repair parts are conveniently available to users; this can be accomplished through distributors as well as, or better than, by branch houses.

Direct sale and delivery of parts may seem to be of some help to the machinery manufacturer in combating pirate parts makers; on the other hand, by depriving distributors of the opportunity to handle the legitimate parts, he may stimulate them to take over marketing of the pirate products. Perhaps a sound policy consists in making sure that parts handling is a profitable business for the distributor and that he carries an adequate, but not burdensome, stock of them.

*What is the firm's size and financial position?* Is the marketer well financed and large, or is he small and without adequate financial backing? If a concern is in a strong financial position, it can support a program of direct distribution that requires the spending of money for sales effort, the long-time investment of funds in branch warehouse facilities, and the tying up of working capital in inventories and accounts receivable. On the other hand, if a firm lacks adequate capital, it must sell its output as quickly as possible after it is produced, get paid for it as soon as it can, and carry on the entire process of distribution at the least possible cost.

The use of distributors or agents helps to achieve these ends. Only a few salesmen are needed to sell to distributors; such outlets carry most of the stocks necessary to serve the trade; and they usually discount their bills. The agent offers the great advantage that while the firm that uses him must generally carry the stock needed to service his customers, it incurs no selling expense until after he has sold some of its goods, and the amount of its selling cost varies with the volume of sales made.

*What are the seller's marketing objectives?* If a manufacturer is marketing his product locally and intends to expand to nationwide distribution, he will need a channel structure which facilitates that expansion. If he plans to diversify his product line, either through development of new products or by acquisition—particularly development—he will need a channel that is flexible in the sense that it can be expanded into new markets simply by adding new units rather than reorganizing to reach each new type of customer. If the objective is to make a profit by skimming the cream of the market through sale of a very high-profit product or provision of the maximum of service, a direct channel is probably most suitable. If the objective is to seek a small profit per unit on a large number of units sold primarily on the price appeal, distributors may be more suitable. Other objectives either of a marketing or company-wide nature also may influence channel structure.

## RELATIONSHIPS IN THE INDIRECT CHANNEL

The manufacturers choice of indirect channel relationships may be separated into those of a strategic nature and those which are matters of policy. In the former instance there are two basic alternatives: *selective* distribution in which the firm sells through but one or a limited number of outlets in each market area or segment, or *intensive*, in which all outlets of a given type in a given area or market segment will be utilized. Policy decisions involve those activities of a service nature which the manufacturer chooses to undertake in support of his strategy.

### Intensive versus selective strategy

The decision to pursue a selective rather than an intensive strategy, or vice versa, hinges on a number of circumstances. Since this is a general text, we will attempt to consider only the more obvious advantages and disadvantages of each alternative.

*Intensive distribution.* If the manufacturer elects to market through all outlets of the chosen type or types that will buy his products, he may be able to gain complete coverage of his total market rather quickly. Merely by the laws of chance at least one outlet in each market area should be willing to handle his product. Moreover, there is apt to be fairly uniform quality of distributor performance throughout a manufacturer's market, since one could expect to find both good and poor distributors in every market area, many of whom would be handling his product. However, the degree of cooperation the manufacturer receives from his several outlets covering the same territory is likely to be small because none receives preferential treatment and each is competing with the others in the sale of the manufacturer's product.

*Selective distribution.* If the manufacturer pursues a selective strategy, he must fit the chosen outlets into a mosiac of areas in which they operate to be sure that all parts of the market are covered. He also has the problem of adjusting claims to territories where the trading areas of two or more selected outlets overlap.

Perhaps the most serious drawback is that the manufacturer puts all his marketing eggs in one or two baskets in each territory. The distributor who looks good on paper or under analysis may disclose clay feet in action, but by then the manufacturer is stuck with him. Usually, it is not possible to get the best distributor in every market; in some areas, it may not even be possible to get a good one unless the manufacturer is himself a prize catch for any distributor. The quality of the manufacturer's marketing performance in an area depends almost entirely on the excellence of his selected distributor there.

The seriousness of this disadvantage is indicated by the high percentage of manufacturer's agents, sales agents, and many distributors who are one-man firms or partnerships. This means that their continuity is highly uncertain. The manufacturer who follows a selective strategy constantly faces the risk of losing an outlet in at least one of his market areas, and in the meantime being without good representation there.

While the manufacturer can designate one distributor as his sole outlet in a given area and make a valid contract to this effect, he cannot legally make a contract that requires the distributor to refrain from handling the products of a competitor if, by so doing, he limits competition. The courts are so rigid in determining when such an agreement limits competition that, for all intents and purposes, all contracts limiting the distributor's choice of suppliers are to be avoided. While the case establishing this legal principle involved the marketing of a consumer good, gasoline, it applies to industrial products as well. The selective strategy when carried to the extent of the so-called exclusive franchise, can be exclusive on only one side, that of the manufacturer. It thus leaves him in a weak position unless his product has unusual attractiveness and potentialities of profit to the distributor.

On the other hand, a selective strategy tends to generate a much closer working relationship with the manufacturer because the selected middleman has a real stake in the manufacturer's success. Consequently, the manufacturer can usually exert a significantly greater degree of control over the distributor of his products under a selective strategy than an intensive one.

The spirit of cooperation between manufacturer and middleman and the recognition of common interest which supports it tend to produce a higher quality of marketing effort by selected distributors and agents than is possible under an intensive strategy. This manifests itself in more aggressive selling effort by the outlet, greater willingness to carry adequate and representative stocks, more active cooperation in promotional programs, and greater willingness to equip himself and his sales force to render the kind of service called for by the manufacturer's strategy. However, the extent to which a manufacturer can expect to enjoy these advantages has definite limits. Within the outlet's operational pattern, the manufacturer's products are still in active conflict with those of other manufacturers for the limited time and effort the agent or distributor has to spend on his entire line.

The manufacturer who pursues a selective strategy can expect some savings in marketing costs. He will have fewer accounts to call on than under an intensive plan. The savings will probably not be commensurate with the reduction in number of accounts, because salesmen's travel time will tend to remain about the same and the average call will tend to be longer. But salesmen can usually spend more of their calling time in constructive effort to move the product into the hands of users and less of it in the struggle to get an order. Since the outlets would be fewer, the average order is likely to be larger, with resulting reductions in order-handling costs.

The selective strategy also is likely to provide the manufacturer with a distributor sales force that is better informed and better equipped to sell his product than would be possible with any other indirect alternative. If a distributor knows that the business he develops for a product in his territory belongs to him and can be served by no one else, it is clearly to his benefit to have his salesmen properly trained by sending them to the producer's factory and by cooperating in other training programs the manufacturer may develop. This is especially important to the maker of highly technical products or those that require technical service.

## Policy questions

An effective strategy requires the support of a well-planned set of policies. These ordinarily include decision rules with regard to how the manufacturer will handle direct sales (house accounts), how much inventory he will expect distributors to carry, how much protection he will afford them, the amount of compensation he will offer outlets, how his products will be priced to them, the kind of marketing assistance he will give and what type of information feedback he wants in return.

*House accounts.* In almost every industry there are certain firms, usually large, that prefer to buy industrial goods direct from the maker; some even refuse to purchase in any other way. Many manufacturers have a few customers whose patronage volume is so great that they cannot afford to take the chance of losing it. Such accounts are usually solicited by executives high up in the marketing organization, even by members of top management. Such customers are often called house accounts, and their denial to the firm's distributors or agents is usually a delicate matter in administering channel relationships.

But most distributors and agents are not without an understanding of the facts of business life, and unless the house account policy is carried to extremes they will usually accept it after due complaint and negotiation. The manufacturer may be able to work out an arrangement with his distributors whereby the outlets carry stocks for, and make deliveries on, blanket contracts with house accounts, and are compensated by receiving an agreed-on portion of their ordinary margin.

When the house-account policy is carried to such an extreme that all the profitable customers are sold direct and the distributor is left with a prospect list composed mainly of cats and dogs, he is likely to view the whole arrangement with something less than unrestrainable enthusiasm. The distributor feels that he is allowed to handle only orders unprofitable for the manufacturer to solicit and deliver; the result would seem to be a situation in which the distributor cannot keep his business alive, let alone make a profit. This is not necessarily true. It is true that most of the customers left to the distributor under this policy will be little ones whose orders for any one manufacturer's goods are too small to be profitable. Yet, when the needs of such a buyer for the products of several manufacturers are lumped, as they are likely to be when placed with a distributor, the resulting total may be big enough to be profitable. It must be admitted, however, that this idea is hard to sell to a distributor who sees the manufacturer depriving him of a large volume of profitable business.

Some manufacturers follow the policy of crediting the distributor with all direct sales they make in his territory and allowing him his regular gross profit on the volume involved in them. In some cases, a selling charge may be assessed against such business, and the distributor credited with the net. Other producers of industrial goods take such orders but turn them over to the distributor for delivery.

*Inventory requirements.* Most makers of industrial products who market through distributors require some assurance that the distributor will carry a stock of the manufacturer's products sufficiently representative of his line and adequate in size to enable the distributor to fill all orders, except the very largest, without delay. This is an ideal earnestly sought but rarely achieved. Most manufacturers recognize that they must maintain stocks at convenient points from which they can supply distributors with goods to satisfy unusually large or emergency demands and requests for products needed infrequently.

If the manufacturer seeks to establish and enforce an inventory requirement that is too heavy, he is liable to lose the cooperation of his distributors. Probably the most sensible policy is that of starting each distributor off with a standard inventory based on the sales experience of the average outlet, and then working out an individual inventory requirement for him on the basis of his own experience during the first year or two after the relationship is established.

A policy of permitting returns of obsolete merchandise as well as overstocks of slow-moving goods is warmly welcomed by many distributors. This can be done during an annual review of distributors' stocks in which distributors and supplier cooperate. Although some manufacturers make a service charge, usually one percent, for returns of overstocks, a policy of allowing returns of overstocked and obsolete items can do much to win distributors' cooperation in any inventory program the manufacturer may wish to establish.

*Protection.* A harmonious relationship within the channel system usually requires that a manufacturer be explicit about the degree of protection he proposes to give intermediaries handling his products. Even marketers pursuing an intensive strategy may limit sales to one group of middlemen—for example, mill supply houses or firms specializing in abrasives—and refuse orders from other distributors who might sell to the same users.

A manufacturer pursuing a selective strategy may market through only one outlet in a given area—an exclusive outlet—or he may select two or three intermediaries as his only outlets in each territory or market segment. By the second practice, of course, he gains the benefit of competition among the selected outlets, but loses the enthusiasm and cooperation that often results when the distributor knows that whatever business he generates for the product belongs to him.

Another matter that involves the manufacturer's willingness to protect his selected dealers is his handling of direct inquiries he receives as a result of advertising or general trade information. If he follows them up with his own marketing facilities and tries to turn them into sales, he is likely to arouse distrust and resentment among his agents or distributors. If, on the other hand, he sends the inquirer the desired information and refers the inquiry to the appropriate selected outlet, together with a copy of his reply, he engenders confidence that he has no intention of undercutting the agent or distributor.

The distributor also wants to know what protection the manufacturer is prepared to offer him on the prices of his floor stocks in case of price reductions. Some manufacturers extend complete protection on all stocks the distributors hold when a price reduction occurs. Then, when the manufacturer reduces his price he simply credits each distributor's account with the amount of the reduction on all stocks held by the outlet. Often the distributor's statement on the amount of such stocks is accepted without checking.

Other manufacturers extend such protection only on stocks the distributor has purchased within the 30-day period immediately preceding the reduction date. Still others notify their distributors of an impending reduction at a set period, often 30 days, prior to the date it is to take effect. This allows the distributor an opportunity to diminish his purchases during the notification period and to approach the effective date with his stock at a minimum. From the standpoint of the manufacturer, this policy has the disadvantage that during the notification period the flow of orders may dry up, followed by a rush of emergency orders to replace stocks on or immediately after the effective date. Also, some distributors inevitably get caught with stocks on hand and are disgruntled. As the effective date approaches, moreover, users of the product are likely to be unable to buy it from distributors who have cut their stocks below the danger point in preparation for the price change.

The notification-period policy also is weak in that it affords an advantage to nonstock-carrying and inadequately stocked distributors selling the goods of a manufacturer who operates on a blanket basis. During the notification period, such a distributor can be very busy taking orders for future delivery at a lower price, while his stock-carrying rivals are trying to work off their inventories at the old price. Users soon become aware that a price reduction is to be made, and they adopt a hand-to-mouth buying policy that tends to defeat the entire purpose of the practice. In addition, the policy penalizes the very distributors most valuable as outlets for the manufacturer's products.

Probably the prime drawback of the notification-period practice is that competitors as well as customers hear about it, and the price-cutting firm loses all the advantages of surprise in its action.

When multiplant users buy centrally, the manufacturers of the goods they purchase must often protect the interests of one selected distributor or agent from infringement by another. This happens when the central buying office of a customer firm located in the territory of one selected distributor or agent makes a contract for equipment or material to be delivered to a branch plant in the territory of another. The second outlet may have done missionary or sales development work on the buying or operating executives of the branch plant, and then each selected agent or distributor feels that he has a claim on some or all of the commission or margin on the sale. Before such situations arise, the manufacturer must work out an equitable basis on which to split margins or commissions between his selected outlets—a basis understood and accepted by all the units in the channel system. It is not necessary that all outlets be enthusiastic about the basis on which splits will be made, but it is essential that all realize it is fair and reasonable, and recognize it as one of the terms of the selective arrangement.

*Compensation.*  The compensation of agents appears chiefly in the form of the commissions paid to them; that of distributors mainly as the margin between the price at which they buy goods and that at which they can sell them.

The percentage an agent gets on sales is apt to be standardized to some extent within trades, although the usual figure may be varied according to the difficulty of selling the product, the volume of sales he expects to realize from it, and the expected duration of the agency relationship. Really, the amount of this percentage is not too important to the manufacturer so long as it is less than the marketing cost-sales volume ratio for which he could get an equally good job by any other means.

Some manufacturers also allow their agents additional compensation for such services as submitting adequate reports of sales calls, carrying on long-range development programs, and other activities which will be beneficial to the manufacturer over the long run but do not result in immediate sales.

The wholesale distributor is interested in the percentage of gross profit he will be able to make on a manufacturer's products. Theoretically, unless an industrial marketer practices price maintenance the distributor can charge whatever price he wants and thus, in some degree, controls the amount of gross profit he receives. In many cases, even when the maker does not legally fix the resale price he may suggest it so strongly that it amounts to a command. This is especially effective when he sells on an exclusive or selective basis. Even when the distributor is free to price an article as he wishes, the prices at which similar products are sold by his competitors fix the limits within which he may choose. In addition, gross-profit percentages are often traditional in a trade; these sometimes command an acceptance equal, or superior, to that enjoyed by legally enforceable price contracts. The net effect is that the prime factor determining the distributor's margin is the price at which the manufacturer sells to him.

*Pricing.* A pricing policy which very much interests distributors is that concerning the way prices are quoted. Some makers of industrial products price their goods net—that is, the figure set down in the price list is the price at which the vendor proposes to sell. Others quote a list price subject to a chain of discounts, such as 40–20–10–10–5 percent. Each of these discounts is subtracted separately from the amount left after the deduction of the previous one.

Thus, in the case just given, if the list price were $1.00 per unit, we would first deduct 40 percent, or 40 cents, leaving 60 cents; we next subtract 20 percent of this, or 12 cents, leaving 48 cents. If we continue this process to the end, we find that the real quoted price is 37 cents. We also may wind up with the suspicion that if we had bargained more ruthlessly we might have forced another 5 or 10 percent discount from the seller. Industrial buyers generally, and especially distributors, prefer the net method of quoting prices. It avoids mistakes and inaccuracies, reduces paper work and laborious computations, and facilitates the computing of resale prices.

The manufacturer who sells through distributors will find it to his advantage to set up a quantity discount system that offers them some price inducement to buy in substantial lots, at least in case or bulk lots, instead of in loose pieces. This is especially desirable when the manufacturer sells on an open-territory basis and so has no contractual means of controlling the lot sizes in which his customers order. Unless he adopts some such pricing system, he is likely to be constantly plagued with the necessity of filling orders for 3, 4, 5, 6, or 8 units when the goods are packed 10 or 12 to the case. Filling such orders is highly expensive. A quantity discount system based on shipping case lots or bulk containers is usually not too difficult to legally defend under the restrictions of the Robinson-Patman Act.

The industrial products manufacturer who markets through distributors will do well to clearly state in his price book the freight allowances and equalization arrangements he is prepared to grant. This matter is equally important to the producer who sells direct, since both the distributor and direct buyer are likely to compute the purchase price of an article on a delivered basis, with freight charges included.

Distributors are divided on what should be the manufacturer's attitude on price-cutting. Of course, every distributor would be very happy if the manufacturers of the products he sells were to prevent other distributors from cutting the prices of those products. He is often not so enthusiastic about an attempt to fix the prices at which he must resell. The manufacturer's practice with respect to price-cutting is not so important when he sells to distributors on a selected basis, for then the distributor does not have to face the price competition of his rivals. It is usually very important to the success of the producer who sells on a blanket basis.

*Marketing assistance.*    Most industrial goods manufacturers who market through agents or distributors find it necessary to mesh their own marketing activities into those of their outlets, and to provide various types of marketing assistance for them. This may involve trivial operating adjustments or elaborate and very costly programs. We will confine our discussion to those most widely used.

*1. Small-order handling.*    Many distributors think the manufacturer whose product is often bought by users in small, broken-package orders should bear some of the cost generated by this characteristic. Some manufacturers make a special allowance to distributors for handling such orders. Others pack their goods two, four, or six units to a shelf package; six, three, or two packages fit into the regular dozen-unit packing case, and each can conveniently be taken out by the distributor and sold as a unit, with considerable reduction in handling cost compared with the cost of breaking open the standard-dozen packing case and handling the items one by one. Sometimes, the greater attractiveness of such packages to the distributor is more than worth the added costs involved.

*2. Advertising.*    A manufacturer can use advertising to promote his distributors' cooperation. This process begins with the preparation of the advertising itself. If it is to mean anything to the distributor, its quality must be such that it will help to sell the manufacturer's goods. Its effectiveness as a tool for securing outlet cooperation will be augmented if it is constructed so that the distributor and his salesmen can use it in their selling work. This will not happen unless those who prepare the copy for the manufacturer study the distributors' sales problems and methods and the buying motives and practices of their customers to know what material will be useful in selling and in what form it will be most useful.

This, in turn, will not happen unless the marketing manager insists on it. The manufacturer must then follow up by merchandising his advertising to the distributors—that is, by showing them how to use it in their sales work and by selling them on using it. But no amount of merchandising work will induce salesmen to use advertising that is not useful in the first place.

The manufacturer who markets through selected distributors can greatly increase the value of his advertising to them by including their names in the copy. The number of selected outlets used by the industrial goods maker is usually small enough so that he can include their names and the cities or areas in which they operate as a regular feature of his copy.

3. *Missionary salesmen.* Missionary salesmen are employed by manufacturers to call on distributors' customers for the purpose of promoting the sale of their products. Although the role of the missionary salesman is more to stimulate interest in the manufacturer's products than to take orders for them, any orders he does receive are usually submitted to the appropriate distributor and the distributor enjoys his regular gross profit margin on them.

The number of missionary men a manufacturer utilizes is usually much smaller than the number of salesmen he would have to employ to market direct. They call on the customer much less frequently than the direct-selling salesman. In many cases, they call only on the largest and most important customers. In others, they may specialize on prospective users whom the distributor finds hard or impossible to sell.

The distributor tends to look on the missionary salesman with mixed emotions. He may be glad for the extra business represented by the orders the missionary man turns over, but he is by no means sure that all turnover sales represent added volume he would not have gotten without the missionary salesman. His own salesmen are usually quite sure that practically all such volume is merely business they would have gotten at the proper time in the course of their usual contacts with the trade. They may develop a feeling that the chief purpose of the missionary man is to show them up. This, in turn, may create a morale problem for the distributor.

The distributor may have a suspicion that the manufacturer's missionary sales force is really a disguised means of developing contact with the market so that at some appropriate future time the producer may shift to direct marketing. Such cases are not lacking. A thin-skinned distributor may feel that a force of missionary men is in itself evidence that the manufacturer suspects he is not doing a good job and is a sort of left-handed insult. But some industrial goods makers have for years marketed through distributors supplemented by missionary men, with confidence and cooperation on both sides. Such an attitude is usually the fruit of a long-continued relationship that supplies a sound basis for it.

The use of missionary men allows the manufacturer to depend on the distributor to supply such services as routine selling, stock carrying, order handling, delivery, and credit extension, while at the same time he may gain through his missionary force some of the benefits of specialized creative selling.

*4. Training.* The industrial marketer who sells his products through distributors usually finds it desirable to provide some sort of training program for his distributors' salesmen. Some such programs are very elaborate; others are quite elementary. Almost all are designed to give the salesmen a better knowledge of the manufacturer's product, how it is made, its technical properties, and how and for what it can be used satisfactorily. Some makers seek to train the salesmen in improved selling techniques, although this is usually left to the distributor.

Many manufacturers offer to train the distributor's salesmen at the factory. A firm that makes industrial tape required its salesmen to hold regular sales training meetings for its distributors' salesmen, mainly to impart product information. The company's salesmen were expected to train the distributors' salesmen in the field in groups of two or three at a time; they also had to help the distributors' men in selling accounts that required unusual technical knowledge or influence.

*Feedback.* Channel relationships are like other human contacts in that areas of frustration and irritation tend to develop. They are also alike in that little sore spots tend to merge and grow into big ones if left untreated.

Therefore, the wise marketing manager tries to provide a feedback of information from the field so that he may know what is happening in his channels and in their contacts with the market. This is not always easy. Sometimes, agents and distributors are not sure in their own minds about the precise sources of dissatisfaction with the relationship. Often, if not too acute, dissatisfaction remains unexpressed. If the source of discontent is trivial or irrational or highly personal and selfish, as it often is, the agent or distributor is loath to bring it out into the open, but tends to rationalize by ascribing it to some logical cause that may be non-existent.

Usually, a proper feedback system will disclose the existence of channel discontent, although not always its causes. Once this area of soreness is located, the manufacturer can set about finding its cause. There are several sources of feedback and diagnostic information.

*1. Correspondence.* Written communication with middlemen will inevitably contain complaints, and every complaint represents a possible point of irritation. Despite the fact that some people are chronic complainers, systematic analysis of correspondence can provide reliable tip-offs about impending trouble.

*2. Representatives.* Those whose responsibility it is to maintain reasonably regular contact with a supplier's middlemen should be an effective source of information feedback. Depending on the size of the manufacturer and the design of the channel structure, his representatives might include sales and marketing managers as well as both regular and missionary salesmen.

3. *The trade grapevine.*  Personal acquaintance with his opposite numbers in competing firms as well as in firms marketing complementary products can provide a manager with important information, particularly if he is willing to reciprocate. Salesmen and advertising personnel are probably on grapevines, too, at least at lower and more specialized levels. While information which comes through them must be examined critically, the truth level of grapevine inputs is often rather high.

4. *Attitude surveys.*  Field surveys are almost always useful sources of information, but expensive. They are particularly effective in determining the exact nature of a problem which has been disclosed by some other source.

## SUMMARY

A channel of distribution can be structured according to one of three general patterns: direct, indirect, and mixed. The direct channel affords the manufacturer a great deal of control but at very high cost. The indirect channel usually involves substantially lower cost but sacrifices the manufacturer's control. The mixed channel offers a way of trading-off control and cost on an area-by-area basis. In any market area or segment in which the marketer decides not to sell direct, he must choose between a selective strategy and an intensive one. He must decide whether he will sell through one or a relatively few outlets or many. Each of these choices has its advantages and drawbacks.

Whatever the strategic choice of the marketer, he must support it with a well-planned set of channel policies. In this regard it is usually desirable for the manufacturer to state his decision rules concerning how he will handle house accounts and the kind of protection his outlets will be offered. It is also important that he be explicit about the inventory obligations of his outlets, the amount of compensation to be allowed, how prices will be quoted, the kind of marketing assistance which will be forthcoming, and the kind of information he needs from his intermediaries.

# 16

# CHANNEL LOGISTICS

THE PRECEDING two chapters emphasized how the structure of the marketing channel and the relationships within it can be fitted to the task of moving a manufacturer's products from his plant to the offices, plants, and job sites of his customers. If this movement is to be achieved with any degree of efficiency, the strategic plan for bringing it about must be supplemented with a plan for coordinating the movement of products through the various intermediaries involved. Coordinating the physical movement of products includes such varied activities as production scheduling, storage, inventory control, materials handling, packaging, order processing, transportation, and plant and warehouse site selection. The analogy between them and the tasks required to supply weapons and material at proper times and places to support military operations is apparent.

The nature of the logistical problem and its bearing on the ultimate success of the strategic plan varies with the type of the product involved as well as with the structure of the channel itself. A manufacturer of heavy equipment engineered for specific applications, for example, is not confronted with the necessity of carrying a finished goods inventory. On the other hand, such a firm may well face problems of scheduling production so as to meet promised delivery dates. Large equipment may also pose transportation problems if units exceed usual railroad or highway size limitations. Companies that do assemble or manufacture for inventory usually face a wide range of problems in storage, stock control, location, order processing, traffic management, and packaging. Success in dealing with such problems requires a comprehensive plan and a system for executing it.

## THE LOGISTICAL PLAN

The concept of physical distribution as an operating subsystem within the larger system represented by total company activity has been current in management thinking since the 1950s. It is now widely recognized that the interdependence of the different distribution functions affords the opportunity for significant cost savings through proper coordination.[1] However, progress in this direction is often slow, due to the practice of splitting physical distribution among traditional functional areas of a company. Executives in charge of these functional areas are understandably concerned with the unique problems of their own departments and do not always take into account the effect of their operations on the business as a whole. This is not a criticism of department managers, because their perception of total system costs and the contribution of various system components to this total is often blurred by the traditional grouping and departmentation of functions.

Production managers, for example, tend to favor long production runs to smooth out operating cycles and to secure low unit manufacturing costs. The effect of such action on the company's inventory burden may not appear to them to be of much consequence. Indeed, if responsibility for inventory is assigned to another department, such as purchasing or materials management, manufacturing executives may have no ready access to data that enable them to compute inventory costs at various levels of production. Moreover, if manufacturing is their sole responsibility, they have little incentive to make such calculations.

By the same token, traffic managers may seek to reduce transportation costs by using relatively slow types of transportation and shipping in large quantities. Without carefully appraising the implication of these decisions, they may seriously weaken the company's competitive position. On the other hand, sales managers often insist on fast delivery service for all customers on all products, without appreciating the effect of such a policy on traffic costs or inventory requirements. Similarly, an economy-minded treasurer who wants to reduce the costs of inventory or prevent an escalation of clerical expense may limit both to the extent that he jeopardizes customer service or prevents the use of modern data processing equipment—which might speed up the operating tempo of the entire organization enough to save far more than its additional cost.

There is mounting evidence, nevertheless, that industrial marketers are becoming increasingly aware of the savings to be realized from careful integration of the various logistical elements of physical distribution into a single system. This is the result not only of a pressing need for increased operating efficiency but also of a growing acceptance of the systems approach to marketing.

---

[1] Several textbooks are now available on this subject. See James A. Constantin, *Principles of Logistics Management* (New York: Appleton-Century-Crofts, 1966); Donald J. Bowersox, Edward W. Smykay, and Bernard J. LaLonda, *Physical Distribution Management* (New York: Macmillan, 1968); and Frank H. Mossman and Newton Morton, *Logistics of Distribution Systems* (Boston: Allyn and Bacon, Inc., 1965).

## The need for efficiency

The importance of physical distribution as a buttress to channel strategy stems from the carrying cost of inventory. In the typical firm, this cost may amount annually to as much as 20 to 30 percent or more of inventory book value. The major contributing factors are labor, interest, space charges, taxes, insurance, obsolescence, and shrinkage. Industrial buyers are therefore motivated to keep inventories as low as possible without causing production stoppages or interruptions in other operations as a result of material shortages. A key element in the success with which inventories can be reduced with only a reasonable risk of shortages is the length and reliability of lead time, i.e., the period that elapses between placement of a purchase order and receipt of the goods ordered. The shorter and more dependable the lead time, the smaller is the inventory needed to reduce the risk of shortage to a given level. For this reason, industrial buyers typically place a high priority on fast delivery of materials carried in inventory, as well as on the certainty of their receipt within a known and definite period of time. Control over inventories can be greatly simplified or vastly complicated by the efficiency with which suppliers perform the logistics function.

The need of industrial buyers for efficient logistical support by suppliers has grown with advances in technology. Increased mechanization and automation of production have motivated manufacturers to push the inventory burden on to suppliers by so scheduling the receipt of purchased materials that they can be moved directly into the production process without passing through a warehouse. As the seller becomes increasingly locked into the buyer's operations, he is increasingly compelled to meet a precise and consistent delivery schedule in order to retain the buyer's patronage. Such arrangements also place a premium on effective quality control by the supplier, because specification tolerances in automated plants tend to be much narrower than in other shops.

Similarly, industrial sellers are motivated by cost factors to keep their inventory investment as low as possible without jeopardizing their ability to meet all reasonable customer demands. Analysis often reveals that no more than 10 to 20 percent of the products offered for sale by a manufacturer account for as much as 80 percent of his total sales, while up to 50 percent of the products carried in inventory may represent less than 5 percent of company sales. Such differing rates of sale cause widely varying inventory costs among products and complicate the problem of inventory control. As a rule, they are the result of product diversification, which, in turn, is often due to intensified competition among sellers and a growing heterogeneity of demand. The last tendency has become more pronounced as industrial buyers themselves have been forced by competition and technology to offer new product lines as well as wider assortments of items within existing lines. A multiplicity of product offerings tends to divide any given level of sales volume into smaller segments and thus increases the inventory burden. For example, increasing the number of products offered from 1 to 3 could increase inventory requirements by 50 percent or more. Even if sales increased, inventory might increase at a faster rate.

Other forces are also at work, prompting industrial sellers to seek greater efficiency in moving their products from assembly line to customer. Perhaps the most important factors are the gradual shrinkage in profit margins over the past decade, important technological changes, and a growing readiness to accept logistics as a basic management function. Profits after taxes (as a percent of sales) for all manufacturing corporations in the United States declined approximately 24 percent from 1965 to 1971, or from 5.6 cents per dollar of sales to 4.2 cents per dollar.[2]

This results not only from increased competition in all its aspects but also from steadily rising costs. The escalation in labor costs, particularly, has prompted recognition that the same type of analysis that reduced these costs in many manufacturing operations might well produce significant savings if applied to materials handling, order processing, packaging, and shipping operations.

Several technological developments have a demonstrated capacity to effect important savings when incorporated into a logistics system. Some of the more striking developments have been the piggyback handling of trucks, fishyback (coordinated truck-ship service), trainship, containerization, and air freight. Improvements in materials handling equipment permit faster and easier handling of palletized and unitized material, both within the warehouse and during order assembly. The availability and use of high-speed computers have made possible the development of wholly new concepts of communication, enabling management to keep abreast of very complicated traffic and inventory situations.

## The logistical system

For discussion purposes, the various physical components of a logistic system can be separated into three broad categories—stationary facilities, the transportation network, and location. A stationary facility may be any geographical location in which there is storage or a transfer of goods from one mode of transportation to another. A transportation network includes all types of carriers—rail, water, pipeline, highway, and air—capable of being linked in the movement of merchandise from

---

[2] U.S. Department of Commerce, *Statistical Abstract of the United States, 1972*, p. 483.

seller to customer. Location involves a choice of geographical points, which makes possible the most efficient utilization of both stationary facilities and the transportation network.

*Stationary facilities.* The major type of stationary facility is the warehouse. It may serve as a storage depot, a transit facility for incoming or outgoing merchandise, or as a terminal facility for a transportation company. Industrial sellers utilize warehouses for a variety of logistical needs, such as storage of goods in process held temporarily outside the immediate production area, and receipt and transshipment of finished goods when located at some point between the company's plant and its customers.

The chief use of storage warehouses generally occurs in relation to, and usually in advance of, various production processes. In the equipment part of the industrial market, it is unusual to store finished goods, ready to be delivered to customers, for any length of time. Situations may develop, though, in which a firm produces or purchases a large quantity of a material or component and must store some portion of it for later sale or use. If such situations occur frequently, or with predictable regularity, some form of stationary storage facility is needed. Makers of parts, auxiliary equipment, and MRO items made to stock instead of on order find it necessary to carry substantial stocks, often at widely scattered points, to service user demand.

Transit warehouses, sometimes referred to as distribution warehouses, serve as transshipment points for bulk breaking, accumulating stocks for larger unit shipment, or transfer from one type of carrier to another. Because of their different function, transit warehouses are designed differently and require more flexible, high-speed equipment for efficient operation than do storage warehouses. Merchandise often remains less than a day in such a facility. Consequently, unless such warehouses are highly mechanized their overhead cost tends to be much higher than that of a storage warehouse for a given level of average inventory.

The terminal and station facilities of transportation companies also serve (sometimes involuntarily) as storage depots for manufacturers as well as transit locations at which shipments can be combined or separated. Although terminal facilities are not under the shipper's control, they are as much a part of a firm's logistic system as the facilities it does control.

*The transportation network.* Available for use as transport components of a manufacturer's logistic system are railroads, trucks, ships, pipelines, and aircraft. Historically, railroads have accounted for the largest share of freight tonnage moved in the United States. The ability of these carriers to move large quantities of merchandise over long distances has assured them the major share of the nation's freight business.

Within the past 35 years, however, the motor truck has grown from a carrier that served limited requirements to the dominant element in the movement of local and regional intercity freight. Moreover, the structure of many individual motor carriers is now transcontinental in scope and includes a variety of services, ranging from city delivery to coast-to-coast operations.

Air freight has also shown significant increases in tonnage carried. This reflects determined effort by air carriers to promote air freight as a regular element of a company's transportation network rather than as an emergency measure limited to rush orders. While air freight has been a satisfactory medium for suppliers of specialty and perishable items, manufacturers of heavy or bulk industrial products are deterred by the higher air rates. However, airline representatives argue that although air freight charges are relatively high its use can often reduce delivery time by enough to enable marketers to cut field inventories and even permit more highly centralized manufacturing operations. Either possibility may effect a significant reduction in the total cost of physical distribution.

In certain instances air freight represents the only practical means of transportation. In providing logistical support for petroleum exploration and drilling operations in the Arctic islands, ice-strengthened freight ships and tankers move drilling rigs, supplies, and fuel during the shipping season to a staging point on Melville Island. From here, aircraft are employed on a year-round basis to haul men and material to operating camp sites. A skycrane helicopter was used effectively in solving the problem of how to transport drilling equipment into an almost impenetrable jungle in Columbia, South America. Several hundred tons of drill equipment, plus a helicopter, were loaded onto a ship and delivered to a point 28 miles from the drill site. The helicopter was reassembled and in ten flight hours offloaded the equipment onto the beach. Then it carried the equipment over the jungle and delivered it where needed. Even the 20,200-pound drawworks were transported and placed with precision on the rig floor. Thus the time and heavy costs of building a road were eliminated and in addition drill rig setup time was substantially reduced.

Water carriers, like the railroads, have lost tonnage to other forms of transportation. They have been faced with restrictions on automation at the waterfront, wage rates in excess of those in other transportation industries, and selective rate cutting by competing carriers. In recent years, though, improved facilities have enabled river barge transportation to capture an increasing share of total traffic. As a group, water carriers still represent a sizable share of total tonnage moved. Pipeline carriers have sharply increased their share of total tonnage moved. Pipeline carriers have sharply increased their share of total transportation revenue since 1950. Due to the demand for economical volume movement of fluids and solids in hydraulic suspension, pipeline carriers have extended their service to areas that as recently as 1950 were not considered feasible for pipeline transportation.

In addition to the carriers themselves, at least two auxiliary agencies constitute an important part of the transportation network. These are freight forwarders and freight pools. The freight forwarder provides a transportation service to the shipper by collecting l.c.l. (less than carload) lots of merchandise at a central point, shipping them in c.l. (carload) lots from there to a distribution station near their destination, and then distributing the goods in l.c.l. lots by truck to their respective destinations. The entire remuneration of the forwarder comes from the difference between the less-than-carload rate he charges the shipper and the carload rate at which he moves the merchandise through most of its journey.

A typical operation involving an l.c.l. shipment from Flint, Michigan, to Key West, Florida, might proceed as follows. The shipment is picked up at Flint by a trucking company under contract with the forwarder, and is carried to an assembly station at Detroit. The forwarder has a truckload of 20,000 pounds going south from Detroit, so he has a trucker carry it to Cincinnati, where he has enough goods consigned to Atlanta or Miami to make up a carload. Therefrom, he ships the goods by rail in a c.l. lot from Cincinnati to one of the southern points. A trucker under contract with the forwarder then carries the shipment to its destination. The shipper has only one contract, with the forwarder, although four transport companies handle the shipment during its journey, and he pays the l.c.l. rate from Flint to Key West, which he would have had to do anyway.

From the standpoint of the shipper, the use of the freight forwarder has several advantages.

1. Speed. The forwarder usually ships in a c.l. lot on the same day on regularly scheduled trains.

2. Flexibility. The forwarder is in a position to use all types of transport to gain the most economical combination of speeds and rates. For example, if the nature of the goods permits, he may ship from an eastern port to Texas by trainship—a trip that requires only one day longer but offers a 50 percent saving in rates.

3. Simplicity. The shipper deals with one shipping company.

4. Savings. The shipper gets special carlot service for l.c.l. rates.

5. Tracing. The forwarder supplies the tracing service desired. Since he is a transport specialist, he can probably perform this task more efficiently than can the shipper.

6. Safety. The forwarder may repack shipments that need such service. He also assumes responsibility for collecting damage claims. His specialized knowledge enables him to do this efficiently.

Freight pools are also very useful devices for industrial manufacturers who habitually ship in l.c.l. lots. The freight pool is an association usually composed of a number of l.c.l. shippers. It is organized in the form of a cooperative, and operates just like a freight forwarder but saves for its members the difference between the c.l. rate at which it ships and the l.c.l. rates the members would have to pay if they shipped separately. That this saving can be substantial is evidenced by a comparison of c.l. and l.c.l. rates per 100 pounds on general drug products from the eastern seaboard to the Pacific Coast. If the l.c.l. rate by rail is given a value of 100, other rates compare as shown in the following table:

|        | Rail | Truck | Forwarder | Cooperative association |
|--------|------|-------|-----------|-------------------------|
| l.c.l. | 100  | 83    | 73        | —                       |
| c.l.   | 44   | 58    | 58        | 55                      |

*Location.*[3]    It is apparent that no seller can be equally near all customers or prospective customers, and that space and time impose significant limitations on the movement of goods from seller to buyer. In consequence, the location of the seller's production and distribution facilities in relation to those of customers is an important factor in his ability to deal with the limitations of time and space.

As a general rule, industrial companies tend to conform to one of four locational orientations: raw materials, labor, market, or power. Depending on the nature of the production process, the type of materials required, the characteristics of the end product, and the tendency of buying companies to cluster in a given area (tire manufacturers in Akron, Ohio; musical instrument makers in Elkhart, Indiana), proximity to raw materials may be an overriding consideration. For other manufacturers, proximity to an adequate labor supply or to customers may be the chief determinant of plant location.

While such factors as customer location, or the availability of power supplies, raw materials, or labor may have a primary influence on site selection, often more than one location would satisfy the primary need. This permits selection of the alternative that represents the most advantageous utilization of the transportation network and the warehouse facilities that have been or are to be acquired. Even if the primary constraints of market, power, labor, and raw material leave little choice among alternatives for plant location, distribution points can be selected to minimize transportation costs while maintaining the desired quality of customer service.

Finding the least-cost combination by trading off (adding and sub-

---

[3] Some of the more recent contributions of basic importance to location theory are published in Gerald J. Karaska and David R. Bramhall, eds., *Locational Analysis for Manufacturing* (Cambridge, Mass.: The M.I.T. Press, 1968).

tracting) one category of cost from another, such as accepting higher transportation costs to realize a proportionately greater reduction in storage costs, is no simple task. Even in the case of small manufacturers, the multiplicity of possible trade-offs can be staggering. Perhaps the most effective technique for dealing with this problem is linear programming—a mathematical formulation that assumes that the most important relationships are linear. For example, if transportation costs are linear in relation to volume, it will cost twice as much as one to transport two items of the same bulk and weight a given distance. While the assumption of linearity is not always tenable, recognition of this limitation to the technique should prevent gross errors in its application. Mathematical models often supplemented by the use of the computer can be used in choosing the most economical locations and sizes for distribution warehouses.

## SYSTEM OPERATIONS

The day-to-day operations of a logistical system involve a coordinated group of functions concerned with the *how much, when,* and *where* of product movement. These are the functions of communication, scheduling, inventory control, materials handling, and traffic.

### Communication

The communication element of logistics has both external and internal dimensions. Externally, communication is concerned with the flow of information not only between the company and its customers but also with independent firms and facilitating agencies that comprise the distribution channel. Internally, communication is concerned with the informational linkage among the various administrative units participating in the firm's logistics system.[4]

*External communication.* Information feedback concerning sales, customer complaints, and operating problems in which the seller may be able to assist the customer are of great importance to a logistics system manager. The seller's exact information needs vary, of course, with the characteristics of the market and the dimensions of his marketing effort. Nevertheless, timely information feedback concerning sales to customers, customer credit, competitive prices, terms of sale, and services are essential for proper management of such functions as inventory control, production scheduling, order processing, and expeditious routing of both finished goods and goods in process within the plant and/or warehouse of the seller as well as through the transportation network.

[4] See Normal L. Enger, *Management Information Systems* (New York: American Management Association, Inc., 1969) and Paul M. Stokes, *A Total Systems Approach to Management Control* (New York: American Management Association, 1968).

The external communication system must also produce an information flow in the opposite direction. Since the customer's satisfaction and continued patronage is the end sought by the seller's entire organization, the customer must also be adequately informed of the seller's actions that affect his own operations. The seller's external communication should be designed to keep customers abreast of such information as expected arrival dates of shipments, any anticipated delays en route, incomplete orders, and substitutions, as well as impending changes in price or design. Such status reporting becomes increasingly unnecessary, though, if the logistics system functions consistently as it is supposed to function. At the time of sale, the customer should be given such information as when the shipment will arrive and whether or not inventories permit immediate completion of the order. The cost of status reporting can reach serious proportions when it must be repeated for hundreds of accounts.

*Internal communication.* The proper functioning of a logistics system requires adequate informational links with the various elements of the system as well as with other functional areas of the firm. This does not mean that every informational detail must be incorporated into a system of formal reports and memoranda. In many instances, verbal communication between the persons involved is the most effective means of information exchange. What is necessary, however, is a recognition of the informational needs and some system of verification to assure that data necessary to the functioning of the system are properly transmitted and received. The most critical information categories are those concerned with product availability (amount and place of inventory), order collection (manner in which orders are placed), order processing, order routing, and credit clearance.

## Scheduling

While responsibility for the logistics function seldom includes in-plant or in-process scheduling, complex logistics problems result if the two operations are not properly synchronized. While it is a marketing responsibility to determine how much the company may expect to sell over a given planning period, the production department usually determines how the products will be made, when they will be made, and in what quantities. A conflict of interest between the marketing and production managers may develop over these decisions because of the inconsistency between efficient production—i.e., production in economic lot sizes—and the maintenance of a finished-goods inventory adequate to meet the requirements of customer service often desired by sales executives. Even if production were scheduled for the economic lot size, as determined by customer service and a defensible investment in inventory, the question of timing would still remain.

Fortunately, production scheduling techniques are sophisticated enough to reflect the influence on total costs of inventory carrying charges, transportation volume-shipping cost breakpoints, purchase discounts, and other costs not directly related to the manufacturing process. Consequently, it is possible to determine the true economic lot size if management decides it should be done. Unfortunately, determining the exact sequence in which the various economic lots should be produced requires the reconciliation of sales forecasts and desired operating standards for customer service, with the lead times required by the production department to manufacture products of the desired specifications. Conceptually, responsibility for this reconciliation belongs in the domain of logistics management. A logistics manager is the proper functionary to inform the production department about what quantities of which products must be produced on what schedule, and to provide the quantity and quality of raw materials at the time necessary to support the schedule. Neither the production manager nor the marketing manager is in a position to appraise the effect of his own actions on the operation of the other.

Proper scheduling of the production function is quite important, because once set, the schedule becomes a fixed element in the design of the logistics system. An utterly inflexible schedule can lead to unnecessary effort and exorbitant overtime costs, while a schedule with too much flexibility can result in idle capacity and numerous forms of wheelspinning. A balance between these extremes can often be achieved by scheduling a relatively continuous level of output, while utilizing various transportation alternatives to either speed or slow the transfer of products from one phase of the system to another as needed to match marketing requirements with manufacturing capability.

### Inventory control

As previous discussion has indicated, finished-goods inventory is the buffer between plant output and market demands. The crux of the inventory problem is to maintain assortments and quantities of finished goods in stock adequate for all reasonable customer demands, while maintaining a turnover rapid enough to keep the cost of inventory at a minimum. This requires a determination of the proper amount of each product to be carried, as well as a system of information feedback that will enable management to regulate the flow of finished products into inventory.

*Determining proper inventory levels.* Since demand can never be predicted with accuracy, more inventory than the manufacturer expects to sell must be carried during any given period. This extra stock provides a cushion or safety factor that can absorb unexpected spurts in demand or interruptions in supply that otherwise would produce stock shortages and lost sales. This safety stock represents the real inventory burden, since it is seldom sold out. In this respect, it resembles a fixed, more than a current, asset. This is apparent in Figure 16–1 which shows the familiar sawtooth pattern of order cycles.

How much safety stock should be carried depends on the variability of sales, the costs of carrying inventory, and the seriousness of a stock-out. A stock-out of a widely used standard item ordinarily represents no serious consequence, because orders can easily be filled in from other sources. While inconvenient and perhaps embarrassing to the seller, the cost of completing an order from other sources of supply is usually nominal. But a specialized machine part with little or no interchange-ability is another matter. Sales fluctuations in these items represent a serious problem of control. How much of a buffer management can afford to maintain against the contingency of a shortage depends in large part on the costs generated by various levels of safety stock.

Although some elements of inventory cost—rent, insurance, taxes, shrinkage—can be readily determined, other costs are more difficult to measure. Interest on invested funds, for example, presents a trouble-some estimate, particularly if no substantial part of the investment represents borrowed capital. There is no consensus on what constitutes an appropriate rate of inputed interest in such cases. Some managers use the rate that would have to be paid on the funds if they were bor-rowed from an available source; others use opportunity cost, i.e., the rate of return that could be earned if the funds invested in stocks were applied to some other opportunity (short-term securities or new equip-ment); and at least a few managers completely ignore interest.

For items of limited life, such as certain types of chemicals, electronic

**FIGURE 16–1.** The order cycle

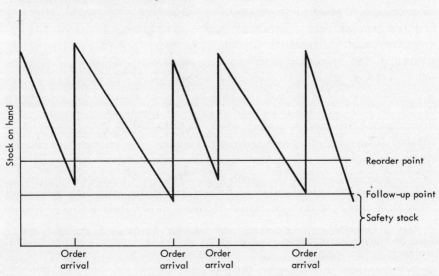

components, and replacement parts, losses that result from obsolescence may be more important than all other costs combined. Unfortunately, obsolescence can be determined with accuracy only after the fact, even though inventory decisions must be made before and during the periods when obsolescence is likely to occur.

Under normal conditions it is important to assign a quantitative value to the seriousness of a stock-out. If the effect is a stoppage on the customer's production line, with consequences that can be estimated, then the cost of a stock-out can be determined at least within a calculable margin of error. If inventory shortages result only in lost current sales and back orders, rather than in lost customers, their cost is the dollar contribution that would have been realized from those sales. Because it is so difficult to estimate the effect of inventory shortages on future sales, the practice of assigning stock-outs a much higher cost value than would be represented by the dollar amount of lost sales is widespread. However, available methods permit fairly accurate estimation of the proper size of the safety stock that should be included in the inventory of an item if realistic values can be assigned to inventory costs and shortages.[5]

In the case of certain products, such as fuel oils, the failure of supply may involve health and safety considerations or may even be a matter of national security. In such instances, reserve stocks must be available without reference to cost, and plans for alternative sources of supply must be prepared to meet the contingency that the in-place logistics system will not be operative.[6]

*The information feedback system.* Information systems for inventory control may take a variety of forms, depending on the number and kinds of items carried, their speed of movement, and the seriousness of a stock-out. Most of the systems, however, can be classified as one of three general types—perpetual, stock count, or visual.

*1. Perpetual.* Perpetual inventory systems provide a continuing picture of the inventory situation, i.e., stock on hand, stock on order, merchandise receipts, and sales. The unique feature of perpetual inventory systems is the collection and posting of sales data for each category of the material or part being controlled. To the stock on hand at the beginning of a period is added receipts of the product, and from their sum are subtracted sales and returns to vendors. The receipts are usually recorded at the end of each working day, while sales and returns are recorded as they occur. The result is a current stock-on-hand figure.

Most manufacturers and industrial distributors who use perpetual inventories keep records in terms of units rather than dollars. A unit

---

[5] See Robert Schlaifer, *Probability and Statistics for Business Decisions* (New York: McGraw-Hill, 1959), chapters 4 and 15.

[6] Planning for emergency conditions is coordinated through the Office of Emergency Preparedness in Washington, D.C.

may be either an individual physical item, such as a centrifugal pump or mechanic's vise, or a standard package, such as a box of washers or keg of nails. It is the lowest common denominator of the inventory practical for counting. Perpetual inventory records on a unit basis afford a complete and current picture of the inventory assortment, as well as the quantities of units in stock, without the need for visual inspection. The dollar value of the inventory can always be ascertained by multiplying the number of units in a given classification by their unit price, and then summing these values for as many classifications as desired.

2. *Stock count.* Stock count systems involve a physical count of products at specified intervals of time. They are, of course, unit systems, and stock on hand can be converted to dollar values by multiplying units by their price. The physical count reveals the stock on hand, items to be reordered, and items in excess supply. The unique feature of this system is that sales are derived from the stock on hand at two different times rather than being recorded separately, as in the perpetual inventory. To the stock on hand at the first count is added the net amount of items received, and from their total the stock on hand at the second count is deducted to determine the quantity sold.

Stock counts are usually made with the aid of a stock list on which is recorded the desired minimum stock of each item, the level at which reorders should be placed, and perhaps the level at which orders should be followed up. The stock on hand is then checked against this list. Since there is no item-by-item record of sales, it is difficult by this system to identify shortages or to determine whether stocks of particular items are being carried in proper relation to expected sales.

3. *Visual.* Although the so-called visual system has many variations, all possess one characteristic in common—the absence of any formal record or list of stock. Typically, the amount of stock that represents the reorder level of an item is physically segregated in some way. When the order picker must go to this segregated stock to fill an order, he is reminded of the need to reorder the item. Sometimes, the segregation is more visual than physical, as when the reorder level is merely indicated by a stripe painted on the side of the bin in which the item is stored.

Even the simplest of information systems entails cost, and any system is of value only when the results obtained from it outweigh the cost of installing and operating it. As a general rule, it is advisable to divide the inventory into classifications based on the urgency of control and to be selective in the application of information systems. For example, an inventory might be divided into thirds, as follows: first part—the 10 percent of the stock that accounts for 30 percent of the company's sales volume; second part—the 30 percent of the stock that accounts for 50 percent of the company's sales volume; third part—the 60 percent of the stock that accounts for 20 percent of the company's sales volume.

These proportions would, of course, vary from one manufacturer to another, but they are not unusual. Depending on the rate of sale and the value of items in these categories, a daily stock count might be used for the items in the first part. These are the fast movers, and the importance of maintaining proper assortments in a fast-moving item as well as the relatively small number of items involved make daily stock counts feasible. A perpetual inventory might be appropriate for items in the second class. These are slower moving than items in the first category, but important enough that a daily on-hand figure is needed. However, they are probably too numerous to justify a daily stock count. Since items in the third part are clearly the slow movers, visual control would probably be adequate for this stock and would be more economical than either of the other alternatives.

### Materials handling

The chief activity conducted in warehouses is materials handling. Like other functional elements of a logistics system, it must be carefully planned and organized so as to mesh properly with the remaining parts of the system. The efficiency with which materials are handled depends in large part on the volume concerned, the degree of fluctuation in volume, local wage rates, the relative cost of space, and the success with which the activity can be organized to minimize idle time, overtime, breakage, breakdowns, and errors. Modern facilities and the latest equipment do not of themselves insure an efficient operation, although they are clearly important contributing factors to efficiency.

A materials-handling system includes not only equipment and various storage aids, but also supporting components and warehouse layout.

*Equipment.* The trend to mechanization in the materials-handling operation continues, and it is to be expected that an increasing number of companies will seek its benefits. The forklift truck came into wide use with the advent of pallets and containers designed to accommodate forklift tines or blades. More recently, the clamp truck, which is capable of picking up and moving loads not palletized or strapped, has received substantial acceptance. Both types of trucks are available in a variety of load capacities, speeds, and widths. Also available is a wide assortment of towing tractors, trains, conveyors, hand-powered equipment, containers, tying devices, bins, drawers, and other storage aids.

*Supporting components.* The pallet or container, together with the storage racks or other equipment required to stock them, are generally referred to as supporting components. It is apparent that the pallet or container size selected must be consistent with the equipment employed and the design of the warehouse or other storage areas used. Many firms have redesigned their product packages or containers to dimensions that permit unitization—simultaneous handling of standard numbers of packages or containers—in the form of a cube or a hexagonal cross section. These two forms are thought to be the most effective for maximum space utilization. Such redesigning can lead to trouble, however, unless the pallet package design also fits into the dimensions of transportation vehicles and the materials-handling systems of customers.

*Warehouse layout.* Layout of the warehouse involves space utilization planning so as to achieve an orderly flow of materials from receiving, to storage, to order selection (which sometimes includes packaging or repackaging), to shipping areas, at minimal cost. Ineffective planning of space utilization can incorporate into materials-handling systems a cost penalty that may be extremely difficult to overcome. As a general rule, space utilization is most efficient if goods can be moved in one direction through the warehouse, while some materials are still permitted to bypass one or more stages of the storage process. For example, it is usually advisable to expedite the handling of materials with a rapid turnover by so arranging layout that they can be moved directly from inbound transportation vehicles to the order selection and assembly area. By the same token, layouts should be planned to avoid crosshauling within areas and to make possible the concentration of the greatest quantity of stock at the point of greatest need. This serves to expedite order picking as well as movement to the next stage of the logistics function.

Layout of the storage area itself includes the pattern of storage locations as well as the surrounding network of aisleways. As a general rule, stock placement should be guided by the activity of the item, size per unit, compatibility with items stored in adjacent locations—e.g., nuts and bolts—and consistency with one-directional traffic flow. The relative emphasis each of these factors should receive is, in turn, influenced by the system of order selection that has been chosen or is under consideration.

Order selection systems tend to belong to one of three general types: out and back, picker, or conveyor. The so-called out and back type of order selection makes use of forklift trucks and is generally appropriate where items are picked in large quantities. Order picker selection, on the other hand, is typically used for the selection of small items, i.e., manpower is used to pick and transport the items selected. Where the activity of the stock warrants a higher degree of automation, conveyors are often used in combination with pickers. In this instance, the pickers are stationed at various intervals along the conveyor, and transfer items ordered from storage racks in their assigned areas by hand to the conveyor.

Which of these selection methods is most appropriate depends on the weight and bulk of the item stored, the number of units typically included in an order, the frequency with which the item is ordered—i.e., activity—and the distance over which it must be transported to reach the next stage in the materials-handling operation. Since each of these factors can usually be assigned a quantitative value, it is possible to develop an index number that can serve as a useful guide in arriving at the best combination of storage pattern and selection procedure.

### Traffic management[7]

The traffic function can be divided into two general areas of responsibility—traffic planning and traffic analysis. Traffic planning is concerned with the use of transportation services, whereas traffic analysis deals with the evaluation of these services in terms of the efficiency of the logistics system. In many firms, the cost of transportation is the largest component in the total cost of logistics. However, the significance of transportation costs should not overshadow the importance of planning the service so that it is compatible with the overall logistics pattern of the firm.

*Traffic planning.* Traffic planning involves the selection of carriers, documentation of shipments, payment of carrier charges, establishment of standards for carrier performance, and designation of action to be taken in the event of substandard performance. The documentation and information feedback, which provide data for specific comparison of traffic performance with standards, are of particular importance.

The basic documents of transportation are the bill of lading, the freight bill, and the freight claim. In general, they provide for proper identification of shipment, billing of freight charges, and adjustment of charges incorrectly billed as well as the settlement of claims resulting from loss or damage to products during shipment. These documents represent the legally enforceable obligation of carrier and shipper to each other, and they supply the information on carrier performance necessary to detect deviations from the shipper's performance standards.

The three most important indexes of carrier performance are billing, delivery time, and condition of delivered goods. Since carriers are not bound by rate quotations or routing promises made by their representatives, shippers must maintain their own traffic files and updated rate lists to assure that the rates they are charged are correct. To minimize the time and effort necessary to audit freight bills, many shippers confine their audits to bills above a certain dollar amount or engage the services of an independent traffic consultant.

In order to stay informed about the performance of hired carriers, traffic managers utilize an assortment of reports. The most common probably are the freight allocation report, the damage report, and the transit time report. Freight allocation reports indicate the amounts of

---

[7] A highly competent treatment of this subject is contained in Charles A. Taff, *Management of Physical Distribution and Transportation* (5th ed., Homewood, Ill.: Richard D. Irwin, Inc., 1972).

freight offered by the shipper to various carriers, and can often be instrumental in exacting the desired level of performance from carriers. Damage reports are usually filed by customers at the request of the shipper, and not only assure that customers are compensated for goods damaged in transit, but also over time produce a record of the carrier's efficiency in handling merchandise.

Transit time reports are also typically submitted by the customer at the request of the shipper in order to reveal the consistency with which the carrier maintains a given delivery schedule. A basic traffic management objective is to standardize transit time from carriers. If the time required to deliver goods from seller to buyer can be predicted with accuracy, one of the variables of inventory control is eliminated for the buyer, and an important sales appeal is created for the seller.

*Traffic analysis.* Over time, the services of a hired carrier may deteriorate, and the shipper may be confronted with the necessity of a through reappraisal of the transportation function. In order to avoid the possibility that such decisions will be made without adequate investigation, a continuous program of traffic analysis is often advisable as an integral part of the logistics function. Such a program might include such projects as periodic estimates of the total cost of transportation, assessing the cost of privately owned transportation, and/or identifying the factors that influence rates as well as the course of rate negotiation.

The total cost of transportation is not reflected in published rates or accessorial charges; it must be estimated. Included in the total cost figure are such items as loading and unloading costs, packaging and dunnage, in-transit loss or damage not covered by carrier liability, obsolescence or deterioration of products due to transit time, and time devoted by management to the control of contract transportation services.

Loading and unloading costs alone could make a low-quoted rate the highest cost between two points. Different carriers require different types of loading facilities, and some offer more loading assistance than others. Moreover, the extra charges for this assistance tend to vary with the type of loading procedure employed by both buyer and shipper. In nearly all cases, no service of this kind is included in published rates.

Although carriers normally prescribe minimum specifications for packaging, the important consideration is the susceptibility of a product to damage. If products are highly susceptible to damage, it may be necessary to provide additional bracing or other protective devices, i.e., dunnage, for safe shipment. While some carriers provide crossbracing and compartmentized vehicles to reduce the possibility of damage, others do not. If not, dunnage must be furnished by the shipper and included in the cost of the transportation function. By the same token, shippers incur additional insurance costs if the carrier has quoted released value rates, i.e., rates under which the carrier's liability in a given shipment is limited to a certain amount.

A continuous program of traffic investigation might also include feasibility studies of owned versus hired transportation, as well as means for negotiating lower quoted rates. To many industrial firms, particularly the larger ones, owned transportation offers significant advantages. It gives the shipper more control over transit time, greater flexibility in adapting the service to the need and special equipment of customers, and a reduction in paper work associated with maintaining tariff files and allocation records, preparing bills of lading, and submitting claims.

Matched against these advantages, though, are costs that require careful appraisal. An owned transportation service requires a capital investment, and both the investment and the manpower needed to operate the service must be efficiently managed. Moreover, the management problems themselves run the gamut from insufficient equipment versus idle time to complex labor relations problems. The labor aspect can be a formidable drawback to a firm with no experience in managing a transportation facility.

Investigating the rate-making process with a view to securing either a downward adjustment of rates or a rate structure that includes more service is probably undertaken to some degree by all large shippers. While rate making is a very complex subject, well beyond the scope of the present discussion, it should suffice to say that rate adjustment is not a panacea for transportation problems, nor are negotiations aimed at securing rate reductions without their elements of risk and cost.

## SUMMARY

Logistics is a function of facilities and their location as well as a transportation network. It is an operation in which such activities as production scheduling, storage, inventory control, order handling, packaging, selection of plant and warehouse sites, and transportation, with their resulting costs, are balanced against the value of customer satisfaction. Customers' needs, the supplier's inventory situation, and the costs and performance of transport agencies must be known. Many firms are making significant savings by holding inventories at a proper level to balance costs against the losses resulting from out-of-stock situations. To do this effectively, management must create and operate a system that enables the manager to know at any time how much inventory there is, where it is, and how much will probably be needed at what locations. The provision of efficient handling equipment is vital.

An effective system of information and communications is also needed to balance the total costs of transportation—not merely freight rates—against the benefits of speed and certainty of delivery. During recent years air transport and pipelines have been increasing their shares of the total movement of goods, although railroads and water carriers are substantially improving their services. Traffic planning and traffic analysis help management make the most efficient use of transportation and assure that transportation services fit the logistics pattern of the firm.

# PART VI

# Marketing strategy:
# The price component

WHILE PRICE is not the only factor influencing the demand for industrial goods and the patronage of industrial buyers, it is an indispensable part of marketing strategy. A price that is too high invites both competition and buyer resistance. While a price that is too low may well discourage competition, it will also deflate profits and may incur losses.

In many instances the prices of industrial goods fall into patterns that are fairly uniform throughout an industry. Nevertheless, a marketer must decide whether or not to follow industry patterns, and if not, how much to deviate from them. These decisions must be made against a background of environmental forces including competition, changing costs, and shifting patterns of demand. We discuss the more important of these forces in chapter 17. The pricing decision itself is treated in chapter 18, and the major choices in pricing policy are the subject of chapter 19.

# 17

## CONDITIONS AFFECTING
## PRICE

LIKE OTHER components of marketing strategy, planning prices involves a substantial input of intelligence concerning environmental as well as operational conditions. Those conditions to which the success of pricing strategy is particularly sensitive are competition, costs, and demand.

## COMPETITION

The nature of competition in industrial markets is influenced by the size of firms, the types of products marketed, their life cycle, and the phenomenon known as price leadership.

### Firm size

In the typical industrial market as few as three or four large firms often account for most of the business. They are usually well financed, active in research, and responsible for developing and introducing most of the technical improvements in the industry. Since they are often organized to market a broad line of products on a mass basis, many of their costs are joint costs. This encourages managers to think in terms of market share and "responsible competition" as strategic goals. While they seek a certain percentage of total sales volume, they rarely take pricing action which results in sudden changes in market share. Product development and customer service represent the chief arenas of competition.

Medium-sized firms often imitate the actions of the larger firms, although their commitments to research generally are much less and their product lines generally more limited. They often concentrate on products too specialized in design or needed in quantities too small to be profitably supplied by larger firms with their less flexible facilities. These businesses seldom initiate price changes. This may be due in part to fear of retaliation, but it is more likely the result of a satisfactory profit position.

Some industries are also characterized by a number of quonset hut or garage operators, who often capture a very small part of the total business but exercise an influence out of all proportion to their market share. Their marketing is usually limited to one or a few products whose technology is simple and whose production does not require expensive equipment or refined operating know-how. Managers typically ride on the technological coattails of the larger firms and know neither the words overhead nor research. Since their customer service is usually rudimentary, price is often their sole appeal. Larger firms can ordinarily do little to meet the price reductions of these enterprises without risking a price war on the one hand or violating antitrust laws on the other.

## Product type

As a result of the influence of firm size, price may occupy a minor place in the total competitive picture of an industry. This often is true for the highly technical, specialized products. It also tends to be true of capital equipment, since a small difference in operating efficiency, aggregated during the life of the machine, can much more than offset a considerable variation in original price.

On the other hand, there are at least two conditions prevalent in many industrial markets which foster price competition. One is the difficulty of achieving product differentiation through advertising; the other is the widespread use of product standards. Since brands, trademarks, and the sheer volume of advertising, in themselves, constitute weak appeals to professional buyers, they provide little protection against price competition and little support for promotional campaigns.

Moreover, many materials and items of equipment are standardized. Some product standards are established by government, as in the case of many materials used in the processing of foods and drugs. Other product standards are set by trade associations, such as NEMA (National Electrical Manufacturers' Association) which has established widely used standards for electric motors. Some product standards, such as those which apply to steel and other metals, are highly complex.

Standards for steel, for example, consist of basic specifications for each type of steel, plus a series of "ons" and "offs" for the addition or omission of certain ingredients, variations in the amounts of ingredients used, or the addition or omission of various treatment processes. Competitors offer for sale substantially the same product in each classification, or a product whose quality equals or exceeds a common level. This substantially eliminates product quality as a competitive element. Consequently, added emphasis is placed on service and price as bases of competition. The result is that the marketer of standardized industrial products is able to use price as a means of gaining objectives much more effectively than can the maker of nonstandardized items.

## Product life cycle

The competitive situation varies widely during the life cycle of an industrial product. This can be illustrated by reference to the different phases in the life cycle of a product shown in Figure 17–1. The most important of these phases from the standpoint of pricing strategy are introduction, growth, and maturity.

FIGURE 17–1.   Product life cycle

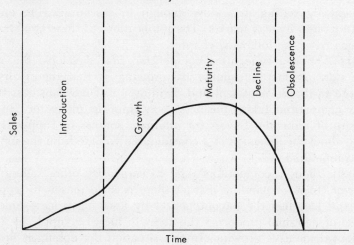

*Introduction.*   When a firm introduces a new material, component part, supply item, or piece of equipment, it may expect to have a monopoly of the market for a period ranging from a few months to a couple of years. During this interval, possible competitors observe the behavior of the new product in use, learn as much as they can about making it, explore the possibility of modifications to increase its efficiency, prepare plans for making and marketing it, and acquire the necessary facilities.

Theoretically, if the innovating firm has a patent on the new product its period of monopoly may last for the life of the patent, 17 years. This rarely happens in practice. It is not easy to get a patent on a material or a supply item, and when one is issued it usually covers the process of making the item rather than the item itself. Rarely is there only one way of making a product. The holder of a process patent often finds that the best way to capitalize on the patent is to license rivals to manufacture and sell under it. This is less true of a patent that applies to a piece of equipment, for it is apt to be much more defensible. But even here the hazards of defending complete exclusiveness are so great that many firms find it desirable to license competitors to manufacture and market the product.

Depending on the innovativeness of the product, strength of the patent protection, the ability of competitors to react, the opportunity for production and/or distribution economies, and the price sensitivity of the market, the manufacturer has the option of pursuing either a high-price or a low-price strategy. That is, management can: (1) accept the risk of encouraging competition by setting a price as high as the traffic will bear in order to maximize profits and achieve a quick recovery of its investment, or (2) accept minimal profits and a slow recovery of its investment by setting price low enough to discourage the entry of competitors into its new market. The implications of these two strategies are discussed in the following chapter.

*Growth.* For a time after competition first develops, the market for the new product is usually still growing so that the rivalry consists more in the development and dividing up of new business than in the new competitors taking business away from the innovator. However, the desire of industrial buyers for alternate sources of supply is likely to bring about the diversion of a considerable volume from the innovator to his competitors.

Initially, though, competitors tend to emphasize other selling points than price. In an expanding market there is little reason to jeopardize profits and lengthen the payout period by lowering prices—unless the entrance of marginal producers threatens to increase supply at a faster pace than demand is growing. In this situation the dominant firm may drop price low enough and long enough to "freeze out" the marginal producers and warn others not to expand capacity too fast.

*Maturity.* As the market develops, use of the product becomes widespread, and as more competitors enter the market, price tends to become more important as a competitive factor. A new supplier can enter the market or an old one increase his market share only by taking part of the market share of another. The temptation to use price as an entering wedge is very strong, since by this time product design is apt to be sufficiently standardized that quality no longer offers an effective basis for competition.

There are exceptions to this general picture. For example, the market for some industrial products, such as metals, basic chemicals, and standardized machines, enjoys a general long-term growth in response to the growth of the ultimate consumer market, although it undergoes minor fluctuations along with the cyclical ebbs and flows of business conditions. The tendency is for competition in these products to stabilize, often permitting a condition of price leadership to develop.

## Price leadership

Price leadership is about what the name implies, one producer in an industry, the dominant one, typically initiates price changes and others follow. Such a condition is most likely to exist when one firm has a clear advantage in cost or production capacity over others and enough financial strength to sustain the losses of a price war without being crippled. The price leader's executives must also be willing to incur the risks of price war in order to establish and maintain leadership.

It may appear that under conditions of price leadership there is no price competition. This is true in the sense that price leadership eliminates violent pricing action to capture individual orders. Such a condition may make individual buyers unhappy, especially when market conditions indicate that prices should be weakening. But this is in part compensated for, because responsible price leadership also affords the buyer a certain amount of protection against price increases when supplies are temporarily limited.

Price leadership has advantages for both the leader and his followers. It also involves disadvantages for them in the form of certain obligations and limitations.

*Advantages.*  Where true price leadership exists, all parties know that destructive price conflicts are not likely to occur. Implicit in the very fact of leadership is a willingness to live and let live. Price wars severe enough to eliminate competitors are likely to be started only by firms that do not recognize the existence of a leadership situation. If such a war starts, the pricing actions of the leader are likely to be designed to discipline the rebel firm and to hold injury to others at a minimum.

The most comforting element to the followers in a price leadership situation probably is their knowledge that so long as they operate within understood limits they are in no danger of price attack. They also avoid most of the really hard pricing decisions. After a situation of price leadership is established, it is probably maintained fully as much by the followers as by the leader. In fact, it is doubtful if under the present rigorous enforcement of the antitrust laws a price leader can take any very effective action to enforce his leadership. He must maintain it by making the right price decisions for the industry as well as for himself.

*Disadvantages.*  Price leadership imposes obligations on the leader as well as on the followers. He can maintain his leadership only by pursuing a definite and consistent pricing strategy, by using his power with restraint, and by recognizing, tacitly at least, the rights of followers to their respective market positions. The history of such situations suggests that actually, over time, the price leader tends to lose relative market position, usually without impairment of his leadership unless the process of attrition goes too far.

Nor does price leadership eliminate the pressures that generate and direct price competition. The threat of independent pricing action is always there, ready to break out if the leader fails to make the right decisions. The leader is always aware that if the followers gang up on him they can probably destroy his position of leadership.

## THE COST FACTOR

Since analytical techniques available to industrial buyers enable them to estimate the costs of many products they buy, cost is an important factor in pricing industrial goods. While the dominant factors in price determination are still on the demand side—what the buyer is willing to pay—the buyer's knowledge, or shrewd guess, of what a product costs is apt to have a considerable influence on what he is willing to pay. Cost is also an important factor in pricing industrial goods, because it represents a floor below which a marketer will not go without strenuous resistance or drastic managerial action to maintain or restore a favorable balance between cost and price.

The importance of cost as a factor in industrial goods pricing varies with the time period under consideration. In terms of the length of time needed to sell goods already produced, cost exercises little influence. At this juncture all costs are sunk in the sense that all money needed to pay for making the goods has already been spent. This is just as true of expenses for materials and direct labor as it is of overhead.

The objective is to get back the money spent, or as much of it as possible. In this situation, both direct and overhead costs have the same effect on pricing—practically none at all. What the buyer will pay becomes almost the sole determining factor, since to hold stocks is not only risky but also costly. The Stanford Research Institute estimates that inventory carrying costs may account for as much as 20 to 30 percent of the value of goods held.[1]

When pricing a product prior to or during its production cycle, costs generated directly by production and marketing should be distinguished from those which arise from the existence of equipment and facilities as well as from those associated with the conduct of business, i.e., true overhead costs. Aside from such considerations as market position and continuous employment for his labor force, the manufacturer must be able to foresee a price that will at least cover direct costs and make some contribution to the replacement of equipment and facilities used to produce his output.

At the inception of a strategic plan for pricing, it is probable that no costs are sunk, except perhaps those of exploration and research. Consequently, the strategy should be designed to recover all such costs, together with a satisfactory return on the investment they represent.

---

[1] National Association of Purchasing Management, Inc., *Materials Management: A Total Control Concept* (PAL 41, 1973).

This entails a recognition of the various direct, indirect, and joint costs involved, as well as their estimation and projection.

While the segregation of direct and indirect costs is a logical step in planning prices, it is also important to recognize costs which are controllable and those which are not, those which are sunk and those which are incremental, as well as those which represent foregone opportunities.

### Direct and indirect (overhead) costs

Direct costs vary more or less proportionally with the volume of production, such as most types of wages, raw material purchases, and income taxes. These expenses are also referred to as variable or operating costs. Sometimes it is possible to identify semi-variable costs—those which change only slightly with the volume of production, such as certain kinds of salary payments and advertising appropriations.

Indirect costs (rent, interest, real estate taxes, insurance, and some types of labor expenses) do not change significantly with the volume of production or sales. They are overhead. Some types of labor expense, i.e., that which is incidental to assembly line or other production operations, tend to behave like overhead within wide ranges of output. Indirect or overhead costs have an important bearing on pricing decisions both in the short and the long run.

*The short run.*  If there is excess capacity, management need not take overhead into consideration so long as the price received for an additional order covers more than its direct costs. Such orders make a contribution to overhead, and net profit will be greater (or net loss less), than if the order had not been accepted.

In deciding whether or not to accept an order or to submit a competitive bid the revenue from which will not cover direct costs and all allocated overhead, the seller must take into account his future relationships with the buyer and the reaction of his competitors. On the one hand, there is danger that a small company which accepts high-volume, low-margin business and expands to meet its production requirements will become dependent on such business and eventually be merely an appendage of the buyer. This is particularly true if the buyer is substantially larger than the seller.

On the other hand, if competitors for a specific order or contract are likely to retaliate against a low offer with an equally low or lower one, the seller may face a price war. If management does not want to risk involvement in what could be a destructive encounter with competitors, it would hesitate to offer a price that does not cover all costs.

*The long run.*  In the long run, all costs become direct in the sense that they must be met if a business is to survive. If sales decline to such an extent that a business cannot meet all costs, those which are controllable may be reduced or deferred. Depreciation charges, for example, need not be met. Repair and maintenance costs can be reduced to a level necessary for day-to-day operation. Reserves of various kinds can be eliminated.

A business may continue in this fashion either until the equipment becomes inoperative and must be sold for scrap or until demand revives to such an extent that overhead costs can again be met. It is often the expectation of revival that keeps a business alive and active through extended periods of unprofitable operation. Indeed, firms have been known to keep their doors open without even meeting direct expenses in order to hold their organizations toegther in anticipation of more prosperous times.

Companies in which a substantial portion of cost is represented by overhead face difficult problems of pricing strategy. What should a firm do whose competitor is selling at a price that does not cover his overhead costs? If the product involved is a major one for the firm but only a secondary or by-product for the price cutter, management faces a difficult decision. The price-cutter may not be aware of his real costs, and therefore cannot be expected to make intelligent pricing decisions.

On the other hand, the price-cutter may be well aware of his costs but is intent on expanding market share and is testing the willingness of other firms to retaliate in kind. This is not an unusual situation in the case of products which cannot be easily differentiated or are typically sold on the basis of standard specifications.

The problem of overhead costs is also a difficult one for the large producer of industrial goods with an expensive R & D program and all the other outlays incidental to being an industry leader. When such a firm must meet the often highly attractive price concessions of one or more quonset hut operators, there is often no alternative but to concede a certain amount of market share. Management must usually console itself that such competitors can supply only a small segment of the market, and they will not grow very much until they will face the same problems of overhead costs as the large firms.

## Controllable and noncontrollable costs

As their name implies, controllable costs are those subject to the manager's discretion. However, their identity varies with different levels of management. For example, the marketing manager has authority to add or not to add a salesman to the sales force. From his standpoint, the expense of operating the new salesman is a controllable cost. However, if he considers doing entirely without salesmen, and relying on advertising and direct mail or on manufacturer's agents to do the selling job, that decision is not likely to be his alone, although he is almost certain to have a hand in it. The expenses of operating a sales force are certainly controllable by top management but usually not by the marketing manager alone.

The logic of this distinction is that the marketing executive is obliged to seek a balance between price and controllable costs that will be most profitable for the company. Sometimes, it will be profitable to increase both price and controllable expenses. Or, price may be increased and controllable costs left unchanged or reduced. If it is impossible to change price, the path to added profit lies through the reduction of controllable expenses. Occasionally, price may be reduced in the hope that added sales volume will more than pay for the same or even added controllable costs.

When the marketing executive deals with noncontrollable expense, i.e., production costs and certain categories of overhead, his field of maneuver is limited. He must manipulate price to cover them or merely cover as many uncontrollables as possible. Heavy noncontrollable costs narrowly limit strategic choices.

### Incremental and sunk costs

Incremental expenses are those added by a given project or program, while sunk costs represent money that has already been spent. The latter can only be recovered by successful operations. When a new product is ready to be introduced, all funds that have been spent on R & D to bring it to the point of market introduction are sunk costs. Money that may be spent to implement a marketing strategy is, at the moment of decision, incremental expense. If special equipment must be purchased to produce the new product, the funds to be invested in it are, up to the moment of purchase, incremental. After the investment has been made, it becomes a sunk cost.

In pricing a new product, the objective should be to cover anticipated costs both sunk and incremental. If estimates have been in error, or something goes wrong after the manufacturer is committed to the new venture, the primary objective then becomes that of recovering sunk costs. This may involve selling at a price that is below full cost as long as it covers incremental expenses with something left over to apply to the recovery of sunk costs.

### Opportunity cost

When a maanger gives up one project in order to pursue another, he incurs an opportunity cost. If he is considering the development of a new product A, he matches the returns he expects from this against those he could expect if he invested the same amount of money, facilities, and time in the development of product B, or in improving the performance capabilities of one or more products already in the product line. When he adopts one venture, the foregone benefits which might have been realized from the next best alternative are an opportunity cost.

This concept has an indirect rather than a direct effect on pricing. It is a factor in the constant series of choices management must make among manipulating price, cutting cost, changing quality, and varying service as alternative means of achieving company objectives. Opportunity cost may cause a firm to continue marketing a product, even though profits are unsatisfactory, if no more fruitful use of capital is available.

## Joint and separable costs

In many manufacturing businesses, the production of one product is inseparable from the production of one or more other products. This results in joint costs. However, when two or more products are made from the same material or are simultaneously processed by the same equipment, one product may need additional processing not required by the other. The expense of this additional processing is a separable cost. For example, cottonseed is produced as a by-product of ginning cotton, and its cost cannot be distinguished from the cost of ginning the cotton. However, the cost of pressing the oil out of the seed is an additional operation, the cost of which is separable.

If a joint product is to be marketed, it must produce a cash flow that is at least equal in value to its separable costs. How much beyond this minimum price it should produce depends on the extent of demand for the product as well as the volume in which the other product is produced. It often happens that over a period of time one product gains in importance while the other loses. The product which gains can be assigned a greater share of the common processing expense. It is not unusual for two such products to completely reverse position over the course of several years; kerosene and gasoline offer a classic example.

A reversal in the importance of two joint products sometimes creates a serious problem. For example, a pharmaceutical firm which manufactured an antibiotic developed an animal-feed additive from residue of the production process. In time the feed additive became more profitable than the antibiotic and its volume grew until more of its essential ingredient was required than could be made available from manufacture of the antibiotic. However, the cost of manufacturing this ingredient independently was prohibitive in relation to the price which could be charged for the feed additive.

There are literally thousands of joint products in the coke industry. Here, the allocation of overhead and joint costs is quite arbitrary, and the pricing of the individual item must depend in very large measure on such factors as the seller's judgment about what the market will bear, his desire to expand the market for a new product, or simply his need to get rid of a certain amount of a given by-product. In certain instances, such as in oil refining, the amounts of the various by-products can be changed within rather narrow limits by alterations in technical processes. Hence, the pricing executive has some room in which to maneuver.

## THE NATURE OF DEMAND

The term "market demand" is used here to refer to the different amounts of a product buyers may be expected to purchase at various prices at a given point in time. An industrial marketer can construct a schedule of demand showing the amounts of a product which might be sold at each of several different prices. Unfortunately, the only facts about demand in which a seller can have much confidence are those represented by the current price of the product and the quantity taken by buyers at that price. The remainder of the demand schedule may be estimated on the basis of anticipated buyer reaction, past experience, or the experience of companies that sell similar products. Since physical volume at different prices must be estimated in order to do any planning at all, it is advisable to make the process as systematic as possible and to recognize the uncertainties inherent in such a schedule.

There is substantial evidence that in the markets for many consumer goods, a higher price will shrink demand and a lower price will stimulate it. This is a result of the valuations buyers place on a product in relation to money. A product priced at 75 cents will be purchased only by consumers who believe it is worth at least that much money. If its price were raised to $1, all consumers who value the product less than they value that much money will be out of the market.

Theory assumes that buyer's attitudes toward the values of money and products are relatively static, that the demand schedule stands still when price changes. This is not always true. The fact that a price change occurs may cause some buyers—sometimes considerable numbers of them—to change their attitudes toward the relative values of product and money. It was explained in a previous chapter that this is likely to be true in the short run with industrial goods. This is due to the professional nature of those who make buying decisions, their familiarity with the market, and the factors that motivate them to purchase or refrain from purchasing.

The value of a product to an industrial user is what it is worth at the time he uses it, and he generally uses it some time after he commits himself to its purchase. So he must constantly think in terms of price in the future—at the end of his purchasing turnaround time, plus his stock turnover period, plus the span of his production cycle—instead of at the current moment. A decline in price, therefore, may cause the industrial buyer to change his mind about probable future prices, and lead him to adopt a waiting policy to see if it will go lower rather than entering the market or increasing his purchases. Thus, a drop in price may, for a time, have the effect of shrinking demand instead of increasing it.

The same sort of change in the reverse direction may occur over the long run. For example, as a result of the drastic increases in the price of steel during the 1950s and 1960s, many industrial buyers who had never given serious thought to substituting plastic or aluminum for steel began to do so. Consequently, there was an increase in the amounts of these products purchased at existing prices and corresponding decreases in the demand for steel products.

If the price of a material drops to a certain level, buyers who previously never thought of using the product begin to investigate possible applications of it in their operations. For example, when the price of vitamins declined far enough, bakers and flour millers began to use them to enrich flour and bread. When the cost of antibiotics fell far enough, the manufacturers of animal and pet foods began to find them useful for stimulating animal health and growth. In both instances, buyers' relative valuations of money and product were changed by events that occurred in the market.

An unusually perceptive economist once remarked that to be truly reflective of actual conditions a demand curve must be drawn with rubber chalk on an undulating blackboard. This may be an overstatement, but it is not a flagrant one for a number of industrial markets.

## The behavior of derived demand

It was observed in an earlier chapter that the demand for industrial goods is derived rather than direct. This means that total demand for an industrial product can increase only as a result of an increase in the purchases of consumer products it is used to produce. Theoretically, if the prices of materials or equipment used in making a consumer product are reduced enough to allow the price of the consumer product to be reduced, its sales may be expected to increase. This in turn will increase demand for the materials and equipment used in its production. Consequently, by reducing price, an industrial marketer may be able not only to increase his share of the market but also to enlarge the total market.

Despite the logic of this relationship, it is apt to occur only if demand for the consumer product is highly elastic. But even if such price elasticity exists, it often happens that a considerable change in the price of an industrial ingredient, component, or piece of equipment will not force or make possible any significant change in the end-product price.

The reason for the sluggishness of price response across markets lies in the nature of derived demand. For example, the cost of purchased materials usually amounts to between 40 and 50 percent of the selling price of the finished product. If one considers an end product sold to the consumer at a price of $1 per unit, with only one material used in making it, the cost-price structure might appear as follows:

```
Retail selling price..........................................  $1.00
    Retailer's gross profit (30%)................................   .30
Wholesaler's price...........................................  $ .70
    Wholesaler's gross profit (15%)............................   .11
Manufacturer's price........................................  $ .59
    Material cost (40%).......................................   .24
    Manufacturer's other costs and profit......................  $ .35
```

If the cost of material is reduced 10 percent while retail and wholesale margins remain the same, the new retail price becomes:

```
Material cost...............................................  $.22
Manufacturer's other costs and profit.......................   .35
Manufacturer's price........................................  $.57
Wholesaler's price (15% margin)..............................   .67
Retailer's price (30% margin)................................   .96
```

A reduction of 10 percent in the price of the material makes possible a reduction of only 4 percent in the price of the end product to the consumer.

But suppose this particular material is responsible for only one fourth of the cost of materials used in making the end product. If its price is reduced 10 percent, the cost-price relationship is altered as follows:

```
Price of original material (¼ of $.24).........................  $.06
Reduced price of original material............................   .05
Other materials ($.24 − .06).................................   .18
Total cost of materials......................................  $.23
Other manufacturer's costs and profits.......................   .35
Manufacturer's price........................................  $.58
Wholesaler's price (15% margin)..............................   .69
Retailer's price (30% margin)................................   .99
```

In this circumstance a reduction of 10 percent in the price of the original material makes possible a reduction in the price of the end product of only 1 percent. This is hardly enough to make much of a dent in the consumer's consciousness or arouse in him any wild enthusiasm to rush out and buy more of it.

This illustration somewhat overstates the case. It ignores the fact that some industrial materials are interchangeable in many uses, such as steel and aluminum. The price of aluminum per ton is higher than that of steel, but it has certain advantages, such as appearance and lightness of weight. As the price of steel increases or that of aluminum falls, it becomes profitable for users to substitute the aluminum for steel for some purposes. By manipulating their prices in relation to those of steel, therefore, aluminum producers may expand their total market by taking over a part of the market for steel.

The fact remains, however, that for many industrial products a marketer's attempt to increase his sales volume by reducing price can succeed only when he takes business away from a competitor. This is so liable to provoke retaliation by the competitor that most industrial marketers are cautious about employing this tactic.

The derived nature of the demand for industrial goods also affects the extent to which it is subject to influence by selling effort. When a manufacturer of a consumer good applies advertising and sales effort to its promotion, he may increase the demand for it in several ways. He may induce a rival's customers to buy from him. He may induce present customers to buy and use more of his product. Or he may persuade people who have never purchased the article to become users of it.

By promotional effort, the manufacturer of an industrial product may hope to take customers away from a competitor. If his promotional work is directed at present users of his product, he can expect to do very little to increase their demand for it. That is conditioned by the demand for the end products it is used to make, and his promotion has no effect on that. A few industrial goods makers find it possible to advertise over the heads of customers to end-product consumers. But this is usually rather expensive because, at best, the manufacturer can hope to get only about 40 to 50 cents of each dollar of new business his promotion may develop, regardless of whether this new business represents increased use by old consumers or the demand of entirely new consumers of the end product. Occasionally, promotion directed at industrial firms may induce a few of them not now making the end product to go into the business; but such pickings are apt to be very slim.

In some cases, through a combination of research and promotion the maker of an industrial product can increase its total sales by developing new users or new end products to be made of or by it. This is true of both materials and equipment. For example, a manufacturer of plastics may work with a customer in a joint program of research to develop a new end product made in part or entirely of a new form of plastic. After a suitable interval, he is usually at liberty to promote and sell the material to other customers for the same purpose.

## SUMMARY

To price intelligently, the industrial marketer must know the type of competition in his industry, the nature of his costs, and the way in which the demand for his products behaves.

The typical industrial market is composed of a small group of large firms, a more numerous group of medium-sized firms, and often a group of very small companies which sell mainly on the basis of price. The first two groups are likely to subscribe to the philosophy of responsible competition. However, the nature and intensity of competition tends to change with changes in the life cycle of products. These conditions often give rise to a phenomenon known as price leadership.

The nature and pricing implications of costs tend to change with different time periods—production cycle, equipment use cycle, or product life cycle. Different kinds of costs—controllable or noncontrollable, incremental or sunk, overhead or direct, incremental, and joint—exercise different influences on pricing.

The derived nature of the demand for industrial goods affects its behavior in response to price change. While it is theoretically possible to stimulate demand for industrial products by lowering their price, increased sales will result only to the extent that prices of related consumer goods can be reduced sufficiently to stimulate their sales. Even in the case of consumer goods with highly elastic demand schedules, two conditions serve to dampen the effect of increases in their sales on demand for the products used in their production. One is the fact that the value of purchased materials amounts to only about 50 percent of the sales value of the finished product. The other is that several products or materials are usually consumed or used in the manufacture of a finished product.

# 18

# PRICING DECISIONS

ONE WAY of treating the formulation of pricing decisions and identifying at least some of the critical factors involved in them is to consider the occasions which require decisions concerning pricing strategy. At the risk of oversimplification, it is useful to distinguish at least three such occasions. The first of these is the introduction of a new product. The second arises when a competitor changes his price or when a new rival enters the market with a price different from that which prevails there. A third occurs when it becomes advantageous for the seller to initiate a change in price. Each of these situations presents its own problems and each calls forth certain responses which have been useful in solving them.

## NEW-PRODUCT INTRODUCTION

At the time a firm introduces a new product it is likely to have a considerable amount of sunk costs invested in it. Activities associated with new-product development, such as research, planning, testing, pilot-plant operation, training salesmen, informing customers, and building stocks of materials as well as finished units, often represent a substantial cash outlay. Unless it is recovered, such an outlay can cause an impairment of the firm's cash position. How fast management should attempt to recover it depends on the financial strength of the company, the presence of other promising projects requiring cash, the anticipated life span of the new product, and the speed with which competition is expected to develop.

Unless recovery of the firm's cash position is a prime consideration management usually has two broad strategy options: (1) to price the new product at a very high level with a substantial gross margin, or (2) to price it at or near the level to which its price would be expected to settle after competition developed, i.e., a low price. Probable price behavior under the two types of strategies is illustrated in Figure 18–1.

FIGURE 18–1.  High- and low-price strategies

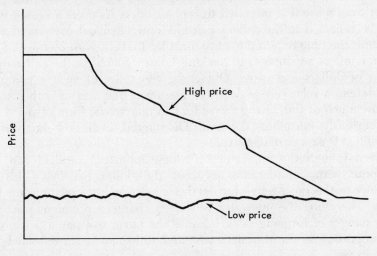

The high-price strategy

The objective of a high-price strategy is not only speedy recovery of a firm's investment but an advantageous cost position over would-be competitors. If the innovating firm can recoup its development costs before competitors enter the market, its income in excess of direct expenses can be applied to improving the product. Competitors who subsequently enter the market must apply part of their cash inflow to the amortization of their own development costs. Unless a competitor achieves a real breakthrough in product design or processing not enjoyed by the innovator, he will probably be at a cost disadvantage relative to the innovating firm.

A high-price strategy can also generate a substantial amount of ill will among customers. But this may be offset or prevented to some extent by timely price reductions before the advent of competition.

Other than financial considerations and the reactions of competitors, there are several conditions which favor a high-price strategy. These are:

- A product which represents a genuine innovation
- The presence of an elite market
- A demand situation which is inelastic
- Uncertainty concerning price sensitivity or comeptitive response
- A relatively short product life span
- A product design that is difficult to copy or produce
- A strong patent position

*Genuine innovation.*  A new product which represents a real technological breakthrough is likely to have substantial value to users. A new machine with a 25 percent higher output and a 30 percent lower power input than those it is intended to replace offers its users a saving which can be reflected in the seller's price. A new chemical compound which shortens the time required to cure meat by 15 days, with no trace of toxic residue, offers advantages to packing houses which can be calculated in terms of dollars and cents. Obviously, the seller of such a compound can defend a relatively high price. The open question in both instances is how much of this saving the seller can take in the form of price without seriously curtailing demand. Discounted cash flow analysis can provide at least a partial answer.

Even though the innovator of a new industrial product can often compute with considerable accuracy the dollar benefit of his new product to the prospective buyer, this may bear little relationship to its costs. Therefore, the innovator can often charge a premium price with little danger of forgoing sales, because the buyer can pay a price out of all proportion to the product's cost and still enjoy a substantial benefit from its use.

*An elite market.*  Firms whose products are of a technical nature, and whose managements are committed to staying in the forefront of their industries, often are undeterred by premium prices. If a new component part or material incorporates a significant advance in product technology, a firm with a reputation for technical leadership in its end products can ill afford the risk of being successfully challenged by a rival while its purchasing department quibbles over price. Such firms can be described as those which require the latest and best and have the financial strength to pay for it.

*An inelastic demand.*  Market conditions may result in demand for a product which is relatively unresponsive to changes in price. In such circumstances, a relatively high price will not act as a deterrent to sales any more than a low price will stimulate them.

*Uncertainty concerning price sensitivity or competitive response.*  In case of real doubt about the impact of a premium price on the volume of sales, or the speed with which a competitor will be able to respond, management must resort to trial and error. A high price is more prudent in this situation than a low price. If the initial price proves to be in error, it is often easier to lower a price that is too high than to raise one that is too low.

*Short life span.*  The shorter the life span of the product the more reason to generate as much profit from its sale as quickly as possible. Otherwise, the innovating firm may never recover its investment. Pharmaceutical firms, whose products sometimes have a life span of less than two years, often have no alternative but to set a price that will recover their development costs in the shortest possible time.

*Product is difficult to copy or produce.*  Product development that is technologically and/or capital-intensive can discourage competition.

If a high level of technology and production know-how are needed to produce a product, it is likely to be difficult and time-consuming for competition to put it into production on an economical basis. In this situation there is good reason to price the product at a premium level. Competitors will probably be slow about deciding whether or not to enter the business and are apt to suffer delays during the process of entry if they do reach an affirmative decision.

*Strong patent position.* Patent protection can give the innovating firm a great deal of latitude in pricing. However, the degree of protection afforded by patents can be easily overemphasized. If the patent holder sets and maintains an exorbitant price, the complaints of gouged buyers may cause the Department of Justice to become interested in all his pricing operations.

Nor are the competitve effects of such a strategy to be ignored. It stimulates competitors to try to find a way to get around the patent. If the patent applies to a product, their efforts usually take the form of developing another machine or material based on a different principle to serve the same purpose. This may not be easy and may prove impossible. If a process patent is involved, as is usually the case with a material, would-be competitors seek a different process to make the same thing. And they are not unlikely to find it. The innovator can minimize the likelihood of both these developments either by setting a price that represents a compromise between the high and low levels, or by licensing other firms to manufacture under the patent, thus providing some measure of competition.

## The low-price strategy

The chief lure of a low-price strategy lies in the strong market position the innovating firm may be able to win before competition develops. Once such a position is achieved, it can be difficult to undermine. This advantage may be weakened somewhat by the desire of buyers to split their orders for the product at the earliest opportunity. However, if this occurs while the product is still in its growth stage, the innovator's loss of market share is apt to be negligible.

The conditions which favor a low-price strategy are about what common sense would suggest—the opposite of those which favor a high-price strategy. In addition, it may be possible to realize substantial economies through volume production and distribution. So, a relatively low price that will stimulate demand and expand sales rapidly is a reasonable strategy.

## Break-even analysis

A useful aid in determining the approximate price level which will balance expenditures and income at various levels of sales is break-even analysis. The technique provides an indication of the effect different pricing decisions will have on the margin between sales dollars coming in and cost dollars going out. By consequence, it enables the seller to identify a price floor below which he should not go. The process of formulating a break-even equation itself can be useful in that it familiarizes a seller with a matter—his own costs—that many of his customers will be attempting to estimate. The method is illustrated in Figures 18–2 and 18–3.

The chart shown in Figure 18–2 represents the break-even technique in its simplest form. The distance between lines AF and CE equals total overhead (fixed) costs, which do not increase as the number of units produced and sold increases. The distance between lines AF and CD equals total costs, both overhead (fixed) and direct (variable). The distance between lines AF and AB equals cash inflow from sales.

The chart indicates that the company makes no profit until line AB intersects and passes above line CD, and that the farther this line extends above CD the more profits the company will realize. For a new product, the best tactic is usually one that will cause AB to pass above CD in the shortest possible time. The best strategy is probably one that will cause AB to extend the greatest distance above CD over the longest period.

This chart can be modified to show the amount of profit (or loss) at different prices and different sales volumes. Such a chart is illustrated in Figure 18–3. Here, 80,000 units is assumed to be capacity production during the first year of operation. Therefore, the horizontal axis is scaled from 0 to 80,000 units.

Costs and sales are measured in dollars on the vertical axis. Fixed costs are assumed to be $500,000 and variable costs $13 per unit. Break-even points are indicated where the sales lines at various trial prices—in

FIGURE 18–2.    Break-even chart

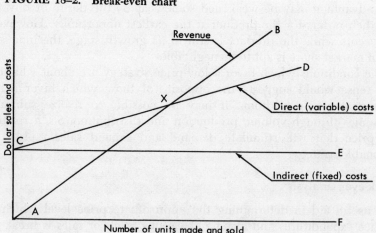

**FIGURE 18–3.  Break-even points**

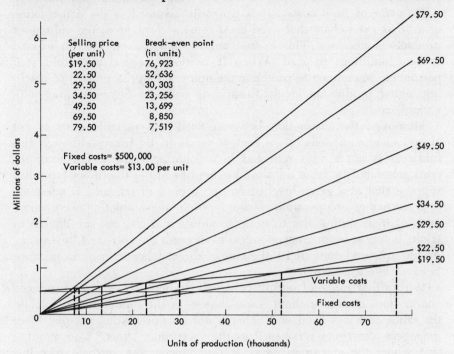

Units of production (thousands)

this example ranging from $19.50 to $79.50 per unit—intersect the total cost line. It can be observed that at a price of $19.50, 76,923 units must be sold in order to break even, whereas at a price of $34.50 only 23,256 need be sold to break even. A break-even point $(X)$ is calculated by substituting a trial price, for example $34.50, in the equation: $PX = FC + VC(X)$, in which $P$ = the trial price, $FC$ = fixed cost, $VC$ = variable cost, and $X$ = the volume of units produced at the break-even point.

$$\$34.50X = 500,000 + \$13X$$
$$21.5X = 500,000$$
$$X = 23,256 \text{ units}$$

Obviously, it is not feasible to calculate break-even volumes for every conceivable price. In choosing trial prices, the seller must rely largely on experience and judgment. An investigation of competitors' prices for similar products can often provide some indication of the practical range of prices. However, this should not be accepted uncritically, because competitors' prices may be more the result of hunch and tradition than analysis. There are also other cautions one should observe in using break-even analysis as an aid in formulating pricing strategy for new products. These regard the behavior of fixed and variable costs, the reliance on historical costs, and the application of the technique to marginal business.

*Behavior of fixed costs.*  It is generally assumed in the construction of a break-even chart that fixed costs remain constant as the volume of production increases. This is true only so long as output can expand without additions to staff. When it becomes necessary to add staff personnel (in contrast to production employees) in the process of reaching higher production levels, fixed costs will also increase along with variable costs.

Moreover, the distinction between fixed and variable costs is not always clear and definite. In fact, it tends to be fuzzy, although this fuzziness is not always reflected in accounting records. For example, costs generated by labor on a production line are of the direct type. But suppose that at a given level of output, a crew of ten men is adequate to perform a given operation efficiently, each one completing one or more parts of it. If output has to undergo substantial change, say double or triple, before it becomes economical to increase the crew to 15 members, or add a second crew of 10, the cost of direct labor in such an instance behaves like fixed costs.

Within that range of output in which the number of units produced can or does change without some change in the input of direct labor, the labor cost is a fixed cost. This is not an unrealistic example. Plant managers sometimes refer to it as the "accordian effect." The moral is that where the accordian effect is pronounced, the varibale cost line should be drawn as a series of ascending steps instead of as a line with an even upward slope.

*Behavior of variable costs.*  It is seldom true, as frequently assumed in the construction of break-even charts, that variable costs increase proportionately with increases in production. In fact, varibale costs per unit often decline, reach a low point, and then increase as production expands. Not only do production costs tend to increase as plant capacity is approached, but selling costs may become prohibitive if management attempts to push sales to a level which corresponds to full production capacity.

*Historical costs.*  Break-even analysis depends heavily on historical costs. However, it is forecasted costs rather than historical costs which are the important consideration, for the seller is pricing for the future not the past. Since forecasted costs seldom materialize exactly, in part because the data on which they are based seldom reflect the accuracy implied by the form in which they appear in the records of account, objectively determined prices require substantial adjustment.

*Marginal business.*  The prospect that sales of a product will never reach the break-even point does not per se condemn it to the scrap heap. The mere effect of spreading overhead may mean that the presence of such products in the line contributes to the profitability of other products. If a product can be sold at a price that generates enough revenue to cover direct costs and make a contribution to overhead, it may enhance the profitability of the product line as long as capacity is available to produce it.

## COMPETITIVE ACTION

The situations in which a seller is most likely to face price moves by competitors is when they are trying to gain entrance to his market or trying to capture a larger share of it. The former situation is one commonly faced by the innovator developing a market for a new product, while the latter is characteristic of established markets.

### New markets

The response of a seller to a competitor's challenge in a new market depends in large part on the pricing strategy he has pursued. If a high-price strategy has been followed, the seller faces a series of decisions, all involving questions of when to reduce price and how much of a reduction to make.

The ideal time to make a downward adjustment in price would be just before competitors' seriously consider entering the market and well before their intentions of doing so are common knowledge. Such a move on the part of the innovator can often be justified on the basis of a reduction in cost due to higher volume operations and improved production know-how, the benefits of which the firm is passing on to its customers. Such action should prevent some of the customer ill will that may arise from the impression that a seller refused to adjust his price downward until forced to do so by competition.

Whatever the timing of the first downward price adjustment, it is probably a good tactic to make it a substantial one. Even a sizable reduction in price that is effected through a series of nibbles is not likely to attract much attention or have much effect on competition. As a general rule, a price cut in this circumstance should be deep enough to mean something to customers and give competitors reason to pause. The more determined competitors will probably be undeterred, but those who are not so determined may lose interest and turn their attention to other markets.

The innovator who has pursued a low-price policy faces a different set of decisions when competition develops. If price has been set at the right level, it is already somewhere near the lowest figure rivals can charge and make a satisfactory profit. Since it is difficult to know where this level is and unlikely that a competitor will accommodate anyone by disclosing it, competition is almost certain to develop in the long run. Consequently, it is important to identify potential competitors and watch them closely enough to sense when market entry might be attempted.

If the innovating firm's own cost/volume relationship is such that further price reduction can be made without jeopardizing a satisfactory profit position, competition may be held at bay for a considerable length of time.

If a competitor resorts to price reductions below cost to gain a foothold in the new market, the innovator must decide whether to fight every encroachment or to accept the loss of a part of his market. The former will obligate the innovator to meet every price cut by a competitor with one of his own. This can soon result in losses to all parties concerned.

Conceding a part of his market to a competitor rather than risk a price war involves the question of how much of the market the innovator is willing to sacrifice. This decision depends to a considerable extent on the innovator's estimate of what share of the market a competitor is willing to accept without resorting to further price cutting. The decision also rests on what share of the market the innovator estimates he can hold on the basis of buyer inertia, the service relations he has been able to establish, and customer's reliance on his superior know-how and longer experience.

### Established markets

In an established market, the price moves of competitors have an immediate bearing on the pricing decisions of the individual seller. It has already been observed that an important ingredient in determining what response should be made to a rival's price change is an understanding of why the change was initiated. Only rarely will all the factors which prompt a competitor's action be known. But a knowledge of market conditions, the competitor's operations, and his current position with regard to finance, inventory, and utilization of capacity is not difficult for trained personnel to acquire. It is the kind of intelligence which can enable them to make some shrewd guesses about competitors' motives.

For example, if a competitor is overstocked or suffering from a poor cash position, the price move may be only temporary until the situation is corrected. On the other hand, if the competitor has been losing market share, because he has been falling behind in technology, the price cut may represent a change in strategy which could continue for a considerable period of time. Consequently, reaction to this price change must be made in terms of its long-run implications, including possible future counter moves by the competitor.

When management concludes that a competitor's price reduction must be met, it must be decided whether to exactly match the competitor's new price, price below it, or above it—but below the former price. As a rule, it is better to do nothing than to meet a competitor's price reduction only halfway. Such action merely calls attention to the competitor's move without really countering it. An exception to this rule would be an ability to offer product quality or service sufficiently superior to that of the competitor that his offering is less attractive despite its lower price. The use of price reductions to screen inferior product quality or service can be readily detected by techniques of vendor and value analysis.

Reducing price below that of a competitor risks a price war, particularly if his new price is a strategic move rather than a tactical ploy. Even though one's analysis revealed that the competitor could not win a price war, the cost of such a contest should also be carefully estimated to be sure the winner could afford his victory.

If a competitor's price reduction reflects a genuine cost advantage, any attempt to match it should be regarded as a holding action until his cost advantage could be neutralized, either through equivalent cost reductions or some premium added to product quality or service. Should the possibility of achieving reductions in cost comparable to that of the competitor appear much more promising than adding a significant premium to the quality of products or service, meeting the competitor's price would be advisable. Although the company undoubtedly would sustain losses until such a cost reduction had been realized, this in itself would serve as a spur to expedite a cost reduction program with all possible dispatch. If the opposite were true, i.e., that a product and service improvement program was most feasible, there would probably be no reason to change price.

In some instances Bayesian analysis can be helpful in tracing through the implications of response to a competitor's pricing action. Its application may be illustrated in the following simplified situation.

A. The manufacturer is selling 1,000,000 pounds of a standardized material per year.
B. He has one competitor whose volume is about the same as his own.
C. The price of the material has been $1 per pound.
D. The manufacturer's total costs are $0.80 per pound and his total profit $200,000 per year.
E. The competitor cuts price to $0.95 per pound.
F. The manufacturer's policy is not to start price wars, and if one begins, to attempt to end it as soon as possible.

Faced with a price reduction by his principal competitor, the manufacturer's options and their consequences might appear to be as follows:

A. If he does nothing, the chances are:
  1. 10 percent that he will suffer no loss of sales and profit will remain unchanged.
  2. 40 percent that sales will decline about 10 percent, production cost will rise to about $0.83 per pound and profit will decline to about $153,000 per year.

3.  30 percent that sales will decline by 25 percent, costs will increase to about $0.88 per pound and profit will decline to $90,000.
4.  20 percent that sales will decline 40 percent, production cost will rise to about $1 per pound and profit will fall to zero.

Summation:

| | | |
|---|---|---|
| 10% of $200,000 | = | $ 20,000 |
| 40% of $153,000 | = | 61,200 |
| 30% of $ 90,000 | = | 27,000 |
| 20% of       0 | = | 0 |
| Value of Alternative A | | $108,200 |

B.  If he matches the competitor's price reduction, total sales of the product could be expected to increase to 2,200,000 pounds annually. Chances are:
1.  60 percent that the competitor will do nothing. Therefore, his sales should rise to about 1,100,000 pounds, costs should decline to about $0.78 per pound, and profit should level off at about $187,000.
2.  30 percent that the competitor will reduce his price to $0.90 per pound. If the manufacturer does not match it, his sales should decline to 900,000 pounds, his costs should rise to about $0.83 per pound and net profit sink to about $108,000.
3.  10 percent that the competitor will return his price to $1. Therefore, the manufacturer would return his price to $1, which should increase sales to about 1,000,000 pounds and annual profits to $200,000.

Summation:

| | | |
|---|---|---|
| 60% of $187,000 | = | $112,200 |
| 30% of  108,000 | = | 32,400 |
| 10% of  200,000 | = | 20,000 |
| Value of Alternative B | | $164,600 |

C.  If he reduces price to $0.90 per pound, the chances are:
1.  70 percent that the competitor will match the new price. Therefore, total industry sales should increase to 2,300,000 pounds, of which he should get half (1,150,000 pounds), costs should fall to $0.777 per pound, and profits should be about $149,500.
2.  10 percent that the competitor will do nothing. Therefore, sales should be about 1,500,000 pounds, costs about $0.75 per pound, and profit about $225,000.
3.  20 percent that the competitor will raise his price to $1 per pound. If the manufacturer does the same, his sales should return to 1,000,000 pounds annually and profits to $200,000.

Summation:

| | | |
|---|---|---|
| 70% of $149,500 | = | $104,650 |
| 10% of  225,000 | = | 22,500 |
| 20% of  200,000 | = | 40,000 |
| Value of Alternative C | | $167,150 |

The three options and their expected values are summarized in a *decision tree* which represents a diagram of the problem. The tree is shown in Figure 18–4. The main branches refer to the three options under consideration. The secondary branches represent the probabilities assigned to different payoffs. The values at the nodes are the payoffs associated with particular options. It is at least clear from this summary that the manufacturer should not sit tight and do nothing when his competitor cuts price.

FIGURE 18–4.    Decision tree—response to a competitor*

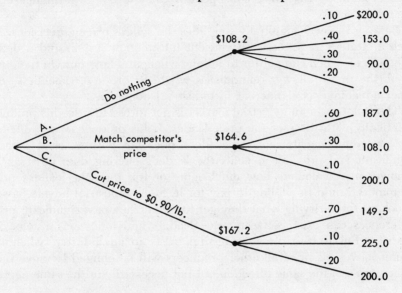

* Payoffs are in thousands of dollars.

This kind of analysis can be extended to include a much wider variety of assumptions, including the presence of more than one competitor. More complex formulations can be developed for analysis by computer to derive the probable effect of each alternative on company profits and to identify the one promising the greatest profit.

## The choice of roles

In principle, the industrial marketer has a choice between a strategy of price leadership and one of following a dominant competitor. In fact, this choice is available only to a few large firms in any given industry. The small and medium-sized firms usually have no such choice. Although their cost structure may be as favorable as that of their bigger rivals, such firms typically lack the financial strength to wage a successful struggle for leadership.

The medium-sized firm may be able to exercise enough influence in a market to make it worthwhile for the price leader to apply disciplinary measures if it refuses to follow. While the very small firm—a garage or quonset hut operator—can never aspire to price leadership, it can usually enjoy a considerable degree of pricing independence. These firms usually have little or no overhead cost. If one of them cuts price, most of the retaliatory counteractions open to the large firms in the industry are either of doubtful legality or very expensive in terms of what can be accomplished. About all the price leader can do is suffer in dignified silence, knowing that the small operator can exercise little influence on the total market.

Being a follower materially simplifies the seller's pricing decisions. All such a strategy requires is an efficient information system and a determination of which competitor to follow, when, and how far. On the other hand, the price follower relinquishes whatever prestige, timeliness, and other advantages are inherent in industry leadership.

The follower in an industrial market is not forced to price his products identically with those of the price leader. If his product-service offering has provable benefits that the leader's does not possess, or if it lacks significant and provable benefits the leader's offering does possess, the follower must calculate how much more or less than the leader's price customers would be willing to pay for it. Since industrial buyers have a penchant for verifying what they get for what they pay, significant price differences can exist between price leaders and followers in some industries. But if true price leadership exists in an industry, when the leader moves his price all other producers will be obliged to move their prices, too—in the same direction but not necessarily in the same degree.

## The use of analogy and hunch

Despite a plethora of statistical data and sound techniques for its analysis and interpretation, the memory of analogous situations undoubtedly forms a highly influential part of the mental and emotional atmosphere in which pricing decisions are made. When confronted by a competitor's price change, it is almost irresistible to recall: "We faced a situation much like this once before and did so and so with pretty good results," or "Company X handled this kind of problem in such and such a manner and got away with it, so why not try the same thing?"

Unfortunately, business situations never duplicate themselves exactly, and seemingly trivial, even unnoticed, variations may cause a pricing action under current conditions to operate in a way entirely different than in the analogous situation. Then, too, there is no assurance that the course of action followed in the analogous case was the best one, and by following it the seller cuts himself off from the possibility of finding a better one.

On the other hand, the hunch of a seasoned executive is not to be regarded with contempt. The feel that a certain price is right or wrong may be compounded of a number of things, such as memories of past experiences, subconscious understanding of competitor and customer emotions and attitudes, an unrealized appreciation of the condition of the market, a nebulous projection of a host of dimly remembered similar situations and decisions in the past, and probably other factors, most of which are pertinent although not clearly understood. In part, this feel may be a result of the working of the subconscious mind, which many people find so helpful in problem solving. In many cases, though, it is something more than this, since the result never rises to the level of the executive's thought processes but manifests itself in his feeling comfortable with one decision and ill at ease with another. Because of the intangible nature of many of the factors that influence pricing decisions, the importance of hunches is probably greater in this area of business decision-making than in most others.

## INITIATING A PRICE CHANGE

Market conditions may offer a number of opportunities to use price change as either a strategic or tactical weapon. Lowering price may be done to expand sales in order to lower unit production costs by a greater degree than the reduction in price, thus strengthening profits. A company may need to strengthen its cash position or to work down finished-goods inventories. A breakthrough in product technology may be of sufficient magnitude to justify an escalation in price. It may be advantageous to use a price change in one product to stimulate sales of another.

Pricing decisions in these and many other situations involve balancing the effect of price on sales and subsequent production costs against expenditures on promotion, service, and other forms of demand stimulation. As a general rule, an increase in sales, and in the amount produced, tends to reduce unit production cost. The greater the importance of overhead expense in the cost structure the more pronounced this effect is likely to be. Therefore, if by reducing price a seller can bring about a considerable increase in sales, it may be that the lower price minus a reduced production cost per unit, multiplied by the increased number of units sold, will create a larger net cash inflow than will a higher price. Whether or not this situation results depends on the reactions of competitors.

Changes in production cost due to shifts in production volume can usually be estimated with reliable accuracy. In the absence of competitors' reactions, the effect of a proposed price change on sales volume also can be estimated, but with somewhat less accuracy. A knowledgeable executive can probably make a reasonable guess as to how competition will react to a given change in price. Combining management's best estimates and informed guesses, the seller's options might appear as follows: *prior to the price reduction*

A.   If price is reduced 5 percent with product sales of $1,000,000 and production costs of $600,000 (ignoring inventories), the probabilities are:

*b*   50 *percent that competitors will not react.* Therefore, net sales of the product should increase about 3 percent, and production costs per unit should decrease about 1.5 percent. This results in an approximate gross profit of $439,000. *469,000*

5 *percent that competitors will cut price, but by less than 5 percent.* In this event net sales should increase about 2 percent and unit production costs decrease about 1.3 percent. This would result in an approximate gross profit of $427,800.

40 *percent that competitors will match the price reduction.* In this event, product sales volume *and* production costs should remain unchanged. *would decline 5 percent, the amount of the price reduction, but*

*This would result in a gross profit of $350,000*

5 *percent that competitors will reduce price more than 5 percent.* In this event, sales volume would decline about 3 percent and unit production costs increase about 2 percent. This results in an approximate gross profit of $358,000.

B.   If price is reduced 10 percent, the probabilities are:

20 *percent that competitors will not react.* Therefore, net sales of the product should increase about 25 percent and unit production cost decline about 5 percent. This would result in an approximate gross profit of $680,000.

10 *percent that competitors will reduce price, but by less than 10 percent.* In this event, sales should rise about 15 percent and unit production costs decline about 4.5 percent. This results in an approximate gross profit of $577,000.

40 *percent that competitors will match the price reduction.* Therefore, sales and unit production costs should remain unchanged. *would decline 10%, the amount of the price reduction but*

*This would result in a gross profit of $300,000*

30 *percent that competitors will reduce price by more than 10 percent.* In this event, product sales volume should decline about 10 percent and unit production costs increase about 5 percent. This would reduce gross profit to approximately $270,000.

The implications of these options are traced in the tree diagram shown in Figure 18–5. As in Figure 18–4, the main branches of the tree refer to the two options under consideration—to reduce price by 5

**FIGURE 18–5.    Decision tree—pricing alternatives***

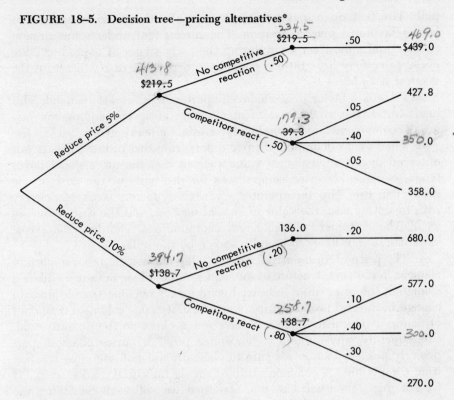

* Payoffs are in thousands of dollars.

*413.8*

percent or reduce it by 10 percent. Since the expected payoff of the former is $219,500 and the latter only $138,700, it is clear that a price reduction of only 5 percent appears to offer greater financial promise than the more spectacular cut of 10 percent *of leaving price unchanged.*

It is true that such analysis involves a tissue of assumptions, only one set of which—those which apply to the effect of output on unit production cost—has any pretense of accuracy. For some products, a statistical analysis of the time relation between a firm's price shifts and its sales volume may also supply some factual basis on which to forecast the effect of proposed price changes on sales. However, there is no escape from formulating a set of assumptions regarding the effects of a number of alternative actions that might be taken in response to each likely reaction by competitors. Without such assumptions, recognized or implicit, no intelligent pricing decisions can be made.

The usefulness of this approach to industrial product pricing is limited by several conditions.

1. Management may have other objectives than maximizing profits. So long as profits are satisfactory, market share, price leadership, image, or growth might be of dominant importance for considerable periods of

time. The best price may be one that enables the marketer to gain or hold a favorable market position. This means that under some circumstances, and almost certainly during the early stages of a product's life cycle, price may bear little resemblance to the one that will return the greatest net profit.

2. Price is a factor of secondary importance in market demand. This tends to be true in the case of many types of special equipment, materials, components, and supplies for reasons already given.

3. The buyer's definition of price differs from that of the seller. It was observed in the discussion of value analysis that the professional buyer tends to make his price comparisons on the basis of the cost of the product in use. This incorporates a variety of factors, such as delivery cost, inventory cost, the value of special services, and the cost of buying itself. The customer's thinking and computations regarding these cost variables are not likely to be fully known by the seller.

4. The price of an industrial product may not constitute an important element in the cost structure of any end product of significance. Unless a change in the price of an industrial good makes possible (or requires) a change in the end product price, and hence, its sales volume, no amount of manipulation of its price will have much effect on the quantity sold. Consequently, any attempt to maximize profit by price changes, particularly price reductions, is sure to elicit prompt and vigorous reaction from competitors. A common attitude among industrial marketers is, "If we cut price, they will cut, too, and then we will each be selling the same tonnage at less profit."

5. The reaction of government agencies must be observed by any firm which makes and markets widely used materials or components. Both the Federal Trade Commission and the Department of Justice are peculiarly sensitive to corporate pricing behavior, and they subscribe to the concept—often acknowledged—of a "fair" price that by no means maximizes profit. A pricing strategy designed to maximize profit will have features which irritate that sensitivity.

It seems to follow that the use of models and complex formulations in pricing decisions is often rendered unrealistic by the intangible factors which exercise so potent an influence on demand for such goods. Their very precision and exactness may mislead the marketer who tries to employ them, unless he is endowed with a rare sense of the intangibles and an unusual power to weigh their importance.

Perhaps it would be useful to conclude this chapter with at least two simple but pragmatic guidelines for establishing profit and price objectives. One frequently used guide is the average rate of return on capital earned by firms in the industry, or the median profit earned by the more successful firms in industry.

The other is the group of needs profits are required to satisfy. For example, profits are needed to pay enough dividends to keep the stockholders satisfied, or at least, quiescent. They are needed to provide capital with which to seek out and exploit opportunities in the form of new products, new markets, or acquisitions. This may be done from retained earnings or by borrowing on favorable terms made possible by a satisfactory rate of earnings on capital already used. Profits also may be needed to build up retained earnings against possible future reverses and to make possible the payment of dividends in spite of them.

It is possible to express all such needs in dollars and thereby set a profit objective toward which the marketer can plan. How far he can go beyond this objective is limited by competition, the possibility of losing customer good will and, with it, market position, and the threat of government action. These limiting conditions, together with a dollar definition of the need for profits, identify a range within which reasonable profit (and, with it, reasonable price) falls.

## SUMMARY

Several situations require pricing decision: when a new product is introduced, when a competitor's price is changed, and when management wishes to use price as a weapon of marketing strategy. The conditions which affect decision are different in each of these situations and each calls for a slightly different analytical approach.

The marketer of a new industrial product may choose a high- or a low-price strategy. Each has its areas of special usefulness and conditions under which it would be appropriate. Despite its limitations, break-even analysis can be an aid in reaching a decision regarding the appropriate pricing strategy.

Response to a competitor's pricing action differs with the market situation in which the action arises. In the case of a developing market for a new product, response to a competitor's price cut would be strongly influenced by whether the innovator has pursued a high-price or a low-price strategy. In the case of an established market, it is important to determine the competitor's motives before planning counter action. This in turn is influenced by whether management has chosen to place the company in the position of a price leader or follower.

The use of pricing change in a company's own marketing strategy involves balancing the effect of price on sales and subsequent production costs against expenditures on promotion, service, and other forms of demand stimulation. How much flexibility a firm will be permitted in working out an optimal balance depends on the reaction of competitors. Bayesian analysis can be helpful in identifying the most probable set of consequences of a proposed price move.

# 19

# PRICING POLICIES

THE BASIC QUESTIONS of pricing policy for many industrial marketers are those regarding the manner in which prices are quoted. This is influenced by the characteristics of the channel system through which a manufacturer's products are distributed as well as by the traditions of the industry. The alternatives usually involve net pricing, the choice of discounts off list price, and the use of geographical reference points or zones.

## NET PRICING

Net price refers to list price less allowances for trade-ins, order pick-up (eliminates delivery), and other cost-significant concessions by the buyer. Net pricing eliminates much of the clerical work, cost, and in some instances, confusion, associated with quoting a list price less a discount or string of discounts. The purchasing officer who negotiates a contract involving a string of discounts is apt to be haunted by the suspicion that if he had bargained just a little harder he might have won an extra 5 percent. Sellers who are sensitive to buyer preferences and free to pursue it probably favor this method of quotation.

## DISCOUNT PRICING

The term *discount* is used here to identify a deduction from the announced list price of a manufacturer. In some industries deductions from announced prices are traditional and, in effect, the seller has policy decided for him. He simply quotes the same discounts as his competitors. Where some latitude in discount policy exists, there are usually at least three alternatives: trade discounts, quantity discounts, and cash discounts. Since all discounts raise questions of legality, the marketing

330

manager who contemplates using them should first consult his company's attorney.

## Trade discounts

When a manufacturer sells all or part of his goods to distributors, he customarily quotes a discount to the distributor which is designed to represent the outlet's operating expenses and profit. If a channel of distribution containing two or more middlemen or levels of customers is used, the price structure may consist of a chain of discounts subtracted successively from each new net price.

Several reasons underlie the use of trade discounts. First, the policy provides a means of suggesting or controlling the resale price. If a flat price were quoted rather than a list price less discount, the result might be a set of differentials in selling prices to final users, depending on the margin added on by each individual distributor. The discount off list, however, automatically defines what the manufacturer thinks the distributor's margin should be and strongly suggests that the outlet's selling price should be the list figure. This reason for trade discounts obviously loses much of its weight in those industries in which price maintenance is widely practiced.

Second, the use of chain trade discounts makes it easier to implement a varying price policy among distributors. For example, a distributor in one district may have facilities for performing certain services that the manufacturer himself must perform in other areas. A simple means of compensating the distributor for these services is to allow him an additional discount. This skirts perilously near the edge of illegality under the antitrust laws.

Third, trade discounts are useful as a way to try to keep actual prices secret, not only among distributors but also from competitors and users. This advantage, however, may be more apparent than real, since an extra discount, like murder, will out however elaborate the measures to conceal it. Finally, expensive catalog revisions are diminished, since nominal list prices may be printed in the catalog and a separate discount sheet made up whenever a price change is desired.

The trade discount may also be used either to protect distributors against direct-buying customers or to deny them their patronage. Large firms often have a policy of purchasing direct whenever possible, in order to avoid paying the distributor's margin. If the product is one the user cannot buy in amounts that are economical for the manufacturer to handle, or if the manufacturer regards distributors as necessary to assure him a satisfactory volume, it would be inadvisable to sell direct. However, refusal to sell direct may prove embarrassing and generate ill will. A trade discount policy of, say, giving 25 percent off list price to distributors and selling at list to all other buyers may be helpful in avoiding such impasses, as the direct buyer would have nothing to gain on the price.

On the other hand, the maker of a component part, such as an electric motor, may want to sell direct to original equipment manufacturers (OEM's) who install the motor in their end products, but indirect to all other buyers. OEM's usually not only buy in large quantities, but their use of a product as a component part creates a replacement market for it. The component part maker can accomplish his purpose by selling to OEM's at the same discount as to distributors, say 25 percent off list, and at list price to all other buyers.

It is important that the trade discount represent as accurately as possible the cost of the distributor's services plus a normal margin of profit. If the discount is too high, it may encourage price-cutting. If it is too low, distributors may well be reluctant to handle the product unless they can sell it above list price, which is not always feasible.

## Quantity discounts

Quantity discounts are price reductions which vary according to the amount purchased. They are very useful to marketers of materials and supplies in dealing with the small-order problem. Firms making and selling these products often find themselves involved in what amounts to a wholesaling business. When selling to a number of hand-to-mouth buyers, the manufacturer is forced into a stock-keeping and bulk-breaking operation which he is seldom organized to conduct profitably.

By instituting a quantity discount policy, the manufacturer offers small-order buyers a tangible incentive to purchase in larger quantities. When the cost of preparing many small orders is added to the higher price per order resulting from the loss of discounts, the savings realized by holding inventories to a minimum begin to disappear. This usually is a more palatable way of controlling the small-order problem than setting a minimum order size, say $50, below which orders will not be accepted.

Quantity discounts may also be used as a means of classifying customers into large-quantity buyers, whom the seller wishes to serve direct, and small-quantity buyers whom he prefers to service through distributors. Since quantity discounts can be so designed that large users find it economical to buy direct and small users do not, the seller can effect a classification of customers into direct buyers and indirect buyers without the administrative detail and embarrassing problems which often accompany more overt customer classification.

Operationally, quantity discounts may be cumulative—based upon total business purchases over some period of time, such as a year or a month—or noncumulative—based on the amount of a single order. In establishing pricing policies, the seller must decide whether his interests are better served by selling at one price to all buyers on a given level of distribution or quoting quantity discounts. If the latter appears most beneficial, he must decide whether cumulative discounts, noncumulative discounts, or both should be offered.

*Noncumulative discounts.* Discounts based on the size of a single order encourage customers to purchase in large quantities rather than small ones. When customers buy in small lots, additional expenses are involved in packing, billing, transportation charges, and broken-package handling. If a buyer is willing to anticipate his needs more carefully and purchase in larger quantities, there is good reason to pass on to him part or all of the resulting savings.

This kind of quantity discount may be expressed as a percentage off list or as a variation in price per unit, as follows:

| Size of order | Percent discount off list | Size of unit | Price per pound |
|---|---|---|---|
| Less than 10 units | 0 | 50 lb. carboy | $0.25 |
| 10 to 19 units | 2 | 100 lb. drum | 0.245 |
| 20 to 29 units | 3 | 250 lb. drum | 0.24 |
| 30 units or more | 4 | 20 × 250 lb. drum | 0.23 |

The per-unit quotation creates somewhat less clerical work than does the percentage-off-list quotation.

*Cumulative discounts.* Discounts based on purchases over a period of time usually have the effect of expanding sales and reducing costs by increasing the amount of business placed by each customer. It also tends to hold the loyalty of the buyer during the discount period. This type of discount policy should be employed when lower distribution cost is a function of size of customer to a greater degree than size of order. An example is provided by the following system used by an abrasives manufacturer in pricing grinding wheels according to the size of the customer's annual purchases.

| | Size of customer's annual purchases | | | | |
|---|---|---|---|---|---|
| | Small | Medium | Medium large | Large | Distributor |
| Size of discount (percent) | 60–5 | 65–5 | 70 | 70–10 | 70–10 |

From the customer's point of view, the cumulative type of discount has the advantage over the noncumulative type in that if the buyer who normally purchases in large quantities wants to order a small emergency shipment from time to time he is not penalized.

When small buyers habitually split their requirements among several sellers, the cumulative quantity discount policy may induce them to concentrate their purchases. By making small customers larger (at the expense of other sellers), the seller enjoys good possibilities for reducing costs. This may be beneficial not only to the customer and to the seller who receives the additional business, but also to competitors who are relieved from handling the unprofitable small orders they would otherwise receive.

### Cash discounts

Cash discounts are deductions the buyer makes from the face of an invoice in return for payment before it is due. Their purpose is to encourage immediate payment, and thus enable the seller to avoid the burden of extending credit. There are also certain positive benefits which accrue to the seller when invoices are paid immediately. These include faster turnover of working capital, the elimination of friction between the company and slow-paying customers, and even increased sales, since customers in good standing are more likely to buy than those in arrears.

Insofar as the savings realized by the seller from immediate payment equal the deduction allowed the buyer, the deduction is a true cash discount. However, if the deduction exceeds this amount, as is sometimes the case, it is not entirely a cash discount. It is rather a trade allowance or a price concession.

The marketer must sometimes adjust his cash discount terms to the accounting practices of his customers. Suppose, for example, a customer follows a policy of paying on the 15th of each month all bills received on or before the 10th, and on the 1st of the month all those received on or before the 25th of the preceding month. The seller will probably be wise to allow him to take his discounts, even though the stated terms are 2 percent, 10 days, net 30 days.

### Legal considerations

In establishing and administering a discount system—in fact, any pricing policy which has the net effect of causing one customer or group of customers to pay a different price from that paid by another—the marketer must be alert to the provisions of federal antitrust laws. The Robinson-Patman amendment to the Clayton Act, which outlaws price discrimination, is particularly important. It is doubtful that the framers of this law intended it to apply to industrial goods. The legislation was designed primarily to protect small retailers and wholesalers against the competition of chain stores. But since the language of the act is couched in very general terms, it is clear that its prohibitions affect the marketing of industrial, as well as consumer, goods.

Under the Robinson-Patman amendment, any treatment or set of terms granted to one buyer and not available to another, and causing a difference in the final costs the two buyers pay for goods, probably falls under the definition of discrimination. Such discrimination is not illegal if:

1.  It is made on the basis of savings resulting from differences in the manner or quantities in which the buyers involved make their purchases;
2.  The goods involved are not of like grade or quality;
3.  The discrimination does not substantially lessen competition;
4.  The goods involved are perishable; or
5.  The discrimination is made in good faith to meet an equally low price of a competitor.

It might appear from these exceptions that the best defense against a charge of price discrimination would be to show a saving. This is true only to a degree. The Federal Trade Commission, which administers the Clayton Act, and the Department of Justice, which enforces it, have made a rather rigïd interpretation of this defense. On the one hand, the seller who offers marketing savings as a defense against price discrimination must do so on the basis of a cost analysis system for marketing which meets the dictates of good accounting practice.

On the other hand, basing a defense on savings in production costs arising from larger transactions is very difficult to support. For example, a seller may be approached by a large buyer whose purchases will double his sales volume, reduce overhead by half, and smooth out seasonal fluctuations in manufacturing—which will further reduce costs. However, the Justice Department has ruled that savings of this type result from the seller's entire volume, not that associated with a single customer, and must be made available to all buyers if it is allowed to any.

Meeting the price of a competitor appears to be the justification for differential pricing that is easiest to defend. Any firm plagued by garage or quonset hut operators can probably defend differential pricing undertaken to meet competition of this sort. But even in this situation the advice of the company attorney should be sought before taking action.

The underlying difficulty is that the law itself is couched in very general and, in some instances, obscure language. The implications of its language are well illustrated by the manufacturer of an industrial material sold to an industry composed of one very large buyer and a number of small to medium-sized ones. The large buyer had customarily purchased a month's supply at a time. One day he approached the material manufacturer with the proposition that if given an appropriate price concession, he would commit himself to the purchase of a definite amount annually. This quantity could be shipped at the discretion of the manufacturer so long as a month's supply of the material was maintained in the buyer's warehouse at all times.

The manufacturer's accounting department was able to verify that the proposal involved significant savings, but also pointed out that the manner in which the savings were computed could raise legal questions. The proposal was then examined by the company's legal department which cautioned that although the company should realize sizable savings as well as profit if the proposal were accepted, the cost of defending it in the courts, should its legality be challenged, would exceed by a substantial margin the amount of anticipated profits.

On the basis of this information, management declined the proposal. The uncertainty of the law in this instance had the effect of blocking a price reduction. Moreover, the refusal of enforcement authorities to make firm commitments regarding the meaning of the law, except as the outcome of hazardous and expensive litigation, discourages good business practice. It handicaps efficient, aggressive competitors, and over the long run probably obliges consumers to pay more for a number of products than would otherwise be necessary.

## GEOGRAPHIC PRICING

Depending on the bulk and weight of a product, the cost of transporting it to the buyer's plant, warehouse, or site may be a significant element of its ultimate price to the buyer. As a result, many industrial marketers include an allowance for transportation cost in their price quotations. Quotations which include such allowances may take two general forms: *factory pricing and freight allowance pricing*.

### Factory pricing

The seller who uses factory pricing almost always ships f.o.b. (free on board) factory or point of origin. This means that the buyer pays all the freight and is responsible for all risks occurring during transport, except those assumed by the carrier.

This method of quotation has several advantages for the marketer. It assures a uniform net price on all shipments, regardless of where they go. It eliminates the necessity of negotiating adjustments of freight overcharges with the carrier. Since, in the absence of agreement to the contrary, title to the goods passes to the buyer when the seller delivers them to the carrier, the seller avoids all risks of damage not assumed by the carrier—chiefly so-called acts of God.

Passage of title at factory also means that the seller assumes no re-

sponsibility for the length of time the carrier takes in delivering a shipment to the buyer's plant. However, this advantage may be more apparent than real, for the professional purchasing officer tends to value
the supplier's delivery service on the basis of his actual turnaround time,
regardless of whose fault it may be that delays, if any, occur.

Due to the bulk and weight of many industrial goods, the expense
of transporting them can be sizable. Consequently, many industrial
marketers cannot be competitive with f.o.b. factory pricing unless they
operate plants in or near their markets. This can be very costly in terms
of duplicate equipment and plants built to less than optimum capacity.
It is often more economical to make some sort of adjustment in the
direction of a delivered, or freight allowance pricing.

## Freight allowance pricing

The industrial marketer who finds it desirable to follow a policy of
freight allowance pricing has several possible methods to choose from.

*F.o.b. destination or delivered prices.* F.o.b. destination means that
the seller pays freight charges and assumes the risks of transport not
taken by the carrier. Title does not pass until the carrier delivers the
goods to the buyer. When this form of quotation is used, the seller may
receive a different net return from every customer. All customers, those
far from the seller's plant and those nearby, pay about the same delivered price for the goods if we ignore other discounts. Minor differentials may occur among customers if shipment is by rail, since those
without spur tracks serving their plants may have to pay a cartage
charge. Even this may be avoided by the use of delivered prices that
contemplate delivery by the seller to the buyer's plant either by some
combination of common carriers or by trucks arranged for by the vendor.

Pricing in this manner enables the seller to compete in all parts of
the market on even-price terms with competitors. This is the most
extreme form of freight allowance pricing.

*F.o.b. shipping point with freight allowance.* Under this policy, the
buyer pays the carrier's charges, and either is allowed a freight discount
or deduction from his invoice or is authorized to pay the freight and
deduct the amount of it from his bill before remitting. This arrangement
relieves the seller from risks of damage and delay in shipment, but it
complicates the paper work of both parties and, if the seller suspects
an overcharge, may lead to disputes between them as to just what the
freight should have been.

*Freight equalization.* This type of quotation is much like f.o.b.
shipping point with freight allowance in its operation. However, it
serves a quite different purpose. Consider a firm with its plant in Newark,
New Jersey, and a competitor in Chicago who sells f.o.b. factory. If
the firm's price is the same as the competitor's and it ships f.o.b.

factory, it is at a freight disadvantage in serving all customers nearer to Chicago than to Newark. It may ship f.o.b. plant and equalize freight with Chicago; then a customer in Fort Wayne, Indiana, pays the freight bill from Newark to Fort Wayne, subtracts from it the freight on an identical shipment from Chicago to Fort Wayne, and deducts the remainder from his invoice before remitting. The Fort Wayne customer thus pays the same freight he would have paid had he bought from the competitor in Chicago.

The purpose of this is obvious; it enables the Newark firm to compete on even delivered-price terms with the Chicago competitor. The firm may have a number of freight equalization arrangements, each one aimed at a specific competitor. The scheme has the advantage of providing quotations tailored with some exactness to the geographic distribution of competitors' shipping points and need not be applied over the entire market. However, implementation of such a policy can become very complicated when competitors are numerous and scattered because of the multiplication of clerical costs and possibilities of error. It may also result in illegal price discrimination if a customer in a freight equalization area competes with one outside any such area in selling his end products.

*Basing point.* This type of quotation is really a form of freight equalization, perhaps identical with it if set up so that it is of unchallenged legality. It is used mainly in the metals industry. Under this system, one point, usually in the area of greatest concentration of the producing industry, is established as the basing point. All prices are then quoted f.o.b. this point, regardless of where the seller may be located. Thus, if Pittsburgh is the basing point for a steel item, a steelmaker in the Chicago area will quote f.o.b. Pittsburgh. This means that the buyer is billed for freight from Pittsburgh to his plant, even though the merchandise is shipped from Chicago. So a buyer located farther from Pittsburgh than from Chicago pays more than the actual cost of transport, while one situated farther from Chicago than from Pittsburgh benefits.

An industry basing point is almost certainly illegal. A basing point established by an individual firm is probably legal so long as competitors have not chosen it for the same use; then the presumption is that the common choice was the result of collusion among them. The whole idea is of such doubtful legality that its use is now very narrowly limited.

The courts and the economists have had much to say about the discriminatory effects of basing point pricing, freight equalization, and freight allowance arrangements. Certainly, the primary intent of the marketer who grants a freight allowance or equalizes freight is not to discriminate among customers but to put himself in a position to compete for their business on a delivered-price basis.

But it is equally certain that regardless of the arrangements the seller may make regarding freight he is bound to discriminate against some-body. If he ships f.o.b. factory, he discriminates against the customers farthest away from his plant. If he ships f.o.b. destination, he favors faraway customers at the expense of those nearby. If he sells f.o.b. factory with an allowance of all freight, he discriminates in the same way; if the allowance is a flat sum, he favors nearby customers who get the allowance without having to pay it all out in freight. If he equalizes freight with certain selected points, he discriminates against customers not within the equalization areas. If he quotes on a basing point system, he favors customers nearer to the basing point than to his plant at the expense of those nearer to his factory than to the basing point.

Since it seems impossible to administer this particular feature of the pricing function without discrimination, the industrial marketer will probably be wise to adjust his freight arrangements with the objective of improving his competitive position rather than of assuring fairness to all customers, to the extent possible without violating legal requirements. All such decisions are subjects for the careful scrutiny of the company attorneys.

## SUMMARY

At the risk of oversimplification, pricing policies for many industrial marketers may be divided into three broad choices: net pricing, discount pricing, and geographic pricing. Net pricing, i.e., list price less trade-in or other allowances, is probably preferred by many buyers and sellers alike, because of its simplicity and ease of administration. In some markets, however, the forces of competition or tradition, or both, may make dis-count pricing a more feasible alternative.

The most common types of discounts, i.e., deductions from list price, are trade discounts, quantity discounts—both cumulative and non-cumulative—and cash discounts. As the names imply, trade discounts are deductions based on functions performed by the buyer, whereas quantity discounts are based on the amount purchased—either in a single order or over time. Cash discounts are deductions for immediate payment. In administering discount policy, the seller must take cognizance of legal as well as commercial considerations.

Geographic pricing is quite common in industrial marketing and tends to be either factory pricing or freight allowance pricing. The former places most of the burden of transportation costs on the buyer whereas the latter places it on the seller. Freight allowance pricing may take several forms, some of which are of doubtful legality.

# PART VII

## Marketing strategy: The promotional component

THE CRUCIAL EVENT in the marketing process is the sale. Within the context of the corporate mission, every component of the marketing strategy is intended to bring it about. But it must be brought about in a way which assures customer satisfaction. This places a special burden on advertising, personal selling, sales promotion, and to a lesser extent, public relations, which are the principal avenues through which direct contact with the customer is made. Each has a unique contribution to make, both in generating sales and in sustaining customer patronage. The intent of the discussion in the following three chapters is to highlight the kind of planning and execution needed to realize the full potential of these activities as well as bring about their proper coordination with each other and with other components of marketing strategy.

# 20

# ADVERTISING

As A COMPONENT of marketing strategy, the effective use of advertising is dependent upon knowing the tasks it can best perform and matching the various elements of the advertising plan to them. These elements include the sales appeals to be used, the media best suited to convey them, the message in which they will be incorporated, and the budget support required by the total endeavor. The collateral topics of publicity, the use of advertising agencies, and the measurement of advertising effectiveness are treated briefly at the end of the chapter.

## ADVERTISING FUNCTIONS

Even a partial listing of the functions which advertising can perform would include such important and varied ones as informing customers and prospects about the seller and his products, identifying new customers, winning recognition, supporting salesmen, motivating distributors, and stimulating primary demand.

### Disseminating information

A primary function of all advertising is to inform people about the products and services of the advertiser. This function is particularly important in industrial marketing because purchases are so frequently made on the basis of facts and logic. If a professional buyer reads an ad at all, he will probably read it carefully, for trade journals and the ads they contain are one of his sources of information about product availability. Consequently, industrial advertising copy is often studded with facts—facts which are precise, documented, and provable. Their presentation is generally colorful, illuminated with personal interest, and embellished with all the skills of the copywriter's art, but facts form the core of the message.

### Identifying new customers

It is very unlikely that an industrial buyer would commit himself to the purchase of a product solely on the basis of information supplied by an advertisement. But buyers frequently can be induced to request additional information about a product or even to order small test lots of it on the basis of information that is presented in a well-written, highly factual advertisement.

Generating inquiries through advertising is a widely practiced method of identifying new customers. Some inquiries may come from present buyers concerning uses or processes with which they are not familiar, and/or from prospects to whom the advertiser's salesmen have failed to gain access. For the most part, however, a well-planned advertising effort designed to probe new markets can be expected to generate inquiries chiefly from firms which currently are not customers of the advertiser.

A very common procedure in dealing with such inquiries is first, to reply by mail or by whatever other means of communication the inquiry is received, and then to turn them over to the salesmen or distributors from whose territories they originated for personal follow-up. It is obviously meaningless to invest in such advertising without a plan for aggressively following up the sales leads it generates. Such a plan should be developed when the advertisement is planned.

This use of advertising is especially important in the introduction of new products. A company which introduced a new cord strapping device advertised it in nine different publications during the first year. About 5,000 inquiries were received as a result of the ads and at a cost of about $10 each. Approximately 40 percent of these leads were subsequently turned into sales. Another company endeavoring to penetrate a new market learned that 23 percent of its new customers attributed their initial interest in the company's product to its advertising. Much advertising is wasted by poor follow-up work.

### Establishing recognition

A resource file containing the names of firms selling products which the company regularly buys is standard equipment in many purchasing departments. This record generally contains pertinent information about each supplier, such as his reputation for quality and service, his financial standing, his price performance, his reliability, and other facts that bear on his usefulness as a source. When bids are to be solicited, invitations to bid may be sent to all names in the file or to a list selected from it. When existing buying relationships are disturbed and new suppliers must be selected, candidate sources are apt to be chosen from the file.

When an industrial goods manufacturer moves into a new market or introduces a new product to be sold to a new group of buyers, one of the first promotional tasks the advertising department faces is to get the company's name in the resource files of as many firms in the new market as possible. Advertisements with well-researched copy in the appropriate trade journals are usually an effective way of accomplishing this end.

Many industrial buyers consult trade journals as a means of keeping their files up to date. Moreover, when a firm changes its manufacturing processes or its product line so as to require unfamiliar equipment or materials, buyers must compile new lists or files of possible suppliers. They are almost certain to consult trade journal advertisements in this process.

Another form of recognition that is important to the industrial seller is that associated with trademarks. A manufacturer of stainless-steel valves learned that, although the product had been on the market for nearly two years, his trademark was relatively unknown. Design engineers, plant managers, and purchasing officers were accustomed to specifying more familiar names when buying new valves or ordering replacements. Distributors did not find the product particularly profitable and, therefore, made no special effort to sell it.

In order to increase sales, the company embarked on an advertising program with two objectives in mind: (1) build an image of product reliability comparable to that enjoyed by its most important competitors, and (2) gain recognition as a leader in the technical development of stainless alloys.

The core of the program consisted of trade journal advertising, with heavy emphasis on institutional copy. A new external house organ was adopted, which featured articles describing the applications of steel valves and castings, as well as the company's association with important industrial users. Industrial catalogs and directories also were used liberally.

Within two years the program began to bear fruit. Distributors who had previously been reluctant to stock the valves were now trying to convince the company of their ability to sell them. Every prospect on the sales department's list of important potential customers had placed an order. The number of inquiries about valve applications had increased 25 percent. Moreover, the company's sales goal had been surpassed by 25 percent. While this kind of success does not accompany every advertising endeavor of this nature, it is not uncommon when the objectives are realistic and the elements of the program fit them.

A favorable company image is also an important aspect of recognition. Although its existence is sometimes difficult to determine, the market impact of an image is nonetheless real. The manufacturer firmly established in one industry may have difficulty penetrating a new industry because its image in the old industry overshadows its entry into the new one. Advertising directed toward the second market may fail to attract the attention or gain the interest of its intended readers, because in their minds the company's image associates it with a different industry.

This problem was faced by a watch manufacturer that sought to establish itself as a supplier of precision components for military weapons systems. A market survey showed that industry buyers thought of the company primarily as a manufacturer of consumer products. In order to create an industry image, the company embarked on a two-pronged campaign, one series of advertisements directed at top management and the other at research, development, and production personnel. The same format appeared in general business publications used to contact top management and in specialized journals read by technically trained individuals. The company name was featured prominently enough to gain the advantage of the goodwill established in the consumer field. At the same time, use of a symbolic drawing or design, with photos and copy describing the company's technical capabilities, served to identify the firm as a manufacturer of precision instruments.

## Supporting salesmen

Advertising can also be effective in preparing prospective customers for salesmen, in reaching personnel inaccessible to them, and in overcoming prejudice about the company or its products.

*Preparing prospective customers.* Advertising can often be instrumental in "opening the door" for salesmen by informing prospective customers of new products, indicating the extent of the advertiser's line of products, and explaining the position of the company in the industry, and its policies toward customers.

Preinforming the buyer in this manner saves the salesman's time and permits him to close sales more quickly. The salesman employed by a company that advertises consistently is likely to be received more cordially, and his selling task is apt to be easier than that of one whose firm does not advertise regularly. Even the small industrial goods manufacturer, through effective use of a limited advertising budget, can open for his salesmen many doors that otherwise would remain closed. It is true that when a salesman has been calling on a customer over a period of time, advertising is relatively less useful, but when he contacts new prospects and, in particular, when his company is reaching out into a new industry, advertising can play an important supporting role in increasing his effectiveness.

*Reaching personnel inaccessible to salesmen.* Advertising may be an effective support when the salesman is unable to contact all individuals in the customer's organization who are influential in making buying decisions. These persons may range from the man on the bench to the research scientist or engineer, or to the outside director who controls the purse strings of the company. Often, the salesman does not know who these key individuals are, and even when they can be identified they may be difficult or impossible to interview. By contacting them through advertising, the marketer may convince them of the virtues of his product or, at least, influence them to the extent that they offer no serious objection to recommendations made by others whom the salesman is able to contact.

Similarly, advertising can be useful in keeping the company's name and product offering before customers between salesmen's calls. "They forget you in a hurry," is true of customers as well as fair-weather friends. Effective selling requires that contact with the customer be made often enough to insure continued association in his mind between the seller and his need for the seller's product. In a competitive market, the seller who overlooks this fact very often finds that sheer weight of competitive contact causes the loss of customers he thought were loyal to him. When there is little difference in quality and price among competitive products, even industrial purchasers are strongly influenced by aggressiveness in marketing. To make the necessary contacts through salesmen's visits is sometimes prohibitively expensive. However, because of advertising's relatively low cost per contact it is well suited to the task of maintaining the required association between salesmen's calls.

When the purpose of the contact is to build goodwill or to keep the product dominant in the eyes of the customer, advertising is often more effective than are personal sales calls. Reminding customers of the advertiser's presence and capabilities is particularly helpful to salesmen in the case of customers whose orders are too small to warrant sales calls as often as they might prefer—yet, whose orders collectively represent a significant volume of business.

*Overcoming prejudice.* Occasionally, advertising can provide valuable support for salesmen by helping to dissipate unfavorable attitudes about the company or its products. Such attitudes may be virulent if the company has produced a lemon or has received a substantial amount of unfavorable publicity as the result of a product failure. Examples of the latter are the West Coast pharmaceutical firm which inadvertently produced and marketed a batch of contaminated polio vaccine, and the Midwest manufacturer of tractors whose machine stalled before millions of television viewers while moving a Saturn rocket from its silo to the launch pad at Cape Kennedy. In both instances public reaction was swift, derogatory, and national in scope.

After the technical fault in such situations has been corrected, advertising may constitute a valuable aid in rebuilding the prestige of the company and its products. It can do this through positive copy which describes the difficulty, indicates how it was met, and stresses the company's past dependability as well as the strong selling features of its products.

When a company develops a synthetic product to compete with a natural one, such as leather, rubber, wool, or cotton, it must expect prejudice from users accustomed to the natural product. Marketers of the natural product are likely to foster this attitude through the implication that the synthetic product is an inferior subsitute. Here, the problem is one of education. Here, advertising may be successful in instructing prospective customers about the product's use and supplying them with technical performance data. In this way, the advertiser may be able to destroy the idea that the new substance is an inferior substitute and establish it as a superior product in its own right.

## Motivating distributors

The industrial goods producer who sells through distributors or manufacturer's agents must convince them to devote sufficient time and energy to his products to sell them successfully. Otherwise, neither the manufacturer nor the middleman will derive much benefit from them. However, commanding adequate attention from middlemen is often difficult because other manufacturers whose products they carry are attempting to do the same thing.

Advertising can be used in several ways to aid a manufacturer competing for middlemen's time. Copy directed at middlemen may point out the advantages of pushing the company's line, such as wide margins, large sales potential, rapid turnover, or the relatively small investment required. The company may identify distributors or agents in regional or national advertising and on direct mailing lists. Sales leads in the form of inquiries obtained through company advertising may be forwarded to the agent or distributor in whose territory the prospective customer is located. It is a common practice to undertake cooperative promotion, either by supplying literature with the imprint of the middleman, which he can mail to his customers, or, less often, by bearing a portion of the cost, typically 50 percent, of space advertising up to a certain percentage of sales.

## Stimulating primary demand

It is sometimes profitable for the industrial goods manufacturer to promote demand for the products of his customers and prospective customers. This may be an effective way of increasing the use of materials or machinery manufactured by the advertiser. Steel companies, for example, have for years placed advertisements in consumer media promoting the virtue of products made of steel. Manufacturers of fibrous glass have pursued the same strategy, using a variety of consumer media to advertise the superiority of fiber-glass reinforced plastic in making such varied products as boat hulls, molded chair bottoms, draperies, automobile bodies, fishing rods, and luggage.

If a material or component part is trademarked, or otherwise retains its identity in the finished end product, its maker may be wise to advertise the product to its end users. In this way, he may be able to induce them to specify end products containing his materials or components. A leading maker of diesel truck engines consistently directs much of its advertising to trucking companies, construction companies, mining companies, and other users of medium and heavy trucks rather than to truck manufacturers themselves. The purpose is to induce these users to specify that their new trucks come equipped with the advertiser's engines. Since truck manufacturers would rather accommodate a buyer's request for a particular engine than lose a sale, this advertising strategy has been very successful.

## SALES APPEALS

Once the decision has been reached regarding the function, or functions, advertising is to fulfill, the advertiser must choose the appeals that will be most effective in implementing them. A sales appeal is an argument, a fact, an idea, or an expression of an attitude or emotion that the advertiser thinks will induce a prospective buyer to react favorably to his message. This appeal is unlikely to have the desired effect unless it promises to help the buyer achieve his own objectives. Consequently, the advertiser must determine the buying motives of his prospective customers—i.e., what they hope to gain through purchasing—before selecting sales appeals.

It may be recalled from earlier discussion that industrial buying motives may be classified as either *basic* or *patronage*. Motives which lead a buyer to purchase a certain type of product, regardless of its form or seller, may be identified as basic. Motives which lead him to prefer one trademark to another or one seller to another may be identified as patronage motives. Although the nature of their responsibility leads one to expect that professional buyers would be more receptive to appeals that involve reason rather than emotion, this does not mean that emotional appeals have no place in industrial advertising. It should be remembered, though, that the purpose of a purchasing officer is to buy and not to be sold. The extent to which he permits himself to be influenced by emotion may render him less effective in getting the best deal for his company.

It is probably true that basic motives are less likely to be influenced by emotion than patronage motives. Materials, parts, supplies, and equipment are impersonal things and do not readily engender strong personal feelings. However, the firms that supply such items are composed of, and represented by, people, and they may readily engender admiration, suspicion, fear, confidence, or any of the other feelings to which man is heir. This implies that while emotional appeals may be of some use in convincing buyers to place a major share of their orders with one firm rather than with its competitors, such appeals are likely to be ineffective in promoting the sale of a generic product.

Earlier discussion has emphasized that a knowledge of these motives may be derived from a study of customers' production systems and organization structure as well as the outlook and attitudes of their executives. This type of research not only discloses the nature of customers' operating problems but the way in which their management perceives them. Some managements are very conservative in their approach to problems, while others are more risk-oriented and willing to experiment with innovative concepts and methods. Some are very price-conscious, while others think chiefly in terms of quality and performance.

A study by Minneapolis-Honeywell Corporation provides an interesting insight into the way motives differ among different groups within the same company. For example, it was learned that:

1.  Upper echelon personnel (vice presidents and above) were most sensitive to a supplier's performance and his record of product innovation.
2.  Purchasing directors were interested in detailed information about products and services.
3.  Production and engineering managers wanted general descriptions of products a supplier made or could make. They preferred to write for the details if they were interested in what he could offer.
4.  Design personnel wanted specific information about technical capacity and competence but showed little interest in anything else.

It is apparent that the advertisers' choice of sales appeals will depend on the particular role assigned to advertising in the firm's promotional strategy, the audience to which they are directed, and the unique characteristics of the featured product. With this kind of direction, the advertiser can formulate sales appeals to which his audience is sensitive because they can relate them to their problems and responsibilities.

## MESSAGE

"Message" is used here to describe both the printed copy and artwork in published media as well as both picture and sound in broadcast media. Two of the more pervasive issues associated with the advertising message are its formulation and policy concerning its content.

### Formulation

The message of a well-designed advertisement for an industrial product generally contains a sequence of elements. A short headline presents an interesting or intriguing idea with enough significance to the reader that he will want to pursue it further. An explanation or amplification of the headline then develops a limited number of specific appeals, which are designed to show the potential user that the product or service can be useful to him and will fulfill an actual need. The message then describes the distinctive features of the product, offering evidence of its desirability and proof of the claims made for it. Finally, the reader is urged to take some action, and, where feasible, specific courses of action are suggested.

It is clearly essential that the copywriter have a precise definition of the audience (or audiences) the advertising must reach. He needs to know what part its various members play in making or influencing the purchasing decision and the kind of information concerning the product and the supplier that each of them will find helpful in the process of decision. Furthermore, the writer of advertising copy should be familiar with the language of his audiences. Engineers, plant managers, and technical researchers are accustomed to technical language and probably prefer it, whereas other managers who are not so technically oriented may prefer plain English.

All promotional statements made in published or broadcast media are subject to the requirements of the Wheeler-Lea amendment to the Federal Trade Commission Act, and to the general prohibition of false claims in the Clayton Act. While these laws were intended primarily to protect consumers, they also apply to the sale of industrial goods. However, it is unlikely that such legislation is of great importance in assuring that industrial advertisers will be truthful. There can be little doubt that confidence, based on sound evidence of reliability, is the sine qua non of patronage for most professional buyers. The technical knowledge, skill, and testing facilities which are often at their command enable them to detect most cases of product misrepresentation that might be made on the part of prospective suppliers. Since the discovery of a vendor's misrepresentation would almost certainly have the effect of destroying his credibility with the buyer, dishonesty is seldom worth the risk it entails.

## Policy

Sensitivity to the risks involved in fraudulent advertising, both legal and economic, as well as cognizance of the problems of management control in large organizations, have produced some rather strict policies regarding the content of advertising messages. The policy statement of a manufacturer of office and data processing equipment is fairly typical:

1. All claims with respect to performance and money-saving must be capable of being substantiated, and must be relevant to a prospect's business requirements.
2. Phases such as "more than" or "less than" must represent a significant amount in relation to the price, savings or product feature described.

3. When testimonials or case histories are used, they must be strictly factual and supportable, with names available on request.

4. At all times, the prospective customer must be given an honest evaluation of what the product represents and how it performs.

5. All promises, stated or implied, must be capable of being fulfilled.

6. Illustrations must be such that the product is shown realistically as to color and size—in a setting which can be characterized as a "standard" business atmosphere, or if not, just silhouetted.

7. A premium must never be used as pure inducement to buy. Premiums, when justified, for one reason or another, should at all times be relevant to the market and low enough in cost so that they may be considered an attention-getter rather than extraneous inducement.

8. Promotion which might compromise the integrity of (the Company) must never be allowed to be mailed.

9. The light-touch approach is acceptable, but only if it can be described as "humor in good taste."

10. Advertising copy with unsupported comparisons—"better"—"faster" —"cheaper," etc., must be avoided.

11. Every promotional piece should be created with each of the following qualities in mind: integrity, good taste, good judgment, honesty.

In order to assure adherence to this policy all advertising is reviewed by the following on a regular basis: Director of Advertising, Divisional Vice Presidents and Marketing Directors, Assistant General Counsel, and the Vice President for Marketing.[1]

Another fundamental issue regarding message content is whether to emphasize trademarks or the company. Proponents of so-called institutional copy argue that it is more important to sell the company—its name, its facilities, and its reputation, than to sell individual product trademarks. Their logic is that given a product's suitability, confidence in its supplier is the most important consideration in the buying decision. Moreover, when the reputation of a company as a reliable supplier has been established, there is no need to develop and promote trademarks.

It may also be contended that as a company diversifies its products, the use of trademarks can result in such a proliferation of names as to confuse customers and seriously dilute promotional effort. When advertising must be spread over a number of different trademarks, it becomes much more difficult to promote any one of them effectively.

However, a commitment to institutional advertising featuring the company rather than specific products or services carries the risk that copy will become generalized and encrusted with platitudes of little or no interest to the reader. Headlining individual products, which is

---

[1] *Corporate Policies and Procedures on Advertising and Promotion,* Report of Sub-Council on Advertising and Promotion of the National Business Council for Consumer Affairs (U.S. Government Printing Office, September 1972), pp. 35 f.

implicit in trademark advertising, gives the advertiser a broad range of opportunity for extracting useful sales ideas. In a sense there is less risk in featuring trademarks, because in the event of a product failure the damage to the company's reputation is likely to be much less than if institutional copy was employed.

A well-known trademark also can be instrumental in building the reputation of a company. It can facilitate entry into areas in which the company name is not well known. Moreover, trademark advertising has the advantage of being easily adapted to testimonials. For example, a firm's message may be introduced by a statement somewhat like, "Here is what X Company did with our product," followed by a description of the manner in which X company fitted the product into its operations and the results it achieved by doing so.

## MEDIA

Marshall McLuhan has said that the medium is the *massage,* implying that the vehicle through which the advertiser's message is carried to its audience has something to do with the effectiveness of the message itself. Indeed, "massage" may be a good description of the contribution of the media. Each medium "rubs" buyers a different way, consequently, the advertiser must select media which reach the proper personnel in the customer's organization with the proper frequency and with the proper "massage." At times, reaching the proper company personnel with the proper frequency may be considered important enough that the media are chosen before the message is formulated. In these cases, the massage precedes the message, and the copywriter must adapt the message to the media.

For the most part, media selection for the industrial advertiser is confined to trade journals, general management publications, catalogs, direct mail, and exhibits. Table 20–1 gives a breakdown of industrial advertising budgets by major items of expenditure, as reported in the *Industrial Marketing* annual survey. While items other than media costs are included, the table affords an insight into the relative importance of various media. The dominance of trade journal space and catalogs is obvious.

It will be observed that some of the items in Table 20–1, such as catalogs and exhibits, are commonly regarded as sales promotion devices. They are included in many industrial advertising budgets, because coordination between advertising and sales promotion is so important that the two are often handled by one organizational unit, usually the advertising department. Another factor that induces management to consolidate the two is the small amount of the total marketing budget the typical industrial firm spends for advertising and promotion, usually one or two percent of sales. Unless a firm is very large, the total amount

**TABLE 20–1. Allocation of advertising expenditures, 1968 and 1972**

| Media | Percent of total budget | |
|---|---|---|
| | *1968* | *1972* |
| Business publications............................... | 39 | 32 |
| Catalogs............................................ | 16 | 21 |
| Administration and salaries......................... | 8 | 8 |
| Trade shows and exhibits............................ | 7 | 8 |
| Direct mail......................................... | 8 | 7 |
| Dealer and distributor materials..................... | 4 | 4 |
| General magazines.................................. | 4 | 4 |
| Publicity and public relations........................ | 4 | 4 |
| Directories......................................... | 2 | 3 |
| Advertising research................................ | 1 | 1 |
| Newspapers........................................ | 2 | 1 |
| Television and radio................................ | 2 | 1 |
| All others.......................................... | 3 | 6 |

Source: *Industrial Marketing* (February 1969 and 1973).

involved in either of the two is not enough to command the interest and justify the expense of a top-notch executive. When they are joined together, this difficulty is diminished.

Newspaper, billboards, national consumer magazines, radio, and television are of very limited usefulness. In rare cases, an industrial goods manufacturer may find it useful to place an advertisement in a newspaper—for example, in the business or real estate sections of the *New York Times* Sunday edition. A few equipment makers maintain displays in airport terminals and some have made limited use of outdoor, i.e., billboard, advertising. But these are clearly exceptional cases.

The choice of media is of course complicated by the number and variety of personnel who influence buying decisions in the typical customer firm. Top management reads one type of publication; operating management, another; design engineers, still another; purchasing officers have their own professional journals; and foremen, supervisors, and factory superintendents look to publications that deal with their peculiar problems. Some journals appeal only to people in one industry but try to offer wide functional coverage within that industry. The editorial and news content of others is directed to one functional group in all industries.

The subscriber and reader distribution of a medium obviously is an important indicator of its suitability for the advertiser. Most publications are prepared to supply detailed breakdowns of their subscriber lists. However, such lists may not give a true indication of readership, due to the practice in many companies of subscribing to one or two issues of a journal and circulating them among a number of personnel.

Some publishing houses research their readership regularly and can supply advertisers with reasonably accurate data concerning the distribution of their publications among different functional groups. When this kind of data is not available, it may be advisable for the advertiser to conduct his own research on the question of readership. The Standard Rate and Data Service, which supplies lists of trade journals classified by the industries and functional groups into which their readers are distributed, can be very helpful in this task.

## BUDGETARY SUPPORT

The amount of money a firm will spend on advertising may be determined by one of several methods. In principle, money should be spent on all marketing activities as long as each dollar spent adds more than a dollar to gross profit. It follows that this dollar expenditure should be allocated to those marketing activities which promise to make the greatest profit contribution. Unfortunately, this is easier to advocate than to do, because it involves a number of variables, most of which are unknown. Sometimes, though, it is possible to quantify these variables. When this can be done, mathematical techniques are available which enable the planner to determine that combination of expenditure allocations which will make the maximum contribution to gross profit. But the result is still uncertain, since it is based on numerous assumptions about factors which are themselves uncertain.

When the purpose of advertising is related to something other than current profits, the principle is also clear. Advertising should be allocated the budget appropriation necessary to accomplish its purpose— provided this amount is less than would be needed to accomplish the purpose by any other means. If the purpose can be achieved in part by advertising and in part by some other activity, advertising should be allocated the amount needed for that part of the total undertaking it can do most effectively and least expensively. This is also very difficult to do in practice. But even though the principle can rarely be applied with anything approximating precision, decisions based on sound principles are more likely to be sound decisions than those which are reached in the absence of any conceptual construct.

As one might expect, what usually happens in practice represents a compromise of sorts. Some firms determine advertising expenditures on the basis of a fixed percentage of sales. The surveys of advertising budgets conducted annually by *Industrial Marketing* magazine and reported in the February issues indicate that between 15 and 20 percent of the reporting firms determine their advertising budgets in this manner. In some instances the sales forecast is the base to which the fixed percentage is applied, in others the base is last year's sales.

Although neither has much to commend it, budgeting a percent of expected sales can be more easily defended than using last year's sales as a base. Both are reminiscent of the mid-19th-century admonition of a Saturday night bath, without regard to time or urgency of need. Neither gives any assurance that either the percentage figure chosen or the base to which it is applied is the one that will result in the greatest profit to the firm or will make the most economical contribution to its non-profit objectives.

Much the same can be said of the practice of budgeting a determined percent of profits—last year's or expected. This practice is probably based on a vague notion that it is a good idea to spend as much as possible on advertising, but not enough to seriously reduce profits.

Slightly more than 40 percent of the firms reporting in the 1973 *Industrial Marketing* survey base their advertising budgets on the task method.[2] Under this method management first decides what functions or tasks advertising is expected to accomplish and then estimates the costs of doing them. If several tasks are to be accomplished, cost estimates would be prepared for each and management would decide which tasks or combination of tasks were worth the cost, and within the limits of the firm's financial resources.

This method has far more to recommend it than the fixed percentage technique, because it forces a determination of advertising's role in the promotional strategy. It involves the process of matching the worth of what one wants to do against the probable cost of doing it. This is an essential feature of business planning. Moreover, it recognizes that advertising should be a means of generating sales or contributing to other company objectives rather than serving as a function of sales or profits, which by implication is its role under the percentage method.

The 1973 *Industrial Marketing* survey also indicates that about 40 percent of the reporting firms determine their advertising budgets by a combination of the task and percentage methods. The survey offers no information regarding the manner in which the two methods are combined. However, it seems probable that chief reliance is placed on the task method, with an upper limit imposed by division or corporate-level management—in the form of a maximum percentage of expected sales—on the amount that can be spent. Whether or not the combination method is really superior to the task method used alone depends on the way the maximum percentage limit is set. If it is arbitrarily fixed and not subject to change, the superiority of the combination method is at least debatable. On the other hand, if the percentage is varied in response to changing circumstances and the changes systematically studied, the combination method clearly has real merit.

## MEASURING ADVERTISING EFFECTIVENESS

The intelligence with which planning is conducted can be greatly enhanced if the planner can measure the results of what has already been

---

[2] "Ad Budgets 1973," *Industrial Marketing* (February 1973), p. 34.

done. This is as true of advertising as it is of any other activity. The essence of measuring advertising effectiveness is to determine what influence, if any, the advertisement has had on the thinking and actions of the people who make or influence buying decisions. Unfortunately, no generally applicable technique for achieving this purpose with assured accuracy has yet been developed.

There would appear to be rather general agreement, though, that attempts to measure advertising effectiveness must be individual to the firm and must begin with a clear understanding of the purposes each advertisement or program is designed to achieve. Methods may then be developed to determine the extent to which each purpose has been accomplished.

For example, if a program was designed to stimulate demand, the flow of orders before and after its initiation could be determined, along with the cost of selling the additional volume. Admittedly, this approach has a few holes in it, the worst being that frequently the influence of advertising cannot be separated from that of other activities going on concurrently. However, if no other activity was in progress to which a given increase in sales could be attributed, the advertising program would appear to be its principal cause.

If the purpose of advertising is to identify new customers, the extent to which it does so can be measured at least in part by the number and kind of inquiries it generated. An inquiry usually contains internal evidence of the stimulus which triggered it. If inquiries obtained by advertising are followed up and result in sales, the cost of the inquiry and the subsequent cost of making the sales can be computed. This makes possible the calculation of an advertising cost per dollar of sales associated with the advertising.

If an advertising program was intended to create an image or dispel a prejudice, an attitude survey conducted before and after the initiation of the program may reveal the extent to which its purpose has been accomplished. Whether or not the purpose, or the extent of its achievement, is worth the cost is much more difficult to determine. However, management must have decided that the purpose was worth at least the amount budgeted for it. Consequently, the cost of complete or partial achievement can be computed and compared with the expenditure originally approved.

Measuring the effect of advertising designed to disseminate information can be done by thorough before-and-after surveys of what sample members of the target audience know about the subject matter presented. The cost and value considerations are the same as those which apply to an image or attitude objective.

While this discussion barely scratches the surface of the subject, its intent is merely to indicate that it is possible to devise methods with which the results of much industrial advertising can be measured with an acceptable degree of accuracy. The cost of measuring performance may, of course, exceed the value of the information it provides. In such cases, one can reasonably question whether or not advertising itself is worth its cost.

## PUBLICITY

Publicity is the "nonpersonal stimulation of demand for a product, service, or business unit, by planting commercially significant news about it in a published medium, or obtaining favorable presentation of it on radio, television, or stage, that is not paid for by the sponsor."[3] Publicity is generally considered to be a promotional activity that supplements advertising. Some industrial goods manufacturers, on the other hand, feel that publicity is a device more effective than advertising, and they look on trade journal advertising as a means of influencing or coercing editors to print free material that will benefit the advertiser. Others argue that editors are continually searching for information of value and interest to their readers, and if such worthwhile information is provided the editor will publish it, whether or not the sponsor has purchased space in his journal.

Some industrial goods manufacturers have been indifferent to publicity. When markets are concentrated and easily reached by salesmen, and when the product is a fabricating material or part or process material that cannot be readily identified in the end product, this policy may have merit. If the company is in a monopoly position, anonymity may aid in protecting that position. It is argued that in these circumstances publicity, at best, can have only limited value and, at worst, may be definitely harmful.

For many industrial marketers, however, publicity represents a useful promotional activity. It can introduce a company to potential customers and cause them to seek it out when they are in the market for products it produces. It can also serve to enhance a company's prestige and to establish it as a leader in its field in the introduction of new products or in communicating information about new developments or improvements in existing products. It can pave the way for salesmen, making the personal selling task easier, more effective, and less costly.

### Securing publicity

Several types of publicity may be distinguished. Probably the most important from the point of view of the industrial goods manufacturer is technical information about the products he makes. It may also be worthwhile to publicize the general merits of the type of product the

---

[3] "Report of the Definitions Committee," American Marketing Association (1960).

company manufactures—for example, plastics, steel, or synthetic rubber —or the type of equipment or service it provides, such as shock and vibration control devices, materials-handling equipment, or special chemicals. News items of general interest about personnel in the firm or interesting information about the company itself, such as plans for expansion, community relations, or programs of customer service, may be beneficial to the company.

The publicity function is often assigned to an individual whose duties consist of gathering and processing newsworthy information within the company or the industry, and making it available to the press. Employees may be encouraged to write technical articles for journals. Some companies have gone a step further and made time available for highly competent employees to write books in their fields. Valuable publicity has been gained by having employees speak before various organizations. Papers on current research or new-product development may be presented before scientific and engineering societies, or talks of a nontechnical nature may be given before civic and social groups. Many companies have found that showing visitors through their plants is an effective means of securing favorable publicity.

Many advertising agencies are organized to handle publicity for their clients, usually on a fee basis. Some companies find it worthwhile to hire a publicity expert who specializes in this type of work; others retain the services of a public relations firm, integrating publicity into their public relations program. The company house organ, when distributed to customers, may be a useful source of publicity.

### Measuring the effectiveness of publicity

Techniques for measuring the effectiveness of publicity are even less adequately developed than those for measuring the effectiveness of advertising. However, useful data can be compiled on the volume and type of publicity secured and whether it was favorable or unfavorable. Most trade journals assist in this effort by mailing published releases to the manufacturers concerned as part of their own promotional programs. Advertising agencies often keep track of such publicity as a service to their clients. Also, clipping service organizations may be employed to gather information, and radio and television monitoring services are available for this purpose.

## THE USE OF ADVERTISING AGENCIES

Advertising agencies are specialist organizations equipped to provide a range of advertising services to their clients. They work on advertising strategy and campaigns, prepare copy and layouts, study markets, select media, and carry out the actual physical production of the advertisement up to the time it is sent to the medium. Agencies usually serve a number of noncompetitive clients.

Most media allow agencies 15 percent on the cost of the space or time purchased. In consumer goods marketing, this commission, plus fees for purchased services, usually represents the total agency income available to cover costs of operation and leave a profit. For many industrial goods marketers, this method of payment does not result in an amount large enough to cover agency costs, and the contract with the agency includes an additional lump-sum payment to compensate for the services wanted. This different relationship of cost to income arises primarily because the space rates charged by business publications are very much lower than those of consumer media with their much larger circulations. Closely coupled with this are the multiple markets involved in the sale of many industrial goods, and the higher cost of preparing a greater number of advertisements, each tailored to a particular group of prospects.

The advertising agency brings to an industrial client a wide breadth of experience in industrial marketing, which can rarely be matched by the experience of a single manufacturing company. It should also be able to provide the qualities of imagination and innovation to an unusual degree. Despite these advantages, agencies probably are not used by industrial marketers to the extent that they are by sellers of consumer goods. There are significant numbers of industrial goods manufacturers whose advertising departments perform all the functions the agency is equipped to handle.

The explanation lies largely in the technical and highly specialized nature of many industrial products. Even when an agency staff includes men with engineering training, a substantial job of education must be done before they are fully conversant with the details of technical products and markets, and are able to prepare accurate and effective copy. Often, copy prepared by the agency must be submitted to the advertiser's technical experts for review. Sometimes, the resulting revisions are so extensive that it would have been more efficient and less costly for the company advertising staff, who are in closer contact with the technical people, to prepare the copy in the first place. Even more difficult for an agency is the preparation of catalogs and direct mail copy; yet these are very important selling tools for the industrial marketer.

There has been an increase in recent years in the number of agencies specializing in industrial accounts. There also has been an increase in the number of agencies which offer their promotional services on a job-shop basis. Both developments have served to increase the usefulness of agencies to the industrial marketer.

There can be no question that the advertising agency can make an important contribution to the promotional strategy of an industrial marketer. It cannot perform some types of activities as well as company personnel, but it can do others better or more economically. The task of the marketing executive is to achieve the most effective integration of company and agency resources.

## SUMMARY

The task of the industrial advertiser is complicated by the multiple buying influence characteristic of many industrial firms, the derived nature of demand for industrial goods, and the fact that many materials, parts, and components lose their identity in the end product. These conditions influence the role of advertising in the firm's promotional strategy, which in turn has a bearing on the purposes which advertising will be called upon to serve. While these purposes vary with the firm and the market situation, several are fairly common. They are: to inform, to identify new customers, to win recognition, to support salesmen, to motivate distributors, and to stimulate demand.

The basic appeals used in advertising copy tend to be rational, emphasizing dollar benefits to the buyer or aid in achieving his non-monetary goals, although appeals to patronage may be more emotional in content. Nevertheless, the most effective advertising copy is probably that which is largely factual, containing claims which are specific and provable.

The most commonly used media for disseminating advertising messages and the sales appeals they contain are trade journals and catalogs, followed by direct mail, exhibits, general publications, and distributor aids. The choice of media is determined by the need to reach the proper personnel in the customer's organization with the proper frequency and with the proper overall impression.

The chief limiting factor underlying the advertising effort is the amount of budgetary support management decides to give it. Sometimes this is determined through the application of a fixed percentage to either last year's sales or anticipated sales. At other times the decision is based on the task assigned to advertising in the general promotional plan or on a combination of both percentage and task methods.

Despite the importance of selecting an appropriate advertising function, the right sales message, proper media, allocating adequate budgetary support, and using the expertise of advertising agencies, measuring results is the indispensable ingredient of effective advertising planning. While this cannot be done with assured accuracy, the development of practically useful methods usually yields to ingenuity and intelligence.

Publicity is commonly regarded as a form of advertising, although it performs a slightly different function and is not paid for by the sponsor. The most effective way to create publicity is to generate newsworthy situations and events. Many advertising agencies are equipped to handle the publicity function for their clients and some actively promote this service. Advertising agencies are probably used less by industrial than by consumer goods marketers to assist in their advertising and publicity. However, this appears to be changing as the number of agencies specializing in industrial accounts increases and the number which offers promotional services on a job-shop basis continues to grow.

# 21

# PERSONAL SELLING

THE USE of personal selling in the promotional strategy involves the selection of salesmen, training them, assigning their tasks, supplying them with home office support, developing a system of compensation, controlling their expenses, providing day-to-day supervision, and motivating them to put forth their best efforts. The characteristics of industrial goods and the circumstances under which they must be sold simplify the performance of some functions and complicate that of others. These functions and the numerous influences that shape their performance are treated under four general headings: selection, training, supervision, and motivation.

## SELECTING SALESMEN

Due to the type of personnel with whom the industrial salesman may have to negotiate, the potential volume of sales his territory may represent, and the technical complexity of problems he may face, he should be carefully chosen and thoroughly trained. The aspects of selection which have almost universal application are the personnel profile sources, and selection aids.

### Personnel profile

The process of selecting an industrial salesman, like that of choosing any other employee, begins with the preparation of a position analysis or man specification. The details of any such specification usually grow out of the nature of the business of the employing company and the kind of selling it has to do. But certain traits and characteristics are common to most industrial marketing firms and grow out of the attitudes of the average buyer, the manner in which he purchases, and the kind of services he wants and expects from the salesmen who call on him. At least the following traits of mind and personality are called for.

1. Initiative and self-discipline. A convincing presentation of a technical product necessitates continual study to up-date one's knowledge, not only that related to his products but to his customers' operations as well. To be alert to new ways of serving them, the salesman must continually search for information and ideas that will benefit them, whether or not such knowledge has direct commercial significance to him.

2. Persistence. A sale is rarely closed the first time an item is presented. A long series of call-backs may be required in selling an expensive piece of equipment. If the buying decision is an important one, the approval of several executives may be required before the order can be placed. This often involves a lengthy period of negotiation and the salesman who continues his selling efforts with persistence and tact, even after the sale seems lost, is sometimes rewarded by seeing the decision process turn in his favor. This means that he must sometimes work for long periods without the emotional lift that comes from getting a buyer's signature on the dotted line.

3. Adaptability. Since the buying decision may be influenced by a number of personnel in the customer firm, an industrial salesman must be able to adapt his manner and his tactics to the individual prospect. In selling an item of specialized equipment, for example, the salesman may have to make his presentation to the man on the bench, the foreman, the shop superintendent, the purchasing agent, and depending on the size of the expenditure the item represents, perhaps to one or more top executives. Obviously, he must be able to speak the language of each.

4. Friendly and considerate. Strong patronage motives on the part of customers are difficult for competitors to break down. To build such motives, not only requires the salesman to be alert to ways in which he can be helpful, but to be personally liked by the people with whom he negotiates.

5. Honesty. This does not preclude enthusiasm in what the salesman says about his product and his company. But when he states a fact about either, it should be provable, and when he makes a promise about what either will do, it should be demonstrable. Misrepresentation by implication or omission destroys the buyer's confidence just as quickly and completely as a blatant untruth.

6. Ability to plan. Due to the relatively small number of prospective customers for many industrial products, the volume of sales each represents, and the number of persons who may influence the buying decision, the industrial salesman is required to plan his activity in some detail. The successful salesmen not only plan their routes and schedules but often their individual calls. Since the salesman should know better than anyone else the kind of opposition and competition he faces, he must do this kind of planning for himself.

Depending on the nature or the marketing policies of the employing firm, other traits or characteristics could be added to this list to complete the profile of the kind of man who is needed. Since there is apt to be a limited number of candidates who match the profile perfectly, it is often a good idea to divide the items included in it into two groups—a Must group and a Would Like group.

## Sources of candidates

Perhaps the most commonly used sources for recruiting industrial salesmen are publications, schools, the existing sales force, other departments of the firm, and competitors. As one might expect, some are better sources than others.

*Publications.* Although the abler type of salesman would probably consult newspaper ads as a last resort, advertisements in the business opportunities section of the *Wall Street Journal* or the *New York Times* often prove fruitful. Trade journals are likely to be a better source than newspapers, particularly for experienced salesmen, because it is probable that they are better known and more regularly consulted by salesmen.

The success with which publications may be used in recruiting depends in large measure on the quality of the advertisement. Common sense would indicate that the copy should be as specific as possible, setting forth the must requirements established by the job analysis as well as the kind of information about the company a prospective employee would like to know.

Although one can find a number of such advertisements which do not identify the advertiser by name, it is probably not advisable to do so. The blind ad may be answered by someone presently in the employ of the advertiser—an embarrassing experience for both. For this reason, salesmen who are contemplating a change in jobs but who are not yet ready to so inform their present employers may hesitate to reply to a blind ad.

*Schools.* Colleges and universities are usually fruitful sources of sales personnel, particularly colleges of engineering and business administration. However, graduates of these schools are almost certain to need extensive training in the practical aspects of selling. Since many such recruits look upon a selling position as a stepping stone to an executive position, a policy of recruiting college graduates for sales positions may result in a high rate of turnover in the sales force.

*Existing sales force.* If salesmen know that their merit ratings will be improved as a result of suggesting suitable candidates for new sales positions, they may be a good source of recruits. The weakness of using the sales force in this way lies in the possibility that salesmen will suggest relatives and friends without regard to their qualifications, or that they will hesitate to suggest anyone at all for fear of eroding their own status in the company if persons they suggest fail to make competent salesmen.

*Other departments of the business.* Candidates from within the firm have advantages in that they enter the sales force with a knowledge of the products and the company, which outsiders must spend a long period of indoctrination in acquiring. Moreover, managers have had an opportunity to observe them and to form sounder judgments of their abilities than is possible through the ordinary selection procedure. Candidates from technical and service departments are especially attractive because they come to sales work with much of the technical information and knowledge of product uses that outsiders gain only after extensive training.

*Competition.* Some firms regularly raid competitors for new additions to their sales forces. In the long run this policy can produce a high rate of personnel turnover, because a man who can be hired away from one firm usually can be hired away from another. Moreover, the hiring firm generally must offer a substantial increase in the salesman's earnings in order to get him. This may mean that his pay is out of line with that of other members of the sales force, a condition that can spell trouble, because it can seldom be concealed. However, hiring an experienced salesman can reduce the need for training, unless he must unlearn a number of the competitor's selling policies and approaches that do not fit his new employer's method of operation.

## Selection aids

Industrial marketers use all the accepted devices for eliminating and choosing candidates when trying to fill sales positions. The nature of their sales problems and methods probably leads them to emphasize the formal application and the personal interview somewhat more than is the general practice.

*The formal application.* The formal application with its record of technical training and experience is the backbone of a selection system. By observing the schools the candidate has attended and the firms by which he has been employed, a fairly reliable picture should emerge of the soundness of his technical preparation, and in what way it has been enriched by experience.

*Tests.* The two most commonly used types of tests probably are technical aptitude tests and sales aptitude tests. There are good reasons to believe that the former are used less extensively than the latter, because industrial salesmen do not need to be technical wizards. But they do need a sufficient technical background to (*a*) recognize the salient aspects of a production, engineering, or chemical problem, (*b*) talk intelligently with the prospective buyer about it, (*c*) realize when they should call for assistance from specialized technical personnel. A man who is a competent scientist is not apt to be a competent salesman; and a salesman who is so interested in the purely technical aspects of the products he sells that he tries to keep abreast of all the developments related to them probably has only a secondary interest in selling.

The aptitude or personal interest test administerd by competent psychologists can be an important aid in identifying candidates who are endowed with the ability to sell as well as the personality, interest, and motivation to use it. Perhaps the real usefulness of such tests lies not so much in their indicating the exact candidates to be chosen as in calling attention to the technically qualified candidates who are not fitted temperamentally or by personality, interest, or aptitude for sales work.

*References.*  The tendency for persons from whom references are requested to report only complimentary information weakens the usefulness of this device as an aid in selecting salesmen. However, a form composed of specific questions, with spaces for answers or a series of columns in which the respondent can rate the candidate on various specified characteristics and traits, may dissipate the inclination to see no evil. A reference who will lie tacitly by omission will probably hesitate to do so overtly. The weakness of such forms is that they may fail to cover the precise area in which the candidate's shortcomings fall.

Some sales managers have been very successful in the use of telephone or personal interviews with persons given as references. The tone of voice, the facial expression, or a tactical hesitation may be more significant than what is said. When the reference gives evidence of an unexpressed reservation, polite probing will sometimes bring it to light.

*The interview.*  The most widely used aid in selecting industrial product salesmen is undoubtedly the interview. Through it, the sales manager can observe at first hand the personality of the candidate and appraise the impression he makes. However, as an aid in selecting salesmen, the interview suffers at least four drawbacks.

1. A man who is excellent at selling a product or service for someone else may not be equally competent in selling himself. It is often taken for granted that a good salesman must be able to sell himself to the prospect and that his ability to do so may be judged to some extent in an employment interview. But selling oneself as an adjunct to a product or service is not the same undertaking as selling oneself alone. A man who is very adroit at the first may be a dismal failure at the second. The reverse is also true.

2. Common sense would suggest that there is always the temptation for a sales manager to favor the candidates who impress him rather than the candidates most likely to impress his firm's customers. The former is a much simpler task than the latter.

3. Without some structure, e.g., an interview form on which the interviewer enters his reactions to specific traits and characteristics of the candidate, the results of an interview may quickly become blurred or confused. Ideally, the information desired about a candidate should be drawn out systematically in a preplanned order rather than being per-

mitted to emerge haphazardly. This requires the kind of planning some managers may be unwilling to give it.

4. Conducting an informative interview requires both skill and talent. It is not something anybody can do well merely because he is in the position to do it. Since few men can wholly escape the bias and unconscious prejudice engendered by their own experience and emotional makeup, it is usually advisable to have a candidate interview several executives—singly or as a group—in the course of employment negotiations. The group interview is frequently used by manufacturers of heavy equipment, because selling such products often requires the sales representative to appear before a group of executives in the prospect firm. Such an interview may afford some notion of the candidate's ability to handle himself in the presence of a group.

## TRAINING

The relatively small number of customers served by industrial marketers and the relatively large size of the typical order lend unusual importance to the training of salesmen. At the same time, the relatively small size of the typical industrial sales force and the high stakes riding on each contact of the marketing firm with its customers render impractical many widely used training methods. Only the large industrial firms, for example, can make very effective use of classroom training. Individualized instruction is probably far more common than any other type. Its essence is that the student salesman works for a time in each of a series of departments or divisions of the company until he has familiarized himself with its products, policies, and operating methods.

The chief disadvantage of such training lies in the likelihood that it will be interrupted. If the student is an able person, he is likely to make himself valuable to one or more of the executives for whom he works. One of them may succeed in keeping the trainee in his own unit, interrupting his progress toward a position in the selling organization. This may have serious consequences for the trainee's career, because substantial sales experience is likely to be a prerequisite for advancement to executive positions in the selling organization. A useful safeguard against such a contingency is to establish definite time limits on the length of a trainee's stay in any one department or division of the business, and then being adamant about enforcing them.

The content of informal training programs varies both with the company and the experience of candidates. The latter is a particularly important consideration of the company.

### Inexperienced trainees

Individualized training programs for inexperienced sales trainees would involve at least four types of subject matter: the company, the product, the customer, and selling techniques.

*The company.*  The new salesman must obviously have a knowledge of his company, its policies, and its methods of operation—particularly those which affect its capacity to serve customers. This knowledge not only equips him to represent the company with a feeling of confidence but serves to create in him a sense of identity with the company. This part of the training may be conducted most effectively in the home or branch office where the trainee might be assigned such tasks as handling and expediting orders, passing on credit applications, processing sales correspondence, answering inquiries, and working in the shipping department.

*The product.*  Much of the information about the company's product line—how it is produced, its technical features, the uses for which it is designed, and its elements of strength and weakness in relation to competing products—can be made available in the form of product or sales manuals. This material is not only useful as text material in the training program but also as reference material when the trainee receives his assignment to the sales force.

A manufacturer of heavy machinery has its prospective salesmen assist with the installation and servicing of its equipment. This experience gives the firm's new salesmen the feel of the product and a very realistic understanding of the circumstances in which it is used. A leading manufacturer of telephone systems and equipment sold to independent telephone companies starts its salesmen as installers. They then graduate to equipment engineers, and after a period of time spent in this work they become salesmen.

*The customer.*  About the only way to know the customer, i.e., what kind of business he operates, how he likes to buy, how he uses the company's products, the kinds of problems he encounters, and what kind of assistance he can use most effectively—is to meet him and deal with him in the field. Traveling with an experienced salesman is perhaps the most usual way of imparting this kind of knowledge.

*Selling techniques.*  As in the case of learning about customers, learning selling techniques must usually be done in the field. Some large firms with sizable sales forces make use of specialized field trainers who spend all their time conducting this type of training. Firms which do not have enough new trainees to support a full-time field trainer rely on branch or regional managers, senior salesmen willing to train new men when the need arises, or even a home office executive if the company has only a few salesmen.

The experience of a good many companies seems to indicate that the most effective way to teach selling techniques is through the procedure of observation, trial, criticism, and perhaps reobservation and retrial. In essence, the new trainee accompanies his instructor and observes what he does. This process may continue for a few calls, or it may go on for months if the average purchase is large and the selling task involved. Eventually, the trainee is given an opportunity to try his own hand at a sales call, either under the observation of his instructor or alone, whichever the personalities and circumstances seem to indicate. In any event the trainee must usually perform in the presence of his instructor at some point in the learning process, and the instructor postmortems his performance and suggests improvements. This process of trial, criticism, and retrial would ordinarily continue until the instructor becomes convinced that his pupil is ready to go on his own.

## Experienced salesmen

The rapid pace of change in both product technology and environmental conditions usually render it desirable to devote some attention to the training of experienced salesmen. This may be done in the field through visits of the branch manager, the supervisor, or the sales manager himself. While such personal contact is probably the most effective method of updating salesmen's knowledge and expertise, it may also be the most expensive and time-consuming. Conferences in the home- or branch-office offer a useful means of imparting such training, although the number of salesmen involved should be small enough to permit an active exchange of ideas among them.

Conventions may also be a productive means of retraining and updating experienced salesmen. A convention can be successful in renewing one's sense of identity with the company. If held at the factory, it can be effective in establishing or maintaining personal relationships among salesmen and the home office personnel with whom they have mail or telephone contact in the course of fulfilling customers' needs. Conventions can also be an effective means of presenting in a short period of time and at low expense the marketing program for a new product, a change in marketing strategy, a new marketing policy, or any other modification in company management of significance to salesmen.

Possible mistakes in running conventions are almost without limit. They are liable to be too long but highly unlikely to be too short. They may be cluttered with speeches of high-ranking company brass with nothing much to say. The occasion should be dignified by the appearance of high company officials; but each should have a significant message to deliver and know when to end it. All presentations should be in terms the salesman can understand and not in highly technical, scientific, or legal language. Salesmen should be given every possible opportunity to participate. Collectively, they are apt to know more about their problems than any company executive could know. The affair should have its social aspects but they should be subordinated—especially the liquid nourishment—to the main business of the meeting. If a convention is worth holding, it deserves the most careful planning and detailed supervision, but few managers relish the assignment.

Much of the really effective work of training experienced salesmen must be done on an individual basis. It consists of diagnosing the man's strengths and weaknesses, trying to show him how to use his strengths more effectively, and inducing him to eliminate his weaknesses or learn to maneuver so that they no longer handicap his performance. Since some of these weaknesses may be in the area of personality, this is a very delicate matter. In the absence of professional psychiatric help, which is a pretty drastic measure, changes in personality traits must be made almost entirely as a result of the efforts of the individual involved. A manager can do little beyond trying to supply the incentive for making them and encouraging the salesman, during what is often a long and frustrating experience. If an undesirable trait is not too ingrained and is not a manifestation of a deep-seated emotional complex, the following procedure used by a number of sales managers may be helpful: (1) compile a personal inventory of the salesman's strengths and weaknesses, (2) determine which weaknesses should be singled out for remedial attention, and (3) initiate remedial action. Each step warrants at least a brief explanation.

*The personal inventory.*    The list of an individual's personality strengths and weaknesses is usually compiled by the man himself with the aid of an interested third party—the sales manager or the company psychologist—who has had an opportunity to observe him. Such an inventory can be a startling revelation. It is perhaps true that most men take themselves for granted, developing undesirable habits and attitudes without realizing it. While a salesman may be partially aware of some of the personal defects which have hindered his sales effectiveness, it is doubtful that he is aware of all of them or has been fully conscious of those he does recognize.

*Identifying traits for correction.*    In singling out traits for remedial attention, it is prudent to concentrate on one or two at a time and to bear in mind that it is usually more fruitful to strengthen relatively strong characteristics than to attempt radical personal changes. For example, it probably would be impossible to change one from an introvert to an extrovert, and very dangerous to attempt, even under professional guidance. But it is possible to compensate for a weakness such as lack of aggressiveness by developing to a higher level of sensitivity such traits as tact, power of observation, willingness to listen, and desire to be of service. If lack of persistence is the weakness, the simple expedient of insisting that a given number of refusals be suffered before an order is given up as lost can elevate the level of a salesman's resolve and perseverance in the pursuit of orders sufficiently to effect a substantial improvement.

*Initiating remedial action.*    Any action taken should follow a plan which has been formulated under the guidance of professional counsel and administered in the same manner. Although self-improvement can only be accomplished by the man himself, no man should attempt it alone. This is true even though the task of self-improvement involves little more than the establishment of good habits of behavior or attitude patterns. Sincerity, helpfulness, consideration, courtesy, honesty, and dependability are not attitudes which can be put on like a mask and then discarded as soon as one leaves the presence of the customer. Even the attempt to strengthen such basic attributes as honesty, courtesy, and dependability should not be attempted by unguided amateurs. Along the path of excessive personal introspection lie many pitfalls of emotional disturbance. A man should be encouraged to reconstruct his personality only under expert guidance and counsel.

## SUPERVISION

Although the exact meaning of supervision varies somewhat from one pundit to another, it includes at least the assignment of tasks, the provision of selling support, and day-to-day guidance in the planning and conduct of negotiation with customers.

### Task assignment

Many industrial marketers find it desirable to define the assignments of their salesmen in terms of customers. While these customers usually include the larger, more important accounts, they may also include small accounts with significant growth potential. If it is desirable to assign geographical areas to salesmen, this is usually done with the understanding that the larger and more important customers in the territory, i.e., the house accounts, will be handled separately by an older, more experienced salesman or even a company executive.

Paper work in the form of report writing is also a part of the usual assignment for salesmen, because of the importance of timely feedback of market information to the home office. Unfortunately, the salesman will not be very thorough in gathering the kind of information he can collect best unless he is trained for it; he will probably not do it unless he is properly motivated; and the information he gathers will not deliver its maximum usefulness to him unless it is properly digested, analyzed, and related to the details of his assignment. Part of the information needed from the field usually must be collected by the headquarters or regional office staffs. Nevertheless, the salesman plays an important role in its collection, and the better he does his part the greater the likelihood that the intelligence which comes back to him from the home or regional office will enable him to make more of a planned and less of a blind approach to his assignment.

### Selling support

Selling support is used here to refer to the various devices with which the salesman may be equipped to help him in making an effective presentation to the customer. These include samples, product models, graphic representations, slides, and films.

*Samples.*  If the product is small in bulk, a display of samples representing the various sizes and designs in which the product is available can be an effective aid in selling. However, care must be taken not to encumber the salesman with an embarrassment of riches. A firm that makes container closures once developed a very compact, ingeniously constructed collection of samples representing each of the several hundred items in its product lines. It was a dismal failure because the salesman found that the prospects' desire to examine all items in the display and to discuss many of them so lengthened the average sales call as to reduce rather than augment his effectiveness. Comparatively few firms selling industrial products are apt to suffer from this difficulty, but as a general rule, selectivity is a more desirable characteristic of a sample display than is completeness.

*Models.*  Firms marketing heavy equipment or machinery often prepare models to demonstrate how the product functions, where it can be installed, and what it is capable of doing. Many purchasing officers probably would welcome more extensive use of such models. However, sales managers often fear that their use tends to cause salesmen to lean too heavily on them to the detriment of their presentation of technical data.

Numerous devices similar to models have also been developed and used with telling effect. A company which makes industrial lubricants prepared a table-top demonstration unit of suitcase size to show its type of lubrication in use, through a system of transparent walls and fluorescent lighting. It was a valuable aid in selling to machine owners and machine builders. A company that makes silencers and motor exhaust mufflers equipped its salesmen with a tape recording device to make recordings of various mufflers or silencing devices on the customer's equipment, which could be played back to the prospective buyer in the quiet of his own office. This was helpful in contrasting the efficiency of the company's equipment with that of competing devices, as well as in selecting the particular type of silencer to do the best job in a specific situation.

*Graphic presentations.*  Pictures of products in action on the job site, charts, graphs, or tables showing performance records, and drawings or blueprints showing their construction are all useful supports for the salesman's efforts. However, they should be of manageable size, and should be placed in the kind of container or case that permits the salesman to present them on the prospect's desk without cluttering or confusion. They also should be placed in such a sequence that the salesman can develop his presentation around them instead of using them as a crutch to fall back on when all else fails.

*Slides and films.*  Increasing use is being made of slides, film strips, and film to support sales presentations. The great advantage of films is that the product can be shown in action, lending the sales presentation an air of realism which can be gained in no other way except by a visit to the user's plant. However, films are expensive to produce, and it may be difficult to justify their cost unless they are to receive a considerable amount of use before their material becomes obsolete.

While slides and film strips lack the dramatic impact of film presentations, they are much less costly to produce and have certain other advantages not possessed by films. For example, an individual frame in a slide or film strip presentation may be kept on the screen while the selling features it illustrates are discussed or while a prospect's questions are answered. This kind of flexibility can lend an atmosphere of informality to a presentation that may substantially enhance its impact.

### Day-to-day guidance

The day-to-day guidance of salesmen has many aspects which vary with the industry, the company, the type of customers, and other variables of the market situation. However, it is almost certain to include such elements as instruction, planning, evaluation, communication, maintaining morale, and the exercise of leadership.

*Instruction.* Salesmen, like other employees, are prone to fall unwares into unproductive habits. It is the task of their immediate superior to be alert to such lapses and seek to correct them. The process of correction usually requires considerable tact and finesse. The industrial salesman is apt to be an able, self-reliant person with strong opinions who does not respond well to direct instruction. Often instructions have to be of an oblique nature which recognizes both the man's intelligence and the uniqueness of his situation.

*Planning and evaluation.* A salesman's immediate superior is often expected to take the lead in planning his work, even to the point of developing with him the approach he will use in negotiating with particular customers. Since able men are likely to be more enthusiastic about carrying out their own plans than someone else's plans, the superior must so draw out his subordinate that he will regard the finished plan as his own and not that of his superior.

Since evaluation is the inevitable accompaniment of planning, the performance of salesmen needs to be evaluated so mistakes can be identified and remedied in the next planning period. The results of evaluation may be formalized with the use of merit ratings which are periodically submitted to headquarters management. Discussion of these ratings with salesmen is a delicate but necessary function of day-to-day guidance if mistakes are to be corrected and each salesman is to develop to his full potential.

*Communication.*   One of the obstacles which frequently obstructs the successful use of personal selling is that men in the field cannot understand why home office management behave in the way they do. Nor does home office management always understand why salesmen harbor some of the complaints and resentments they sometimes do. An essential part of the day-to-day guidance of salesmen is to explain company policies and decisions to them and explain their problems, doubts, and feelings to management. The close coordination necessary among different specialized groups whose actions can influence sales depends upon the existence of mutual understanding among them.

*Maintain morale and discipline.*   High morale is indispensable for sustained high levels of performance, but it cannot be taken for granted. The industrial salesman is particularly vulnerable to "giveupitis." He often must go for long periods between sales. He must call on some prospective customers for weeks or months or years before a break comes that gives him a chance at the business. Much of the time he must negotiate with men further up in the business hierarchy than he is. Some of them have greater technical competence than his. And all of them regard him and his product and his services with critical eyes, and often speak of them with critical tongues. All these things tend to deflate the ego. And the ego is very important in maintaining the enthusiasm that is so important for sustained effort in any undertaking.

While there are no panaceas which apply to every situation, a fundamental requirement is a superior *who* the salesman knows *has* confidence in his abilities and *to whom* he knows he can turn for constructive and sympathetic advice. The cause of poor performance or of some condition that is creating low morale may, of course, be traced to the salesman himself, i.e., to carelessness, disregard of instructions, or poor judgment. In such instances, some degree of discipline must be applied, but it should be applied in doses compounded to fit the diagnosis of each individual case.

*Leadership.*   Without leadership, little of consequence would happen. Yet what constitutes leadership and how it is exercised has never been fully explained. George S. Patton—conceited, arrogant, profane, unpredictable, brash, and dictatorial—was a great leader. Omar N. Bradley—quiet, modest to the point of shyness, steady as a rock, without either dash or color—was a great leader. It is difficult to understand what traits they held in common. Indeed, one is virtually forced into the expedient of defining leadership in terms of its results rather than its innate characteristics.

Perhaps it can be said that leadership is the quality of a manager that makes his subordinates proud of him and proud of the organization to which they belong. It is that quality of a superior that lifts the men under him out of their limitations and stirs them to performance that matches their true abilities. If this is leadership, the supervisor of salesmen should have some measure of it, because it has a powerful effect on the enthusiasm and drive the men will put into their selling effort.

## COMPENSATION

The circumstances under which many industrial products are sold render the straight salary, or some modification of it, the logical method of compensating salesmen. The infrequent and irregular intervals at which orders are received would result in a feast or famine for them if income was related to sales. Moreover, the large proportion of salesmen's time that is spent in development and service work, neither of which results in immediate sales, and the cooperative effort needed in selling to customers with numerous plants requires a compensation plan that recognizes work as well as sales. The salary augmented by a commission schedule or with bonuses is widely used by industrial firms whose marketing strategy emphasizes personal selling. Nonmonetary incentives are also used in conjunction with salaries, but probably to a much lesser extent than either commissions or bonuses.

### Commissions

Obviously, the function of the salary is to afford the salesman continuity of income. The commission gives him some incentive to increase his total sales volume or rewards him for the results of successful development or service work done previously. The effectiveness with which the salary-commission plan functions depends upon how well it is drawn. The longer the period between sales and the more development and service work the company expects the salesman to do, the larger the salary should loom in his total compensation. But the commission must be large enough to afford an incentive to increase volume.

Sometimes the commission plan will include a drawing account against commissions. For example, a salesman may be authorized to draw $600 at the beginning of each month and to receive a 2 percent commission on sales. If his sales during a given month amounted to $60,000, his total income for the month would be $1800 (.02 × 60,000 plus $600). However, any month in which his commission was less than his drawing account, the difference would be deducted from future commissions. That is, if the man's sales volume was only $25,000 in a given month, his income for the month would be $1100 ($600 plus his commission of $500), but $100 would be deducted from next month's commissions.

In the event the salesman encounters a period of bad luck that persists for, say, a year, his commission arrears may be adjusted or written off. This will enable him to begin the new year without handicap.

However, this kind of beneficence ordinarily can be expected only when management is convinced that circumstances were beyond the salesman's control.

A commission plan may also incorporate a series of weights to induce salesmen to allocate proportionately greater effort to products requiring extensive development work. This may be done by setting different commission rates for different products as well as by using weights. The latter system is illustrated in the following example. Here the salesman's commission would be 2 percent of $140,000, or $2,800.

| Product | Monthly sales | Incentive factor | Adjusted monthly sales |
|---|---|---|---|
| A | $ 38,000 | 1.00 | $ 38,000 |
| B | 200,000 | .20 | 40,000 |
| C | 80,000 | .40 | 32,000 |
| D | 15,000 | 2.00 | 30,000 |
| Adjusted total | | | $140,000 |

## Bonuses

Bonuses are frequently based on sales volume, either in absolute dollars or in relation to a quota or estimate of territory potential. They may also be based on net profits, either of the company or of the particular division or territory to which the salesman is assigned. Bonuses may also be based on a rating system which is intended to reward the more intangible elements of his performance. Such a system was devised by the sales manager of a large firm. The following substantially abridged version of the system is illustrative.

1. Supplying an important customer with extra service was rewarded with a letter of commendation from the sales manager with a check for $50.

2. Supplying an important customer with an unusual form of service that resulted in increased profit was recognized with a letter of commendation from the marketing manager with a check for $250.

3. Action that saved a very important customer from a competitor or added a similar one to the customer list was recognized with a letter of commendation from the executive vice president with a $500 check.

4. Developing a new application of one of the company's products to a customer's operations, which increased the customer's purchases and profitability, was rewarded with a letter of commendation from the president with a check for $1,000.

The kind of performance for which each type of award would be given was explained in considerable detail and made known to the salesmen. The system had the advantage of offering two kinds of incentives in one package, recognition and money.

Sales managers often experience great difficulty in administering bonus systems. The difficulty usually arises when the system becomes so complex that its operation cannot be readily understood by those for whom it has been designed. Misunderstanding then leads to doubt and doubt to suspicion or apathy. A cardinal principle in planning and administering a bonus system is that the bonus should be paid for a specifically defined action and the definition should be clear enough that every salesman understands exactly what he must do to earn the reward. If the system is beyond the ready comprehension of any fully qualified member of the sales force, it is probably too complicated. On the other hand, a bonus should not be in the nature of a Christmas present, whose payment or amount depends on the state of the manager's ulcers or emotions at the moment of decision.

## EXPENSE CONTROL

While a salesman's expense account is not a part of the company's compensation or incentive system, it may affect his take-home pay, and certainly affects the enthusiasm he has for his job and his company. If a firm's policy regarding expense accounts is too rigid or niggardly, its salesmen may have to pay part of their expenses out of their regular compensation. Such a contingency is certain to affect morale. If, on the other hand, expense account policy is too liberal or is carelessly administered, the expense account may become a source of supplementary income to the salesmen who choose to make it so.

Expense control is complicated by the need to adhere to the rulings of the Internal Revenue Service (IRS), which will not permit what it regards as excessive expense allowances to be treated as costs in computing profits. Such allowances may also constitute a problem to the salesman in preparing his own tax reports. The expenses usually involved are the cost of travel, food, lodging, expenses incidental to living away from home, and entertainment. Entertainment is an especially tricky item—so much so, in fact, that it is often treated as a separate problem.

There are at least three basic methods used by industrial marketers to control salesmen's expenses: automatic allowance, per diem allowance, and reimbursement. While each is subject to innumerable variations, there are significant features that distinguish one from the other. Also, each has certain advantages and disadvantages.

### Automatic allowance

Under this method the salesman pays his own expenses out of his regular compensation, which supposedly contains an increment to cover them. This has the advantages that the firm is saved considerable record-keeping expense, a source of administrative friction is eliminated, and the man's expenses tend to be frugally managed.

On the other hand, since the management has no records from which to learn how much a salesman should spend or actually does spend, it is apt to be somewhat in the dark when it sets the increment added to the basic remuneration to cover expenses. This plan may also result in the man's managing his expenses too frugally for the company's benefit, since it is often difficult for him to understand that to make money he must spend money.

## Per diem allowance

Under this method the salesman is permitted a lump sum per day or, if considerable travel is involved, per mile. This avoids the hardship to the salesman of having to pay money from his own pocket in doing development work that does not result in immediate sales to cover its cost. Here too, it is not easy for management to decide just how much the lump sum should be. Moreover, having received the lump sum, the salesman may try to skimp on expense corners to save some of it, with the result that he may not do the aggressive selling management expects. Finally, IRS believes in specifics and prefers to allow as costs against profits only the expenses actually incurred.

## Reimbursement

This is the method preferred by the Internal Revenue Service. The salesman maintains a detailed expense account which he submits to his employer for reimbursement. The salesman is reimbursed only for expenses actually paid. This method does not discourage a salesman from spending more if by so doing he can sell more, but management can audit and review his expenditures in order to keep them within reasonable bounds.

On the other hand, anyone who has traveled on an expense account knows that it is difficult to include all the extra outlays incident to living away from home, each trivial in itself but adding up to a considerable sum. Then, too, salesmen show a truly remarkable ingenuity in developing schemes for beating the rules. If expense control is too rigid, precious thought and imagination will be spent on doctoring the expense account, when they would materially increase sales if properly applied. Sales managers are usually convinced that salesmen's expense accounts contain some of the purest and most creative fiction to be found in the language. Probably the essence of good expense control is the manager's recognition that some salesmen will beat the game, and that he can only try to keep the overages within reasonable bounds. Due to the high quality and relatively high income level of industrial salesmen, their tendency to pad expense accounts is probably less pervading and urgent than among their consumer goods counterparts; but, by the same token, they do a more finished job of it when provoked to try it.

Reimbursement for entertainment expenses is a special target for the attention of IRS. Probably, the soundest policy for controlling it is to require full reporting of such expenses and to allow only those which can reasonably be expected to contribute to sales. Especially to be avoided are the spectacular forms of entertainment and any with a predominately amusement aspect.

## SUMMARY

The personal selling component of promotional strategy involves the selection, training, supervision, and compensation of salesmen, plus control of their expenses. The selection procedure begins with development of a profile of desired traits and abilities against which candidates can be measured. The major sources of candidates for selling positions are trade journal advertising, colleges and universities, and nonselling divisions of the company. Sources of lesser importance are newspaper advertising, suggestions of present salesmen, and competitors. In the process of selection the formal application and the interview are probably most useful, although psychological tests and references can contribute valuable help if properly conducted.

The training of salesmen differs with the amount of selling experience they possess. Informal methods are widely used with trainees who have had little or no selling experience. The subject matter in such training is apt to be technical and customer-oriented. Experienced salesmen are likely to be trained on an individual rather than a group basis.

The supervision of salesmen includes assignment of their tasks, providing them with support for their selling efforts, and day-to-day guidance in the planning and conduct of negotiations with customers. Industrial salesmen are often assigned lists of customers on whom to call, although they may also be given assignments on the basis of geographical territories. Supporting them in the field usually takes the form of selling-aids such as product samples, models, pictures, performance records, slides, film strips, and films. The day-to-day guidance called for involves instructions concerning work habits, evaluation of their performance, interpreting home office policies (and interpreting salesmen's behavior to the home office), maintaining their morale, and providing leadership.

Compensation systems for industrial salesmen usually emphasize the salary or drawing account to provide continuity of income and to pay for development work. Commissions, bonus arrangements, and even nonmonetary rewards can be employed to provide incentives. Control of salesmen's expenses requires a nice balance between excessive rigidity, which stimulates evasion, and excessive benevolence, which wastes the firm's money and invites trouble with the Internal Revenue Service.

# 22

# SALES PROMOTION AND PUBLIC RELATIONS

SALES PROMOTION is used here to include those items or activities which are used in direct support of personal selling efforts. While some of these have already been touched upon in the preceding chapters, the more important ones such as trade shows, catalogs, and samples are given fuller treatment here, along with such secondary activities as promotional letters, novelties, and entertainment. Public relations and publicity also have a part in the promotional strategy of a number of industrial marketers. They are briefly discussed at the end of the chapter.

## TRADE SHOWS AND EXHIBITS

The modern trade show, which traces its antecedents to the medieval fair, is an important promotional element in industrial marketing. It offers manufacturers an opportunity to display and demonstrate their products to a large number of prospects within a short period of time, which would otherwise be difficult to do because of the widespread nature of many industrial markets.

### Exhibitors' objectives

Since it is well nigh impossible to trace sales that result from this type of promotion, the trade show's value to the exhibitor must often be measured in terms of more limited objectives. Some of the more important purposes which can be served by exhibiting at trade shows are meeting potential customers, building prospect lists, building goodwill among present customers, discovering new product applications, introducing new products, demonstrating nonportable equipment, aiding and attracting new dealers, and meeting competitive effort.

*Meeting potential customers.* A trade show offers an excellent opportunity for the exhibitor to contact special groups within potential customer firms who are interested in his products. These include supervisory, technical staff, and executive personnel, who are difficult to reach in their plants or offices, but who are usually influential in making purchasing decisions.

*Building prospect lists.* While sales are rarely consummated at a trade show, the exhibitor who keeps a record of visitors to his booth may expect to glean from it substantial additions of interested firms and persons for his prospect file.

*Building goodwill.* For some exhibitors the primary value of a trade show lies in the opportunity it affords to build goodwill among customers or among customer employees who will eventually be in a position to influence purchases. In many instances, such an occasion is the only time office personnel of the exhibiting firm are able to meet persons within customers' organizations with whom they correspond or communicate by telephone. This element of personal contact can serve to create a preferential position for the exhibitor in the minds of customers' personnel and also smooth relations with them.

*Discovering new product applications.* Exhibiting at trade shows can sometimes enable the marketer to discover new applications for his products. Visitors often come to trade shows with a specific problem in mind, and they spend a considerable portion of their time there in looking for a product that will solve it. The possible application of a product to new needs may be unknown to the manufacturer until pointed out by potential users. From this source of information, for example, a sewing machine manufacturer got the idea that with a slight modification his machines had multiple uses in the light plastics industry.

*Introducing new products.* When a new industrial product is developed, the trade show offers an excellent opportunity to present, within a day or two, complete facts on a new product that could be brought to the attention of the same audience through individual contact only over a period of many months. Exhibitors often regard this as a primary function of trade shows, and they make a special effort to have new developments ready for exhibition at such affairs.

*Demonstrating nonportable equipment.* Many industrial goods are too large or complicated to be set up and demonstrated in each prospect's plant by the salesman or manufacturer's representative. But the manufacturer can afford to display such equipment at a trade show, where he has reasonable assurance that his exhibit will be seen by a number of prospects.

*Meeting competitive effort.* That competitors are exhibiting at a trade show is a subtle, but nonetheless realistic, reason for taking part. While a leading company in its field may choose not to enter a particular show and will suffer no detrimental effects, a lesser-known company may find that its lack of representation reflects on its competitive position. Even the leader may suffer if he stays out too long. When there are readily observable quality differences in favor of a company's product, it is often desirable to exhibit so that direct comparison may be made with competitors' products.

*Aiding and attracting new dealers.*    The trade show gives the exhibitor an opportunity to introduce new dealers or distributors to established clientele as well as to prospective customers. By having these representatives in the booth with his own personnel, the marketer can emphasize their relationship with his organization, thus aiding their selling efforts. An equally important function is to attract new dealers or representatives. These intermediaries often visit trade shows to look for new connections or new products to add to their lines.

## Exhibition scheduling and planning

Selecting the proper trade show can sometimes present a difficult problem, particularly for the manufacturer whose products are sold in several different industries. Very often management finds itself under pressure from groups of customers to buy space in a particular trade show. Frequently, their customers' real motive is to secure a contribution in support of the trade association sponsoring the show. A number of trade shows are sponsored by trade associations and are sometimes held in conjunction with a national convention. Others are promoted by exposition management firms and may be either national or local in appeal.

The manufacturer should carefully evaluate the shows that cover the markets in which he is interested to determine which ones most nearly meet his requirements. Such information as the nature of the audience, the show's acceptance in the industry, management's reputation for good publicity and sound operating policies, the rates charged for space, restrictions on exhibitors, and the anticipated number of exhibitors are important in evaluating the suitability of a trade show for the marketer's promotional strategy.

Planning participation in a trade show usually is the responsibility of the advertising department. Plans should include selection and dramatization of a theme, as well as the preparation of displays, headlines, illustrations, and copy that will attract and interest prospective customers. In addition, the booth must be designed and built or purchased, and provision made for packing, shipping, and setting up the exhibit at the exposition site.

Planning exhibits can involve a bewildering array of detail, especially for the company which exhibits a full line of a particular kind of equipment. PERT (Program Evaluation and Review Technique) has proven to be a useful planning and control device for such tasks and is increasingly employed by industrial marketers. Its application to small, less-complex projects has been overshadowed by its initial use for large, com-

**FIGURE 22–1. Application of PERT to planning an exhibition of construction machinery**

A.  PERT chart developed from computer printout in (B). The original chart was six feet square.

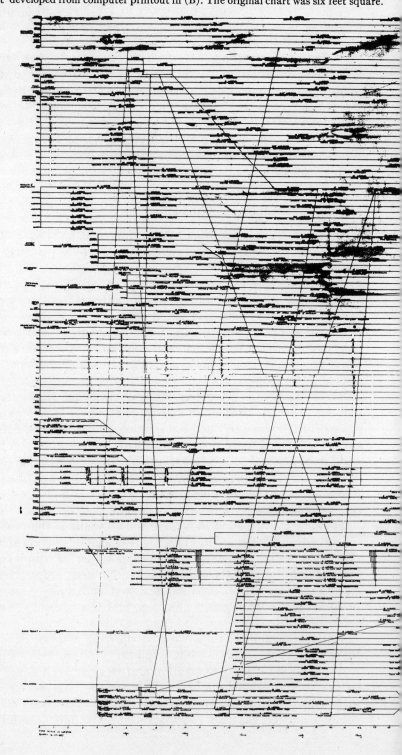

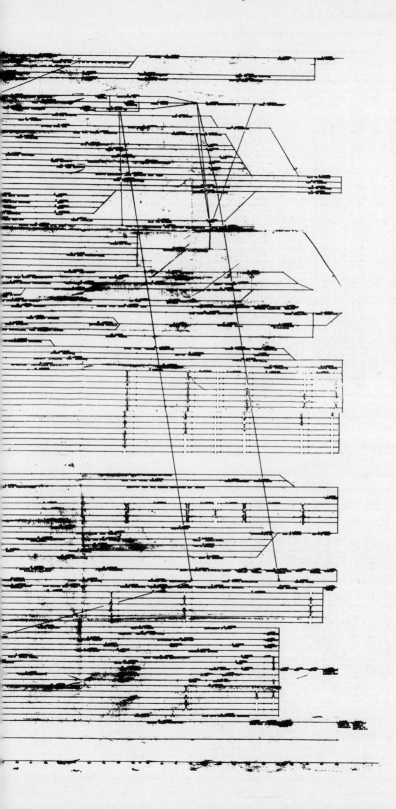

## FIGURE 22-1. (Continued)

B. Computer printout used to develop PERT chart in (A).

A 0000  07-09-68 02-15-68 02-21-69    CONEXPO 69          FILE 0002

| | | | | | | | |
|---|---|---|---|---|---|---|---|
| 0001 | MH001 | MH002 | 08.0 08.0 08.0 | 05-17-68 | SECURE EST OF HOUSING REC | C |
| 0002 | MH002 | MH003 | 08.0 C8.0 C8.0 | – – | MAKE ROOM ASSIGNMENTS | |
| 0003 | MH003 | MH004 | 03.C 03.0 03.0 | – – | DETERM MP REQUIR | |
| 0004 | MH004 | MP031 | 00.0 00.0 00.0 | – – | REQ MANPOWER FROM MP | |
| 0005 | MH004 | MH005 | 04.0 C4.0 04.0 | – – | SECURE MANPOWER LIST | |
| 0006 | MH005 | MH006 | 02.C 02.0 02.0 | – – | MAKE MP ASSIGNMENTS | |
| C007 | MH006 | MP033 | 00.0 00.0 00.0 | – – | INFO TC MP | |
| 0008 | MH006 | MH007 | 12.C 12.0 12.0 | – – | FIRM VISITCR LIST FROM DL | |
| 0009 | MH007 | MH008 | 06.C 06.0 06.0 | – – | ROOM ASSIG CONFIRM RESERV | |
| 0010 | MH008 | DL022 | 00.0 00.0 00.0 | – – | FIRM DLR RM ASSIGN TO CL | |
| 0011 | MH008 | RSDD | 03.C 03.0 03.0 | – – | MAKE MP ASSIGN ANC BRIEF | |
| 0012 | MH009 | MH010 | 06.C 06.0 06.0 | 03-01-68 | RESERVE RCCMS SHERMAN | C |
| 0013 | MH010 | MH011 | 04.C C4.0 04.0 | C5-20-68 | ORDER HOSP ROOMS SHERM | C |
| CC14 | MH011 | MH012 | 28.C 28.0 28.0 | – – | ORDER CATERING DECCR SHER | |
| 0015 | MH012 | MH024 | 06.C 06.0 06.C | – – | REVIEW PLANS | |
| 0016 | MH024 | RSDD | 03.C 03.0 03.0 | – – | CHI MP ASSIG ANC BRIEF | |
| 0017 | MH013 | MH014 | 06.C 06.0 06.C | 03-01-68 | RESERVE RCCMS BISMARK | C |
| 0018 | MH014 | MH015 | 04.C 04.0 04.0 | 05-20-68 | CRDER HOSP ROOP BISMARK | C |
| 0019 | MH015 | MH016 | 28.C 28.0 28.0 | – – | ORDER CATERING DECCR BISM | |
| 0020 | MH016 | MH024 | 06.C 06.0 06.C | – – | REVIEW PLANS WITH HOTELS | |
| 0021 | MH017 | MH018 | 06.C 06.0 06.C | C4-29-68 | RESERVE RCCMS SHERATCN | C |
| 0022 | MH018 | MH019 | 04.C C4.0 04.0 | 05-20-68 | CRDER HOSP ROOMS SHERATCN | C |
| 0023 | MP001 | MP002 | 04.C C4.0 04.0 | 03-26-68 | REVIEW NEEDS ALL SUPVRS | C |
| 0024 | MP002 | AVO26 | 00.C 00.0 00.0 | – – | NAME TAG REQ TO AV | |
| 0025 | MP002 | MP003 | 10.C 10.0 10.0 | C5-08-68 | SOURCES PERSONNEL SURVEY | |
| 0026 | MP003 | MP004 | 00.0 00.0 00.0 | 06-24-68 | SPLIT REQUIREMENTS PRESHO | C |
| 0027 | MP003 | MP035 | 00.0 00.0 00.0 | C6-24-68 | SPLIT REQUIREMENTS TRAVS | C |
| 0028 | MP003 | MP027 | 00.0 00.0 00.0 | 06-24-68 | SPLIT REQUIREMENTS MM | C |
| 0029 | MP003 | MP013 | 00.0 00.0 00.0 | 04-03-68 | SPLIT REQUIREMENTS INTERP | C |
| 0030 | MP003 | MP006 | 00.0 00.0 00.0 | 06-21-68 | SPLIT REQUIREMENTS FT | C |
| 0031 | MP006 | MP007 | 14.C 14.0 14.0 | 06-24-68 | DET FACTORY TRIPS MP NEED | C |
| 0032 | MP007 | MP008 | 02.C 02.0 02.0 | – – | SELECT ESCCRTS | |
| 0033 | MP008 | AVO28 | 00.0 00.0 C0.0 | – – | ESC NAME TAGS REC TO AV | |
| 0034 | MP008 | MP009 | 01.0 01.0 01.0 | – – | INFORM FT ESCORTS | |
| 0035 | MPC09 | FTO11A | 01.C 01.0 01.0 | – – | INFO TC FT CCORD | |
| 0036 | MP009 | MP010 | 04.C 04.0 04.0 | – – | INFO TC RS COORD | |
| 0037 | MP01C | MP011 | 01.C C1.0 01.0 | – – | REVIEW ROUTES | |
| 0038 | MP011 | MP012 | 08.C 08.0 08.0 | – – | FIRM ASSIGNMENTS ESCORTS | |
| 0039 | MP012 | RSDD | 01.0 01.0 C1.0 | – – | BRIEF ESCCRTS | |
| 0040 | MP013 | MP014 | 02.C 02.0 02.0 | 04-03-68 | DET INTERP REQ | C |
| 0041 | MP014 | MP015 | 12.0 12.0 12.0 | – – | SELECT INTERPRETERS | |
| 0042 | MP015 | AVO28 | 00.C 00.0 00.0 | – – | INT NAME TAGS REC TO AV | |
| 0043 | MP015 | MP016 | 01.C 01.0 01.0 | – – | INFCRM INTERPS | |
| 0044 | MP016 | MP017 | 03.C C3.0 03.0 | – – | CRG INTERP WORK SCHED | |
| 0045 | MP017 | MP018 | 02.C 02.0 02.0 | – – | ARR INTERP MOUSING | |

| REPORT | START | SCHEDULE | | | |
|---|---|---|---|---|---|
| DATE | DATE | DATE | . . . NETWORK DESCRIPTICN . . . | FILE   2 | PAGE 01 |

07-09-68  02-15-68  02-21-69    CONEXPO 69

| BEGIN EVENT | END EVENT | ACTIVITY RANK | END SERIAL | TOPOLCGY . . . . . ACTIVITY . . . DESCRIPTICN . . | ACTIVITY TIME | EARLIEST CATE | ACTIVITY ESTIMATES . . . . . COMPLETION . . LATEST DATE | SLACK | SCHEDULE DATE | PROB |
|---|---|---|---|---|---|---|---|---|---|---|
| AD001 | AD054 | 1 | 1089 | CATALOG AVAILABLE D4C | 35.0 | 35.0 10-16-68 | 36.4 10-25-68 | 1.4 | | |
| AD001 | AD056 | 1 | 1C90 | CATALOG AVAILABLE C6C | 35.0 | 35.0 10-16-68 | 35.4 10-18-68 | .4 | | |
| AD002 | AD003 | 1 | 626 | CCMP OUTLINE SHCW PROG | 4.0 | 5.2 04-18-68 | 22.4 07-19-68 | 13.2 | | |
| AD003 | AD004 | 2 | 627 | ORDER PHCTCS SHCW PROG | 2.0 | 11.2 05-02-68 | 24.4 08-02-68 | 13.2 | | |
| AD004 | AD005 | 3 | 628 | WRITE 1ST DRFT SHCW PROG | 8.0 | 19.2 06-27-68 | 32.4 09-27-68 | 13.2 | | |
| AD005 | AD006 | 4 | 632 | CCMP ROUTING SHCW PROG | 6.0 | 25.2 C8-08-68 | 38.4 11-08-68 | 13.2 | | |
| AD006 | AD007 | 5 | 633 | APP FINAL ART SHCW PROG | 4.C | 29.2 09-05-68 | 42.4 12-06-68 | 13.2 | | |
| AD007 | AD008 | 6 | 634 | PRINT SHOW PROG | 8.C | 37.2 10-31-68 | 50.4 01-31-69 | 13.2 | | |
| ADC08 | RSDD | 15 | 687 | SHIP TO CHICAGO SHOW PROG | 2.0 | 57.2 C3-20-69 | 52.4 02-14-69 | 13.2 | | |
| AD009 | AD010 | 1 | 1096 | GATHER SPECS ALL SPEC SHT | 10.0 | 11.2 C5-30-68 | 34.0 09-13-68 | 15.2 | | |
| AD010 | AD011 | 2 | 1097 | WRITE SPEC SHEETS | 4.C | 19.2 06-27-68 | 34.4 10-11-68 | 15.2 | | |
| AD011 | AD012 | 3 | 1098 | CCMP RCUT SPEC SHTS | 8.C | 27.2 C8-22-68 | 42.4 12-06-68 | 15.2 | | |
| AD012 | AD013 | 4 | 1099 | PRINT SPEC SHEETS | 4.0 | 33.2 10-03-68 | 48.4 01-17-69 | 15.2 | | |
| AD013 | RSDD | 15 | 685 | SHIP TO CHICAGO SPEC SHTS | 4.C | 57.2 C3-20-69 | 52.4 02-14-69 | 15.2 | | |
| AD014 | AD015 | 14 | 609 | CCMF REWRITE PRCC CAT | 16.C | 23.2 C7-25-68 | 24.4 08-02-68 | 1.2 | | |
| AD015 | AC016 | 2 | 610 | RENCRK ART PRCC CAT | 8.0 | 31.2 C9-19-68 | 32.4 05-27-68 | 1.2 | | |
| AD016 | AC017 | 3 | 611 | CCMP RCUT PRCC CAT | 4.0 | 35.2 10-17-68 | 36.4 10-25-68 | 1.2 | | |
| AD017 | AC018 | 4 | 612 | APP FINAL ART PROD CAT | 4.0 | 39.2 11-14-68 | 40.4 11-22-68 | 1.2 | | |
| AD018 | AD019 | 5 | 613 | PRINT CATALCG | 8.0 | 47.2 01-09-69 | 48.4 01-17-69 | 1.2 | | |
| AD019 | RSDD | 15 | 686 | SHIP TO CHICAGO PROD CAT | 4.C | 57.2 C3-20-69 | 52.4 02-14-69 | 1.2 | | |
| AD020 | AD021 | 1 | 635 | WRITE BRIEF 992 | 14.0 | 19.2 C6-27-68 | 23.4 07-26-68 | 4.2 | | |
| AD021 | AD022 | 2 | 643 | CCMP ROUTING 992 BRIEF | 8.0 | 27.2 C8-22-68 | 31.4 C9-20-68 | 4.2 | | |
| AD022 | AD023 | 3 | 653 | PRINT BRIEF 992 | 6.0 | 33.2 1C-C3-68 | 37.4 11-01-68 | 4.2 | | |
| AD023 | AD024 | 4 | 660 | HOLC SHIPPING 992 BRIEF | 13.0 | 46.2 01-02-69 | 5C.4 01-31-69 | 4.2 | | |
| AD024 | RSDD | 15 | 688 | SHIP TO CHICAGO 992 BRIEF | 2.0 | 57.2 03-20-69 | 52.4 02-14-69 | 4.2 | | |
| AD025 | ADC26 | 1 | 636 | WRITE CATALCG 930 | 20.C | 25.2 C8-08-68 | 28.4 08-30-68 | 3.2 | | |
| AD026 | AD027 | 2 | 644 | CCMP ROUTING 930 CAT | 10.0 | 35.2 10-17-68 | 38.4 11-08-68 | 3.2 | | |
| AD027 | AD028 | 3 | 654 | PRINT CATALCG 930 | 12.0 | 47.2 C1-C9-69 | 5C.4 01-31-69 | 3.2 | | |
| AD028 | RSDD | 15 | 689 | SHIP TC CHICAGO 930 CAT | 2.0 | 57.2 C3-2C-69 | 52.4 02-14-69 | 3.2 | | |
| AD029 | AC030 | 1 | 637 | WRITE BRIEF 920 | 24.0 | 29.2 C9-05-68 | 32.4 05-27-68 | 3.2 | | |
| AD030 | AD031 | 2 | 645 | CCMP ROUTING 92C BRIEF | 8.C | 37.2 1C-31-68 | 40.4 11-22-68 | 3.2 | | |
| AD031 | AD032 | 3 | 655 | PRINT BRIEF 920 | 10.0 | 47.2 C1-09-69 | 5C.4 01-31-69 | 3.2 | | |
| AD032 | RSDD | 15 | 690 | SHIP TO CHICAGO 92C BRIEF | 2.C | 57.2 C3-2C-69 | 52.4 02-14-69 | 3.2 | | |
| AD036 | AD037 | 1 | 661 | HOLC SHIPPING 941 CAT | 5.0 | 23.4 C7-26-68 | 49.4 01-24-69 | 26.0 | | |
| AD037 | RSDD | 15 | 691 | SHIP TC CHICAGO 941 CAT | 3.0 | 57.2 03-2C-69 | 52.4 02-14-69 | 26.0 | | |
| AD038 | AD039 | 1 | 639 | WRITE BRIEF 627 | 15.0 | 20.2 07-04-68 | 23.4 07-20-68 | 3.2 | | |
| AD039 | AD040 | 2 | 647 | CCMP ROUTING 627 BRIEF | 8.0 | 28.2 08-29-68 | 31.4 09-20-68 | 3.2 | | |
| AD040 | AD041 | 3 | 657 | PRINT BRIEF 627 | 6.0 | 34.2 10-17-68 | 37.4 11-01-68 | 3.2 | | |
| AD041 | AD042 | 4 | 662 | HOLC SHIPPING 627 BRIEF | 12.0 | 46.2 01-02-69 | 49.4 01-31-69 | 3.2 | | |
| AD042 | RSDD | 15 | 692 | SHIP TO CHICAGO 627 BRIEF | 3.0 | 57.2 03-20-69 | 52.4 02-14-69 | 3.2 | | |
| AD045 | AC046 | 1 | 664 | WRITE INFO #12 ADD | 6.0 | 21.8 C7-16-68 | 23.4 07-26-68 | 1.6 | | |
| AD046 | AD047 | 2 | 665 | WRITE ADDENDUM #12 | 6.0 | 27.8 08-27-68 | 29.4 09-06-68 | 1.6 | | |
| AD047 | AD048 | 3 | 666 | COLLATE ADDENDUM #12 | 20.0 | 47.8 01-14-69 | 49.4 01-31-69 | 1.6 | | |
| AD048 | RSDD | 15 | 693 | SHIP TO CHICAGO #12 CAT | 3.0 | 57.2 03-20-69 | 52.4 02-14-69 | 1.6 | | |
| AD051 | AD052 | 1 | 658 | PRINT CATALOG 824C | 6.0 | 21.8 07-16-68 | 23.4 07-26-68 | 1.6 | | |

# FIGURE 22-1. (Concluded)

| REPORT DATE | START DATE | SCHEDULE DATE | . . . . NETWORK DESCRIPTION . . . . | FILE 2 | PAGE 01 |
|---|---|---|---|---|---|
| 07-09-68 | 02-15-68 | 02-21-69 | CONEXPO 69 | | |

| BEGIN EVENT | END EVENT | END RANK | SERIAL | . . ACTIVITY DESCRIPTION . . | TIME | EARLIEST DATE | LATEST | COMPLETION DATE | SLACK | SCHEDULE DATE | PROB |
|---|---|---|---|---|---|---|---|---|---|---|---|
| HH002 | HH003 | 1 | 2 | MAKE ROOM ASSIGNMENTS | 8.0 | 21.6 07-15-68 | 21.4 | 07-12-68 | .2- | | |
| FT016 | FT017 | 1 | 86 | FINALIZE AUR DISPLAY PLAN | 3.0 | 21.6 07-15-68 | 21.4 | 07-12-68 | .2- | | |
| FT023 | FT024 | 1 | 87 | FINALIZE MAP DISPLAY PLAN | 3.0 | 21.6 07-15-68 | 21.4 | 07-12-68 | .2- | | |
| FTC30 | FTO31 | 1 | 88 | FINALIZE IC DISPLAY PLAN | 3.C | 21.6 C7-15-68 | 21.4 | 07-12-68 | .2- | | |
| FT037 | FT038 | 1 | 89 | FINALIZE TECH CENT DISP | 3.0 | 21.6 07-15-68 | 21.4 | 07-12-68 | .2- | | |
| FT044 | FT045 | 1 | 90 | FINALIZE ACM CISPLAY PLAN | 3.0 | 21.6 C7-15-68 | 21.4 | 07-12-68 | .2- | | |
| FT051 | FT052 | 1 | 91 | FINALIZE EP DISPLAY PLAN | 3.0 | 21.6 07-15-68 | 21.4 | 07-12-68 | .2- | | |
| PS007 | PS008 | 1 | 200 | OUTLINE SCRIPT   VISUALS | 14.0 | 23.6 C7-29-68 | 23.4 | 07-26-68 | .2- | | |
| EWC09 | EW010 | 1 | 256 | PRELIM SHIFT ASSIGNMENTS | 12.0 | 32.6 C9-30-68 | 32.4 | 09-27-68 | .2- | | |
| ID011 | ID012 | 1 | 375 | FIRM IN PLANT CISPLAY | 12.0 | 28.6 C9-02-68 | 28.4 | 08-30-68 | .2- | | |
| ID017 | IC018 | 1 | 384 | ORDER STANDS D399 | 5.0 | 22.6 07-22-68 | 22.4 | 07-19-68 | .2- | | |
| ID027 | ID028 | 1 | 396 | ORDER 310C | 4.0 | 22.6 07-22-68 | 22.4 | 07-19-68 | .2- | | |
| ID038 | IC039 | 1 | 408 | CRDER D348 | 4.0 | 22.6 07-22-68 | 22.4 | 07-19-68 | .2- | | |
| ID049 | ID050 | 1 | 420 | ORDER 5310 | 4.0 | 22.6 C7-22-68 | 22.4 | 07-19-68 | .2- | | |
| MR007 | MR008 | 1 | 560 | BEGIN PRODUCTION 779 | 16.C | 33.6 1C-07-68 | 33.4 | 10-04-68 | .2- | | |
| MR018 | MR019 | 1 | 561 | BEGIN PRODUCTION 992 | 16.C | 33.6 1C-07-68 | 33.4 | 10-04-68 | .2- | | |
| MRC29 | MR030 | 1 | 562 | BEGIN PRODUCTION 930 | 16.C | 33.6 1C-07-68 | 33.4 | 10-04-68 | .2- | | |
| MRC40 | MR041 | 1 | 563 | BEGIN PRCDUCTICN 920 | 16.C | 33.6 1C-07-68 | 33.4 | 10-04-68 | .2- | | |
| MR051 | MRC52 | 1 | 564 | BEGIN PRODUCTION 983 | 16.C | 33.6 1C-07-68 | 33.4 | 10-04-68 | .2- | | |
| MR062 | MR063 | 1 | 565 | BEGIN PRODUCTION 941 | 16.C | 33.6 10-07-68 | 33.4 | 10-04-68 | .2- | | |
| MR073 | MRC74 | 1 | 566 | BEGIN PRCDLCTICN C9G | 16.C | 33.6 1C-07-68 | 33.4 | 10-04-68 | .2- | | |
| MR084 | MR085 | 1 | 567 | BEGIN PRCDUCTICN D6C | 16.C | 33.6 1C-07-68 | 33.4 | 10-04-68 | .2- | | |
| MR095 | MR096 | 1 | 568 | BEGIN PRODUCTION C4C | 16.C | 33.6 1C-07-68 | 33.4 | 10-04-68 | .2- | | |
| MR106 | MR107 | 1 | 569 | BEGIN PRCDLCTICN 651 | 16.C | 33.6 1C-07-68 | 33.4 | 10-04-68 | .2- | | |
| MR117 | MR118 | 1 | 570 | BEGIN PRODUCTION 627 | 16.C | 33.6 10-07-68 | 33.4 | 10-04-68 | .2- | | |
| MR128 | MR129 | 1 | 571 | BEGIN PRODUCTION J611 | 16.C | 33.6 1C-07-68 | 33.4 | 10-04-68 | .2- | | |
| MR139 | MR140 | 1 | 572 | BEGIN PRODUCTION #12 | 16.C | 33.6 1C-07-68 | 33.4 | 10-04-68 | .2- | | |
| MR150 | MR151 | 1 | 573 | BEGIN PRCDLCTION 824C | 16.C | 33.6 1C-07-68 | 33.4 | 10-04-68 | .2- | | |
| DP016 | DP017 | 1 | 723 | COMPLETE DESIGN RAMP | 8.0 | 28.6 C9-02-68 | 28.4 | 08-30-68 | .2- | | |
| DP022 | DP023 | 1 | 727 | COMP DESIGN INFO BOCTHS | 8.0 | 25.6 C8-C9-68 | 25.4 | 08-09-68 | .2- | | |
| DP034 | CP035 | 1 | 728 | COMP CESIGN CUSH HITCH | 8.0 | 22.6 C7-22-68 | 22.4 | 07-19-68 | .2- | | |
| DP071 | DP072 | 1 | 751 | ORD PARTS 11CO CUT | 10.0 | 24.6 C8-05-68 | 24.4 | 08-02-68 | .2- | | |
| DP083 | DP084 | 1 | 753 | ORD PARTS MG CONT CUT | 10.0 | 24.6 C8-05-68 | 24.4 | 08-02-68 | .2- | | |
| DP095 | DP096 | 1 | 755 | ORD PARTS 5310 CUT | 10.0 | 24.6 C8-05-68 | 24.4 | 08-02-68 | .2- | | |
| MR209 | MR210 | 1 | 1030 | ASSEMBLE SHIP PRODUCT | 17.0 | 25.6 C9-02-68 | 29.4 | 09-06-68 | .2- | | |
| HH003 | HH004 | 2 | 3 | DETERM MP REQUIR | 3.0 | 24.6 C8-05-68 | 24.4 | 09-06-68 | .2- | | |
| PS008 | PS009 | 2 | 201 | WRITE RT 1ST CRFT PRES MA | 6.0 | 25.6 C5-05-68 | 29.4 | 09-06-68 | .2- | | |
| EW010 | EW011 | 2 | 257 | COCRD RM   SHIFT ASSIGN | 4.0 | 36.6 1C-28-68 | 36.4 | 10-25-68 | .2- | | |
| ID012 | ID013 | 2 | 377 | FIRM ESCORT ASSIGNMENTS | 4.0 | 34.6 1C-14-68 | 34.4 | 10-11-68 | .2- | | |
| ID018 | ID019 | 2 | 385 | DETERMINE TRANS REQ D399 | 4.0 | 26.6 C8-16-68 | 26.4 | 08-16-68 | .2- | | |
| ID028 | ID029 | 2 | 397 | ORDER STANDS 3100 | 5.0 | 27.6 08-26-68 | 27.4 | 08-23-68 | .2- | | |
| ID039 | ID040 | 2 | 409 | ORDER STANDS D348 | 5.0 | 27.6 C8-26-68 | 27.4 | 08-23-68 | .2- | | |
| ID050 | ID051 | 2 | 421 | ORDER STANDS 5310 | 5.0 | 27.6 C8-26-68 | 27.4 | 08-23-68 | .2- | | |
| MR008 | MR009 | 2 | 578 | MOUNT ALL ATTACH 779 | 4.0 | 37.6 11-04-68 | 37.4 | 11-01-68 | .2- | | |
| MR019 | MR020 | 2 | 579 | MOUNT ALL ATTACH 992 | 4.0 | 37.6 11-04-68 | 37.4 | 11-01-68 | .2- | | |

| REPORT DATE | START DATE | SCHEDULE DATE | . . . . NETWORK DESCRIPTION . . . . | FILE 2 | PAGE 01 |
|---|---|---|---|---|---|
| 07-09-68 | 02-15-68 | 02-21-69 | CCNEXPO 69 | | |

| BEGIN EVENT | END EVENT | END RANK | SERIAL | . . ACTIVITY DESCRIPTION . . | TIME | EARLIEST DATE | LATEST | COMPLETION DATE | SLACK | SCHEDULE DATE | PROB |
|---|---|---|---|---|---|---|---|---|---|---|---|
| ID085 | ID086 | 1 | 946 | OUTLINE PRESENTATIONS | 8.0 | 19.2 C6-27-68 | 14.4 | 05-24-68 | 4.8- | | |
| TRC02 | TRC12 | 1 | 162 | PERSCNNEL TRANSPCRT REQIR | 8.0 | 16.4 06-07-68 | 2C.4 | 07-05-68 | 4.0 | | |
| ID0C1 | ICC58 | 1 | 429 | SEC REQ PARTS 5310 C&T | 12.0 | 12.0 05-08-68 | 2C.4 | 07-05-68 | 8.4 | | |
| AVOC3 | AVOC4 | 1 | 6Q7 | CCMP RCUGH DRAFT W/VISUAL | 12.0 | 2C.4 C7-C5-68 | 20.4 | 07-05-68 | .0 | | |
| DP0O4 | DP063 | 1 | 712 | COMP ART CO DIVERS DISP | 14.C | 14.4 05-24-68 | 2C.4 | 07-05-68 | 6.0 | | |
| ID076 | ICC77 | 1 | 935 | WRITE CATALGGS | 12.C | 17.00 06-12-68 | 2C.4 | 07-05-68 | 3.4 | | |
| HMC02 | HH003 | 1 | 2 | MAKE ROOM ASSIGNMENTS | 8.0 | 21.6 07-15-68 | 21.4 | 07-12-68 | .2- | | |
| FT016 | FT017 | 1 | 86 | FINALIZE ALR DISPLAY PLAN | 3.0 | 21.6 07-15-68 | 21.4 | 07-12-68 | .2- | | |
| FT023 | FT024 | 1 | 87 | FINALIZE MAP DISPLAY PLAN | 3.0 | 21.6 07-15-68 | 21.4 | 07-12-68 | .2- | | |
| FT030 | FT031 | 1 | 88 | FINALIZE ID DISPLAY PLAN | 3.0 | 21.6 07-15-68 | 21.4 | 07-12-68 | .2- | Activities |
| FT037 | FT038 | 1 | 89 | FINALIZE TECH CENT CISP | 3.0 | 21.6 07-15-68 | 21.4 | 07-12-68 | .2- | above the |
| FT044 | FT045 | 1 | 90 | FINALIZE ACM CISPLAY PLAN | 3.C | 21.6 07-15-68 | 21.4 | 07-12-68 | .2- | line must |
| FT051 | FT052 | 1 | 91 | FINALIZE EP DISPLAY PLAN | 3.0 | 21.6 07-15-68 | 21.4 | 07-12-68 | .2- | be completed |
| PR003 | PR004 | 1 | 175 | MAIL FTG RES FORMS | 2.0 | 14.C 05-24-68 | 21.4 | 07-12-68 | 7.4 | by this |
| ID070 | ICC71 | 1 | 923 | LIST AVAIL PERSONNEL | 6.0 | 14.4 05-24-68 | 21.4 | 07-12-68 | 7.0 | date |
| MR201 | MR204 | 1 | 1021 | DETER PP AVAIL | 8.0 | 17.6 06-31-68 | 21.4 | (07-12-68) | 3.8 | |
| ID017 | ID018 | 1 | 384 | ORDER STANDS D399 | 5.0 | 22.6 07-22-68 | 22.4 | 07-19-68 | .2- | | |
| ID027 | ID028 | 1 | 396 | ORDER 310C | 4.0 | 22.6 07-22-68 | 22.4 | 07-19-68 | .2- | | |
| ID038 | IC039 | 1 | 408 | CRDER D348 | 4.0 | 22.6 07-22-68 | 22.4 | 07-19-68 | .2- | | |
| ID049 | ID05C | 1 | 420 | CRDER 5310 | 4.0 | 22.6 07-22-68 | 22.4 | 07-19-68 | .2- | | |
| MR158 | MR159 | 1 | 502 | CRDER PACH D399 | 4.0 | 21.6 07-15-68 | 22.4 | 07-19-68 | .8 | | |
| MR169 | MR17C | 1 | 503 | ORDER MACH 3100 | 4.0 | 22.0 07-17-68 | 22.4 | 07-19-68 | .4 | | |
| MR180 | MR181 | 1 | 504 | ORDER MACH D348 | 4.0 | 22.4 07-17-68 | 22.4 | 07-19-68 | .4 | | |
| MR191 | MR192 | 1 | 505 | ORDER MACH 5310 | 4.0 | 21.6 07-15-68 | 22.4 | 07-19-68 | .8 | | |
| ADC02 | ADC03 | 1 | 626 | CCMP OUTLINE SHC& PROG | 4.0 | 5.2 C4-18-68 | 22.4 | 07-19-68 | 13.2 | | |
| DPC34 | CP035 | 1 | 728 | COMP CESIGN CUSH HITCH | 8.0 | 22.6 C7-22-68 | 22.4 | 07-19-68 | .2- | | |
| AVC13 | AVC14 | 1 | 830 | COMP FIRST CRAFT EMP GUID | 4.0 | 21.6 07-15-68 | 22.4 | 07-19-68 | .8 | | |
| AVC20 | AVC21 | 1 | 837 | CCMP FIRST DRAFT VIS GUID | 4.0 | 21.6 07-15-68 | 22.4 | 07-19-68 | .8 | | |
| TRC12 | TRC13 | 2 | 163 | SELECT CARRIERS PERS | 2.0 | 18.4 06-21-68 | 22.4 | 07-19-68 | 4.0 | | |
| ICC58 | ICC59 | 2 | 430 | SENC CISPLAY TC VENDCR | 2.0 | 14.0 05-22-68 | 22.4 | 07-19-68 | 8.4 | | |
| MR159 | MR160 | 2 | 520 | SURVEY SAFETY ITEMS D399 | .0 | 21.6 07-15-68 | 22.4 | 07-19-68 | .8 | | |
| MR170 | MR171 | 2 | 521 | SURV SAFE ITEMS C334 3100 | .0 | 22.0 07-17-68 | 22.4 | 07-19-68 | .4 | | |
| MR181 | MR182 | 2 | 522 | SURV SAFE ITEMS 110C D348 | .C | 22.0 07-17-68 | 22.4 | 07-19-68 | .4 | | |
| MR192 | MR193 | 2 | 523 | SURVEY SAFETY ITEMS 5310 | .C | 21.6 07-15-68 | 22.4 | 07-19-68 | .8 | | |
| ID086 | ID087 | 2 | 947 | WRITE PRESENTATICN MATL | 8.0 | 27.2 08-22-68 | 22.4 | 07-19-68 | 4.8- | | |
| PS007 | PS008 | 2 | 20C | OUTLINE SCRIPT   VISUALS | 14.0 | 23.6 07-29-68 | 23.4 | C7-26-68 | .2- | | |
| ADC20 | AD021 | 1 | 635 | WRITE BRIEF 992 | 14.0 | 19.2 C6-27-68 | 23.4 | 07-26-68 | 4.2 | | |
| ADC38 | AD039 | 1 | 639 | WRITE BRIEF 627 | 15.0 | 2C.2 07-04-68 | 23.4 | 07-26-68 | 3.2 | | |
| AD051 | ACC52 | 1 | 658 | PRINT CATALOG 824C | 6.0 | 21.8 07-16-68 | 23.4 | 07-26-68 | 1.6 | | |
| AD045 | AD046 | 1 | 664 | WRITE INFO 812 ADD | 6.0 | 21.8 07-16-68 | 23.4 | 07-26-68 | 1.6 | | |
| FT005 | FT007 | 2 | 71 | DET TOTAL MANPCWER REQUIR | 4.0 | 22.0 07-17-68 | 23.4 | 07-26-68 | 1.4 | | |
| PR004 | PR005 | 2 | 176 | DET CONT   QUAN PR FCLDER | 2.0 | 22.0 07-17-68 | 23.4 | 07-26-68 | 1.4 | | |
| MR204 | FTCO7 | 2 | 1022 | MANPOWER INFO TO FT | 2.0 | 22.6 07-22-68 | 23.4 | 07-26-68 | 3.8 | | |
| ADC14 | ACC15 | 1 | 609 | CCMP REWRITE PROC CAT | 18.0 | 23.2 07-25-68 | 24.4 | 08-02-68 | 1.2 | | |
| AD068 | AD069 | 1 | 67C | SECURE INFC 781 BRIEF | 14.C | 21.2 07-11-68 | 24.4 | 08-02-68 | 3.2 | | |

plex undertakings in military weapons systems and space exploration.

Two requirements must be met in order to apply PERT to a marketing problem. First, fundamentals of the technique such as work breakdown structure, networking, and time estimation must be mastered. Second, managerial requirements, the problem's complexity, and the time and cost involved in its accomplishment must be recognized. PERT not only reveals the significant relationships between tasks which must be performed in order to complete a project on time, but highlights exactly where trouble spots are likely to occur.

The preceding excerpt from a computer printout illustrates both the application of PERT to a marketing project and the amount of detail involved in planning an exhibition. It was provided by a large manufacturer of construction machinery.

## CATALOGS

Firms with an extensive assortment of products which can be distinguished by size, shape, or other features that affect the precise uses to which they can be adapted are probably well advised to publish catalogs. For example, a medium-sized company making electrical components listed in its 1,000 page catalog some 10,000 items. The book cost $10 a copy, and 50,000 copies were distributed to firms that might be expected to buy electrical components. This is a lot of money to spend on one promotional medium. However, if properly distributed, it was probably in the catalog file of every significant firm buying electrical components in the company's market area.

Catalogs tend to be either general or special in content. The former would include all the products of a company, whereas the latter would be limited to those products of interest to particular groups of customers or industries. Sometimes, a general catalog is sectionalized according to customer groups so that each section or a combination of several sections can be distributed to the appropriate group as a specialized catalog. Otherwise, the entire document can be distributed as a general catalog. Although general and special catalogs can fulfill a number of different purposes for the marketer, their preparation and distribution follow a fairly common pattern.

### Reasons for using catalogs

The specific reasons for using catalogs differ from industry to industry and among individual companies. The most common, perhaps, are to produce orders, to develop recognition by buyers, to generate requests for information, to stimulate invitations to bid, and to get specifications adopted.

*Produce orders.*  With the exception of products in the maintenance, repair, and operations category, it is doubtful that many orders are placed on the basis of a catalog description without the intervention of some other form of promotional effort, such as a salesman's visit. A more usual occurrence is that someone in a position to influence buying will recommend a product that he has seen with supporting information in a catalog. Then, too, a catalog can sometimes reach an influential person in a company who is not readily accessible to salesmen. Informative catalogs can facilitate the process of approval by providing adequate product data to those who must give the approval. If marketing management knows who such people are, they can forward catalogs directly to them.

*Develop recognition.*  Buyers frequently rely on catalogs to determine who makes what. Consequently catalogs can be useful in assuring that when a prospective customer wants the kind of product the marketer sells, he stands a reasonably good chance of being considered as a possible supplier. It is doubtful, though, that many firms find it profitable to rely entirely on the catalog for this purpose.

*Generate requests for information.*  It is difficult, if not impossible, to include in a catalog all the information about a product that a prospective buyer might desire, especially if the product is highly technical in nature. But enough facts usually can be given to induce a prospective buyer to request more. This opens the door to wider contact through correspondence or salesmen's calls. Through this means the salesman often can establish contact with engineers, maintenance men, and operating executives whom he probably would find difficult to reach without the catalog-inspired request as a door opener. Purchasing officers are not always willing to allow such contacts, but they are hard to refuse when initiated by persons from within the company.

*Stimulate invitations to bid.*  When a buyer is asked to purchase an unfamiliar product, he is likely to consult his catalog file to discover who makes such products. From this information he would probably compile a bidders list of select firms he would ask to submit bids. If the buyer did not request bids, he probably would request quotations or other product and service information. The catalog thus affords the manufacturer a chance at all available business, but he cannot safely rely on it as the sole means of getting most of the available business.

*Specification adoptions.*  When products are purchased on the basis of specifications prepared by the buyer, it is important to a potential supplier that the specifications are compatible with those of his own product. If a firm's catalog describes its products by specification and the buyer wants the firm as a possible supplier, he may make an effort to have his own specifications drawn so as to be compatible with those of the supplier. Then, too, in drawing specifications for an unfamiliar product, the purchaser's engineers may begin with those of suppliers, if they are available. If the supplier's catalog specifications are used as a model, there is a good chance that his product will be the only one, or one of only a few, which can meet the buyer's specifications when they are completed.

## Catalog preparation

The initial step in preparing a catalog is to determine which functional groups in customer firms are likely to use it and what kinds of information they are likely to want. Purchasing officers of customer firms are almost certain to be prime catalog users. In fact, the purchasing department is often the recognized custodian of the company catalog file. The engineering staff, particularly that part of it engaged in product design, also is likely to need catalogs. For certain kinds of products, maintenance personnel and the factory management group are frequent users. The technical research staff may have occasional need to consult general catalogs and more or less constant need for laboratory equipment and supply catalogs.

The types of information these groups commonly seek in catalogs are: who makes and sells what; product specifications and operating characteristics; application possibilities; performance data; service requirements; methods of fabrication or assembly; illustrations or drawings; cost data; warranties; the maker's facilities and services; and if the product is marketed through distributors, the names and addresses of local suppliers. A firm with an extensive product line could not present all such information within the covers of a catalog without producing a document of indescribable bulk and withering cost. But it may be possible to summarize the most significant information in each category and indicate the person to contact for additional data. As a general rule, the most effective catalog is one which represents a compromise between bulk and cost on the one hand and completeness of information on the other.

## Catalog distribution

Distributing the catalog is a key operation. If it fails to reach the hands of those who will use it, the effort is wasted. The identity of such personnel may not always be readily ascertained and when it is, they may not be readily accessible, at least to salesmen. For this reason many firms make no effort to distribute catalogs to small buyers whose possible volume of purchases may be insufficient to justify the cost. This may be a short-sighted policy, because small firms have a way of growing into big ones, and their management may then resent having been ignored during the firm's early years of development. Since catalogs usually cost so much, it is almost always beneficial to research the market in which they will be distributed in order to positively identify the names, affiliations, and titles of persons to whom they should be given.

A number of industrial marketers have received valuable assistance in the preparation and distribution of their catalogs from Sweets Catalog Service. This is a New York–based firm which maintains a staff highly skilled in preparing and printing catalogs. In addition, it is prepared to undertake distribution of the book to key personnel of important buying firms in six functional areas: light construction, architecture, industrial construction, plant engineering, product design, and machine tools. Distribution is made not simply to firms in these areas, but to specific individuals, by name and title, who are most likely to use the catalog. Many firms apparently find that this specialized service enables them to prepare, produce, and distribute their books either more cheaply or more efficiently, or both, than they could with their own facilities and manpower.

## SAMPLES

Samples are widely used in the promotion of products which are compact, light, and relatively inexpensive. Sample lots of newly developed chemicals are typically made available to prospective users as a phase of the product development program. Such programs typically seek to develop information regarding (1) possible uses and performance, (2) bugs that may not have been discovered in preliminary use tests, (3) the existence of a market, and (4) the extent of such a market. The distribution of samples to interested firms is an effective way of accomplishing this end.

Samples are also extensively used as a means of gaining an entrée to new customers. For example, the pharmaceuticals detailer, a missionary salesman who calls on physicians, regularly carries samples of the products he wants to influence the physician to prescribe. In return for their time, many physicians expect to receive such free goods to distribute to indigent patients who could not otherwise afford proper medication. Many process and fabricating materials, parts, and operating supplies can be sold almost entirely through the use of samples, due to the ease with which their use can be demonstrated during the salesman's call. Indeed, samples are often part of the sales contract. When samples are written into the contract, the seller guarantees that they are representative of the lot to be delivered, thus simplifying the inspection and testing the buyer is obliged to do.

Samples may be distributed in a variety of ways, depending on how they are to be used. They may simply be mailed to a list of prospective users with covering promotional literature. This procedure, while insuring adequate coverage of the market, suffers from the disadvantage that recipients may not examine, or perhaps even notice, an item that comes to them unsolicited through the mails. For this reason, some manufacturers follow the practice of advertising samples either through trade journals or by direct mail. Response is increased by inserting a coupon or return card for the interested party's use in requesting a sample. A number of industrial marketers believe that it is sound practice to make a nominal charge for samples as a means of imparting a value to the product, thereby insuring its careful examination and avoiding waste. The waste problem may also be handled by distributing samples through salesmen, who are instructed to leave them only when the prospect appears genuinely interested. In many industries, the trade show offers an excellent opportunity to distribute samples to substantial numbers of interested potential customers within a short time.

The use of samples may be criticized on the grounds that it is costly, that it has been overdone to such an extent that buyers no longer pay much attention to them. It is also argued that something received for nothing, or only a token payment, is considered of little worth, and that the great proportion of samples are taken by the sample hound, who is not a genuine prospect for the product. These arguments undoubtedly have an element of truth.

Like other forms of promotion, samples can be misused. They are obviously inappropriate for many industrial products, because of the product's cost, weight, bulk, toxicity, intricate design, or other quality. However, for products which lend themselves to this form of promotion, either because of their physical properties or qualities which possess dramatic appeal, samples may be the most economical way to get real promotional impact. Since the cost of manufacturing samples is really an incremental expense, the use of samples should be relatively inexpensive, particularly if waste can be avoided through proper distribution.

## PROMOTIONAL LETTERS

The work of industrial salesmen can be greatly facilitated through the use of promotional letters. For example, a letter of introduction preceding a salesman's first visit will identify him with his company and help break down the natural barrier between strangers. Letters dictated for individual customers and timed to arrive between periodic visits of the salesman may be an effective method of keeping in touch with the customer. This is particularly important in selling heavy machinery and other types of products purchased infrequently. When the buyer is in the market only once in four or five years, the cost of continuous personal contact is apt to be excessive; yet the seller cannot safely assume that the buyer will get in touch with him when he wants to make such a purchase. A well-organized correspondence program can materially reduce the cost of sales solicitation in such a market.

Mailing pieces, such as advertising reprints, brochures, catalogs, and technical data sheets probably receive much more attention when accompanied by an individualized covering letter than when received without one. Salesmen might be expected to perform this task, since they are in the best position to know where, when, and to whom such mailing pieces should be directed. However, the disadvantage of relying upon salesmen to perform this function is that many salesmen do not have time, cannot write well, or simply do not care for paper work.

A plan that has been successful for some companies is to organize a special correspondence section to handle promotional letters. Salesmen can then instruct this section by means of a card form regarding the kinds of promotional literature which should be sent to which customers and what should be said in the covering letter.

Perhaps the most important area in which correspondence can influence sales is that of handling inquiries. These may be impersonal, in the form of coupons or cards supplied by the seller, or they may be personal letters asking for detailed information. In general, the response should correspond to the degree of formality of the inquiry. While form letters or printed material may be adequate for the more general kind of inquiry, a personalized letter is required for the personal inquiry. In any case, the reply should be prompt. If adequate information cannot be supplied on the day following receipt of the inquiry, a letter of acknowledgment should be forwarded, indicating when complete and specific information may be expected. No effort should be spared in making each letter an effective sales presentation. Results of this type of promotion can be improved by maintaining a tickler file system on sales inquiries and renewing contact with them at suitable intervals.

The possibilities of injecting salesmanship into other types of business correspondence should not be overlooked. In adjustment and collection letters, the emphasis should be on reselling a product so as to successfully conclude the sale and lay the groundwork for future sales. The credit manager has many opportunities to exercise positive salesmanship by inviting desirable prospects to open accounts, by encouraging the use of credit, and by writing letters of appreciation for the use made of accounts.

Letters following the receipt of an order furnish an excellent opportunity to promote sales, especially in new accounts, accounts that have been inactive, and large orders. All business correspondence, no matter how routine, should have as its major objective promotion of the idea that the company is a good one with which to do business. The relatively small outlay required to improve company correspondence as compared with other promotional expenditures should pay large dividends to the industrial goods manufacturer in strengthening his competitive position.

The correspondence function may be the responsibility of the individual or company division most directly concerned or assigned to a special section. In favor of the former, i.e., decentralized organization, is the likelihood that the writer will have the most accurate and timely knowledge about the subject of the letter. On the other hand, when the work load becomes heavy, correspondence may be slighted in favor of other, more pressing, responsibilities.

Under a centralized arrangement, promotional letters would be the primary responsibility of a special correspondence section. The advantage of this is the strong probability that letters composed by specialized staff would be more effective communications than those dictated by salesmen, sales managers, or other company officials not primarily concerned with, or skilled in, letter writing. A correspondence section is also better equipped to write letters that concern several departments of a business and to maintain uniform company policy in correspondence. By virtue of its specialized staff and equipment, a correspondence section can probably manage volume correspondence more efficiently than any other unit in an organization.

## PROMOTIONAL NOVELTIES

Advertising novelties are small, interesting, or personally useful items on which are imprinted the name and perhaps an advertising message of the issuing company. Their purpose is to keep buyers, and those who influence buying, constantly aware of the supplier's identity and of the general nature of the products he offers. Unlike premiums, which are used extensively in consumer marketing, promotional novelties are seldom associated with special merchandise offers, nor are they generally used to specifically induce a purchase. Rather, they are generally given away without obligation.

An effective promotional novelty should meet at least four requirements.

1. Inexpensive. If it appears to be costly, it may be looked upon with suspicion at least by the purchasing agent, who recognizes that its cost must be included in the price of the products its donor is in business to sell.

2. Unusual and eye-catching. A ball-point pen used as a promotional novelty by a petroleum company is a good example of an unusual, eye-catching novelty. The upper part of the barrel of the pen was made of transparent plastic filled with heavy clear oil. Inside the barrel was a cylindrical sinker that slowly moved through the oil as the vertical plane of the pen was changed. The company name was imprinted on the sinker.

3. Multiple impact. The company name and whatever promotional message accompanies it should be seen by a number of people over a period of time. The more exposure it receives the better. This is one reason so many industrial marketers give away thousands of calendars

each year. A calendar placed in a customer's office or plant will expose the donor's name and promotional message to a substantial number of persons connected with the customer for a year.

4. Useful. A novelty which has no conceivable use for the recipient is likely to be discarded soon after he receives it. On the other hand, one which possesses some measure of utility, such as a pocket slide rule for an engineer or an atomic weight scale for a chemist, may be retained (and mentioned in conversation) for a considerable length of time.

## ENTERTAINMENT

There is an old adage that more business is transacted on the golf course than over a desk. The industrial marketer who overlooks the element of truth in this statement is being something less than realistic. Whether or not to entertain and the funds which should be committed to it depend on the types of products involved and the nature of the circumstances as well as on the stipulations of the Internal Revenue Service. The marketer of products manufactured to standard specifications and sold in bulk may give entertainment his primary promotional emphasis because it appears to be as effective as any other form of sales promotion. However, the marketer of a highly differentiated product, or one with an established market position, would have difficulty finding a rationale for much customer entertainment.

The possibility that entertainment could have a negative effect is almost always present. Personnel of the customer firm may regard an offer of entertainment as contrary to good business practice or, at best, as bordering on impropriety. The former is illustrated by an example of entertainment that backfired.

A group of buyers visiting New York City were entertained lavishly at a banquet and taken to a heavyweight title fight by a firm interested in gaining their patronage. The next day, a competitor solicited the same group of buyers with the approach that as a matter of policy it never entertained customers. The competitor got the business by showing that because of this and other operating economies he was able to produce an identical product at a lower price.

The same sort of reasoning applies to the practice of giving gifts to customers. Gift giving may occur ostensibly to express gratitude at the signing of an important contract or at the fulfillment of obligations under it. It is most likely to occur at Christmas or on the buyer's birthday or some similar occasion deemed appropriate. However, expensive, or even modestly ostentatious, gifts may pose an embarrassing problem for the recipients. To return them smacks of ingratitude. To keep them may arouse suspicions about the buyer's ability to remain completely objective in future negotiations with the donor. Consequently, many companies have firm policies forbidding their employees to either give to, or accept gifts from, anyone soliciting or doing business with the company. Others limit gifts, either offered or accepted, to something a person can eat, drink, or smoke in a day. There is an old adage to the effect that business which can be bought with a valuable gift can be bought by a competitor with a more valuable gift.

## PUBLIC RELATIONS

Public relations may be defined as a planned program of policies and conduct that will build public confidence in and increase public understanding of its sponsor. It differs from publicity in that it is much broader in scope; in fact, it has been said that public relations is 90 percent doing right and 10 percent talking about it. One may question whether public relations should properly be considered as a method of promoting sales, since many who have dedicated themselves to the field look on public relations as a way of corporate living. Some go so far as to place the building of public confidence and understanding above the profit motive as a basic business objective. Few would deny, however, that there is, at least, a close relationship between a sound public relations program and a sound, long-range sales promotion program.

It is generally believed that to be effective, public relations effort must be directed at some specific, reasonably homogeneous group. The general public is not such a group; rather, it is a series of groups each having its own problems and interests, and each of which must be met on a different plane. Each group may be bound together by a number of forces, including such factors as racial, religious, occupational, political, professional, economic, patriotic, fraternal, and educational interests. A useful classification of so-called publics, prepared by the Committee on Industrial Practices of the National Association of Manufacturers, is as follows:

1. Customers
2. Suppliers
3. Competitors
4. Employees
5. Stockholders
6. Creditors
7. Local community
8. The government

The relative importance of these publics differs with each industry and, in fact, with each company within an industry. It is doubtful that the various classes of publics are mutually exclusive. One individual, for example, might be a customer, a supplier, and a creditor, as well as a member of the local community. Despite these complications, an important first step in public relations is to define as specifically as possible the various publics whose confidence and understanding are to be sought.

## Planning the public relations program

Public relations planning involves at least two stages: (1) defining the problem, and (2) determining the action to be taken in order to solve the problem. Very often, company management becomes aware of a problem only after it has resulted in some major difficulty, such as a proposal for new legislation, detrimental to the company's interest, which is designed to correct a real or fancied fault. It is therefore important to conduct research that will illumine the inevitable blind spots, which every management suffers, and provide a clear, reliable picture of the ideas specific publics have about the company.

In conducting this research, two basic techniques are available—the historic method of impressionistic observation and the more objective method of opinion sampling. The historic method depends for its success on the experience and perception, or the political or social sense, of the individual making the observation. To the skilled observer, it provides a means of quickly sizing up a situation with a minimum of effort. Difficulty arises when two impressionistic observers arrive at different conclusions. Action may be blocked, since there is no sound means of reconciling their differences.

The opinion-sampling technique, while less flexible and obviously more costly, will undoubtedly yield more accurate results if properly applied. In place of opinion about opinions, the survey provides facts about opinions. The intangible qualitative data of which public opinion is composed are reduced to a form that can be charted, analyzed into classes or groups, and made more meaningful to management. The process involves defining the public, selecting a representative sample, designing a questionnaire that will yield unbiased results, obtaining the interviews, and then tabulating and analyzing the results.

Having gathered the facts and defined the problem, management is in a position to undertake the second stage of the planning program—determining what to do on the basis of the facts. This is a top-management decision of vital importance. In determining the course of action, executives must carefully weigh the objectives of the company, the facilities available, the size of the task to be accomplished, the cost, and the value of the end result. When the relative importance of these factors has been determined, a basic plan can be formulated to meet the situation. This plan may then be issued as a major policy of the company and, as such, becomes the backbone of future public relations work. Day-to-day tactics must conform to the overall strategy and contribute to its successful achievement. Such a plan is a requirement for concerted and coordinated action throughout the company, which is necessary in order to insure the success of the public relations program. However, the plan must not be too rigid. Public opinion is continually changing as it reacts to what is seen, heard, read, and experienced; therefore, the basic strategy must be open to review and revision as events dictate.

## Implementing the program

The basic philosophy underlying public relations is sound performance in the public interest. No company can boast of a performance record that cannot be improved to some degree. Research may indicate that the company's products could be made cheaper or better. It may show that the company's waste disposal system pollutes the local water supply, that excessive smoke creates a health hazard, or that unsightly factory buildings depress local real estate values. A common source of public relations problems lies in the continual effort of operating officials in a large corporation to make the best possible showing on the current profit-and-loss statement, which sometimes results, despite top-management policy to the contrary, in taking unfair advantage of small suppliers and competitors. Before any attempt is made to meet a public relations problem through communication, every effort should be made to insure that actual performance with respect to that problem is sound. This involves management's acceptance of the thesis that, in general, the social interest and long-run company interest coincide.

## Tools and media

A sound public relations program, no matter how carefully formulated, will fall short of its objectives if not implemented with effective media. For example, the so-called open-door policy may provide a valuable way of keeping in touch with employee opinion. In many instances, however, the open door has proved to be a barrier rather than an avenue for communication. Such machinery as the grievance committee or depth interviewing by an outside organization is probably more effective in revealing workers' sentiments. In getting management's story across to employees, more positive media include the indoctrination handbook, bulletin board, payroll insert, newsletter, and house organ. Some companies have successfully used public address systems in building employee morale.

In reaching the community where the plant is located, the local press offers the advantage of adequate coverage at minimum cost. In addition, the various types of publicity are available for improving community relations. But, in the final analysis, nothing is so effective as personal contact with community leaders.

In dealing with customers and potential customers, smaller industrial goods manufacturers rely heavily on trade journals and direct mail, while the large corporation has made increasing use of national consumer media, including radio and television. Finally, in reaching the stockholder the trend has been toward dressing up the annual report to make it more interesting and informative, providing dividend check enclosures that explain company operation and policy, and encouraging direct communication with stockholders at the annual meeting.

Public relations is not a specific marketing activity that may be expected to result in immediate sales. Rather, it is a means of creating an atmosphere or a climate that is hospitable to the marketing efforts of a firm and tends to cause them to be more fruitful. So far as it does this, the activity represents a valuable contribution to the firm's total marketing strategy.

## SUMMARY

The most significant sales promotion activities for many industrial marketers are trade show exhibits, catalogs, samples, promotional letters, promotional novelties, and entertainment. Trade show exhibits are generally used to meet potential customers, discover new product applications, introduce new products, demonstrate nonportable equipment, aid and attract new dealers, and match competitive efforts. To be successful, participation in trade shows must be planned in considerable detail.

Catalogs are another important component of promotional strategy for a number of industrial marketers. The purposes that catalogs are chiefly employed to serve include producing orders, developing recognition, generating requests for information, stimulating invitations to bid, and getting the marketer's product specifications adopted by as many firms as possible. In preparing catalogs, the marketer needs to know who are their principal users and what kinds of information they hope to find in them. If properly distributed, the catalog may reach buying influences very difficult to contact by any other means.

Samples are especially useful in promoting new products, as well as being a general aid to the salesman. Due to their expense, the distribution of samples needs to be well planned.

Letters are also a useful sales promotion activity if properly composed and properly timed. If not, they may have a negative effect. It is probably advisable to place responsibility for promotional letters in a specialized unit, although almost every division and department of a business usually participates by supplying information to the unit.

Promotional novelties are a secondary means of sales promotion but are often effective as continuing reminders of the marketer and his products. Both promotional novelties and entertainment can be useful in smoothing the process of market development as well as negotiations with customers.

The essence of public relations is the proper conduct of a firm's relationship with the various subgroups which compose its general public. This requires thorough study of the way in which the company's operation affects each of these groups and a comprehensive program for responding in a positive way to each of them.

# PART VIII

## Marketing control

THE PRECEDING SECTIONS on marketing strategy have treated it in a conceptual sense, identifying its constituent parts and discussing how each functions in the context of a total plan. There is little reason to formulate a marketing strategy, however, unless an effort is made to assure that it will be followed. Systems designed for this purpose are commonly identified with the label of control. Since strategy is intended to implement the corporate mission, any system for controlling it must be mission related.

It is apparent that implementation of marketing strategy calls for the joint effort of a number of people within a firm. Consequently, it must be directed in terms of clearly defined long- and short-term objectives. These objectives not only serve as the focal point of strategy but also as the primary element of any system for controlling it. The formulation of strategic goals within the context of the corporate mission is discussed in chapter 23. The tenor of this chapter, of necessity, differs sharply from that of preceding ones. Since goals that serve as focal points of planning must be measurable, techniques for their determination may be quantitative to the point of being tedious. To some extent this is true of the techniques discussed here, which are more statistical than mathematical. Nevertheless, their use is widespread and they represent basic methods of market prediction.

The translation of these goals into operating standards and the different elements of control that operate to enforce them are the subject of chapter 24.

# 23

## STRATEGIC GOALS

IT HAS ALREADY been observed that the task facing management in setting objectives and goals is that of balancing the desirable against the feasible. Without attempting to argue the point, it is probably true that few managers have much difficulty identifying ends they would like to achieve. The hopes, desires, and ambitions of company officers and owners are often readily apparent. But to set goals, however desirable, that do not have a chance of attainment is to invite waste and apathy.

The feasibility of an objective is sure to be influenced by a number of conditions, the nature of which are sure to vary with each individual company. For most marketing objectives, however, the possibility of attainment is ultimately determined by two primary elements: (1) the nature of market opportunity, and (2) the capacity of an organization to exploit it. The measurement of market opportunity and ways of formulating objectives that reflect it are discussed in this chapter. The translation of marketing goals into performance standards and the design of control systems based on them are treated in the following chapter.

### IDENTIFYING MARKET OPPORTUNITY

Market opportunity is used here to refer to the capacity of a market for a given product which the firm can be competitive in supplying. Techniques for identifying industries and market segments with the most promising growth and demand potential have already been discussed (chapters 8 and 9), along with the types of analysis which can be useful in revealing the competitive strengths and weaknesses of a company (chapter 10). When accompanied by the insight that executive experience and acumen provide, these methods can be successful in singling out the industries and customer groups which should be the targets for the firm's marketing effort.

Logically, these target markets should be ranked in some order of priority, to assure that markets representing the greatest opportunity receive the largest commitment of resources. This practice may sometimes be difficult to "sell" to top management, particularly if markets which represent the most promising opportunities are not currently producing the greatest volume of sales. Nevertheless, it is difficult to deny the argument that resources should be allocated to markets in relation to the amount of anticipated long-term payoff each represents. These evaluations provide the background for setting long- and short-term marketing objectives.

In this discussion, long-term objectives refer to those which pertain to a three- to five-year time span and represent a strategic choice. Short-term objectives pertain to a period not exceeding one year and represent operational choices. Since different industries and market segments represent different degrees of opportunity, it is necessary to formulate strategic and operational goals for each. The goals for different industries and market segments are then summed to give strategic and operational goals for the company.

Depending on the extent of a company's experience in a target market, long-range goals may be determined on the basis of projections of past sales as well as market share. Obviously, if a target market is not one in which the company has previously been active, there can be no projection of past sales.

Projections are usually formulated in two phases. The first is a statistical extrapolation of past experience that has been reduced to a time series. The second phase is the adjustment of this extrapolation for conditions anticipated in the future that did not exist in the past and could not be reflected in the extrapolation.

## GOALS BASED ON MARKET SHARE

An estimate of market share begins with a projection of total sales for an industry or market segment, after which an estimate is made of the share of that total the company is expected to command.

### Projecting industry sales

Numerous techniques have been developed by individual companies and by trade associations to estimate total expected sales of an industry. However, information concerning the details of these methods and the success with which they have been used is very sketchy. Discussion here will therefore be limited to the better-known methods which are based on projections of trend.

To appreciate the usefulness and limitations of trend projection requires some familiarity with the mechanics of trend fitting. When using trend for purposes of prediction, it is usually advisable to employ some technique that permits the description of trend in terms of a mathematical formula. This lends more objectivity to the extension of trend, without removing the subjective element from trend fitting. Regardless of the method employed, the fitted trend line or curve should appear logical and reasonable in view of what is known about forces affecting industry sales. In essence, one should begin by fitting a freehand trend line, exercising the best judgment possible, and then choose the mathematical method that appears most consistent with the nature of this line.

Value of shipments in the paint, varnish, and lacquer industry from 1962 to 1972 are shown in Figures 23–1 and 23–2. It is apparent that the path of the series could be described with reasonable accuracy by a straight line drawn freehand. However, everyone who attempted to draw such a line would probably draw a slightly different one, with the result that when the line was extended to make a forecast, no two people would get the same answer. Consequently, it is usually advisable to supplement a freehand projection with a mathematically determined one. Indeed, the series shown in Figure 23–1 might be described by either a straight line or a curve.

*Straight-line trend.* A straight line is described by the equation $Yc = a + bX$. The origin or beginning of the line is indicated by the symbol $a$. The value of $a$ indicates how high above the $X$ (horizontal) axis the trend line of a plotted series begins. The slope of the line is represented by the symbol $b$, whose value indicates how much the trend line rises or falls from one unit of time to the next. Since their values must be determined for each series being studied, $a$ and $b$ are referred to as *unknowns*. They are also *constants*, because their *values* do not change.

The symbol $Yc$ refers to a point or points along the trend line. The letter $Y$ is used because the trend line will be expressed in the same units as appear on the $Y$ (vertical) axis of the graph—in this illustra-

**FIGURE 23–1. Value of shipments of paints, varnish, and lacquer, 1962–72 (millions of dollars)**

| Calendar year | Factory shipments |
|---|---|
| 1962 | $1,831.8 |
| 1963 | 1,206.7 |
| 1964 | 1,281.6 |
| 1965 | 2,196.2 |
| 1966 | 2,100.0 |
| 1967 | 2,348.2 |
| 1968 | 2,587.1 |
| 1969 | 2,776.7 |
| 1970 | 2,737.1 |
| 1971 | 2,830.9 |
| 1972 | 3,009.2 |

Source: *Survey of Current Business*, January, 1973.

**FIGURE 23–2.   Value of shipments of paints, varnish, and lacquer, 1962–72  (straight-line trend)**

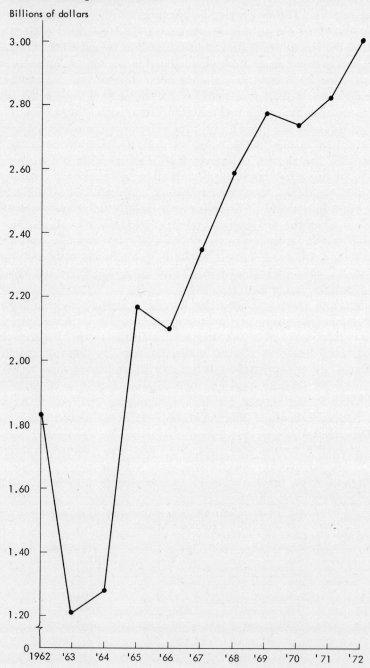

tion, millions of dollars. The small letter $c$ is added to show that the $Y$ values are computed. The symbol $X$ refers to units of time, plotted along the $X$ axis.

It is generally agreed that if a series can be described by a straight line, the least squares method is the best way to compute it. This method determines the line from which the values in a series deviate the least. If the vertical deviation of each value in a series is given a plus or minus sign, plus if the value is above the line and minus if it is below it, the sum of the deviations will be zero. Then, if the deviation of each value in the series from this line is squared, the sum of these squares will be less than the sum of the squared deviations of these values from any other line that might be drawn. A least squares trend line, therefore, describes the line of balance through the original data.

In order to draw a least squares trend line, values for $a$ and $b$ in the straight line equation must be found. Since values for $X$ are known (they refer to units of time), calculation can be simplified by merely designating them as 0, 1, 2, 3, and so on. Then using the two equations (called "normal" equations), $Y = Na + b\Sigma X$ and $\Sigma XY = a\Sigma X + b\Sigma X^2$, substitutions may easily be made which permit solving for the unknowns. The symbol $N$ in the first equation refers to the number of values in the series. The procedure of substitution and solution is accomplished in two steps:

1. Arrangement of the data to satisfy the terms of the normal equations, and
2. Substitution of values in the normal equations and solving for unknowns.

These steps are illustrated in Figure 23–3. Values for $a$ and $b$ are substituted in step three of this figure. Since the trend line is represented by a formula, it can be extended as far into the future as the analyst deems suitable. The projection of factory shipments of paint, varnish, and lacquer for 1977 would be $3,943,000,000, i.e., $Yc = 2.263 + 0.168(10)$.

*Curvilinear trend.* Despite the appropriate manner in which a straight line appears to describe the trend in factory shipments of paint, varnish, and lacquer, the series does seem to have a slight bend in it. In such instances, it is usually revealing to determine whether a second-degree curve fits the series as well or better than a straight line. Such a curve can also be extended mathematically.

A curve, of course, differs from a straight line in that its slope is continually changing. Consequently, the formula for a second-degree curve (one with a single bend in it) involves a third term and a third unknown. The equation $YC = a + bX + cX^2$, in which the symbol $a$ indicates the point above the $X$ scale where the curve begins (the value of $Y$ when $X$ is zero); $b$ indicates the amount and direction of the slope

**FIGURE 23–3.    Computation of trend values, using least squares method (value of shipments of paints, varnish, and lacquer, 1962–72)**

Step 1.    Arrangement of data to satisfy terms of normal equations.*

| Calendar year | X | Value of shipments (billions of dollars) Y | XY | X² |
|---|---|---|---|---|
| 1962 | −5 | 1.83 | −9.15 | 25 |
| 1963 | −4 | 1.21 | −4.84 | 16 |
| 1964 | −3 | 1.28 | −3.84 | 9 |
| 1965 | −2 | 2.17 | −4.34 | 4 |
| 1966 | −1 | 2.10 | −2.10 | 1 |
| 1967 | 0 | 2.35 | 0 | 0 |
| 1968 | 1 | 2.59 | 2.59 | 1 |
| 1969 | 2 | 2.78 | 5.56 | 4 |
| 1970 | 3 | 2.74 | 8.22 | 9 |
| 1971 | 4 | 2.83 | 11.32 | 16 |
| 1972 | 5 | 3.01 | 15.05 | 25 |
|  | $\Sigma X = 0$ | $\Sigma Y = 24.89$ | $\Sigma XY = 18.47$ | $\Sigma X^2 = 110$ |

Step 2.    Substitute values in normal equations and solve for unknowns.

$$Y = Na + bX \quad \text{or} \quad 24.89 = 11a + 0$$
$$XY = aX + bX^2 \quad \text{or} \quad 18.47 = 0 + 110b$$
$$a = 2.263$$
$$b = 0.168$$

Step 3.    Compute trend, using formula $Yc = a + bX$ or $Yc = 2.263 + .168X$ (origin 1962; $X$ units, one year; $Yc$ units in value of shipments in millions of dollars).

| Calendar year | a | b | X | Yc |
|---|---|---|---|---|
| 1962 | 2.263 | + 0.168 | −5 | = 1.423 |
| 1963 | " | " | −4 | = 1.591 |
| 1964 | " | " | −3 | = 1.759 |
| 1965 | " | " | −2 | = 1.927 |
| 1966 | " | " | −1 | = 2.095 |
| 1967 | " | " | 0 | = 2.263 |
| 1968 | " | " | 1 | = 2.431 |
| 1969 | " | " | 2 | = 2.599 |
| 1970 | " | " | 3 | = 2.767 |
| 1971 | " | " | 4 | = 2.935 |
| 1972 | " | " | 5 | = 3.103 |

* Computation here is by the so-called short method in which the origin of the trend line is placed in the center of the X scale, i.e., in the middle year of the series instead of the first year. The years in the first half of the series are then designated as −1, −2, −3, and so on, beginning with the middle year which is 0; the years in the second half of the series are designated as +1, +2, +3, and so on, beginning with the middle year. This simple manipulation of the X scale eliminates a term from each of the normal equations, thus simplifying the computation.

at the point $X$ equals zero; and $c$ indicates the amount of change in the slope of the curve from one unit of $X$ (time) to the next. The problem, then, is to find appropriate values for $a$, $b$, and $c$.

As in the use of the straight-line formula, solving for the unknowns involves the substitution of values in normal equations. The normal equations for the second-degree curve are:

I       $\Sigma Y = Na + b\Sigma X + c\Sigma X^2$

II     $\Sigma XY = a\Sigma X + b\Sigma X^2 + c\Sigma X^3$

III    $\Sigma X^2Y = a\Sigma X^2 + b\Sigma X^3 + c\Sigma X^4$

The procedure for using these equations is the same as that for linear trend. It is demonstrated in Figure 23–4. A comparison of straight-line and curvilinear trends is shown in Figure 23–5. Since the origin is taken at the middle of the time period, $X = 0$, and $X^3 = 0$. Thus the three normal equations become:

I       $\Sigma Y = Na + c\Sigma X^2$

II     $\Sigma XY = b\Sigma X^2$

III    $\Sigma X^2Y = a\Sigma X^2 + c\Sigma X^4$

The projection of factory shipments of paint, varnish, and lacquer to 1977 is \$3,610,000,000—a difference of \$333,000,000 from the projection derived from a straight-line trend. While this is a statistically significant amount, the two projections provide the analyst with a range whose limits have been objectively determined and within which actual industry sales in 1977 are likely to fall. Projections of paint, varnish, and lacquer industry sales to 1980, using both straight-line and curvilinear trends, are shown in Figure 23–6. Whether or not industry sales in 1977 are likely to be nearer the \$3.9 billion figure or \$3.6 billions depends on the effect of economic, legal, and other environmental factors on the level of industry output and demand.

There are other curves which could be fitted to industry sales data for the purpose of developing a prediction of future sales volume. These have features which permit them to be fitted to series whose curvatures cannot be accurately described by the second-degree curve. However, the discussion of the second-degree curve should suffice to indicate the nature of curve fitting and demonstrate the usefulness of this technique in deriving forecasts.

## Adjusting projections

It is almost always necessary to modify trend projections as the result of anticipated conditions for which statistical techniques make no allowance. The probable effect on industry sales of such factors as the expected level of business activity, changes in the structure of inter-industry competition, and promotional efforts of the industry need to be weighed and incorporated into the final estimate. Since the significance of such factors can seldom be determined by quantitative measures, their proper evaluation in terms of industry sales depends in large measure upon the business acumen and judgment of the analyst. Businessmen can receive valuable assistance in appraising the impact on their industry of anticipated economic and other environmental conditions from industry trade associations, the U.S. Department of Commerce, publications of the Federal Reserve Banks, studies of University

**FIGURE 23–4.** Computation of trend values, using second-degree curve (value of shipments of paints, varnishes, and lacquer, 1962–1972; S.I.C. 2851)

Step 1.   Arrangement of data to satisfy normal equations.

*Calendar*

| year | $X$ | $Y$ | $XY$ | $X^2$ | $X^2Y$ | $X^4$ |
|------|-----|-----|------|-------|--------|-------|
| 1962 | −5 | 1.83 | −9.15 | 25 | 45.75 | 625 |
| 1963 | −4 | 1.21 | −4.84 | 16 | 19.36 | 256 |
| 1964 | −3 | 1.28 | −3.84 | 9 | 11.52 | 81 |
| 1965 | −2 | 2.17 | −4.34 | 4 | 8.68 | 16 |
| 1966 | −1 | 2.10 | −2.10 | 1 | 2.10 | 1 |
| 1967 | 0 | 2.35 | 0 | 0 | 0 | 0 |
| 1968 | 1 | 2.59 | 2.59 | 1 | 2.59 | 1 |
| 1969 | 2 | 2.78 | 5.56 | 4 | 11.12 | 16 |
| 1970 | 3 | 2.74 | 8.22 | 9 | 24.66 | 81 |
| 1971 | 4 | 2.83 | 11.32 | 16 | 45.28 | 256 |
| 1972 | 5 | 3.01 | 15.05 | 25 | 75.25 | 625 |
|      |   | 24.89 | 18.47 | 110 | 246.31 | 1,958 |

Step 2.   Substitute values in normal equations and solve for unknowns.

$$\Sigma Y = Na + c\Sigma X^2 \quad \text{or} \quad 24.89 = 11a + 110c$$
$$2X^2Y = a\Sigma X^2 + c\Sigma X^4 \quad \text{or} \quad 246.31 = 110a + 1958c$$

Eliminate $a$ by multiplying the first equation by 110 and the second by 11, then subtract the second from the first to derive the value of $c$:

$$2737.90 = 1210a + 12100c$$
$$\underline{2709.41 = 1210a + 21538c}$$
$$28.49 = \qquad\quad -9438c$$
$$c = -.003$$

Determine value of $b$ and $a$ by solving remaining normal equations.

$$\Sigma XY = b\Sigma X^2 \qquad\qquad \Sigma Y = Na + c\Sigma X^2$$
$$18.47 = 110b \qquad\qquad 24.89 = 11a - .003(110)$$
$$b = .168 \qquad\qquad a = 2.23$$

Step 3.   Compute trends, using formula $Yc = a + bX + cX^2$ or $Yc = 2.23 + .168X - .003X^2$ (origin 1967; $X$ units, 1 year; $Yc$ units, factory shipments in billions of dollars)

*Calendar*

| year | $a$ | $b$ | $X$ | $c$ | $X^2$ | $Yc$ |
|------|-----|-----|-----|-----|-------|------|
| 1962 | 2.23 | + .168 | (−5) | − .003 | (25) | = 1.31 |
| 1963 | " | + " | (−4) | − " | (16) | = 1.51 |
| 1964 | " | + " | (−3) | − " | (9) | = 1.70 |
| 1965 | " | + " | (−2) | − " | (4) | = 1.88 |
| 1966 | " | + " | (−1) | − " | (1) | = 2.06 |
| 1967 | " | + " | (0) | − " | (0) | = 2.23 |
| 1968 | " | + " | (1) | − " | (1) | = 2.40 |
| 1969 | " | + " | (2) | − " | (4) | = 2.55 |
| 1970 | " | + " | (3) | − " | (9) | = 2.71 |
| 1971 | " | + " | (4) | − " | (16) | = 2.85 |
| 1972 | " | + " | (5) | − " | (25) | = 2.99 |
| 1977 | " | + " | (10) | − " | (100) | = 3.61 |

**FIGURE 23–5.** Comparison of straight-line and curvilinear trends (value of shipments of paints, varnish, and lacquer, 1962–72)

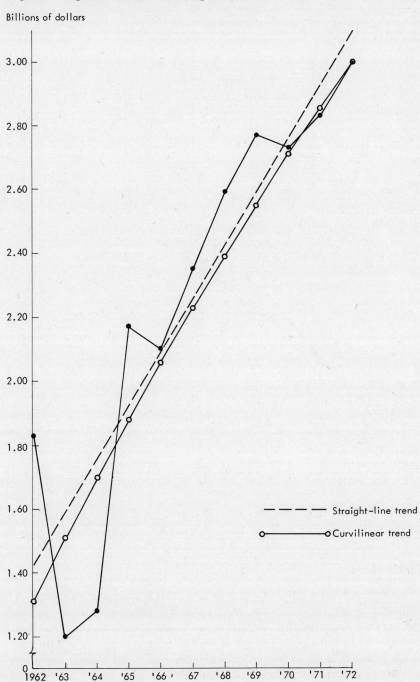

**FIGURE 23–6.   Value of shipments of paints, varnish, and lacquer, projection to 1980**

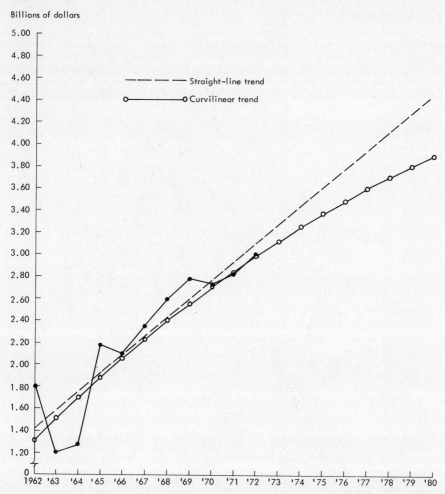

Billions of dollars

Bureaus of Economic and Business Research, and surveys published by the business press as well as from numerous private consulting firms.

## Market share

Predicting what share of total industry sales a company will be able to command is largely a matter of managerial judgment. It is not only necessary to appraise the effectiveness of management's own marketing strategy but to anticipate actions of competitors and assess whether they are likely to be more or less successful than one's own efforts. A competitor who has made substantial additions to his sales force, another who has expanded his production facilities, a third who has completed a

program of vertical integration will all have an impact on the allocation of buyer patronage.

Obviously, this is not the kind of situation that is subject to direct
statistical measurement. However, it is almost always advisable to determine market share over a sufficient period of time in the past to identify
any persistent characteristics in its behavior. This at least supplies a
benchmark from which to judge the reasonableness of alternative possibilities. Where a discernible trend is evident, the market share prediction may be based on the assumption that it will continue, providing
the appraisal of competitors' actions and reactions does not lead one to
the opposite conclusion.

**FIGURE 23–7.**   **Market share of a manufacturer of paints and lacquer
( 1963–72)**

| (1) | (2) | (3) | (4) |
|---|---|---|---|
| | Total value of shipments paints, varnish & lacquer (billions | Manufacturer shipments (billions of | Market shares (%) |
| Year | of dollars) | dollars) | (Col. 3 ÷ Col. 2) |
| 1962 | 1.83 | .024888 | 1.36 |
| 1963 | 1.21 | .016214 | 1.34 |
| 1964 | 1.28 | .018432 | 1.44 |
| 1965 | 2.17 | .029512 | 1.36 |
| 1966 | 2.10 | .026880 | 1.28 |
| 1967 | 2.35 | .029610 | 1.26 |
| 1968 | 2.59 | .033929 | 1.31 |
| 1969 | 2.78 | .035862 | 1.29 |
| 1970 | 2.74 | .034798 | 1.27 |
| 1971 | 2.83 | .034809 | 1.23 |
| 1972 | 3.01 | .038528 | 1.28 |
| Average market share, last five years | | | 1.28% |
| Industry sales forecast, 1977 | | | $3,750,000,000 |
| Sales objective, 1977 | | | 47,000,000 |

An example of market share prediction is given in Figure 23–7 for a
manufacturer of paints and lacquer sold to the building trades. Since
industry sales typically can be forecast with greater assurance of accuracy than individual company sales, the market share method of
prediction is basic in the definition of strategic marketing goals.

The 1977 sales objective of $47,000,000 represents a strategic market-
ing goal based on a market share prediction of 1.28 percent, average
market share during the most recent five-year period, and an industry
sales prediction of $3,750,000,000. The latter figure represents the mid-
point between the high and low projections shown in Figure 23–6 and
was chosen for purposes of illustration.

## GOALS BASED ON SALES FORECASTS

It is generally advisable for companies which have sales experience in an industry or market segment to supplement a marketing goal based on anticipated market share with one based on a forecast of sales. Habit, loyalty, and simple inertia insure that next year's sales will be related to this year's sales and to the sales of all preceding years. Consequently, trend projection is as useful and appropriate in predicting future company sales as in predicting industry sales. It should be emphasized that "projection" is not the same as prediction. As indicated earlier, projections indicate what will happen if past relationships, or assumptions concerning them, continue to be valid. A trend projection must therefore be refined and sharpened through further analysis before it may be accepted as a firm prediction.

The steps involved in fitting a trend line to industry sales and extending it into the future would also apply to company sales. Sales of an individual company, however, are often much more erratic in their behavior than the sales of an industry. This is understandable in view of the fact that decreases in sales suffered by one company are frequently offset in the total picture by sales increases of its competitors. Except for a one product company, or one whose different products have similar marketing characteristics, separate forecasts are likely to be developed for each major product. The different product forecasts are then combined into a total company sales forecast.

Fitting a trend line to the sales of an individual product or the experience of an individual enterprise may therefore require more sensitive techniques than those discussed in the preceding section. Representative of such techniques are the higher-degree polynomial curves, asymptotic curves, and weighted moving averages.

### Higher-degree polynomials

It has been shown that a second-degree curve has one bend in it and, consequently, involves one more constant in its estimating equation than does the straight line. Third- and fourth-degree curves have two and three bends in them respectively, and accordingly involve additional constants in their estimating equations. In contrast to a second-degree curve which slopes in a negative direction at one stage and in a positive direction at another, a third-degree curve changes direction three times. Fourth- and fifth-degree curves may change their direction of slope four and five times, respectively. By adding another constant to the estimating equation, one more bend is added to the trend curve. Estimating equations for third-, fourth-, and fifth-degree curves are given below:

Third degree.........$Yc = a + bX + cX^2 + dX^3$
Fourth degree........$Yc = a + bX + cX^2 + dX^3 + eX^4$
Fifth degree.........$Yc = a + bX + cX^2 + dX^3 + eX^4 + fX^5$

If the origin is taken at the middle of the period to which the trend line is to be fitted, four normal equations are required for a third-degree curve:

$$\text{I} \qquad \Sigma Y = Na + c\Sigma X^2$$
$$\text{II} \qquad \Sigma XY = b\Sigma X^2 + d\Sigma X^4$$
$$\text{III} \qquad \Sigma X^2 Y = a\Sigma X^2 + c\Sigma X^4$$
$$\text{IV} \qquad \Sigma X^3 Y = b\Sigma X^4 + d\Sigma X^6$$

Solving equations I and III simultaneously will yield values for $a$ and $c$, while solving equations II and IV simultaneously will yield values for $b$ and $d$. Computing the needed values of $X$ and $Y$ requires only one more column of figures than is used for the second-degree curve. This is a column necessary to obtain $\Sigma X^3 Y$. When values for the constants have been obtained, substitution in the estimating equation will provide trend values for the period desired.

A fourth-degree curve involves the following equations, assuming the origin is taken at the middle of the period.

$$\text{I} \qquad \Sigma Y = Na + c\Sigma X^2 + e\Sigma X^4$$
$$\text{II} \qquad \Sigma XY = b\Sigma X^2 + d\Sigma X^4$$
$$\text{III} \qquad \Sigma X^2 Y = a\Sigma X^2 + c\Sigma X^4 + c\Sigma X^6$$
$$\text{IV} \qquad \Sigma X^3 Y = b\Sigma X^4 + d\Sigma X^6$$
$$\text{V} \qquad \Sigma X^4 Y = a\Sigma X^4 + c\Sigma X^6 + c\Sigma X^8$$

Solving equations II and IV simultaneously gives values for $b$ and $d$, while the simultaneous solution of equations I, III, and V gives values for $a$, $c$, and $e$.

## Asymptotic curves

Sales performance which appears to be approaching a high point or ceiling at which it is "leveling out," or which is declining at a decreasing rate, can usually be best described and projected by one of the asymptotic curves. While the second-degree curve would also "fit" a series which is increasing or decreasing by decreasing increments, it would not flatten out at the top (or bottom) as such a series would tend to do. Consequently, to describe the trend of a series which is increasing by smaller and smaller increments requires a curve that will level out in its latter stages. Curves whose formulas give them this property are called "asymptotic" because they approach, but never quite reach, a limit, or asymptote.

The properties of an asymptotic curve are illustrated in Figures 23–8 and 23–9. It can be observed here that a series will tend to "level out" when the proportional change in its increments of growth or decline is less than 1. Curves of this type which are most commonly used in projections of sales data are the modified exponential and the Gompertz curves.

**FIGURE 23–8.** Illustration of two series of data that are approaching a limit, or asymptote

| Units of time | $Y$ | Incremental change | Proportional change in increment | $Y'$ | Incremental change | Proportional change in increment |
|---|---|---|---|---|---|---|
| 0 | 100 | | | 100 | | |
| 1 | 120 | 20 | | 80 | −20 | |
| 2 | 130 | 10 | 50% | 70 | −10 | 50% |
| 3 | 135 | 5 | " | 65 | − 5 | " |
| 4 | 137.5 | 2.5 | " | 62.5 | − 2.5 | " |
| 5 | 138.75 | 1.25 | " | 61.25 | − 1.25 | " |
| 6 | 139.375 | .625 | " | 60.625 | − .625 | " |
| 7 | 139.6875 | .3125 | " | 60.3125 | − .3125 | " |
| 8 | 139.15625 | .15625 | " | 60.15625 | − .15625 | " |

*The modified exponential.* The modified exponential formula describes a curve whose absolute change is decreasing by a constant proportion. The common exponential or compound interest curve is described by the formula $Yc = ab^x$, in which $a$ is the first-year trend value, $b$ is the rate of change in $a$ for each time interval, and $x$ is the time interval from the first year of the series. If $b$ is a positive number greater than 1, the curve will have a positive slope which increases at a uniform rate. If $b$ is a positive number less than 1, the reverse will be true, and the amount of change will approach 0 as a limit.

If the equation is modified by adding another constant, $K$, making it $Yc = K + ab^x$, then this constant will be the limit which the curve approaches rather than 0. With the equation so modified, $a$ is now the difference between the first-year trend value and the value of $K$, $b$ is the rate at which $a$ is adjusted for each time interval, and $x$ is the time interval from the first year of the series.

Since the modified formula has three constants, three equations are required to fit it to a series. These equations are usually expressed as follows:

$$\text{I} \qquad b^n = \frac{\Sigma_3 Y - \Sigma_2 Y}{\Sigma_2 Y - \Sigma_1 Y}$$

$$\text{II} \qquad a = (\Sigma_2 Y - \Sigma_1 Y)\frac{b - 1}{(b^n - 1)^2}$$

$$\text{III} \qquad K = \frac{1}{n}\left[\Sigma_1 Y - \left(\frac{b^n - 1}{b - 1}\right)a\right]$$

Arranging data to satisfy these equations requires that the given series first be divided into three equal sections as is done in Figure 23–10. The $Y$ values in each section are summed giving, in this illustration, the following partial totals:

$$\Sigma_1 Y = 694$$
$$\Sigma_2 Y = 812$$
$$\Sigma_3 Y = 856$$

**FIGURE 23–9. Two series approaching limits, or asymptotes (rate of change in increments, 50%)**

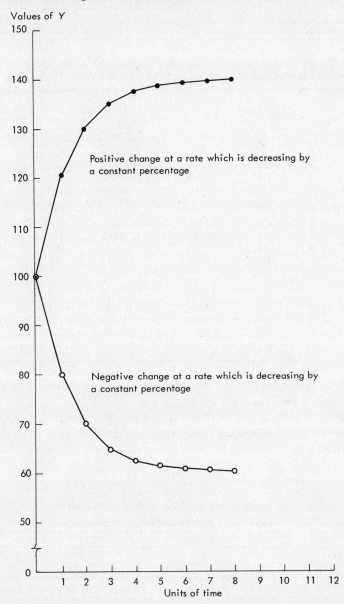

The curve is fitted by setting the corresponding partial totals of the computed $Y$ values equal to the partial totals of the original data. The preceding equations give values for the constants which accomplish this. It is always advisable to verify the accuracy of these computations by comparing the value of $b^n$ obtained in the solution of equation I (shown in the next paragraph) with the computed value of $b^n$ in the table. The partial totals of the $Yc$ values should also equal the corresponding partial totals of the original data. These values are marked by asterisks in Figure 23–10.

FIGURE 23–10.    Computation of modified exponential trend values fitted to a pharmaceutical manufacturer's sales of antibiotics, 1961–1972 (millions of dollars)

| (1) | (2) | (3) Sales of antibiotics | (4) | (5) | (6) | (7) |
|---|---|---|---|---|---|---|
| Year | X | Y | $b^x$ | $ab^x$ $b^x(-65.57968)$ | $K + ab^x$ 220.54014 + $ab^x$ | Yc |
| 1961 | 0 | 156 | 1.00000 | −65.57968 | 154.96046 | 155.0 |
| 1962 | 1 | 188 | * .78144 | −51.24593 | 169.29421 | 169.3 |
| 1963 | 2 | 174 | .61063 | −40.04492 | 180.49522 | 180.5 |
| 1964 | 3 | 176 | .47717 | −31.29266 | 189.24748 | 189.2 |
| $\Sigma_1 Y$ | | 694* | | | 693.99737* | |
| 1965 | 4 | 196 | .37288 | −24.45335 | 196.08679 | 196.1 |
| 1966 | 5 | 198 | .29138 | −19.10861 | 201.43153 | 201.4 |
| 1967 | 6 | 206 | .22769 | −14.93184 | 205.60830 | 206.6 |
| 1968 | 7 | 212 | .17793 | −11.66859 | 208.87155 | 209.9 |
| $\Sigma_2 Y$ | | 812* | | | 811.99817* | |
| 1969 | 8 | 214 | .13904 | −9.11820 | 211.42194 | 211.4 |
| 1970 | 9 | 216 | .10865 | −7.12523 | 213.41491 | 213.4 |
| 1971 | 10 | 222 | .08490 | −5.56771 | 214.97243 | 215.0 |
| 1972 | 11 | 204 | .06634 | −4.35055 | 216.18959 | 216.2 |
| $\Sigma_3 Y$ | | 856* | | | 855.99887* | |

Substituting the three partial totals $\Sigma_1 Y$, $\Sigma_2 Y$, $\Sigma_3 Y$ in equation I gives the value of $b$ shown below. The symbol $n$ refers to the number of observations in each section of data. Logarithms[1] are used to extract the fourth root of $b^4$.

$$b^4 = \frac{856 - 812}{812 - 694} = \frac{44}{118} = .37288$$
$$4 \log b = \log .37288 = 9.57157 - 10$$
$$\log b = 9.89289 - 10$$
$$b = .78144$$

[1] To take the root of a logarithm may require some manipulation of the number itself. Dividing 9.57157–10 by 4 would result in a fractional characteristic, which would be extremely awkward to convert to an antilogarithm. Either of two procedures may be employed to avert this difficulty: (1) increase the characteristic by a sufficient amount to give an even-numbered quotient when divided by the coefficient of log $b$, e.g., 39.57157–40. Now, 39.57157–40 divided by 4 gives a quotient of 9.89289–10, or (2) eliminate the characteristic of the logarithm by subtracting the logarithm from another logarithm whose mantissa is 0, such as 10.00000–10. Thus, 10,00000–10 less 9.57157–10 gives −.42843, which is the same logarithm without its characteristic. Dividing −.42843 by 4 gives −.107107. To return the characteristic to the logarithm add 10.00000–10, which gives 9.89289–10.

Equation II may be solved by substituting the value of $b$. Thus,

$$a = (812 - 694)\frac{.78143 - 1}{(.37288 - 1)^2} = \left(\frac{-.21857}{.39328}\right)$$
$$a = -118(.55576) = -65.57968$$

The value of $K$ may now be found by substituting the values for $a$ and $b$ in equation III.

$$K = \frac{1}{4}\left[694 - \left(\frac{.37288 - 1}{.78143 - 1}\right)(-65.57968)\right]$$
$$= \frac{1}{4}\left[694 - \left(\frac{-.62712}{-.21857}\right)(-65.57968)\right]$$
$$K = \frac{1}{4}[694 - (2.86919)(-65.57968)] = \frac{1}{4}(694 + 188.16058)$$
$$K = \frac{882.16058}{4} = 220.54014$$

Substituting the values of $a$, $b$, and $K$ in the modified exponential equation, $Yc = K - ab^x$, gives the estimating equation: $Yc = 220.54014 - 65.57968(.78143)^x$. The trend values for 1961 through 1972 are shown in column 7 of Figure 23–10. Projection of this trend to 1977 is computed here. The fitted modified exponential trend line and its projection are shown in Figure 23–11.

| Year | K | | a | $b^x$ | | Yc |
|------|---|---|---|-------|---|-----|
| 1973 | 220.54014 | — | 65.57968 | $(.78143)^{12}$ | = | 217.1 |
| 1974 | " | | " | $(.78143)^{13}$ | = | 217.8 |
| 1975 | " | | " | $(.78143)^{14}$ | = | 218.5 |
| 1976 | " | | " | $(.78143)^{15}$ | = | 218.9 |
| 1977 | " | | " | $(.78143)^{16}$ | = | 219.3 |

*The Gompertz curve.* This curve describes a series in which the absolute values are increasing at a decreasing rate, but not at a rate that is uniform or constant. The Gompertz curve, therefore, represents a variation of the modified exponential. This is accomplished by converting the natural values of a series to logarithms. While the increments of change in the logarithms decline by a constant percentage, the increments in the natural numbers of these logarithms vary in both absolute and relative amounts. It is this characteristic of the Gompertz curve which makes it a somewhat more practical instrument than the modified exponential, since the latter describes a curve whose absolute rate of increase is decreasing at a constant percentage.

The formula for the Gompertz curve may be written $Yc = Ka^{b^x}$. Ex-

**FIGURE 23–11. Modified exponential trend line fitted to a pharmaceutical manu-facturer's sales of antibiotics (projected to 1979)**

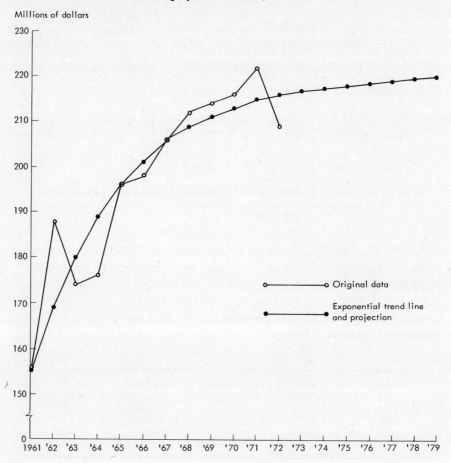

Millions of dollars

pressed logarithmically the formula becomes $\log Yc = \log K + (\log a^{b\,x,}$ in which $\log K$ is the logarithm of the maximum value or limit toward which the curve is expanding (or contracting), $\log a$ (which will have a value between 0 and 1) is the logarithm of the amount by which the trend value falls short of this limit, and $b$ is the rate at which $a$ is adjusted for each time interval. The constant $x$ is the time interval from the first year of the series.

The procedure employed in fitting the Gompertz curve to a series involves the conversion of values in the series to logarithms, division of the series into three equal parts, and taking the sum of the logarithms of each part. These partial totals are then substituted in the following equations to derive values for the three constants:

I $\qquad b^n = \dfrac{\Sigma_3 \log Y - \Sigma_2 \log Y}{\Sigma_2 \log Y - \Sigma_1 \log Y}$

II $\qquad \log a = (\Sigma_2 \log Y - \Sigma_1 \log Y) \dfrac{b - 1}{(b^n - 1)^2}$

III $\qquad \log K = \dfrac{1}{n} \left[ \Sigma_1 \log Y - \left( \dfrac{b^n - 1}{b - 1} \right) \log a \right]$

The procedure for solving the equations is the same as that followed in fitting the modified exponential. Substituting the partial totals of log $Y$ in equation I will give the value of $b$. The value of log $a$ is then found by substituting the value of $b$ and the appropriate partial totals in equation II. Equation III is solved by similar substitutions. The solution of the three equations is shown below:

1. Solving for $b$.

$$b^6 = \frac{14.326789 - 13.436763}{13.436763 - 11.878214} = \frac{.890026}{1.558549} = .571061$$

$\log b^6 = 9.756692 - 10$

$\log b = 9.959449 - 10$

$b = .910850$

2. Solving for log $a$.

$$\log a = 1.558549 \frac{.910850 - 1}{(.571061 - 1)^2} = 1.558549 \frac{-.089150}{(-.428939)^2}$$

$$\log a = 1.558549 \frac{-.089150}{.183989} = 1.558549 \,(-.484540)$$

$$\log a = -.755179$$

3. Solving for log $K$

$$\log K = \tfrac{1}{6} \left[ 11.878214 - \left( \frac{-.428939}{-.089150} \right)(-.755179) \right]$$

$\log K = \tfrac{1}{6}[11.878214 - (4.811430)(-.755179)]$

$\log K = \tfrac{1}{6}[11.878214 - (-3.633491)] = \tfrac{1}{6}(11.878214 + 3.633491)$

$\log K = \tfrac{1}{6}(15.511705) = 2.585284$

The computations required in fitting the Gompertz curve to sales data and projecting it are shown in Figure 23–12. The fitted trend line and its extension are shown in Figure 23–13.

### Weighted moving average

Since a moving average implies no "law of growth," as do the asymptotic curves, and requires no prior decision regarding the linearity of a

**FIGURE 23–12.   Computation of Gompertz curve fitted to a manufacturer's sales of portable power tools (millions of dollars)**

| Year | X | Sales of power tools Y | Log Y | $b^x$ (b = .910850) | (Log a)$b^x$ (Log a = −.755179) | Log K + (log a)$b^x$ (Log K = 2.585284) | Yc |
|------|---|------|----------|----------|----------|----------|-------|
| 1954 | 0 | 72 | 1.857332 | 1.000000 | −.755179 | 1.830105 | 67.6 |
| 1955 | 1 | 97 | 1.986772 | .910850 | −.687855 | 1.897429 | 79.0 |
| 1956 | 2 | 100 | 2.000000 | .829648 | −.626533 | 1.958751 | 90.0 |
| 1957 | 3 | 105 | 2.021189 | .755685 | −.570677 | 2.014607 | 103.4 |
| 1958 | 4 | 101 | 2.004321 | .688316 | −.519802 | 2.065482 | 116.3 |
| 1959 | 5 | 102 | 2.008600 | .626953 | −.473462 | 2.111822 | 129.4 |
|  |  |  | 11.878214 |  |  | 11.878196 |  |
| 1960 | 6 | 122 | 2.086360 | .571060 | −.431252 | 2.154032 | 142.6 |
| 1961 | 7 | 160 | 2.204120 | .520150 | −.392806 | 2.192478 | 155.8 |
| 1962 | 8 | 188 | 2.274158 | .473779 | −.357788 | 2.227496 | 168.8 |
| 1963 | 9 | 174 | 2.240549 | .431542 | −.325891 | 2.259393 | 181.7 |
| 1964 | 10 | 201 | 2.303196 | .393070 | −.296838 | 2.288446 | 194.3 |
| 1965 | 11 | 213 | 2.328380 | .358028 | −.270375 | 2.314909 | 206.5 |
|  |  |  | 13.436763 |  |  | 13.436754 |  |
| 1966 | 12 | 224 | 2.350248 | .326110 | −.246271 | 2.339013 | 218.3 |
| 1967 | 13 | 248 | 2.394452 | .297037 | −.224316 | 2.360968 | 229.6 |
| 1968 | 14 | 230 | 2.361728 | .270556 | −.204318 | 2.380966 | 240.4 |
| 1969 | 15 | 251 | 2.399674 | .246436 | −.186103 | 2.399181 | 250.7 |
| 1970 | 16 | 246 | 2.390935 | .224466 | −.169512 | 2.415772 | 260.5 |
| 1971 | 17 | 269 | 2.429752 | .204455 | −.154400 | 2.430884 | 269.7 |
|  |  |  | 14.326789 |  |  | 14.326784 |  |
| 1972 | 18 |  |  | .186228 | −.140635 | 2.44649 | 278.4 |
| 1973 | 19 |  |  | .169626 | −.128098 | 2.457186 | 286.5 |
| 1974 | 20 |  |  | .154504 | −.116678 | 2.468606 | 294.2 |
| 1975 | 21 |  |  | .140730 | −.106276 | 2.479008 | 301.3 |
| 1976 | 22 |  |  | .128184 | −.096802 | 2.488482 | 307.9 |
| 1977 | 23 |  |  | .116756 | −.088172 | 2.497112 | 314.2 |
| 1978 | 24 |  |  | .106347 | −.080311 | 2.504973 | 319.8 |
| 1979 | 25 |  |  | .096866 | −.073151 | 2.512133 | 325.2 |
| 1980 | 26 |  |  | .088230 | −.066629 | 2.518655 | 330.1 |

series, as do the polynomial curves, it sometimes offers a useful alternative in trend projection. By introducing weights in the computation of the moving average, it is possible to get a smoother trend line and consequently a more reliable freehand projection.

The usual type of weighting is binomial, in which the weights are given by the coefficients of $a$ and $b$ in the expansion of the binomial. If $N$ is the number of years averaged, the number of factors in the binomial expansion would be $N - 1$, or $(a + b)^{N-1}$. To compute a weighted three-year moving average, for example, one expands $(a + b)^2$, which is $a^2 + 2ab + b^2$, giving weights of 1, 2, and 1. The middle year

**FIGURE 23–13.** Gompertz curve fitted to a manufacturer's sales of portable power tools (with projection to 1980)

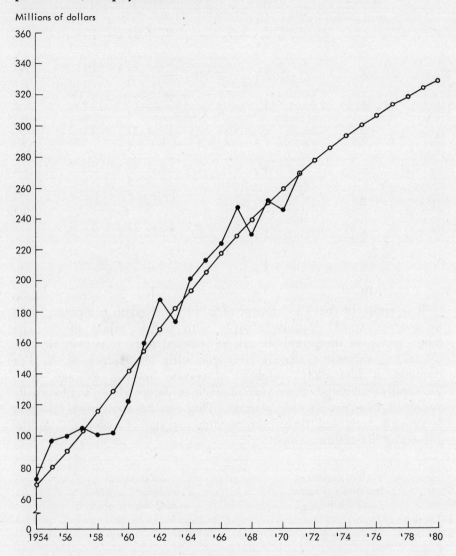

receives twice the weight of the other two. A binomially weighted four-year moving average would have weights of 1, 3, 3, and 1, and coefficients of $a$ and $b$ in the expansion of the binomial $(a + b)^3$.

The procedure for computing a binomially weighted moving average is shown below, where $N = 3$. The number in the denominator in column 3 is of course the sum of the weights.

| (1) | (2) | (3) |
|-----|-----|-----|
| Year | Sales | Moving average |
| 1 | $Y_1$ | |
| 2 | $Y_2$ | $\dfrac{Y_1 + 2Y_2 + Y_3}{4}$ |
| 3 | $Y_3$ | $\dfrac{Y_2 + 2Y_3 + Y_4}{4}$ |
| 4 | $Y_4$ | $\dfrac{Y_3 + 2Y_4 + Y_5}{4}$ |
| 5 | $Y_5$ | $\dfrac{Y_4 + 2Y_5 + Y_6}{4}$ |
| 6 | $Y_6$ | $\dfrac{Y_5 + 2Y_6 + Y_7}{4}$ |
| 7 | $Y_7$ | $\dfrac{Y_6 + 2Y_7 + Y_8}{4}$ |
| 8 | $Y_8$ | $\dfrac{Y_7 + 2Y_8 + Y_9}{4}$ |
| 9 | $Y_9$ | $\dfrac{Y_8 + 2Y_9 + Y_{10}}{4}$ |
| 10 | $Y_{10}$ | |

It is apparent that the amount of labor involved in computing such an average would increase sharply with higher values of $N$. The laboriousness of the procedure can be lessened to some degree, though, by taking successive moving averages with low values of $N$. For example, a binomially weighted three-year moving average of a binomially weighted three-year moving average gives a binomially weighted five-year moving average. This can be shown by taking a binomially weighted three-year moving average of column 3 in the preceding illustration. Thus,

| (1) | (2) | (3) |
|-----|-----|-----|
| Original values | Three-year binomially weighted moving average | Three-year binomially weighted moving average of col. 2 |

$$Y_1$$
$$Y_2 \quad \frac{Y_1 + 2Y_2 + Y_3}{4}$$
$$Y_3 \quad \frac{Y_2 + 2Y_3 + Y_4}{4} \quad \left(\frac{Y_1 + 2Y_2 + Y_3}{4}\right) + 2\left(\frac{Y_2 + 2Y_3 + Y_4}{4}\right) + \left(\frac{Y_3 + 2Y_4 + Y_5}{4}\right)$$
$$Y_4 \quad \frac{Y_3 + 2Y_4 + Y_5}{4}$$
$$Y_5 \quad \frac{Y_4 + 2Y_5 + Y_6}{4}$$

Consolidating the values in column 3, above, the expression becomes

$$\frac{1Y_1 + 4Y_2 + 6Y_3 + 4Y_4 + 1Y_5}{16}$$

a binomially weighted five-year moving average. By the same logic, it can be demonstrated that a six-year binomially weighted moving average can be obtained by taking a four-year binomially weighted moving average of a three-year binomially weighted moving average. This process can be continued until an average with the desired weights is found.

As a practical matter, the desired weighting may be determined by plotting the results of each weighted moving average until a trend line of satisfactory smoothness has been obtained. Plotting will also bring to light any significant errors in computation. This smoothing results from the fact that the binomial weighting system allows the influence exerted on the average by a single value to gradually increase and then gradually diminish. In an unweighted six-year moving average, for example, the influence of any given value on the result is always $\frac{1}{6}$. In a binomially weighted six-year moving average, on the other hand, the influence of a given value on the result increases from $\frac{1}{32}$ to approximately $\frac{1}{3}$ and then diminishes to $\frac{1}{32}$. While there are other types of weight patterns than the binomial, the even progression of binomial weights usually produces a smooth trend line, particularly with higher values of $N$. It is the one most commonly used.

The computations required in smoothing a moving average by using binomial weights are shown in Figure 23–14. Three of the resulting series of trend values are fitted to the original data in Figure 23–15. It can be observed here that the greater the span of years included in the average, i.e., the higher the value of $N$, the smoother the curve. This smoothness is achieved, of course, at the expense of losing values at each end of the trend line. It is sometimes possible to "save" some of these end values and still get satisfactory results by doing the initial smoothing with a small-term binomial moving average and the final smoothing freehand. Since the projection of a moving average trend line will be freehand anyway, it is not illogical to do the final smoothing in this manner—particularly by a person who is familiar with the data and the characteristics of the market. This should not be attempted by one who is a novice or does not have the feel of the market.

### Adjusting projections

It has already been observed that statistical projections must always be examined and usually modified to reflect the interplay of forces which are not represented in the original data. Adjusting statistical projections of company sales or individual product sales before they are combined into a company forecast, involves much the same considerations as in estimating market share. The impact of one's own strategy on the allocation of buyer patronage and the reaction of competitors to it are basic questions.

**FIGURE 23–14.  Computation of binomially weighted eleven-year moving average of dial light sales by a manufacturer of electronic components**

|  |  |  |  | 1949–72 | | |
|---|---|---|---|---|---|---|
| (1) | (2) | (3) | (4) | (5) | (6) | (7) |
|  | Dial light | | | Binomially weighted moving averages | | |
| Year | sales | Three-year | Five-year* | Seven-year† | Nine-year‡ | Eleven-year§ |
| 1949 | 10,515 | | | | | |
| 1950 | 9,578 | 10,393 | | | | |
| 1951 | 11,903 | 12,280 | 12,166 | | | |
| 1952 | 15,737 | 13,710 | 13,307 | 13,053 | | |
| 1953 | 11,465 | 13,530 | 13,433 | 13,305 | 13,283 | |
| 1954 | 15,450 | 12,961 | 13,049 | 13,468 | 13,855 | 14,167 |
| 1955 | 9,480 | 12,746 | 14,340 | 15,180 | 15,675 | 15,997 |
| 1956 | 16,576 | 18,906 | 18,991 | 18,874 | 18,785 | 18,741 |
| 1957 | 32,991 | 25,406 | 23,174 | 22,214 | 21,720 | 21,484 |
| 1958 | 19,067 | 22,978 | 23,516 | 23,581 | 23,713 | 23,577 |
| 1959 | 20,788 | 22,702 | 24,117 | 24,853 | 25,165 | 25,325 |
| 1960 | 30,167 | 28,469 | 27,661 | 27,375 | 27,258 | 27,178 |
| 1961 | 32,755 | 31,003 | 30,061 | 29,430 | 29,032 | 28,772 |
| 1962 | 28,333 | 29,771 | 29,936 | 29,892 | 29,766 | 29,615 |
| 1963 | 29,663 | 29,201 | 29,637 | 29,850 | 29,897 | 29,793 |
| 1964 | 29,145 | 30,376 | 30,191 | 29,998 | 29,613 | 29,531 |
| 1965 | 33,552 | 30,813 | 29,974 | 28,606 | 29,001 | 29,083 |
| 1966 | 27,003 | 27,893 | 28,489 | 28,796 | 28,718 | 28,846 |
| 1967 | 24,017 | 27,356 | 28,234 | 28,675 | 28,948 | 29,068 |
| 1968 | 34,386 | 30,332 | 29,745 | 29,646 | 29,660 | |
| 1969 | 28,541 | 30,961 | 30,861 | 30,673 | | |
| 1970 | 32,375 | 31,192 | 31,226 | | | |
| 1971 | 31,476 | 31,558 | | | | |
| 1972 | 30,905 | | | | | |

\* Three-year binomially weighted moving average of column 3.
† Three-year binomially weighted moving average of column 4.
‡ Three-year binomially weighted moving average of column 5.
§ Three-year binomially weighted moving average of column 6.

## GOAL DEFINITION

In any industry or market segment in which a company has sufficient experience to be developed into a sales prediction, it is advisable to have predictions based both on sales experience and market share expectations. This provides the management team with two forecasts of sales volume, each formulated differently, which can be compared and appraised in light of all relevant economic and environmental forces expected to be present over the next three- to five-year period. Unless both forecasts produce the same results, which is unlikely, management will have a high forecast and low forecast which should substantially narrow the range within which it must rely upon judgment and intuition in reaching a decision concerning a long-range sales goal.

Strategic goals may also be expressed in other terms than sales volume or market share. Management may wish to establish a company image which will serve to distinguish what the company is and does from its

**FIGURE 23-15.** Binomially weighted moving averages fitted to annual sales of dial lights by a manufacturer of electronic components (with projection to 1978)

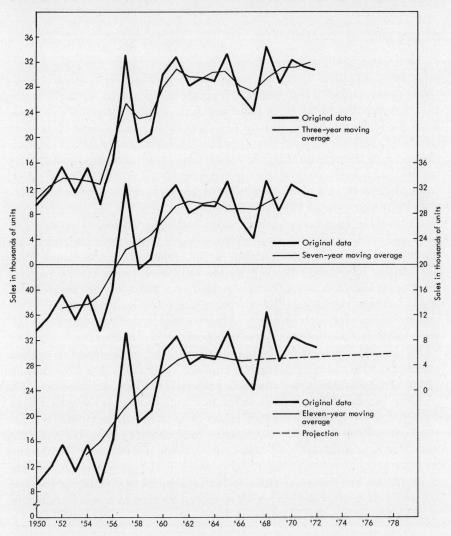

major competitors. It may also wish to achieve a given level of growth through acquisition, or to realize a given level of return on investment. Unless circumstances were such that one of these objectives could only be realized at the expense of one or more of the others, all could be incorporated into the statement of long-run ends to be achieved. As a concise definition of what a company will seek to accomplish, a strategic goal may subsum several other goals. It is indispensable, though, that the subgoals be ones which are subject to measurement. Otherwise, the degree of success achieved by a strategy cannot be determined. Such a situation lessens considerably the value of experience in facilitating subsequent planning efforts.

## SUMMARY

Long-term goals are the focal points for strategic planning. They provide a definition of results to be achieved which is consistent with the corporate mission and specific enough to be measured. Their formulation is a process of balancing the desirable against the feasible. Goals must obviously represent accomplishment which management regards as desirable. But they must also represent achievement which is within the grasp of the organization. Although long-term marketing goals might include such ends as establishing a particular image, reaching a given level of growth, or a given return on investment, market share and sales volume usually are of prime importance.

Developing long-range market share and sales volume objectives can be done with statistical projections of past experience modified by anticipated environmental conditions not reflected in the projections. Ordinarily, long-range market share and sales objectives would be developed for each industry or segment composing a company's total market. These would then be compared, adjusted, and combined into a single forecast for each industry or market segment. Summing these objectives gives the strategic marketing goal for the enterprise.

Market share projections begin with forecasts of industry sales against which a market share percentage is applied. This results in a sales volume figure. Probably the most common projective techniques used for this purpose are the least squares trend line and the second-degree curve. Except for one-product companies, or companies whose products have similar marketing characteristics, sales projections tend to be done for each major product and combined into a company forecast. Due to the more erratic behavior of individual product or company sales, it may be desirable to use more sensitive techniques, such as the higher degree polynomials, asymptotic curves, or weighted moving averages in developing the company sales projections.

# 24

# PERFORMANCE STANDARDS AND INSTRUMENTS OF CONTROL

PERFORMANCE STANDARDS are the month-by-month objectives which must be met if annual, and eventually, strategic goals are to be realized. They are derived from strategic goals frequently by using the first year of a three-to-five-year projection modified in light of anticipated economic and other environmental factors. These short-term, annual objectives are almost always incorporated into an operating budget as well as translated into operating standards which can be linked to a network of enforcement activities.

## SHORT-TERM GOALS

Since it may be possible to anticipate internal conditions one year ahead with some degree of confidence, it is sometimes useful to derive a short-term sales prediction from expense and profit expectations. Comparison of a sales forecast derived from a trend projection with one that will be necessary to meet expected expenses and desired profits can be a sobering revelation. A trend-based sales goal may appear completely unrealistic as the result of such a comparison. If it does, management is at least alerted to be ready for rough weather. There may be no choice but to trim expenses, lower profit expectations, and strain to get every ounce of productivity out of the sales force. On the other hand, the comparison may reveal what could be done with a greater commitment of resources to advertising and selling.

In some instances it also may be possible to make use of correlation techniques in developing a short-term sales prediction which can be compared with a trend-based prediction. If factors which are known to have a definite bearing on company sales can be identified and predicted with an acceptable degree of accuracy in the short run, a correlation-based sales prediction can be very revealing. If the presence of variable costs render an expense-based prediction impractical, the possibility of using correlation should be seriously investigated.

## Expense-based goals

The projection of expenses as a means of establishing short-run sales objectives rests on the assumption of a unique functional relationship between costs and sales. Once total costs have been estimated, this functional relationship makes it possible to determine the volume of sales necessary to defray them and realize the desired margin of profit. It is perhaps needless to mention that this approach is limited to firms in which the variable cost component of total operating cost is negligible. While such a limitation renders expense projection impractical for many manufacturers, the major expense categories of some are relatively fixed, at least in the short run.

*Expense estimate.* An analysis of expenses, category by category, should reveal that use of this method is limited to firms in which the variable cost component of total operating cost is negligible. While such a limitation renders expense projection impractical for many firms, it does not prevent its use by all. Small enterprises, particularly, often discover that most of their expense categories are relatively fixed, at least in the short run.

The mechanics of the expense-oriented sales projection generally involve four steps: (1) an estimate of expenses for the future period in question, (2) anticipated gross margin for this period, (3) selection of a profit goal, and (4) application of the expense ratio (estimated gross margin minus profit goal) to estimated total expenses.

## Estimate of future expenses

A careful analysis of expenses, category by category, should reveal which are likely to increase, to decrease, or to remain unchanged during the coming budget period. This analysis must, of course, include a recognition of the effect on future costs of such nonrecurrent factors as a special promotional campaign, the redecoration of offices and display rooms, and the purchase of new equipment, as well as the savings expected from the use of new equipment and the institution of more efficient procedures. In some instances, fitting a trend line to past expenses and extending it into the future is a logical way of estimating the probable change in a given expense category. The changes which seem reasonably certain may then be noted, and a new listing of expenses applicable to the coming period compiled.

*Gross margin and net profit objectives.* An estimate of gross margin for a given future period may rest simply on what the firm has realized

during the immediate past. Barring any unusual circumstances, a manufacturer may reasonably assume that his gross margin cannot be much
better or much worse than it was last year. Accordingly, this figure is
often taken as a legitimate planning objective for next year. While this
method of selection has the advantage of simplicity, a better method is to
list the annual realized gross margins over a long enough period to
reveal any persistent characteristic in its behavior. Next year's figure
may then be determined in light of what has been accomplished in the
past as well as any new conditions which are expected to enter the
situation.

However the anticipated gross margin is established, it is usually enlightening to compare it with the margins earned by other manufacturers
of similar size in the same kind of business. Such information is available
in the Census of Business for census years, and from Dun and Bradstreet
and a number of trade associations for current years. If anticipated
gross margin is below the average of the industry, or of similar businesses
of similar size, an effort should be made to unearth an explanation. Poor
profit performance may be, and often is, symptomatic of internal weaknesses which management should identify and correct with all possible
speed.

Much the same comment may be made regarding the selection of a
net profit objective. While current net profits almost inevitably influence
the choice of next year's goal, many managers prefer to set their net
profit objectives "somewhere near" the average ratio earned by firms of
the same general class as their own. Nevertheless, an examination of the
past trend in net profit performance is usually helpful in determining a
figure which is desirable as well as realistic.

*Application of the expense ratio.* If anticipated gross margin for the
coming year is 20.5 percent and the profit goal is 8.3 percent, then 12.2
percent of net sales will be available for selling, administrative, and other
expenses. If total expenses are estimated at $24.6 million, the volume of
sales required to meet them and profit expectations can be determined
as follows:

Sales objective next year . . . . . . . . $X$
Then $.122X$ must equal $24.6 million
Therefore, $X$ must equal $201.6 million.

## Correlation-determined goals

With the advent and increasing use of automatic data-processing
equipment, correlation techniques, perhaps, offer the greatest promise of
improved short-run sales forecasting. Every variable known to have a
material influence on the success of marketing efforts can be included in
the computation and given a weight commensurate with its influence.

Although the use of multiple correlation entails nothing beyond simple algebra, the statistical procedure is rather involved. To fully explain its application in the formulation of a company sales forecast would require an involvement in statistical detail that is beyond the scope of the present chapter. However, a discussion of multiple correlation and a demonstration of its application is treated in a number of standard texts on business statistics. Those who have an interest in exploring the operation of this technique may pursue it there.

## THE MARKETING BUDGET

It is sometimes assumed that control is impossible without budgets. This is an exaggeration, for in small firms managed by one or two persons it is often possible to obtain a high degree of control without formal budgeting. In a small, closely knit organization, plans can be relatively short-term and easily adjusted when conditions change. Consequently, performance can often be readily gauged by standards which exist in the minds of the managers.

A business does not have to attain great size, however, to render informal methods inadequate for effective control. Even if formal budgets are not employed, it is seldom possible to achieve control over sales and expenses without utilizing budgetary principles.

### The sales budget

Since the sales budget represents a component of the overall company budget, the various parts of it correspond to the different categories in the company budget. Depending on the manner in which the marketing effort is organized, it may be advisable to separate expenses into those which pertain to inside selling and those which pertain to outside selling. If the sales manager, for example, spends a third of his time "in the field" selling, a third of his salary and traveling expense should be charged to outside selling rather than to administration. It may also be desirable to separate expenses into variable, semivariable, and fixed categories.

Variable expenses, of course, change from month to month with sales volume, and often involve touchy problems of estimation. Fixed expenses —which can usually be forecast with more confidence, e.g., automobile licenses, insurance, and depreciation—are often "written off" in equal monthly installments throughout the year. Some items, of course, contain elements of both fixed and variable expense and also may present perplexing estimating problems. Anticipated expenses for inside and outside selling activities can be summed to give totals for the company.

Two important measures of performance, in addition to monthly sales objectives and expense limits, are: (1) contribution to overhead, and (2) selling expense as a percent of total sales. The sales department's projected contribution to overhead and profits may be estimated by subtracting planned sales expense from gross profit. In some instances, management may prefer to begin with a specific contribution objective and endeavor to reduce departmental costs to levels which will permit this contribution with the forecasted volume of sales.

Total sales expense expressed as a percent of planned sales is an equally significant performance standard. It not only indicates the amount of sales expense relative to income, but provides an index of comparison both with past company performance and with industry averages. Since selling expense is generally one of the largest categories of cost, it is a key performance indicator.

The general format of the sales budget is shown in Figure 24–1. It will be observed that columns pertaining to each month and to year-to-date are labeled *planned* and *actual*. This enables the sales manager to

**FIGURE 24–1. Six-months sales budget form**

| SALES BUDGET - JANUARY 1 TO JUNE | | | | | | |
|---|---|---|---|---|---|---|
| | JANUARY | | JUNE | | YEAR TO DATE | |
| | PLANNED | ACTUAL | PLANNED | ACTUAL | PLANNED | ACTUAL |
| NET SALES | | | | | | |
| Gross sales less returns | | | | | | |
| and allowances | | | | | | |
| COST OF GOODS SOLD | | | | | | |
| Beginning inventory plus net | | | | | | |
| purchases (including infreight | | | | | | |
| and transportation) less closing | | | | | | |
| inventory. | | | | | | |
| GROSS PROFIT | | | | | | |
| | | | | | | |
| OUTSIDE SELLING EXPENSE | | | | | | |
| Sales administration | | | | | | |
| Salaries commissions, bonuses | | | | | | |
| Payroll taxes | | | | | | |
| Automobile (insurance, licenses, taxes, depreciation) | | | | | | |
| Contributions to group insurance and pension plan | | | | | | |
| Promotional literature (including catalogues) | | | | | | |
| Miscellaneous expense | | | | | | |
| TOTAL | | | | | | |
| INSIDE SELLING EXPENSE | | | | | | |
| Sales administration | | | | | | |
| Wages, salaries, commissions, bonuses | | | | | | |
| Payroll taxes | | | | | | |
| Depreciation on display fixtures | | | | | | |
| Insurance on display fixtures | | | | | | |
| Contribution to group insurance, etc. | | | | | | |
| Sales promotion (including catalogues) | | | | | | |
| Miscellaneous expense | | | | | | |
| TOTAL | | | | | | |
| | | | | | | |
| TOTAL SELLING EXPENSE | | | | | | |
| | | | | | | |
| CONTRIBUTION TO OVERHEAD | | | | | | |
| | | | | | | |
| TOTAL SELLING EXPENSE/TOTAL SALES | | | | | | |
| | | | | | | |
| | | | | | | |

compare monthly and cumulative performance with budgeted amounts. Even a cursory inspection of these columns gives management an illuminating picture. If selling expenses exceed budgeted figures for a given month, management can quickly determine whether it is outside or inside selling which is responsible and consult the detail within the particular category to determine specifically where the trouble lies. As a practical matter, the ratio of selling expense to total sales provides the chief performance standard. If sales exceed the forecast by a substantial figure, the absolute amount of variable expenses would, of course, be increased. But the ratio of selling expense to sales that is considered as satisfactory would be unaffected.

Other comparisons are also possible. For example, management may want to know how the performance of a given month compares with that of the same month a year ago, or how the year-to-date performance compares with that of the same period last year. Even in relatively small firms, periodic reports of planned versus actual performance that follow the same format as the budget are necessary to keep managers properly informed. Any commentary, however general, pertaining to the known or probable causes of conspicuous failures to meet budget standards can be of great assistance in preparing the following year's sales budget. A rather common format for sales budget reports is shown in Figure 24–2. If it is desired to know the ratio of each expense item to sales, it is a simple matter to divide the appropriate value by the net sales figure. These examples merely illustrate a form that is basic and fairly common.

In the last analysis, circumstances peculiar to the individual firm determine the form which the sales budget (or other budgets) should take. Form is not particularly important anyway so long as the statement of expected sales and desired selling expenses are clearly, definitely, and completely recorded. Good format simply provides greater assurance that these characteristics of a good plan will be incorporated into the budget and that any significant errors, conflicts, or omissions will be readily detected.

*Budgetary units.* Although management, particularly the treasurer or controller, thinks in terms of dollars, the marketing manager must think

**FIGURE 24–2.  Sales budget report form**

| MONTHLY SALES BUDGET REPORT | | | | For the month of _____ | |
|---|---|---|---|---|---|
| | LAST YEAR | BUDGET | ACTUAL | OVER (-) UNDER (-) | COMMENT |
| NET SALES | | | | | |
| COST OF GOODS SOLD | | | | | |
| GROSS PROFIT | | | | | |
| OUTSIDE SELLING EXPENSE   SALES ADMINISTRATION | | | | | |

in terms of products. A sales budget expressed in dollars, consequently, has less meaning to a sales manager and his staff than one expressed in physical units of merchandise. Obviously, a sales budget expressed in physical units must be limited to the sales plan. But this is important, because it is necessary to coordinate the sales plan with production plans, and due to changing margins and special prices, physical units are the most practical denominator. Moreover, separating physical volume from dollar volume makes it possible to draw a sharper distinction between satisfactory and unsatisfactory performance. Sales performance in physical units escapes the distortion which affects dollar figures when prices are changed or margins adjusted.

The exception to this general rule would be the firm with so many lines and such varied assortments within lines as to make complete budgeting on a physical unit basis too tedious and time-consuming for practical use. However, as is often the case, a major portion of the dollar sales volume is contributed by a relatively small number of lines. In this instance, major lines may be grouped separately and their performance standards expressed in physical units while standards for the remaining lines may be expressed in dollars only.

### The expense budget

Performance standards for costs are especially important because they place sales performance in better perspective. If these standards reflect consideration of past experience and all pertinent anticipated conditions affecting sales, costs, and profit, they represent limits on operating expense beyond which individuals responsible for marketing efforts should not go without approval from higher authority.

In principle there can be as many separate budgets as there are administrative units within the marketing department or expense classifications in the department's chart of accounts. Expense budgets may be developed for warehousing, sales, and service operations; or for individual categories of expense such as wages and salaries, supplies, promotion, training, delivery, and insurance. In some instances a department manager may prefer to budget only major items of expense and lump together other items in summary form. As a general rule, though, it is advisable to treat any item of expense separately where it is clear that to do so is the only sure way of affording the manager directly responsible for it a means of keeping actual outlays in line with planned outlays. If, for example, the warehouse superintendent is expected to make but one out-of-town business trip next year at a cost of $120, it would have little meaning for purposes of control to budget $10 each month for his traveling expenses.

Total fixed, total variable, and total semivariable expenses are logical control points, particularly if they are expressed as percents of net sales. When actual expenses in any of these classifications are expressed as a percent of actual net sales, and do not correspond to the planned ratio, actual expenses in the various subclassifications can be examined to identify both the type of expense and the functional unit contributing to the divergence of actual and planned figures. To facilitate such comparisons it is important that expense reports which highlight differences between actual and planned expenses be submitted to management on a regular schedule. The form that such a report might take is illustrated in Figure 24–3.

Sometimes it is desirable to prepare expense budgets for sales volumes of 10 to 15 percent above and below that which is forecast. This is commonly known as a flexible budget, since it provides alternative cost expectations in the event that sales vary from the forecast. An analysis of past differences in costs associated with different levels of sales should indicate how much variable and semivariable expenses could be expected to change with a given change in sales. Simple correlation is a very useful tool in identifying the relationship between variation in a given item of expense and variation in sales.

### Practicing budgetary control

If budgetary controls over sales and expenses are to achieve the results for which they are designed, management must recognize that they are only tools and not substitutes for management itself. Like all tools, controls should be chosen for the task at hand and the results obtained with them are determined by the skill of the user. It is axiomatic that skill in the use of budgets comes with experience both in their preparation and administration. Just as wide organizational participation is advisable for assuring that plans are understood and workable, so budget making, since it is planning, is more likely to be successful if line managers are permitted to have a part in it.

Of particular importance in successful budgetary control is avoiding the inflexibility that robs a manager of his freedom to manage. At the other extreme, of course, is the budget which lumps all of a department's allowable expenditures together and permits the department manager to decide how this lump sum is to be distributed. Although the latter approach has much to commend it, it should be possible to allow the department manager a reasonable degree of latitude in changing the budget pertaining to his activities, and in shifting funds, without giving him complete discretional authority to partition a lump sum. Too much flexibility can be as much of an obstacle to effective control as too little.

It is also essential that budget making be accompanied by constant reexamination and reevaluation of the various bases by which plans are translated into numerical terms. Budgets have a way of perpetuating precedents. If a certain amount was spent for supplies during an earlier period, this tends to become prima facie evidence for its reasonableness

**FIGURE 24-3.  Summary expense budget report form**

COMPANY BUDGET REPORT

For the month of _____

| INCOME AND EXPENSE CATEGORIES | THIS MONTH | | | YEAR TO DATE | | | THIS MONTH LAST YEAR | | | COMMENT |
|---|---|---|---|---|---|---|---|---|---|---|
| | BUDGET | ACTUAL | OVER (+) UNDER (–) | BUDGET | ACTUAL | OVER (+) UNDER (–) | BUDGET | ACTUAL | OVER (+) UNDER (–) | |
| GROSS SALES | | | | | | | | | | |
| Less returns and allowances | | | | | | | | | | |
| NET SALES | | | | | | | | | | |
| Less cost of goods sold | | | | | | | | | | |
| GROSS PROFIT | | | | | | | | | | |
| EXPENSES | | | | | | | | | | |
| FIXED EXPENSES | | | | | | | | | | |
| Rent (or equivalent) | | | | | | | | | | |
| Taxes – property | | | | | | | | | | |
| Depreciation | | | | | | | | | | |
| Maintenance and repair | | | | | | | | | | |
| Interest | | | | | | | | | | |
| TOTAL | | | | | | | | | | |

in a current period. Precedents once established tend to become fixed floors and may soon transform a budget into a cloak for inefficiency. The somewhat deceptive definiteness of reducing plans to quantitative values, and objectives to specific standards, should never be permitted to over-shadow the basic purpose of planning and control. Nor should the im-mediacy of budget standards be permitted to blind one to the primacy of company objectives under any circumstance in which the two might appear to be in conflict.

## THE PROCESS OF CONTROL

It has already been observed that marketing control consists of per-formance standards, which are often incorporated into formal budgets, and a feedback system utilizing sales and expense reports. While there is really no satisfactory substitute for direct observation and personal con-tact, particularly when it is necessary to appraise matters of an intangible nature, the backbone of any information feedback system is usually the formal report. However, no control will result simply because reports have been submitted. It is necessary to have not only regular comparison of performance with standards but also delegation of sufficient authority to take needed action when significant deviations of results from standards are revealed.

### The reporting system

Although the subject of reports and their preparation is beyond the scope of a general discussion, there are aspects of formal reporting of such elementary significance that they should not be ignored even in a general discussion. Efficient communication requires that the information transmitted be concise, adequate, and timely. It is equally important, though, that the right type of report be used at the most appropriate time and under conditions for which it is best suited. Writing a mem-orandum is needless if a phone call will suffice. Similarly, it is reckless to convey information by telephone if the receiver needs it for later reference or to verify other information. Reports should be suited to the occasion, they should be timely, and they should focus attention on the matters requiring action.

*Suitability.* It is axiomatic that the language and format of a report match the work habits and mental aptitudes of the manager who receives it. Because the major functions of the manager are planning and decision making, he must receive the information on which he bases his planning and decision in a form which will permit him to assimilate and compre-hend it in the shortest possible time. While some managers prefer lengthy statistical compilations and can distill their significance without undue effort, others regard any message longer than a page as too detailed.

As a general rule, the detail contained in a report should reflect the level of management to which the report is directed. The lower the echelon, the more detail that is warranted because responsibilities are more detailed. The higher the echelon for which a report is being prepared, the more condensed it should be. Reports should nevertheless contain a comparison of performance with standards at the particular control points with which the executive is concerned. An explanation of any discrepancies between performance and standard is also usually desirable. Ideally, control reports should contain suggestions for corrective action, if in the opinion of the subordinate preparing the report action is called for. This would not be advisable, of course, if making such suggestions was outside the responsibility of the person preparing the report, or if their inclusion would unduly delay its transmittal.

*Timeliness.* The timing of reports should reflect as nearly as possible the frequency with which the information they contain is used. Accordingly, the lapse of time between the initiation of a report and its delivery should correspond to the capacity of the reporting unit to complete the report without a frantic, last-minute rush. To assure smooth operation of the reporting system, it is sometimes helpful to classify reports as special, or recurring. For special reports, the lead time is often set by reporting units, whereas in the case of recurring reports it is set by standard procedure.

It is also apparent that the promptness with which discrepancies between standards and performance is reported has much to do with the effectiveness of control. A report received in May showing that salesmen's traveling expenses were substantially higher than budget for the month of March has lost some of its usefulness. Two months later it may be difficult for the salesman concerned to reconstruct the situation that accounted for this discrepancy. As a general rule, the longer the time lag between an undesirable event and the reporting of it, the more difficulty the responsible manager is likely to have in diagnosing the trouble and deciding on proper corrective action.

The effort to report information promptly, though, very often results in some inaccuracy. Data must almost invariably be drawn from the accounting system well in advance of any formal accounting statement. Shipments, sales, certain items of cost, and other operating data must often be reported orally. But since trends rather than absolute measurements are of prime significance, the accuracy required in formal end-of-period summarizations is unnecessary. Revised data can be supplied later as they are needed for accounting statements or statistical analyses.

*Focus.* Control reports should be so constructed that they direct attention to matters requiring action. Ordinarily, their purpose should be as definite and as limited as possible so that the reader is immediately alerted to their significance. The use of charts often serves admirably to focus attention on important relationships and contributes to the simplicity and clarity of the content. Although simplicity and clarity are relative matters, the trend of any quantitative factors should be obvious to interested parties. The significance of information is the important consideration, rather than the information itself.

## Comparing standards and performance

If performance standards have been properly defined, and if the reporting system enables executives to know how operations are being conducted, designing procedures that will bring discrepancies between standards and performance to the attention of executives should present few problems. Usually these procedures spell out the timetable for initiation and submission of control reports, assign responsibility for compiling the text of the report, identify the admnistrative units which are to contribute to the report, and specify the sequence in which these units will participate.

If both standards of performance and information regarding performance are adequate, appraising the two and deciding on appropriate action can be fairly simple. When objective performance is measured against objective standards—as in the case of sales, costs, inventories, physical handling, and clerical work—discrepancies can ordinarily be quickly identified and their implications readily appreciated. In other instances drawing accurate comparisons and reaching a decision regarding what corrective action, if any, is required may be quite difficult. This is often the case in exercising control over the activity of particular individuals, such as salesmen.

It is difficult to determine, for example, whether a salesman is devoting as much attention to development work as management desires. Unless his calls are monitored in some way, or management is in close personal touch with a number of customers, it is difficult to know exactly what a salesman does during a call. When the accomplishment of a task moves away from an order assembly line, a machine, or a routine of some sort, the exercise of control becomes more difficult and often more important.

## Corrective action

Setting performance standards, getting an adequate feedback of information, and comparing performance with standards are really preliminary steps. They can be done expertly and no control will result unless someone acts to correct operations which have deviated from standards, or acts to prevent such deviations from occurring. But such action can be taken only by persons who hold the requisite authority. For this reason, control can be fully effective only when persons directly responsible for operations not only have adequate standards and sufficient information on which to base action, but the authority to act.

Well-conceived organizational structure and clearly defined duties aid in identifying the individual or individuals responsible for a particular activity. How much responsibility these individuals 'have for meeting specific objectives or standards, however, is a function of the degree of decentralization which is practiced. The only person who can really control an activity is the one who has direct authority over it. There is little a salesman can do, for example, to control telephone expense in his territory if the sales manager has instructed him to telephone his orders rather than submit them at the end of the day. Similarly, a warehouse superintendent is limited in his ability to control order-picking and assembly costs, if it is company policy to fill all orders no matter how small. Limitations on the amount of authority that can reasonably be granted an individual have to be recognized in planning controls.

Given the requisite authority, corrective action may take several forms. It may consist of making adjustments for unforeseen circumstances. Since performance standards are directly related to operating objectives and these are, in turn, based on forecasts, anyone in charge of controlling an activity must be ready to make adjustments or take steps which will make actual conditions conform to those anticipated in the forecasts. For example, most forecasts would presuppose the existence of accurate records and normal operating routine. But undue delay in posting sales and merchandise receipts will produce inaccurate stock records, and a backlog of orders could seriously interrupt warehouse routine. When such conditions threaten, merely requesting clerical personnel to work overtime may be sufficient corrective action. Or, it may be necessary to revise operating procedures, assign additional personnel to the operations concerned, install additional equipment, or some combination of these alternatives.

Of all the conditions assumed in forecasts there are many that a manager has no power to change or adjust. The availability of personnel, competitors' tactics, suppliers' shipping schedules, business conditions, and product innovations are all conditions which have to be taken as given. Consequently, when they change unexpectedly there is seldom any alternative but to revise plans in terms of these changes. Schedules may have to be revised, work reassigned, performance standards altered, or policies reshaped to more accurately reflect the environment in which they have to be enforced. For example, unexpected delays in shipments from suppliers may reduce inventory levels so near minimum points that customers have to be placed on a priority basis or rush orders sent to alternative sources of supply. If the condition should persist, avoiding inconvenience to customers might require a change in inventory standards, a reassessment of present suppliers, or a different policy concerning delivery.

Corrective action frequently involves changes in the supervision of personnel. All too often failure to meet standards can be traced to faulty direction. Moreover, the problem may lie deeper than a simple misunderstanding of instructions. Personnel whose performance is at fault may lack the necessary training and experience for their assignment. In such instances corrective action may consist of instituting a training program as quickly as possible. Or, if the required know-how must be acquired chiefly through experience, corrective action may consist of transferring the errant individual or individuals to other positions and replacing them with better-qualified employees. Although a reassignment of tasks may correct the difficulty, it may also have repercussions on morale for those who are transferred to positions of lower status or compensation. Those who need additional experience to regain their former positions or assignments should, of course, be so placed that they will have the opportunity to acquire this experience. This is a fair resolution of such a matter, since the one who is really at fault is the manager who originally assigned persons to tasks for which their experience did not qualify them.

Sometimes performance does not conform to standards because persons assigned to tasks simply lack the desire to discharge them satisfactorily. In such situations corrective action must be directed toward stimulating and motivating employees. Ideally, of course, remedial action is preferable to corrective action. For control should imply more than a ferreting out of trouble and temporarily correcting it. Alert managers seek to anticipate unsatisfactory performance and prevent it by antecedent action. In this way subordinates are more apt to look upon control as an aid rather than a policing action.

## SUMMARY

The exercise of guiding and restraining action in conformity with established plans is identified as control. It represents the final phase in the continuing cycle of planning, organizing, coordinating, and directing which defines the responsibilities of a manager. However, the line between control and other phases of management is not always clear because many of the objectives which serve as guides for planning become operating standards for control. This is particularly true of short-term objectives.

Since a short-term sales goal is often derived from the first year of a long-term projection, it is almost always advisable to compare it to other short-term goals which have been developed by different techniques. Two forecasting methods widely used for this purpose are the expense projection method and statistical correlation. The reconciliation of two or more sales forecasts derived by different methods should produce an annual sales goal in which management can place some confidence.

The annual sales goal is generally translated into a series of performance standards which indicate what sales performance must be month-by-month if the annual goal is to be realized. Similarly, the annual sales goal itself represents a performance standard which must be met if that particular year is to make its planned contribution to the long-term (strategic) goal. Since sales performance is much more meaningful in light of the costs incurred to achieve it, marketing control includes standards for expenses as well as sales.

Any action to bring about compliance of operations with plans presupposes the requisite authority to prescribe such action. This has to be defined by organization, and those with the authority to prescribe corrective action must direct subordinates to take it.

Although this process is closely interwoven with other phases of management and can almost never be identified apart from them, it has been treated separately here for purposes of simplicity. The exercise of control therefore involves four essential steps or phases: (1) the definition of standards of satisfactory performance, (2) the development of an information feedback or reporting system, (3) the establishment of procedures for reporting and comparing performance with the standards, and (4) the delegation of authority to take appropriate remedial action.

# Cases

# ACME CHEMICAL COMPANY

The Acme Chemical Company, located in New England, manufactured a great variety of products and distributed them through its 12 sales divisions, which were roughly broken down along product lines. The company initiated a study of its sales operations to determine distribution costs. A breakdown of the 12 sales divisions, showing the percentage of customers purchasing less than $100 during a typical year, was as shown in Exhibit 1. This study focused attention on Division 16, the coverings division, and supplied information useful to the division sales manager, Mr. Bowden, about the relative profitability of customers, products, and orders. Since this study indicated the existence of relatively large numbers of low-profit-margin customers and product lines in the division, Mr. Bowden had to determine what action, if any, he should take.

As shown in Exhibit 1, 62 percent of the division's customers accounted for only 2 percent of its gross sales, which totaled $608,000 for the year. A more detailed breakdown of gross sales by customer size was as shown in Exhibit 2. This breakdown revealed that sales during the year to 12 customers (1.5 percent of the total number) were $306,000, which represented 50.3 percent of total volume for that year.

In order to get a better idea of the profitability of customers with low annual sales, Mr. Bowden requested the market research department to undertake an analysis of the minimum average order cost. Determination of the cost of an order was complicated by the different types of costs involved—variable, semivariable, and fixed. Furthermore, no clear-cut line of demarcation existed between these types. If fixed costs, such as rent, taxes, and depreciation, were to be considered, they had to be arbitrarily allocated. Furthermore, a serious question usually existed as to the propriety of the allocation, because even if the coverings division eliminated a substantial portion of its orders the fixed costs would continue at the same rate.

Therefore, the market research director, Eliot Snow, decided that a reasonable approach was to disregard fixed costs and to consider only the direct or out-of-pocket costs. These expenses increased or decreased in total as the number of orders increased or decreased. If the gross mar-

**EXHIBIT 1**

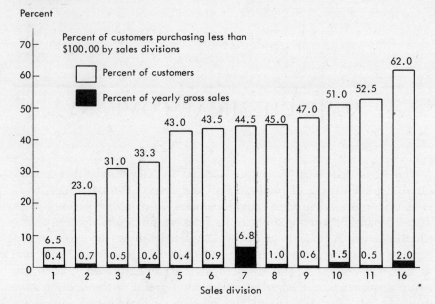

Percent

Percent of customers purchasing less than
$100.00 by sales divisions

☐ Percent of customers

■ Percent of yearly gross sales

**EXHIBIT 2.  Division 16, coverings division (gross sales by customer size)**

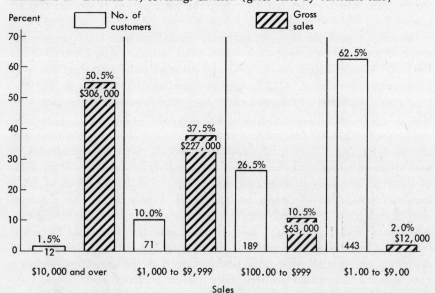

Percent     ☐ No. of customers     ▨ Gross sales

50.5%  $306,000

37.5%  $227,000

26.5%

10.0%

10.5%  $63,000

62.5%

1.5%  12

71

189

443

2.0%  $12,000

$10,000 and over     $1,000 to $9,999     $100.00 to $999     $1.00 to $9.00

Sales

**EXHIBIT 3.** Average items per invoice (orders typed by order and billing department for month of May)

| Division | Total invoices May | Total items | Average items per invoice |
|---|---|---|---|
| 16—coverings........................ | 237 | 338 | 1.42 |
| 1................................... | 222 | 258 | 1.16 |
| 2................................... | 221 | 271 | 1.22 |
| 3................................... | 8 | 12 | 1.50 |
| 4................................... | 123 | 151 | 1.22 |
| 5................................... | 245 | 319 | 1.30 |
| 6................................... | 106 | 212 | 2.00 |
| 7................................... | 19 | 54 | 2.84 |
| 8................................... | 214 | 234 | 1.10 |
| 9................................... | 82 | 133 | 1.62 |
| 10.................................. | 187 | 314 | 1.67 |
| 11.................................. | 13 | 17 | 1.30 |
| 12.................................. | 57 | 71 | 1.24 |
| 13.................................. | 74 | 110 | 1.48 |
| 14.................................. | 6 | 7 | 1.16 |
| 15.................................. | 135 | 237 | 1.75 |
| Total, all orders............... | 1,949 | 2,738 | 1.40 |

gin exceeded the cost of processing and filling an order, the excess revenue contributed to the reduction of overhead; therefore, the order was worth handling.

The cost of processing an invoice depended largely on the number of items on the invoice. Mr. Snow made an approximation of an average number of items per invoice, as shown in Exhibit 3. The average items

**EXHIBIT 4.** Cost of processing an order, excluding shipping department handling (total company invoices typed January 1 through July 31: 22,666)

I. *Payroll:*

| | | |
|---|---|---|
| Allocable to order and billing................... | $ 9,940 | |
| Allocable to accounting....................... | 6,986 | |
| Allocable to IBM operations................... | 357 | |
| All benefits at $0.068/$100 payroll.............. | 12 | |
| Total.................................... | $17,295 | |
| Payroll per order—$17,295/22,666.............. | | $0.7630 |

II. *Cost of paper:*

| | Per invoice | |
|---|---|---|
| Invoice set.................................... | $0.0450 | |
| IBM cards.................................... | 0.0055 | |
| Bills of lading............................... | 0.0155 | |
| File folder.................................... | 0.0188 | |
| Three-cent stamp............................. | 0.0300 | |
| Invoice envelope.............................. | 0.0362 | |
| Total....................................... | | 0.1510 |

III. *IBM rental*....................................... 0.0385

Total Cost.............................. $0.9525

**EXHIBIT 5.  Cost of handling for shipment**

| Container | Handling cost |
|---|---|
| Single shipments................................. | $0.221 |
| 55-gallon drums.................................. | 0.292 |
| 30-gallon drums.................................. | 0.237 |
| 15-gallon drums.................................. | 0.174 |
| 5-gallon pail..................................... | 0.077 |
| 1 gallon or smaller............................... | 0.104 |
| No. 10 can case................................... | 0.043 |
| Barrels—4 and 6 hoop sugar...................... | 0.050 |
| Bags—burlap and paper.......................... | 0.072 |
| Cartons, fiberboard............................... | 0.208 |
| 5-gallon keg..................................... | 0.122 |
| Rolls insole...................................... | 0.226 |
| Empty drums.................................... | 0.050 |
| Empty pails...................................... | 0.014 |
| Miscellaneous shipments.......................... | 0.472 |

per invoice for the coverings division was 1.42, as compared with an overall company average of 1.40.

The average cost of handling an order, based upon total invoices received by the company from January 1 to July 31, excluding the necessary handling in the shipping department, was 95 cents, as shown in Exhibit 4. The cost of handling for shipment varied widely, as indicated in Exhibit 5, depending on both the size of the order and the type of container. However, in order to arrive at an average total cost figure, Mr. Snow computed the average handling cost for a single shipment as 22 cents, which added to the 95-cent processing cost gave $1.17 as the total cost of handling an average order.

Exhibits 6 and 7 revealed that 12 percent of all orders in this division were for less than $5, with an average gross margin of $2, and as many as 30 percent were orders for less than $10 worth of merchandise.

In comparison with other company divisions, this percentage of small orders was high. As shown in Exhibit 6, the preponderance of these small orders was in the product classes AB, AC, and AD. Large orders, on the

**EXHIBIT 6.  Coverings division (sizes of orders by product—April, May, and June—total orders: 472)**

| Product | Number of orders | $0–$5 | $5.01–$10 | $10.01–$20 | $20.01–$50 | $50.01–$100 | $100–$500 | Over $500 |
|---|---|---|---|---|---|---|---|---|
| AB. | 144 | 19.5% | 31.2% | 13.9% | 21.5% | 12.5% | 1.4% | ... |
| AC. | 61 | 18.5 | 18.5 | 11.8 | 24.1 | 11.1 | 12.3 | 3.7% |
| AD. | 54 | 24.1 | 22.3 | 5.5 | 40.8 | 5.5 | 1.8 | ... |
| AE. | 24 | ... | 12.5 | 33.3 | 29.2 | 25.0 | ... | ... |
| AF. | 16 | ... | 31.3 | 12.5 | 37.5 | 6.2 | 12.5 | ... |
| AG. | 5 | ... | ... | 40.00 | ... | ... | 60.0 | ... |
| AH. | 2 | ... | ... | ... | 100.0 | ... | ... | ... |
| AI. | 40 | ... | ... | ... | 15.0 | 7.5 | 57.5 | 20.0 |
| AJ. | 126 | 1.6 | 7.9 | 5.6 | 7.1 | 20.6 | 53.2 | 4.0 |
| All products. | 472 | 12.2 | 18.0 | 9.0 | 21.0 | 14.0 | 23.0 | 3.0 |

**EXHIBIT 7. Coverings division—April, May, June (gross margin by size of orders)**

| Product | $0–$5 | | | $5.01–$10 | | | $10.01–$20 | | | $20.01–$50 | | |
|---|---|---|---|---|---|---|---|---|---|---|---|---|
| | Total G.M. | No. of orders | Aver. G.M. | Total G.M. | No. of orders | Aver. G.M. | Total G.M. | No. of orders | Aver. G.M. | Total G.M. | No. of orders | Aver. G.M. |
| AB | $ 52.65 | 28 | $1.88 | $189.20 | 45 | $4.20 | $138.74 | 20 | $6.93 | $ 481.65 | 31 | $15.50 |
| AC | 35.98 | 17 | 2.11 | 28.29 | 10 | 2.83 | 4.20 | 1 | 4.20 | 201.03 | 13 | 15.50 |
| AD | 24.80 | 13 | 1.91 | 37.55 | 12 | 3.12 | 18.12 | 3 | 6.04 | 278.44 | 22 | 12.70 |
| AE | .... | .... | .... | 13.99 | 3 | 4.66 | 62.78 | 8 | 7.85 | 119.74 | 7 | 17.11 |
| AF | .... | .... | .... | 9.84 | 5 | 1.96 | 8.13 | 2 | 4.06 | 69.56 | 6 | 11.59 |
| AG | .... | .... | .... | .... | .... | .... | 16.75 | 2 | 8.37 | .... | .... | .... |
| AH | .... | .... | .... | .... | .... | .... | .... | .... | .... | 17.88 | 2 | 8.94 |
| AI | .... | .... | .... | .... | .... | .... | .... | .... | .... | 82.10 | 6 | 13.68 |
| AJ | 6.44 | 2 | 3.22 | 40.54 | 10 | 4.05 | 40.00 | 7 | 5.71 | 146.34 | 9 | 16.26 |
| All Products | $119.87 | 60 | 2.00 | $319.41 | 85 | 3.76 | $288.72 | 43 | 6.72 | $1,396.74 | 96 | 14.34 |

| Product | $50.01–$100 | | | $100.01–$500 | | | Over $500 | | |
|---|---|---|---|---|---|---|---|---|---|
| | Total G.M. | No. of orders | Aver. G.M. | Total G.M. | No. of orders | Aver. G.M. | Total G.M. | No. of orders | Aver. G.M. |
| AB | $ 626.41 | 18 | $34.60 | $ 118.00 | 2 | $ 59.00 | .... | .... | .... |
| AC | 176.23 | 6 | 29.37 | 851.45 | 12 | 71.00 | $ 705.04 | 2 | $ 352.52 |
| AD | 97.63 | 3 | 32.54 | 49.92 | 1 | 49.92 | .... | .... | .... |
| AE | 186.36 | 6 | 31.06 | .... | .... | .... | .... | .... | .... |
| AF | 15.00 | 1 | 15.00 | 97.40 | 2 | 48.70 | .... | .... | .... |
| AG | .... | .... | .... | 168.70 | 3 | 56.23 | .... | .... | .... |
| AH | .... | .... | .... | .... | .... | .... | .... | .... | .... |
| AI | 68.80 | 3 | 22.93 | 3,263.47 | 23 | 142.00 | 2,430.59 | 8 | 303.82 |
| AJ | 1,009.51 | 26 | 38.80 | 7,392.56 | 67 | 110.50 | 2,025.46 | 5 | 405.09 |
| All Products | $ 2,179.94 | 63 | 34.50 | $11,941.50 | 110 | 108.50 | $5,161.09 | 15 | 344.00 |

*Totals:*

| | |
|---|---|
| AJ | $10,660.85 |
| AI | 5,844.96 |
| All Other | 4,901.00 |

(AJ and AI contributed $16,505 in gross margin. All remaining products contributed only $4,901 gross margin)

other hand, were received for the classes of products AJ and AI; these two were by far the most profitable in the division. Exhibit 7 shows that from April through June, AJ contributed $10,660 in gross margin, AI contributed $5,845, and all remaining products yielded only $4,901.

The AI product class was probably the most profitable in the division, since selling expense and research costs were properly allocable to AJ, and research costs were allocable to AB, AC, and AD. The AI product class had had no research expense during recent years, and it had practically no selling expense, since customers for that product ordered direct from the Acme Company and were seldom solicited by company salesmen. Thus, the class of products on which the coverings division directed the least effort—the AI group—yielded a greater profit than any other group of products in the division.

---

# AGEX OIL COMPANY (A)

The marketing executives of the Agex Oil Company were reviewing its sales organization with particular reference to the position of industrial salesmen.

The company's operating territories included most of the Atlantic seaboard area and several adjacent states. Its marketing organization consisted of three regions, as shown in Exhibit 1. The three regions were made up of 11 sales divisions, which, in turn, were broken down into 55 districts. Typical division and district organizations at that time were as shown in Exhibit 2. Not all districts had assistant district managers.

Industrial salesmen and dealer salesmen were paid on a straight salary basis. The industrial salesmen received training in industrial lubricants and specialty products, as well as general background on company organization, refining processes, and the marketing of company products to industry. Their jobs were considered highly specialized, and their training was broader and more intensive than that of other sales groups.

While the general salesmen reported to and were under direct authority of the district manager, the industrial salesmen reported to the industrial products manager on the divisional level and, consequently, were not directly under the authority of the district managers in their respective territories.

This organization of the sales function resulted in many disadvantages. The fact that district managers were not directly in control of all the

**EXHIBIT 1**

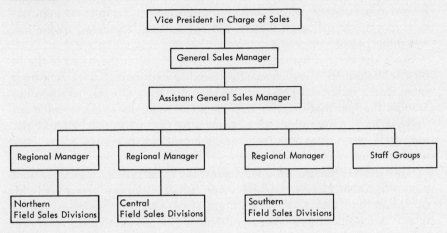

**EXHIBIT 2**

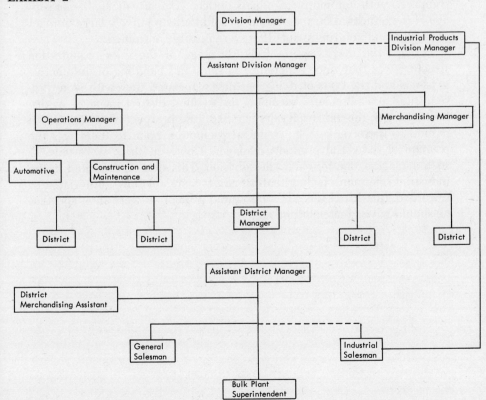

activities in their districts resulted in some communication difficulty and lack of coordination, with overlapping effort. For example, an industrial salesman might call on a firm to sell automotive lubricants, motor fuel, and other petroleum products.

Since the district managers did not have direct authority over the industrial salesmen, they were often neither acquainted with nor interested in the industrial phase of the business. This attitude was accentuated by the fact that over 90 percent of the company's sales volume was derived from automotive sales. Many division managers believed that industrial sales were relatively unimportant when compared to other product lines.

This was misleading, in a way, since the total sales of the Agex Company was about $1 billion, which made its industrial business a fairly big operation in its own right. The margin of net profit on the industrial volume was considerably higher than that on the automotive business. The industrial market was also geographically concentrated, although there were some industrial customers in every sales district. The bulk of the industrial volume was sold to large users who were few in number as compared with automotive products outlets. A relatively small percentage of the industrial business could be sold to the relatively large number of small manufacturing plants that were possible customers.

Perhaps the most important disadvantage of the sales organization structure was that since experience in sales and handling of automotive products and the costs of doing business associated therewith were prerequisites to a salesman's becoming an assistant district manager or district manager, the industrial salesman had little prospect of attaining promotion to these ranks. The principal promotion open to them was the position of industrial products manager. However, there were only 11 such managers, one for each sales division. This situation resulted in the industrial salesman's feeling that his efforts were not fully appreciated or rewarded, that his chances for substantial promotion were slim, and that he should have greater incentive.

# AGEX OIL COMPANY (B)

The executives of Agex Oil Company, a large integrated firm, were reviewing the training program for the company's industrial salesmen.

During its early history, the company had no training program for its industrial salesmen, so the men lacked adequate knowledge about specifications on many products in the line. About 30 years ago, a vice president of sales developed and instituted an industrial sales training course. During this three-week course, given at the company refinery, the trainees learned how industrial lubricants were manufactured and blended, and familiarized themselves with detailed product specifications. The trainees also received some sales product training in the refinery by means of a machinery audit, during which each trainee determined the type of lubricant required by a particular machine and attempted to sell the selected product to the plant superintendent. When these trainees returned to their districts, they were better informed about many products than their sales managers. To correct this situation, the company then made the product data and specifications used in the training course available to all sales personnel.

About 10 years later, company executives developed a series of lectures to be presented to industrial salesmen over a period of six months. One executive suggested that the lectures be printed in textbooks and used for class discussion groups to meet in New York City during a three-month period, with industrial sales staff men in the New York office as instructors. Several discussion groups were held, and the text material later formed the basis of a correspondence course for industrial salesmen, which the company adopted. The material covered practically all phases of the petroleum industry, including geology, production, refining, transportation, combustion, lubrication principles, product specifications and testing, prime movers, industrial lubricants, and other subjects.

The company suggested, but did not require, that its industrial salesmen take the correspondence course. The company furnished each division with a complete set of the various textbooks for each salesman enrolled in the course, as well as a list of questions on each book. The division supplied the salesman with only one book at a time, and he was supposed to submit written answers to the questions before being supplied with additional text material. The salesmen were required to submit a total of 85 papers, to be graded and returned. Initially, the New York office staff graded the papers; later, a model list of answers was developed and sent to each division office, and the paper grading was then handled on the divisional level. Although most salesmen turned in one to two papers per month, the company imposed no limit for completion of the course.

The division manager of industrial sales, or a delegated assistant, usually graded the papers. For better instruction, the company naturally desired that the paper grader should write comments on the papers, explaining why a given answer was incorrect. Such attention required considerable time and effort on the part of graders, but most divisions handled this function reasonably well.

This correspondence course underwent several improvements: the papers were later assigned on a more definite schedule, plant visits were included, and the divisional industrial sales manager spoke to the salesmen after they completed a part of the course. The text material was revised to eliminate overlapping, and the subject matter on geology, production, refining, and transportation was eliminated. The revised course was called The Technical Sales Course.

For over a decade, the company used The Technical Sales Course in training its industrial salesmen. Gradually, the executives came to feel that this correspondence type of training needed to be supplemented with two additional courses—a basic industrial sales course and an advanced industrial sales course. Company executives believed that the basic industrial sales course should represent the minimum essential knowledge required for industrial sales work by providing up-to-date information on the technical aspects of the company's products, information on company research and development, and an analysis of its marketing operations. The proposed basic course covered general background on company organization, information on production, transportation, and refinery manufacturing processes concerning fuels, lubricants, and specialties. In addition, it provided some study of industrial marketing operations, sales techniques, laboratory work, and public speaking, as well as inspection trips to nearby plants. The executives believed that this type of training could best be given on a full-time study basis, which would require a two-month course. The basic course was not intended to provide detailed information on specific industries.

Company executives believed that the advanced industrial sales course should be a refresher course designed for industrial salesmen with extensive experience or for men who had taken the basic eight-week course at least two years previously. The course was to be of two weeks' duration on a full-time study basis, and was to provide up-to-date information on the latest petroleum developments in the industrial field. In addition to some information included in the basic course, the advanced course covered certain new areas, such as making a lubrication survey of a new power station, new developments in the machinery field, market analysis of industrial potential, study of laboratory analysis of used oils, sales demonstrations, study of additives, new synethetic lubricants, and study of more specialized products, including cutting oils, hydraulic oils, transmission oils, petroleum solvents, liquefied gases, drawing compounds, quenching and tempering oils, and process oils.

Although company executives were in accord regarding the need for both a basic and an advanced industrial sales training course, there was some difference of opinion about the method through which these courses should be taught. Some executives favored division-level instruction by specially trained instructors from the New York offices to be sent to the company's 11 divisions. These instructors would themselves receive training in educational and teaching methods, as well as in the subject matter they taught. Executives favoring the instruction of salesmen on the division level believed that the basic two-month industrial sales training course should be taught on a full-time basis, but that the two-week advanced course might be taught on either a full-time or part-time basis.

Other company executives believed that both the basic and advanced courses should be taught at some central training center established by the company. Under this plan, both courses would be limited to a maximum of 20 salesmen, who would be selected from the various divisions. It was argued that by locating the central training center close to New York City, the instruction might be supplemented by management personnel from the headquarters office. Under this plan, the trainees participating in both courses would be housed convenient to the training center and would remain there through the duration of the course.

Under both alternative methods of instruction, the division managers would select salesmen to participate in the courses, and their selections would be subject to approval by sales management in New York City.

# AGEX OIL COMPANY (C)

The Agex Oil Company operated large refineries in the New York area and in the Gulf, and conducted marketing operations contiguous to these manufacturing sources. The development of a considerable concentration of steel plants along the middle eastern seaboard made it desirable for the company to reevaluate its marketing operations as they pertained to the steel industry. The company's marketing organization is shown in Exhibits 1 and 2.

The company manufactured almost every kind of petroleum product. The industrial product line included a wide variety of lubricants and other petroleum products, many specifically engineered and blended for specialized end uses. The importance of specialized engineering service to customers had increased greatly in recent years, since there was a growing tendency for industrial customers to evaluate competitive suppliers by the quality of such service rendered.

**EXHIBIT 1**

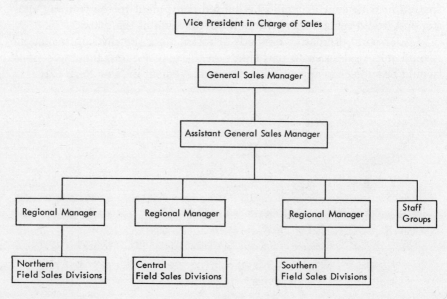

**EXHIBIT 2.   Typical division organization**

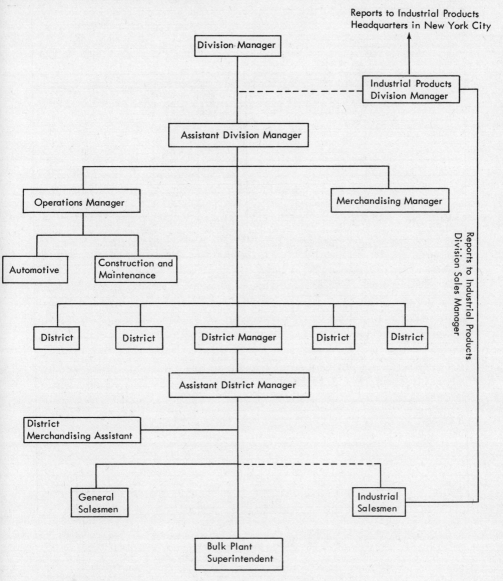

The company sold its industrial products through a sales force of more than 80 industrial salesmen, who worked out of district offices and were paid on a straight salary basis. An increasing percentage of these salesmen were graduate chemists and engineers, and were considered both salesmen and technical experts. A salesman sometimes encountered technical problems that demanded greater experience than he possessed;

**EXHIBIT 3**

| Company Name | | | | | | Indus. Code | | | P   O   R | | |
|---|---|---|---|---|---|---|---|---|---|---|---|
| | | | | | | | | | FO  N   G | | |

| Office | Street | | | | Plant | Street | | | | | |
|---|---|---|---|---|---|---|---|---|---|---|---|
| | City | | Ph. | | | City | | | Ph. | | |

| Contacts | | Title | | | | | |
|---|---|---|---|---|---|---|---|

| Lubricating Oils (Bbls.) | | | | | Grease, wax, pet. & Spec. (Bbls.) | | | | |
|---|---|---|---|---|---|---|---|---|---|
| Competitive Name Comp. | Competitive E.Y.C. | Our E.Y.C. | Dely. Meth. | Brand Names | Competitive Name Comp. | Competitive E.Y.C. | Our E.Y.C. | Dely. Meth. | Brand Names |
| | | | | | | | | | |
| | | | | | | | | | |
| | | | | | | | | | |
| | | | | | | | | | |
| | | | | | | | | | |
| | | | | | | | | | |
| | | | | | | | | | |
| Totals | | | Grand Total | | Totals | | | Grand Total | |
| Contract Expires | | | | | Contract Expires | | | | |

**Fuel Oils (Inc. Diesel)**

| Grade | Dely. Meth. | Total E.Y.C. | Supplier | Cont. Exp. | Use, Spec. Requirements, Etc. |
|---|---|---|---|---|---|
| | | | | | |
| | | | | | |
| | | | | | |

**Naphthas and Solvents**

| Grade | Dely. Meth. | Total E.Y.C. | Supplier | Cont. Exp. | Use, Spec. Requirements, Etc. |
|---|---|---|---|---|---|
| | | | | | |
| | | | | | |
| | | | | | |

**Automotive, Aviation and Marine**

| Grade | Dely. Meth. | Total E.Y.C. | Supplier | Cont. Exp. | Use, Spec. |
|---|---|---|---|---|---|
| | | | | | |
| | | | | | |
| | | | | | |

**L.D.E. Record**

| Equip. Number & Type | Dispensing Pumps | Barrel Pumps | Lube Tanks | Grease Outfits | Underground Tanks |
|---|---|---|---|---|---|
| Process | | | | | |
| Products | | | | | |

Remarks:

| Division | Salesman | Date of S-110 |
|---|---|---|

E.Y.C.—Estimated Yearly Consumption.
L.D.E.—Lubricant Dispensing Equipment.

therefore, he occasionally had to call on the headquarters organization in New York City for assistance in solving them. The engineers assigned to the New York headquarters devoted their attention to customer engineering service and did not actively sell industrial products.

Company salesmen were required to submit a trade report (Exhibit 3) for each customer. These trade reports provided data concerning customer purchases, supplies, units purchased, and, where obtainable, the price per unit.

**EXHIBIT 3** (*Continued*)

| Sales 19 | | | |
|---|---|---|---|
| Code No. | | | |
| Product | | | |
| Delivery Pt. | | | |
| January | | | |
| February | | | |
| March | | | |
| April | | | |
| May | | | |
| June | | | |
| 6 Mo. Total | | | |
| July | | | |
| August | | | |
| September | | | |
| October | | | |
| November | | | |
| December | | | |
| 12 Mo. Total | | | |

| Sales 19 | | | |
|---|---|---|---|
| Code No. | | | |
| Product | | | |
| Delivery Pt. | | | |
| January | | | |
| February | | | |
| March | | | |
| April | | | |
| May | | | |
| June | | | |
| 6 Mo. Total | | | |
| July | | | |
| August | | | |
| September | | | |
| October | | | |
| November | | | |
| December | | | |
| 12 Mo. Total | | | |

| Sales 19 | | | |
|---|---|---|---|
| Code No. | | | |
| Product | | | |
| Delivery Pt. | | | |
| January | | | |
| February | | | |
| March | | | |
| April | | | |
| May | | | |
| June | | | |
| 6 Mo. Total | | | |
| July | | | |
| August | | | |
| September | | | |
| October | | | |
| November | | | |
| December | | | |
| 12 Mo. Total | | | |

Each industrial salesman also submitted a monthly progress report (Exhibit 4) to his division office. This report gave information on business the salesman had gained or lost during the preceding month.

Company executives believed that the shift in the steel mill industry made it desirable for the company to determine its position in this industry with regard to share of the market, end use of products, relative profits on different products, and volume. It was also necessary to deter-

**EXHIBIT 4**

PROGRESS REPORT
(Show all quantities in Bbls.)

Salesman _____    Month _____    19___

| | | | Business Gained | | | | |
|---|---|---|---|---|---|---|---|
| NAME OF ACCOUNT | ADDRESS | OUR PRODUCT | CURRENT RESULTS | E.Y.C. | NEW OR REPLACE-MENT* | COMPETITOR | REMARKS |
| NEW BUSINESS CONTACT | | | | | (*N for New:  R for Replacement) | | |
| | | | | | | | |
| | | | | | | | |
| | | | | | | | |
| | | | | | | | |
| ADDITIONAL BUSINESS--CONTRACT CUSTOMERS | | | | | | | |
| | | | | | | | |
| | | | | | | | |
| | | | | | | | |
| | | | | | | | |
| | | | | | | | |
| SPOT OR OPEN MARKET | * | (*Indicate by X Whether Item Purchased Before) | | | | | |
| | | | | | | | |
| | | | | | | | |
| | | | | | | | |
| | | | | | | | |
| | | | | | | | |

| | | | Business Lost | | | |
|---|---|---|---|---|---|---|
| CONTRACT | ADDRESS | OUR PRODUCT | ACTUAL 12 MOS. SALES | | COMPETITOR | REASON FOR LOSS |
| | | | | | | |
| | | | | | | |
| | | | | | | |
| ITEMS--CONTRACT CUSTOMER | | | | | | |
| | | | | | | |
| | | | | | | |
| SPOT OR OPEN MARKET | | | | | | |
| | | | | | | |
| | | | | | | |

| | | | Products under Test | | | | |
|---|---|---|---|---|---|---|---|
| CUSTOMER | ADDRESS | PRODUCT | QUANTITY DELIVERED | E.Y.C. | COMPETI-TOR | OUR OR COMPETI-TIVE ACCOUNT | RESULTS |
| | | | | | | | |
| | | | | | | | |
| | | | | | | | |
| | | | | | | | |
| | | | | | | | |

mine what, if any, personnel changes were required in order to intelligently solicit business of a new type in certain marketing territories, and to determine whether the company should make certain steel mill lubricants at other refineries situated closer to the market.

While the trade reports and progress reports provided a general guide, they did not furnish all the information required for a complete evaluation of the market in the steel industry. Therefore, a special survey form (Exhibit 5) was prepared. From trade directories and other sources of information, the marketing department in New York prepared a list

**EXHIBIT 4** (*Continued*)

| | | | Contracts | | |
|---|---|---|---|---|---|
| CUSTOMER | ADDRESS | EXPIRATION DATE | RENEWED (Check ✓) | PENDING (Check ✓) | REMARKS |
| | | | | | |
| | | | | | |
| | | | | | |
| | | | | | |
| | | | | | |
| | | | | | |
| | | | | | |
| | | | | | |
| | | | | | |
| | | | | | |
| | | | | | |
| | | | | | |

| | Competitive Prices | | | | | | |
|---|---|---|---|---|---|---|---|
| CUSTOMER | COMPETITIVE PRODUCT BRAND | PRICE | E.Y.C. | DELY METHOD | OUR REPLACEMENT | PRICE | RECOMMENDATION |
| | | | | | | | |
| | | | | | | | |
| | | | | | | | |
| | | | | | | | |

**Competitive Practices**

**Business Conditions and Trends**

**Special Sales Activities**

that set forth the name of each customer, or potential customer, and the name and location of the customer's plants for which full information was desired. The list was prepared in triplicate and sent to appropriate sales division offices. The industrial salesman concerned filled in a survey form for each company listed in his territory; the industrial sales manager in the division office reviewed the survey forms and sent a completed copy of each to the New York office. The survey covered all steel accounts, including mills, fabricators, and processors.

This survey covered not only lubricants but also other petroleum products and specialties purchased by the steel industry, such as aromatic and aliphatic solvents, gasoline, kerosene, diesel fuel, distillate fuel, residual fuel, and liquefied petroleum gas (LPG). The survey indicated the various classifications of products used in each steel mill; showed

## EXHIBIT 5

Customer _____

Plant _____

Location _____

### CLASSIFICATION OF STEEL MILL LUBRICANTS AND FUELS

| Classification | Explanatory Remarks | Supplier* | Brand | Consumption Bbls. per Year | Price | Remarks |
|---|---|---|---|---|---|---|
| Absorbent Oil | Used only in by-product coke plants | 1.<br>2. | | | | |
| Transformer Oil | Transformers and circuit breakers | 1.<br>2. | | | | |
| Light Process Oil | Slushing or rust preventive oil<br>Coal Spray Oil<br>Quenching Oil<br>Uncompounded roll oil<br>Flushing Oil<br>Light noninhibited hydraulic oil<br>Low viscosity air filter oil | 1.<br>2.<br>3.<br>4.<br>5. | | | | |
| High Quality, Low Viscosity Lubricating Oil | Turbine oil<br>Electric motor oil<br>Hydraulic oil<br>Low viscosity oil for circulating systems<br>Air compressor oil | 1.<br>2.<br>3.<br>4. | | | | |
| Engine Oil | General purpose, medium viscosity lubricating oil<br>Air filter oil<br>Hydraulic oil | 1.<br>2.<br>3.<br>4. | | | | |
| High quality, high viscosity straight oil | Circulating systems serving backing roll bearings or gear and bearing systems where lubricant is continuously reused and EP properties are not required | 1.<br>2.<br>3.<br>4. | | | | |
| Black Oil | Rough journal bearings<br>Low cost lubricating oil for once through application in old equipment | 1.<br>2.<br>3.<br>4. | | | | |

(3)

| Classification | Explanatory Remarks | Supplier* | Brand | Consumption Bbls. per Year | Price | Remarks |
|---|---|---|---|---|---|---|
| Open Gear Lubricants | Wire rope and open gear lubrication--to include solvent cutbacks and other specialties of type | 1.<br>2.<br>3.<br>4. | | | | |
| Multi-Purpose Grease | Generally used throughout a plant to simplify grease lubrication practices | 1.<br>2. | | | | |
| Miscellaneous Greases | Block greases<br>Hot neck greases<br>Cold sett greases<br>Plug valve lubricants<br>Pipe thread lubricants<br>Wool yarn greases<br>Replenishing grease<br>Wire rope manufacturing lubricant<br>Launching lubricants | 1.<br>2.<br>3.<br>4.<br>5.<br>6.<br>7.<br>8. | | | | |
| Specialties | Soluble and compounded cutting oils<br>Drawing and forging compounds<br>Tableway lubricants<br>Compounded rust preventives and rust preventive bases<br>Compounded roll oils and roll cleaners<br>Palm oil substitutes<br>Coating oils<br>Petrolatum and wax | 1.<br>2<br>3.<br>4.<br>5.<br>6.<br>7.<br>8.<br>9.<br>10. | | | | |

## EXHIBIT 5 (*Continued*)

| Classification | Explanatory Remarks | Supplier* | Brand | Consumption Bbls. per Year | Price | (2) Remarks |
|---|---|---|---|---|---|---|
| Cylinder Oil | To include both compounded and uncompounded cylinder oils<br>Tempering oil<br>Circulating oil for old gear and pinion sets not requiring EP lubricants | 1.<br>2.<br>3.<br>4. | | | | |
| Detergent Motor Oil | Diesel engines<br>Automotive engines<br>Blowing engines | 1.<br>2.<br>3.<br>4. | | | | |
| Mild EP Leaded Gear Oils | Gear and bearing systems requiring extreme pressure properties and suitability for long-time service | 1<br>2.<br>3.<br>4. | | | | |
| Conventional EP Roller Bearing Grease | Rolling mill and highly loaded bearings | 1.<br>2.<br>3. | | | | |
| High Temperature EP Roller Bearing Grease | Rolling mill and highly loaded bearings | 1.<br>2.<br>3. | | | | |
| Lime Base General Purpose Grease | Miscellaneous bearings | 1.<br>2.<br>3 | | | | |
| Electric Motor and High Temperature Grease | Soap type | 1.<br>2<br>3. | | | | |
| Electric Motor and High Temperature Grease | Nonsoap type | 1.<br>2. | | | | |
| Graphite Grease | Plate and blooming mill bearings<br>Hydraulic plungers<br>Miscellaneous journal bearings | 1.<br>2.<br>3. | | | | |

| Classification | Explanatory Remarks | Supplier* | Brand | Consumption Bbls. per Year | Price | (4) Remarks |
|---|---|---|---|---|---|---|
| Fuels and Solvents**<br>LPG | | 1.<br>2.<br>3. | | | | |
| Solvents<br>(a) Aliphatic | | 1.<br>2.<br>3. | | | | |
| (b) Aromatic | | 1.<br>2.<br>3. | | | | |
| Gasoline | | 1.<br>2.<br>3. | | | | |
| Kerosene | | 1.<br>2.<br>3. | | | | |
| Diesel Fuel | | 1.<br>2.<br>3. | | | | |
| Distillate Fuel | | 1.<br>2.<br>3. | | | | |
| Residual Fuel | | 1.<br>2.<br>3. | | | | |

*To include Company sales.

**Remarks should indicate special restrictions as sulfur content, etc. LPG remarks should indicate whether used in conjunction with Natural Gas and any trend toward or away from the use of Natural Gas.

those steel mills and marketing territories in which the company had a satisfactory share of the business, as well as those in which the company was not well represented; provided a factual basis for evaluating and realigning the sales personnel in the various marketing territories; and indicated company products that were performing satisfactorily, products that should be improved to give optimum operating results, and new products that might be needed in the product line.

The elapsed time required to conduct the survey was four months—the time span between development of the survey form and tabulation and analysis of the completed forms in the New York office. The salesmen returned approximately 300 completed forms to the New York office, each form representing a separate steel company within the company's marketing territory.

This was the first such survey conducted by the company, and the management was well satisfied with the results obtained. One executive suggested that the company conduct similar surveys in other industries, such as textiles, chemicals, public utilities, and paper mills.

# ASPHALT CORPORATION OF AMERICA

The Asphalt Corporation of America (to be identified as ACA) manufactured a line of industrial adhesives, mastics, weather stripping, sewer pipe gaskets, bridge bearings, and various types of expansion joints for roads, concrete buildings, and jet runways. These products were sold to a wide spectrum of manufacturing and construction enterprises throughout the United States. In the mid-1960s ACA management found itself confronted with two classic marketing problems: how to react to price-cutting competitors on an established product, and how to determine the best price at which to introduce a new one.

The adhesive resin introduced by the company in 1958 for cementing corrugated fiberglass-reinforced plastic panels was an immediate success. ACA's adhesive not only possessed certain advantages over those currently in use but was priced below the two market leaders. Although there was no reaction by manufacturers of the two leading products initially, both sharply reduced their prices as soon as it became apparent that ACA's adhesive was commanding a significant share of the market. ACA's management did not want to lose market share. This would mean a shrinkage in volume that would exert upward pressure on unit costs.

To attempt to maintain their low-price position in the face of such a challenge would risk a price war with two larger competitors.

The company also was preparing at this time to introduce a new type of composition rubber expansion joint to be used in concrete block construction. Expansion joints are devices inserted between concrete blocks used in wall construction to prevent cracking due to settling or to contraction and expansion as a result of temperature changes. ACA executives believed their new joint to be superior to other types of expansion joints on the market and thought that it should be introduced without delay. However, they were not sure whether the new product should be priced above, below, or the same as joints with which it would be in direct competition.

## Plastic panel adhesives

Corrugated, fiberglass reinforced plastic (FRP) panels were first introduced in the late 1940s and soon achieved wide use as awnings, canopies, carport covers, and porch roofs and also as exterior siding for buildings and as interior partitions. Their light weight, strength, durability, permanence of color (panels soon were available in a variety of colors), and ease of handling made FRP panels very popular and generated a substantial demand for products used with them, such as adhesives.

In order to join panels securely, an adhesive was applied in a strip along the edges of panels which were then overlapped to form a continuous surface. The adhesive usually consisted of a bonding agent (resin) dissolved in a solvent. When applied, the solvent evaporated leaving the bonding agent. While an adhesive with a high density of bonding agent produced a stronger bond between panels, the speed with which the solvent evaporated made such adhesives difficult to apply.

ACA's adhesive was designed to overcome this disadvantage by employing the solvent, toluene, which had a relatively slow rate of evaporation. This permitted a higher density of the bonding agent without affecting ease of application. The ACA adhesive contained about 44 percent resin as compared with 30 percent resin content in competing products.

Toluene was manufactured by ACA, using a secret process which had been developed in the company's own laboratories. Due to the volatile and combustible nature of its ingredients, toluene was a difficult chemical to produce. In order to impart a relatively low volatility to the resulting solvent, the ingredients had to be mixed within very narrow heat tolerances. If the mixing temperature was too low, the chemical process would abort and the resulting product would be useless. Other adhesive manufacturers who used toluene produced it with a different formulation that did not require the narrow heat tolerances but which did impart a higher volatility to the solvent.

For satisfactory results, plastic panel adhesives also had to be light stable. Otherwise the resin would discolor under the ultraviolet rays of the sun, producing unsightly streaks where the opaque panels had been cemented together. Light stability could only be achieved with use of the correct stabilizers combined in the proper proportions. ACA's chemists had developed a formulation and a process that resulted in an adhesive that could be guaranteed to retain its light stability for the life of the panel on which it was used. Other manufacturers had difficulty matching this warranty.

In addition to these advantages, ACA's adhesive was packaged in a resealable container, which made it more convenient and somewhat more economical to use. Unlike competitors' products, a partially used container of ACA adhesive could be resealed tightly enough to prevent the remaining contents from drying out before being used.

*Pricing.* ACA had adopted a pricing formula for its products that resulted in a selling price that was roughly five times raw material costs. The formula was based on an analysis of the firm's costs which revealed that the average sales dollar included the following direct and indirect expenses.

> Raw materials...................... $ .20
> Labor.............................   .40
> Overhead, incl. profits.............   .40
> Total..............................  $1.00

Raw material cost for the plastic panel adhesives was 66 cents per gallon. On the basis of its formula, the company priced the adhesive at $3.30 per gallon. This was the price to manufacturers who bought directly from ACA. The company also sold the product to independent distributors, who in turn resold it to dealers and contractors. Since it was established practice in the industry to allow direct purchasers a 50 percent discount (off list price) and distributors a 26 percent discount, list price was set at $6.60 per gallon and the following price schedule adopted.

> List price (to dealers and contractors)..................... $6.60
> Distributors' price (26⅔% discount).....................   4.95
> Manufacturers' price, i.e., direct purchase
> price (50% discount)...............................   3.30

*Distribution.* ACA's distribution system for adhesives and mastics was a mixture of direct and indirect channels (Exhibit 1). These products were regularly sold to about 600 accounts, 70 of which were manufacturers of FRP panels, 200 of which were independent distributors (i.e., merchant wholesalers), and the remainder were dealers (mostly lumberyards, hardware, and paint stores) and contractors.

ACA's outside salesmen call on the approximately 12 manufacturers who accounted for 85 percent of the FRP panel business and about 25 large building materials distributors, such as Cadillac Glass Company in Chicago and T. C. Essen Company in Milwaukee. Salesmen also made direct calls on tract builders, big end-user accounts (such as U.S. Steel

**EXHIBIT 1.  Distribution system for adhesives and mastics**

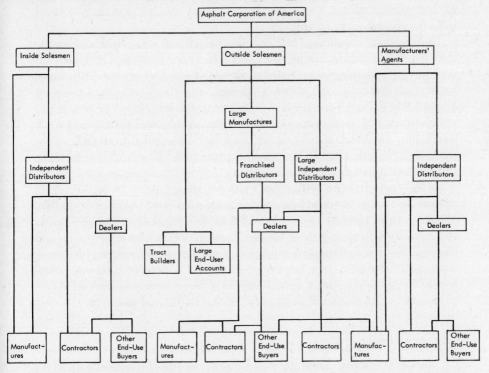

and Anheuser-Busch, who used FRP panels for shed roofs and skylights in plant roofs and operated their own construction crews), and large contractors, such as American Bridge. Seven manufacturers' agents located in Chicago, Cleveland, Los Angeles, Dallas, Toronto, Atlanta, and Hackensack, N.J., called on the remaining manufacturers and distributors. Inside salesmen at ACA contacted by telephone manufacturers and distributors who represented prospective customers but who were located outside manufacturers agents' territories.

Manufacturers resold most of the adhesives they purchased, and other accessories such as special nails and drilling tools, to their own distributors and dealers so that they would have the materials and equipment needed to install FRP panels. Distributors who bought adhesives from ACA salesmen or agents generally resold them to dealers and to contractors too small to warrant the attention of ACA salesmen or agents.

The company supported these selling efforts with an advertising program which included full-page ads in *Construction News* and *Engineering News Record,* direct mail, and point-of-purchase materials. Direct mail literature was made available to both distributors and dealers with space for distributor/dealer imprint. Point-of-purchase materials were also made available to all distributors and dealers to encourage their use in showroom displays. The company budgeted about 3 percent of annual sales for the advertising program.

*Competitors' reaction.*   At the time the adhesive was introduced the lowest-priced comparable product was selling for $3.63 per gallon to direct buying manufacturers. Sales of the ACA product rose steadily until its market share reached about 8 percent, which was a sales volume of about 1,000 gallons per month. At this point, the largest of the two major competitors, Borden Chemical, cut the price of its panel adhesive to $3.30 per gallon on direct purchases by manufacturers and introduced a new discount schedule that yielded a new price of $3.00 per gallon to large direct-buying users.

ACA countered this action by reducing its list price to $6.00, which placed its price to direct-buying manufacturers at $3.00 per gallon. Within a short time, the second of the major competitors, Tremco Corp., reduced its adhesive prices to the same level as those of ACA and Borden. Borden thereupon announced a *supplemental quantity discount.* This permitted very large buyers an additional 5 percent discount below the $3.00 per gallon price and allowed all orders received over a 30-day period to be accumulated to qualify for the additional discount.

### Expansion joints

The new type expansion joint had been developed in cooperation with the Cedar Rapids Block Joint Company, a manufacturer and distributor of *Durawall* (steel reinforcing rods welded into a 12-foot by 16-foot net) and other materials used in masonry construction. While expansion joints were no guarantee against cracking, their capacity to expand or be compressed with slight shifting or settling of a concrete block wall reduced the likelihood of serious damage to the wall through cracking. The use of these joints required a special type of concrete block, known in the trade as a steel sash block. This type of block was made with a vertical groove in one end. The blocks were originally made for use with steel frames, the end groove providing a space into which the frame, or sash, could be fitted. When the grooved ends of two such blocks were butted together, the resulting slot, or trough, formed a space into which the expansion joint could be fitted (Exhibit 2).

A concrete block wall built to U.S. Government specifications, for example, would have to have an expansion joint about every 12 feet in each row of blocks. Some builders regarded the 12-foot requirement as excessive and believed the same effect could be achieved by placing expansion joints as far as 25 to 30 feet apart. Blocks not having expansion joints were laid in place with mortar in the time-honored fashion.

The differences between ACA's expansion joint and those of competitors were its shape and dimensions (Exhibits 3 and 4) as well as the

**EXHIBIT 2.  Steel sash block showing matching grooves**

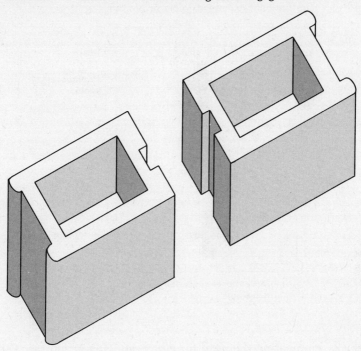

material from which it was made. Steel sash concrete blocks were typically 8 inches high, 8 inches thick, and 16 inches in length. While conventional expansion joints were thick enough to fill the "short" space between blocks, most were only 2¼ to 2½ inches wide and did not fill the "long" space (that at right angles to the wall) between blocks. Since blocks were 8 inches thick, this left approximately 3¾ inches of space on either side of the expansion joint which had to be filled with mortar or caulking.

There was some disagreement in the trade as to whether this space needed to be completely filled. Most builders filled it with caulking to achieve greater protection against moisture seepage and to give the joint a neater appearance. Others only filled the space along the edges of the blocks that would show and left the remainder unfilled. ACA's expansion joint avoided this problem because it was 8 inches wide and completely filled both "short" and "long" space between blocks.

The superior feature of the ACA joint was not simply its longer dimensions, but its unique combination of hard and soft composition rubber. The nature of the material was such that it expanded or was compressed as required to fit the contour of the space between adjacent steel

**EXHIBIT 3.   Sash blocks showing ACA and conventional expansion joints in position**

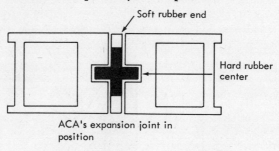

ACA's expansion joint in position

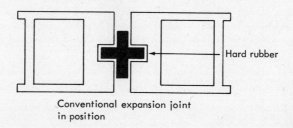

Conventional expansion joint in position

sash blocks, eliminating the need for either caulking or mortar. The technique for bonding in a single joint two types of rubber of substantially different degrees of hardness had been developed by ACA chemists.[1] It was a closely guarded corporate secret. Nevertheless, company executives were certain that competitors would make a determined effort to imitate their product and wanted to market it over as wide an area as quickly as possible.

*Marketing plans.*   Available information from trade and industry sources indicated that current use of any type of expansion joint in concrete block construction was rather limited. Nevertheless, company officials believed that their inclusion in U.S. Government building specifications and the growing number of state and local building codes which specified them would expand the existing market substantially. ACA's market research department estimated that total sales of expansion joints of all types was about 2 million linear feet annually. This volume was divided about equally among three manufacturers.

It had been agreed that the Cedar Rapids Block Joint Company would distribute the new joint to concrete block manufacturers. Cedar Rapids had 30 salesmen who sold reinforcing rods to these manufacturers

---

[1] Hardness in rubber is measured in durometers. The higher the durometer value of a substance the greater its hardness. While the interior part of the ACA joint had a durometer value of 50 to 75, the part of the joint which fitted into the outside space between blocks was only 5 to 10 durometers. This gave the outside edges of the joint a very spongy but also a very durable quality.

**EXHIBIT 4.  Different dimensions of ACA and conventional expansion joints**

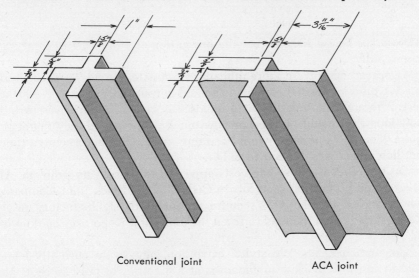

Conventional joint                    ACA joint

throughout the United States and had established a good rapport with their purchasing departments. However, these manufacturers were predominately small, local businesses, because the bulk and weight of concrete blocks made their shipment too costly over any but short distances. The local nature of their market limited the selling effort most were willing to put behind such accessories as reinforcing rods and expansion joints. There was little reason to assume that they would do more than stock the new joint.

In light of these conditions it was decided that selling efforts should be directed primarily at contractors and architects. Since most architects specified reinforcing rods and expansion joints in concrete block structures, contractors who built architect-designed buildings were required to use them. However, it was known that a sizable amount of concrete-block construction was done without the guidance of an architect and that in these cases reinforcing rods and expansion joints were frequently omitted. In some instances the omission was due to ignorance. Consequently, both contractors and architects appeared to represent key promotional targets.

The decision regarding the price at which the new product should be introduced raised the familiar questions of cost, volume, value to customer, and competitive response. Expansion joints were molded in long strips and then cut into the proper lengths. ACA had approximately $12,000 invested in molds and another $5,000 sunk in development costs. Direct manufacturing cost per linear foot was estimated at 36 cents in production runs of 100,000 to 300,000 feet. This included the following raw material and labor costs:

Raw materials............... $0.12
Labor..................... 0.24
Total..................... $0.36

At volumes below 100,000 feet the proportion of labor cost to total cost rose rapidly.

Overhead costs were more difficult to estimate. No additional factory space would be needed so long as annual output did not exceed 300,000 feet. Although the investment in molds was known, no one was certain how long they could be used or how much maintenance they might require. The new operation would certainly demand some executive time, but how much was difficult to judge.

On the other hand, selling costs appeared to present no problem. All sales would be in truck-load lots to Cedar Rapids Block Joint Company, which agreed to take ACA's entire output at the f.o.b. factory price. Cedar Rapids then planned to resell the joints at a 25 percent markup on its cost.

Conventional, i.e., "old style," expansion joints were currently being sold to concrete block manufacturers at a list price of only 25 cents per linear foot. However, the ACA joint had significant economic advantages for the contractor. It provided a better seal, thus reducing the possibility of moisture seepage and subsequent complaints by users or buyers of the structure. Since no caulking or mortar was needed where the ACA joint was used, both construction time and material cost could be saved. Ordinarily, it required a "block man" about one minute to fully caulk or mortar a joint. Current wage rates for "block men" in the Midwest varied from $4.50 to $5.25 per hour. The cost of mortar or caulking saved was estimated at about 12 cents per joint (the space between two butted steel sash blocks).

---

# ATLANTIC PULLEY LAGGING COMPANY

The L. M. Robbins Company operates a combination distributor and manufacturers' agent business in Philadelphia which markets conveyor belts. The belts are available in a variety of fabrics including cotton, synthetic fiber, metal mesh, and rubber. Customers are mainly in the greater Philadelphia area, although some are headquartered there, with plants in various parts of the country.

In 1968, Mr. Robbins established the Atlantic Pulley Lagging Company as a part-time venture to sell lagging for conveyor and elevator pulleys. Not only was Mr. Robbin's participation in the business a part-time affair, but so was that of the firm's other employees—a superintendent, a factory worker, a secretary, an accountant, and a salesman. The accountant worked one evening each week, and the salesman, who had a full-time job elsewhere during the late afternoon and early evening, devoted what time he could to the lagging business.

Lagging is a ribbed rubber composition material that is applied to the surface of cylindrical pulleys. Its purpose is to provide traction in the operation of various types of moving belts looped around the pulleys. The various types of lagging sold by Atlantic are shown in Exhibits 1, 2, and 3.

The ordinary type of lagging, Mark II, is shown in Exhibit 1. This product is used primarily on packaging machinery and in food processing plants. It accounts for about half of Atlantic's total sales. Mark II is made to Atlantic's specifications by the Continental Rubber Works of Hanover, Germany.

A special kind of lagging known as slide, or panel, lagging is shown in Exhibit 2. This is made by the Holz Rubber Company of Lodi, California. It is available in five different styles and three tread designs to meet a wide variety of pulley requirements. Atlantic is the sole distributor of slide lagging in eastern Pennsylvania and southern New Jersey.

A new lagging design known as Mark IVB, originated by Atlantic, is shown in Exhibit 3. It consists of a central section with the ribs running at right angles to the belt direction and side sections in which the ribs run circumferentially. This design has the advantage of keeping the belt centered on the pulley cylinder. Although still in the experimental stage, the product has been enthusiastically endorsed by three large users and Mr. Robbins believes it has considerable potential. He plans to apply for a patent in the near future.

Since lagging wears out and has to be replaced, Atlantic operates a shop that is equipped to strip old lagging from pulleys and attach new to them. About 15 to 20 percent of the company's business is of this type, and Mr. Robbins would like very much to increase it. In his words, "If we can get firms accustomed to sending their pulleys to us to lag, we should be able to develop a thriving repeat business, as they will get out of the habit of stocking lagging and will soon lose the technique of installing it." This event would make them more dependent upon Atlantic.

### The market for lagging

It is difficult to measure the total market for lagging. Mr. Robbins estimates that in the eastern half of the U.S. total sales of lagging by all sellers probably amount to about $200,000 annually. He also estimates

EXHIBIT 1.   Promotional material showing Atlantic Mark II lagging

*Attention Plant Superintendent –*

**BEFORE**

**AFTER**

# PULLEYS NEED NEW LAGGING?

We'll remove old lagging and recover with the Atlantic Mark II lagging. It is self cleaning, oil and waterproof.

Or, if desired, we can ship new lagging for you to apply in your own shop.

## ATLANTIC PULLEY LAGGING CO.
**8 NORTH 3rd STREET**
**EMMAUS, PA. (Near Allentown) 18049**
**(215) 967-3377**

EXHIBIT 2.   Promotional material showing slide lagging

**EXHIBIT 2** (*Continued*)

# "SLIDE-LAG" the sound investment

## DOWN-TIME COSTS MONEY!

### "SLIDE-LAG" Saves Money

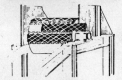

SLIDE - LAG saves money because it reduces down-time previously spent to install other types of lagging, to practically nothing.

Why! Because SLIDE-LAG is so easy to install—just like one-two-three **and . . . NO BOLTS, SCREWS or ADHESIVES.**

Simply weld a retainer strip, lay in a pad, weld in another strip, lay in another pad, etc. until the job is finished.

Installation takes but a few hours.

Replacement can be done in minutes—simply by sliding the pads in or out from the ends of the pulley—

WITHOUT REMOVING THE PULLEY FROM THE CONVEYOR

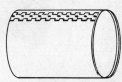

ONE

### "SLIDE-LAG" Saves Time

SLIDE-LAG is available for both crowned and straight faced pulleys.

The built-in crown is an exclusive feature available only in Style No. 1 SLIDE-LAG. It permits converting straight faced pulleys to crown face and quicker replacement of traction pads.

SLIDE-LAG can be compactly stored and makes substitute pulleys entirely unnecessary.

TWO

### "SLIDE-LAG" Solves Maintenance Problems

Because SLIDE-LAG is so easily and quickly installed or replaced, emergencies can be reduced to simple maintenance.

SLIDE-LAG is invaluable for complicated installations where removal of head-shaft pulleys is difficult due to drive mechanism, structural obstructions or height.

SLIDE-LAG is invaluable for automated conveyor systems where continuous flow is essential.

SLIDE-LAG is also invaluable for installations located in remote places such as mines or quarries.

THREE

## SLIDE-LAG MAKES ALL OTHER

Page 2

# *for maintaining continuous production.*

**SLIDE - LAG
OUT - PERFORMS
ALL OTHER
PULLEY LAGGING**

SLIDE-LAG offers performance that is far superior to any other type of pulley lagging, especially under severe operating conditions.

**"SLIDE-LAG" Offers Superior Traction**

This by reason of: 1) high traction type rubber; 2) skillfully engineered "Gear Tooth" spacings between traction pads; 3) Slide-Lag's unique tread design, combining diagonal grooves, wide channels and narrow squeegee action slits. No slippage, wet or dry.

**"SLIDE-LAG" Is Self - Cleaning**

The combination of grooves and wide channels between traction pads allows loose foreign particles to work themselves out before they get the chance to injure the belt covering.

**"SLIDE-LAG" Is Rugged**

SLIDE-LAG pads are constructed of specially compounded abrasion resistant rubber, integrally molded and vulcanized under high pressure (700 p.s.i.) to a heavy gauge steel backing plate which is preformed to the pulley diameter. This method neutralizes internal stresses and provides optimum (permanent) bond in addition to higher rubber density for maximum strength and longer wear.

The retainer strips, also of heavy gauge pressed steel, are accurately formed so that when assembled, the traction pads are firmly keyed to the pulley face.

**FULL SIZE SECTION
SLIDE-LAG PULLEY TRACTION PAD
AND STEEL RETAINER STRIPS**

## *PULLEY LAGGING OBSOLETE*

Page 3

**EXHIBIT 2** (*Concluded*)

that sales of slide lagging probably add another $200,000 to $300,000 to the market.

Atlantic's competition seems to come not so much from other companies selling lagging as from rubber belting distributors and their customers. In Mr. Robbins's opinion, about 90 percent of industrial plants in the East lag their pulleys with ordinary rubber belt or rubber rough top belt. They simply spiral the belting around the pulley using sunken head rivets to attach it at each end. While such improvisation functions satisfactorily in many cases, prepared lagging is a more durable covering, provides greater traction as a result of its ribbed construction, can be easily cleaned, and is impervious to oil and water.

The superior qualities of prepared lagging are real but difficult to prove, except in cases in which prospective buyers have experienced serious problems in moving materials by belt. The lagging is such a small part of a conveyor or elevator system that it is difficult to focus buyer attention on it. It is so simple and easy to wrap ordinary belting around a pulley, cement or rivet it fast, and hope for the best, that a salesman typically encounters a wall of indifference when attempting to sell lagging. As Mr. Robbins observed, "Nobody ever sees the lagging. It is under the conveyor belt and such a small item that selling the material on a quality basis is very difficult."

## Marketing performance

The L. M. Robbins Company acts as sales agent for the Atlantic Pulley Lagging Company. The Robbins Company sales force consists of Mr. Robbins, one full-time salesman, and a man who works on a part-time commission basis. The three members of the sales force receive a 15 percent commission on sales to industrial users and a 10 percent commission on sales to original-equipment manufacturers and to distributors. Atlantic buys and stocks the lagging.

During the first full year of operation, sales of the Atlantic Company were $12,000, resulting in a small loss. The second year of operation brought sales of $25,000 and a profit of $800. During the third year sales rose to about $39,000 with profits of $1,300. The Robbins Company also received about $3,000 in commissions that year on the Atlantic business it handled. An operating statement for nine months of the 1970–71 fiscal year is shown in Exhibit 4, and a balance sheet as of May 31, 1971, is given in Exhibit 5.

Mr. Robbins is not satisfied with the results of his venture in lagging. "This business has not taken off in the way I thought it might," he remarked. "It really has been quite a disappointment. On the other hand, it has not been a financial drain. I might actually make a little money if I were to liquidate it now."

The possibilities of expanding the business are not promising. The

**EXHIBIT 3.  Promotional material showing the new Atlantic Mark IVB lagging**

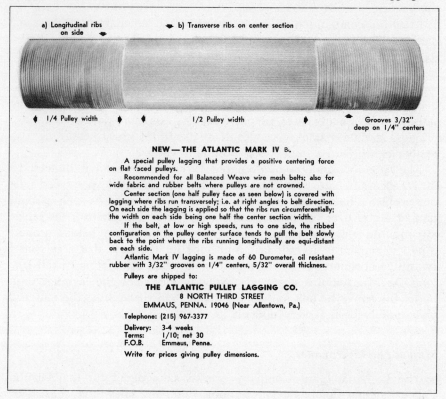

a) Longitudinal ribs on side

b) Transverse ribs on center section

1/4 Pulley width          1/2 Pulley width          Grooves 3/32" deep on 1/4" centers

### NEW — THE ATLANTIC MARK IV B.

A special pulley lagging that provides a positive centering force on flat faced pulleys.

Recommended for all Balanced Weave wire mesh belts; also for wide fabric and rubber belts where pulleys are not crowned.

Center section (one half pulley face as seen below) is covered with lagging where ribs run transversely; i.e. at right angles to belt direction. On each side the lagging is applied so that the ribs run circumferentially; the width on each side being one half the center section width.

If the belt, at low or high speeds, runs to one side, the ribbed configuration on the pulley center surface tends to pull the belt slowly back to the point where the ribs running longitudinally are equi-distant on each side.

Atlantic Mark IV lagging is made of 60 Durometer, oil resistant rubber with 3/32" grooves on 1/4" centers, 5/32" overall thickness.

Pulleys are shipped to:

**THE ATLANTIC PULLEY LAGGING CO.**
8 NORTH THIRD STREET
EMMAUS, PENNA. 19046 (Near Allentown, Pa.)

Telephone: (215) 967-3377

Delivery:   3-4 weeks
Terms:      1/10; net 30
F.O.B.      Emmaus, Penna.

Write for prices giving pulley dimensions.

company is limited by its agency agreement with Holz to eastern Pennsylvania and southern New Jersey in the sale of slide lagging. If it should attempt to market Mark II and Mark IVB lagging through distributors or agents in other parts of the country, the incomplete line of lagging would handicap selling efforts. It was Mr. Robbins's opinion that no agent or distributor would spend very much time on a small volume item like lagging unless there was a sizable profit in it or some other significant advantage in handling it. "I can imagine no such inducement with regard to this product," he remarked.

On the other hand, Mr. Robbins wonders if a considerable volume could not be developed by direct mail. He observed that the need for lagging is likely to arise in any particular plant only once or twice a year. Unless a salesman should happen to make a call at the plant on the particular day the need arose, he would be unlikely to get an order. A continuous direct mail program might succeed in keeping the advantages of lagging before purchasing officers so that when conveyor or belting problems arose, they would think of lagging. Such a program probably could be managed on a part-time basis. However, it would take time to organize and might prove costly.

**EXHIBIT 4**

ATLANTIC PULLEY LAGGING COMPANY
Operating Statement
Nine months to May 31, 1971

| | | | |
|---|---|---|---|
| Net Sales | | | $32,256.65 |
| Cost of Goods Sold | | | |
| Inventory 9/1/70 | $ 8,302.70 | | |
| Purchases | 21,924.00 | | |
| Total | 30,226.70 | | |
| Inventory 5/31/71 | 13,158.07 | | |
| Material used or sold | | $17,068.63 | |
| Supplies used | | 1,471.35 | |
| Cost of labor | | 4,315.57 | |
| Total | | | 22,855.55 |
| Gross Profit | | | $ 9,401.10 |
| Other Operating Expenses | | | |
| Commissions | | $3,659.91 | |
| Payroll taxes | | 228.97 | |
| Office expense | | 540.76 | |
| Parcel post, freight | | 828.96 | |
| Telephone | | 217.70 | |
| Rent | | 660.00 | |
| Advertising | | 30.00 | |
| Travel | | 43.20 | |
| Depreciation | | 175.81 | |
| Insurance | | 58.00 | |
| Miscellaneous | | 15.78 | |
| Total | | $6,459.09 | 6,459.09 |
| Net Profit | | | $ 2,942.01 |

Tentative figures for the last three months of the fiscal year indicate a loss of about $1,700, leaving a net profit of about $1,242 for the year.

**EXHIBIT 5**

ATLANTIC PULLEY LAGGING COMPANY
Balance Sheet
May 31, 1971

*Assets*

| | | |
|---|---|---|
| Cash...................................... | | $    532.98 |
| Accounts receivable....................... | | 7,739.71 |
| Inventory................................ | | 13,158.07 |
| Equipment............................... | | 1,392.74 |
| Reserve.................................. | | 351.41 |
| Total Assets............................ | | $23,174.91 |

*Liabilities*

| | | |
|---|---|---|
| Accounts payable | | |
| L. M. Robbins........................... | | $13,572.98 |
| Others.................................. | | 2,357.86 |
| Commissions payable....................... | | 137.26 |
| Accrued taxes............................ | | 205.90 |
| Total Liabilities....................... | | $16,274.00 |

*Net Worth*

| | | |
|---|---|---|
| Capital.................................. | $3,290.68 | |
| Retained profits.......................... | 3,610.23 | |
| Total Net Worth........................ | | 6,900.91 |
| Total Liabilities and Net Worth.......... | | $23,174.91 |

# BEECHCRAFT HAWKER CORPORATION

The Beechcraft Hawker Corporation was organized in 1970 as a wholly owned subsidiary of Beech Aircraft Corporation of Wichita, Kansas, to market in North America the business jets produced by Hawker Siddeley Aviation Ltd. of London, England. Under terms of the agreement, the new corporation acquired the aviation assets and personnel of Hawker Siddeley International, Inc., a subsidiary of the Hawker Siddeley Group in North America. The acquisition offered important advantages to both parties. While Beech possessed a strong distribution system in the U.S., the company had no jet aircraft to market through it. Hawker Siddeley had jets, but its access to the U.S. market was limited to two independent distributors, Atlantic Aviation and AiResearch Aviation. Beech now had a jet and Hawker Siddeley a much more extensive outlet to the U.S. market.

Like executives of many new corporations, those at Beechcraft Hawker faced some perplexing problems at the very outset of operations. While no one had entertained any illusions about walking off with the business jet market unopposed, competition proved to be formidable. A viable promotional program for selling business jets had to be developed.

Experience indicated that the most effective way to sell private aircraft was to demonstrate them to prospective buyers together with a presentation concerning the economics of their use. Most aircraft companies, including Beech, and such giants as Grumman and Lockheed, based their promotional efforts on the demonstration ride and personal presentation. Beechcraft Hawker also adopted this approach. The company placed full-page ads in *Business Week,* the *Wall Street Journal* and *Fortune, Flying,* and *Business and Commercial Aviation,* which not only touted its business jet but announced that a prospective buyer could arrange for a demonstration by calling the nearest Beechcraft Hawker representative, or the president of the corporation. Some examples of these ads are shown in Exhibits 4, 5, 6, and 7. However, no one had a reliable formula for motivating prospective buyers to request demonstration rides.

The contract between Beechcraft Hawker and Hawker Siddeley also stipulated that the development of future business jet aircraft would be conducted as a joint venture. This raised the question of product design that would give Beechcraft Hawker a unique position in the business jet market as well as that of proper timing in the phaseout of an existing model and the introduction of a new one. The speed with which technology advanced and the strength of competition made decisions concerning product policy and market positioning particularly urgent.

An unexpected problem with ominous implications occurred in the autumn of 1973 when the Arab oil embargo plunged the nation into an energy crisis unprecedented in its peacetime history. Although the extent to which the supply of fuel available for general aviation, as opposed to commercial aviation, was unknown, the future of all private plane manufacturers was suddenly clouded with uncertainty.

## Beech strategy

Beech Aircraft Corporation was generally regarded as the Rolls-Royce of the General Aviation Industry. It had dominated the market for turbo-prop business aircraft and air taxis for a number of years. The company's 175 sales outlets in the United States represented the most extensive sales and service network in the industry geared to the sale of large corporate aircraft. While Beech executives considered the development and manufacture of business jets as early as the late 1950s, the project did not receive serious attention until the following decade when Beech customers began expressing strong interest in jet power.

Conversations between executives at Beech and Hawker Siddeley Aviation Ltd. were opened in 1961 concerning some type of marketing or manufacturing arrangement involving jet aircraft. Contacts between the two firms continued intermittently until 1969 when two events brought the decision on business jets to the forefront of Beech planning. The first was an announcement by archrival, Cessna Aircraft, that it would have a twin jet business plane ready for delivery by 1972. The second was a sharp decline in Beech Aircraft profits as a result of the debilitating effect of a 26-day strike at midyear and a downturn in the U.S. economy that produced swollen inventories of unsold planes. Earnings per share of common stock tumbled to 28 cents in 1969, from a high of $1.28 in 1967.[1] Under pressure of these events as well as of that exerted by both customers and dealers eager to enter the jet age, Beech President Frank E. Hedrick and Board Chairman Olive Ann Beech decided that the company could no longer postpone its entry into the business jet market.

The timing of the decision was not particularly advantageous for Beech. Soaring costs and the company's financial condition made it impractical for the firm to attempt to develop its own jet, even though it was believed that a Beech jet would be appreciably different from the one developed and manufactured by Hawker Siddeley. The imminence

---

[1] Annual Report, Beech Aircraft Corporation (1973), p. 4.

of competition and the time that would be required to develop a new plane virtually from scratch also made such a venture impractical. To extricate the company from this impasse, Mr. Hedrick and Mrs. Beech decided to negotiate an accommodation with Hawker Siddeley. Their efforts culminated in the acquisition agreement.

In essence, the agreement gave Beech Aircraft Corporation the aviation assets of Hawker Siddeley International Corporation in return for which Mr. Hedrick and Mrs. Beech agreed to market Hawker Siddeley's business jet through Beech's North American sales outlets. The Beechcraft Hawker Corporation was subsequently established to implement the stipulations of the agreement. This strategy enabled Beech to enter the business jet market in its initial growth phase while minimizing its capital risk and conserving its financial resources. The move not only enabled Beech to escape substantial development costs, but unlike rival Cessna, whose plane was new and untried, Beech acquired a tested and successful business jet in the 9–14-passenger (depending upon seating arrangements) Hawker Siddeley HS 125. The plane was subsequently redesignated in North America as the Beechcraft-Hawker BH 125.

One of the significant advantages of the BH 125 was its short-field performance. It could both take off and land on a 3400-foot runway with full payload, making hundreds of small, close-in remote airports accessible. Moreover, such landing performance was achieved without the use of costly and heavy thrust reversers, which require additional maintenance.

As Mr. Hedrick described the arrangement, "Hawker has the hardware and we have the marketing organization."[2] Nor did marketing someone else's plane concern him. "Real growth in general aviation is dependent solely on marketing," Mr. Hedrick commented. "To be very candid about it, if you turned loose different engineers to design a plane of a certain horsepower and size, the end results would be very similar."[3] He predicted the BH 125 would take one third of the business jet market.

Hawker Siddeley had sold 28 jets in the United States in 1969 with only two distributors. This was about equal to sales of Pan American's Falcon and North American's Saberliner but well behind the 61 Lear Jets sold by Gates Learjet Corporation in 1969. However, Mr. Hedrick was confident that the strength of the Beech distribution system would be sufficient to place sales of the BH 125 substantially ahead of both the Falcon and the Saberliner, its two main competitors.

### The relationship between Beechcraft Hawker and Hawker Siddeley

At the time Beechcraft Hawker was organized, the BH 125–400, an enlarged and improved version of the BH 125, was in production, and

---

[2] "Beech Makes Its Move," Forbes (February 1, 1970), p. 21.
[3] Ibid.

development of the BH 125–600, a slightly stretched version of the BH 125–400, was nearing completion. Hawker-Siddeley served as prime contractor for these planes, which were purchased by Beechcraft Hawker. The aircraft were delivered to Beechcraft Hawker's Wichita facility minus interiors and avionics, which were installed there to customers' specifications. Beech engineers subsequently did collaborate with the Hawker Siddeley design group on certain modifications in the two aircraft, such as weight reduction, improved door assemblies, and instrument panel layout.

The BH 125–600 was in the preliminary design stage in 1970, so Beech expected to have some influence on the final development of this plane. As Mr. Hedrick phrased it, the Beech contribution to the development of the BH 125–600 would be primarily that of "Americanizing" its design.[4] It was important that the plane's specifications fit the requirements of the U.S. market. As the market for this plane developed, Beechcraft Hawker might also become a production subcontractor for some of its components, but Hawker Siddeley would continue to be responsible for the major part of its production, including final assembly. As in the case of the BH 125–400's, it was planned to fly the basic BH–600 aircraft from England to Wichita where their interiors and avionics would be installed to customer specifications.

Beechcraft Hawker also assumed support in 1970 for the approximately 130 HS 125's previously sold by Hawker Siddeley in the United States, Canada, and Mexico. Contracts with Hawker Siddeley's two North American HS 125 distributors, Atlantic Aviation and AiResearch were renegotiated. Since Atlantic Aviation was already a franchised Beech distributor, it was agreed that the firm would continue to sell and service the BH 125 along with other planes of the Beech Aircraft Corporation. However, AiResearch sold planes which were directly competitive with both Beechcraft Hawker and the Beech Aircraft Corporation lines. Due to well-established relations with Beech competitors, AiResearch management decided to dissociate their firm with the sales of Beech products but continue to operate as a service facility for the BH 125.

At the close of 1973, the Beechcraft Hawker line consisted of two planes, the BH 125–400, which was scheduled to be phased out, and the BH 125–600. Although production and marketing of the original "125" had already been discontinued, the planes still in operation were serviced by Beechcraft Hawker distributors. The BH 125–400 had a maximum capacity of 11 passengers, depending on the amount of cabin space and seating arrangements requested by the buyer. It was powered by two Rolls-Royce/Bristol Viper 522 engines which developed 3,360 pounds static thrust per engine. This gave the plane a maximum cruise speed of

---

[4] Erwin J. Bulban, "HS-125 Paves Way for Beech Expansion," *Aviation Week & Space Technology* (January 5, 1970), p. 21.

**The BH 125–400 business jet**

**The BH 125–600 business jet**

434 knots[5] at 31,000 feet and power to climb to an altitude of 35,000 feet in 25 minutes with a 23,300-pound load (maximum payload plus fuel). The manufacturer's suggested list price for the aircraft, fully equipped, was $1.2 million.

The BH 125–600, introduced in September 1972, extended both the capacity and performance of the BH 125/400. While it was only 3 feet longer (50 feet, 5-¾ inches overall length) and seated up to 3 more passengers than the "400," the new plane incorporated some significant improvements. Its two Viper 601 turbojet engines developed 3,750 pounds static thrust per engine, which gave it a 20 percent greater payload, a 24 percent faster climb, an increase in range of about 10 percent, and nearly 5 percent greater speed than the "400." Maximum takeoff

---

[5] A knot equals a speed of 1 nautical mile per hour. A nautical mile equals 6,080.20 feet.

weight (maximum payload plus fuel) was also increased (by 1700 pounds) to 25,000 pounds. Manufacturer's suggested list price for the "600" was $1.5 million. The company had announced late in 1972 that first-year production of the BH 125–600 would be 30 units, 20 of which were to be sold to customers in North America.

Introduction of the "600" series raised the question of what would become of the "400" series. Beechcraft Hawker executives wanted to retain the 400's to compete with Rockwell's Sabre 400 and, to a lesser degree, with the Falcon 10 and the Learjet 25 (see Exhibit 1). However, it was reported in the trade press in November 1972 that Hawker Siddeley had stopped production of the 400's, and if production were resumed start-up costs would drive their price up close to that of the 600's.[6]

## The U.S. aircraft market

The total market for aircraft in the United States is divided into three large components: General Aviation, Commercial Aviation (scheduled flights), and Military Aviation (Government). The market for business aircraft is a major segment of the General Aviation market and the market for business jets is a subsegment of the business aircraft market.

## General aviation[7]

In 1971 scheduled airlines served only 542 of the nation's 10,639 airports, boarding more than 90 percent of their passengers at only 100 cities. All scheduled airlines combined operated with only 2,642 aircraft. By contrast, the approximately 131,149 aircraft operating in U.S. since 1968 belonging to the General Aviation category have carried as many people each year as were carried by all scheduled airlines combined and even today carry one of every three inter-city passengers. Moreover, general aviation pilots logged 25.4 million hours in 1971, four times as many as all commercial airline pilots.

This important category of domestic civil aviation is composed of business aircraft, nonscheduled commercial aircraft, agricultural aircraft, personal aircraft, and aircraft used for instructional purposes.

*Business aircraft.* This segment includes all aircraft flown by a business firm for transportation required by its operations. In many instances these planes are flown by professional pilots, although they may be flown by properly licensed company executives. As a rule, the larger higher-performance planes are flown by professional pilots. Aircraft owned by

---

[6] *Business and Commercial Aviation* (November 1972), p. 49.

[7] Sources: *FAA Statistical Handbook,* Department of Transportation, Federal Aviation Administration (1972), pp. 47, 101, 212. *Handbook of Airline Statistics,* Civil Aeronautics Board (1971), p. 407.

**EXHIBIT 1.   Business and nonscheduled commercial jet aircraft, 1973**

| Manufacturer | Model | Passenger capacity | Payload WMF (lb.) | Field Length (ft.) | Cruising altitude (ft.) | Basic price ($) |
|---|---|---|---|---|---|---|
| Cessna.................... | Citation | 7–8 | 1,109 | 3,575 | 35,000 | 725,000 |
| Gates Learjet............... | 24D | 8 | 934 | 3,917 | 45,000 | 863,000 |
| Gates Learjet............... | 25B | 10 | 1,719 | 5,186 | 45,000 | 966,765 |
| Gates Learjet............... | 25C | 6 | 579 | 5,186 | 45,000 | 1,026,085 |
| Hansa..................... | HFB320 | 12 | 1,067 | 5,500 | 38,000 | 890,000 |
| Israel..................... | Westwind 1123 | 8–10 | 589 | 5,350 | 41,000 | 1,050,000 |
| Rockwell.................. | Sabre 40A | 10 | 2,110 | 4,900 | 40,000 | 1,145,000 |
| Rockwell.................. | Sabre 60 | 9 | 2,110 | 5,050 | 41,000 | 1,496,000 |
| Rockwell.................. | Sabre 75 | 12 | 2,320 | 5,400 | 39,000 | 1,800,000 |
| Falcon.................... | 10 | 7 | 1,817 | 5,050 | n.a. | n.a. |
| Falcon.................... | E | 10 | 2,880 | 6,400 | 35,000 | 1,700,000 |
| Falcon.................... | F | 10 | 2,210 | 5,250 | 35,000 | 1,750,000 |
| Beechcraft Hawker.......... | 125–400 | 7–11 | 1,861 | 5,450 | 41,000 | 1,300,000 |
| Beechcraft Hawker.......... | 125–600 | 9–14 | 2,263 | 5,350 | 41,000 | 1,592,000 |
| Lockheed.................. | Jetstar | 12 | 2,604 | 6,000 | 35,000 | 1,750,000 |
| BAC...................... | 111S400 | 25–84 | 3,598 | 7,200 | 31,000 | 2,000,000 |
| BAC...................... | 111S500 | 25–114 | 10,998 | 7,900 | 31,000 | 5,200,000 |
| Douglas................... | DC–9S10 | 20–90 | 1,350 | 5,700 | 35,000 | 2,970,000 |
| Douglas................... | DC–9S20 | 20–90 | 3,396 | 4,750 | 35,000 | 3,520,000 |
| Grumman.................. | Gulfstream II | 19 | 3,600 | 5,000 | 43,000 | 3,204,000 |
| Fokker.................... | F–28 | 20 | 1,019 | 5,500 | 31,000 | n.a. |
| Boeing.................... | 737–200 | 20 | 6,600 | 6,570 | 30,000 | n.a. |
| Boeing.................... | 727–100 | 20 | 6,810 | 7,760 | 30,000 | n.a. |

SOURCE: Compiled from *Business and Commercial Aviation* (April 1973), pp. 60–63.

company executives that are flown primarily on company business also would be included in this category.

The 1.3 billion miles flown by business aircraft in 1971 constituted 36 percent of the total miles flown by general aviation craft, making this the most important segment of the general aviation market. General aviation statistics published by FAA in 1972 indicated that of the 18,035 multi-engine aircraft in the general aviation category, 65 percent were used for some phase of business and executive transportation. In the opinion of FAA, business aviation constitutes the most promising and fertile growth segment of civil aviation.

> The attractiveness of aircraft for business transportation, coupled with the introduction of less expensive smaller-type turbine aircraft, substantiates the premise that the more significant areas of growth in civil aviation will emanate mainly from the business aviation segment.[8]

Business aircraft include a variety of planes of different passenger capacities, performance characteristics, and price. For marketing purposes they can be divided into four classes: single and multiengine piston aircraft, turboprops, jets, and helicopters. Although single and multiengine

[8] *FAA Statistical Handbook of Aviation* (1966), pp. 92 f.

piston craft represent the most important class in terms of the total number of planes in operation, turboprops and jets have shown the fastest rate of growth over the past ten years. The distribution of aircraft ownership among the 1300 largest corporations in the United States is shown in Exhibit 2. The largest corporations are, of course, but a fraction of the approximately 2 million corporations doing business in the United States in 1972.

*Nonscheduled commercial aircraft.* Planes included in this classification are those used in air-taxi operations, crop dusting, and other agriculturally related operations, and such specialized commercial applications as aerial photography, mapping, and weather reconnaissance.

*Personal aircraft.* These are planes owned by individuals for their own pleasure rather than for business, and are not for hire.

*Instructional aircraft.* Planes operated by university and private flying schools, which are not part of a charter service, generally belong to this category.

**EXHIBIT 2.** Distribution of business aircraft ownership, 1972

| Aircraft type | 1,000 Largest industrial corporations* | 300 Largest nonindustrial corporations† | Total |
|---|---|---|---|
| Single and multiengine.................... | 421 | 62 | 483 |
| Turboprop............................. | 408 | 64 | 472 |
| Jets.................................. | 468 | 88 | 556 |
| Helicopter............................ | 55 | 13 | 68 |
| All types............................. | 1,352 | 227 | 1,579 |

\* Only 432 of the 1,000 largest industrial corporations operate private aircraft. SOURCE: *Business and Commercial Aviation* (November 1972), pp. 57–67.

† Only 78 of the 300 largest nonindustrial corporations operate private aircraft. SOURCE: Ibid. (September 1972), pp. 64–71.

The jet segment of the business aviation market is composed of 15 manufacturers which in 1973 offered 24 models for sale. Comparative data on configuration, performance, and prices are given in Exhibit 1. At the low end of the price scale (about $700,000) jets compete with turboprops that have comparable seating capacity, superior short-field performance, and greater fuel economy, but lack the speed and prestige of the jets.

There are several types of business jets, but due to performance, cost, seating capacity, and other features all are not in direct competition with each other. For example, the Learjet is smaller and less expensive than the BH 125, which would place it in a slightly different market segment. The larger size and higher price of the BH 125 would generally restrict it to larger companies with greater aviation needs than those whose requirements could be met by the Learjet and other smaller business jets. This circumstance tends to limit the market potential of the BH 125.

A widespread practice in the purchase of business aircraft is the use of competitive bids. Through the investigation of published material, perhaps supplemented by interviews with salesmen and consultation with other company personnel, and sometimes outside aviation consultants, the purchasing department of a company assembles a set of specifications which define the passenger capacity, payload capability, and performance characteristics desired. Those in a company who are thought to have the most influence on these specifications are the professional pilots who fly company planes, pilot executives who may fly company-owned planes, and the nonpilot executives whose responsibilities require frequent air travel.

When assembled and properly approved, the "specs" are then circulated to a number of manufacturers who are invited to submit bids. The manufacturer who can meet the buyer's specifications at the lowest price generally receives the order.[9] Specifications which include price ceilings may eliminate some manufacturers from consideration. Otherwise, several manufacturers might be invited to participate in the bidding.

Specifications drawn up by a purchasing department are likely to be influenced by economic considerations such as the lowest total cost per nautical mile consistent with requirements for safety and convenience. Although a person can be transported less expensively an a scheduled airliner than a private plane, he is obliged to match his own schedule with that of the airline. Since this can rarely be a perfect match, travel by scheduled airline is almost invariably accompanied by hours of waiting at terminals. A variety of distractions and inconveniences make it difficult for even the most experienced traveler to use such time productively. As a result, much of it is wasted. A private plane, particularly one spacious enough to permit on-board conferences, not only can conserve substantial amounts of executive time but affords the kind of convenience which fosters more productive use of the time which cannot be saved.

Since scheduled airlines serve only 542 of the nation's 12,639 airports, business jets with short-field capability offer the advantage of air transportation to cities inaccessible by commercial airline. Avoiding travel by train and personal automobile saves executive time and constitutes an important economic consideration.

If economy is the dominant motive, turboprops are strongly competitive with jets. Turboprops in the 7 to 12 passenger range are available from $429,000 to $700,000. A "top-of-the-line" turboprop is about equal to the lowest priced jet. So far as interiors and instrumentation are concerned, there is little difference between the two types of aircraft, although the turboprop is usually a larger aircraft than the small jet. Both can be equipped to suit the preference of the buyer.

---

[9] The lowest bid might not receive the order if the buyer's previous experience with the vendor had not been favorable and there was little difference among the lowest bids.

Economy may not be the dominant factor influencing the buyer's specifications. Since business executives are mortals, economy may well share priority with another motive dear to the hearts of mortals—prestige. The stronger this motive, the more likely specifications are to stress speed, operating range, and high altitude ceilings associated with jet aircraft. The personal preferences of a company's chief executive also play an important part in determining specifications.

The prestige of the jets stems in part from the new technology they represent. The turboprop, for example, was first introduced in the early 1960s and is the echo of yesterday's technology, not today's. Since jets are faster and quieter than turboprops, they do offer greater savings in travel time and greater comfort during travel than turboprops of comparable size. Moreover, jet planes do have some compensating cost advantages, such as slower depreciation (because they are newer) and lower maintenance costs.

The availability of competent ground support service at convenient locations also is a factor likely to be emphasized by purchasing departments. On the other hand, short-field performance, a forte of the turboprops, may be a dominant factor if the company's plants or branches are widely dispersed and/or located in communities with limited airport facilities.

## Beechcraft Hawker marketing

The foundation of marketing strategy at Beechcraft Hawker has been product performance and the company's unmatched ground support. The former has been highlighted by such copy headlines as "the no-compromise jet" and "the best dollar-for-dollar value anywhere in corporate aviation." In North America Beechcraft Hawker jets have been sold through 20 distributors, 7 of which combine sales and service. Within this network 13 are independent sales agents who also sell planes of other manufacturers, while 7 are either owned or controlled by Beechcraft Hawker. The location of these outlets and service facilities is shown in Exhibit 3.

The major problem facing those who plan marketing at Beechcraft Hawker is that of identifying the real decision makers in companies that are prospective buyers of private jet planes. It was known from the analysis of past sales, for example, that the person who made the initial inquiry regarding a purchase usually was not the one who signed the purchase order or authorized payment. Moreover, a third or fourth person typically was included in the demonstration ride or otherwise consulted regarding the purchase. In some instances the plane was not even registered in the name of the company whose personnel had negotiated the transaction, but in the name of a subsidiary company.

It was believed that many such aircraft were purchased solely on economic grounds. Typically, companies interested in purchasing a busi-

EXHIBIT 3. Beechcraft Hawker jet sales and service network in North America

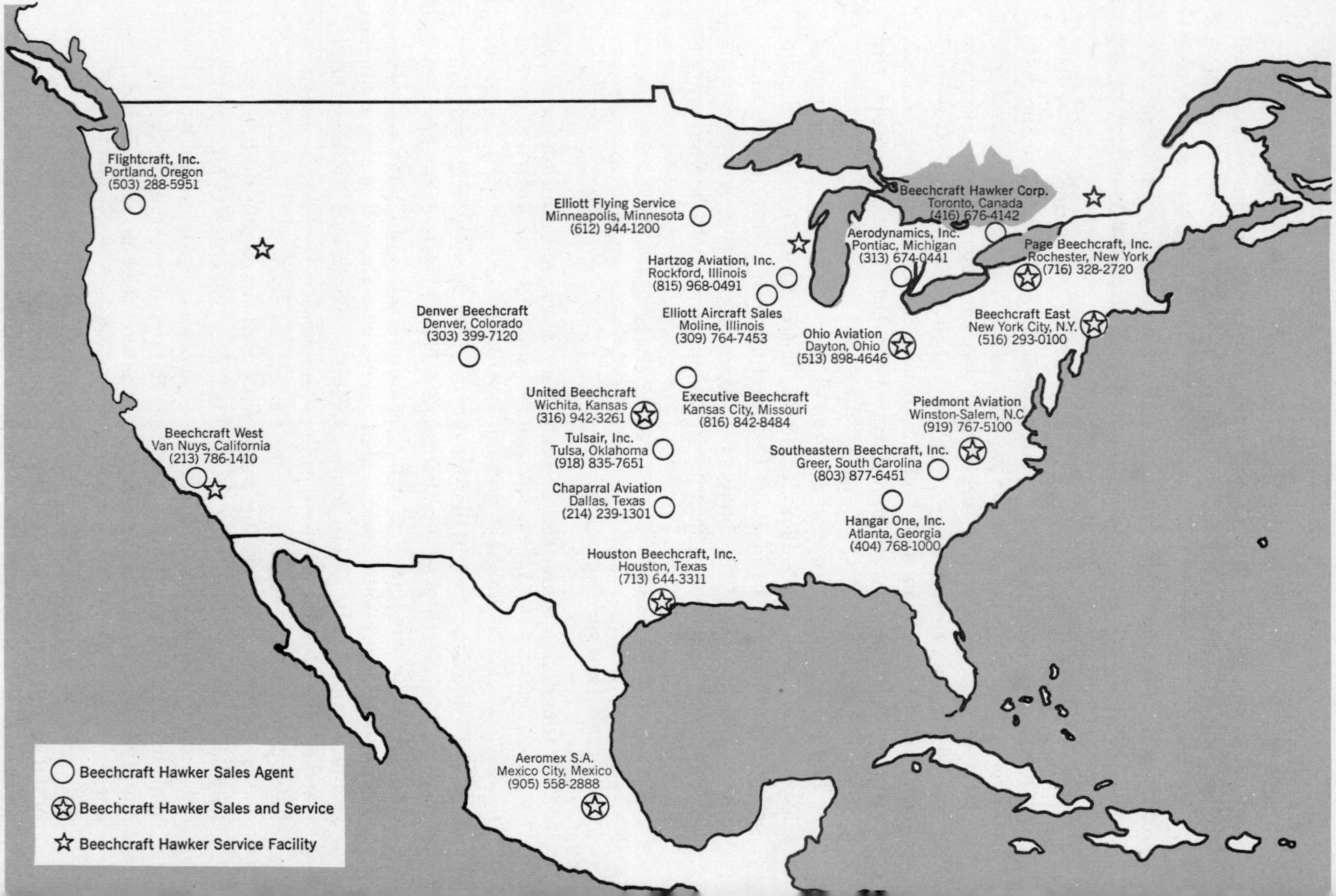

Beechcraft Hawker Corp.
Toronto, Canada
(416) 676-6142

Page Beechcraft, Inc.
Rochester, New York
(716) 328-2720

Beechcraft East
New York City, N.Y.
(516) 293-0100

Aerodynamics, Inc.
Pontiac, Michigan
(313) 674-0441

Piedmont Aviation
Winston-Salem, N.C.
(919) 767-5100

Ohio Aviation
Dayton, Ohio
(513) 898-4646

Southeastern Beechcraft, Inc.
Green, South Carolina
(803) 877-6451

Hangar One, Inc.
Atlanta, Georgia
(404) 768-1000

Hartzog Aviation, Inc.
Rockford, Illinois
(815) 968-0491

Elliott Aircraft Sales
Moline, Illinois
(309) 764-7453

Executive Beechcraft
Kansas City, Missouri
(816) 842-8484

Elliott Flying Service
Minneapolis, Minnesota
(612) 944-1200

United Beechcraft
Wichita, Kansas
(316) 942-3261

Tulsair, Inc.
Tulsa, Oklahoma
(918) 835-7651

Houston Beechcraft, Inc.
Houston, Texas
(713) 644-3311

Denver Beechcraft
Denver, Colorado
(303) 399-7120

Chaparral Aviation
Dallas, Texas
(214) 239-1301

Aeromex S.A.
Mexico City, Mexico
(905) 558-2888

Beechcraft West
Van Nuys, California
(213) 786-1410

Flightcraft, Inc.
Portland, Oregon
(503) 288-5951

○ Beechcraft Hawker Sales Agent

⊛ Beechcraft Hawker Sales and Service

☆ Beechcraft Hawker Service Facility

**EXHIBIT 4**

**EXHIBIT 5**

# Five things you can tel

# your boss about value:

First of all, you'll probably want to mention the inherent value of the Beechcraft Hawker Jet 125-600. He'll be interested in the fact that you can fly a 1,600 nm trip with all 8 passenger chairs filled.

Simply stated (you can tell him), your "full fuel" range with the BH 125-600 is the same as your "full passengers" range...a unique feature that is one of the reasons the BH 125-600 is the best dollar-for-dollar value anywhere in corporate aviation.

The second thing you can tell your boss about value is the importance of mission flexibility...the ability to go wherever there's a need to go.

Short fields, unimproved strips, and high elevation...a combination that could be a problem with other business jets.

Again, your boss will immediately see the unquestioned value of the BH 125-600's unique lift-dump flap system that permits FAR 91 landings at typical landing weight (17,000 lbs.) in distances as short as 2,130 ft. ...without the problems and limitations of thrust reversers.

And the value of being able to operate to and from dirt and gravel strips.

And the value of the power that permits a balanced field length for takeoff of 5,350 ft. at full gross weight.

Third: Tell him how important it is to have a well-designed, efficient and comfortable flight deck, like the BH 125-600's.

And point out that handling ease becomes a major factor to a pilot, particularly during the approach phase.

Are these things of value to him? You bet they are, because they make your job easier.

Fourth: Impress upon him the significance of design simplicity and fail-safe engineering in the areas of maintenance and safety. And use the BH 125-600 as an excellent example of what a corporate airplane should be like under the skin.

The fifth thing you can tell your boss about value is "Be comfortable."

He's probably got his own ideas about comfort, but you've seen a lot of corporate jets and you know that there's not another one in the same price range that can compare with the BH 125-600 in terms of headroom, shoulder-room or legroom.

Or individual passenger comfort, as reflected in the fine leathers, fabrics and carpeting. And the incredibly quiet cabin.

Or passenger convenience, as shown by the completely private lavatory, the separate baggage compartment, the completely equipped galley.

Value.

Value in five significant areas that are vitally important to your corporate top management. And yet there's still more to BH 125-600 story.

Get the full colorful and impressive story by calling Lloyd W. Harris, President, Beechcraft Hawker Corporation, today (316) 685-6211. Or write on your company letterhead, requesting information on the Beechcraft Hawker Jet 125-600...the best dollar-for-dollar value anywhere in corporate aviation.

Beechcraft Hawker Corporation
A subsidiary of
Beech Aircraft Corporation
Wichita, Kansas 67201

**EXHIBIT 6**

# The No-Compromise Business Jet.

Most companies...maybe yours...have been compromising on their business missions for years. Not compromising safety, of course, but sacrificing a little here in order to gain something else there.

For instance: Maybe you've been making a number of sacrifices to get speed alone. Or maybe you've been giving up comfort to get all-around performance. Or performance to get economy. Or perhaps you've reluctantly given up economy for comfort.

That's over now.

Because with the Beechcraft Hawker 125-600...the No-Compromise Business Jet...you can now apply your own high standards of impeccable quality to your business flying activities

With the 600, you can have it all: true jet performance, true operating economy, true executive comfort.

For instance:

The Beechcraft Hawker 600 can consistently achieve cruise speeds up to 517 mph.

The 600 can fly 1,850 miles nonstop, putting your business destinations within quick, easy reach.

The 600 can climb directly to 41,000 ft. to cruise over the weather in smooth, maximum performance air.

The 600 can operate from almost any kind of airport, including those with unpaved strips.

And, because of the 600's outstanding short-field

performance, you can utilize countless shorter strips you probably don't even consider now.

With this superior performance and mission flexibility, you might expect to compromise on passenger capacity or comfort...but you don't. The 600 will go with eight to ten passengers, a crew of two and baggage for everyone.

Furthermore, your Beechcraft Hawker 600's private cabin will be exquisitely handcrafted to meet your own personal preferences in cabinetry, fabrics and colors...as well as options and accessories.

One important, indisputable fact emerges from all of this: the 600 offers the most remarkable combination of performance, comfort and economy to appear in many years.

That's why the Beechcraft Hawker 600 represents the best value for money available anywhere to travel-oriented businessmen.

See the No-Compromise Business Jet soon. And stop compromising on your business missions.

**600 Demonstrator On Tour Now!** To make it easier for you to ask the questions you probably want to ask, Beechcraft Hawker has launched a continuous continental tour through the United States, Canada and Mexico with the 600 Demonstrator. To schedule the 600 for a private demonstration mission, call Lloyd Harris, President, Beechcraft Hawker Corp. at (316) 685-6211 today.

## Beechcraft Hawker Corporation

A subsidiary of Beech Aircraft Corporation, Wichita, Kansas 67201

EXHIBIT 7

**This is the best value-for-money available today to travel-oriented businessmen:**

**Beechcraft Hawker Jet 125-600**

ness jet evaluate several different types to determine which plane's capability best matches the needs of the company. Yet, sales representatives often expressed the view that occasionally emotion was a factor in the decision to buy a particular plane, for planes have a natural appeal to an individual's desire for pleasure and prestige.

Corporate marketing personnel doubted that emotion and prestige were any but minor aspects in the decision to purchase a particular business jet. They regarded the business/pleasure/prestige syndrome as so involved and entwined as to render fruitless any attempt to determine which element exercised the dominant influence in a particular purchase transaction.

As a result of these uncertainties concerning purchase motivations, Beechcraft Hawker advertising stressed the themes of performance, convenience, and economy. Typical ad copy included such statements as the following (see Exhibits 4, 5, 6, 7):

You can carry a full complement of passengers, crew and baggage and still achieve the maximum, non-stop range of 1850 miles.

The 600 can climb directly to 41,000 feet to cruise over the weather in smooth, maximum performance air.

The 600 can operate from almost any kind of airport, including those with unpaved strips.

. . . because of the 600's outstanding short-field performance, you can utilize countless shorter strips you probably don't even consider now.

In addition, copy typically emphasized the ability to make one's own flight schedule and go wherever there was a need to go, and also the comfort of traveling in a quiet cabin with plenty of headroom, shoulder-room and legroom. The copy "punch line" was an invitation to the reader to ask about a demonstration ride by calling the company president directly or writing to him on one's company letterhead. Beechcraft Hawker's ad agency also prepared a richly illustrated brochure containing detailed performance data on Beechcraft-Hawker planes and explaining the various options available in interiors and avionics.

Marketing effort was not limited to the demonstration ride, personal presentation, and promotional literature, because the flight characteristics of most jet aircraft are quite similar. Consequently, it was also necessary to systematically research potential customers in order to identify their particular needs. This placed a great deal of importance on coordination between research and sales. Since the capability profile of a plane must fit the particular needs of a customer, a detailed marketing program must be developed for each bona fide prospect. The development of such programs represent the principal thrust of marketing effort at Beechcraft Hawker.

# THE CATERPILLAR TRACTOR COMPANY

In 1965 the Caterpillar Tractor Company, through an exchange of stock, acquired the Towmotor Corporation, a pioneer in the field of industrial lift trucks. When the merger was completed, Caterpillar management was faced with the problem of how the two companies, both with extensive but different distribution systems, would operate under one corporate umbrella. Since both systems served the entire United States, some way must be found to satisfactorily integrate them.

The legal environment posed a different question. The Occupational Safety and Health Act (OSHA) passed by Congress in 1970 established comprehensive in-plant and equipment safety standards which included in their coverage materials-handling equipment. Materials-handling always had been a safety-conscious industry, but OSHA standards represented minimal ones, and provisions of the act permitted the several states to develop and enforce their own safety standards. State safety regulations were to be consistent with federal ones, but they could also be more stringent. Companies with national distribution systems were thus faced with the possibility of having to comply with as many as 50 different sets of safety specifications in designing their products.

While different safety specifications could undoubtedly be met, the necessity of doing so would place the national producer at a disadvantage in competing with the small regional producer. Varying safety standards would have the effect of forcing a firm like Towmotor, which competed with a number of smaller producers, to either (a) conform to the most stringent set of standards, charging customers in states with less-stringent safety specifications for designs they could legally forgo, or (b) introduce additional lines (or a string of options), which could seriously compromise the economies of scale that represent the large manufacturer's chief advantage.

## THE COMPANIES

Caterpillar at this time was the largest American firm engaged in the manufacture and sale of earthmoving equipment. Company sales in 1965 were $1.3 billion, which represented about 65 percent of total U.S.

volume of this kind of machinery. During recent years the company had diversified into the manufacture and marketing of diesel engines, gas turbines, electric sets, and welding equipment, in addition to expanding its line of earthmoving equipment. But it was still essentially an earthmoving equipment company. Sales were running well ahead of production capacity and the firm was committed to a $600-million building program over the 1966–69 period.

Towmotor, with annual sales of about $75 million, was a family-owned firm. It had manufactured the first forklift truck in 1933 and for the next decade had enjoyed a steady growth. World War II placed tremendous emphasis on methods of materials handling that were quick and economical of manpower. This emphasis continued after the war and Towmotor sales benefited from it. During the middle 1960s total U.S. sales of lift trucks grew substantially but at a decreasing rate, as shown in the following table.

**Change in total U.S. sales of lift trucks 1963–66)**

| Year | Percentage increase |
|------|---------------------|
| 1963 | 36 |
| 1964 | 21 |
| 1965 | 20 |
| 1966 | 18 |

Four firms accounted for 80 percent of the industrial lift truck market in 1965. Clark Equipment Company (Industrial Truck Division) was the dominant supplier in the market, followed by Hyster Company (Industrial Truck Operations), Eaton Corporation (Industrial Truck Division), and Towmotor—in that order.

Towmotor did not make or sell electric lift trucks, which put it at some disadvantage where fumes or noise were important factors. The company also was weak in foreign sales. Only about 10 percent of its volume was marketed abroad. On the other hand, almost half of Caterpillar's volume was in foreign sales. Probably this was a significant factor in bringing about the merger.

## INDUSTRY CHARACTERISTICS, 1970

Materials-handling equipment may be divided into four broad product categories: elevators (S.I.C. 3534), conveyors (S.I.C. 3535), cranes, hoists, and monorails (S.I.C. 3536), and industrial trucks (S.I.C. 3537). A profile of the industry is given in Exhibit 1.

The various models of industrial lift trucks are identified in Exhibit 2. A relatively few models of this equipment account for most of the sales. The proliferation of models is explained by the early practice of virtually custom-building any type of vehicle wanted by the customer. This was

**EXHIBIT 1.   Materials-handling industry, 1970**

Value of U.S. shipments (millions of dollars)..................... 2,560
Number of establishments..................................... 1,082
Employment (thousands)......................................    87
Exports as percent of U.S. shipments..........................   8.0
Imports as percent of estimated U.S. purchases.................   4.2
Annual growth rates, 1963–70 (percent)
    Value of product shipments (current dollars).................   8.5
    Value of exports (current dollars)...........................   8.1
    Value of imports (current dollars)...........................  28.0
    Employment...............................................   5.4
Major producing areas.......... Middle Atlantic, North Central,
                       and Western states.

the only way some of the smaller manufacturers could break into the market, and once a new type of vehicle was available, larger manufacturers were under pressure to add a similar model or option to their own lines. For example, electric-powered, counterbalanced, rider forklift trucks may be purchased with either solid or pneumatic tires. Most of these vehicles are equipped with solid tires, however, because pneumatic tires are advantageous only for outdoor, off-road applications, and electric trucks offer superior performance in indoor applications where solid tires are preferred. Yet, if one manufacturer of electric trucks offers a tire-wheel option, others are under pressure to do so.

Very few of the 70-odd manufacturers of industrial lift trucks, the largest of which are listed in Exhibit 3, started their businesses with these vehicles. Most were initially in other types of businesses and diversified into the lift truck market. Allis Chalmers, for example, was initially in heavy equipment, Otis Materials Company was initially a maker of elevators and conveyors, and the Eaton Corporation started business as a producer of automotive components.

Lift trucks are typically purchased as a fleet item and replaced on a regular basis. In terms of service, maintenance, operator training, and record keeping, it is advantageous for the user to have a "clean fleet" of one maker rather than an assortment of machines from a variety of manufacturers. This practice has worked to the advantage of manufacturers who entered the market early but to the disadvantage of those who later tried to gain a foothold in it. The "clean fleet" preference also has made it difficult to increase market share. Consequently, growth opportunities have been limited largely to new customers or new applications.

Another significant industry characteristic is that lift truck users tend to look to distributors for service and spare parts rather than to manufacturers. Although the market for lift truck spare parts is not as active as that for construction equipment, because the average wear and tear is not as great, the lift truck aftermarket is nevertheless a significant one. This is evidenced by the number of nongenuine parts manufactures active in the industry both here and abroad. Since many users of lift

**EXHIBIT 2.  Model assortment of industrial truck line**

### SOME REPRESENTATIVE TOWMOTOR MODELS

Powered Trucks (see drawings in this exhibit)
  Fork Lift Trucks (rider)
    Counterbalanced (electric, solid-tired)
    Counterbalanced (electric, pneumatic-tired)
    Counterbalanced (I.C.E., solid-tired)*
    Counterbalanced (I.C.E., pneumatic-tired)*
    Outrigger (electric)
    Side-Loader (electric)
    Side-Loader (I.C.E.)
    High-Lifter Loaders (extendable reach)
  Fork Lift Trucks (walkie)
    Counterbalanced (electric)
    Counterbalanced (I.C.E.)
    Outrigger (electric)
    Side-Loader (electric)
  Platform Trucks (rider)
    High-Lift (electric)
    High-Lift (I.C.E.)
    Low-Lift (electric)
    Low-Lift (I.C.E.)
    Low-Lift (electronically controlled)
  Platform Trucks (walkie)
    High-Lift (electric)
    Low-Lift (electric and I.C.E.)
  Straddle Carriers
    With Rigid Shoes*
    With Swinging Shoes*
    End Straddle
    With Crane and Trolley
    Straddle-Type Highway Trailer Frame
  Front-End Loaders
    Pneumatic-Tired†
    Crawler
  Non-Elevating Trucks
    Platform Trucks (rider)
    Platform Trucks (walkie)
  Special-Purpose Trucks
    Die Handling*
    Stock Selector*
    Vacuum Lift
    Maintenance–Production*
    Other
Auxiliary Attachments for Industrial Trucks (see drawings in this exhibit)
  Towmotor makes almost entire line of attachments.
Accessories for Industrial Trucks
  Towmotor makes cabs, overhead frame guards, operator foot guards, and
  mechanical back-up alarms.
Auxiliary Power Equipment
Non-Powered Trucks
  Two-wheel Hand Trucks
  Platform Hand Trucks
  Hand Lift Trucks
  Wheeled Shop Containers
  Dollies
Industrial Trailers
Industrial Tractors†
Components
  Wheels and Tires
  Casters
  Drives

* Product area of Towmotor.
† Product area of Caterpillar.
Notes: Counterbalanced, Outrigger, Side-Loader, and High-Lift Fork Lift
trucks can come in various combinations of telescoping or nontelescoping masts
that are tilting or nontilting.
  See drawings on following pages of powered industrial trucks and accessories
for powered industrial trucks.

**EXHIBIT 2.**    (*Continued*)

SOME REPRESENTATIVE TOWMOTOR MODELS

Model 860P
Gasoline or LP Gas

Model V41
Gasoline or LP Gas

Model T50B
Gasoline or LP Gas

Model AH–60
Diesel Powered

**EXHIBIT 2.**   (*Concluded*)

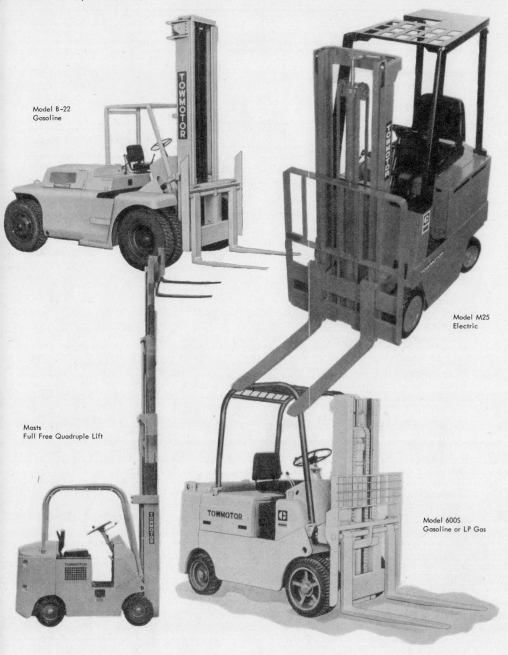

Model B-22
Gasoline

Model M25
Electric

Masts
Full Free Quadruple Lift

Model 600S
Gasoline or LP Gas

## EXHIBIT 3.  Companies competing with Towmotor in 1970

| Firms | Product Codes |
|---|---|
| Air Technical | 9, 12, 13 |
| Allis Chalmers | 1, 3, 5, 7, 9 |
| Alfab | 12 |
| American Pulley | 9, 13 |
| Barrett Cravens | 9, 12 |
| Camet | 5, 6 |
| Case | 5 |
| Champ | 5, 6, 7, 8, |
| Clark Equipment | 1, 2, 5, 6, 7, 9, 10, 11, 15 |
| Colson | 9, 15 |
| Crown Controls | 9, 12, 13, 15 |
| Blue Giant | 9, 15 |
| Datsun I.C.E. | 1, 2, 3, 4, 5, 6, 7, 8 |
| Deere | 5 |
| Drott | 10, 11 |
| Dunbar | 5, 6, 7, 8 |
| Eaton | 1, 2, 3, 4, 5, 6, 7, 8, 9, 10, 12, 13 |
| Economy | 13 |
| Elwell-Parker | 12, 13, 15 |
| Erickson | 5, 6, 7, 8, 12, 13 |
| E-Z Way | 1 |
| Ferguson | 10 |
| Grand Specialties | 9, 12, 13, 14, 15 |
| Harlo | 1 |
| Hartman | 15 |
| Hydromation | 13 |
| Henry | 5 |
| Hyster | 1, 5, 7, 11, |
| International Harvester | 1, 5 |
| Knickerbocker | 1, 2, 3, 4, 5, 6, 7, 8, 12 |
| Lange | 12, 13 |
| Lectro Lift | 1, 5 |
| Le Tourneau | 7 |
| Lewis Shepard | 9 |
| Lift Trucks | 9 |
| Loft-a-Lift | 15 |
| Lull | 5, 15 |
| Maycoa | 14 |
| Morgan Manufacturing | 5 |
| North American Manufacturing | 1 |
| Otis Material Handling | 1, 2, 3, 4, 5, 6, 7, 8, 12, 13 |
| P C M (Div Koehring) | 5 |
| Pettibone Mercury | 1, 2, 3, 4, 5, 12 |
| Prime Mover | 9 |
| Raymond | 9, 12, 13 |
| Revolator | 9, 12, 13 |
| Silent Hoist | 1, 2, 3, 4, 5, 6, 7, 8, 12 |
| Selma | 7, 10, 11, 15 |
| Southworth | 12 |
| Stratton | 9, 12, 15 |
| Taylor Machine Works | 7 |
| United Tractor | 15 |
| Warner & Swasey | 5 |
| West Bend | 9, 12, 14, 15 |
| White Industry | 1, 2, 3, 4, 5, 6, 7, 8, |
| Wright Hibbard | 12, 13 |

**EXHIBIT 3.** (*Continued*)

*Product codes:*

*Fork lift truck (rider), counterbalanced*

1.  solid-tire, telescoping mast, tilting
2.  solid-tire, telescoping mast, nontilting
3.  solid-tire, nontelescoping mast, tilting
4.  solid-tire, nontelescoping mast, nontilting
5.  pneumatic-tire, telescoping mast, tilting
6.  pneumatic-tire, telescoping mast, nontilting
7.  pneumatic-tire, nontelescoping mast, tilting
8.  pneumatic-tire, nontelescoping mast, nontilting

*Other types of industrial lift trucks*

9.  Platform Lift Truck, walkie, low-lift, electric
10. Straddle carriers, rigid shoe
11. Straddle carriers, swinging shoe
12. Die Handling truck (rider), high-lift, platform, w/mechanical die movers
13. Die Handling truck (rider), high-lift, platform, w/hydralic die movers
14. Stock Selector Truck w/right and left angle stocking
15. Maintenance–Production truck, combination platform truck and crane

SOURCE: "Buyer's Guide," *Modern Materials Handling*, June 1970.

trucks are small and look to one distributor for all their materials-handling needs, few distributors will agree to handle the trucks of one manufacturer exclusively.

Foreign competition comes chiefly from Japanese firms, particularly Datsun, Toyota, TMC (tradename of Togo Umpanki Co., Ltd.), and Komatzu. However, their presence is largely concentrated on the West Coast and their efforts center more in the used than the new truck market.

The most significant factor influencing demand for lift trucks would appear to be capital spending, which in turn is influenced by depreciation allowances, investment tax credits, and business optimism. Both data and common sense indicate that demand for this equipment varies inversely with labor productivity. The demand prediction for lift trucks in Asia is nil, but future expectations of growth for this market in Europe and the U.S. are optimistic. In the U.S. where wage rates are increasing faster than productivity, it is anticipated that strenuous efforts will be made to narrow or close this gap, and lift trucks are a significant factor in such effort. The Department of Commerce projections of demand for materials-handling equipment indicate that sales will reach $3.25 billion in 1975, compared to $2.55 billion in 1970, and will climb to $4.56 billion by 1980, an increase of 6 percent over 1970.

## THE PRODUCTS

Caterpillar products are strictly big-ticket items, varying in price from $17,500 to $186,000 per unit. They are technically complex and involve a high level of engineering know-how. Their purchase is apt to require a major decision by executives of the customer firm.

The major markets in which Caterpillar machines and equipment are sold include agriculture and forestry; local, state, and federal governments; mining; pipe lines; water management; and general construction. Although the average life of a piece of earthmoving equipment is about five years, many are in use for much longer periods of time. Such equipment usually gets rough use and repair, and maintenance service is constantly needed. During its working life, a piece of heavy machinery often requires spare parts and maintenance, the aggregate cost of which about equals its initial purchase price. Caterpillar makes and supplies about 150,000 different replacement parts for the machinery and equipment it manufactures. Other firms also are active in making and selling parts for Caterpillar-built products.

Caterpillar engines are used to power its own equipment and also are for sale as components to other equipment manufacturers, i.e., the OEM[1] market. Typically, the OEM customers handle the replacement parts and service requirements for diesel engines.

Towmotor products are much less expensive, much less complex, and are offered in a narrower assortment of models than that of Caterpillar. Towmotor lift trucks and straddle carriers are produced in about 65 different models, as compared with a Caterpillar product line of about 105 models. Five of the best-selling forklift models are shown in their typical work environments in Exhibit 4. As indicated here, the need for Towmotor products centers around the manufacturing, warehousing, and transportation industries.

While the aftermarket has been less important to Towmotor than to Caterpillar, replacement parts and service still represent significant sources of Towmotor revenue. The company maintains six factory-owned service outlets, located in New York, Chicago, Detroit, Philadelphia, Cleveland, and Newark. These outlets carry a complete parts inventory for the best-selling models and can handle any repair or maintenance problem except rebuilding motors.

## MARKETING ORGANIZATION

Towmotor marketed its products through about 90 manufacturers' agents, most of whom were located east of the Mississippi River. An agent often represented as many as 25 or 30 principals, who manufactured a variety of materials-handling equipment, such as walkie trucks, electric-powered trucks, conveyors, bins, shelving, and overhead buckets. Each operated within geographically limited territories.

Towmotor agents represented practically every conceivable variation

---

[1] Original Equipment Manufacturers.

**EXHIBIT 4.   Five popular Towmotor models**

in size and service capability. The large agents sold as many as 100 trucks per year, operated a lease business, sold service contracts on all equipment as a matter of policy, maintained a number of models on display, and carried a limited parts inventory for the most popular models. No more than 15 agents could be included in this category. At the other extreme were agents that sold no more than 1 or 2 trucks a year, had no models on display, carried no parts inventory, did not offer leasing contracts, and represented as few as 12 principals. All agents, large or small, located in the same city as a Towmotor service outlet typically referred all repair jobs to the service outlet rather than attempting to make the repairs themselves.

An agent's contract could be cancelled by either party within six

**EXHIBIT 5.    U.S. Commercial Division**

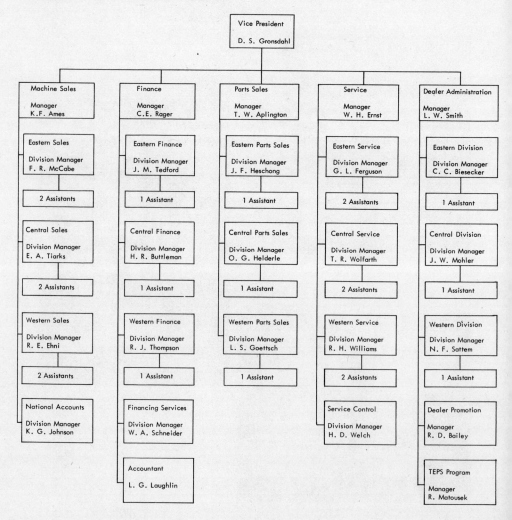

months after proper notification. But whether an agent who had held an agency for a number of years could be cancelled without compensation presented a touchy legal question and whether he *should* be dropped, except for due cause, involved a nice ethical question. Nor could the public relations aspect of such action be ignored.

Caterpillar had about 98 independent domestic distributor-dealers with about 305 outlets. This meant that the typical distributor had about two branches. In addition there were 19 agricultural supply houses with 20 outlets and one engine distributor. In all they employed about 12,000 people. The sales force of the average dealer numbered between six and eight salesmen. Average annual sales per dealer was about $12,400,000. Typically, a distributor-dealer had to have about $2,600,000 of his own money invested in the business in addition to a line of credit of about $3,300,000. Average return on a dealer's investment was about 20 percent.

**EXHIBIT 6.   Market Development Division**

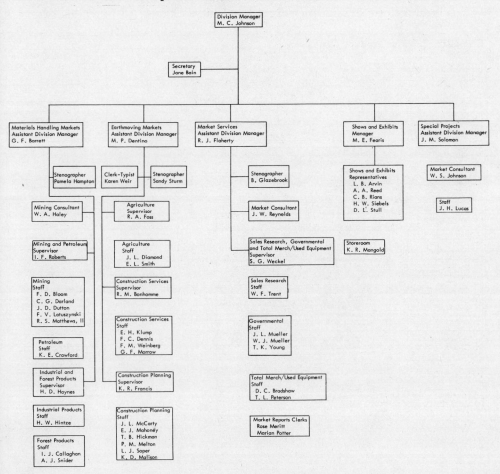

Caterpillar protected its distributors by refusing to sell direct, a policy which had been enforced consistently over a long period of time. As a result of this policy and of the general attractiveness of the Caterpillar line, the company's relations with many of its distributors were long standing, most of the distributorships were old established businesses, and distributor turnover was very low. Typically, a distributor handled only Caterpillar products except where additional lines were needed to meet competition. A number of Caterpillar distributors had for many years handled Hyster forklift trucks and enjoyed very amicable working relations with the Hyster Company.

Caterpillar's domestic marketing organization included the Commercial Division under a vice president and the General Offices Marketing Department, also under a vice president. The head of the Commercial Division supervised the work of five functional department managers for finance, parts sales service, machine sales, and dealer administration, as shown in Exhibit 5. Additionally, each function was divided geographically into three divisions covering the United States. All functional de-

**EXHIBIT 7.  The Product Division**

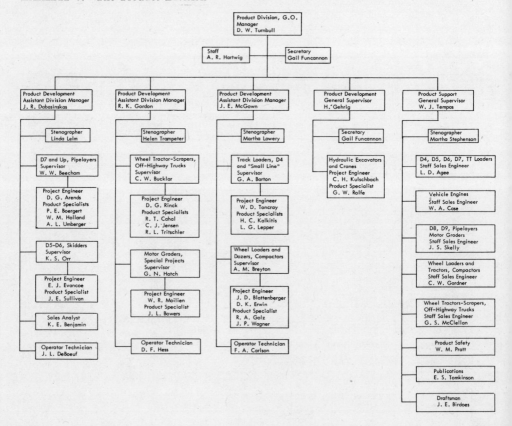

# EXHIBIT 8. Sales Training Division

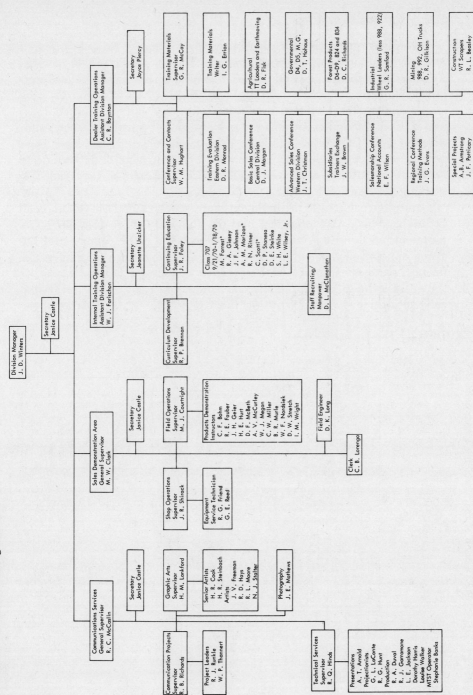

* Cat Overseas Employees.

**EXHIBIT 9. Advertising Division of the Marketing Department**

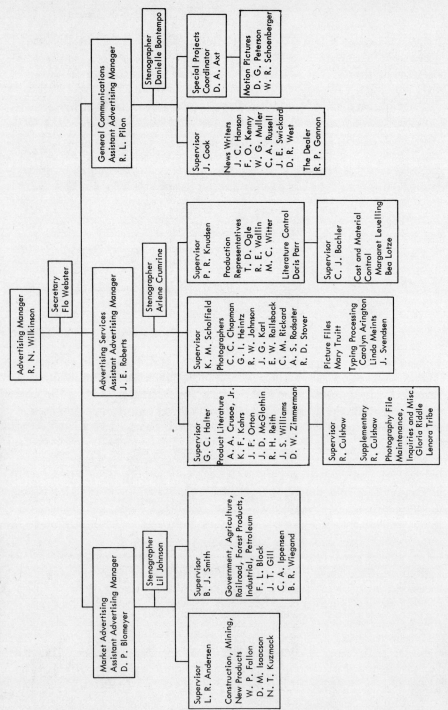

\* On medical leave.

partments except finance had field representatives living in the field, where they maintained continuous contact with dealers and customers. These field representatives served in an advisory capacity to dealers, each working in his area of functional responsibility.

The General Offices Marketing Department was a staff function which consisted of the Market Development Division (Exhibit 6), the Product Division (Exhibit 7), the Sales Training Division (Exhibit 8), and the Advertising Division (Exhibit 9). Each of these divisions had worldwide responsibility for providing assistance and functional direction to its counterparts at the various Caterpillar marketing subsidiaries throughout the world.

# COLLIS COMPANY

The Collis Company, located in Cincinnati, Ohio, manufactured a variety of paper products, both consumer and industrial, among the nine divisions within the company. Alarmed that the company's gross profit margin had dropped 10 percent in the previous two years and believing that their sales expenses were excessive, the management introduced in November a new system of sales reporting and trade analysis. This system, which gave necessary and useful information of sales costs, as well as competition and market potential, was adopted by several divisions of the company but resisted by others. The industrial specialties division, particularly, objected strenuously to the new sales reporting system. Six months after its introduction A. M. Plumley, general manager of sales, was considering the best means of securing the complete cooperation of the various sales divisions, especially the industrial specialties division.

The Collis Company manufactured among its nine divisions corrugated and solid fiber shipping containers, corrugated and solid fiber packing materials, grocery bags and sacks, folding cartons, wrapping paper, asphalt laminated paper, folding paraffined cartons, and a line of industrial specialties, including insulating material and board and paper specialties.

During the previous ten years, the company had greatly expanded its plant and equipment. At the beginning of the period, 72 percent of the company's output was used for food packaging, but after that year the company tried to achieve stability through product diversification. The result was that by the end of the period no one industry consumed more than 32 percent of the output.

The typical sales organization for a division included a divisional sales manager, in charge of all selling activities within the division, and under him at least one senior and one junior salesman.

The old sales reporting form had remained essentially unchanged since its introduction 18 years before. This sales report consisted of five duplicate copies in colors white, yellow, red, blue, and green, routed by color as office copy, salesman's copy, laboratory copy, file copy, and the copy to the vice president of sales. These reports were very unsatisfactory, because they gave only the barest information, such as the firm called on, date, salesman, person interviewed, and brief resumé of the interview. These resumés varied greatly, including such extraneous material as guest entertainment as well as desired information on customer needs, purchases, and so forth.

This sales reporting system was unsatisfactory in that the report gave little market data of value; difficulty was encountered in that the salesmen failed to use common units of measurement; and the form was not conducive to an orderly account of the interview. Also, since the company required every salesman to submit a sales report for each call made, the resulting number of reports was such that the sales managers did not have sufficient time to examine them in detail. The salesmen themselves soon realized that their reports were not being read, and many of them neglected to fill out the forms, or did so only in a perfunctory manner. Several top executives agreed that the company needed a new sales report form that would be more accurate, more flexible, more easily prepared by the salesmen, and would provide adequate market data.

Several of the executives concerned also felt that the company's weekly expense report needed revision, since it neglected certain data and was too detailed on other items, such as automobile expenses.

After thorough study of forms used by similar companies, Robert S. Dearfield, director of marketing research, developed a new trade report, shown in Exhibits 1 and 2. Every Collis Company salesman was required to fill out this trade report once a year for each of his customers.

Mr. Dearfield also developed a new combined weekly call and expense report; on one side was printed the expense report, and on the reverse side (Exhibit 2) the weekly call report. The weekly call report summarized a salesman's weekly calls, and each salesman was to send it to his sales manager at the end of the week. Combining the expense and weekly call reports into one form was considered advantageous, not only in that the company could more easily correlate a salesman's expenses to his trips and calls made, but also in that the use of this new form required the Collis Company salesmen to complete their weekly call reports before they could submit their expense reports for repayment. Salesmen were not reimbursed for expenses until they completed the reports.

The market research department transferred the data from the annual customer trade reports to sort cards for ready reference and to punch cards for machine analysis. Thus, for each customer, the Collis Company had available data on type of customer (manufacturer, processor, distributor), annual requirements, size, salesman handling the account,

**EXHIBIT 1A**

Salesman

Date of Interview

COLLIS COMPANY

Date Written

Trade Report

Firm

Interviewed

Sales, Service or Development Information, Summary first, then details

| |
|---|
| Sales Admin. |
| Sales Div. |
| Laboratory |
| File |
| Patent Dept. |
| Cincinnati |

Routing

| |
|---|
| 1 |
| 2 |
| 3 |
| 4 |

| |
|---|
| Initial Report |
| Revised Data |
| Service Call |

Typed by

---------------

Date ----------

Confirmed
by Letter of

---------------

Is Market Information up to date? Check Reverse Side.

customer code number, major supplier, locations, Standard Industrial Classification Code, products purchased from the company, and the end use of purchases.

The major problem in the use of these new report forms lay in selling the idea to the salesmen and gaining their willing cooperation. While his department was preparing the new system for use throughout the company, Mr. Dearfield met with C. J. Cox, vice president in charge of sales, Mr. Plumley, general manager of sales, and the sales managers of the nine divisions to explain the plan, what it had accomplished in previous trial uses in selected company divisions, and its potential value on a company-wide basis.

Mr. Dearfield then presented the completed trade analysis system at

**EXHIBIT 1B**

---

COLLIS COMPANY

Market Information

This Market Data required only on initial call or to show revisions or additions.

KEY PERSONNEL
(Names & Titles) _____

_____

_____

PRODUCTS MADE OR SOLD _____

_____

| | |
|---|---|
| Manufacturer | |
| Processor | |
| Distributor | |

Employees _____

Annual Sales _____

Floor Space _____

COMPETITIVE INFORMATION: Report below purchases of all products in Collis Company's field.

| Products Purchased (Name, Type and Grade) | Use | Supplier of Products | Yearly Purchases (Units) | Price & Unit |
|---|---|---|---|---|
| | | | | |

Sales, Service or Development Information-- (Continued from Front)

a quarterly meeting of the top 20 men in the marketing department, including Cox, Plumley, and all division sales managers. He explained the market and expense data, shown in Exhibit 3, to be obtained from the proposed system through the use of discussions supplemented by bar charts, slides, and other visual demonstrations.

Meetings of a division sales manager and his salesmen were called at the discretion of the sales manager, usually about every two weeks. Many of these division sales managers recognized the necessity of selling the system to their salesmen, and used skits, charts showing the flow of information from salesmen to market research department and back

**EXHIBIT 2**

| | | | | | |
|---|---|---|---|---|---|
| COLLIS COMPANY | | | | | |
| Weekly Call Report | | | | | |
| Date | Company and Individual | Customer | Prospect | Records* | Purpose and Results of Call |
| | | | | | |

*Records: (Are records up to date?)
　　N  New prospect. Trade report sent in.
　　C  Correction. Trade report showing change sent in.
　　　 File data is complete. No change necessary.

to salesmen, question and answer periods, and other selling devices. Mr. Dearfield attended many of these meetings and contributed to the further understanding of the new system.

One reason for the salesmen's resistance to the proposed changes was that very few of them had worked with other companies. Thus, they were not familiar with the similar sales reporting systems used by other companies and resisted changes in their own routine. The most prevalent reason for dislike of the new system was that the salesmen believed such reporting was not properly their job as salesmen, and they feared they would become paper-form handlers. The salesmen also believed that dollar sales figures were most important, and they were not interested in the origin of the sales or the dimensions of the market potential. They felt that they had operated satisfactorily under the old system, and they

**EXHIBIT 3.   Collis Company, marketing and expense data from expense, call, and trade reports**

| | | Type of report | | | |
|---|---|:---:|:---:|:---:|:---:|
| Type of data | | Expense | Call | Trade | Sales* analysis |
| I. | Selling expense data | | | | |
| | Analyses of selling and call expense: | | | | |
| | By territories | x | x | .... | x |
| | By salesmen | x | x | .... | x |
| | By customers or prospects | x | x | .... | x |
| | By customer size | x | x | x | x |
| | By class of trade and industry group | x | x | x | x |
| | Entertainment cost by types of customers | .... | .... | .... | .... |
| II. | Sales control data | | | | |
| | Analyses of sales coverage: | | | | |
| | By territories, by salesmen | x | x | .... | x |
| | By customers or prospects | x | x | .... | x |
| | By class of trade, by industry | x | x | x | x |
| | By types of customers, by customer size | x | x | x | x |
| | Analysis of sales per call | .... | x | .... | x |
| | Qualitative analysis of calls | .... | x | .... | x |
| III. | Market data | | | | |
| | Analyses of product potentials: | | | | |
| | By class of trade | .... | .... | x | x |
| | Analyses of competition: | | | | |
| | By company size | .... | .... | x | x |
| | Analyses of Collis Company's share: | | | | |
| | By geographic area (territories) | .... | .... | x | x |
| | Trends in product consumption: | | | | |
| | By industries (markets) | .... | .... | x | x |
| | By customers or prospects | .... | x | x | x |
| | By product and usage | .... | .... | x | x |
| | By product types and grades | .... | .... | x | x |
| | By consumption units | .... | .... | x | x |
| | By prices of products consumed | .... | .... | x | x |
| | Key personnel and changes in personnel | .... | .... | x | .... |
| | Plant capacities | .... | .... | x | .... |

* Prepared by the Marketing Research Department from the expense, call, and trade reports.

regarded the weekly call report as a device for checking on their activities, indicating a lack of confidence and trust in them on the part of the sales executives.

Although most top executives generally favored the new system, several thought the existing system was satisfactory. Mr. Plumley wholeheartedly endorsed it and was its strongest supporter. Mr. Cox, his superior and director of marketing, supported the program primarily because he placed great confidence in Mr. Plumley's judgment and usually supported his decisions. The top-level decisions on the trade analysis system were under the jurisdiction of these two men.

Three of the nine divisions within the company cooperated fully. Three divisions were undecided about the new system, and although they complied to the extent of supplying the desired information, they were not enthusiastic but waited to see the turn of events. Two other divisions resisted weakly, one primarily because the manager had been with the company for over 30 years, and claimed he knew the desired information and could see no use for the new forms in his division. The remaining division, industrial specialties, represented the major source of resistance to the new plan. The personnel of this division consisted of the sales manager, H. D. Miner, and three salesmen, ranging in ages between 35 and 40. All had been with the company 15 to 20 years. These men were not college graduates, as were the majority of the company's salesmen, but they were excellent salesmen who had joined the company on graduation from high school.

Mr. Miner, who was 35 years old, was a college graduate who had been with the company for 10 years. He would not attempt to force the new sales reporting system on his salesmen against their wills, but stated that it was Mr. Dearfield's task to convince his (Miner's) salesmen of the merits of the new plan.

Mr. Plumley, general manager of sales, had been the industrial specialties sales manager prior to Mr. Miner. Mr. Plumley, in turn, had taken over the division when it was beset with problems of morale and low sales, primarily the result of mismanagement by his predecessor, Mr. Griffith. Griffith had been a stubborn and strong-willed sales manager, and although he had had close personal and social contact with his men, his leadership often resulted in discontent among them.

Mr. Griffith had left the company three years ago, and Mr. Plumley had become the industrial specialties division sales manager. He attempted to establish better coordination and communication between his division and the company, and he greatly improved morale. When Mr. Plumley was promoted to general manager of sales two years later, Mr. Miner took over as sales manager, but Mr. Plumley continued in close contact with the division. Mr. Miner maintained closer personal and social contact with his salesmen than Mr. Plumley had.

The industrial specialties division salesmen were paid on straight salary, which was often a source of discontent, since salesmen in certain other divisions earned larger remuneration on the basis of an incentive payment plan.

When the company introduced the trade analysis system, the industrial specialties salesmen complained bitterly about the weekly call report. Mr. Miner invited Mr. Dearfield to discuss this report with his salesmen, but the discussion proved unsuccessful, largely because Mr. Miner had misrepresented the plan to his salesmen, and they voiced many loud, but ungrounded, objections. Whether Mr. Miner had done this intentionally, Mr. Dearfield did not know.

Mr. Dearfield then prepared a new presentation on the weekly call report, but when he appeared before these salesmen a second time to discuss it, the salesmen transferred their objections from the call report to the customer trade report. They objected that filling out the trade report would take too much time and that the information obtained would not be really valuable. Mr. Dearfield countered that it should not take more than five minutes to correctly fill out the report, and he explained how the company would use the data obtained. Nevertheless, the industrial specialties salesmen did not fill out the trade reports, and eight months after the introduction of the new trade analysis system the marketing research department had not received a single trade report from the salesmen of this division. While other divisions did not cooperate as fully as desired, industrial specialties was the only division that offered flat resistance to the trade report. Of necessity, the salesmen of this division turned in their weekly call and expense reports, since the company required these before it would repay the salesmen's traveling expenses.

Although Mr. Plumley strongly supported the new plan and spoke in favor of it at meetings with his sales managers, Mr. Dearfield hesitated to ask him to take coercive action against reluctant sales managers, since he believed that voluntary cooperation was most important. Therefore, aside from his endorsement of the trade analysis system at meetings with his sales managers, Mr. Plumley took no action to force compliance, although he felt that company efficiency and morale were reduced by what he considered unreasonable resistance.

# THE CUMMINS ENGINE COMPANY

At the end of 1967 the Cummins Engine Company was in trouble. Sales had fallen off; costs were rising, and profits had slipped badly. While the industry was in a slump, Cummins seemed to have suffered more than most competitors and there were ominous signs that the reversal of fortune represented more than a mere temporary decline.

## The Company

The Cummins Engine Company was founded in 1919 to make and sell diesel engines, which were then largely an untried product. The original organizers of the enterprise were William G. Irwin, a Columbus, Indiana, industrialist, and Clessie L. Cummins, his chauffeur and mechanic. Both believed in the potential of the unwieldy "oil" engine and by the mid-1920s had developed a diesel power plant suitable for marine use, particularly for large pleasure craft. This market virtually disappeared in the economic debacle of the early 1930s, and management turned its attention to the on-highway truck market. Here, the economy and durability of the diesel engine was beginning to be recognized, and the company hit pay dirt. Following its first sale of truck engines to Purity Foods, which operated a sizable fleet of trucks, Cummins rode the crest of the boom in diesel-powered equipment that developed shortly before World War II.

The rising status of "Cummins Dependable Diesels" was indicated in 1948 when the first public issue of Cummins common stock reached the over-the-counter market. The company pioneered a number of innovations and improvements on the diesel during the 1930s and 1940s, mainly applicable for trucks. By the mid-1950s, its innovative thrust made the company one of the nation's leading suppliers of diesel power plants for on-highway trucks.

As a result of its success an aggressive program of expansion and diversification was initiated in 1956, which represented a dramatic break with the company's one-product, one-plant structure of the past. Its new engine plant in Shotts, Scotland, was the first facility built by an American diesel manufacturer in the United Kingdom. This was followed in the early 1960s with a licensing agreement with Komatsu in Tokyo, Japan, for the production of engines to be used in earthmoving equipment; with a joint venture with Kirloskar, in Poona, India, for the production of in-line engines; the construction of an engine plant in Melbourne, Australia; and a licensing agreement with Diesel Nacional (DINA) in Sahagun, Mexico, for the production of both in-line and V engines.

During this period, the company also built or acquired five additional facilities in the United States. The Atlas Crankshaft Company in Fostoria, Ohio, produced crankshafts, valves, piston pins, and precision-machined capscrews. Frigiking Division in Dallas, Texas, manufactured and marketed truck-cab and passenger-car air conditioners. Fleetguard Division in Cookeville, Tennessee, produced air, lube, and fuel filters for heavy-duty equipment and passenger cars. Cummins ReCon Division, in Memphis, Tennessee, reconditioned fuel injectors, heads, water pumps, and other engine parts for distribution through the Cummins distributor organization.

One of the historic strengths of the company has been its extensive distributor and OEM dealer network. At the time of this case, the Cummins distribution system provided sales and service through approximately 140 distributors, all but a few of which were independently owned, and 1500 dealer outlets. This network was supported by a force of sales engineers who operated out of 11 regional offices. The company also maintained a factory training school at Columbus, Indiana, which was regularly attended by distributor and dealer service personnel to keep abreast of the most recent operating, maintaining, and repairing techniques for Cummins engines.

From the early years of its history, Cummins strategy has been to remain independent and to limit diversification to businesses closely related to diesel engines. Development work on gas turbine engines has been the only major exception. Implementing this strategy has brought management face to face with the marketing problem that any independent supplier of components must solve when he goes into someone else's end products. This problem is how to create enough demand among ultimate users of his product to compete not only with other suppliers of the same product but also with the end-product makers' own similar component.

Two conditions complicated the problem for Cummins. The first was that the diesel was a more expensive power plant than the gasoline engine with which it competed. The concept of a lightweight, heavy-duty diesel that was more economical in the *long run* than a gasoline engine was not easy to sell. The second complication was that many equipment manufacturers produced their own gasoline engines and were not interested in seeing diesel engines replace their own engines in their own equipment.

Management attempted to surmount the first of these obstacles through an intensive R & D effort aimed at increasing the diesel engine's horsepower output and reducing its weight. This effort proved very successful. The second obstacle was attacked by going over the heads of equipment manufacturers to their customers and selling them on the diesel as a replacement engine for their present equipment. In this latter undertaking, Cummins enjoyed some significant advantages.

As Board Chairman J. Irwin Miller observed some years ago, a diesel engine was not just another major component. It was the heart of a piece of equipment. While it was high-priced, this was less important from a user's point of view than its operating and maintenance costs, reliability, and performance. Trade surveys indicated that a high percentage of diesel-powered equipment users specified the kind of engine they wanted in their equipment, because it was so vital to their operations.

This gave Cummins an opportunity to sell what it had to sell—a tough, high-performance, close-tolerance engine with low operating costs. Customer preference for the Cummins engine became so pronounced that even GM's Euclid Division offered it as optional equipment.

Another advantage enjoyed by Cummins was that it sold nothing on which its engines were used. Consequently, competitors of equipment manufacturers that made both engines and equipment tended to prefer the noncompeting Cummins for original installation.

At the time of this case, Cummins offered 23 basic automotive diesels, ranging in output from 140 to 420 horsepower. A variety of accessory equipment was also available to allow buyers to adapt these engines to their own specialized applications and individual needs. These accessories included:

| | |
|---|---|
| Air compressors | Starting systems |
| Heat exchangers | Torque converters |
| Industrial clutches | Reduction gear units |
| Bases | Fuel tanks |
| Air precleaners | Instrument panels |
| Gauges | Enclosures |
| Safety controls | Heavy-duty dust-protection |
| Corrosion resistors | devices |

## Changing fortunes

During the late 1950s and early 1960s the production of diesel trucks grew by leaps and bounds, increasing by about 400 percent in the ten-year period. This made a tempting market, and competition moved in. Through its Detroit Diesel Division, General Motors had for some time made its own diesel truck engines; Mack Truck had done likewise. Late in the 1950s the Detroit Diesel Division abandoned the policy of making engines only for General Motors trucks and began to sell on the open market.

Other truck manufacturers began to make their own diesel engines as did several makers of heavy equipment, such as Caterpillar, which set up its own engine division that also sold on the general market. General Motors Detroit Diesel Division was the most active of the new competitors, multiplying its share of the market three times in a period of ten years. As a result of all this Cummins lost ground until in 1967 it had only a little over one third of the market instead of the well over half, which it had held ten years before.

In 1967 the bottom dropped out. Sales fell from $331,000,000 to $306,000,000 and earnings dropped from about $16,000,000 to $3,600,000. This decline, however, was only about eight percent in comparison with an industry decline of about 13 percent in physical units sold. So it was not too alarming. What was more sinister was a report that the White Motor Company, which took about one third of the Cummins output, was planning to build its own diesels.

Until rather recently Cummins had specialized on the truck market and most of its research, production, and marketing thinking was still oriented toward that market. Diesel engines had many other applications, such as in air compressors, agricultural implements, cranes, earthmoving equipment, pumps, tractors, airport sweepers, crushing machinery, drilling equipment, generators, mixers, pile drivers, locomotives, forklift trucks, hoists, logging and lumber-handling equipment, and many other uses. Recently Cummins had made some attempts to exploit these markets but without conspicuous success.

The Company has maintained a fairly heavy program of research. The annual expenditures for research and development grew from about six million dollars in 1960 to $17,125,000 in 1967. In spite of these heavy outlays for research, Cummins no longer held the lead in technological breakthroughs and improvements that it had only recently enjoyed. Perhaps this was because competitors were also researching heavily, and in many cases were beating Cummins to the punch. Perhaps it was because the technology was sufficiently advanced so that spectacular breakthroughs were no longer possible. On the other hand, it may have been due to the fact that the increase in research effort had been too recent to have borne results yet.

During the first half of 1968, the market for engines recovered and Cummins bounced back, pushing its market share above 40 percent and its profits to near the level of 1966, a record year. But the tendency of big truck companies and power-equipment firms to make their own engines and to bid for a share of the noncaptive diesel-engine market still hung over Cummins management.

Some typical Cummins engine models are shown in Exhibits 1 through 4.

**EXHIBIT 1.   Cummins V-504-C engine**

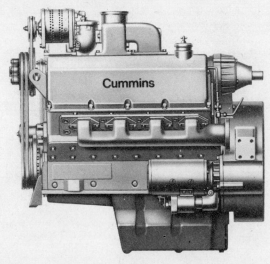

This is an 8-cylinder engine that develops 210 horse-power at 3,300 rpm. Net weight with standard accessories is 1,460 pounds.

**EXHIBIT 2.   Cummins V-903-C engine**

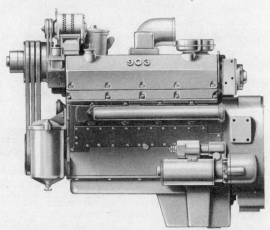

This is a 4-cycle, 8-cylinder engine that develops 320 horsepower at 2,600 rpm. Net weight with standard accessories is 2,200 pounds.

**EXHIBIT 3.   Cummins NT-855-C engine**

This is a 4-cycle, 6-cylinder engine with a power range from 280 horsepower to 335 horsepower at 2,100 rpm. Its net weight with standard accessories is 2,770 pounds.

**EXHIBIT 4.   Cummins VT-1710-C engine**

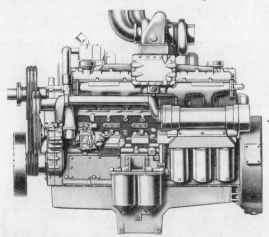

This is a 4-cycle, 12-cylinder engine that develops 635 horsepower at 2,100 rpm. Its net weight with standard accessories is 5,780 pounds. This engine had not yet been introduced at the time of the case.

**EXHIBIT 5.  Cummins Engine Company organization chart**

**A. Officers and staff**

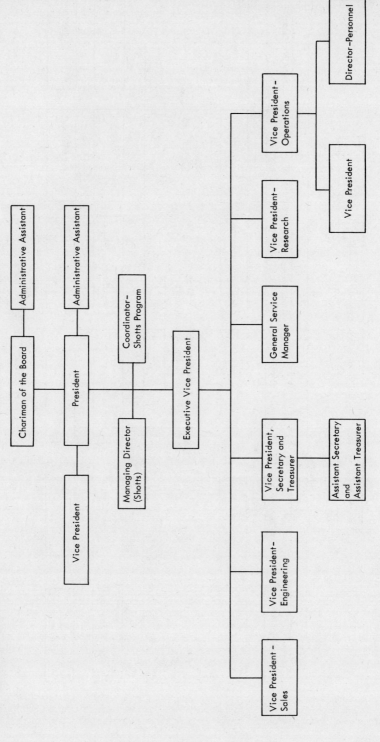

**EXHIBIT 5.** (*Continued*)

B. Manufacturing division

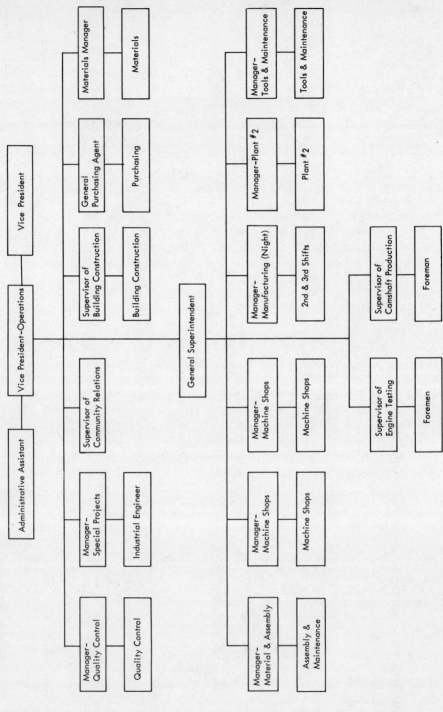

# THE CUNDY-BETTS CORPORATION

The Cundy-Betts Corporation, one of the large wholesalers of electrical and electronic supplies, apparatus, and appliances, has grown with the industrial expansion of the Midwest. Like most electrical distributors, this company stocks a considerable variety of goods. Its inventory of supplies and apparatus includes small items, such as wire, cables, switches, fittings, conduit, radio speakers, amplifiers, and residential and industrial lighting fixtures, as well as such major equipment as air conditioners, heating units, motors, transformers, and power tools. The company also carries a full line of small and major appliances, including TV sets. About 45 percent of gross sales comes from supplies and apparatus; the remainder is accounted for by appliances and TV.

Cundy-Betts has grown considerably since its 1922 beginning in a barn converted to a warehouse and only one full-time salesman. Today, it employs 65 salesmen, who sell to 20,000 accounts in a 5-state area. To serve these accounts, the company maintains 15 warehouses, with an average floor space of about 18,000 square feet. Stocked in these warehouses are some 30,000 items from nearly 3,000 suppliers. Sales volume last year was around $7.5 million.

Competition in this 5-state area comes from some 200 other independent electrical wholesalers, as well as a number of direct-selling manufacturers. In recent years, the most aggressive competition has been from manufacturers, who maintain local warehouses and ship on consignment. This competition has not only resulted in the loss of some customers, but has also served to reduce throughout the area much of the selling appeal of Cundy-Betts' own complete local stocks. Moreover, the willingness of these manufacturers to sell on consignment and drop ship has encouraged a number of marginal operators to enter electrical wholesaling. Equipped with no more than a telephone and a list of prospects, these operators have been able to quote prices considerably below those of the established service wholesaler.

The company is faced with a difficult decision. It may retrench on inventories and services, and thus join the discounters in taking advantage of manufacturer's stocks and direct shipments to customers. While this step may enable the company to meet the lowest prices of competitors, it will eventually reduce the organization to the role of a broker. On the other hand, it is not difficult to appreciate the electrical manufacurers' position. To get the most out of their enormous productive capacity, volume selling is imperative. Yet, the weak-kneed selling efforts of many wholesalers and their failure to maintain adequate stocks are well known. This plus the natural craving of each manufacturer for a bigger share of the total market are the ingredients of an explosive situation.

It seems evident to company management that their growth has been sustained by a wide and deep product coverage combined with quality service. Moreover, because of the new electrical products and the changes in old ones constantly being introduced, it seems all the more necessary to carry extensive stocks. It also has been the salesmen's experience that when customers want merchandise, they want it at once. As one salesman expressed it, "If our customers have to wait while we order merchandise from Chicago, they may as well order it themselves." At the same time, financial and inventory records have revealed a disturbing situation. Although gross sales have nearly doubled in the last ten years, gross and net profits and dollar earnings have declined steadily. The number of items classified as "slow" has doubled in two years, and turnover has declined for the fourth consecutive year.

In order to tighten up their operating efficiency without compromising what were regarded as the essentials of wholesaling, the following policy revisions were adopted.

1. Complete inventories but fewer sources of supply. Complete stocks were considered necessary to insure prompt delivery—an essential in wholesaling. While the same variety of items was maintained, the number of manufacturers represented was sharply reduced. The decision on which manufacturers to eliminate was made only after a careful analysis of vendors on the basis of sales, lead time, price, adjustments, and complaints.

2. Systematic and formalized training of salesmen. Although the company had always stressed knowledge as well as method in selling, there had been no organized attempt to instill these qualities in its sales force. A plan was therefore devised to bring every salesman to the home office every year for two weeks of formal training. When asked to supply representatives and educational aids for this training program, the manufacturers' response was immediate and enthusiastic.

3. Specialized selling. To make the fullest use of the individual salesman's competence and capacity, the company separated its supplies and apparatus business from appliances and TV. Each of these divisions was given its own sales force and its own warehouses.

4. Selective distribution. Management had known for some time that, on the average, 30 percent of its customers accounted for 70 percent of its business, but this circumstance had never influenced policy. Now

a determined effort was made to recruit big-order business as well as business less affected by price competition. The number of retailers that company salesmen contacted was also cut in half so that they could concentrate on the high-volume outlets.

5. Full-service package. This included assistance to manufacturers in sales promotion and other selling campaigns, as well as specialized services to nonretail customers. For example, the company organized a complete lighting service, offered at cost to contractors and architects.

Putting these policy revisions into effect, however, created some perplexing adjustment problems. The gradual elimination of low-volume buyers and the solicitation of larger accounts involved disadvantages as well as advantages. Large buyers were more sensitive to quality, more demanding about service, and more conscious of price, generally speaking, than were small buyers. While the separation of appliances and TV sales from supplies and apparatus was logical from a product and customer standpoint, the significantly higher ratio of expenses to sales in the supplies and apparatus came as a distinct surprise to management. Indeed, the division had failed to show a net profit since its establishment. Although substantial increases in sales had been achieved, they had been largely offset by increases in selling expense.

This situation was largely attributed to the greater technical competence, longer period of training, higher salaries, more sales calls per sale, and greater emphasis on development work required of industrial salesmen as opposed to salesmen in the appliance and TV division. In order to meet the competition of direct-selling manufacturers for big-volume accounts, it was also necessary to establish an engineering department within the supplies and apparatus division. The old service division, which had been very successful in dealing with the repair and maintenance needs of small accounts, simply did not have the personnel capable of handling the production and design problems encountered in large establishments.

Although most Cundy-Betts suppliers provided technical assistance to end users of their products, this assistance was seldom available as quickly as customers demanded it. Moreover, most buyers expected satisfactory service from the distributor who had sold the product rather than from the product maker. While these facts helped to explain the poor profit performance of the supplies and apparatus division, they did not make it any easier for management to accept.

Mr. Dean, who had been appointed manager of the supplies and apparatus division, found it necessary to spend about half of his time with the new engineering department. He thought the change in the company's organizational structure from a functional to a more product-oriented basis was logical in view of the revision in company policies. In his judgment, though, these changes had been pushed too rapidly. He thought that giving marketing a greater voice in management decisions and more influence over company budgets was more important than separating it into essentially consumer and industrial divisions. It was also his contention that the engineering department was woefully understaffed. He pointed out that it had only a quarter of the personnel and a fifth of the budget of the old service division—to carry out an assignment too big for the old division.

In the final analysis, he thought, it was the technical service man who brought in the repeat business. Consequently, the engineering department should, at least, be placed on an equal footing in terms of numbers, salaries, and prestige with the old service division and eventually with the sales force itself. However, management did not see the role of the engineering department in quite the same light as Mr. Dean, so he was unable to get a sufficient increase in the division's budget to add substantially to the strength of the department.

The general manager of Cundy-Betts was J. G. Van Allen. He had been with the firm for about 20 years, first as a salesman of appliances, then of television, and later as manager of the newly formed appliance and television sales division. When the top executive position became vacant in 1960 because of retirement, Mr. Van Allen was appointed to that office. Before becoming general manager, he had made no secret of his belief that the supplies and apparatus division constituted the company's foremost problem. On his appointment as chief administrative officer, he stated that his first objective would be to place this division on a paying basis.

Mr. Van Allen thought that one of the division's major weaknesses was inventory control. No one in the division knew, he declared, when deliveries were received, where they were stored, or how much of an item was on hand. Returned goods were accepted without inspection, damaged goods were not accounted for, and, worst of all, orders were not processed in any systematic way. The last condition, he insisted, frequently caused embarrassing situations with customers, and he cited several letters of complaint he had received from manufacturers regarding Cundy-Betts' allegedly unreliable delivery service.

The second major weakness of this division, Mr. Van Allen argued, was its failure to properly plan its product lines. While he conceded that stock turnover had improved and the ratio of inventory to net working capital had been lowered over the past four years, streamlining the inventory in a quantitative sense was not enough. Inventory must also be streamlined qualitatively, he stated, by adding new products with high demand potential and by weeding out old products that were no longer paying their way.

He reminded Mr. Dean that although every industry the division served was spending millions on product research and development, Cundy-Betts had not added a half-dozen new products to its industrial lines in the past 10 years. For example, the National Building Material

Distributors' Association had estimated that in the Midwest alone over 50,000 homeowners would install automatically operated garage doors in the next 3 years, and another 30,000 homes would be either built with or converted to electric heat. Yet, Mr. Van Allen pointed out, the supplies and apparatus division did not carry a single piece of equipment that could be used in either type of installation. By contrast, over 50 percent of the sales volume in the appliances and television division came from products the company did not stock 10 years ago. He cited upright freezers, transistor radios, tape recorders, color television, electric can openers, and battery-operated clocks as a few examples of such products.

Mr. Dean hotly contested this diagnosis of the supplies and apparatus division. His comments are quoted below.

This division has made every possible effort to tighten inventory control. There is a limit to what we can do, however, because the real responsibility for this function rests with the purchasing division. All inventory records are maintained by the purchasing staff, and we simply tell them what products we want and when we want them; what happens after this is out of our hands. However, we have adopted a new simplified order form for salesmen, which replaces the old multicopy, snap-out form with a single punch card. This card has all the pertinent information about a product prepunched in it, and requires only the salesman's signature to authorize shipment. Use of the punched card not only reduces the time required to process an order, because the processing procedure can be mechanized, but also permits the recording of more complete information about the product and customer. Faster order handling with more product information should make possible more efficient control over inventory. If purchasing is not doing a satisfactory job of maintaining proper inventory levels and assortments, it is they who should answer for this and not us.

Complaints about the unreliability of delivery service on industrial products are news to me. My salesmen send their orders directly to the purchasing department, where the merchandise sold is deducted from the stock-on-hand and the new stock-on-hand figure posted. Four copies of the order card are then reproduced; three are sent to the warehousing division and one to us. Warehousing immediately sends one of these cards—it is labeled "invoice" and has all pertinent information printed on it—to the purchaser to acknowledge receipt of his order. When the order is shipped, the second card is sent to the accounting division, and the third is retained for warehouse records. The accounting department then bills the customer for the amount of the order less discounts at the end of the month. If delivery service is unreliable, it is because of a time lag between mailing of the order-acknowledgment card and shipment of the order.

Frankly, this is the first time I have heard of complaints about our delivery service. Why a company would write to the general manager of a supplier about such a complaint rather than bring it to the attention of the salesman who took the order is more than I can understand. Besides, when we sell more than 8,000 accounts annually I can't be very upset about a half-dozen complaints. I think that is a pretty good record of service. When Mr. Van Allen brought these letters to my attention, I personally checked all our call reports for the past year. None of the salesmen had reported any complaints about delivery. They would have no reason to withhold such information, because poor delivery service would be no reflection on them. Making delivery is the responsibility of the warehousing division.

The allegation that our product lines are poorly planned because we have failed to add enough new products and to eliminate enough old products reveals Mr. Van Allen's abysmal ignorance of this division and the market it serves. Manufacturers *are* spending a lot of money on product development, but our customers are not gadget-happy. They will not replace an old piece of equipment or apparatus with a new one simply because the new one is better looking or possesses greater snob appeal. The new product must be demonstrably superior in a profit sense before it has a Chinaman's chance of displacing an established product. Based on Department of Commerce statistics, a new product introduced today has only 1 chance in 50 of being accepted by the market. In other words, approximately 98 percent of the new products introduced fail to win acceptance in the marketplace. This means that somebody gets stuck with a lot of unsalable merchandise. And this division's record of increasing stock turnover and decreasing ratios of inventory to net working capital indicates that we have been successful in avoiding this pitfall.

It is true that the division has eliminated suppliers rather than lines, but we are not carrying a single product for which we do not have buyers. We are also cautiously adding some new lines—notably, television focusing magnets, coin boxes for pay television, telephone-answering devices, and color television scanning equipment. Admittedly, these lines do not represent a very substantial portion of our total sales, but they are growth lines for which there is an established demand.

We do not stock parts for automatically operated garage doors or control equipment and devices for electrically heated homes because these items are typically installed by builders. We have never sold to building contractors because we have never regarded the construction industry as a very healthy market. Not only is it subject to severe seasonal and cyclical swings, but also most builders are small- to medium-sized operators, whose prime consideration is almost always price and who never seem able to pay on time.

We could undoubtedly get more volume if we chose to enter the construction market. But we would be obliged to add new lines, which I presume would please Mr. Van Allen, and increase the amount of working capital committed to inventory, which I presume would not please him. Since our present sales force is spread about as thin as we dare to spread it, entering a new market would most assuredly require an expansion of the field sales force and additional promotion; the net result, at least in the short run, would be to increase expenses by a greater proportion than sales. Moreover, the price situation in the construction market is about as bad as I have seen in my lifetime. To penetrate it we would have to be prepared to reduce prices to the level of drop shippers and other non-stock-carrying middlemen. This would mean taking losses as high as 20 percent on some lines. No company can afford to sell inventory at 80 cents on the dollar to get more business.

Industrial selling requires a competent engineering service department as well as a competent field sales force. Neither can be created overnight. While this company has always sold in the industrial market, it has never attempted to systematically recruit, train, and promote industrial sales personnel. As a result, whenever one of our men develops into a really competent salesman one of our suppliers hires him away from us. In fact, a really ambitious man will not stay with us because he soon realizes that there is no place to go in this organization. It is the consumer product salesmen who have always received the promotions to managerial positions. And there are few career salesmen in this business, the work is too hard, the hours are too long, and the weekends on the road too frequent. As this division develops, however, with its own field offices and warehouses, there will soon be some attractive management positions to hold our good men. We will not have the men to fill these positions, though, unless the program of systematic personnel recruitment and training I have begun is continued. If a profit-making sales and service staff is to be developed in this division, the company must be willing to make a substantial investment in it. This, Mr. Van Allen seems unwilling to do.

The executive in charge of all purchasing at Cundy-Betts was Louis Schlarmann. The purchasing department staff included 25 buyers who specialized by product line and about 20 clerk-secretaries who handled correspondence and maintained inventory records. Mr. Schlarmann was aided by four assistant division managers. One manager supervised industrial goods purchases, another supervised consumer goods purchases, a third was responsible for inventory control, and the fourth was office manager.

Mr. Schlarmann did not believe the inventory situation was either so confused as Mr. Van Allen thought or so completely the purchasing department's responsibility as Mr. Dean seemed to think. He admitted that some confusion probably did exist when industrial product sales were separated from consumer sales and separate warehouses were established for each division. But he was not aware that any misunderstanding still existed regarding merchandise receipts, stock-on-hand, and stock location. His remarks were essentially as follows.

Initially, only the fastest moving lines were stocked in the field warehouses. The slow movers of both divisions were carried in our main warehouse at the home office. The reason was that we were obliged to use rented warehouse space until we could construct our own facilities. During this period, there were delays in making delivery whenever a salesman sent in an order listing some items warehoused locally and others warehoused at the home office. In these cases, the customer received his order in two installments. Since customers usually want their entire order as soon as possible, our classification of slow-moving and fast-moving goods didn't give them much satisfaction. A customer is understandably confused when part of his order is delivered in four days and the remainder doesn't arrive for another week. It seems to me, though, that the salesmen could have done more to explain this situation to our customers. Complaints about delivery eventually filter back to us and we endeavor to give the customer a reasonable explanation, together with an apology. I don't recall how many such complaints we handled last year, but it wasn't enough to be alarming.

There was also apparently some misunderstanding on the part of our personnel about which items were classified as slow moving and which as fast moving. As a result, items were occasionally reported as out-of-stock at local warehouses when they were actually in the main warehouse. Since we now have adequate storage space, we have abandoned the slow-moving–fast-moving classifications and carry complete stocks at our field warehouses. This source of confusion has therefore been largely eliminated. There are probably still some delays when an order received at a division warehouse contains items stocked by the other division. For example, one of Mr. Dean's salesmen might submit an order for a freezer or an electric can opener to be used in a company's kitchen. Neither of these items are stocked in the apparatus and equipment division, although salesmen in this division may take orders for them. Such orders must be sent to the nearest consumer products field warehouse or to the main warehouse.

However, we now have in operation a rather effective system of cross-listing all items carried by the company. It enables the stock pickers at any field warehouse to determine quickly where any item not in their own facility is located. If a telephone call to this warehouse reveals that the item is in stock, the order is sent there and filled immediately. As you may know, we have a division office at each warehouse, and every item stocked has a separate punch card, prepared when the item is received. The card is stored in a tub file until the item is sold. That is, we maintain a perpetual inventory of items by keeping a physical inventory of cards. An order clerk can determine in a matter of minutes whether an item is in stock and where it is located if not carried in that particular warehouse.

The only factor currently causing delays in delivery is an out-of-stock situation. Since our buying is done on the basis of forecasts formulated by the sales divisions, we can do nothing if these forecasts are in error. The forecasts submitted by Mr. Dean's division have frequently been too conservative on a number of products. Consequently, in a number of instances we have been obliged to place emergency orders with suppliers in order to fill orders submitted by his division. This is not only an expensive way to order—it usually means a long-distance telephone call or a telegram—but it also delays delivery to the customer.

We in purchasing have nothing to do with the planning of product lines, either quantitatively or qualitatively, as Mr. Van Allen phrases it. The sales divisions tell us what products they want us to stock, and we endeavor to secure these on the most advantageous terms. When we recently discontinued a number of our former suppliers, the names of the firms to be dropped were submitted to us by the sales divisions. Our function is exclusively that of serving other divisions of the company. We make no decisions with regard to what is purchased or from whom; we fill orders, we do not initiate them. The only product decisions solely ours concern the proper quantity to order, the most economical ratio of stock to sales, and the various terms of purchase, that is, price, delivery, scheduling, discounts, insurance, and so on.

The company controller was Dale Torrence, who was also secretary of the board of directors. He explained that the organizational changes, while not affecting his department directly, made it impossible to allocate costs. He had estimated the company's break-even volume at about $7 million. While break-even estimates for the two divisions were still provisional, he felt that the break-even point for the supplies and apparatus division would not be much less than $3 million. Although sales for the division had not yet reached this figure, results for the present year were expected to slightly exceed the break-even volume. Mr. Torrence also stated that company sales had exceeded break-even volume every year because of appliance and television sales to retail dealers. The accounting division charged all direct expenses against the division that incurred them, and allocated overhead on the basis of nonselling personnel or square feet of floor space, as appropriate.

Mr. Torrence thought the difficulties plaguing Mr. Dean stemmed from his zeal to increase sales on the assumption that volume beyond the break-even point was pure profit. The controller observed that additional sales volume invariably requires more inventory and more money invested in accounts receivable. Cundy-Betts simply did not have the working capital for such an expansion, and borrowing was proving to be expensive. As Mr. Torrence expressed it, borrowing working capital "eats up profits faster than they can be made." The situation became critical recently when the company lost $200,000 in 4 months, but fortunately this experience has not been repeated. He added that he would like to see sales level off at about $7.5 million until earnings provided enough capital to support further expansion.

Mr. Torrence was also interested in Mr. Van Allen's views concerning product-line programming, i.e., the addition of new products and the elimination of old ones. During the past year, the accounting staff had endeavored to make some distribution cost analyses to ascertain the contributions various products were making to company overhead. The sales tabulation they assembled is shown in Exhibit 1.

Due to the expense of making a comprehensive study of all products, Mr. Torrence's cost analysis was of a fragmentary nature. Nevertheless,

**EXHIBIT 1.  Sales trends by product group (supplies and apparatus division)**

| Product group | Percentage of total company sales volume | | |
|---|---|---|---|
|  | 1964 | 1966 | 1968 |
| Power tools..................... | 35.7 | 28.0 | 21.7 |
| Heating units.................. | 13.3 | 12.6 | 10.1 |
| Color scanners................. | * | 1.5 | 3.0 |
| Lighting fixtures............... | 11.3 | 10.4 | 5.3 |
| Switches...................... | 7.6 | 8.0 | 6.1 |
| Wire recorders................. | 4.0 | 5.0 | 4.1 |
| General-purpose tape recorders... | 5.3 | 4.5 | 5.6 |
| Type A speakers................ | 5.7 | 8.0 | 10.0 |
| Type B speakers................ | 13.1 | 15.0 | 18.2 |
| Conduit........................ | 4.0 | 7.0 | 10.9 |
| Focusing magnets.............. | * | * | 1.5 |
| Coin boxes.................... | * | * | .5 |
| Automotive parts.............. | * | * | 2.0 |
| Telephone parts................ | * | * | 1.0 |
| Total product sales............ | 100.0 | 100.0 | 100.0 |

* Not stocked that year.

it disclosed that several of the company's products were priced at figures that put them in the red on a gross profit basis or resulted in no contribution to net profit and general overhead after estimated selling costs were deducted from gross profit. Mr. Dean, however, had defended the company's pricing policy on the basis that some of these loss products constituted an element of considerable importance in the cost structure of the typical buyer, and that these buyers also purchased other products on which the firm made a profit. He was unable to say whether or not this was true of all products on which his division was sustaining losses.

Mr. Torrence's conclusion was that it would be ridiculous to add new products without first eliminating some of the unprofitable ones now carried in the supplies and apparatus division. He warned that the company's financial position would not permit the continued sale of products at a loss. He was not prepared to say, though, which of the losing products should be discontinued.

# THE DELTA DISTRIBUTING COMPANY

The Delta Distributing Company was first established in Orlando, Florida, in 1935 by a prominent local family. It was organized for the purpose of supplying building materials (mainly roofing and allied products) to lumberyards, building material dealers, hardware stores, and contractors within Orange County and the immediately adjoining counties. The company was forced to suspend operations in 1942, however, because it was unable to secure inventory. The production of all nonessential civilian goods was sharply curtailed during the war emergency which followed the bombing of Pearl Harbor, and when the last of the "prewar" inventory had been sold, the enterprise was forced to close.

The owners did not reestablish the business as a stock-carrying wholesale distributor after VJ Day. They had become interested in other commercial activities and decided to operate their former business as a dropshipper. In this capacity it sold only in full truckload and carload lots, but provided credit, billing services, and technical assistance. As a dropshipper the Delta Company did not develop any substantial volume of business. In fact, no effort was made to advertise or otherwise promote the company and its products. Most sales were made to the larger prewar customers who had had a long association with its management.

The firm continued in this way until 1959 when the business of a merchant wholesaler in Lakeland, a city some 50 miles southwest of Orlando, was destroyed by fire. For several reasons, ill health of the owner being prominent among them, the Lakeland firm was not reopened. It had handled several of the lines sold by Delta, and since this left some of the firm's suppliers without representation in the area, Delta management was subsequently approached by them with an offer of a franchise for the Lakeland territory. Only one string was attached to the offer, and that was that Delta would have to lease and operate a warehouse in Lakeland. In short, Delta would have to operate as a merchant wholesaler instead of as a drop-shipper. Moreover, these suppliers wanted an answer quickly, so they could take steps to secure other representation should Delta decline their offer.

This presented Delta management with a perplexing decision. There was no time to conduct an extensive market survey. The company had no one on its present staff who was equipped by either training or experience to undertake such a study with confidence. Inquiries made of consulting firms in Miami, Jacksonville, and Atlanta indicated that no reputable firm could undertake the study and assure its completion in less than six weeks. This was more of a delay than the suppliers were willing to grant. But to accept the offer to lease a warehouse and invest in inventory to serve a market of uncertain potential was loaded with risks.

On the other hand, there were some very positive factors in this situation that could not be ignored but the significance of which was difficult to appraise. First, the established territory of the Lakeland company was available to Delta without the financial consideration usually involved in the transfer of established territory from one company to another. Second, the services of the assistant manager of a defunct Lakeland wholesaler, a highly regarded and competent young man, were available to Delta, provided he was offered the opportunity to purchase stock in the new company. Third, the sales manager of the Lakeland company was willing to become affiliated with the new enterprise, thereby providing continuity between established customers and the new company. Fourth, management was familiar with the general line of building materials for which it was offered the franchise. Fifth, the company had a number of customers in the southwestern part of its territory whose accounts could be transferred to the Lakeland concern.

On the basis of these considerations plus management's "feel" of the market situation, it was decided to accept the franchise offer and reactivate its stock-carrying operation in Lakeland. The owners succeeded in establishing a line of credit with two different Orlando banks totaling $250,000. With financial support assured, the new venture was begun.

A vacant two-story building was secured in Lakeland to serve as a warehouse and office. The ground floor of this building, containing 12,000 square feet of space, was well adapted for a combination sales office and display room, and two heavy-duty elevators permitted easy access to the second floor storage area. In addition a rear yard was available for the storage of materials unaffected by weather. Furthermore, the location of the warehouse itself afforded certain advantages: (1) it was on a railroad siding and adjacent to a U.S. highway, and (2) it was within a few blocks of two other building material distributors. This latter characteristic was important because of the convenience to pick-up customers, of which there were thought to be quite a number. If one distributor did not have wanted materials, the customer would find it relatively easy to drive to a second outlet. Also, it was known that some customers followed a practice of making purchases from a prescribed list, i.e., buying specific items and brands from different distributors. In this respect, proximity to other distributors represented a significant advantage.

The territory taken over by the Delta Distributing Company included an area within approximately a 35-mile radius of Lakeland. This was by no means a large-volume market, but at least in past years it had produced a steady demand for building materials. In addition to this contiguous area there were a few islands of activity beyond these limits, notably at Sebring and Sarasota. The principal source of volume sales, as well as competition, was Greater Tampa.

The weight and bulk of building material places limitations on the extent to which a territory can be expanded. As a general rule, a building material distributor can expand outward from his warehouse only to the point at which delivery costs make it impossible to remain competitive in price. Realizing these limitations, management decided that the company should seek to consolidate and improve its position in this area through quality and efficient service rather than by expansion into new territories. Although there had not been sufficient time to conduct a market study prior to the decision to undertake the new venture, a study was undertaken as soon as the various legal details connected with the opening of the enterprise had been completed. The purpose of the study was to accumulate sufficient information about the territory to establish policy concerning products to be carried, services to be offered, and types of customers to be served. Since the firm would soon be ready for business, it was decided to combine the survey with a promotional campaign. A set of objectives which the survey should accomplish and some suggestions regarding procedure were drawn up by the president and submitted to the general manager. These are given in Exhibit 1.

**EXHIBIT 1. Guide for promotional and market research project**
The object of this survey is to promote business for the Delta Distributing Company and to secure information regarding market potential in the area presently covered by the company's delivery service.

The specific objectives are:

1. To promote the use of the services provided by the Delta Distributing Company to the firms called on and particularly to impress upon them the fact that Delta is a permanent, established company in business to provide all the services desired by its customers.

2. To inquire of potential customers as to what services and specific items of material they have difficulty obtaining and would like for the company to handle.

3. To make suggestions as to possible products which Delta might handle and get favorable or unfavorable reactions concerning them. These products might include guttering and sheet metal supplies, floor tile, Orangeburg pipe, ornamental iron railings, precast brick siding, aluminum siding, aluminum guttering, built-up roofing and all products and equipment connected with it, plastic dome skylights, etc. (A complete list to be attached.)

**EXHIBIT 1** (*Continued*)

4. In addition to lumber yards, information should be obtained as to the need for material and services by sheet metal shops, roofing and siding applicators, floor tile applicators, and hardware stores. In connection with this objective, information should be obtained as to what other suppliers in the area are handling products and services for this type of potential customer. In particular, it is desirable to find out if sheet metal supplies are being actively and properly wholesaled in the area. The next most important product is asphalt tile.

Suggestions for procedure in obtaining the above information:

1. It first should be decided if every potential company of all types and classifications in a town or area should be contacted or whether one specific classification should be contacted over the entire territory first, followed by each other classification in order.

2. Next, lists should be obtained, where possible, of the names and addresses of all companies in all classifications listed for the entire area.

3. We cannot expect the lists in Item 2 to be complete; therefore, it is suggested that in each town the phone book be consulted and lists drawn up for use. These lists should be kept for follow-up direct-mail advertising.

4. It would be desirable to have a direct-mail piece to go out to all potential customers before individual contact is made; however, this may not be possible due to the time shortage.

5. A slightly different approach should be made to existing customers and to customers who have never traded with the company. This type of customer should first be thanked for past patronage and then questioned as to his satisfaction with the services and opinions on the new products and services.

6. With potential customers who have not used our company before, some information on the status of the company would have to be obtained before questions could be asked.

7. It should be explained to all people contacted that you are not attempting to sell anything at this time and that you are not fully acquainted with all of the products of the company so that you cannot give specific information as to products, but that you are primarily interested in getting information which will be of service to the potential customer.

General helpful information:

1. Why should they trade with a wholesaler? The wholesaler is in business to make them money. He does this by keeping informed of all existing and new products and keeping a complete inventory of all styles and colors of these products so that it will not be necessary for the retailer to tie up his money and his space.

The territory to be surveyed was enlarged slightly and the types of potential customers to be contacted within that territory were indicated. A marketing professor at a local college was retained to conduct the survey and was given a thorough briefing on the company's situation. His instructions were to obtain sufficient information about the market to make an estimate of its potential and to acquaint potential customers with the products and services to be offered. Samples of products *not handled* by Delta were also presented, to determine the extent of customers' interest in competing products.

Firms contacted during the survey included building material dealers, home modernization companies, hardware stores, contractors, farm cooperatives, and certain selected industrial purchasers, such as railroads and utility companies, which have their own construction crews. These firms were located primarily through telephone directories and inquiries made at local banks. In small towns, the local farm cooperative often operates as a combination building material dealer and hardware store. Also, the general hardware store would often be the home modernization contractor. Special emphasis was placed on the potential business in small towns, because it was found that the large lumberyards in the metropolitan areas tended to have direct buying arrangements with manufacturers.

The interviewers carried a Stenorette portable tape recorder and made a complete report of each interview. This report was made while he drove to the next interview. In this manner, much detailed information was obtained which was later transcribed. In addition to the standard data obtained, there were numerous small items of information which proved of value. For example, it was found that nine out of ten purchasing agents interviewed knew the Delta sales manager and liked him. To convey the nature of interviews, a few are reproduced in Exhibit 2.

As a result of the information obtained from this survey, a number of benchmarks were established which served as a frame of reference for policy formulation. For example:

1. It was estimated that the potential represented by the territory was ample, although this conclusion was based on estimated purchases of the firms interviewed, which were neither a random sample of the total buyers in the territory nor a complete census of them.

2. Additional product lines were added. A lively interest was discovered in ten categories of products which neither Delta nor the former company had discovered.

3. Two categories of products were discontinued. It was discovered that these lines were being purchased direct from manufacturers by most of the firms interviewed. Since these were lines which required little in the way of service, buying from Delta offered no real advantage over buying direct.

4. Delivery service and its reliability were important, but daily ship-

EXHIBIT 2.   Excerpts from transcribed interviews selected from the Market Survey made by the Delta Company*

It is now 1:17

"Name deleted. He sells building materials. I noticed he had Celotex shingle samples and ceiling, continental nails—but he wasn't there. Talked to his wife. She says she knows he would be interested in a price list and would like to be on our mailing list. He has his office in his home at this time and is contemplating building a warehouse and putting an office in part of it."

It is now 1:50

"Name deleted. This is a co-op deal and is the building material outlet here. He handles some shingles and nails and little wire—right in his grain office. He's been getting it out of Dealers Supply in Danville; however, this guy should be on our mailing list."

It is now 4:21

"Name deleted. I talked to Mr. ——. He is the owner and manager. He said, "Boy, you came in at just the right time. I need 8 sqs. of pastel red shurlocks, Flintcote brand." He said he would call tomorrow. He seemed very interested in our line. Buys from everyone. He looked at our price list, looked it over carefully and said he will want the new issues as they come out. This is the hottest prospect I found today."

It is now 11:30

"Name deleted. I left price list. He said he'd like to be on the mailing list. Keystone wire, Can't Sag Gates. Interested in our delivery service. Interested in galvanized roofing. I think he'll do some business with us."

It is now 11:55

"Flat tire."

It is now 2:50

"Name deleted. He is glad to know about Versa Iron. Said he would buy gutter if we have it in stock. He has our FK samples on display and will probably sell some for us."

It is now 12:00

"Name deleted. Talked to manager—he'd like to be on mailing list. Wants salesman to drop by. He's glad to hear we have a line of FK and cold process roofing. Think we might do some business.

It is now 4:40

"Starting to pour down rain, heading for home."

* Survey made during January, February, and March, 1960. Approximately 200 interviews. The items represent only short excerpts from longer interviews.

ments were not necessary. It was decided to organize a delivery service on the basis of routes, so that a different route would be covered each day of the week and every customer could expect delivery every week on the same day.

5. The mailing list was expanded to three times the size of that formerly maintained by the company in Lakeland.

6. Customer buying habits were revealed. Information was collected relating to customers' appraisal of various competing suppliers, their plans for growth and development, and the progressiveness of their management.

The Delta Company sales office and operating personnel were moved to Lakeland, although the accounting staff remained in Orlando. This was considered necessary for purposes of control. This staff maintained the financial records of the Delta enterprise as well as those of the family's other commercial interests. Since these interests were centered in Orlando, facilities and equipment for the maintenance of the financial and tax records were available there. Separating the financial administration of the company from other aspects of its management was not regarded as an unsatisfactory arrangement. All sales receipts, purchase orders, cash receipts (in excess of that needed for petty cash), and miscellaneous charges were forwarded daily to Orlando. A summary of financial transactions and a cash position report was prepared weekly in Orlando and sent to the Delta president. A record of receipts and disbursements was also maintained by a clerk at Lakeland. Otherwise, the Delta company operated as an independent, self-supporting business in Lakeland.

The Delta staff consisted of 14 people: a president, general manager and purchasing agent, assistant general manager, warehouse superintendent, sales manager, four salesmen, two truck drivers (who also served as order pickers between runs), two secretaries, and a clerk-typist. Each employee had specific duties and the limits of his authority were well understood. An organization chart is given in Exhibit 3.

*The President,* who resides in Orlando, has been occupied with investigating new product possibilities, capital budgeting, and top-level supervision. Once each week he holds a meeting with his key people in Lakeland, i.e., the general manager and his assistant, the sales manager, and the warehouse superintendent. If the need arises, he is usually free to drive to Lakeland on short notice. For occasions that may require his personal attention between visits, his company car is equipped with a two-way telephone.

*The General Manager* is responsible for day-to-day operations of the new company. He is apparently a very capable man who is not beyond assisting a driver to load his truck if the need arises. Although he is in charge of purchasing, a substantial part of his time is devoted to pro-

**EXHIBIT 3.  Organization chart of the Delta Distributing Company**

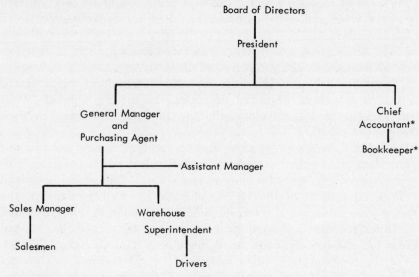

\* Located in Orlando.

motional work with customers and prospects; so much of the administrative routine of his office is handled by an assistant.

*The Assistant General Manager* is the "inside man" of the company. His work consists of maintaining all records and submitting the daily reports to Orlando, following up purchase orders, interviewing vendor representatives in the absence of the general manager, dealing with customer complaints, and interviewing customers in the absence of the sales manager.

*The Sales Manager* works both in and out of the office. About two thirds of his time is spent "on the road." His job is to contact current and potential customers, supervise the other salesmen, and sell. Each salesman makes out a daily report of all contacts (see Exhibit 4); each writes his own orders.

*The Warehouse Superintendent* is responsible for the proper storage and handling of all material. He also supervises the physical count of inventory and is directly responsible for the inventory control system.

The merchandising policies of Delta were patterned after those recommended by the Natural Building Material Distributors Association (see Exhibit 5). They provide the general guide which management follows in its planning and operations. There is no price cutting. A standard price list is issued monthly, giving the most recent price changes instituted by suppliers as well as any adjustments in price resulting from a favorable supply situation or a special promotion. There is no deviation from the

**EXHIBIT 4.   Salesman's daily report**

Name_____                          Date_____

| Name | Address | Call again | Interested in | Remarks |
|------|---------|------------|---------------|---------|
|      |         |            |               |         |
|      |         |            |               |         |
|      |         |            |               |         |
|      |         |            |               |         |
|      |         |            |               |         |

Speedometer reading in morning at home_____

Time of first call_____ o'clock              Last call_____o'clock

Speedometer reading in evening at home_____

Use reverse side for any additional information

prices quoted on these lists. The company does allow a 2 percent discount on all accounts paid by the tenth of the month following receipt of the order. The net amount is charged until 30 days from receipt of an order, after which the account is overdue. Regular deliveries are made once each week to every customer without charge. A nominal charge is made for customers who request more frequent delivery.

All of Delta's suppliers have salesmen and technical personnel available for service problems. They are contacted when needed. For example, the representative of one major supplier spends about half his time in the Delta territory traveling with Delta's salesmen, assisting them with their contact work, and giving counsel on specific merchandising and technical problems. From time to time Delta holds a sales and technical information meeting to which customers are invited. At one such meeting recently, the subject of aluminum siding was to be discussed and Delta's supplier of this siding sent its top technical adviser to participate in it. About 85 percent of the customers invited attended.

**EXHIBIT 5. Merchandising policy of the Delta Distributing Company**
It is the policy of our company to sell only to dealers, applicators, and industrial accounts that give us satisfactory evidence of their financial strength; and for the reasons shown herewith, following his classification, is generally known to be a dealer, applicator, or industrial account.

We will carry in stock a range of building materials which are sold to the following classes of trade:

1. Lumber and/or Building Material Dealers
2. Specialty Building Material Dealers
3. Heating, Plumbing, and Sheet Metal Shops
4. Floor and Wall Covering and Kitchen Dealers
5. Hardware and Paint Stores
6. Built-up Roofing Contractors
7. Specialty Applicators
8. Industrials
9. Federal Projects

As direct representatives of major manufacturers, we conform with the sales and merchandising policies of those manufacturers—with certain restrictions in cases where the manufacturer's policy is more liberal than our own.

As a general yardstick of our policy as applied to the above classes of recognized wholesale buyers, we make the following statements:

(1) Lumber and Building Material Dealers

We recognize the lumber dealers as completely integrated suppliers of building materials of all kinds and for that reason will sell the recognized lumber dealer any product we carry in stock, or available by direct shipment from our manufacturer suppliers.

(2) Specialty Building Material Dealers and Cabinet Shops

We recognize that the specialty building material dealer has recently come into existence. This dealer will specialize in a particular phase of building materials and stock and sell a limited group of items. We will sell to this group of dealers only the items he regularly stocks and offers for sale to the retail trade.

(3) Heating, Plumbing, and Sheet Metal Shops

We sell to these retailers such products as fabricated steel, insulation, and such other products as are definitely used in that business. Many sheet metal shops are engaged in the roofing business and to those so engaged, we will sell roofing and waterproofing products.

(4) Floor and Wall Covering and Kitchen Dealers

To these dealers, we sell floor and wall tile products, underlayment materials, adhesives, metal mouldings, kitchen cabinets, bathroom cabinets and accessories, etc.

**EXHIBIT 5** (*Continued*)

(5)    Hardware and Paint Stores

These dealers may purchase from us such products as are normally carried in stock and sold by hardware and paint stores. The products normally purchased from us by hardware stores are nails, guttering materials, lock sets, cabinet hardware, caulking, roofing cements, paints, building paper, roll roofing (we do not sell shingles or insulation materials to hardware stores).

(6)    Built-up Roofing Contractors

These are specialized contractors engaged in roofing and waterproofing commercial and industrial buildings. To them, we sell pitch, asphalt, roofing materials of all kinds, galvanized flat sheets, roof drains, roof insulation and other materials identified with that type of business.

(7)    Specialty Applicators

These are specialized contractors engaged in selling certain materials on an applied basis.

(a)    Roofing and Siding Applicators
These applicators are engaged exclusively in the sale, on an applied basis, of roofing, siding, insulation, guttering, combination windows, awnings, etc.

(b)    Floor and Wall Tile Applicators
These applicators are engaged exclusively in the sale, on an applied basis, of floor tile and wall tile and such other products as may be identified with their business. They must not be engaged in general construction work.

To the above specialized applicators, we will sell such products as are used in their respective types of business. We will not recognize new, specialty applicators unless they maintain an office and warehouse and show financial responsibility.

(8)    Industrials

We will sell to industrials or manufacturers only such materials as are used in the production of a finished product and sold by those manufacturers through their normal sales channels. We will not sell to industrials any product to be used for maintenance or new construction by their own workmen.

(9)    Federal Projects

We reserve the right to sell directly to the contractors of federal projects when competitive practices justify.

We reserve the right at all times to refuse to sell any dealer for any reason.

We are occasionally requested by customers to supply them for their own personal use materials which would not normally be sold

**EXHIBIT 5** (*Continued*)

to them. To avoid giving offense to loyal and deserving customers by refusing them the right to purchase for their own home (not their business) materials not identified with their business, we have adopted the policy of selling them such materials at a mark up of 20 percent over the regular dealer price. This markup is passed on in the form of a credit memorandum to our nearest customer who handles the type of material sold.

We welcome the suggestions and advice of all of our customers in all classes of trade in the development of a sound and equitable sales policy.

Terms and Conditions of Sale

Coverage: Our trade area is covered by our salesmen on a regularly scheduled program not exceeding three-week intervals.

Distribution Points: Unless specifically noted to the contrary, all prices shown in our price lists are for materials F.O.B. our warehouse. We also make shipments of materials on a "direct sales" basis which are on a basis of direct from manufacturer to dealer. These are made on F.O.B. shipping point and on freight allowed.

Direct Shipments: When we ship carloads or truckloads direct from our source of supply to the customer, our terms and prices are those extended by the specific supplier of the materials shipped, unless specifically agreed upon to the contrary.

Freight Allowances: All products are sold F.O.B. our warehouses or other distribution point, whichever is the point of origin. Some of our products are sold with all or a portion of the freight charges allowed. We may make express or parcel post shipments at the customer's request and expense.

Crating, Boxing, and Bagging: If any item in its normal packaging has to be specifically packaged in some way for shipment for the customer's convenience, or if portions of regular packages are shipped, we reserve the right to make a special charge for crating, boxing, or bagging involved.

Damage in Transit: Our company assumes no liability for damage or loss after the materials have been delivered to the carrier. Claims should be filed by the consignee.

Returned Materials: Merchandise returned to our warehouse will be subject to a charge of 10 percent to cover the cost of handling and reconditioning, or to the actual cost of handling and reconditioning when in excess of 10 percent. Customers will also be charged for any transportation costs incurred by us on the original shipment or the return. No returns will be accepted without prior permission.

Terms: Two percent cash discount 10th, net 30 days, past due thereafter. Cash discounts on direct shipments are same as by manufacturers making shipments. Cash discount granted providing no past-due balance

**EXHIBIT 5** (*Concluded*)

is left on our books. No cash discount allowed on freight charges prepaid or allowed by us. Interest charged on past-due accounts.

Credit: All orders shall at all times be subject to the approval of our credit department, and we shall reserve the right to require a full or partial payment in advance.

Prices and Specifications: All prices and specifications herein, or as later revised, are subject to change without notice. Prices in effect at time of shipment from our warehouse or distribution point will apply. All orders and sales contracts are subject to contingencies of manufacture, strikes or labor trouble or shortages, fires embargoes, or Government acts, regulations or requests, delays in transportation, inability to obtain necessary materials and other causes beyond our control.

Guarantees: We are not manufacturers or fabricators so have no control over the way any item is made. Therefore, we are assuming no responsibility for the failure, or resulting damage, that may occur due to the proper or improper application or use of any product we sell. We shall, however, attempt to buy only from reliable manufacturers and should any complaint arise regarding any product we sell, we will gladly do our utmost to have the manufacturer of the given product make a quick inspection and/or adjustment.


The company's main effort to stimulate sales is exerted through the dissemination of information by the salesmen. This includes various types of brochures, pamphlets, and mail stuffers which are distributed to customers to be passed on to ultimate users. This type of promotion has been supplemented and supported by a direct-mail program. This program has consisted of three elements. First, the company issues a monthly descriptive price list which is mailed to all customers and prospects. Secondly, a monthly newsletter is mailed separately to the same firms and is designed to provide information about the company, the personnel, the products and services offered, and other items of interest. Third, special promotional literature supplied by manufacturers is sent out periodically to announce new products and spearhead special selling campaigns or to tie in with national advertising.

With the exception of three office girls, all members of the Delta organization have been sent to various plants of suppliers to be given the latest information about products and manufacturing processes. In addition, most manufacturers' area representatives conduct meetings with the entire staff every two weeks to acquaint them with the company's financial standing, progress toward sales objectives, and any problems currently facing the organization. Communication is thought to be good.

The company is nevertheless faced with some problems. It now accepts all orders regardless of size. This has been done, of course, to acquire new business and to provide the type of service which would induce new customers to become permanent accounts. But small orders are seldom profitable and there are growing indications that the company is accepting business it should refuse. The question is how to increase order size without losing customers.

Warehousing is also becoming a problem. The present facilities are rapidly approaching their capacity, and there is no room for their expansion. It would not be feasible to add another floor to the present building. There are other warehouse sites available; this would not only entail building costs, but also none are as advantageously located as the present site. In this respect, there is also some concern that the building boom this area has been experiencing may suddenly level off. The construction industry, particularly in Florida, has in the past been plagued with severe cyclical fluctuations. No one is very confident in predictions of the duration of the present upswing. Consequently, capital commitments must be made with caution.

A particular touchy problem was that the chief executive of the company was a part-time administrator. He combined the responsibility of his position in Delta with interests in other commercial ventures. Yet managing a going business, even a small business, is a full-time occupation. It would be rather difficult for one of his subordinates to tell him this. Both the general manager and the sales manager were deeply concerned about the demands which the president's other interests placed upon his time. He held the purse strings of the enterprise and had to approve every change in basic strategy and clear all decisions of a policy nature, but he was not on hand to watch and study the situations which made changes in policy and strategy necessary. Consequently, the general manager was obliged to spend much of his time in communication with the president, keeping him abreast of what was happening, although he felt he could more profitably be devoting himself to the problems of small orders, warehouse facilities, and market development.

At the end of its first year of operation the company sustained a loss of some $20,000 on sales of $325,000. Average inventory investment for the year was just under $65,000 at wholesale list. All but 15 percent of this volume represented sales from inventory. The latter were divided among the following product groups: (a) 50 percent in roofing and allied products, (b) 25 percent in steel products, i.e., nails, fencing, metal roofing, and (c) 25 percent in specialty items, i.e., ladders, fixtures, aluminum siding and gutters. While this performance was disappointing to the president and other company personnel, it came as no shock. The first year of operations for almost any type of business included expenses which will not have to be repeated, and mistakes are sure to be committed which will be avoided in the future. Consequently, optimism was still high.

Shortly after the first year's results had been compiled and management was assessing the situation, a large wholesaling combine in Georgia with branches in Jacksonville, Miami, Daytona Beach, and Tampa offered to buy the Delta enterprise. Their first offer was $100,000 plus a dollar-for-dollar exchange of the combine's common stock for the remaining value of Delta assets. The offer was refused. Six months later the combine made a new offer in which it proposed to buy Delta assets at their present book value, plus $20,000 in cash and common stock equal in value to Delta's franchises in the territory as determined by the manufacturers who had granted those franchises.

The decision facing the president was rather clear. If he sold the company, he would be giving up the future profits that the enterprise might be able to produce. On the other hand, he regarded the last offer as a fair one, and one that would enable the owners to recover their original investment plus a modest claim on the earnings of another company whose survival ability had already been demonstrated.

---

# THE FRANKLIN ELECTRIC COMPANY

The executives of the Franklin Electric Company were wrestling with the problem of a new product which, although it seemed to have very attractive potential, was not going satisfactorily. The problem was complicated by the fact that the new product appealed to a market that was entirely different from that with which Franklin personnel were familiar.

## Company background

The Franklin Electric Company was founded in 1944 to build and market small electric motors designed to meet individual customer needs. This concept was contrary to the standard industry practice of adapting mass-produced motors to each application. The enterprise was initially organized as a partnership by Edward J. Schaefer and T. Wayne Kehoe, two former General Electric Company engineers, with a total capitalization of $19,500. Responsibility for engineering and design was assumed by Mr. Schaefer; responsibility for sales was assumed by Mr. Kehoe.

The firm's first customer was the U.S. Army Signal Corps, which purchased a number of electric generators for military use. With the end of World War II, the partners turned their attention to building a civilian market for electric motors. Concentrating on the manufacture of pump motors, they succeeded in winning orders from some of the nation's largest pump manufacturers. This required not only a quality product, but the ability to meet difficult deadlines. On one occasion the partners worked continuously for 72 hours to handcraft a specially designed motor for a prospective customer. On another occasion the entire work force disregarded normal working hours and produced 1,000 sump pump motors in four days, at a time when maximum output of motors of all types was only 350 units per day.

The partnership arrangement soon proved to be inadequate and the enterprise was incorporated in 1946. Mr. Schaefer became president, treasurer, and chairman of the board, while Mr. Kehoe became vice president, general sales manager, and a director. Among other directors on the board were the wives of the former partners and a certified public accountant. Leadership remained in the hands of an "inside" board through the decade of the sixties. The founder of the company was still its president and chief executive officer. His entire experience as well as that of most members of the firm's operating management was in the electric business.

By 1967 the company had scored some significant technical breakthroughs. Franklin engineers were the first to develop a small, compact motor with a stator which could be used for many different horsepower ratings, and they were the first with a commercial line of aluminum-frame motors for use where weight was an important factor. The company also developed the first practical submersible electric motor which used water for lubrication. Gear motors in both fractional and integral horsepower sizes were introduced in 1964, together with a line of food-packaging machinery that could wrap and label packages of varying dimensions without adjustment. The latter represented almost a million dollars in development costs.

At the time this case was written, the product line included four items:

1. Standard fractional and integral horsepower motors
2. Submersible motors
3. Gear motors
4. Automatic food-packaging machines

The company served three broad markets with these products: motor drive systems, water resources, and food-processing machinery. The motor drive systems market involved a variety of motor applications in compressors, air conditioners, business machines, data processing equipment, conveyors, and other industrial products. These utilized Franklin's fractional and integral horsepower motors as well as its line of gear motors.

The water resources market was the principal outlet for its submersible motors which powered submersible pumps, the most economical method of obtaining groundwater. Groundwater constitutes about 97% of the world's supply of fresh water. Franklin was the world's largest producer of submersible motors, which accounted for the major share of company sales. Their most common application was in domestic water systems.

Franklin's line of food-packaging machinery was purchased primarily by supermarkets for use in their meat departments. It was the first such system available to supermarkets. Research was under way on an automatic computing scale to be used in conjunction with this machinery.

Research and development work was also in progress on a number of products in the field of oceanography. Management believed that its experience in submersible technology afforded the firm a real competitive advantage in this comparatively new industry.

Table 1 shows certain operating and financial statistics of the company for the year to which this case refers.

### TABLE 1

| | |
|---|---:|
| Net sales | $18,178,000 |
| Income before taxes | 2,793,000 |
| Net income | 1,433,000 |
| Working capital | 6,146,000 |
| Current ratio | 3.7 to 1 |
| Net property, plant, equipment | 3,338,000 |
| Capital expenditures | 425,000 |
| Depreciation and amortization | 413,000 |
| Total assets | 11,906,000 |
| Long-term debt | 1,720,000 |
| Common stockholders' equity | 7,882,000 |
| Employee wages and benefits | 6,371,000 |
| Number of employees | 900 |

## Product development

Some years ago Franklin executives became worried by the fact that its business was so largely dependent on the market for motors, especially motors used in pumping liquids. In an attempt to diversify, Franklin acquired the rights to an automatic packaging machine that had been developed by a local inventor. The machine, which was in the prototype stage, was further developed by Franklin engineers into a commercially feasible production model. The product had been on the market several years at the time of this case, but sales and profit results were much less than had been anticipated for it.

Most fresh meat sold in supermarkets and chain stores must be encased in an envelope of cellophane or plastic film. The process of preparing it for sale includes several steps. First, the meat must be sliced into cuts of the size and type customers will wish to buy. Each cut must be trimmed to remove excess fat, gristle, and the like. These cuts are then placed in a plastic tray and wrapped in cellophane or plastic film. Finally, each package must be weighed and labeled before it is transferred to the self-service display case on the selling floor.

Traditionally, each of these steps or operations and the transfer of meat from one to another was done by hand. In the course of time some of the work of cutting was done by machinery, although it remained a highly skilled operation. There seemed to be no way to mechanize trimming. When self-service meat departments first came into operation, cuts were wrapped in cellophane and the open ends of the wrap sealed on an iron (the same kind as an iron used for ironing clothes) turned upside down in a slot on the work table.

The clumsiness of this operation soon resulted in the designing of a work table with a hot plate in the center and a rheostat on the front to control the temperature of the plate. A later refinement included an attachment for a roll of film, making the hot-plate table into a self-contained handwrap station. Tables of this type were first marketed by J. B. Dove & Sons, Inc., a Midwest packaging machinery manufacturer. With such tables a more sophisticated system then evolved, in which two or more handwrap stations were used in conjunction with a power conveyor that carried packages from the wrap stations to a scale, and an automatic labeling machine that moved them from the conveyor across the scale.

Although semiautomatic machines were introduced that eliminated much of the handling involved in the packaging process, Franklin's was the first fully automatic machine that wrapped and labeled in one continuous operation. Toledo Scale and Hobart also were known to be working on automatic packaging machines. It was anticipated that in time a machine would be developed that would package, weigh, and label automatically in one operation.

The percentage distribution of labor costs incurred in retailing meats was about as follows:

|  | *Percent* |  |
|---|---|---|
| Cutting | 38 |  |
| Packaging, weighing, labeling | 29 | (mostly packaging) |
| Stocking sales cases | 13 |  |
| Customer service | 9 |  |
| Cleaning | 4 |  |
| Receiving | 3 |  |
| Ordering and clerical | 2 |  |
| Supervision | 2 |  |

The shelf life of packaged fresh meats is limited to about three days. After that time the seal loosens, the meat loses its "bloom," becomes less attractive in appearance and no longer sells readily. When this begins to happen, the meat must be unwrapped, retrimmed and rewrapped, or perhaps converted into ground meat or hamburger and rewrapped. This rewrapping operation is very costly, sometimes running as high as $0.125 per package.

The effect of all this is complicated and multiplied by the fact that 70 percent of all retail meat sales are made on Thursday, Friday, and Saturday. This means that wrapping cannot be a continuous uniform operation, but must run light on Monday, Tuesday, and Wednesday, and heavy on the last three days of the week. This tends to complicate problems of organization and supervision and increase costs. It increases the desirability of equipment that will provide speed and flexibility in packaging.

One student of the subject reported the labor costs of wrapping a package of meat as follows:

$$
\begin{array}{ll}
\text{Hand wrap} & 1.04\text{¢} \\
\text{Semiautomatic} & .52 \\
\text{Automatic} & .23 \\
\end{array}
$$

Another study indicated that to wrap an average-sized package by hand required approximately 10 seconds, a rate of 6 packages per minute per person. With a semiautomatic machine the rate increased to 12–15 packages per minute, and with a fully automatic machine 30–35 packages could be wrapped per minute.

The importance of the cost saving feature is emphasized by these facts: (1) meat is usually a low profit or losing item in the store, and (2) meat is an item that draws and holds customer traffic. The process of handwrapping also requires a lot of highly expensive store space that could otherwise be used in selling.

## Market development

The market for the automatic meat-packaging machine consists mainly of supermarkets. But not all supermarkets find it profitable to use the machinery. The volume of meat sales is a primary determining factor. On a purely statistical basis, the break-even volume seems to be somewhere between $10,000 and $15,000 of meat sales per week. A store with this much business or more will find it less costly to use a fully automatic machine than to package by hand or semiautomatic means. This dollar limitation of course takes no account of the advantage of having more freshly packaged meat in the display sales cases nor of the saving in space. Of course if Franklin could achieve a sufficient savings in production costs to warrant a reduction in the machine's existing price of $6,388, these break-even figures would be lower.

Statistics of supermarket stores compiled by *Progressive Grocer* were as follows:

| *Annual sales* | *Number of stores* |
|---|---|
| $500,000 to $1,000,000............................ | 13,125 |
| $1,000,000 to $2,000,000......................... | 12,155 |
| Over $2,000,000................................. | 5,620 |

Meat sales constituted about 25 percent of the volume of the average supermarket. Of the 5,620 stores having sales of two million dollars or more, 3,670 were members of chains and 1,950 were independents.

It would be possible for a chain system to cut and package meat in a central warehouse and distribute it from there to the individual stores. Practically, this is not usually feasible, because the manager of the meat department of a store finds it very difficult, if not impossible, to forecast a day ahead of time exactly how much of each cut of meat customers will wish to buy. This procedure would also require daily deliveries from the central warehouse if the meat is to be fresh. Most chains do not find it economical to deliver this often.

It is estimated that about 1,800 new supermarket stores are opened each year. This includes newly constructed stores, old stores that are remodeled or replaced by larger ones, and old stores whose volume has grown to the supermarket minimum level of $500,000 annual sales. Most of the newly opened stores are large outlets.

The company's marketing research department made the following estimates of the total market for automatic packaging machines on the basis of several assumptions:

Assumption A—Central processing plants will serve all superettes (27,800 stores), and all supermarkets except those doing over two million dollars annually, and each central plant will serve 40 stores. (Each central plant having two machines.)

| | | |
|---|---|---|
| Supermarkets over $2,000,000..................................... | 5,620 | machines |
| All other supers (25,280 divided by 40) × 2........................ | 1,260 | " |
| Superettes (27,800 divided by 40) × 2............................ | 1,400 | " |
| Total............................................................ | 8,280 | " |

Assumption B—Central plants will serve all supermarkets and superettes (each central plant having two machines).

| | | |
|---|---|---|
| Supermarkets (30,900 divided by 40) × 2.:........................ | 1,540 | machines |
| Superettes (27,800 divided by 40) × 2............................ | 1,400 | " |
| Total........................................................... | 2,940 | " |

Assumption C—Price reductions on automatic machines are made which make it economically feasible for 50% of the supermarkets in the one to two million dollar category to use the equipment.

| | | |
|---|---|---|
| Supermarkets over $2,000,000..................................... | 5,620 | machines |
| Half of $1–$2,000,000 group..................................... | 6,077 | " |
| Total........................................................... | 11,697 | " |

There were a number of obstacles to the introduction of automatic meat-packaging machines. For one thing the back room personnel of the typical store were not mechanically minded and could hardly be expected to take readily to the operation of such a machine. There were also technical problems of fitting the machine into the space, routine, and operating conditions of the individual store. Expert help was often needed to install the machine and train employees to operate it.

Then too, the idea of machine operation was foreign to the whole tempo and atmosphere of a retail store. So it was not easy to convince management that automatic packaging of so individualistic a product as meat was practical. This difficulty was compounded by the fact that many stores had no cost analysis that would segregate the expense of packaging from other costs of meat handling. So they had no way of knowing how much savings automatic packaging might yield. In some areas labor unions opposed the introduction of automatic machines. It is also probable that the potential of the machine to eliminate some jobs did not endear workroom personnel to its use. Moreover, an operator who was in the mood to do so could easily sabotage it.

The price of the machine, $6,388, as against $2,500 for semiautomatic equipment and $400 for a handwrap station acted as a deterrent to purchase. The average supermarket had an annual budget of $11,000 for new equipment. The purchase of an automatic packaging machine would exhaust well over half of this total.

Franklin's efforts to sell the cooperative and voluntary chain-store groups were handicapped by the machine's flat pricing structure with no discounts. A member store of a cooperative or a voluntary chain system could buy one machine at the same unit price group headquarters would pay for a dozen. Since many of the chain and voluntary group headquarters organizations looked to quantity discounts to finance their operations or to sell their services to members, the Franklin price structure did not invite these headquarters groups to push the sale of automatic packaging machines enthusiastically.

Many of these obstacles could be overcome or minimized by proper personal selling and effective technical and training service. The attitude of unions varied from one area to another. In St. Louis, for example, the Amalgamated Meatcutters and Butcher Workmen of North America threatened to strike if any automatic wrapping machines were installed.

The executives of Franklin Electric were uncertain about what channels to use to reach the market. There was a general feeling that it could best be cultivated by Franklin salesmen and a Franklin service force. But this would involve a considerable overhead expense and there was some question as to whether the probable sales volume would support it. About this time the Hobart Company bought a small manufacturer of semiautomatic packaging machinery and began handling its marketing with a Hobart sales force. As a result a number of manufacturers' agents who had previously represented the small manufacturer were left without a product line. This circumstance seemed to offer Franklin a ready-made channel system, for these agents represented experienced sales coverage which would take Franklin a long time to develop on its own.

Consequently, it was decided to retain a sufficient number of these agents to handle sales of the new product on the East and West Coasts and in Canada. Marketing in the central U.S. would be done through Franklin's own sales and service organization. The plan was to reach all of Canada and three-fourths of the U.S. market through agents. Since agents made available by the Hobart move covered only about half of this vast territory, Franklin was obliged to recruit additional agents.

It was anticipated that product service would present a problem. Management therefore retained two local independent service organizations, one in New York and one in Chicago, and signed a contract with the Radio Corporation of America to provide product service and technical backup over the remainder of the nation. Franklin agreed to train the salesmen of the agents as well as the service men of R.C.A. and the two local organizations based in New York and Chicago.

In addition, Franklin obtained a list of supermarkets by city of location from *Supermarket News,* which was shared with the manufacturers' agents; prepared exhibits for the annual meetings of the Supermarket Institute; and placed ads in various trade media. Both the list of supermarkets and the names of persons who visited the exhibits proved to be fruitful sources of prospective customers. On the other hand, the media advertising done by Franklin did not prove very effective in generating contacts with prospective customers, and there were serious doubts that it could be made so.

In operation this plan proved to be less than satisfactory. Only 190 machines were sold during the first two years of marketing effort, a figure which represented less than 3 percent of estimated market potential. Such performance was especially disturbing, because it was important that Franklin capture a strong position in this market before Toledo Scale and Hobart succeeded in introducing a similar machine.

The Franklin marketing department had found that the sale of an automatic packaging machine was usually a multiple contact process. The persons with buying influences who had to be contacted and "sold" in the average chain or cooperative organization included at least the following:

*The store's meat manager,* who was primarily interested in how the machine would fit into his existing facilities and its effect on his operations and his costs.

*The store manager,* who was interested in the machine's effect on the overall budget of the store.

*The headquarters' meat manager,* who was interested in about the same things as his store counterpart.

*The equipment buyer,* who wanted to know about price, delivery, discounts, service, and the reliability of the supplier.

*The research team* that conducted use tests.
*The people who would operate the machine.*
A *financial officer,* in some cases, who was interested in such matters as the effect of the machine on cash flow, amortization, and depreciation.

The marketing department felt that it had also found the most effective selling methods to be:

a.  Demonstration
b.  Trial
c.  Back room layout advice and assistance

Demonstration was necessary to convince the store's meat manager that the machine would work. Many did not think that automatic packaging was feasible. A visit to a store where an automatic packaging machine was in use proved to be the most effective way of overcoming such skepticism. This prompted the policy of making machines available on a 30-day trial basis.

Implementing this policy required careful administration. The machine would not function properly unless it was properly installed and properly integrated into the meat room layout. Sometimes this required changes in the layout. The machine had to be handled correctly by operating personnel. This required training. Since an untrained, careless, or antagonistic operator could render the machine useless, it was often necessary for either a salesman or a serviceman, or both, to spend considerable time demonstrating the effectiveness of the machine when properly operated. Consequently, the provision of back room layout service and training assistance by R.C.A. and the two independent firms had to be carefully coordinated with the work of salesmen. With three different firms involved, coordination of sales and service effort often proved very difficult.

It became clear that if Franklin was to get proper distribution, it must have complete control of both the selling and service functions. Unfortunately, this was easier to decide than to accomplish. In its efforts to structure a more tightly controlled distribution system capable of contacting and servicing supermarkets, Franklin suffered from the narrowness of its product line. It sold only one item of equipment out of many that were needed to operate a supermarket meat department.

For example, one firm in the industry offered in its catalog the following extensive line of back room equipment:

| | |
|---|---|
| semiautomatic packaging machines | shrink tunnels |
| conveyor sealing systems | power belt conveyors |
| console meat-wrapping systems | accumulator turntables and bins |
| | tray sealers |

multideck meat-wrapping
  systems
table-top wrapping systems
produce-wrapping systems
tubular frame bases
film dispensers
trim stations
label activators
roll label dispensers
platters and pans
platter and pan carts and
  racks

bag sealers
offal-packaging systems
hot plates
hand sealers
utility tables
stretch net systems
meat-dusting machines (to
  brush off bone fragments)
meat lugs
stocker trucks

The possession of a complete line of equipment such as this affords several advantages to the marketer of automatic packaging machines.

First, it would provide a volume large enough to support the sales and service organization needed to market automatic packaging equipment effectively. There was doubt that the volume of an automatic packaging machine alone would be sufficient to do this.

Second, an extensive assortment of equipment to sell would give salesmen a profitable entrée into supermarkets of all sizes and types. Once "inside the door," they would have an opportunity to study the store's operations to discover whether or not the use of automatic packaging machinery would be feasible.

Third, a full line of equipment gave a firm prestige and standing in the industry. To personnel in the supermarket industry, a firm (such as Franklin), without an assortment of related equipment to sell was viewed as an outsider dabbling in the retail meat business. No matter what degree of efficiency could be claimed for its product, such a firm was still looked upon as an opportunist whose main interest was not in the meat business.

### The options

Franklin had at least four alternatives which might be pursued in an effort to resolve the question of what to do with its automatic packaging machine. The company could *build and market a line of equipment* to serve the back room requirements of the supermarket industry. However, this would represent a long and slow process both to build the needed assortment of products and to develop standing and prestige in the industry. The latter would probably be the more difficult and time-consuming because it would involve the recruiting and training of a sales and service force and then the slow winning of confidence by performance.

On the other hand, Franklin could *attempt to merge with or acquire a firm already in the business* with an established product line and an operating sales and service force. Several companies matched these criteria. There were, of course, the two giants of the industry, Toledo Scale and Hobart. Both of these firms sold and serviced a complete line of equipment (including handwrap and semiautomatic wrapping machines, labelers, conveyors, scales, grinders, choppers, and saws), but neither had at this time a fully automatic packaging machine comparable to Franklin's.

It was known that both Toledo and Hobart recognized the need for automatic weighing and labeling equipment that could be linked with an automatic packaging machine to perform the series of packaging functions—wrapping, weighing, and labeling—in a single operation. Franklin was already engaged in research and development of such equipment, but so were Toledo and Hobart. The closer these firms were to a "breakthrough" in their R & D efforts, the less interest a merger with Franklin would have for them. If a real breakthrough seemed some distance into the future, Franklin's head start with one functioning automatic element of the three, probably would stimulate interest in a possible merger with it. No one at Franklin professed to know the true situation.

There were also a number of smaller firms which manufactured and marketed more limited lines of back room equipment. A representative sample of them would include the following:

1.  J. B. Dove and Sons, Inc., producing handwrap and semiautomatic packaging equipment, as well as a variety of materials-handling equipment associated with back room operations.
2.  The Wrapping Machinery Company, specializing in semiautomatic wrapping equipment and offering a respectable assortment of models.
3.  Sturtevant Industries, specializing in labelers of various types and sizes.
4.  Lasar Manufacturing Company, specializing in meat saws of various types and sizes.
5.  The Biro Manufacturing Company, also specializing in meat saws.

Mergers and acquisitions both present knotty problems, not the least of which are financing and organization. How long their resolution will require depends upon a number of variables, some of which cannot be fully recognized beforehand. Parties to merger and acquisition agreements invariably approach such moves with great caution. Franklin should do no less.

Then, too, *the company could continue on its present course,* trying to weld its present agents and contract services into a more cohesive marketing system. In this, management at least has the advantage of knowing where the problems lie and of having had some experience in coping with them.

Franklin could also *sell or lease the patent rights to its packaging machine* to another manufacturer and concentrate its efforts in markets in which it has a greater competitive advantage and more experience. While this option might be looked upon as defeatist, it does offer the possibility of an eventual recovery of the company's original investment in the product and precludes further investment in a difficult venture.

**EXHIBIT 1.   Franklin Electric's automatic packaging machine**

Shrink Tunnel:
Requires separate 230 volt, single phase
60 cycle, 20 amp receptacle.

F-510 SHRINK WRAPPING MACHINE

Physical size: F-510

8'-3" overall length
2'-4¼" overall width
4'-8½" overall height

Electrical requirements:

208-230 volts, single phase, 50/60 cycle
20 amp outlet within 10 feet of point
(see drawing)
30 amp supply recommended

Film roll size:

9" wide, 3" I.D. core – minimum
18" wide, 10" diameter — maximum

Meat cuts of varying sizes placed on the track at the left of the machine are carried through it. A film envelope is fitted to each cut by a shrinking process that produces a tough, nearly skin-tight wrapping.

# THE HANCOCK COMPANY (A)

The Hancock Chemical Company is a manufacturer of fine chemicals and drug materials. At the time of this case its annual sales volume was between $60 and $80 million. The company makes about 1,000 products, some 200 of which are responsible for 70 to 80 percent of its sales volume. The company conducts an extensive program of chemical, pharmacological, and medical research, and is firmly committed to the proposition that such research is vital to leadership in the fine chemical business. About 60 percent of its present sales volume is in products developed through research during the past 15 years. Its present sales volume is about 5 times that of 15 years ago.

The importance of different products or groups of products in the sales volume pattern of the company varies widely from year to year as is shown by the following table.

| Product group | Percentage of total company sales volume | | |
| | 1945 | 1955 | 1965 |
|---|---|---|---|
| A | 11.3 | 10 | 5 |
| B | 9.6 | 8 | 5 |
| C | 7.7 | 2 | * |
| D | 7.3 | 5 | 1 |
| E | 7.0 | 12 | 0.5 |
| F | 6.9 | 3 | 2 |
| G | 3.9 | 4 | 3 |
| H | 3.9 | 2 | 0.3 |
| I | 3.8 | 4 | 1 |
| J | * | 15 | 27 |
| K | * | 7 | 6 |
| L | * | * | 15 |
| M | * | * | 12 |
| N | * | * | 9 |

* Not in the line.

The products of the company can be grouped in the following classes:

a. Antibiotics (penicillin, etc.)     e. Agricultural
b. Medicinal chemicals     f. Food
c. Vitamins     g. Industrial
d. Hormones     h. General

While the research and production problems of each group differ from those of the other groups, they do not differ too much from one another in the methods or problems of selling.

The products of the company are sold to the following types of buyers:

a. Pharmaceutical manufacturers, who use them in compounding preparations sold chiefly under their brands over the retail counter. Some of these preparations are sold only on doctor's prescription. There are about 900 such manufacturers—about a dozen very large, most small. They are heavily concentrated around New York, Chicago, and St. Louis, although there are a few in all parts of the country.

b. Veterinary houses, which use Hancock products to compound medicines sold chiefly under their own brands for use in treating animals. There are about 200 such houses.

c. Cosmetic manufacturers, about 1,000, who use certain Hancock products in preparations sold under their own brands.

d. Industrial buyers, who purchase Hancock products for a variety of uses; the most important is the vitamin enrichment of foods and animal and poultry feeds. About 15,000 industrial firms can use Hancock products; only about 6,000 can use them in sufficient quantity to justify direct sales service. These firms must be canvassed by salesmen qualified to offer technical advice and service.

e. Laboratories of industrial firms and educational institutions, about 1,000 of significance. Most of them buy from laboratory supply distributors, of which about 30 are of any real importance. This business is declining in volume.

f. Chemical supply and laboratory supply and equipment wholesalers, about 200 worth carrying on the company's customer list.

g. Governmental units, buying mainly for health and hospital work. They purchase chiefly on bids.

h. Competing manufacturers, who buy from Hancock items that Hancock can make more cheaply than they can. Hancock also purchases certain items from them. There are about 30 of these, a half-dozen really important. It is very important to maintain cordial relations with some of these firms.

Gross profits are usually about 40 percent on sales, although the gross profit figure on individual items fluctuates widely, from as much as 90 percent on sales to a minus quantity. Selling and other distribution expenses are generally about 6 percent of sales. Net profit before taxes usually averages about 15 percent of sales, and after taxes about 7 percent of sales. Both selling expenses and net profit percentages vary widely among the different products as percentages of sales.

The introduction of a new product into the line is usually an expensive process. It often happens that during the test-tube and pilot plant stages, costs of as much as several millions accrue against a possible new product. Sometimes these costs must be written off to profit and loss when it proves impossible to develop a prospective new product to the marketable point. If a new product gives evidence that it will be demanded in considerable quantities, it may be necessary to build or buy new equipment, sometimes costing several millions. The firm usually has a large sum of money invested in a product in the form of sunk costs before a nickel's worth of it is ready to be sold on the market.

The officials of the firm feel that three aspects of the company's pricing policies and practices should be reexamined.

1. In the chemical business, as in several others, there are two schools of thought about pricing policy and practice on a new product. When a firm brings out a new product, it usually has a virtual monopoly for a period varying from a few months to one and one-half or two years. During the early part of this period, competitors may be expected to watch the product's reception on the market and to attempt to appraise its market possibilities. After they become convinced that its production and sale will be a profitable venture, they must spend considerable time in procuring or developing equipment with which to make it, and in developing production and selling know-how by a process of trial and error.

During this period of monopoly, some firms follow the policy of pricing the product at the highest figure they can get for their supply, which is usually limited in relation to the demand. Sometimes the gross profit on such an item will run as high as 80 or 90 percent on sales during this period.

Other companies prefer the policy of trying to compute the level at which the price of the product will settle when it has become an established member of the line and after competition has developed. Such a firm then fixes its initial price at or near this level.

The Hancock Company has followed the first of these policies, but some of the executives are dissatisfied with it. They feel that it tends to invite competition, to cause embarrassment because of the deep price cuts that must be made when competition appears and begins to be established, and to create customer ill will because buyers feel that during the early stages of product marketing they were gouged by unreasonably high prices. It is usually not easy to explain the theory underlying such a policy, because many customers find it hard to believe that developmental costs are as high as they really are. Nor is it usually desirable to disclose such costs to customers in detail.

2. The company is one of the oldest in the field and commands great prestige throughout the industry. From the beginning, it has been meticulous in maintaining the most exhaustive system of checks and tests to assure the quality of its products. Hancock quality is a byword in the trade. It has also placed great emphasis on service, both in the form of delivery and in technical aid and advice on the use of its products.

As a result, there has been a feeling among some company executives that it is beneath Hancock's dignity to engage in too active price competition. The outcome of this has been a certain slowness in meeting competitors' price cuts. When a competitor cuts the price of an item, Hancock has a tendency to assume a somewhat haughty and righteous air, designed to indicate that such cheap practices are beneath its dignity and standing in the industry. Often, this attitude is maintained until the competitor makes serious inroads into the Hancock volume; then price is reduced to the level set by the competitor. The salesmen then have to struggle mightily to recapture customers enticed away by the lower price.

The routine necessary to initiate a price reduction may also have contributed to this slowness of response to competitive price cuts. Price changes are originated in the marketing department by the manager of price policy, who reports to the vice president in charge of marketing. A recommendation of the price policy manager must be approved by the vice president for marketing, who transmits it to the executive vice president and the president, without whose approval it cannot become effective. One of these men is a graduate of sales and the other of controllership; both are very much interested in pricing and carefully study proposed price changes. Their studies sometimes require considerable time.

Several of the younger executives feel that both the system and the policy should be changed in some way so as to bring about a quicker, more responsive, and more competitively effective pattern of pricing policy and practice.

3. Various cost-of-distribution studies have disclosed that many of the company's products are priced at figures that put them in the red on a gross profit basis, or result in no contribution to net profit and general overhead after distribution costs are deducted from gross profits. A few of these products are items that the company sells in considerable volume and are footballs of competition. They constitute an element of considerable significance in the cost structure of the typical customer who buys them. Most of them, however, are sold in small volume. The average customer who buys such an item purchases only a few dollars, or at most a few hundreds of dollars, worth of it a year. It constitutes no significant element in his cost structure. A few are articles whose prices are closely watched as barometers of price movements and indicators of competitive price position in the trade.

Some of these loss items are bought by customers who purchase from the Hancock Company significant volumes of profitable products. Others are bought largely by customers who purchase nothing else from the company.

Several executives of the company feel that this entire area of the company's pricing policy and practice should be studied, and that certain general principles and procedures should be established to administer prices of individual items belonging to this unprofitable group.

# THE HANCOCK COMPANY (B)

The Hancock Company is a chemical manufacturer. Its products are sold for use by pharmaceutical and drug manufacturing concerns, veterinary products manufacturers, food and beverage manufacturing houses, educational, commercial, and industrial laboratories, industrial establishments, and ultimate consumers, to whom they are dispensed by hospitals or physicians or on physician's prescription through retail drugstores.

The company's sales have grown very rapidly from $8.1 million in 1929 to $55.4 million in 1946, $108.5 million in 1952, and over $200 million in the 1960s.

No small part of this great expansion of sales is the fruit of the extensive research program, which the company began in the early thirties and has continued to the present time. This research work is organized under a separate department; its chief reports directly to the company president and is a member of the operations committee, which includes the chief operating officials of the firm. This department contains units specializing in organic and biochemical research, microbiological research, and physical and inorganic chemical research. It also includes a development unit, which specializes in problems of chemical technology and production and has control of the pilot plant operations involved in carrying a new product from the test tube to the factory processing stage.

During one period of the company's development, there was considerable dispute between the research group and the engineering group over which should have charge of carrying a new product through the pilot plant stage of its development and readying it for full-scale plant processing operations. The research men felt that since they had lived with the idea from its inception and knew all its past history they were best qualified to carry its development right through to the floor of the factory and supervise the ironing out of all the difficulties that might occur in integrating it as a full-fledged member of the line. The engineering group felt, on the other hand, that since the umbilical cord binding a new product to research had to be cut at some time, and that since the test tube was the scale of operations at which the research men functioned best, while plant operation was the particular province of the engineers, the new product should be transferred to the control of the engineering department when it entered the pilot plant stage. The engineers finally won out, and the development section of the research department was transferred to the engineering department. While the research department members were not exactly happy about the outcome, they gradually became reconciled to it, more readily perhaps because the engineering department was under the leadership of a new chief who gave better technical service in the work of introducing new products than the research group had formerly been able to do.

But this happy resolution of the company's attempt to organize the technical aspects of new product work failed to solve all the problems connected with it. When a new article is ready for production and commercial use, it still must undergo the procedure of being tested and released for distribution by the Food and Drug Administration, and must be worked into the sales line as a full-fledged member of the company family of products. If this work were left until the test-tube and pilot plant stages were completed, the ultimate results from a profit standpoint might prove to be far from satisfactory. The commercial aspects of a new product need to be explored concurrently with its technical features. Current stories in the industry tell of a firm that spent $500,000 developing a new product, only to find that its total possible sales were about $50,000 a year. The sales department was too heavily burdened with the day-to-day crises that attend the work of capturing and holding customers to do much with the task of exploring the market possibilities of a new product, let alone that of appraising its probable effect on the cost and profit structure of the firm.

Top management felt that a separate unit of the company was needed to do this work. As a result, a product development department was established. Mr. Stanton, the head of the new department, set out to explore the areas within which his unit might operate to the profit of the company.

Mr. Stanton soon felt himself handicapped by what seemed to him a lack of product policy on the part of the company. For example, there seemed to be no clear-cut determination on the extent to which the company should sell such products as insecticides, which were somewhat outside the drug field. There also seemed to be some confusion of policy about the question of whether the company should develop a line of products to be sold over the retail drug counter under the Hancock label. Mr. Stanton finally worked out the following statement of the responsibilities and authority of his department for inclusion in the organization manual of the company.

### MANAGER PRODUCT DEVELOPMENT DEPARTMENT

Reports to: The President

In carrying out his responsibilities he:

1. Correlates and directs all matters related to the establishment of new products by the company.

2. Surveys and analyzes the sales and market possibilities for present and new products in existing and new fields.

3. Determines sales potentials for products in development or suggested for development.

4. On the basis of market surveys and analysis, recommends development or production of new products.

5. Estimates actual sales of new products to guide the planning of necessary production and sales facilities.

6. Coordinates the company's efforts in developing new products, including the recommending of manufacturing capacity, sales programs, and distribution plans.

7. When necessary, carries out initial sales of new products prior to turning them over to the marketing division.

8. Studies and reports on the probable effects of the introduction of new products on the financial, cost, and profit structure of the company.

Mr. Stanton attempted to build up the organization of the product development department and to expand its activities. In the process, he engendered antagonism among several of the operating divisions to such a point that neither he nor his assistants were able to obtain the cooperation so vitally necessary to the proper performance of the department's functions. For example, he urged that the product development department employ a small force of specialty salesmen with whom to conduct pilot marketing programs when introducing new products to the market, and he thought most new products should not be turned over to the marketing division until in the course of such pilot programs the bugs had been worked out of their distribution and production systems. This did not exactly serve to endear his department to members of the marketing division. After about ten years, Mr. Stanton made a connection elsewhere and left the company. His place was taken by Mr. Boyle, a very able young man with excellent technical and business training, pleasing personality, and great vigor and drive. He previously had been an executive of a smaller company.

About this time, at the suggestion of the administrative vice president Mr. Ross, careful study was given to the problem of establishing a marketing research department. This step was finally decided on at about the time Mr. Boyle assumed direction of the product development department, now elevated in the organization hierarchy to the status of a division. The new department was made a part of the enlarged division. Since Mr. Boyle was not immediately able to dissipate the lack of sympathy between his division and the marketing group, and since the tasks of sales analysis and making sales estimates still remained in the sales planning department, a unit of the marketing division, the work of the marketing research department was confined mainly to market explorations for new products and to economic studies for top management.

The large number of products made by the company and their diversified nature caused other complications. Each product, or at least each group of them, possessed problems of its own with respect to its improvement, the control of its quality, its production, and its marketing. For example, the problems involved in handling narcotics were especially unique in the rigid control required because of governmental regulations and the socially dangerous nature of the products themselves. The management decided that these problems required special attention, so a product manager was appointed to devote all his attention to the narcotics line. Other persons were assigned to this type of work, and in due course there were 10 product managers, each dealing with the problems of a separate group of products.

An executive of the company described the duties and authority of a product manager as follows.

> The general responsibility of a product manager is that of a business manager for a specific product or group of products. He is responsible for coordinating all activities that have an effect on the profit contributions of the product or products assigned to him. Acting in a staff capacity, he works closely with operating and staff executives to maintain and improve the position of the product or products and the profits.
>
> While he has no line authority, he has the responsibility of keeping top management informed on important operating problems and also on such other information as industry trends, the company's competitive position, sales forecasts, and any other significant matters. He makes recommendations on policies and practices that will improve the profit position, and assists operating executives in carrying out programs in accordance with instructions from the operations committee.

At first, each product manager reported directly to the chairman of the operations committee. Later, conterol of their activities was concentrated under a director of product managers, Mr. Angus, who reported to the chairman of the operations committee.

The responsibilities of a product manager were described in the organization manual of the company as follows.

> The product manager is responsible for assisting general management and operating executives in improving the profit contribution of the products assigned to him. Acting in a staff capacity, he is responsible for continuous analysis, evaluation, and coordination of all company activities affecting these products, including sales, production, scientific, purchasing, engineering, financial and related matters. Serving as a focal point in the company for information about his products, he makes recommendations, after close collaboration with interested operating departments, on policies and programs designed to strengthen their competitive position and increase their profits. He is responsible for assisting in the management of contracts affecting the products, and for maintaining outside contacts and relationships as assigned.

The results were not always happy. The operating executives sometimes complained that the product managers got in their hair. For example, a product manager often felt the need of visiting members of customer trades in order to get a more realistic idea of the market conditions for his products than could be obtained from a desk in Baltimore, headquarters of the company. This was resented and opposed by the marketing division executives, who felt that relations with a customer were a delicate matter and should not be disturbed by other representatives of the company whose questions might raise embarrassing doubts in the customers' minds. Likewise, the sales executives were sometimes embarrassed by the estimates of sales possibilities issued by product managers. In estimating the sales of a product, the product manager usually dealt in terms of sales potentials—the volume Hancock would get if it got all the sales of the product there were to get. When the sales executives submitted their estimates of what they actually expected to sell during a coming budgetary period, general management sometimes did not remember to distinguish between the differing bases upon which the estimates were made, to the chagrin of the marketing group.

Some overlapping also developed between the work of the product managers and that of the product development division. For example, the head of the product development division felt that his unit should have primary responsibility for all new products, even when there was a product manager assigned to the general group of products to which the new product belonged. The director of product managers felt, on the other hand, that when a product manager was assigned a group of products he should be held primarily responsible for all new products developed in his group, and that the product development division should get into the picture only on request of the product manager. On the other hand, the director of product development was of the opinion that, of necessity, his group should interest itself in existing as well as new products. He expressed his attitude as follows.

> Product development is not merely a matter of taking new products proffered by research, coordinating the various matters relating to initial sale, and then dropping them. It must be concerned on a continuing basis with the various product lines, their profitability and competitive strength, the long-time as well as the short-run picture, changes in the economic position of industries served by Hancock products, and the relation of existing and potential facilities to demand.
>
> In order to properly evaluate the position of a potential new product, it is essential that those studying the problem be thoroughly informed about the past and present history of similar products, and the development in the line of products of which the new product will be a part.
>
> Furthermore, once all the necessary work has been done to understand whether a new product should be added to the line and what its competitive position should be, it seems to me wasteful at that point for the individual who has conducted the preliminary study to drop the item and no longer be concerned with it. This individual should follow

and keep in touch with the inventory position and markets and prices and costs of the article, not for the purpose of exerting line authority over the operating departments, but to be able to warn of significant trouble ahead or to interpret accumulating inventories, changing costs, and other factors of the competitive situation and the need for the development of new or improved products or the abandonment of existing products or product lines.

The establishment of product managers in addition to the product development division cannot help but result in duplication and extra overhead for the company. To be competent in his field, a product manager must give consideration to the competitive position of his assigned products and to the development of new products to strengthen the line within his field of responsibility. He must, therefore, overlap the responsibilities of product development. On the other hand, in order to consider new products intelligently and to evaluate their profitability and proper distribution, product development must keep informed of the status of existing product lines, thereby duplicating the work of the product managers.

These conflicting attitudes led to the development of the following personnel picture (secretarial help excluded).

| Product or activity group | Product development | | Product managers | |
|---|---|---|---|---|
| | Men | Money | Men | Money |
| General administration................... | 1 | $15,000 | 1 | $12,000 |
| Miscellaneous products................... | 1 | 10,000 | | |
| Industrial products....................... | 1 | 8,500 | | |
| Narcotics and vitamins................... | 1 | 8,500 | 3 | 18,000 |
| Veterinary products.: .................... | 1 | 8,500 | 1 | 8,500 |
| Pharmaceutical products................. | 2 | 17,000 | 1 | 8,500 |
| Specialties............................... | 1 | 4,000 | | |
| Antibiotics.............................. | | | 3 | 19,500 |
| Laboratory chemicals..................... | | | 1 | 8,500 |
| Inorganic chemicals...................... | 1 | 8,500 | | |
| Total............................... | 9 | $80,000 | 10 | $75,000 |

This resulted in an overlapping of about $37,000 in the salaries of men in the two groups who were performing identical functions with respect to the same products.

Top management felt that the time had come to attempt to eliminate as much as possible of the overlapping and misunderstanding that resulted from this situation.

The director of product managers and the director of the product development division suggested that they be allowed to work together to divide up the area between them and set limits to their respective fields of authority and responsibility. In fact, they had made tentative steps in that direction, although they had not been able to agree on substantial areas.

Mr. Ross suggested that both product managers and the product development division be abolished, and a director of merchandising be set up. The responsibilities of this new official would include:

1. Studying the product line as to sales, profits, and competition.
2. Evaluating the outlook for the company's products in all commercial aspects.
3. Deleting or modifying existing products.
4. Studying containers and labels in order to reconcile the interests of sales, production, and scientific divisions.
5. Evaluating the markets and all commercial aspects of new products, and making decisions with respect to all new products involving a financial outlay of less than a fixed amount; recommending with respect to other proposed new products.
6. Studying inventories of finished goods and recommending policies in order to reconcile the interests of sales, production, and finance.
7. Studying price policies and practices.
8. Acting as a focal point for all company information about products.
9. Making decisions about finished inventory levels within limits of established policy.

In making this proposal, Mr. Ross sought to solve another problem that had long been a matter of vexation—the control of inventory. From time to time, the operations committee established overall policy on the amount and composition of inventory, both of materials and finished goods. This policy was carried out by the manufacturing planning department, which also made the necessary decision in the absence of a policy decision to cover a specific situation not of major importance. On occasion, a series of such minor decisions on inventory had worked into a policy pattern of major import. Mr. Ross felt that the inventory management was a matter in which at least three major operating parts of the company—production, sales, and finance—had an interest, and that, therefore, it should not be under the control of the production division.

EXHIBIT 1. The Hancock Company

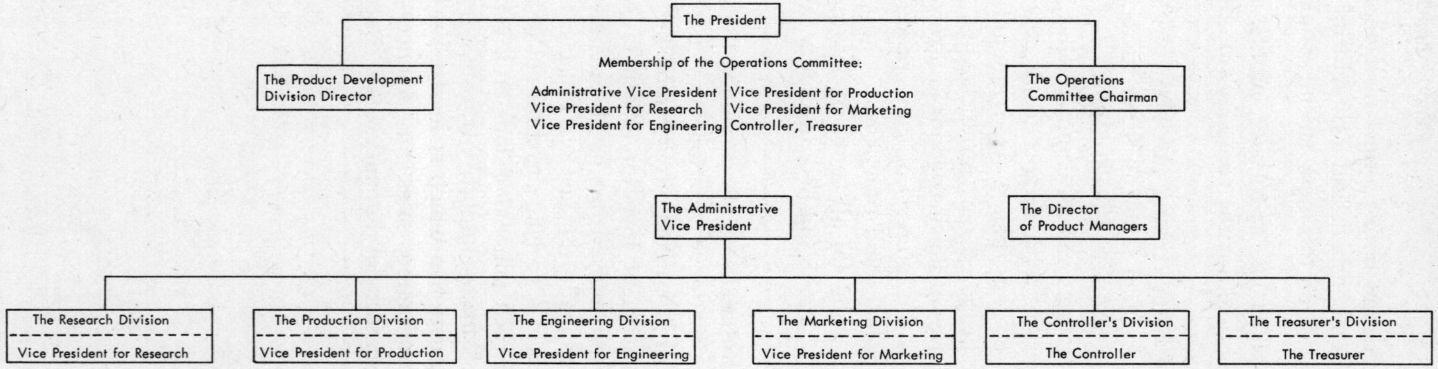

# THE HAYS-HILLIARD CORPORATION

The Hays-Hilliard Corporation is a distributor of industrial equipment, machinery, and heavy hardware located in Milwaukee, Wisconsin. The company's six branches, each with a sizable warehouse facility, are located in Chicago, St. Louis, Cincinnati, South Bend, Indianapolis, and Evansville. Sales in 1972 amounted to slightly more than $18 million, an increase of about 20 percent over the preceding three years. The Chicago branch, which was the largest, accounted for about $4.5 million of the total, whereas the smallest branch, at Evansville, accounted for about $700,000. Although all branches have shown sales increases over the most recent three-year period, sales at Chicago and Milwaukee have made the greatest contribution to the overall 20 percent figure.

While a period of continued growth and expansion had produced increased sales, earnings had shown an ominous tendency to shrink. Highly competitive markets made it impossible for the company to pass on to customers anything approximating 100 percent of the increases in costs with which it had been faced over the past five years. The remedy appeared to be tighter controls administered through a more closely knit organizational structure with greater centralized authority.

There was no opposition to the institution of these reforms. It was widely agreed that they were needed. Implementing them, however, produced sharp disagreements, particularly between the president and the manager of the Chicago branch. The latter regarded them as meddlesome and unworkable. Although performance at the Chicago branch had been satisfactory, the president feared that making an exception for it would create hard feelings among managers of other branches. On the other hand, any uniform relaxation of the requirements that specific control procedures be followed and reports be submitted regularly might impair the whole cost control program. It was also feared that forcing compliance with top management's directives would precipitate a serious morale problem among branch managers, which at worst could result in the loss of some experienced management personnel. The outline of a control system that would be both effective in controlling costs and acceptable in application was not readily apparent to the president and his staff.

## Company background

Hays-Hilliard functions both as a manufacturer's agent and merchant wholesaler. Approximately 60 percent of total sales in 1972 were made on a commission basis. However, sales from inventory have shown a steady upward trend since the formation of the present corporation in 1957, through a merger of the Hays Equipment Company and Hilliard Associates. The Hays Equipment Company had been an old and well-established wholesaler of machinery and heavy hardware. The company was organized in Indianapolis in 1901 and during the twenties had established branches in Evansville and South Bend. It was a family-owned concern, and the son of the founder had been managing the company very successfully since the mid-thirties. However, he suffered a heart attack in 1952 and for reasons of health was forced to relinquish much of his managerial responsibilities to a salaried administrator. Since the "young" Mr. Hays had no heirs who desired to enter the business and follow in his footsteps, he decided to sell it.

Unfortunately, he was unable to find anyone, or any group, with sufficient interest in a wholesaling business and sufficient capital to take over his company. So, as his health improved with rest and semi-retirement, he was contemplating a return to active business life when a banker friend introduced him to Frank Hilliard of Milwaukee. Mr. Hilliard was senior partner of a highly successful and rapidly growing organization that served some of the leading producers of heavy industrial equipment as a manufacturer's agent. Mr. Hilliard and two other former equipment salesmen organized a partnership in the late 1930s to sell on a commission basis a line of heavy-duty gas and air compressors. The venture was successful and expanded both in territory and principals represented. The first branch office was opened in Chicago in 1941, and as the result of encouragement and assistance from three large principals, additional branches were opened in St. Louis and Cincinnati shortly after the close of World War II.

Hilliard and his partners did not have a great deal of surplus capital, but their business had a high going-concern value and they were eager to expand. After some lengthy negotiation, Mr. Hilliard persuaded Mr. Hays to retain his financial interest in Hays Equipment Company, pool his assets with those of Hilliard and his partners, and form a corporation. In this way, Hilliard pointed out, Mr. Hays could be assured of a reasonably substantial income without the risk and worry of reinvesting a sizable sum of money. Moreover, he could be as active or inactive as he desired. Mr. Hays agreed, and the new corporation was formed in 1957 with Hays receiving 45 percent of the outstanding stock, the remainder being divided equally among Hilliard and his former partners. Mr. Hays became chairman of the board of the new corporation and Mr. Hilliard became its president.

The first endeavor of the new enterprise was to acquire by purchase or construction suitable warehouse facilities in Cincinnati, St. Louis, Chicago, and Milwaukee. To finance this acquisition the company managed to secure a long-term loan from a large life-insurance company in Milwaukee. Mr. Hilliard was certain that the ability to promise fast delivery on items in constant demand would give a substantial boost to sales volume. By 1972, the company carried from 5,000 to 7,000 items in inventory. These ranged from certain types of nuts and bolts, selling for a few cents each, to high-capacity compressors selling for as much as $16,000 each. On all of them lead time was usually important in closing a sale.

In 1971 Mr. Hays decided to retire altogether from business life, and was succeeded as chairman of the board by Mr. Hilliard, who also continued as president of the firm. The choice of Mr. Hilliard was unanimous. Opinion of him is pretty well summed up in the following remark by one of the directors: "Frank not only knows how to get things organized, but he has a real talent for spotting opportunities to increase efficiency and volume. He is also a good judge of men and knows how to make them work hard without making them sore. That's really all it takes in this business."

The Chicago branch is the largest of the Hays-Hilliard operations in terms of sales, although the Indianapolis branch moves the largest volume of units. The Chicago branch also has shown the fastest rate of growth. It is headed by Mr. W. W. Walton, who started as a salesman with Hilliard Associates when their St. Louis office was opened. Mr. Hilliard regarded Wig, as Mr. Walton is known to his colleagues, as a competent salesman and the kind of "go-getter" who could build the Chicago branch into the dominant supplier of its type in the area. Wig was promoted to general manager of the Chicago branch in 1970. It was already one of the major sources of supply for retail hardware stores, the contract construction industry, many commercial enterprises, and the state highway department. With a new warehouse (completed in 1970), which would permit same-day delivery of high-demand items, and a seasoned, sales-minded manager, Mr. Hilliard was confident the branch could also get a handsome share of orders placed by industrial plants in the Chicago area.

## Organizational changes

When Hilliard decided to move Walton to the Chicago branch, he drew up the job description for branch general manager shown in Exhibit 1. Mr. Hilliard had spent a number of years in the Chicago area, both as a salesman and as manager of the Hilliard Associates office there. Even as president of Hays-Hilliard he had taken an active part in expanding the facilities of the branch. Consequently, he had a deep

### EXHIBIT 1.  Job description, Branch General Manager

1.  The branch general manager is responsible for all operations of his facility and has direct authority over all persons employed at this facility.

2.  The branch general manager is responsible for the formulation of semiannual sales, expense, merchandise, and capital budgets covering the operation of his facility. These budgets must be submitted to the president of the corporation for review and approval no later than May 15 and November 15 of each calendar year.

3.  The branch general manager is responsible for the formulation of all sales and operating policies and procedures which he deems necessary for the efficient administration of his facility. These policies and procedures are subject to review by the corporation president, but each branch is considered autonomous within the general framework of corporation policy.

4.  The branch general manager is responsible for and has authority to establish jobs and positions necessary to maintain the efficient operation of his facility and to hire persons to fill these jobs and positions. It shall also be the responsibility of the branch general manager to determine the qualifications needed by persons who fill these jobs and positions. Any additions to the budget required by these jobs and positions are subject to review and approval by the home office.

5.  The branch general manager is responsible for determining wage and salary schedules and for devising any incentive-compensation plans which he believes will contribute to the efficiency of his facility. Such plans and schedules must be consistent with corporation policy regarding compensation.

6.  The branch general manager is directly responsible to the president of the corporation and will render to that officer such reports as he may from time to time request.

personal interest in the development of this outlet as well as a rather thorough knowledge of the operating and marketing problems its management involved. He was known to believe that the branch would have to undergo some major organizational changes in order to realize its full potential.

Mr. Walton had scarcely taken over management of the branch when he and Mr. Hilliard began to have differences as to what organizational changes were needed. Mr. Walton thought that he should be able to purchase all the merchandise sold by the branch with the possible exception of items which could not be purchased in sufficient volume to earn quantity discounts, or items on which manufacturer's minimum order quantities were too large relative to the branch's rate of sale. In other words, when the Chicago branch purchased pipe and rod cutters in sufficient volume to qualify for quantity discounts, Walton saw no reason why these or other items ordered in quantity should be requisitioned through the Milwaukee office. He did not think centralized purchasing made any sense except on merchandise on which manufacturers placed high volume requirements.

Mr. Hilliard, on the other hand, was an advocate of centralized purchasing. He was afraid that decentralizing the function would tend to cause inventories to pile up in branch warehouses, with consequent heavier carrying costs and working-capital requirements. He was also afraid that the corporation's prestige with well-known vendors would suffer unless large orders were handled centrally. Moreover, Mr. Hilliard suspected that Walton was not managing his inventory investment as well as he should. Although Mr. Hilliard confessed that he had no clear evidence to substantiate this suspicion, he did notice that on the last two semiannual budget reports stock–sales ratios at the Chicago branch exceeded those at both the Milwaukee and the St. Louis branches in almost every classification. This would seem to indicate, so Mr. Hilliard concluded, that Walton was either ordering in larger quantities than necessary or was ordering too far in advance. He had suggested to Walton that it would be a good idea for each branch to submit a monthly inventory report to the home office on the 500 fastest-moving items.

Since Mr. Walton had never responded to this suggestion, Hilliard instructed the manager of purchasing for the corporation to draw up an inventory control plan which would assure that all branches would keep their inventory investment and risk in inventory at a minimum. Hilliard was convinced that close, centralized control over inventory was one of the ways to make money in wholesaling. The purchasing manager's report is shown in Exhibit 2.

At the same time Mr. Hilliard assigned the inventory project to the purchasing manager, he assigned a similar project to the personnel manager, Mr. Ralph (Buck) Rogers. Mr. Rogers was instructed to draw up a set of personnel policies for the corporation that would assure the maximum in employee cooperation. Hilliard believed that enlightened employee relations was another key to success in wholesaling. He was confident that Hays-Hilliard could make significant gains over its competitors by reducing waste, pilferage, damage, and employee turnover, and by building the confidence of employees in the fairness and competence of Hays-Hilliard management.

Before putting any recommendations on paper, Mr. Rogers visited all the branches and talked with virtually every supervisor, foreman, and employee on the company payroll. He also spent a substantial amount of time discussing the subject of personnel relations with branch managers as well as with Mr. Hilliard. In addition to these extended visits with company employees and executives, Rogers also consulted

**EXHIBIT 2.    Summary of report on recommended central inventory control**

In order to keep the total cost of inventory at a minimum, it is necessary to equate the costs of storage (insurance, interest, rent, taxes, and handling) with the costs of acquisition (communication, purchasing agent's salary, clerical expense, and travel). Branches should therefore design their accounting systems so that it is possible to identify and determine each of these classes of expense. The amount of each class of expense should then be related to each item carried in inventory in the following manner and reported annually to the home office.

Interest—average monthly value of the item inventory.
Rent—number of square feet of warehouse space utilized by item.
Taxes—average monthly value of goods in stock.
Handling costs—annual turnover.
Acquisition costs—lumped together and allocated on the basis of number of invoice lines devoted annually to item.

The home office will then compute the value of annual purchases, the reorder quantity, and the order frequency that will assure minimum total costs of inventory. From unit- and dollar-sales reports submitted by branches, the Milwaukee purchasing staff can determine when the stock on hand of any given item has reached the reorder point and place an order for the proper quantity. In this way, reordering will become automatic. There would be no need for branch purchasing agents to file requisitions with the home office as in the past. But it would be advisable to make some changes in current sales-reporting procedure. Instead of the sales summaries which are now submitted monthly, there should be a daily sales report on the fastest-moving items (sales in excess of 50 units per week), biweekly reports on items with a movement of 20 to 49 units per week, and monthly reports on all other items.

A perpetual inventory record would be maintained at the home office on all items carried in stock by all branches. To verify the accuracy of the book inventory, branches would be requested to take a physical inventory twice each year and submit dollar and unit stock-on-hand figures with their semiannual budgets. By centralizing inventory management at the home office, both purchasing and stock control can be more scientific. The volume of work would also be great enough that complete mechanization of the process would be feasible. Savings in branch acquisition costs alone should be sufficient to offset the added expense of more frequent reporting. Closer regulation of purchases and tighter control over stocks-on-hand should result in a substantial reduction of the possession cost of inventory.

The following suggested sales-reporting form would provide sufficient information for centralized inventory control.

**EXHIBIT 2** (*Continued*)

HAYS-HILLIARD CORPORATION

<u>Sales Report</u>

Branch_____Week beginning_____ Week ending_____

| Item number | Volume class | Quantity sold | | Unit price |
|---|---|---|---|---|
| | | Units | Dollars | |
| | | | | |

relevant publications of the American Management Association and the Industrial Relations Research Association. On the basis of the information he gathered from these sources, he compiled a policy manual containing about 40 working rules that he thought each branch manager should try to enforce. These rules were organized under six headings: selection and indoctrination, training, compensation, benefits, discipline, and termination.

After the few minor changes suggested by Mr. Hilliard were incorporated into the policy statements, the manual was duplicated and a copy sent to each branch manager, director, and foreman in the company. Attached to each copy of the manual was a personal memorandum from Mr. Hilliard stating that the contents of the manual represented official corporation policy regarding personnel administration. Also included in the memorandum was the statement that Mr. Rogers would visit each branch periodically to assist in any way he could with the interpretation and implementation of the directives contained in the manual.

On the first visit that Mr. Rogers made to the Chicago branch he discovered that two directives which he regarded of paramount importance had apparently been overlooked by Mr. Walton. These were the directives that all branch managers should (1) hold meetings of all foreman, directors, and employees once each month to discuss problems of mutual interest and (2) hold a meeting of all salesmen once each week to go over new-product promotions, customer relations, progress toward quotas, and other matters of mutual concern. Mr. Rogers reported on his conversation with Mr. Walton as follows:

> Wig and I had a very pleasant and amicable visit until the subject of weekly and monthly meetings came up. He said that on the whole he appreciated the manual on policy and thought that it would put some structure into operating procedures. But he continually referred to the tendency of large businesses to put middle management in a strait-jacket and he expressed the hope that Hays-Hilliard wasn't getting that big. Finally, I gathered the impression that despite his comments to the contrary, Wig deeply resents this policy manual and especially my efforts to induce him to follow it. He argues that it isn't necessary for him to hold monthly meetings with his operating staff and employees because he is in almost daily contact with them anyway. He thought that such meetings would just be a waste of time, because there simply wouldn't be that much to communicate. Wig was confident that he could keep in touch with his men quite adequately through day-to-day contact. I tried to explain to him that while this might be true now, systematic employee relations could easily get lost in the shuffle in an expanding enterprise. He seemed impressed with this thought, but I don't know whether he was sufficiently impressed to attempt to do anything about it. Only time will tell.

Mr. Hilliard was not particularly disturbed by this report. The Chicago branch had been showing consistently good performance, both in sales and profits, and he was inclined to think that Walton had just been too busy to organize a schedule of meetings. After all, if 38 of the 40-odd policy directives were implemented within the first year, this was a pretty good progress. He told Rogers to wait another six months or so and give Wig time to "pull in his horns."

Mr. Rogers did not visit the Chicago branch again until after seven and a half months, at the end of a series of visits at the other five branches. When he learned that Walton had still not held a meeting with his staff, salesmen, or other employees, Rogers determined to find out whether Walton planned to give these policies a try or whether he was intending to drag his feet just as long as he could get away with it. This time he spent several hours with Walton, during which he went over in some detail how regular meetings with middle management, salesmen, and employees had been paying off in the other branches. He also emphasized to Walton that all the research in industrial relations that he, Rogers, knew about underscored the importance of regular meetings with personnel.

Again, Mr. Walton offered no objection to Rogers's argument. He simply insisted that each branch had unique problems that managers had to solve in their own way. He did not think that the fact that other branch managers found regular meetings with personnel to be beneficial was proof that he would find them equally so. Mr. Walton admitted that he had as many problems as any branch manager, but said that they were not communication problems. He said that if communication with staff and sales force or with employees developed into a problem, he would certainly institute a series of meetings as well as try everything else he could think of to effect a solution.

Mr. Walton's interpretation of the policy manual was that it should be followed *in general,* but that the branch manager had the prerogative of making exceptions where, in his opinion, a given policy statement did not apply to his situation. In Walton's opinion this was the only interpretation that made any sense. If the details of branch operation were to be dictated by top management, then why not save a lot of money and simply put a foreman in charge of a branch instead of a manager. Walton said that he could not conceive of any way a manager could manage unless he had freedom to make decisions regarding operating plans and short-run strategy.

Mr. Rogers endeavored to explain that branch managers had complete freedom to make decisions regarding operating plans and strategy within the general confines of corporate policy. The reason for the personnel policy manual was top management's conviction that this was an area in which there was tremendous untapped potential for increased operating efficiency. Moreover, Mr. Rogers contended that the policy manual had been very carefully developed and that Walton himself had contributed a good share of the ideas that were included in it. Furthermore, he reminded Mr. Walton that Mr. Hilliard would be greatly disturbed to learn that after nearly two years corporate policies were still not being fully enforced at the Chicago branch.

Upon his return to Milwaukee, Mr. Rogers reported on the situation he had found at the different branches. Although each had its share of perplexing problems and blind alleys, Mr. Rogers was most distressed with the situation he had found in Chicago. He considered Walton's attitude as little short of mutinous, and reported the substance of his lengthy conversation with Walton to Mr. Hilliard. Since there was a routine branch managers' meeting to be held in Milwaukee within the next few weeks, Rogers requested Mr. Hilliard to take this opportunity to have a talk with Walton. Mr. Hilliard agreed, but added that he thought it would be a good idea for Rogers to join the conversation too.

During the branch managers' meeting, Mr. Hilliard asked Walton if he could speak with him, and an appointment was arranged. Mr. Rogers was alerted to be present and at the appointed time the three met in Mr. Hilliard's office. Hilliard opened the conversation:

*Hilliard:* Wig, I wanted to talk to you and Buck about the problem we have been having in getting some of our personnel policies into operation. I don't want you to think that I've called you in to bawl you out or criticize you in any way. I realize you branch managers have a lot on your minds and simply do not have time to study and try to understand why we at the home office request some of the things we do. It's really asking too much of you fellows to insist that you see everything exactly as we do, even things that we regard as vitally important.

*Walton:* I couldn't argue with that, Mr. Hilliard. We have our hands full in Chicago just doing well what we have to do to keep abreast of this fast-moving market. When I think about what we have accomplished in improved efficiency and increased sales, I feel pretty good. But when I think of what we should have done and what we're going to have to do, I get as jumpy as a long-tailed cat in a room full of rocking chairs.

*Hilliard:* I can certainly appreciate that, Wig. And I want to commend you on your sales performance the first half of this year. I noticed that first quarter sales were up 11 percent over last year. That's not bad in a sagging market. But frankly, Wig, I'm not surprised. I have never had any doubts about your ability to produce sales. I am a little concerned, though, that some of our personnel policies aren't being carried out at your branch. This is important, too, for our long-term growth and continued ability to operate efficiently. Manpower is our most costly resource, and we cannot leave its management to chance.

*Walton:* I can't argue with that either. I doubt that you could find anybody in this organization who is more thoroughly convinced of the importance of good employee relations than I am. I spend a good deal more of my time on my feet consulting with and personally directing my staff and my salesmen than I spend on my fanny behind a desk. Our communication is so good and our personal relationships so direct and cordial that there is really no need for a program of formal meetings such as Buck, and apparently you, advocate. I give training and instructions to people who need it when they need it and as frequently as they need it. To schedule regular meetings, as suggested in the policy manual, would be unnecessarily time-consuming and would really contribute nothing to the good employee relations we already have. In fact, I fear that such meetings might even detract from them by introducing an element of formality and stuffiness into our contacts.

*Hilliard:* Well, I take my hat off to you, Wig. The company is fortunate in having a branch manager who recognizes the importance of good contacts with his staff and sales force as clearly as you do, and who is capable of maintaining them. But we here at the home office are desperately afraid that such necessary elements of good personal relations as employee benefits, work rules, merit rating, and compensation schedules will be ignored in the pressure to get other things done which at the moment seem more urgent. I know you would agree that when employees are fully aware of their benefits, understand the factors which determine their ratings and salary, and appreciate that management has a personal concern for their welfare and their future with the company they will be better employees. I know you would agree that employees who know the rules and policies of a company are easier to lead.

*Walton:* I wouldn't disagree with that for a moment.

*Hilliard:* What we are proposing, Wig, is good for you and good for the company. Take it from somebody who has been in this business 35 years, systematic coverage of employee benefits, ratings, compensation, quotas, and other matters affecting personnel in regular, periodic meetings pays real dividends in operating efficiency. Its simply impossible to do this effectively unless management sets aside a specific time each week for personnel meetings and allows sufficient time in executives' schedules to prepare for these meetings. Obviously, the latter will be much easier to do if executives know that a given time is always reserved for personnel meetings or conferences. Buck, you know more about this than most of us, what do you think?

*Rogers:* Wig, everybody of any reputation who has studied this question—and some of the best minds in the country have wrestled with it—say there is simply no substitute for organized, systematic personnel conferences, particularly where field salesmen and servicemen are involved. I have not seen a single survey which did not point up the near abysmal ignorance of most employees regarding the value of their benefits and the reasons for particular goals and quotas. This is no fault of management, in most cases, except that management has not provided a means to clearly and forcefully convey its message. I'm not trying to tell you how to run your branch, Wig, but merely suggesting that you can profit by taking action which will avoid these pitfalls in human relations which other companies have found it so easy to fall into. Wouldn't you agree that it's important for all employees to know exactly what is expected of them and why it is expected of them, and to know exactly what the benefits of high-level performance are to them in terms that they can understand, namely dollars and cents?

*Walton:* Yes, indeed, this is important, Buck. And it has to be done in the most effective way management can find to do it.

*Hilliard:* Well, fine! I knew there was no real disagreement here. We're all shooting at the same target and we all realize that we can't hit it without good communication and good relations with our service and sales staff—in fact with all our employees. Buck, you will continue to work with Wig, won't you, and give him any assistance you can? And both of you know that you can call on me anytime you think I might be able to contribute anything.

*Rogers:* Yes, indeed, Mr. Hilliard. Wig and I do not always use the same words, but we speak the same language.

*Hilliard:* Now that we have this personnel business settled, there are some other items of business I wanted to go over with you, Wig—the sales forecast for the next six months, and a couple of items in your capital budget. Buck, did you have anything else in mind?

*Rogers:* No, Mr. Hilliard. Wig is doing a great job. Glad I had a chance to visit with you again, Wig, even if it wasn't very long.

*Walton:* Same here, Buck. Come down and see us more often. It's only about a ninety-minute drive from here, you know.

About six months after the meeting in Milwaukee, Mr. Rogers visited the Chicago branch again to talk to Walton about a new incentive-compensation plan for the sales and service staff. Since it was a rather involved scheme, requiring some adjustment in wage and salary levels for virtually every job classification, Rogers wanted to go over the details with Walton before recommending specific wage and salary ranges for the Chicago branch. During this visit the subject of personnel meetings was mentioned, and Rogers discovered that no such meetings had been held. Moreover, there was no indication from Walton's remarks that anything had been done to arrange for any such meetings in the foreseeable future. In view of the urgency and detail of the compensation plan, Rogers decided not to reopen the question of personnel meetings with Walton at this time.

On his return to Milwaukee, however, Rogers decided to add a supplement to his policy manual, namely a requirement that each branch manager submit a report each quarter indicating the number of personnel meetings held and the nature of each meeting, including a list of topics discussed. When Mr. Hilliard approved the additional requirement, a copy of it was mailed to all branch managers with instructions to insert it in their policy manual. When Mr. Walton received this policy supplement, he made the following comment about it in a conversation with the branch sales manager, John McVey:

> Well, Buck has finally lowered the boom. Why is it that as soon as a fellow gets to be a top executive, he isn't happy unless he is throwing his weight around and generating a lot of reports to read. You would think these guys enjoyed nothing more than sitting at a desk shuffling paper. I'll tell you one thing, John, Buck will get his meetings, as often and as many as he wants. And if he wants me to hire a clown to keep my men awake at these meetings, I'll do that, too. From now on I'm going to run this place by the book; everything the boys in Milwaukee want, they're going to get. Hilliard and Rogers have both made up their minds that there is no substitute for formal meetings in maintaining good personnel relations. I think they are both dead wrong, but there is nothing I can do but go along with them. It will be a cold day in Purgatory when I put any faith in formality and folderol to get people to do things.

## Operations at the Chicago branch

Sales performance at the Chicago branch had been entirely satisfactory. To a man, the sales force was enthusiastic about the formation of Hays-Hilliard Corporation and seemed to take genuine pride in belonging to the largest unit of the enterprise. Increases in the volume of orders taken ranged from 10 to 25 percent per man within a year after Walton had become branch manager. This caught Mr. Hilliard's attention and he was interested in discovering the reason for such a spurt in performance, so that whatever incentive accounted for it could be utilized at other branches.

From all that he had been able to learn, a great deal of the credit was due to Mr. Walton. Walton, he learned, would sit down with each salesman once a month and go over his plans for the following month—new accounts to be called on, items to be pushed, customer complaints to be handled, contemplated changes in number of sales calls or routes, and so on. In particular, Walton always took great pains in helping salesmen plan their calls so as to avoid backtracking and crisscrossing their territory and also helped them allocate their time to customers in proportion to the potential business the customer represented. He did not hesitate to tell a salesman when he was not satisfied with the number of calls made, the volume of orders per call, or any other aspect of the salesman's performance. Walton also kept abreast of what salesmen at other branches were doing and let his men know when men at other branches were outselling them. He also found out as much as he could about the techniques and approaches used at other branches and passed any new ideas along to his own men.

Mr. Rogers reported, however, that salesmen at the Chicago branch were apparently not in full agreement regarding their opinion of Mr. Walton's supervision. Three of the nineteen field salesmen at Chicago indicated that Walton gave them too much direction and they expressed the hope that they could be given a little more freedom to exercise their own initiative. One of these three commented that Walton treated them "like kids." Two other men had complained that Walton did not know much about the market outside the Chicago area, and was unreasonable in some of his demands, because he knew so little of the obstacles and selling problems in the outlying territories. "It all looks the same on a map," one of them commented. These two men were assigned to downstate Illinois. A majority of the sales force, however, seemed to regard Walton as a capable administrator and voiced no discontent with his leadership.

There was no question that Walton is "on his feet" most of the time and takes a personal interest in all operating departments of his branch. For example, he set down a list of rules for operating the warehouse, such as "always keep inflammables in the south end of the main building" (this part of the structure was windowless and of all-masonry construction), and "store all items with a movement of more than 50 units per week in a special section adjacent to the shipping and receiving dock." Moreover, he tours the warehouse at least once a week to see that the rules are being carried out and to study ways for more efficient handling.

The type of equipment to be used and the handling methods to be followed for each major classification of merchandise carried in inventory are specified by Mr. Boling, who is in charge of all warehousing for the corporation. These and other instructions pertaining to the proper handling, storage, and shipment of merchandise are contained in a warehouseman's manual prepared by Mr. Boling and distributed to all branches. The manual was based on expert study of the most advanced techniques in materials handling and with particular effort to adapt these techniques to the type of commodities carried by Hays-Hilliard. Walton had mixed feelings about the value of the manual, however, and frankly admitted that he followed some of the instructions in it but ignored others.

Mr. Hilliard commented privately that he was aware of rather widespread flouting of Boling's instructions, but believed that problems of integration would have to be tackled one at a time. He said that once personnel administration was functioning smoothly, it would be necessary to have a man check all branches to be sure there was reasonable uniformity in materials-handling methods. Otherwise, he said, branch managers would not have the advantage of low-cost warehouse operations provided by expertly designed methods.

About this same time, Walton also became irritated with the kind of reports requested by Mr. Haring, the corporation controller. Twice each year the home office provided each branch with a forecast of total industry sales within its designated trading area. The branch manager was instructed to multiply this figure by the percent of the total he estimated his branch could account for. With this objective in mind, he was then instructed to submit an expense budget, indicating in detail the amount of various classes of expenditures (40 in all) that were regarded as necessary to reach this sales-volume goal. In addition, any needed capital expenditures also had to be indicated in a separate capital budget, which included six categories of capital outlay. A full explanation had to accompany every proposed capital outlay except for working capital.

Walton has become increasingly outspoken in his objection to estimating 40 separate categories of expense every six months. He insists that as long as his profits as a percent of sales and as a percent of invested capital are satisfactory, there is no reason for the home office to know how much he has spent on advertising, utilities, salesmen's salaries, office salaries, telephone service, and 35 other categories. In other words, if a branch is profitable, why worry about whether its profit is the result of increasing sales, decreasing costs, or something else?

### The president's position

Mr. Hilliard is convinced of the need for centralized capital and expense control. He is able to cite a number of cases of what he regards as examples of capable executives being so carried away with their own operations that they lose their objectivity. These range all the way from requests for capital expenditures that didn't pay off to requests for extra personnel who were not needed. He recalls that three years ago, the Indianapolis branch submitted a request for $50,000 to be used for an extension of the shipping and receiving dock. After consideration of the traffic expected to result from estimated sales increases, the request was denied. Since profit and sales performance of the branch have improved steadily, Mr. Hilliard concluded that this proved the request for increased dock space to have been unreasonable and extravagant. He also recalls a request by the St. Louis branch manager some time ago for additional office equipment and office personnel, both of which were denied after comparing the resulting ratio of equipment and personnel to space and sales volume at this and other branches. The denial of this request resulted in no problems or difficulties at the St. Louis branch, so far as anyone had been able to determine.

These and similar circumstances reinforced Mr. Hilliard's belief that executives are typically under pressure from their own subordinates and employees to add more people and more equipment because employees instinctively resist efforts to step up their efficiency. Their first reaction to such efforts is invariably to demand more help and more or better equipment. When they have been convinced that neither are going to be forthcoming, they are more willing to adjust to tighter operating procedures. "There is more rationalization than reason in most of these requests for more selling staff, too." Mr. Hilliard has recently commented. "If every salesman could be induced to make one more sales call *after* he is ready to quit for the day, this in itself would be tantamount to increasing our sales force by 15 or 20 percent." "When an executive is under pressure from subordinates to add more equipment and people, it's always easier to go along with them than to try to convince them that they are wrong. Then, too, it is always a great temptation to pass the buck."

The logical time to turn down such requests and keep expenditures from getting completely out of line, Hilliard thought, was during budget review. Consequently, it was necessary to have detailed budget breakdowns for each branch for each budget period. He contended that control had to go beyond the profit figure. Even though he fully expected the branch managers to object to this kind of scrutiny by the home office, he was convinced they would see the value of it in the long run.

**EXHIBIT 3.  Hays-Hilliard Corporation organization chart**

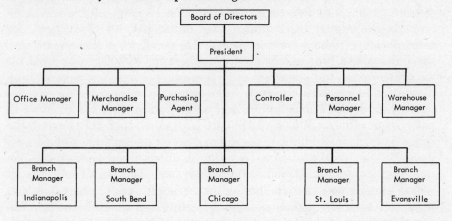

**EXHIBIT 4.  Organization chart, Chicago branch**

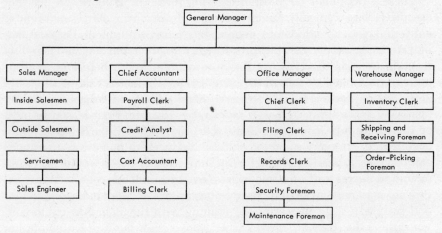

# THE HEFLIN CHEMICAL SUPPLY COMPANY (A)

The Heflin Chemical Supply Company is a large distributor of agricultural chemicals, fertilizers, and animal medicines. It is located in Ohio and sells through a force of some 40 salesmen. One of the company's most successful products is a medicinal powder, trade-named Promaine. When added to animal feed, Promaine not only protects the animal against certain diseases but stimulates growth as well. The company holds a manufacturer's franchise on the product which makes it the exclusive supplier in a territory including western Ohio, most of Indiana, and eastern Illinois.

The chief purchasers of Promaine are feed manufacturers: large hog and beef cattle raisers who prepare their own feed mixtures; country elevators which do custom mixing of feeds for farmers; and farm supply stores. Since Promaine is a potent drug, only a few ounces need to be added to a 100-pound batch of feed to obtain the desired results in growth stimulation and disease prevention. While use in excess of recommended quantities has no harmful effect on animals or the consumer end products obtained from them, neither does it provide any additional benefit. Consequently, failure to follow directions in mixing represents a waste to the user.

The principal competing product is a preparation made by the Roudebush Chemical Corporation of Buffalo, New York. It is marketed under the trade name Viotin, and is sold throughout the Midwest chiefly by manufacturers' agents. Viotin is a crystalline compound of considerably greater bulk than Promaine powder. Its price is somewhat less per pound than Promaine, but it must be used in larger proportions to achieve the same results. Other preparations with medicinal characteristics similar to those of Promaine and Viotin are also on the market. Some are in dry crystalline form to be used as feed additives, others are in liquid or tablet form to be added to the animals' drinking water. Promaine, however, is the only powdered form in which such preparations are available.

Laboratory tests by the manufacturer have indicated that in comparison to Promaine, the use of other feed additives increases the cost of a

100-pound batch of feed from 10 to 15 percent when the same degree of potency is achieved. Tests conducted by agricultural experiment stations corroborate this and have established the fact that there is no difference in mixing qualities between the powdered and crystalline forms of such preparations. Either form becomes uniformly distributed through a batch of feed when ordinary types of mixing machinery are used. Tests by experiment stations also confirmed the superior effectiveness of Promaine in reducing the incidence of certain animal diseases. The same tests further proved the growth-stimulating properties of Promaine to be equal to that of other similar feed additives, including Viotin.

Recently, the Hoosier Feed and Milling Company, a well-established manufacturer of livestock feeds and an important customer of the Heflin Company, circulated the announcement shown below in its monthly promotional letter. This letter is sent to a substantial list of farmers, feeders, elevator operators, and farm supply stores in the Midwest.

> During the coming year we plan to discontinue the use of all growth and disease preventatives in our line of Banquet Feeds except the drug Viotin. Our reasons for this decision are the proven facts that:
>
> a.  only crystalline preparations, such as Viotin, can be uniformly mixed in the batching process because a certain amount of bulk is needed in relation to potency.
> b.  the action of Viotin is less severe than other preparations; Viotin has no harmful aftereffect on animals, and
> c.  the lower price per unit of active ingredient in Viotin will permit us to supply our customers with Banquet Feeds at lower prices than we would otherwise be obliged to charge.
>
> It is our considered judgment that Viotin is the only feed additive whose potency and safety have been scientifically proven and laboratory tested. We are confident that this change, made in the interest of the many farmers and feeders who use our product, will meet with their approval. We believe that our demonstrated policy of supplying only the finest feeds will further the confidence that Midwest farmers and livestock men have always placed in products of the Hoosier Feed and Milling Company.

This announcement came as a complete surprise to Heflin management. Although sales records had indicated that Hoosier Feed and Milling placed no orders for Promaine for a period of about ten weeks prior to their announcement, this had not been regarded as significant. The company had never ordered more frequently than once every two or three months. These orders were ordinarily large enough so that the Heflin company typically drop-shipped them to give Hoosier Feed and Milling the best possible discount. Call reports submitted by the salesman serving this account indicated no dissatisfaction with Promaine and no complaints from its users.

Heflin management immediately retained a law firm to study the situation and advise them as to what legal steps, if any, they should take. Legal counsel later reported that sufficient evidence existed for Heflin to bring suit against Hoosier Feed and Milling with every expectation of recovering heavy damages. There was no indication whatever that the Roudebush Company or any agent representing it had anything to do with the action of Hoosier Feed and Milling except to sell it Viotin.

Soon after the appearance of the announcement, Hoosier Feed and Milling's chief competitor, the Garver Feed Company, approached Heflin management with a proposal. The Garver president thought that this situation presented his company with a golden opportunity to discredit Hoosier Feed and Milling by exposing its brazen misrepresentation. The plan was to accomplish this exposé with an extensive direct mail campaign as well as space advertising in local newspapers throughout the market area served by the two feed companies. Without specifically naming Hoosier Feed and Milling, the advertisements would recite Hoosier's claim and then refute it by presenting the true facts of the matter, supported by quotations from technical bulletins of the agricultural experiment stations. The Garver Company and Heflin would split the costs of the campaign.

The Garver company had used Promaine in its feed since the product was first introduced and, like Hoosier Feed and Milling, had been one of Heflin's best accounts. It was a somewhat smaller firm than Hoosier Feed and Milling but well managed by a young and agressive staff. The marketing area served by both companies included most of Indiana, east central Illinois and western Ohio.

At a meeting of the Heflin executive group several other suggestions for dealing with the situation were also forthcoming. One proposal was to try to get the Roudebush Company to bring pressure on Hoosier to clean up its advertising. From all that could be ascertained, Roudebush had had nothing to do with the Hoosier announcement. Consequently, it was argued that until further information indicated the contrary to be true, it would be reasonable to proceed on the assumption that Roudebush was a reputable company whose management would not condone outright misrepresentation. If all the facts of the matter were laid before the Roudebush Company, it would be in a position to exert pressure on Hoosier Feed and Milling to either retract their statement or at least to refrain from making any further such statements.

Moreover, those who advocated this alternative emphasized that Hoosier Feed and Milling was still a potential customer. If Heflin sued them or entered into a "plot" with one of their competitors to discredit them, their patronage would be lost for all time. It was suggested that the objective in dealing with this problem should be to keep Hoosier Feed and Milling as a customer, not to punish them. There was general agreement that Hoosier Feed and Milling should be brought back "into the fold," if that were possible. There was some skepticism, however, that Roudebush would have any incentive to correct their customer's misinformation—if indeed that was really the cause of the trouble. And even if Roudebush should urge them to make a retraction, it was doubtful whether a manufacturer could exert much influence over a customer anyway. Once a product has passed from the hands of the manufacturer to those of the customer, the manufacturer no longer has much control over what the customer does with it or says about it.

Another suggestion was that Heflin should approach Hoosier Feed and Milling at the highest administrative level and candidly discuss the whole affair. This would at least shed some light on what prompted the announcement and afford Heflin an opportunity to "call any bluff" Hoosier might be running. There could be nothing lost in letting Hoosier management know in a tactful way that Heflin executives were aware of the insecurity of Hoosier's legal position. Moreover, restitution could be made at such a meeting without any loss of face for either party.

If such a meeting were approached in a constructive and positive manner, it was argued, Heflin could do a real selling job at the policy making level of the Hoosier organization—an opportunity seldom afforded a salesman. On the other hand, if such a meeting should reveal Hoosier management to be truculent and unwilling to consider the affair objectively, then it would at least be clear that more forceful measures would have to be used. The position of those who advocated this approach was that every effort should be made to settle the disagreement as amicably and peacefully as possible. Only when such efforts proved to be fruitless should action be taken that would produce an altercation with Heflin's former customer.

A final suggestion was that Heflin undertake an extensive promotional campaign, entirely on its own, that would place before the market the verified facts about Promaine's performance for all to see. It was argued that no one who had been in the feed business as long as the men who were managing Hoosier Feed and Milling could be that misinformed about two such widely used products. Therefore, Heflin might as well accept the fact that Hoosier executives were being influenced by ulterior motives. And, it was argued, the most effective way to combat such deliberate deception as that being attempted by Hoosier, was with the truth. A campaign to spread the truth could embrace space advertising, pamphlets, direct mail, and all other appropriate promotional media. Salesmen could be briefed on the situation and be supplied with experiment station reports and other documentary evidence for distribution to customers on regular sales calls.

The particular virtue of this alternative, its advocates stressed, was that it could be implemented quickly and without setting any dangerous precedents—as in the case of the Garver proposal. It was important that any erroneous impressions created in the minds of customers by the Hoosier announcements be emphatically corrected. It was also important that this be done without creating the impression that the company was playing favorites or trying to take advantage of an awkward situation. An aggressive, factual, and comprehensive promotional campaign would meet both needs—or so the proponents of this alternative believed.

The president listened patiently to these suggestions and to the various arguments advanced for and against each. He then adjourned the meeting and retired to his office to mull over the different alternatives and try to reach a decision.

# THE HEFLIN CHEMICAL SUPPLY COMPANY (B)

The Heflin Chemical Supply Company is a large distributor of agricultural chemicals, fertilizer, and animal medicines located in Ohio. Its operations are divided into four functional divisions: warehousing, finance, sales, and maintenance. The warehousing division is responsible for all receipts, shipments, storage, and internal movement of merchandise, for physical inventory, and for custody of all equipment used in handling merchandise. The maintenance division is responsible for the physical operation, repair, and service of office and warehouse facilities. All accounting records including dollar and unit inventory records, costing, budgetary control, the authorization of monetary receipts and disbursements, the management of credit and insurance, office services, and the custody of petty cash are the responsibility of the finance division. The sales division is responsible for all activities connected with the buying and selling of merchandise with the exception of pricing, which is shared with the finance division.

The sales division is headed by R. G. Dunn, who started with the company 34 years ago as a bulk fertilizer salesman. He is a firm believer in the "personal touch" in matters of supervision, and in permitting salesmen as much individual initiative as possible in the administration of their territories. Consequently, each salesman is assigned a specific territory in which he can operate pretty much as he pleases. In his territory, a salesman is virtually an independent businessman with Heflin supplying the capital. All that Dunn insists upon is that each territory contribute its fair share of company profit.

This does not mean that a Heflin salesman can operate with complete freedom from budgetary control. But he does develop his own budget of anticipated expense and revenue for his territory, which he submits each year to the company's administrative board. The board, which is composed of the four division heads and the president, compares each salesman's budget with a budget which has been developed independently for his territory by the finance staff. This latter budget is based on statistical projections of past cost and revenue experience together with what influence anticipated business conditions, competitors' tactics, or Heflin's own plans would be thought to have on costs and revenues in the territory.

If the two budgets involve substantial differences, a conference is arranged between the salesman and a member of the finance staff to reconcile the points of difference. If this meeting fails to produce agreement, the matter is then referred back to the administrative board for a decision. Since the sales plan contained in the territorial budget becomes, upon approval, the salesman's quota, most disagreements arise over projected increases in the sales plan. Salesmen have tended to be distrustful of the statistical procedures employed by the finance staff and are apt to challenge any sales projection which exceeds last year's sales by more than 10 percent. Over the last 3 or 4 years, however, the administrative board has been obliged to make the final decision in only 3 cases out of 10.

Each salesman's territory includes about 11 counties. The largest territory includes 13 counties and the smallest 8. Salesmen whose territories are in northern Ohio, Indiana, and Illinois reside there, and typically maintain sales offices in their homes. Although there is no formal procedure with regard to visiting the home office, Mr. Dunn customarily holds a general sales meeting each year in January. He also calls salesmen to the home office for individual consultation any time a situation arises which either the salesman or management regards as requiring a change in plans for the territory.

Marketing and financial plans are formulated for each calendar year. Requests are usually sent to salesmen for their preliminary estimates of costs and revenue in September and firm plans are to be ready for top management approval in December. The master plan for the coming year is then usually introduced to the organization at the general sales meeting in January. Also at this time any additional training which would be called for by the plan is conducted. However, the general sales meeting is not entirely a business affair. It is looked upon as a social occasion as well and a good deal of entertainment and levity are included in the program. Wives are welcome to accompany their husbands to these affairs, and a number of them do, sometimes against the wishes of their husbands—so it is rumored. Other than the studied attention given to a review of the operating details of the plan, the general sales meeting is a gala occasion.

In addition to this annual meeting and periodic visits of salesmen to the home office, Mr. Dunn also visits each territory at least once each year. During these visits, which typically last two or three days, he makes calls with salesmen and endeavors to get a first-hand picture of conditions in the field. He believes that such visits not only give him the best indication of how well salesmen handle customers, but also serve to impress both salesmen and customers with the sincerity of management's interest in them.

Although Mr. Dunn personally directs the sales force and contributes a number of the promotional ideas employed, he has a merchandising manager who develops and plans all activity of a promotional nature. He is also aided by a field service manager. The latter handles those customers whose service needs are beyond the knowledge of the salesman. The merchandise manager supervises a staff of six, five of whom give their full attention to advertising and other promotional work. The sixth man devotes most of his time to the assembly, analysis, and presentation of information contained in sales reports. His primary responsibility is the operation of the sales reporting system. The field service manager has one assistant.

Most of Heflin's salesmen have been with the company for a number of years. Their average length of service would probably be at least ten or twelve years. Only one, the youngest of the group, holds a college degree. The others are graduates of the school of experience and hard knocks, an accomplishment which is not to be disparaged. Their morale is considered by Mr. Dunn to be very high. He has seldom found it necessary to discipline anyone in his division and turnover is practically zero. Salesmen are paid a straight salary plus a bonus. The bonus is based on a weighted average of three factors: number of years of service with the company, percent by which territorial sales exceed quota (a negative weight is used if territorial sales fall below quota), and company net profits after taxes.

Dunn has become increasingly concerned in the past few months with evidence that the feedback of information from field salesmen has been faulty. Recently the company had inaugurated what was thought to be a well designed sales reporting system. It consisted of a weekly call report, a weekly expense report, and a monthly summary report. The call report summarized the salesman's activity for that particular week giving the names and addresses of firms or farmers called on, whether the salesman had ever called on the party previously, the type of activity in which the firm or farmer was engaged, and the purpose of the call. If the purpose was to make a sale, the salesman was asked to report the results of the sales efforts. If the call was of a service nature, or a combination of sales and service, the salesman was asked to report the nature of the service problem.

The expense report included the customary items of meals, lodging, automobile expense, and entertainment. It covered the same period and was due at the same time as the weekly call report. In fact, salesmen were not reimbursed for their expenses until the weekly call report had been received. Upon receipt of the reports the office staff transferred the data they contained to punch cards and compiled a master summary with details classified by territory. Thus, Heflin had a master punch card for each customer containing data on type of customer (feeder, elevator, farm supply store, etc.), location, annual requirements, size, salesman handling the account, customer code number, products purchased, and other suppliers serving the customer, as well as a territorial breakdown of expenses.

While information supplied by the call reports seemed to be fairly complete, suspicion was aroused that salesmen were careless in filling out the reports. A detailed comparison of orders taken with information contained in call reports following difficulties with one of the company's best accounts confirmed these suspicions. The problem now arose as to what should be done about this situation. As an initial step management proceeded to hold a series of conferences with each salesman at which the discrepancies between the record of orders submitted and information contained in call reports were tactfully called to his attention. Almost all salesmen were guilty of some carelessness in completing call reports. While results of these conferences were mixed, three conclusions seemed to stand out: (1) design of the call report form could be improved with a view to lessening the amount of time required to complete it, (2) salesmen generally did not realize the importance of information requested in the call report to management, and (3) the sales force was spread so thin over the Heflin market area that time which otherwise might be available for filling out reports was usually spent in traveling.

Redesigning call report forms and educating salesmen with regard to the importance of completing them accurately were largely matters of internal adjustment. Dunn thought that these problems could probably be worked out satisfactorily by his own staff working in cooperation with salesmen. What to do about an overetxended sales force, however, was another question. Two alternatives were available: (1) to increase the size of the sales force, or (2) redesign the sales territories with a view to identifying areas of greatest potential and limiting the use of salesmen to them. Areas of low potential could either be served by mail order or ignored altogether.

The first alternative did not have much appeal to any member of the administrative board. To recruit and train additional salesmen without any real assurance that a larger sales force would increase sales volume faster than it would increase costs bordered on recklessness. Whether the increased accuracy of sales reporting and the more effective administration to which this should contribute would be worth the cost of an enlarged sales force was very difficult to answer. Also difficult to answer was the question of how many additional salesmen should be hired if this alternative were chosen.

In view of the urgency of the problem and the weight attached to the disadvantages of expanding the sales force, it was decided to experiment with the second alternative J. R. Osborn, the man in charge of the sales reporting system, was given the task of assembling all pertinent data needed for the measurement of market potential. An additional secretary was assigned to his office and he was told to proceed with the job in any way he wished, but to get it done as quickly as possible.

The original territorial boundaries had been drawn with a view to equalizing travel distances as well as to make it convenient for salesmen to cover their territories from their homes. Osborn therefore decided to first try to measure the potential within each territory. He proposed to determine the areas of greatest and least potential within each one so that the territorial boundaries could be adjusted with least disruption of the present pattern. Since the basic geographic unit was the county, Osborn planned to rank each county in each territory on the basis of its potential. When each county had been ranked, territorial boundaries could then be easily redrawn so that each salesman would have a territory of roughly the same potential which in most instances he should be able to serve without changing his present location.

Osborn decided to begin his analysis with the central Illinois territory, which was the one farthest west. This territory was assigned to R. M. Barnett and included Iroquois, Ford, Livingston, McLean, DeWitt, Piatt, Macon, Moultrie, Douglas, Edgar, Champaign, and Vermillion counties. It covers an area of approximately 8800 square miles and was thought to include counties of widely differing market potential. The data pertaining to these counties assembled by Osborn are shown in Exhibits 1 and 2.

In addition to unpublished data provided by the state departments of agriculture in Ohio, Indiana, and Illinois, Osborn utilized material from the following standard references.

U.S. Census of Agriculture, 1958, Vol 1, *Counties.*

U.S. Department of Commerce, 1959, *City and County Data Book,* 1962.

U.S. Census of Manufactures, 1958, *Location of Manufacturing Plants.*

U.S. Census of Business, 1958, Vol. II *Retail Trade Illinois Agriculture Statistics,* 1959, Bulletin 59–1.

**EXHIBIT 1. Statistical analysis of farms and farm products**

| | Cham- paign | DeWitt | Douglas | Edgar | Ford | Iroquois | Liv- ingston | Macon | McLean | Moultrie | Piatt | Ver- milion |
|---|---|---|---|---|---|---|---|---|---|---|---|---|
| Employment in agriculture | 3,405 | 1,155 | 1,338 | 1,915 | 1,457 | 3,318 | 3,119 | 1,750 | 4,119 | 963 | 1,247 | 2,621 |
| Number of farms | 2,620 | 1,094 | 1,136 | 1,611 | 1,207 | 2,976 | 2,825 | 1,540 | 3,189 | 996 | 1,966 | 2,435 |
| Size of county (sq. mi.) | 1,000 | 399 | 420 | 628 | 458 | 1,122 | 1,043 | 1,173 | 576 | 345 | 437 | 898 |
| Percent of total land area in farms | 93.8 | 95.2 | 92.1 | 92.1 | 95.8 | 94.0 | 95.5 | 89.4 | 96.2 | 92.9 | 98.6 | 87.3 |
| Average size of farms (acres) | 229 | 222 | 219 | 230 | 248 | 227 | 226 | 214 | 227 | 206 | 262 | 206 |
| Value, land & buildings ($1,000) | 128 | 107 | 114 | 88 | 104 | 90 | 96 | 112 | 106 | 101 | 127 | 78 |
| Value of crops ($1,000) | 24.6 | 9.7 | 10.9 | 13.0 | 10.2 | 24.4 | 24.4 | 15.3 | 27.2 | 8.8 | 13.4 | 19.1 |
| Commercial fertilizer used (T) | 32.6 | 8.7 | 15.8 | 17.2 | 10.2 | 33.7 | 27.3 | 19.2 | 36.0 | 10.2 | 18.1 | 29.1 |
| Value of livestock & livestock products sold ($1,000) | 8,047 | 3,787 | 2,445 | 5,893 | 4,836 | 9,383 | 10,229 | 3,733 | 19,197 | 1,882 | 4,375 | 8,699 |
| Value of poultry & poultry products sold ($1,000) | 868 | 141 | 397 | 276 | 519 | 1,479 | 2,122 | 199 | 860 | 164 | 418 | 377 |
| Number of livestock farms | 227 | 156 | 66 | 331 | 183 | 278 | 354 | 130 | 662 | 55 | 98 | 354 |
| Number of poultry farms | 30 | 10 | — | 5 | 10 | 50 | 56 | 5 | 20 | 10 | 6 | 10 |
| Cattle and calves (1,000 head) | 41 | 20 | 14 | 29 | 29 | 55 | 64 | 21 | 90 | 13 | 21 | 40 |
| Hogs and pigs (1,000 head) | 50 | 42 | 31 | 70 | 42 | 85 | 86 | 36 | 185 | 15 | 28 | 72 |
| Chickens (1,000 head) | 181 | 31 | 89 | 80 | 178 | 372 | 564 | 57 | 248 | 44 | 54 | 103 |

EXHIBIT 2.  Statistical analysis of agricultural supply and service establishments

| | Champaign | DeWitt | Douglas | Edgar | Ford | Iroquois | Livingston | Macon | McLean | Moultrie | Piatt | Vermilion |
|---|---|---|---|---|---|---|---|---|---|---|---|---|
| Number of grain elevators | 0 | 0 | 2 | 1 | 1 | 3 | 3 | 3 | 2 | 1 | — | 1 |
| Number of farm, garden supply and feed stores | 26 | — | — | 1 | — | — | 31 | 17 | 29 | — | — | 27 |
| Total sales of farm, garden, supply & feed stores ($1,000) | 1,583 | — | — | 10 | — | — | 3,574 | 1,282 | 4,198 | — | — | 4,856 |
| Number of feed manufacturing plants | 7 | 4 | 3 | 1 | 4 | 6 | 7 | 7 | 10 | 4 | 3 | 14 |
| 1–99 employees | 1 | — | — | — | 2 | 2 | 2 | 2 | 1 | — | 1 | 3 |
| 100–250 employees | — | — | — | — | — | — | 1 | — | 1 | — | — | — |
| 1 product | 3 | 1 | 1 | — | — | 2 | 1 | 2 | 2 | 1 | — | 4 |
| 2–3 products | 3 | 3 | 1 | — | — | 1 | 1 | 1 | 2 | 2 | 1 | 3 |
| 4–6 products | — | — | 1 | 1 | 1 | 1 | 1 | 1 | 2 | 2 | 1 | 3 |
| 7 or more products | — | — | — | — | 2 | — | 1 | 1 | 1 | — | — | 1 |

# THE HOOKER CHEMICAL COMPANY

Early in 1968 executives of the Hooker Chemical Company were considering the introduction of a solvent-based resin system for shrink-proofing woolen materials. It was believed that imparting complete machine launderability to items made of wool would dramatically stimulate demand for wool fiber, and hence, for the chemicals used to treat it. All-wool goods that were labeled machine-washable still required special washday handling and lacked the easy-care characteristics of garments made with synthetic fibers or with blends of wool and other fibers. If completely launderable all-wool fabrics were available, they would reduce apparel maintenance costs for consumers while still affording them the well-known serviceability and aesthetic values of wool. Completely launderable all-wool garments would also eliminate the easy-care advantage over woolens of clothing made from synthetic fibers.

Although the technical feasibility of Hooker's resination process seemed assured and a preliminary marketing strategy had been formulated, strong doubts were being expressed about the wisdom of proceeding further with the project. The long-term demand for wool, the proper direction for the company's growth, its ability to compete in the textile market, and the questionable strength of its patent position were some of the issues dividing management. Some executives felt that the availability of nonshrinkable, launderable woolen materials might slow or reverse the apparent trend of the demand away from woolens. It was also argued that the introduction of the new product might afford Hooker an entering wedge into the textile chemicals market.

## Growth and development of the Company

The Hooker Chemical Company was organized in 1909 by the Hooker family to produce chlorine, caustic soda and derivative products in the Niagara Falls area. Through the years, it has broadened its product mix, always staying within the general area of chemical technology. In 1967 the distribution of its sales volume among the several product groups was as follows:

| Product group | Percent |
|---|---|
| Plastics | 20 |
| Farm chemicals | 19 |
| Chemical intermediates | 15 |
| Pulp & paper chemicals | 10 |
| Metal treatment chemicals | 10 |
| International | 8 |
| Other chemicals | 8 |
| Detergent & dry cleaning chemicals | 7 |
| Protective coatings | 3 |

The company operates three majority or wholly owned subsidiaries and five divisions, each with a high degree of autonomy (see Exhibit 1). The Industrial Division which produces a variety of widely used industrial chemicals in 11 plants is the largest of the divisions. It is the third largest producer of chlorine in North America; this output is supplemented with some 150 specialized chemicals ranging from "Alkali Special 928," a bottle-washing compound, to "Tetrakis (Hydroxy-methol) Phosphonium Chloride 80%" used in producing durable, fire-retardant finishes on cotton, rayon, paper and other cellulosic materials. In addition, the division produces a number of custom chemicals that are used by pharmaceutical manufacturers and by other chemical companies in the production of dyes, weed killers, insecticides, pesticides, and solvents of all types.

The Durez Division produces plastic molding compounds, various types of resins, and polyurethane foam used in the automotive and aerospace industries. The division's Hetron polyesters, plastics that replace metal, have users in such areas as building construction, corrosion-resistant industrial ductwork, aircraft fuselages, and truck cabs.

The Ruco Division, which originally produced a line of rubber chemicals, now manufactures polyvinyl chloride and urethane-based fabrics. The former is used to make plastic bottles, film, plastic pipe, and rigid plastic extrusions. The man-made fabrics can be made to look and feel like top-grade leather, including suede. They are produced in a variety of colors, patterns, and surface finishes and find application in shoes, clothing, luggage, upholstery, and even conveyor belts, tents and tarpaulins.

The Parker Division produces a variety of chemicals and processes for the cleaning, treatment, and protection of metal surfaces. A particular strength of the division is Bonderite coatings, which are used in the preparation of metal surfaces to insure rust resistance and longer paint life. Such coatings are used extensively by steel mills to treat the continuous strip stock sold to metal fabricators. The Parker Division also produces and markets the solvent, trichlorethylene, a widely used metal-degreasing agent.

The Puerto Rico Chemical Division is largely a specialty producer of

**EXHIBIT 1. Hooker Chemical Company Organization**

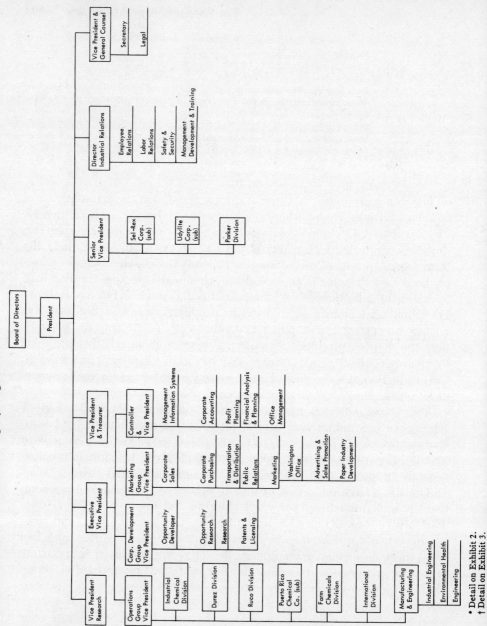

* Detail on Exhibit 2.
† Detail on Exhibit 3.

**EXHIBIT 2.   Organization of Central Research Laboratory**

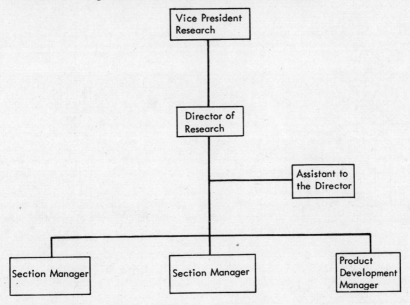

phthalic anhydride, a basic chemical used in the manufacture of alkyd resins, plasticizers and polyester resins.

The Udylite Division is the world's leading supplier of machines, chemicals, accessories and supplies for electroplating, electropainting, and related treating processes for nonprecious metal. The Udylite coating and finishing process is applied to such diverse bright metal-plated products as automobile bumpers, golf clubs, and electric toasters. Udylite's sister division, Sel-Rex, is one of the largest suppliers of precious-

**EXHIBIT 3.   Organization of Industrial Chemicals Division**

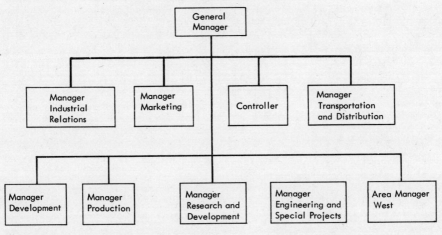

EXHIBIT 4. Development plan (PERT diagram) wool stabilization—product resin 409

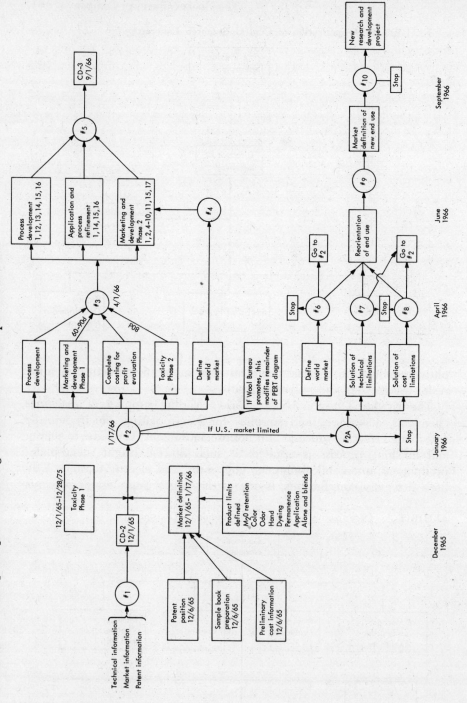

metal plating compositions and equipment, particularly gold. These products find applications in jewelry finishes, data processing equipment, computers, telecommunications equipment, missiles and other electronic devices.

The Farm Chemicals Division is one of the world's leading producers of diammonium phosphate, used as fertilizer throughout the United States, Latin America and the Far East. The division is also an important supplier of phosphate nutrients. The latter are used in the manufacture of livestock and poultry feeds. The division also makes a wide range of chemical intermediates used in the manufacture of pesticides.

The International Division offers for export sales the products of the other divisions. In addition it operates manufacturing plants in Belgium, Mexico, Argentina, Australia, and Japan.

Each division and subsidiary is operated as a cost–profit center and has its own factories as well as its own marketing and market development departments. Each division is headed by a Division General Manager and each subsidiary by a President or Vice President. Within the general framework of corporate strategy and policy these officers are fairly autonomous. Their operations are subject to review by at least one of three corporate vice presidents, two of whom have direct responsibility for several divisions or subsidiaries (Exhibit 1).

The corporate headquarters staff issues statements of policy and procedure designed to clarify the authority relationships among divisions and subsidiaries as well as between them and corporate headquarters. Exhibit A-1 in the Appendix gives an example of such a statement with respect to policy governing the commercialization of new products. Exhibit A-2, Appendix, gives an example of a statement of procedure. The steps outlined here are particularly helpful in understanding what is expected to happen to a new product during its research, development, and introduction phases as well as what alternative courses it may follow if the normal route is blocked or disturbed. Standard procedures to be followed in initiating a market evaluation of a new product, reaching a decision concerning its commercialization, and planning the development of its market are shown in Exhibits A-8, A-9, and A-10 (Appendix).

## Expansion into the textile market

Before the early 1960s Hooker had not been interested in the business of providing chemicals used by the textile industry other than soaps and cleansers. Some time prior to 1965, the Central Research Laboratory, seeking to broaden the scope of the Company's operations, hired a research chemist with considerable background and experience in the area of processing materials used by the textile industry.

This man began experimenting with some polymer types developed by Hooker Laboratories for use in other markets, seeking to determine their applicability either "as was" or in modified form to the textile applications with which he was familiar. His early results seemed promising enough to justify a research project costing about $25,000 a month and extending over a period of some months. No significant preliminary studies had been made of the market for textile chemicals nor was top management in any way committed to entering the market. Company policy did envisage the goal of expanding Hooker's product mix within the general industrial chemicals area.

The subsequent history of the project was about as follows:

*July 1965.*  Hooker's textile laboratory submitted to the Wool Bureau[1] for shrinkproof testing a number of worsted flannel swatches. Each of the swatches had been treated with one of three polymer shrinkproofing resins developed by Central Research. In addition to machine washing and drying, the resin-treated fabrics were also tested for their ability to accept dye. The results indicated that each of the three resins imparted excellent shrinkage control to the fabrics tested, without affecting materially their wool-like feel, appearance, or subsequent dyeability.

Impressed by the initial performance of Hooker's resins and the apparent simplicity of their application, Wool Bureau technicians requested and received permission to do some experiments with the Hooker method, using both worsted and wool flannel. These would be conducted at the Bureau's technical laboratories in Lowell, Massachusetts. If the outcome of the experiments was encouraging, Hooker and Wool Bureau technicians would begin serious discussion about commercial development and promotion of the method. None of the methods presently available to shrinkproof wool were completely satisfactory, due in some cases to the unappealing appearance and feel of the treated fabric (it no longer looked or felt like wool) and in other cases to the difficulty of dying treated fabric.

Wool Bureau people believed the time was right for the introduction of an effective shrinkproofing formulation which would not alter the aesthetic qualities and dyeability of the fabric. They estimated the future U.S. market for wool to be about 90 million pounds annually (equivalent to about $8 million in sales at $3.00/lb. of resin), but stressed the importance of the foreign market. This was attributable to the more extensive use of wool in apparel there and to the purchase by a single firm of all foreign rights to the Wurlan process[2] which had restricted its use both in Europe and the Orient.

The Wool Bureau was interested in promoting anything which would enhance the marketability of wool. The "Wool Mark" was currently being

---

[1] The Wool Bureau is the U.S. arm of the International Wool Secretariat, a nonprofit organization supported by wool growers throughout the world to promote the use of wool. Its U.S. headquarters is located in New York City.

[2] This was thought to be clearly the most effective wool shrinkproofing process currently available.

promoted by the Bureau on 100 percent virgin wool garments that met certain high quality standards. The following year it could be used on knit goods only if they were washable.

*August 1965.* The experiments at Lowell, Massachusetts, were very encouraging. Central Research circulated a memorandum to Product Development and other interested central units that it had evolved a new method for shrinkproofing woolen cloth. The memorandum reported findings which indicated that garments made of wool treated with the Hooker process could be subjected to conventional home washing and tumble drying. Shrinkage during extended laundering proved to be in the same range as that encountered with cotton or synthetic fabrics. While the aesthetic qualities of treated fabrics (the feel of wool) were slightly altered, experts in the field did not consider the degree of alteration as unacceptable. Neither the strength properties nor the appearance of treated fabrics were altered. Ability of treated fabrics to accept dye was actually enhanced. Patent coverage was thought to be attainable.

*October 1965.* The Product Development Department began a preliminary study of the wool textile market to determine:

a.  Whether the market would be receptive to the new process.
b.  What competitive processes there were, and the extent of demand for them.
c.  How these processes compared with the new Hooker process chemically and in cost/benefit results.

*November 1965.* Product Development's preliminary study produced the following information:

a. Market receptiveness—U.S. wool consumption in 1965 was estimated at 375 million pounds.[3] This represented an increase of 8 percent over wool consumption the previous year, but a decrease of about 13 percent compared with wool consumption in 1962 of 429 million pounds.[4] It was thought that only about one third of total wool consumption would be considered for shrinkproofing. Due to the preliminary nature of the investigation, this figure did not include possible use of shrink-resistant wool in blankets, military applications, or wool-blend fabrics.

If the process proved to be successful on a production basis, the Wool Bureau offered to promote it and provide the needed technical service in every industrialized nation where per capita consumption of wool exceeded that of the United States and was still growing.

b. Competitive situation—Three processes were discovered to be directly competitive with that developed by Hooker: oxidative systems, interfacial polymerization, and single resin treatment.

---

[3] *America's Textile Reporter* (October 28, 1965).
[4] *Statistical Abstract of United States, 1964,* p. 797.

*Oxidative systems* had gained the widest current acceptance and were reported to be used on 5–10 million pounds of wool in 1965. The Wool Bureau was currently promoting one such system, the so-called WB-7 process.

*Interfacial polymerization,* the "Wurlan" process, was developed by the Western Regional Research Laboratories of the United States Department of Agriculture. It was considered to be the most effective system for shrinkproofing wool. Despite its demonstrated effectiveness and relatively low cost, a complex application procedure had discouraged its use. Only one major firm was known to be making even limited application of the process.

*Single resin treatment* utilized a polyethylene polymer which was a member of a new series of ionomers[5] recently introduced by one of the large chemical companies. Its ability to shrinkproof wool was an apparently unexpected use for the chemical. The process employing it was effective without altering the feel or appearance of treated woolen fabric. However, treated fabric did not always accept dye with evenness and uniformity. Only one major woolen mill was reportedly producing resin-treated fabric, although another was said to be investigating its possible use.

*c.* Comparison of chemistry and cost/benefit results with Hooker process—*Oxidative systems,* as their name implies, involve the oxidation (combining with oxygen) of wool usually by immersion in a permanganate solution. Permanganic acid is a powerful oxidizer in aqueous solutions, but erodes 2–3 percent of the wool fiber during the oxidation process. When the value of the wool loss is added to the basic chemical cost of the permanganate solution, \$0.04/lb. of wool, total cost of the process was estimated at \$0.06/lb. of wool.

None of the oxidative processes produced a completely launderable wool but merely reduced shrinkage over a limited number of washings. Their chief advantages were ease of processing and no alteration in the woollike feel or appearance of the treated fabric.

*Interfacial polymerization* required two impregnations of wool fiber: the first with an aqueous solution of hexamethylene diamine and the second with an organic solution of sebacoyle chloride. This process was quite complex, necessitating close control of bath conditions and molecular sieves for drying. Cost was estimated at \$0.55/lb. of wool.

*In the single resin treatment,* resin is applied in diluted form, using a chlorinated solvent as a diluent. Processing is simply a matter of applying a chlorinated solvent solution of the resin to wool, then drying and heat-curing. Basic chemical costs were thought to be in the range of \$0.07–

---

[5] These are chemical agents which adhere to fibers as the result of the electrical charge they carry rather than as the result of chemical action with the fiber.

0.10/lb. of wool, exclusive of the solvent. The J. C. Penney Company was known to be offering yard goods treated with resin at $3.00/yd., which was the normal price of untreated wool.

In comparison, the Hooker process appeared to have significant advantages and few disadvantages. Processing was simple and could be accomplished in any one of several wet processing steps to which wool is normally subjected. Like all resin systems, solvent recovery was a disadvantage, but there was hope of eliminating this through further development work. Chemical costs were competitive with other systems.

*December 1965.* Product Development Department completed a development plan for the wool shrinkproofing project which is outlined in the PERT diagram shown in Exhibit 4. As indicated in the diagram, the first major assignment of Phase I of the plan was market definition. For this assignment sample books of treated and untreated fabric were prepared for distribution to woolen mills, patent position was to be clarified, and full cost information obtained. The initial phase of a toxicity program would also begin.

It was thought that Product Development would be able to tell Management reasonably soon what the U.S. market for wool shrinkage materials actually was, as well as define the strengths and weaknesses of the Wool Bureau in promoting the product. The present plan did not envision Wool Bureau promotion of the product.

The second decision phase of the plan called for the completion of toxicity tests (including the use of human subjects) and the beginning of a marketing and development plan, complete costing for profit evaluation, and definition of the world market. If the number 3 decision were "go," the plan would move into its final phase.

*January 1966.* The first field reports prepared by Product Development personnel concerning the market for wool shrinkproofing material were submitted to departmental management soon after the first of the year. Excerpts from typical reports follow:

> Chief of Textile Laboratories—Woolen
> U.S. Army Quartermaster Corp.
>
> Army use of wool declining. Wool stabilization treatment probably limited to socks and blankets. Wool use in blankets would probably be discontinued within two years in preference to polyester filling encased in nylon.
>
> Observed that there are already 9 or 10 competitive processes available, many quite inexpensive; thinks it would be a mistake to spend any development money in this area. He believed Wurlan process to be the best at present, but would be interested in examining Hooker process if it were equal to Wurlan. Only one mill at present was producing stabilized wool using the Wurlan process and USQMC is wary of contracting with a single supplier.

Sales Manager, Men's Wear
Large Woolen Mill

He believed washable wool market would be limited to women's wear and style-centered teen wear. His company's sales of stabilized woolen yardage in women's wear last year was 960,000–1,200,000 yards. Potential usage in men's wear would be limited to no more than 2–5 percent of the casual slack market in his opinion. He thought the washable wool potential for children's wear was nil due to the higher price required by stabilization.

The mill's sales of washable wool this year were twice that of last year. He estimated present washable wool market to be in the vicinity of 10–12 million yards (10 oz. cloth). He was interested in the Hooker process but did not care to see lab samples. In his opinion mill trials of the resin were the only real test.

President
Large Woolen Mill in Northeastern U.S.

His mill's production of stabilized wool last year using single resin system was 1.5 million yards. Output would have been greater had processing problems not developed. He believes he could easily sell 5 million yards next year with a reliable stabilization system. Estimates the potential of his own company in this market at 10 million yards annually, mostly for use in women's and children's wear. Two large retail chains are "clamoring" for washable wool garments, but he cannot at present produce the fabric in the quantities in which they want to buy.

He would like to test the Hooker process, and if satisfied with it, will commit his company to cooperate fully with us in perfecting mass production processing. He also supplied the names of two other firms whose management might be interested in working with us on mill runs of the process.

Men's Wear Product Development Manager
Large Woolen Mill in Southeastern U.S.

Predicted that his company would sell 5 million yards of washable wool next year, mostly for women's wear. He thought the company had about 20% of the market.

A cellulose-wool blend is currently under development and he is very interested in a reliable stabilization system to shrinkproof the wool portion of the fabric. The existing market for this blend is estimated at 30–40 million yards with a strong growth potential.

He inspected Hooker's lab samples and was impressed with their feel and appearance. On the basis of our process description, he will move to get a meeting between his staff technicians and ours to discuss mill trials.

Consumers Union
Mt. Vernon, New York

CU has never made a survey of consumer reaction to a "washable wool" but are planning to do a study on wool treatment in general. No date has been set for the study. CU officials want information on the Hooker process if we decide to "go" with it.

Due to the oversell which currently plagues the wash-n-wear market, they believe consumer reaction to a new "washable" wool would be skepticism. The term "washable" is surrounded by confusion. Will such fabric need ironing after washing? Will it dry wrinkle-free? In their opinion any restrictive instructions, e.g., DO NOT DRYCLEAN, would be "suicide." This would create sales resistance and bury the concept of "care-free" garments.

The feel and appearance of Hooker treated fabrics was considered excellent but opinions about future markets were more guarded. In children's garments the shift is toward synthetics. Many sweaters are already washable if special precautions are taken and consumers generally accept these restrictions.

In their opinion promotion of the process would have to be essentially educational in nature punctuated by specific claims to promote confidence. They suggested airline stewardesses as good models to demonstrate the quality of fabrics treated by the Hooker process.

Research Staff
Large Textile Merchandising Firm

Although this firm does not manufacture anything, it is strictly a merchandising company, the top brass have good relations with all the major textile firms. They are keenly aware of market demand and should be able to give us an honest appraisal of the potential for Resin 409. We also wanted to explore ways of working with them on the development of the product if they were interested in it. It was explained that our Management was not yet committed to a "go" on this project and that there was a possibility that we might not proceed with it. They asked if Hooker would consider manufacturing the resin and allow someone else to market it. We answered that this was a possibility but would require a decision at a higher level than we represented.

They outlined three different arrangements their company has used in promoting new products like Resin 409.

1. Buy all patents and rights to the product and assume full responsibility for manufacturing and marketing it.
2. Purchase product from the manufacturer with exclusive rights to market it.
3. Share marketing and related expenses with manufacturer. In their opinion marketing costs on a product like Resin 409 could be as much as two and one half times manufactured cost.

Following this preliminary discussion, we presented our data on the performance of Resin 409. We also passed around for inspection treated sweaters and test fabrics which had been exposed to various cycles of home washings. Their reactions were as follows:

1. Garments and fabrics had a harsh feel, but they admitted that this could be overcome through chemical and mechanical manipulation.

2. Our performance data were considered insufficient for them to reach a decision concerning use at present. On the basis of our data, they do not regard Resin 409 as significantly better than competitive products. Moreover, they contend that with solvent-recovery cost plus our estimated price of $3.50 per pound, the cost of treating could be 16¢ to 17¢ per pound of wool. This is quite high.

3. They admit we have an interesting development and are willing to cooperate with us in its commercial development if we decide to "go" with it. They can supply an extensive sample of styles in both woven and knitted type fabrics to a worldwide market. They would also be willing to test fabrics treated with our process for compatibility with chemicals ordinarily involved in textile processing. Their interest would decrease considerably if our process were applicable only to woven fabrics.

*March 1966.*  The results of this survey were reported to the Vice President for Research and Development. The gist of the report was that while the existing market for washable woolens was small, it could probably be expanded readily since there seemed to be a strong latent consumer desire for such garments. The Hooker process seemed to have definite technological and financial advantages over competing processes.

Management was aware that several of these conclusions were based only on performance data developed in the laboratory under carefully controlled conditions and on a small scale. Results on a large scale and under factory conditions might be quite different, so it was agreed that the next step should be to arrange with a woolen mill for full-scale mill trials in order to develop more reliable performance records, to discover "bugs" in the process, and possibly modify the technology to eliminate them.

This was easier decided than done. The Hooker process involved resination from a solvent base. Historically, the industry had been set up for aqueous processing and very few firms used the resination method of shrinkproofing. It was necessary, therefore, to find a firm with resination equipment and know-how and proper solvent-recovery equipment. Nor were all customer firms willing to tolerate the disturbances of their own operating routines that would inevitably accompany their functioning as a pilot or field development laboratory for Hooker. In this relationship Hooker's technical people would necessarily have access to many of the details of the customer's operating methods and know-how which he would rather not have generally known.

In due course, Carleton Woolen Mills, which was using a competitor's solvent-based resination process agreed to cooperate in trying out the new Hooker product. Carleton Mills management had experienced several difficulties in using the competitive process and hoped that the Hooker process would offer a solution.

*Late 1966 and early 1967.* Over a period of several months, cooperative experiments were conducted in Carleton's plant. As was to be expected, factory-scale use of the process disclosed a number of "bugs." For example, the first trial run resulted in a fabric unpleasantly heavy to the touch but it also showed that the Hooker process was much simpler to operate and had technical advantages over the best competitive process. After four trials and subsequent modifications, Carleton felt the new process was good enough to justify dropping the competitive product and relying entirely on the new one. At this point Hooker management felt that the new product–process was ready for regular commercial development.

*February 1967.* The Central Research and Development Department prepared a form CD-3, Exhibit A-8 (Appendix), which transferred responsibility for the project to the Development Department of the Industrial Chemical Division. In its commercial development work during succeeding months, this division encountered several discouraging developments.

The shrinkproofing material was applied during the finishing process by means of a pad roll including a device called an elastometer which came in contact with the solvent and was attacked by it. For some reason this difficulty had not shown up in the previous Carleton experiments.

The Division's market development department made a cursory market research study and came up with a very negative report. Their limited contacts with the trade indicated that the makers of woven wool goods would not be very much interested in shrinkproofing their products. For example, the blanket market was moving so rapidly toward synthetics that blanket makers could see no point in improving items that produced a dwindling part of their volume.

Another consideration was the fact that the textile market was a new one for Hooker and that neither the Industrial Chemical Division nor any other division of the company had a sales force trained to contact the textile industry. While Central R & D tended to regard the shrinkproofing process as an entering wedge into a market which in time might even justify a separate division, the Industrial Chemical Division was bound to view the matter more from the standpoint of the possibilities of the particular product.

*July 1967.* The project was referred back from the Industrial Chemical Division to Central Research and Development for further development work or abandonment.

Central R & D went to work on the application problem. It was discovered that the Dow Chemical Company had for sale a machine which applied chemicals to textiles by means of a spray instead of a pad roll. This machine had never been used for applying resin and it was feared that slight variations in application might result in streaking when the fiber was dyed. Experiments were conducted during the fall of 1967 and by November they were reassuring enough to convince Carleton management that it was a "reasonable gamble" to install a Dow machine.

During this period Central R & D also uncovered another possible market in the treatment of worsted fabrics which are used in great volume in making men's suits. Ordinarily, before this fabric is made into garments it must be preshrunk by sponging at a cost of between five and seven cents a yard. Hooker process shrinkproofing which stabilized worsted materials dimensionally would eliminate the loss of from three to six percent in fabric area normally incurred by the previous preshrinking method. Since the cost of manufactured worsted fabrics ordinarily runs from $5 to $15 a yard, this saving would vary from 15 cents to 90 cents a yard.

*February 1968.* At this point Central Research and Development was in the following position:

1. Apparently it had eliminated most of the production and usage "bugs" and had a product that was viable technically.
2. It had filed a series of patent applications on the technology involved, but no patents had been issued.
3. The chemistry involved was novel but not so complex as to preclude or even seriously handicap copiers. So far it had protected its technology by close control of all lots of the chemical.
4. It had one customer, Carleton Mills, whose annual take of the product was about $46,500.
5. It had a limited liaison with about a dozen other possible customer concerns but no firm relations with them.
6. It could see a possible market for dimensional stabilization materials and processes not only in the treatment of worsted, single-knit goods and double-knit goods, but also for various types of blended fabrics and synthetics.

At this point also Central R & D had several alternatives:

a. It could abandon the project.
b. It could have another go at transferring it to the Industrial Chemical Division.
c. It could start commercial development of the product and carry it far enough that the project would either prove to be a failure or the Industrial Chemical Division become anxious to take it over.

If the last of these was adopted, a marketing strategy had to be developed. The Product Development group of Central R & D saw a number of factors that needed to be given careful consideration in formulating a strategy.

a. The amount of resin sold for shrinkproofing would depend on the consumer demand for textile products that did not shrink.

b. The logical and economical point of application was in the mill that produced the textile fabrics from which consumer products were made.

c. Hooker's market protection was very uncertain. Many chemical houses could make resins. Hooker's contribution and hence its advantage lay in the novelty of the process for applying the resin to the cloth and its know-how in such application. The best Hooker could hope for in the way of legal protection was a process patent which is notoriously hard to defend.

d. Both the textile market and the textile chemical market were highly competitive and competition tended to emphasize price. For example, a couple of years earlier a new textile processing chemical had been introduced which at first sold for 38 cents a pound. Within a year, the price had been driven down to 13 cents a pound.

One school of thought in the group favored selling the product to any textile mill that could be persuaded to buy it and to pass on Hooker's application know-how to customers through a well-trained technical service staff. They felt that being the first in the field would put the company in a situation to use its superior technical service to capture a market position which would be hard for competitors to attack with the price appeal alone.

Another group urged that protection be sought by branding the process and advertising it widely in ultimate consumer media after the manner of Sanforizing and Simonizing. Mills using the Hooker Process could be permitted to mark their fabrics with the "Hookerized" label which consumer textile product makers and marketers in turn could use in their sales promotion.

A third proposal which was strongly advocated was that Hooker sell textile mills under a dual contract, one part of which authorized the mill to apply the process and use the know-how and technology under a secrecy clause and the other part of which involved the purchase of the resin. The mill would pay a price for the resin and a royalty per pound of fabric treated.

There was also a hot dispute about price. One school of thought urged that the initial price be placed very high, absorbing about two thirds of the estimated customer benefit and allowing plenty of room for reductions to discourage competition. The estimated cost and consumer benefit data indicated that the price tag could be set at a figure that would carry a very attractive profit. Another group was equally positive that the initial price should be only slightly more than the figure at which the price might be expected to settle under competitive conditions.

## Appendix: Excerpts from Policy and Procedure Manual

### EXHIBIT A–1:    Marketing policy—New-Product Commercialization

A.  *General Statement of Policy*

The development and commercialization of new products will be planned to be consistent with long-range corporate and division objectives. Specific procedures will be established to assure efficient development of new products to commercial success.

B.  *Authorization*

This policy is authorized by the President.

C.  *Administration*

This policy will be administered by the Vice President—Research and Development, Division General Managers, and Director of Marketing.

D.  *Application of Policy*

1.  A "new" product is defined as a product not presently being marketed by the Corporation and not similar enough to an existing product or product group to be considered simply as an addition to the product line.

2.  New products may originate in Research, in the Divisions, or may be brought into the company from outside sources by Research or by the Divisions. All company components have a responsibility to identify new product opportunities needed to achieve long-range business objectives.

3.  For new products originating in Research, except when determined otherwise for specific cases, the Corporate Research and Development Department will have responsibility through market evaluation on the commercial side and through semiworks production on the process and production side. Divisions will have responsibility for market development, commercial production, and commercial sale.

4.  For new products originating in the Divisions, the Division will normally have responsibility for all development functions, unless specific assignment is made to Research.

5.  Market development for new products not assigned to a Division will be the responsibility of the Director of Marketing.

6.  The long-range plans of the Divisions and the Corporation will be used as a guide to help in planning the research and development program.

7.  Commercial prices for products new to the Corporation will be recommended by Division General Managers and approved by the Vice President—Divisions.

8.  Sales commitments will not be made to customers on new products without prior Corporate approval of funds for any necessary production facilities.

9.  Development of procedures for the commercialization of new products is the responsibility of the Director of Marketing. Procedures will provide for assignment of individual responsibilities and for a reporting system that will assure efficient and rapid commercialization.

**EXHIBIT A–2.  Procedures for commercialization of new products**

The following prescribes a general procedure and also outlines the major functions involved in commercializing a new product. For the sake of clarity and brevity, only general rules are set down. Since a variety of exceptions must be made according to the origin of the product, its nature, the market situation, and other variables, a detailed procedure might easily become incomprehensible. If these general rules are well understood, it becomes a relatively simple matter to steer the unusual case through the needed steps.

Exhibit A-3 depicts the flow of the product and the responsibility therefore from an idea in Research to an item of commerce. This is split into two streams, showing on the right those groups handling marketing or commercial responsibilities. Other groups on the left function to produce needed technology for design and needed materials for the groups on the right. Those groups above the dotted line make up Corporate Research and Development while those below represent the Division interested in the new product. In specific cases different assignment of responsibility between Research and Development and the Division may be made. At this date, for example, there are two exceptions: market evaluation responsibility for pesticide chemicals and for organophosphites is assigned to the Eastern Chemical Division rather than to Research and Development.

Exhibits A-4, 5, 6, and 9 more fully illustrate the communications systems necessary and also outline the major activities and responsibilities in each of the four development phases.

The basic objective of this procedure is to move development projects to full commercialization successfully, and as rapidly and efficiently as possible. The focus, always, is on the final phase: commercial production marketed by field sales.

The normal steps through which a development becomes commercial are described in this procedure. However, since the commercial phase is our focus, judicious short cuts and by-passing of intermediate phases is encouraged. Such accelerated scheduling on both the production and commercial side is a management responsibility at each of the key decision points in the procedure, and at any intervening point when appropriate. The key decision points are the following:

| Decision Points | Responsibility | Control |
|---|---|---|
| Establishment of Research Project | VP—R & D | Research Project Proposal Form #3 |
| Initiation of Market Evaluation | VP—R & D | CD-2 |
| Pilot Plant Expense Exceeds $5000 | VP—R & D | CD-3 Progress Review |
| Decision to Commercialize | Div Gen Mgr | CD-3 |

**EXHIBIT A–2** (*Continued*)

| *Decision Points* | *Responsibility* | *Control* |
|---|---|---|
| Beginning of Market Development........ | Div Gen Mgr | CD-4 |
| Decision to Provide Commercial-Scale Facilities.......... | Div Gen Mgr w/ Corporate approval | Appropriation Request |

Examples of desirable short cuts in the standard procedure might be developments such as the following:

a.  A custom chemical might move directly from Research to Field Sales and *Product Management* on the commercial side, but go through all or most of the phases on the production side.

b.  A new product for which process technology and facilities are available might skip all or most of the production phases, but go through all of the commercial phases.

**EXHIBIT A–3**

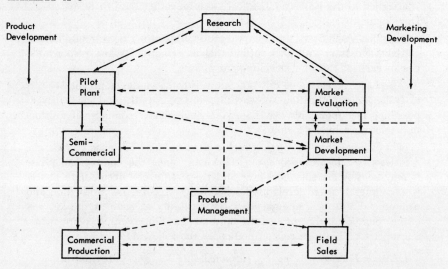

*Notes:* Titles in boxes represent functions rather than organization components. For example, Product Development in Research and Development is responsible for Market Evaluation function; the Market Development function may, depending on the division, be handled by Market Development, Product Management, or Sales Management.

Solid arrows indicate flow of responsibility through various phases.

Dotted arrows indicate flow of communication.

Dashed line shows division of responsibility between Divisions and Research and Development Department.

**EXHIBIT A–4.  Research phase**

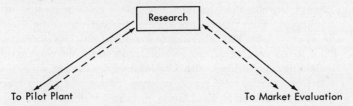

Major Activities and Responsibilities

a.  Research receives and screens, with Market Evaluation, laboratory developments, ideas, suggestions, and market needs from all sources.

b.  The long-range plans of the Divisions and the Corporation are to be used as a guide in determining content and scope of Research programs.

c.  Research formally initiates research project on those items passing the screening tests.

d.  Research initiates preliminary cost studies.

e.  Research initiates preliminary patent studies.

f.  Research prepares patent disclosures.

g.  After responsibilities pass to other functions shown above, Research performs such additional work as may be needed by these functions.

h.  Research terminates any project when cogent reasons develop.

i.  Research, with Market Evaluation, prepares Form CD-2, transferring project to Market Evaluation phase.

**EXHIBIT A–5.  Market evaluation phase**

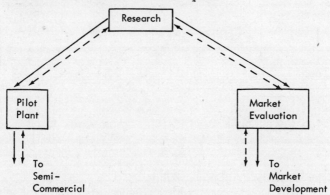

Major Activities and Responsibilities

a.  CD-2 issued by Market Evaluation. CD-2 serves as authorization for further development work.

b.  Market Evaluation investigates market to determine information required by Form CD-3. The program for the required market investigation is planned according to a PERT type of schedule with periodic (at least quarterly) reviews.

**EXHIBIT A–5** (*Continued*)

c.   Process Development initiates pilot plant work at request of Market Evaluation. Pilot plant work on any project exceeding $5,000 is to be approved by Vice President, Research and Development.

d.   Pilot plant group explores feasible routes and develops engineering technology, consulting with Corporate Engineering.

e.   Either Research, pilot plant, or semi-commercial group meets sample needs of Market Evaluation, this to be determined by circumstances.

f.   Project is dropped if development data indicates lack of opportunity for commercial success.

g.   For promising projects, Process Development conducts further economic studies as required for CD-3.

h.   Market Evaluation distributes samples for evaluation no charge or sells them according to research sample price schedules established by the Research and Development Department and calculated to be significantly above probable commercial prices.

i.   Market Evaluation with Divisional approval quotes prospective customers the anticipated commercial price range.

j.   Patent Department makes patent review of product and contemplated process or processes.

k.   Market Evaluation completes CD-3.

l.   With Division having commercial responsibility, project is dropped or moved on to Market Development upon review of CD-3.

**EXHIBIT A–6.   Market development phase**

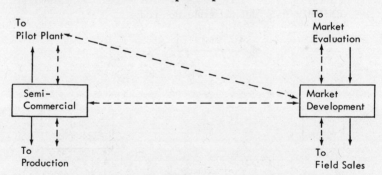

Major Activities and Responsibilities

a.   Market Development with assistance from Market Evaluation and from Marketing Research prepares CD-4 marketing plan.

b.   Pilot plant work may continue throughout this period.

c.   Process Development provides further cost studies with Engineering assistance upon request.

d.   From results of CD-4 marketing plan, Market Development revises CD-3 updating the Market Evaluation Report. If new information indicates changes in probable success, project is modified, expanded, or discontinued—according to the market opportunity.

e. Process Development provides semi-works facilities upon recommendation of Market Development with approval of Division General Manager, needed quantities to be provided by most convenient means. Capital Appropriation Request to be prepared if required for semi-works facilities.

f. Sales commitments are not to be made to customers without prior Corporate approval of funds for facilities that will be required.

g. Market Development Manager or Sales Manager requests the preparation of an evaluation grade capital estimate, manufacturing costs, economics, and time requirements.

h. Market Development will recommend firm prices for decision by the Sales Manager and the Division General Manager, and approval by Corporate management.

i. The Division General Manager, with concurrence from Corporate management, makes the decision to provide commercial facilities or to discontinue commercialization.

j. The Division General Manager or Plant Manager secures appropriation grade capital estimate from Engineering, sales and price projections and competitive evaluation from Market Development, and secures a review of manufacturing costs and economics from the Division Controller.

k. The Division General Manager submits a completely documented proposal to Corporate management.

## EXHIBIT A–7

Procedure for Initiating Market Evaluation of a New Product,
Form CD-2

Project No: _____

Name of Project: _____

Division Assignment: _____

Report Prepared By: _____

Date: _____

### Product Considerations

1. Technical achievement:

### Market Considerations

2. Anticipated markets and applications:

3. Summary of competitive situation for above markets and applications, as known at this time:

### Project Plan and Costs

4. Project cost to date:

5. Product Development plan:
    Projected CD-3 completion date:
    Estimated costs to obtain CD-3:
       Market investigation:
       Pilot plant and process investigation:

**EXHIBIT A–8**

Procedure for Appraising Feasibility of New Product Commercialization,
Form CD-3

Project No: _____
Name of Project: _____
Division Assignment: _____
Report Prepared By: _____
Date: _____

## Product Considerations

1. Product specifications:
2. Relation to existing products or product lines:
3. Patent position: (Statement from Director of Patents and Licensing to be obtained and attached.)

## Market Considerations

4. Industry markets in which product will be sold: (Give present market potential and growth possibilities for product in each industry market.)
5. Potential major customers:
6. Potential major applications: (Summarize each major application describing present and anticipated competition in each. Consider competition from same products, alternative products, alternative processes, etc.)
7. Product application development: (Extent to which each major application has been proved out; work remaining to be done.)
8. Competitive situation: (Describe competing companies, products, processes, prices. For competing companies give information as appropriate on comparative proprietary position, degree of integration, volume, cost position, and marketing capabilities.)
9. Relation to markets now served:
10. Pricing plan:* (Show development prices and anticipated commercial price range.)
11. Forecast price and sales volume:

|  | AV. SP | Total Sales | |
|---|---|---|---|
|  |  | Quantity | Dollars |
| 1st year of commercial sales |  |  |  |
| 2nd year  "        "        " |  |  |  |
| 5th year  "        "        " |  |  |  |
| 10th year  "        "        " |  |  |  |

## Manufacturing Considerations

12. Brief description of process:
13. Raw materials used:
14. Process development plan: (Describe what process development work must be done for successful commercialization.)

**EXHIBIT A–8** (*Continued*)

### Financial Considerations

15. Project costs to date:
    a.  Research:
    b.  Market Evaluation:
16. Probable plant investment:
17. Probable profitability:

| | 1st Yr | 2nd Yr | 5th Yr | 10th Yr |
|---|---|---|---|---|
| | 19___ | 19___ | 19___ | 19___ |

    Sales
        Av SP
        Units (Pounds, Tons, Gals)
        Dollars
    Mfg and Shipping Cost
    Gross Profit
    S G A
    Net Income Before Taxes
    Total Assets Used
    Net Income Ratios
        To Sales
        To Assets Used

\* Requires Divisional approval.

**EXHIBIT A–9**

### Procedure for Preparing Marketing Plan for New Products, Form CD-4

Project No: _____
Name of Project: _____
Plan Prepared By: _____
Date: _____

### Marketing Plan

(To be prepared at beginning of Market Development stage and revised as appropriate during Market Development. When project is transferred to Sales, a Marketing Plan for the Commercial Phase is to be prepared. This Marketing Plan outline can also be used as a guide for preparing marketing plans for existing products.)

1. Five-year forecast of selling price and sales volume.
2. Hooker commercial approach: (Identify major markets and major benefits offered, then summarize basic strategy for developing the market.)
3. Product availability: (Quantities available now and over the next few months, where produced, how scheduled, sample policy.)
4. Pricing: (Current price schedule, forecast future prices.)
5. Market Research: (Further market data needed and plan for obtaining it.)
6. Field Sales: (Who will do sales work, what customers and prospects will be called on.)

**EXHIBIT A–9** (*Continued*)

7. Customer service: (How will orders, invoicing, scheduling, shipping, and correspondence relating thereto be handled.)
8. Technical service: (Who will do technical service and product application work, how much will be required, and plan for developing any needed application, processing or use data.)
9. Literature and promotion: (What materials will be produced, by whom, and how will they be used.)
   Publications:
   Publicity:
   Selling Aids:
   Advertising:
10. Distribution plan: (Will sales be direct to users, through distributors, export. Describe plan.)
11. Trademarks: (Will any present or new trademarks be used? How?)
12. Patents: (Policy on licensing Hooker patents, evaluation of adversely held patents)
13. Product planning program: (What continuing product development work will be needed.)

**EXHIBIT A–10.   Commercial phase**

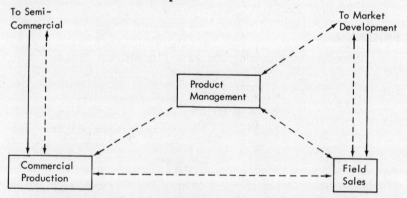

Major Activities and Responsibilities
a. Facilities are designed and constructed either by Corporate Engineering working with the Division, or by Division Engineering as appropriate.
b. Product Manager prepares marketing plan CD-4.
c. Commercial operations begin.

# THE MARGEANN CHEMICAL COMPANY

Some years ago, an executive of the Margeann Chemical Company on a visit to Japan was told of a compound, gibberellin, which when sprinkled on certain plants stimulated growth and caused considerable increases in foliage, fruit, and seeds. He brought a sample back to America. Small-scale experiments indicated that the reports he had received from his Japanese friends were justified.

The Margeann Chemical Company made and marketed bulk chemicals to the pharmaceutical manufacturing industry, the veterinary trade, the food business, the animal food industry, makers of plant protective and growth-promoting compounds, and to general industrial houses. All Margeann products were used by the buying firms as materials in their end products. Total sales were about $100 million. The management was aggressive and definitely growth minded. The firm had financial resources to enable it to launch any new venture of reasonable proportions. During recent years, corporate earnings had averaged about 14 percent (before taxes) on investment.

The marketing research department and the product development group were instructed to study the gibberellins as a possible addition to the product line.

The product development report stated that the Margeann Company had existing production facilities to make the product. While initial costs of producing small amounts would be high, the costs of making it in quantity should be somewhere between $30 and $50 a pound. The product could be applied to plants in five ways:

1. As a spray on the foliage.
2. As a paste in an inert carrier.
3. As a dust composed of the compound and a carrier.
4. As a dip solution.
5. As a solution in which seeds could be soaked.

Each of these methods required that the material be compounded with other ingredients, since the amount needed for any one application was almost infinitesimally small.

Provable claims showed that gibberellin caused certain kinds of flowers and ornamental plants to grow much larger, with more foliage and more luxuriant flowers. To exploit this market, the product had to be packed in very small units suitable for the retail trade, and the company would have to advertise it to ultimate consumer-users and develop channels of distribution to reach them. The company was neither experienced nor skilled in this kind of business.

Field tests in west Texas indicated that the application of 8 grams per acre to cotton plants on well-irrigated land increased the yield about 20 percent. The average yield per untreated acre was about 3.5 bales. These results indicated nothing about the effect of the material when used on cotton planted on land that was not well irrigated, or what it could do in cotton areas other than west Texas. About half of the two million west Texas acres planted to cotton were well irrigated. Cotton acreage in the country totaled about 10 million. In addition, the treatment of cottonseed with a special form of the material at the rate of ½ gram per 100 pounds of seed considerably shortened the germination period and greatly increased the percentage of the seed that germinated. About 20 pounds of seed were planted per acre.

Field tests in the grape-growing area of California also showed that application of the material to vines increased the size of the fruit so that it commanded a higher price on the market and increased the output per acre. During one season, treated grapes sold for $8.80 per 24-pound lug as against $5.78 per lug for the untreated fruit. From the grower's standpoint, the economics of its use in the California area worked out about as shown in Table 1.

In addition, use of the material relieved the table-grape grower of the necessity of girdling, at about $15 an acre, and thinning, at about $200 an acre in Coachella Valley and about $45 an acre in San Joaquin Valley. Some growers were afraid of the effect that continued application of gibberellin might have on the vines, which took from 10 to 15 years to grow to bearing maturity. For example, no one knew whether the increased productivity it generated would exhaust the plants before their

**TABLE 1.  Experience with grapes**

| Kind of grapes | Per acre without treatment | | | Per acre with treatment | | Material used per acre (grams) | Total Number of acres planted to grapes |
| | Costs | Returns | | Cost of applying | Gross returns | | |
| | | Gross | Net | | | | |
| Table (in Coachella Valley): | $800 | $1,200 | $400 | $145 | $1,800 | 16 | 7,000 |
| Table (in San Joaquin Valley): | 645 | 875 | 230 | 75 | 1,250 | 8 | 18,000 |
| Raisin | 375 | 550 | 175 | 50 | 605 | 8 | 119,000 |
| Wine | 375 | 500 | 125 | 50 | 600 | 8 | 52,000 |
| Canning | 375 | 600 | 225 | 50 | 660 | 8 | 4,000 |

normal time or whether it might prove poisonous to them if applied over a number of years. About 500,000 acres were planted to grapes in the United States. While the results shown in the table above might be representative of the possible effects of gibberellin wherever applied to grapes, no valid claims of effectiveness could be made outside the California area.

It might be expected that the application of gibberellin to some other crops would yield results justifying exploration. To find out which crops would respond to it enough to justify commercial development was a costly process, requiring several years of experimentation and controlled field tests. So the management of the Margeann Company decided to pursue a vigorous campaign to capture the markets represented by the California grape growers and the west Texas cotton planters. It was hoped that the cash inflow from these operations might provide some of the funds needed to explore the effectiveness of the product on other crops and to develop provable claims for its use.

A study of the market indicated that a sales force to distribute the product directly to users or even to local dealers would be entirely too expensive. Such a force would have only one product to sell and there was no reasonable assurance that the company could develop within the near future a plant product line with enough volume to make possible direct distribution. Furthermore, management was aware that its skills did not lie in the direction of marketing to some millions of farmers through the various types of dealers who served them.

It was decided, therefore, to market the product as a bulk item to formulator distributors who either resold it without change of form or mixed it with carriers needed to assure convenience and control of application. It was estimated that about 25 to 30 such formulator distributors would be needed to provide adequate coverage throughout the country. The formulator-distributor could be expected to resell the product at a price about 50 percent above the figure at which Margeann sold it to him. The local dealer would probably add about 33 percent to the price he paid the formulator-distributor to arrive at his selling price. Thus, if Margeann's price for a given amount of the product were $1, the formulator-distributor would probably charge about $1.50, and the local dealer, $2 for the same amount.

It was known that at least three other companies were interested in developing the business of making and selling gibberellins to the agricultural trade. According to all reports, Margeann was about a year or a year and a half ahead of the rest of them in its developmental work. Two of the rival firms were hard-hitting and aggressive, but none of them were habitual price cutters. It was certain that the process of developing the market for the product in any crop area would be slow—from three to six years—and costly. Margeann management did not feel that for some years, at least, price would become a very decisive patronage appeal.

The executive vice president asked the director of marketing to recommend a specific price or structure of prices at which Margeann should offer the product. He also requested the formulation of a pricing policy to be followed as the market was developed and competition became active. Margeann's general policy had been to try to be price competitive without being either a price cutter or a price leader.

---

# OLIN MATHIESON

Mr. James F. Towey, vice president of Olin Mathieson Chemical Corporation and General Manager of its Brass Division, was wrestling with the problem of what to do about the firm's metal cladding business. What had looked like a very promising source of income had, by a single decision of the Federal Government, been turned into a business of doubtful future.

Olin Mathieson Company is the result of the combination of Olin Industries, founded in 1892 to manufacture explosives for use in the coal mines and later expanded into the production of firearms and ammunition, and the Mathieson Company, established at about the same time to make and sell alkalies and later expanded into the production and vending of caustic soda, chlorine, synthetic ammonia and into the fine and kraft paper business. The name of the firm was subsequently shortened to Olin Industries.

At the time of this case the organization structure of the firm was as shown in Exhibit 1, which includes not only the organizational relationships within the company but the product groupings into which its business was divided.

Each division is operated as a more or less autonomous unit and is expected to return a satisfactory profit and to improve its position in the industry to which it belongs. Each division is under the direction of a vice president and general manager with broad powers and responsibility.

## THE BRASS DIVISION

The Brass Division was the outgrowth of World War I, which caused a shortage of brass for cartridge cases and primers. As a prime producer of munitions, Olin Industries started a brass mill in East Alton, Illinois.

**EXHIBIT 1**

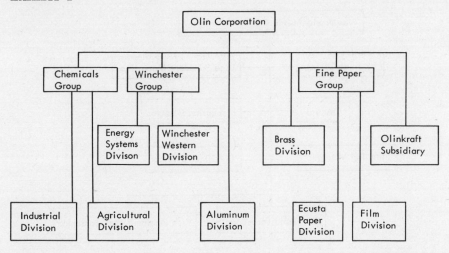

When the war ended, Management faced the problem of capturing a share of peacetime demand for brass products.

The going was tough. The brass industry, composed mainly of firms that had been in business a half century or more, was concentrated in the Connecticut Valley and the average user never thought to look for a supplier in the Middle West. The Western Cartridge Company, the Olin subsidiary that handled the brass business had no connections in the user market and very little knowledge of it.

Management accepted these handicaps as a challenge instead of a deterrent and set out to find a niche into which its brass business could fit. A study showed that brass was made according to standard specifications drawn to describe the products of the most efficient production processes. The result was that brass users were obliged to design their products to use the standard alloys instead of seeking materials to fit what they wanted to make.

Olin therefore adopted a policy of tailoring the brass to fit the use instead of forcing the user to tailor the use to the brass. Company engineers and salesmen sought out users with special needs and developed materials specifications to fit the needs and then tried to develop processes to make brass to fit the specifications. This was not always easy to do. But intelligent persistence solved most of the problems, and Olin developed a reputation for its "tailored brass" upon which it prides itself to this day. The Brass Division has a reputation for developing products suited to the specialized needs of users. As a result the division now holds a significant share of the commercial copper-alloy market.

The general organization structure of the Brass Division is shown in Exhibit 2.

**EXHIBIT 2.   Olin Brass Division**

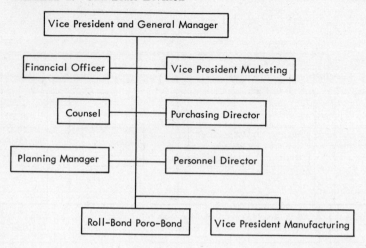

The products made and sold by the Brass Division may be divided into seven groups:

1.  Mill sheet and strip (copper and copper alloys)
2.  Fineweld tubes (electronically welded copper-alloy tubes)
3.  Somers thin strip (close-tolerance and critical-finish copper alloys, nickel and stainless steel)
4.  Posit-Bond products (metallurgically bonded strip of two or more dissimilar metals—clad metals)
5.  New alloys (high-strength and corrosion-resistant modified copper)
6.  Roll-Bond, Poro-Bond (a clad product using aluminum in panel form instead of in coils)
7.  Fabricated products (stamped and drawn parts made from brass, aluminum, stainless steel or low-carbon steel)

In marketing these products the organization structure in Exhibit 3 was used.

The salesmen operated out of 15 major cities that were centers of the copper-alloy using industries. Each product-group sales manager headed a group of technical service men, market development engineers, customer service men, and correspondents. His job included coordinating and directing all marketing activities for his products, which were sold through the general salesmen reporting to the Director of Field Sales. The product-group sales manager was also responsible for pricing, scheduling, order handling, market development, and the provision of technical service.

To clad a metal is to cover it with another metal by bonding. The process is essentially the application of pressure by rolling. While the

**EXHIBIT 3.    Marketing Department (Brass Division)**

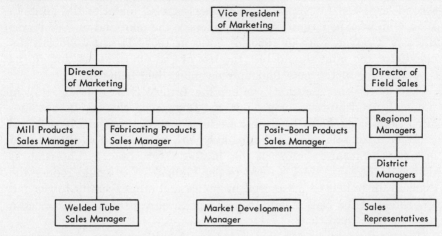

process itself may be simple, a high degree of technology is involved in its application.

The name, Posit-Bond, is a registered trademark of the Olin Mathieson Company and it refers to clad metals in strip form. It is composed of two or more wrought metals metallurgically bonded without the use of a bonding agent. This process results in a composite metal that will not peel and that has other desirable properties. It is available in strips, tubes, and plates.

The process of cladding metals is an old one. But before the time of this case it was used mainly in the jewelry industry where gold was cladded to a baser metal to conserve the supply of the more precious metal and in the thermostatic bimetal industry which cladded two metals with different expansion reactions to heat. For a number of years the laboratory of the Brass Division had been working on the development of processes for metalurgically cladding dissimilar metals so as to develop composites suitable for a wider range of industrial uses. No startling discoveries had resulted, although the researchers learned a lot about cladding.

For several years the Brass Division had been supplying the United States mint with cupro-nickel for the coinage of nickels, and bronze for pennies. Through this connection the Marketing Vice President in 1965 learned that the mint intended to coin dimes and quarters composed of a copper base clad on both sides with an alloy of 75 percent copper and 25 percent nickel. This composite would retain the silvery appearance the public demanded in dimes and quarters, would satisfy vending machine requirements, and would cause no drain on the silver supply.

The research laboratory of the Division went into high gear on the project and within a few weeks developed a sample composite that met the requirements of the mint. The resulting contract made Olin the second largest of four approved suppliers of clad metal to the mint. In 1966, Olin was the largest of two suppliers to the mint and in 1967 it was the sole supplier. Late in 1966, or early in 1967, Treasury officials decided that the mint should buy the use of the Olin process and do its own cladding at the new Philadelphia mint, then being built.

This raised the question whether the Brass Division should stay in the clad metal business or get out of it, scrapping thereby its accumulated experience, know-how, and productive capacity. The Division had contracts to supply ammunition makers with bronze-clad steel for bullet jackets. The future volume of this business was about as uncertain as that with the mint, since an end to the Vietnam War would reduce the demand for bullets to those used by police and other security forces and sportsmen. If the clad metal business was to be worthwhile, it needed a broader base than that.

Division executives felt that there was a tendency among design engineers to be more "materials conscious" and to demand more specialized properties in metal materials, as their designs became increasingly sophisticated in the attempt to achieve more miniaturization and greater reliability. During recent years more metal composites seemed to have been designed than ever before. These materials were "application engineered," in the sense that each was designed for a specific application and use.

When two metals are properly bonded, they behave as one metal under stress and cannot be separated by pulling the components. The whole composite strip will break first. This cohesiveness of the composite offers certain advantages. For example, a metal that resists corrosion may be clad to the surface of a lower-cost corrosive metal to make a cheaper corrosion-resistant material; or a corrosive-resistant metal may be bonded to the outside of a current-carrying material to get a long-lasting, current-carrying composite. Two metals that respond differently to heat and cold can be bonded to get a composite useful for control purposes. Division executives felt that there was increasing need in industry for materials of such versatility. Most of them would have to be "tailored" to fit the specific use.

When the Treasury announced its decision to clad its own materials for quarters and dimes after 1969, the executives of the Brass Division took steps to explore the possible commercial market for clad metals. A task force was organized with a membership of market research, market development, research and development, cost analysis, and manufacturing personnel to study the matter. This group was to seek answers to the following questions:

1. Is there a large volume commercial market?
2. If so, what equipment and facilities would we need to cultivate this market?

3. If so, does the potential revenue constitute a satisfactory return on investment?
4. Can Olin get a satisfactory share of the business?
5. If the answers to the preceding questions are encouraging, how should Olin organize to develop the market?
   a.  Establish a clad metal division?
   b.  Have the clad metal business handled by either the Brass Division or the Aluminum Division and, if so, by which one?

The task force made a careful study of the potential volume of clad metals in each of the primary metals markets. It also estimated Olin's share of each market and probable prices. From these data and production cost estimates a picture of the possible clad metal business was developed, showing equipment requirements, manufacturing processes, and anticipated return on investment.

The net of the report was that the long-run prospects were good. There were a number of large-volume potential markets for clad metals that, if properly developed, would earn Olin a good return on investment. Since most of these markets were in copper-base alloy products, the task force recommended that responsibility for the business be assigned to the Brass Division. Also, the Brass Division had more experience and know-how in metals-bonding than the Aluminum Division did.

But the short-run prospects were not so promising. The task force found little existing demand for clad metal products. An expensive and time-consuming exploration of the various markets was needed to develop "tailor-made" materials to suit the various use requirements in each market. The task force report gave no satisfactory estimates of the timing and quantity of the development of demand and of equipment and facilities needed to satisfy it.

The Brass Division established a Posit-Bond Marketing Department with two primary missions. Its first goal was to develop a firm forecast of demand based on achievable penetration of potential clad-metal markets to guide the procurement of facilities. The second goal was to exploit these markets. Since the achievement of the first of these goals required the development of close working contacts with firms in each market, the accomplishment of the first mission could be carried out through the conduct of the first stages of the second. The organization of the new department is shown in Exhibit 4.

Customer service included pricing, scheduling, order handling, policies and procedures. The technical service manager was to direct and coordinate all market development and technical service work. Selling was to be done through the regular Brass Division sales force.

The field salesman and the market development engineer operate as a team in doing market development work. The salesman, knowing his customers, chooses the firms most likely to have possible uses for clad metals and tries to set up with each of them a joint meeting of himself

**EXHIBIT 4.   Posit-Bond products marketing**

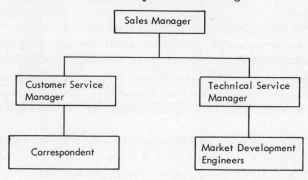

and the Olin development engineer with the purchasing officer and design engineer of the prospective customer. In such a face-to-face encounter the development engineer and the design engineer can often work out specific applications that would be missed without the interflow of knowledge and interests that results from personal contact.

Of course the discussion of specifics usually follows a presentation by the development engineer of a description of the possible role of clad materials in making product improvements and reducing costs. The goal of the contact is to get the customer's agreement to try out clad metal in a specific process in his plant. When this happens, the following procedure is set in motion:

1.   Product specifications are sent to the Olin plant where the feasibility of making the composite is determined.
2.   If the product can be made, a process for doing so is developed.
3.   The costs of the product are determined.
4.   A sample of the product is made and sent to the customer for evaluation. There is no charge for the sample.

The salesman or the development engineer follows up with an attempt to get a report from the customer as to how well the materials performed in the application. The intent is to get the customer involved in the project and to develop a quick flow of information about the usefulness of the clad materials. The salesman can probably supply the names of other customers likely to require similar applications.

In getting the customer involved Olin runs the risk that he will also learn about any problems the Brass Division runs into in developing a material for the application. Also, at the initial contact the customer can be given little assurance that a composite can be developed to suit his purpose or as to the cost of it if it can be developed.

The procedure is not always as simple as it sounds. Clad metal is almost always two or more stages away from the end product and sometimes its use requires significant changes in the design or specifications of the end product. For example, a customer may make radiator tanks to be included in the cooling system of an automobile or a truck. Or he may make wire terminals sold to an electrical systems manufacturer or maker of subassemblies to be included in machines or appliances. If the use of the clad metal requires a change in the design of the cooling system or the subassembly, the procedure can become quite complicated and frustrating, because design engineers tend to be very cautious about making changes in an assembly that is working satisfactorily. Since several designers usually work on any one design, many contacts must be made and a number of persons must be convinced before the project can proceed. The salesman and the development engineer must make these contacts and develop relations of confidence and cooperation. This usually takes a long time and a lot of work.

## COMPETITION

Most of the numerous firms capable of cladding metals specialize in precious metals for the jewelry industry and neglect industrial applications. Only one of the few interested in the industrial market is large enough and has enough technical know-how to offer serious competition to Olin. This company has been active in the business for two years. The Olin sales-engineer teams have become aware of its activity in the field.

They have found its efforts both a help and a hindrance. In many parts of the market it has established an awareness of and a knowledge of clad metals that would not otherwise have existed. Some design engineers are thus more receptive to their use than they would otherwise have been. On the other hand, this company has expanded its sales force very rapidly and many of its salesmen do not know as much about cladding processing techniques and applications as they should. In some cases the Olin representatives find that they must resell design engineers who have been oversold and disappointed by results or who have been unsold by aggressive and ill-informed tactics.

Mr. Towey is impressed by the difficulties to be met in developing the market for clad metals and with the length of time over which Olin will probably have to pour cash into development without adequate return. On the other hand, he is attracted by the market that seems to be there if it can be developed.

# OWENS-CORNING
# FIBERGLAS CORPORATION (A)

The executives of the Supply and Contracting Division of the Owens-Corning Fiberglas Company were considering a proposal of the Ace Fiberglas Products Company that the Division take over the job of marketing Ace's fiberglas concrete dome business in 11 western states. The considerations that apparently moved the Ace Company to make this proposal were about as follows:

*a.* The dome part of the business required facilities and skilled service quite different from those needed for the rest of the Company's business.

*b.* The Ace Company did not have the needed facilities and skilled personnel. In most parts of the country the potential volume of the dome business was enough to justify the Company in providing the facilities and personnel. This was not true of the 11 states in question.

*c.* The Supply and Contracting Division of Owens-Corning had in the area facilities that could readily be used and personnel whose existing technical background could readily be augmented to provide the services required. The Division has 24 branch units, either in the 11 states involved or situated so that they can serve customers in those states.

A concrete forming dome is a form used in building construction. These forms are needed to support the concrete ceilings in the various stories of multiple-story buildings during the hardening process. These forms are put in place before the concrete is poured and are allowed to remain supporting the ceiling until the material sets and cures, after which they are removed, and can be used again. These forms had traditionally been made of steel. The Ace Company made them of plastic reinforced by fiberglas. The plastic forms have a number of advantages which we will discuss later. (See Exhibits 1 and 2.)

## OWENS-CORNING FIBERGLAS COMPANY

The Owens-Corning Fiberglas Company was started in 1935 as a joint venture of the Owens-Illinois Glass Company and the Corning Glass Company to exploit the market potential of glass fiber developed

**EXHIBIT 1.**  Fiberglas concrete forming domes "on location"

by their laboratories. In spite of the heavy competition of such long-established basic materials industries as steel, ceramics, aluminum, wood, and natural and synthetic fibers, its growth has been very rapid. Sales volume grew from about $4,000,000 during its first full year to about $374,000,000 in 1966. Although other companies, such as Johns-Manville and Pittsburg Plate Glass have moved into the business, Owens-Corning still retains about 70 percent of the volume. Operating statistics of the Company are shown in Exhibits 3 and 4. Much of this growth has

EXHIBIT 2.  Waffle-type ceiling patterns

probably been due to a very active and effective research program and to a highly flexible and hard-hitting marketing performance.

The organization structure of the corporation at the time of this case is shown in chart form in Exhibits 5, 6, and 7. An examination of Exhibit 6 suggests that the marketing organization is set up on the basis of customer or user groups rather than products. Each of these customer divisions is a semiautonomous unit whose head makes his own decisions, subject to central company policy. As a result, the company makes use of a variety of marketing channels, each suited to the job of reaching a specific customer or user group market.

The general policy of the Company has been to avoid going into the manufacture of end products but to try to link up with or even develop competent fabricators to whom it can sell fiber glass and with whom it can share its technical know-how in making and marketing end products from it. It is also Company policy to sell to the industrial and commercial construction industry through local independent distributors and/or contractor customers wherever they are available. Where such outlets are not available the Company establishes branch units to handle the business.

The operation of these branch units constitutes a function of the Supply and Contracting Division. As a result of the fact that this Division is a sort of fill-in or troubleshooting unit, its method of operation is very flexible. When conditions are right the Division markets through distributors or contractors; under other conditions it may sell direct to users and itself act as a contractor. Its general objective is to expand the use of fiber glass by any legitimate means. In carrying out this objective, the Division may buy products or materials from the Company or an outside supplier and resell them. It operates on a nationwide basis through 58 branch locations, most of which include facilities and personnel for warehousing, selling, and servicing the items handled. These facilities include warehouse space, trucks, scaffolding, and other construction contracting equipment. The branch staff includes engineers, experienced contract estimators, field superintendents who manage jobs in the field, and qualified carpenters and asbestos workers who apply insulating materials.

On a resale basis the Division handled a full range of insulating and acoustical products. Through its construction contracting section the Division was equipped to handle acoustical ceilings, plumbing insulation, heating and air-conditioning insulation, cold-storage insulation, and marine insulation. Its customers were all in the industrial, commercial, and residential sectors of the construction business and included distributors, owners, architects, general contractors, and subcontractors.

Several Company policies have a bearing on the operations of the Supply and Contracting Division. They were summarized as follows:

1. Volume use of Fiberglas. The S and C Division will aggressively assist in the volume utilization of Fiberglas materials, including products manufactured by customers of the Company.

2. Profit. The Division and each of its units must earn a profit return on capital employed that is better than that of competitive firms in the geographic area.

3. Capital expenditures. Any proposal for capital expenditures to be made for the Division must compete with all other new venture proposals from any other part of the Company.

**EXHIBIT 3**

OWENS-CORNING FIBERGLAS CORPORATION AND
CONSOLIDATED SUBSIDIARIES
Consolidated Balance Sheet
December 31, 1966 and 1965

|  | *1966* | *1965* |
|---|---|---|
| ASSETS | | |
| *Current Assets* | | |
| Cash............................................. | $ 13,406,431 | $ 13,510,304 |
| Time deposits....................................... | — | 10,100,000 |
| U.S. Government and other securities, at cost (approximates market)............................. | — | 5,435,351 |
| Receivables, less allowance (1966—$1,750,000, 1965—$1,500,000) for collection losses................ | 54,588,908 | 51,542,594 |
| Inventories, at lower of cost (first-in, first-out basis) or market— | | |
| Finished products.:................................ | 29,112,713 | 24,168,760 |
| Materials and supplies............................. | 8,429,441 | 7,257,223 |
| Costs on contracts in progress, less billings (1966—$8,180,649, 1965—$8,662,171)................ | 314,259 | (671,191) |
| Total Current Assets.:.......................... | $105,851,752 | $111,343,041 |
| *Other Assets* | | |
| Investments in and advances to foreign companies, at cost (Note 2)........................................... | $ 8,069,561 | $ 5,949,237 |
| Prepaid expenses, other investments, etc................. | 3,630,093 | 4,780,775 |
| Patents, at cost less amortization..................... | 720,378 | 958,126 |
|  | $ 12,420,032 | $ 11,688,138 |
| *Plant and Equipment, at cost* | | |
| Land and buildings................................. | $ 63,258,021 | $ 59,716,678 |
| Machinery and equipment............................ | 196,986,054 | 163,834,493 |
| Precious metals.................................... | 28,017,681 | 21,268,508 |
| Construction in progress............................ | 27,967,441 | 18,191,775 |
|  | $316,229,197 | $263,011,454 |
| Less—Reserves for depreciation and deferred investment credit (1966—$5,407,674, 1965—$3,431, 861)............ | 132,810,537 | 119,515,320 |
|  | $183,418,660 | $143,496,134 |
|  | $301,690,444 | $266,527,313 |

**EXHIBIT 3** (*Continued*)

|  | 1966 | 1965 |
|---|---|---|
| **LIABILITIES AND STOCKHOLDERS' EQUITY** | | |
| *Current Liabilities* | | |
| Accounts payable and accrued liabilities.:............... | $ 23,939,366 | $ 23,110,669 |
| Accrued U.S. and foreign income taxes................. | 5,213,160 | 9,869,938 |
| Dividends payable.................................... | 2,365,196 | 2,353,051 |
| Total Current Liabilities....................... | $ 31,517,722 | $ 35,333,658 |

*Long-Term Notes Payable*

Domestic operations—

| | | |
|---|---|---|
| Due June 1, 1988, 4.2%, subject to annual prepayments of $4,150,000 commencing June 1, 1977.:............... | $ 50,000,000 | $ 50,000,000 |
| Due under Revolving Credit Agreement, 6%, convertible through April 1, 1969, to 5-year term loans at an interest rate ¼% above the prime rate then in effect.......... | 23,000,000 | — |

Foreign operations—

| | | |
|---|---|---|
| Due December 15, 1980, 5.75%, subject to annual prepayments of $715,000 commencing December 15, 1972.:.... | 6,500,000 | 6,500,000 |
| Due December 31, 1974, 7% (less 4% subsidy through 1970 granted by Belgian Government), subject to annual prepayments of $223,200 commencing December 31, 1969...................................... | 1,340,000 | — |
| Due June 30, 1973, 6.8% (less 3% subsidy through 1968 granted by Belgian Government), subject to prepayments of $750,000 on June 30, 1968, and $1,050,000 annually thereafter............................... | 6,000,000 | 6,000,000 |
| Due November 1, 1968 and 1969, 9%................ | 579,900 | — |
| | $ 87,419,900 | $ 62,500,000 |

| | | |
|---|---|---|
| *Reserve for Rebuilding Furnaces and Reconditioning Machines* | $  2,853,638 | $  3,273,694 |

*Stockholders' Equity*

| | | |
|---|---|---|
| Common stock, par value $1 per share; authorized 8,000,000 shares (Note 3), outstanding 1966—6,757,702 shares, 1965—6,723,004 shares............................. | $ 50,214,076 | $ 48,229,968 |
| Retained earnings.................................... | 129,685,108 | 117,189,993 |
| | $179,899,184 | $165,419,961 |
| | $301,690,444 | $266,527,313 |

**EXHIBIT 4**

OWENS-CORNING FIBERGLAS CORPORATION AND
CONSOLIDATED SUBSIDIARIES
Consolidated Statement of Income
For the Years Ended December 31, 1966 and 1965

|  | 1966 | 1965 |
|---|---|---|
| *Net Sales* | $373,673,079 | $335,337,976 |
| *Costs and Expenses* | | |
| Cost of sales | $276,389,515 | $250,483,653 |
| Marketing expenses | 28,709,840 | 25,378,405 |
| General and administrative expenses | 15,244,021 | 12,687,287 |
| Research and development expenses | 7,773,368 | 7,632,605 |
| Total costs and expenses (including depreciation of $15,106,564 in 1966 and $13,446,181 in 1965) | $328,116,744 | $296,181,950 |
| Income from operations | $ 45,556,335 | $ 39,156,026 |
| *Gross Revenue from Royalties* | 2,076,659 | 1,957,880 |
|  | $ 47,632,994 | $ 41,113,906 |
| *Other Charges* | | |
| Cost of borrowed funds | $  3,263,386 | $  2,102,832 |
| State income and franchise taxes | 1,777,645 | 1,335,317 |
| Other (net) | 816,987 | 554,902 |
|  | $  5,858,018 | $  3,993,051 |
| *Income Before Provision for Income Taxes* | $ 41,774,976 | $ 37,120,855 |
| Provision for U.S. and foreign income taxes | 19,844,000 | 17,606,000 |
| *Net Income* | $ 21,930,976 | $ 19,514,855 |
| Per share on common stock outstanding December 31 | $3.25 | $2.90 |

4. Prices. The prices of all contract work will be fixed by the manager of the Supply and Contracting Division Unit involved. Units vending resale items must price them within limits established to protect the Company's relations with customers or possible customers.

## THE ACE COMPANY

The Ace Fiberglas Products Company, which has approached the Supply and Contracting Division to take over the marketing of its fiber glass-reinforced-plastic concrete forming domes in the western territory, was started in 1946 to make and sell fiber glass reinforced plastic products. Currently it made and sold a wide variety of such products through eight product divisions:

1. Division A—Products for the transportation industry sold to automobile and truck manufacturers.
2. Fabricating Division—General fiber glass custom moldings sold to a wide variety of customers.

**EXHIBIT 5. General organization**

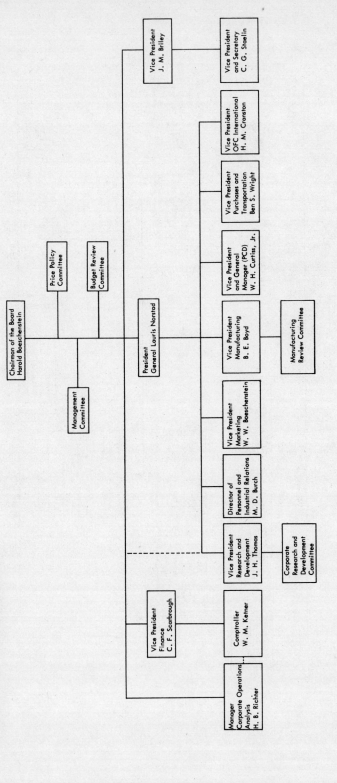

**EXHIBIT 6. Marketing organization** (*Toledo*)

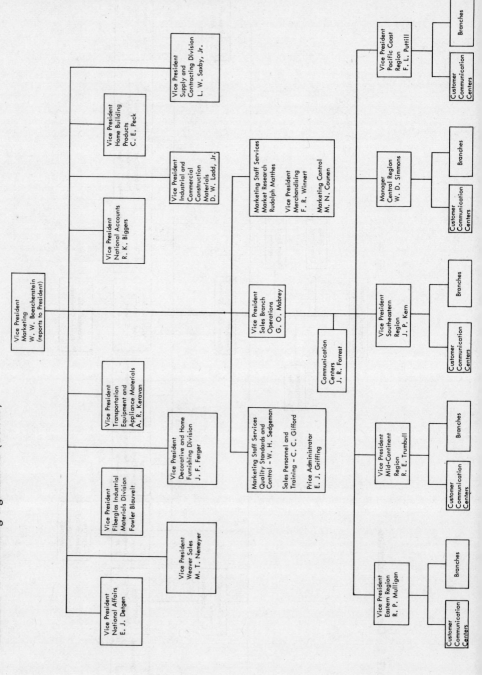

**EXHIBIT 7.  Supply & contracting division (*Toledo*)**

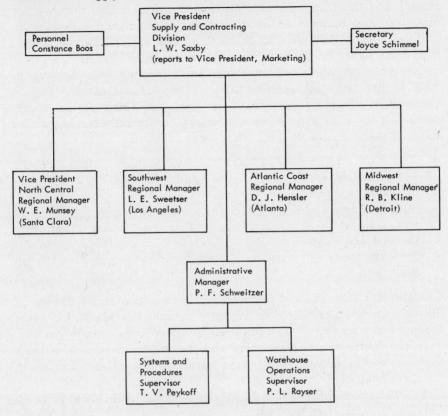

3. Resin Division—Polyester resin for captive use by the Ace Company.
4. Boat Division A—Fishing, outboard, outdrive, and sailboats sold through boat dealers.
5. Boat Division B— Fiber glass and aluminum boats also sold through boat dealers.
6. Ace Midwest Division—General fiber glass custom moldings sold to a variety of customers in the midwestern states.
7. Tray Division—Material-handling items, such as trays and tote boxes, sold through manufacturers' agents to materials-handling companies-users.
8. Dome Division—Concrete forming domes leased to building contractors.

Although the Ace Company sells all over the United States, its business is heavily concentrated in the midwestern states.

Each of the product divisions listed above is relatively autonomous, being headed by a vice President and General Manager and with its own manufacturing and marketing facilities and personnel. The Vice President of the Division makes his own decisions within the limits of objectives and budgets finally determined by Company management.

Total sales in 1966 were $23,937,000, an increase of about $3 million from 1965. Other financial statistics are shown in Exhibit 8.

The Ace Company went into the concrete forming dome business in 1962. It first made an experimental lot of domes and enlisted the co-operation of a building contractor to try them out. This experiment indicated that the fiber glass dome had several important advantages over the steel dome commonly used. They were as follows:

a. The labor cost of placing and stripping the form is less, since its lighter weight enables one man to handle it instead of the two required for the steel dome.
b. Since the forms will not bend (as steel does), they can be used more times at lower maintenance cost than steel, if they are properly handled and cleaned.
c. Since the forms will not rust, they can be stored outdoors on the job site.

Additional technical and semitechnical information about the use of fiber glass forms is presented in Exhibit 9, compiled by Mr. A. J. Forbes, the manufacturer's agent who has been handling Ace domes in Arizona.

In the course of this experiment and the market development work that followed it, the Ace management learned several other things about the dome business.

1. Satisfaction in the use of domes depended on their being properly installed, properly stripped after the concrete was set, and properly cleaned between uses.

2. Contractors preferred to obtain their dome forms on lease instead of by purchase. This cut down on their investment and avoided the need to carry expensive equipment that was used only during a relatively short part of the construction period.

3. The forms can be used about once per month. It takes about 30 days to place the forms, pour and cure the concrete, and strip the forms. In the West, this turn-around time is nearer 20 days. On jobs involving several uses of the forms it is wise to allow about 30 days additional on each job to provide for delays between uses.

4. A form is good for about 30 uses before it must be discarded.

With these facts in hand the Ace management decided to move into the dome business in a serious way. It set up a separate division to handle the business and began to manufacture a stock of domes for lease. The division manager decided to try to reach contractor-erectors through manufacturer's agents on a commission basis. By the end of 1966 the Company had $1,600,000 invested in a stock of dome forms, which generated a cash inflow of $1,300,000 annually from leases.

**EXHIBIT 8**

## ACE FIBERGLAS COMPANY
Balance Sheet
August 27, 1966, and August 28, 1965, and comparison

|  | August 27, 1966 | August 28, 1965 | Increase (Decrease) |
|---|---|---|---|
| **FINANCIAL POSITION** | | | |
| *Current Assets* | | | |
| Cash..................................... | $ 253,327 | $ 236,434 | $ 16,893 |
| Accounts receivable: | | | |
| Trade................................. | 1,615,453 | 1,704,173 | (88,720) |
| Floor-plan notes....................... | 272,476 | 393,721 | (121,245) |
| Allowance for doubtful accounts.......... | (27,000) | (62,000) | 35,000 |
| Other................................. | 228,449 | 127,813 | 100,636 |
| Customer dies-in-process.::.............. | 162,892 | 305,100 | (142,208) |
| Inventories: | | | |
| Raw materials and supplies.............. | 1,201,699 | 1,030,184 | 171,515 |
| Work-in-process and finished goods........ | 1,287,545 | 1,124,078 | 163,467 |
| Prepaid expenses......................... | 88,451 | 65,972 | 22,479 |
| Total Current Assets:................ | 5,083,292 | 4,925,475 | 157,817 |
| | | | |
| *Investment in Reco* | | | |
| Capital stock, at cost..................... | 1,500 | 1,500 | –0– |
| Note receivable.:......................... | 160,000 | –0– | 160,000 |
| Total.:.:......................... | 161,500 | 1,500 | 160,000 |
| | | | |
| *Property, Plant, and Equipment, at cost* | | | |
| Land and improvements................... | 114,959 | 101,151 | 13,808 |
| Buildings and improvements............... | 3,741,438 | 3,437,083 | 304,355 |
| Less: Accumulated depreciation.......... | 1,066,919 | 825,239 | 241,680 |
| Net................................... | 2,674,519 | 2,611,844 | 62,675 |
| Machinery, equipment, etc................. | 7,036,632 | 6,115,168 | 921,464 |
| Less: Accumulated depreciation.......... | 4,087,619 | 3,314,645 | 772,974 |
| Net................................... | 2,949,013 | 2,800,523 | 148,490 |
| Construction in Progress.::.............. | –0– | 50,460 | (50,460) |
| Property, plant, and equip.—Net.......... | 5,738,491 | 5,563,978 | 174,513 |
| | | | |
| *Other Assets* | | | |
| Insurance and rent deposits................ | 76,441 | 75,339 | 1,102 |
| Deferred development costs................. | 151,470 | 114,834 | 36,636 |
| Total Other Assets.:................. | 227,911 | 190,173 | 37,738 |
| Total Assets....................... | $11,211,194 | $10,681,126 | $ 530,068 |

**EXHIBIT 8** (*Continued*)

FINANCIAL POSITION (continued)

|  | August 27, 1966 | August 28, 1965 | Increase (Decrease) |
|---|---|---|---|
| *Current Liabilities* | | | |
| Notes payable to banks..................... | $ 1,075,000 | $ 1,503,907 | $(428,907) |
| Current portion of long-term debt | | | |
| Banks................................. | 700,000 | 344,200 | 355,800 |
| Equipment purchase obligation:........... | 115,478 | 58,816 | 56,662 |
| Other................................. | 12,816 | 16,188 | (3,372) |
| Accounts payable | | | |
| Trade................................. | 1,283,982 | 1,711,502 | (427,520) |
| Payroll deductions...................... | 53,013 | 74,310 | (21,297) |
| Other................................. | 45,286 | 92,472 | (47,186) |
| Accrued liabilities | | | |
| Federal income taxes.................... | 689,529 | 9,988 | 679,541 |
| Wages, salaries, commissions.............. | 341,840 | 260,566 | 81,274 |
| Pension contribution..................... | 120,474 | 129,737 | (9,263) |
| Payroll taxes............................ | 43,662 | 46,561 | (2,899) |
| Other taxes............................ | 59,123 | 64,394 | (5,271) |
| Interest................................ | 10,963 | 54,584 | (43,621) |
| Other................................. | 24,246 | 63,753 | (39,507) |
| Total Current Liabilities.::.............. | 4,575,412 | 4,430,978 | 144,434 |
| *Long-Term Debt* | | | |
| Mellon National Bank.::::................. | 50,000 | 717,200 | (667,200) |
| Security-Peoples Trust..................... | 100,000 | –0– | 100,000 |
| Equipment purchase obligation:............. | 913,705 | 811,183 | 102,522 |
| Other................................. | 4,291 | 12,929 | (8,638) |
| Total Long-Term Debt................ | 1,067,996 | 1,541,312 | (473,316) |
| *Stockholders Equity* | | | |
| Common stock, par value $3.00, Authorized—300,000 shares Outstanding—202,899 shares.............. | 608,697 | 608,697 | –0– |
| Additional paid-in capital.................. | 547,662 | 547,662 | –0– |
| Retained earnings........................ | 4,411,427 | 3,552,477 | 858,950 |
| Total Stockholder's Equity.::::.......... | 5,567,786 | 4,708,836 | 858,950 |
| Total Liabilities...................... | $11,211,194 | $10,681,126 | $ 530,069 |

**EXHIBIT 9.** Molded fiber glass forms for reinforced concrete construction with special application to Southwestern states (A. J. Forbes)

There is increasing interest in concrete structures among industrial, commercial, and institutional architects in the United States with the ever increasing potential of schools, warehouses, office buildings, etc. in Arizona.

The availability of concrete forming materials has a bright future. There are many types of concrete forms available on the market today. There is the flange type form in steel, long forms in steel and in wood, and single piece steel dome forms and plastic forms. The product outlined in this survey is the use of the single piece molded fiber glass form. The maximum reuse of any concrete form is basic to economy. The designer can achieve real economy for concrete joist construction by establishing joist depth and spacings which allows the maximum reuse of concrete forms for all floors including the roof. Depth and width of the joist must be set in accordance with the average load and span requirements. After the depth and spacing of forms have been established, they should be used in their relative position in the floors and also in the roof to obtain maximum economy. Experience has proved that changing the depth of concrete joist systems from floor to roof because of the usual difference in superimposed loads does not result in the savings anticipated.

The molded fiber glass dome form is a new developed form for forming two-way dome slab construction sometimes known as "Waffle-Type Construction." It is a one-piece form designed especially for exposed concrete joist ceilings. This type of form must be so set on centering so that it is removed by air pressure. Using this type of removal it eliminates prying and results in a smooth and undamaged concrete finish. High quality architectural concrete work is consistent because the molded fiber glass form remains uniform in shape throughout construction. The waffle-type construction is ever increasing because of the savings it offers in concrete construction.

Wide column spacing for open floor area is easily achieved because of the (1) basic economy of two-way construction and (2) the savings of dead load through the use of joist framing systems. Story heights are decreased by the elimination of beams which are required in one-way joist construction where wide column spacings are required. The two-way joist system also gives uniformity to ceiling height which simplifies the installation of pipes, air-conditioning, strip lighting, and other equipment that is usually installed against the ceiling. Also, aesthetically pleasing ceilings of exposed concrete are obtained by the use of dome forms.

The superiority of molded fiber glass forms over the steel forms which have been used in the industry for some time are as follows:

1. The low cost of tooling in molded fiber glass in relationship to the high cost of tooling for steel forms. Molded fiber glass is practically impervious to corrosion, while the steel forms require expensive cleaning before use. Rust stains the concrete, resulting in expensive concrete finishing, and oil is necessary to prevent rusting which, during a slow down in construction, allows dust to be picked up resulting in a rough dirt-stained concrete surface after the concrete is poured.

2. The molded fiber glass form does not require any oiling; however, occasional waxing gives an opportunity for longer use and easier removal of the form after the pouring of the concrete. Due to the perfection in the technique

**EXHIBIT 9** (*Continued*)

of dies, the molded fiber glass form is almost a perfect uniform surface over the entire surface area of the dome that is in contact with the concrete.

In steel forms, you find indentations which lead to imperfections in the concrete poured against it. Also, during the handling of dome forms, steel corners get bent which must be straightened out which sometimes lead to irregularities in the joints between the forms. Due to the uniformity of the dies, this is eliminated in the use of molded fiber glass forms. In the area of high cost labor, the molded fiber glass form offers great savings in handling. A molded fiber glass form weighs approximately 40 percent less than a steel form of a similar size. Also, in the area of labor there is a safety factor in the use of molded fiber glass domes. Not only its light weight, but the elimination of sharp corners in fiber glass results in the lower opportunity of man injuries on any job. A steel dome dropped can gash a foot due to its weight and sharp corners. Also during the time the domes are being removed for reuse, occasionally it can fall free during the stripping of the scaffolding and can seriously injure a man on the head or shoulders if the form is metal. However, due to the lightness of weight, this hazard is reduced, so the overall advantages of molded fiber glass has shown ever increasing use in concrete forming.

The normal method used in concrete forming of this type is that they are handled by a qualified specialist in the area of setting and removal of this form. The reason for this is as follows:

> Usually, due to long experience, the men for a forming contractor's crew can save time in the removal and placing of concrete forms. Also, due to required maintenance on steel forms for long use and quality forming, the forms must be maintained in perfect condition. Leasing the forms to a general contractor leads to abuse which requires costly maintenance and shortens the life of the equipment. Our proposal would be to lease the forms, including labor, to the general contractor. This is a normal industry practice throughout concrete forming equipment.

In order to project the use of this form, we need to look at what has transpired in the last three (3) years. Three years ago, the dome had its introduction to the Arizona market in the Mountain States Telephone and Telegraph Building at McDowell Rd. and Central Ave. The area utilizing the domes comprised approximately 60,000 square feet. The next year, the interest in this building was expressed by additional structures being designed on a system using this type of form, bringing the use to approximately 150,000 square feet. Last year with the high school in Scottsdale, two buildings at Arizona State University, and other smaller jobs, the use exceeded 350,000 square feet. Since January 1, 1962, additional work has been done that exceeded 200,000 square feet for the first six months of this year. In the next six months, an additional 300,000 square feet went out for bids, bringing the total use for 1962 and early 1963 to over 500,000 square feet. At the present time, competitive situation is very good. The availability of equipment is from approximately three sources throughout the United States and with the ever-growing popularity, due to the low cost of this type of structural system, the equipment is in constant demand, not only in our area, but in others, which leads to a healthy economic picture for the next three to five years at least.

**EXHIBIT 9** (*Concluded*)

Due to the potential profit opportunity and the conservative estimate used in this life of the equipment, we feel that it is almost imperative that the opportunity to enter the market be taken now.

The basic problem in handling this equipment is cash flow. The average use of the equipment based on the initial inventory would be approximately between eight and ten times per year requiring three years for depreciating the equipment. However, due to its nature, you would be utilizing the equipment very heavily for short periods of time and then have it back in inventory not working for other periods of time which makes a projection on an ordinary pay-out basis difficult. It might be possible to utilize financing on a job basis in order to achieve a cash flow that would not jeopardize ordinary business operation. As an adjunct to the leasing or rental of this type of equipment to the general contractor, is the framing or understructure which is utilized in this type of construction. This is a service that can be performed by sub-contractor or by the general contractor himself. Due to the amount of equipment it takes in this field, many of the general contractors have started the use of a specialty service so that their capitalization is not as heavy. At the present time, we have available approximately 40,000 square feet of this type of equipment which would give us a very competitive edge in bidding this service to the general contractor. The entire program has good growth opportunity at a very exceptional margin to the ever increasing labor costs. This looks to be a very bright spot in the construction industry.

The needs for additional equipment to service the industry will have some immediate cash flow since no additional forms will be purchased until there is a contract that has an immediate use.


On the whole the dome business proved satisfactorily profitable except in 11 western states. While the Ace Company operated throughout the country, its business was heavily concentrated in the Midwest area, and its volume in the Far Western states did not justify the maintenance of the facilities needed to serve forming-dome customers adequately. Management was loath to forgo the business in this area entirely and hit upon the idea of offering Owens-Corning—which covers the area adequately with branch facilities—a deal whereby its Supply and Contracting Division would buy domes made by Ace and lease and service them in the area. In this way Ace would enjoy a manufacturing profit and the Supply and Contracting Division would reap a marketing profit. This was the proposal which the Division executives were considering early in 1967.


## THE DEAL

Management felt that if the Division accepted the deal, it would be necessary to obtain the services of someone who knew something about the dome business and who was familiar with the concrete construction industry in the western area to operate the business there. The agent who had been handling the dome business for the Ace Company there seemed to be a likely candidate, so he was interviewed for the ostensible purpose of obtaining information.

He estimated that the total dome business of all kinds in the 11 states amounted to between $15,000,000 and $16,000,000 a year with an ultimate potential much higher. Practically all of this was in the hands of firms handling steel forms. Three of these operated over the entire area:

1. Ceco Steel Company, with about $8,000,000 invested in steel dome forms.
2. Steel Form Contracting Company, whose investment was unknown.
3. Soule Steel Company, with an inventory of between 7,000 and 8,000 steel forms.

In addition there were four significant steel dome firms that operated on a local basis:

1. Mercer Steel in Seattle
2. The Hiller Company in Los Angeles
3. Pattock-Hiller in San Francisco
4. J and B Products in San Francisco

Ace's western agent had on consignment in his headquarters city, Phoenix, Arizona, about 10,000 fiber glass forms. Another 8,000 domes were in use on current jobs. The agent felt that about 17,000 additional forms would be needed to service the area properly. Ace proposed that the Supply and Contracting Division buy the 18,000 forms in stock and in use for about $250,000. The 17,000 new forms would cost about $450,000. The Division would thus have a total investment in forms of about $700,000.

The agent further reported that the average construction job required about 1,500 forms on a three-use basis. The leased billing on such a job would be about $8,100. He also stated that Ace was currently securing about 25 percent of the jobs on which he bid. Transportation was a primary element of cost. The forms were generally delivered to the job site by truck, about 500 to 600 per vehicle. They could be shipped to some jobs by rail, about 975 per boxcar at a somewhat lower rate. Ace had been spending on transportation about 20 percent of total rental billings. By carrying stocks at strategic branch locations, the Supply and Contracting Division could probably reduce this somewhat.

Facilities had to be provided to clean and repair the forms from time to time. This might be done either in the field or at service centers. Ace had been shipping many forms back to the factory for this purpose. The S and C Division could probably do the work in its branch facilities, although considerable savings were possible from performing certain operations, such as repainting, on a quantity basis.

In the preliminary negotiations, the Ace management gave the Vice

President of the S and C Division a price list at which Ace proposed to sell new domes of different sizes to the Division. When Mr. Saxby, the Vice President, expressed some reservations about the validity of these prices, the Ace managers submitted a justification for them in the form of a breakdown of cost and other elements that made up each price. This is presented in Exhibit 10. Mr. Saxby felt that since Ace would sell large quantities of forms to the Division in one contract, the marketing cost should be eliminated or materially reduced. There was also some question as to whether painting would really be needed.

**EXHIBIT 10.  Ace Company price list (setting up and operating Dome Division)**

| Dome size | Cost | Paint cost | Total mfg'd. cost | G A&S* cost 40% | Die amort. | Total cost | Profit 11.1% | Total price net |
|---|---|---|---|---|---|---|---|---|
| 19x19x6 | $ 5.11 | $ .63 | $ 5.74 | $ 2.30 | $ .50 | $ 8.54 | $ .95 | $ 9.49 |
| 19x19x8 | 5.46 | .70 | 6.16 | 2.46 | .50 | 9.12 | 1.01 | 10.13 |
| 19x19x10 | 5.77 | .80 | 6.57 | 2.63 | .75 | 9.95 | 1.10 | 11.05 |
| 19x19x12 | 6.21 | .90 | 7.11 | 2.84 | .75 | 10.70 | 1.19 | 11.89 |
| 19x19x14 | 6.77 | .93 | 7.70 | 3.08 | .75 | 11.53 | 1.28 | 12.81 |
| 19x19x16 | 7.20 | 1.01 | 8.21 | 3.28 | .75 | 12.24 | 1.36 | 13.60 |
| | | | | | | | | |
| 24x24x8 | 8.03 | .94 | 8.97 | 3.59 | 1.00 | 13.56 | 1.51 | 15.07 |
| 24x24x10 | 8.60 | 1.07 | 9.67 | 3.87 | 1.00 | 14.54 | 1.61 | 16.15 |
| 24x24x12 | 9.13 | 1.12 | 10.25 | 4.10 | 1.00 | 15.35 | 1.70 | 17.05 |
| 24x24x14 | 9.81 | 1.23 | 11.04 | 4.42 | 1.00 | 16.46 | 1.83 | 18.29 |
| 24x24x16 | 10.40 | 1.35 | 11.75 | 4.70 | 1.25 | 17.70 | 1.96 | 19.66 |
| | | | | | | | | |
| 30x30x8 | 11.07 | 1.31 | 12.38 | 4.95 | 1.25 | 18.58 | 2.06 | 20.64 |
| 30x30x10 | 11.72 | 1.42 | 13.14 | 5.26 | 1.25 | 19.65 | 2.18 | 21.83 |
| 30x30x12 | 12.32 | 1.55 | 13.87 | 5.55 | 1.25 | 20.67 | 2.29 | 22.96 |
| 30x30x14 | 12.97 | 1.70 | 14.67 | 5.87 | 1.25 | 21.79 | 2.42 | 24.21 |
| 30x30x16 | 13.92 | 1.79 | 15.71 | 6.28 | 1.50 | 23.49 | 2.61 | 26.10 |
| 30x30x18 | 14.44 | 1.90 | 16.34 | 6.54 | 1.50 | 24.38 | 2.71 | 27.09 |
| 30x30x20 | 15.16 | 2.00 | 17.16 | 6.86 | 1.50 | 25.52 | 2.83 | 28.35 |
| | | | | | | | | |
| 30x20x8 | 8.49 | 1.11 | 9.60 | 3.84 | 3.00 | 16.44 | 1.82 | 18.26 |
| 30x20x10 | 9.09 | 1.23 | 10.32 | 4.13 | 3.00 | 17.45 | 1.94 | 19.39 |
| 30x20x12 | 9.62 | 1.34 | 10.96 | 4.38 | 3.00 | 18.34 | 2.04 | 20.38 |
| 30x20x14 | 10.42 | 1.44 | 11.86 | 4.74 | 3.00 | 19.60 | 2.18 | 21.78 |
| 30x20x16 | 11.22 | 1.53 | 12.75 | 5.10 | 3.00 | 20.85 | 2.31 | 23.16 |
| | | | | | | | | |
| 41x41x12 | 19.60 | 1.72 | 21.32 | 8.53 | 3.00 | 32.85 | 3.65 | 36.50 |
| 41x41x14 | 20.34 | 1.84 | 22.18 | 8.87 | 3.00 | 34.05 | 3.78 | 37.82 |
| 41x41x16 | 21.38 | 2.02 | 23.40 | 9.36 | 3.00 | 35.76 | 3.97 | 39.73 |
| 41x41x18 | 22.44 | 2.20 | 24.64 | 9.86 | 3.00 | 37.50 | 4.16 | 41.66 |
| 41x41x20 | 23.82 | 2.40 | 26.22 | 10.49 | 3.00 | 39.71 | 4.41 | 44.12 |
| 41x41x22 | 24.93 | 2.65 | 27.58 | 11.03 | 3.00 | 41.61 | 4.62 | 46.23 |
| 41x41x24 | 26.69 | 2.90 | 29.59 | 11.84 | 3.00 | 44.43 | 4.93 | 49.36 |

The above prices do not include any commission for an agent nor any allowance for reconditioning the domes after use in the field. The above prices are what the Dome Division should get if it sold domes outright, and what Ace should realize on each dome net to DD after all other expenses.

* General, administrative, and marketing costs.

Several officials of the S and C Division felt that the deal as proposed by Ace was one-sided in that the Division was allocated only a group of "cat and dog" customers in a particular area that Ace could not service profitably. They argued that if the Division took over the dome business in the western states, the agreement should provide that at some future time the Division could at its option take over and handle the business on a nationwide basis.

From fragments of information gathered from the Ace executives, Ace's manufacturer's agent in the Western territory, and some field investigations by the Division's salesmen, Mr. Saxby's assistant was able to piece together the following estimates of cost and other factors that would have to go into the leasing rental for each use of a dome. For purposes of illustration he based his calculations on a dome which the Division bought from Ace at a price of $20.00.

| | | |
|---|---|---|
| Price from Ace............................................. | $20.00 | |
| Depreciation (on basis of 30 uses)............................ | .67 | per use |
| Maintenance and repair.:..................................., | .21 | per use |
| Basic Cost of Dome......................................... | .88 " " | |
| Overhead cost on dome (15% of basic cost):::................... | .13 " " | |
| Profit on dome (25% of all previous costs)..................... | .25 " " | |
|    Total Dome Costs.::....................................... | 1.26 " " | |
| Layout and setting......................................... | .36 " " | |
| Overhead (15% of layout and setting)......................... | .05 " " | |
| Profit (25% of layout and setting plus overhead).:............... | .10 " " | |
|    Total Labor and Handling................................ | .51 " " | |
|    Total Costs.::........................................... | 1.77 " " | |
| Estimated transportation (20% of above)...................... | .35 " " | |
|    Bid Rental Per Dome.:::................................... | 2.12 " " | |

Perhaps it would be better to bid $1.77 per use per dome plus actual transportation from and to nearest S and C Division branch or from point of preceding use, whichever was the lower. This would put the Division in a favorable competitive position in relation to steel domes.

# OWENS-CORNING
# FIBERGLAS CORPORATION (B)

In an effort to find new uses for fibrous glass following World War II, the Owens-Corning Fiberglas Corporation gave increased attention to developing applications for the material in consumer products. By the end of 1960 a considerable amount of development work had gone into fiberglass furniture, draperies, luggage, fishing rods, gun stocks, trays, boats, car bodies, construction, and archery equipment.

In its search for new opportunities, management was guided by a long-standing basic policy expressed as follows:

> Either our materials must do a job that no other materials can do effectively
>
> Or for the same price they must perform better than competitive materials
>
> Or at a lower price they must do as good a job as alternative materials
>
> Or their unique characteristics must enable the manufacturer using Fiberglas to make corollary savings not possible with other materials.

An application in which the high-strength, lightweight characteristics of fiberglass gave it a significant advantage over other materials was luggage. The net value of shipments by manufacturers of leather luggage alone amounted to more than $200,000,000 in 1960. At an average price of $50 per unit, this represented an annual production of 4 million units. It was estimated that, on the average, as much as 3½ pounds of fiberglass would be required for each piece of luggage. This volume represented an attractive marketing opportunity. Despite efforts to convince luggage manufacturers of the advantages of fibrous glass as early as 1953, sales of the material for this purpose never exceeded 500,000 pounds annually.

## The Company

Owens-Corning Fiberglas Corporation was organized in 1935 as a joint venture of the Owens-Illinois Glass Company and the Corning Glass Company to expand the market potential of glass fiber developed by their laboratories. In spite of the heavy competition of such long-established materials as steel, ceramics, aluminum, wood, and natural, as well as synthetic, fibers, the use of fibrous glass has grown very rapidly. The company's sales volume rose from about $4,000,000 during its first full year of operation to about $374,000,000 in 1966. Sales reached $500,000,000 in 1971 and $615,000,000 in 1972. Although other companies, such as Johns-Manville and Pittsburgh Plate Glass have moved into the business, Owens-Corning still retains about 70 percent of the total market.

The organizational structure of the company is set up on the basis of customer or user markets rather than products. Included in this structure are divisions for national accounts, industrial materials, transportation equipment and appliances, home furnishings, home building products, industrial and commercial construction materials, and weavers. Each of these divisions is a semiautonomous unit, whose head makes his own decisions, subject to general company policy. As a result, the company makes use of a variety of marketing channels, each suited to the job of reaching a specific customer or user-group market.

The general policy of the Company has been to avoid going into the manufacture of end products but to try to link up with, or even develop, competent fabricators to whom it can sell fiberglass and with whom it can share its technical know-how in making and marketing end products from it. It is also company policy to sell to the industrial and commercial construction industry through local independent distributors and/or contractor customers wherever they are available. Where such outlets are not available, the Company establishes branch units to handle the business.

### Early attempts at market development for luggage

The Company's first development work in the luggage market was done in cooperation with a firm that had manufactured leather luggage for many years. The high price of leather, its susceptibility to damage, and the restrictions on weight imposed by increased air travel had prompted this company to experiment with other materials for its product. By 1953 the company's design department, working in cooperation with personnel at the Owens-Corning Technical Center at Newark, Ohio, had developed a new line of luggage with outside shells made of fiberglass reinforced plastic (FRP). Edging and hinges were made of extruded aluminum and the inside of the case was lined with vinyl plastic. The new line included five sizes and was offered in seven different colors. While market acceptance was encouraging, some frustrating problems were encountered.

In designing a case that would have exceptionally high impact strength, engineers failed to take full advantage of the strength/weight ratio of fiberglass. As a result the new line of luggage weighed slightly more than leather luggage of comparable capacity. Due to a miscalculation concerning manufacturing cost, it had to be sold at prices nearly as high. Management's intention of penetrating the volume luggage market with a superior product achieved no significant measure of success. Nevertheless, the company did succeed in selling its limited production of the new line at a satisfactory profit.

Impressed by the extent of consumer response to FRP luggage, even at premium prices, a number of smaller luggage makers contracted with plastic molders to make luggage shells of this material. By 1960 there were a number of custom molders actively seeking this type of business. Unfortunately, they represented widely varying degrees of experience with FRP, and many encountered serious problems. The most common of these were keeping the color shade constant in each shell and controlling the quality of the surface finish. Due to the high rate of rejections by luggage firms with whom they had contracts, a number of molders suffered such heavy financial losses that they abandoned all work with FRP material.

Inexperience with FRP on the part of luggage manufacturers themselves produced some blunders in styling, which gave FRP luggage a bad image in some markets. For example, one large department-store chain that was considering the purchase of FRP luggage marketed by a well-known maker discovered serious flaws in several of the company's models. Store buyers discovered that neither the suitcases nor the attaché cases could pass minimum impact-strength tests established by the U.S. Bureau of Standards. In one of these tests a piece of luggage is dropped on each of its four corners and its handle from a specified height. A dent, crack, or break on any part of the luggage tested disqualified the product.

There were also other problems. The leading manufacturer of low-priced luggage refused to consider FRP for its products, because the firm's production manager considered present techniques of forming FRP luggage shells to be too slow. He argued that the company's plant was not only geared to higher-volume production than would be possible with FRP, but new equipment would also be needed to process it. Moreover, the firm's design engineer did not believe that FRP luggage shells offered enough of an advantage over their present vinyl-covered plywood shell to justify the equipment and start-up costs necessary to use it.

FRP luggage shells were typically made by what was known as the air preform process, which might employ either automatic or manual equipment. Automatic equipment consisted of a plenum chamber (Exhibit 1) into which chopped glass fibers one to two inches in length were blown, to be collected on a perforated metal screen shaped like a luggage shell. An air current through the plenum chamber and the perforations of the metal screen was generated by a fan. The fibers carried

**EXHIBIT 1.   Schematic drawing of air preform plenum chamber**

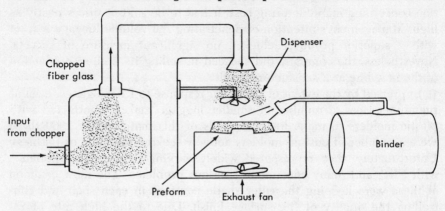

by this air current were dispersed uniformly over the screen by means of a rotating distributor. A resinous binder was applied to the fibers as they collected on the screen. When the preform reached the proper thickness, it was removed from the plenum chamber and placed in an oven (Exhibit 2). Here, water in the binder was driven off and the preform cured.

The manual equipment consisted of a preform screen mounted on a rotating ring. An operator directed the flow of chopped glass fibers and binder onto the rotating metal screen. When the preform reached its proper thickness, it was placed in an oven to cure as shown in Exhibit 2.

Compared with other plastic-molding processes, such as injection molding, compression molding, low-pressure forming, high-pressure forming, and extrusion, this process was rather slow. One luggage shell every five minutes was a fairly rapid rate of production. This rate could

**EXHIBIT 2.   Schematic drawing of preform oven**

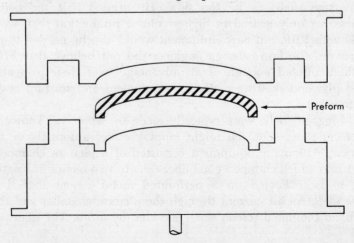

be doubled only by doubling the investment in equipment. A machine for making preforms might cost between $6,000 and $8,000; a press, about $25,000, and a set of matched dies, about $15,000, depending on the capacity of the equipment and whether it was single stage or multistage.

## Marketing strategy

It was apparent from the first contacts with luggage manufacturers that convincing them of the merits of FRP for luggage would require personal selling of a very high order and involve a considerable amount of technical information. Manufacturers would not only have to be convinced of the superiority of FRP material over leather, plywood, and metal, but be assured of enough technical assistance to make the transition to FRP relatively smooth and within justifiable cost limits. Since there was not an unlimited pool of manpower at Owens-Corning from which to draw, it was decided to restrict initial contacts to leading luggage makers and the custom molders whom they might mention as possible primary or back-up suppliers.

The Company's long-standing policy against knowingly competing with its customers ruled out any attempt to manufacture and market FRP end products. However, this left management free to give customers as much help as possible in processing FRP materials, identifying market opportunities, and promoting their products. Management also encouraged custom molders to make use of the name "Fiberglas," the copyrighted Owens-Corning trademark, in building markets for their own products incorporating the material.

While the Company carried out a vigorous advertising campaign highlighting the exceptional qualities of fiberglass and illustrating various end products, including luggage, the names of manufacturers were never mentioned. This policy was intended to avoid the situation of having to advertise for all customers if advertising was done for one, and to avoid the hard feelings which might arise if such a program, once begun, was discontinued. Furthermore, the Company did not want customers to believe that Fiberglas prices were set at a level that made possible an advertising slush fund. Finally, it was thought wise to avoid any implication that Owens-Corning was "underwriting" the success of its customers' operations.

Salesmen who called on luggage manufacturers were indoctrinated in custom molding techniques at the Company's Technical Center. Instruction was given by authorities on various aspects of plastic processing. In addition to formal instruction, numerous demonstrations were conducted involving products and processes related to the plastics industry. Refresher courses were given about every two to three years.

Most salesmen called on other users of FRP in their respective territories rather than limiting their attention to custom molders. None were specialists in plastic molding, although through their training and home study most had acquired enough information about processing techniques to "talk the language" of the molders. Only a few had been instructed to devote the whole of their efforts to molded products. These were men whose territories included significant concentrations of custom molders.

The activities of all salesmen operating in the luggage market were directed by the Textile Products Sales Manager. He was responsible both to the Vice President of Marketing at corporate level and to the Vice President of the Industrial Materials Division.

Although these salesmen were qualified to answer most questions about the use of FRP materials, they were encouraged to call on the applications engineering staff at Newark for assistance. In some instances the only assistance needed was new technical data not included in the salesman's kit. In other instances an engineer would be asked to visit an interested luggage maker with the salesman, or members of the luggage maker's engineering or production staff would be invited to visit the Newark facility for the observation of tests or other demonstrations.

### Market performance

The first piece of popular-priced FRP luggage was marketed in 1953 by one of the nation's leading makers of high-quality luggage. It met with no enthusiastic public response. The pieces were priced from $19 to $35 and were available in a variety of colors and sizes. However, in an effort to give its new luggage line an image of modernity and youth, the company's styling was apparently too radical to appeal to consumer tastes prevailing at the time.

There can be little doubt that a properly executed test market would have revealed the error in design. Plans for a test market were abandoned, however, when it was learned that start-up costs would be so high that the total cost of producing a few hundred samples would not be significantly less than a full production run of several thousand pieces. This was because the investment required for molds and other plastic-processing equipment resulted in substantial economies only with volume output.

Unfortunately, the manufacturer's design was faulty as well as radical. Most of the luggage shipped to department stores that sold its more expensive line did not pass minimum impact-strength tests established by the U.S. Bureau of Standards. Despite the number of pieces of this luggage which were rejected by store buyers and returned to the manufacturer, the product was nevertheless promoted vigorously by the stores as the lightest and strongest they had ever sold. The Owens-Corning trademark, "Fiberglas," was used prominently both in store displays and newspaper advertising. However, the fact that so many substandard pieces of the luggage had to be returned apparently so dampened the enthusiasm of sales clerks that few encouraged customers to buy it.

Before Owens-Corning management could reach a decision on the best way to deal with this problem, a blatant case of product misrepresentation came to their attention. The salesman in New York City forwarded to the Textile Products Sales Manager copies of a full-page ad in the *New York Times* featuring a well-known TV personality testifying to the ruggedness and lightness of his new Fiberglas luggage. The ad quoted the TV personality as saying that he dropped his new piece of luggage, kicked it around, and jumped on it without scuffing it, warping it, denting it, or puncturing it. Full use was made of the Owens-Corning Fiberglas name.

It was known that this particular luggage manufacturer made luggage of plywood covered with a vinyl sheet laminated to cardboard. A phone call to the luggage department of the New York department store that placed the ad disclosed some interesting information. The store's luggage buyer had approached this particular manufacturer with a request that he make a line of luggage that would incorporate enough fibrous glass that it could be advertised as Fiberglas luggage. Eager to get the additional business but having no experience with fibrous glass, the firm contracted with its vinyl supplier to laminate clear vinyl sheets to thin Fiberglas mats. This material was then laminated by the manufacturer to cardboard to make a covering for its plywood luggage shells.

The luggage not only could be advertised as made of Fiberglas, and hence tie in with the Owens-Corning promotion of the Fiberglas label, but also possessed other advantages. The Fiberglas mat, pressed into the clear vinyl, presented an attractive "jackstraws" appearance, which was very much in fashion at the time. The Fiberglas mat also increased the tear resistance of the vinyl surface and stopped any rips from traveling once they had started. However, it was obvious that no luggage with a plywood shell could take much dropping, kicking, and stomping without sustaining severe damage.

This, and similar experiences, raised the question whether some Owens-Corning customers should be discouraged from manufacturing FRP luggage. One highly placed executive recommended a program to evaluate customers' products before permitting them to use the Fiberglas name. This program envisaged the establishment of an evaluation committee within the company to test products submitted by customer firms. Products submitted would be tested against he Bureau of Standards minimum specifications as well as against competitive products in the same price and performance class. The manufacturers of products approved by the committee would be permitted to use the Fiberglas name in their advertising and would be supplied with "Made of Owens-Corning Fiberglas" labels, which could be affixed to their products.

The Company was also approached at about this time by several manufacturers expressing great interest in making products of Fiberglas mat laminated to vinyl film or sheeting. Managers of these firms believed this was an ideal material for the manufacture of nonrigid-type luggage, and that a good market even existed for wallets and handbags made of the material.

Before Owens-Corning could react to either of these situations, the Industrial Materials Division began to send disturbing reports of the vigorous competition its textile salesmen in the luggage field were encountering from the newly developed ABS plastics. This family of compounds when molded into various shapes possessed all the properties of ruggedness, impact strength, and scuff resistance characteristic of FRP materials, but within a relatively narrow temperature range—about 32° to 90° Fahrenheit. Above 90°, ABS plastic luggage begins to lose some of its rigidity and resistance to scuffing. Below 32° the material begins to develop brittleness, which increases markedly at lower temperatures.

In the 32°–90° temperature range, ABS plastics perform as well as FRP and at significantly lower prices. However, ABS luggage is slightly heavier than FRP luggage of the same size and performance characteristics. The manufacturer cannot shift readily from one of these processes to the other, because each requires different equipment, the cost of which is high enough to be a deterrent.

It appeared that the vigorous efforts by Owens-Corning in behalf of FRP had succeeded in getting nearly all of the nation's luggage makers converted to molded luggage shells just in time to enable them to take advantage of the lower-cost ABS plastics in the manufacture of their products. As the Textile Products Sales Manager nervously expressed it, "This luggage business is a completely new ball game, and we had better come up with a completely new game plan."

# PROCTER & GAMBLE

## GENERAL BACKGROUND

The Procter & Gamble Company was developing a new aerosol antiperspirant spray deodorant to be marketed under the brand name *Secret*. The package for containing the product was to be a glass bottle with an external coating of plastic which would give the bottle an appealing appearance and feel. The bottle would require a cap of a snap-on style. It would be necessary that, on the one hand, the cap fit tightly enough to prevent its separating from the bottle if the bottle were picked up by the cap. On the other hand, the cap would have to fit loosely enough to be removed with relative ease. Consequently, a very precisely made cap would be required.

In the process of this product development effort, it became apparent to those involved that, in order to attain the aesthetic and the convenience qualities desired for the package, a cover cap would be needed which would be larger and closer fitting than the standard stock item available in the marketplace.

Development of such a cap would require the participation of people from various P&G corporate departments. The organization structure involved was as shown in Exhibit 1.

The function of each department may be described as follows:

1. The Toilet Goods Division Advertising Department is subdivided into Brand Groups which are concerned with the merchandizing aspects of a product line, with Brand Managers guiding the merchandizing activities of particular brands such as *Secret*. A Brand Manager is quite interested in the package concept since its cost, availability, technical characteristics, and consumer acceptability can affect the marketing plans for the product. Therefore, while he does not direct the efforts of those involved in packaging development, the Brand Manager must be involved.

2. The Toilet Goods Division Product Development Department is responsible for formulating new products or improvements of existing

**EXHIBIT 1**

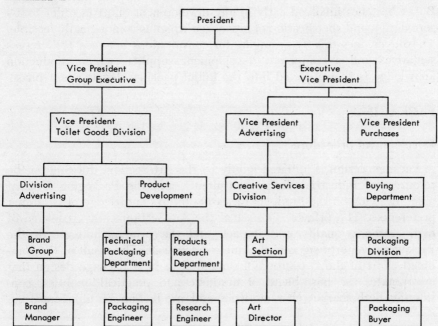

Toilet Goods items for the purpose of gaining a technical advantage over competing products. Product Development is subdivided into various functions including the Technical Packaging and Product Research functions, with the Technical Packaging Engineer doing development work on the package for the product and the Research Engineer evaluating this work from a consumer-use standpoint. The Technical Packaging Engineer and the Research Engineer work closely together, since the activities of one will affect the efforts of the other. In total, they develop an effective and workable package within the cost limits of competitive marketing. The Technical Packaging Department is responsible for writing specifications for the package.

3. The Art Section is responsible for creating the package image, or appearance. Within the Art Section, there are Art Directors assigned to the various brands. The Art Directors generally work with outside consultants to achieve the desired package image.

4. The Buying Department's function is to make a contribution to Company profits on a continuing basis by furnishing raw materials, supplies (including packaging materials), and equipment to the plants when needed; by actively encouraging suppliers to compete for P&G business; and by working effectively with other departments (e.g., Manufacturing, Product Development, Engineering, Advertising) to assure maximum value for what is spent. This activity includes assisting in selecting packaging-material suppliers who will do development work on new items in cooperation with P&G Engineers, as well as negotiating with suppliers for normal or current requirements of existing packages. The Buyer becomes involved early in any development effort in order to assure design and specification of a package which is commercially feasible. The Buyer does this by arranging for consultations between P&G representatives and a competent development supplier, whose production knowledge is then injected into the initial package development phase.

## PACKAGING

### Development procedure

Package design is initiated jointly by the Art Section, drawing on the resources of industrial design consultants, and the Packaging Department, drawing on the Products Research group's knowledge of consumer preferences. The primary interest of the Art Section is in a package of high aesthetic quality and impact, and the primary interest of the Packaging Department is in its functional aspects. The result of the combined effort of the two groups is intended to be a package design that incorporates the best blend of aesthetic and practical qualities, considering both market characteristics and production requirements.

After the package concept has been defined, the Packaging Engineers submit specifications to the Buying Department. Then the Buyer investigates potential sources of the item required and solicits proposals from those who, in his judgment and that of the Packaging Engineer, are qualified to be development suppliers. During these initial phases of the search for a development supplier, the Buyer is the primary contact with the suppliers. However, the efforts of the Buyer are supplemented very substantially by those of the Packaging Engineer and, in some cases, the two jointly visit potential suppliers whose proposals are attractive, in order to confirm their development capabilities, particularly if those suppliers have no record of demonstrated performance for P&G. Once a development supplier is selected, the Packaging Engineer is in close contact with the supplier, particularly during the time when the tooling is under construction and test production is being technically evaluated.

In the case of a typical cap development, the development phase includes constructing a relatively inexpensive test mold[1] according to cap specifications provided by the Packaging Engineer, and then producing sample caps from it. Such a mold, which has only a single cavity, is capable of making only one cap at a time, and costs about $1,000.

Test mold samples are extensively tested by the P&G Packaging Engineer before approval. Following approval, work begins on a production mold, which is capable of producing a large number of caps in a single cycle of operation. During this phase of eliminating the "bugs" and moving to the larger, more expensive production mold, many man hours of consultation are spent on the technical aspects of the development.

Once the production mold is constructed, trial runs are conducted and caps from this production mold evaluated in P&G laboratories and plants. This testing is the responsibility of the Packaging Engineer; and upon successful conclusion of the evaluations and tests, the mold is approved for use.

The Buyer then enters orders with the supplier for manufacture of whatever quantities of caps are necessary to support production of the new item in its market test.

## Expansion procedure

If market tests establish the desirability of expanding the product into national distribution, the Buyer solicits proposals from possible suppliers to cover the potential packaging requirements. The development supplier is among those solicted. Because of his close acquaintance with the problems and difficulties of production, the development supplier

---

[1] Also referred to as unit mold.

has the advantage of experience in making his proposal for expansion requirements. This experience gives him no assurance of the expansion business, however, since his proposal is judged on its total competitive merits, of which development performance is only one, though an important, element.

Essentially, the Buyer operates on the basis of soliciting bids from a group of manufacturers. This is called an "inquiry." The premise is that broad competition among suppliers and materials will establish values most favorable to the Company for the near term as well as for the long pull. Business is awarded among manufacturers who earn their business by the value they offer P&G.

Value may be defined as a function of the interrelationship of several variable factors:

1. Those pertaining to specifications, which affect the function, appearance, and performance of the item.
2. Those pertaining to costs, which include various individual charges such as material, labor, discounts, setup charges, mold or die charges, terms of payment, freight, and so on.
3. Those pertaining to service, such as proximity, type of delivery, the reliability and flexibility of the supplier, and other aspects of his performance as a supplier.

This emphasizes the importance of the Buyer's working effectively with those in other departments so as to be able to recognize what constitutes maximum value and to assure that proper action is taken to secure it for the Company.

The following are some of the considerations for handling the placement of business:

1. The Buyer prefers stability of sources to the maximum possible degree consistent with maintaining effective competition among suppliers.
2. Past performance is a known value that is considered by the Buyer.
3. The value of having more than one supplier is recognized.
4. If a current supplier does not offer the best value, he may still be permitted to retain a portion of his volume.
5. The Buyer will not disclose prices of either successful or unsuccessful bidders. All suppliers' prices and information will be held in confidence.

## SELECTING THE DEVELOPMENT SUPPLIER
## FOR THE *SECRET* CAP

Selection of the development supplier for the *Secret* cap began when the Buying Department received a memo (Exhibit 2), together with drawings (Exhibit 3) of the proposed cap, requesting that a development supplier for the project be recommended.

**EXHIBIT 2**

8.

# INTERDEPARTMENTAL CORRESPONDENCE

FROM  Toilet Goods Technical Packaging Department     **DATE**  March 16, 1966

TO  Buying Department                                  **ATTENTION**  Mr. T. S. Grey

SUBJECT  SECRET "S" OR "AP" OVERCAP     **IN REPLY TO LETTER OF**

In order to facilitate use of a large directional actuator on the Secret "AP" glass aerosol, the cover cap currently used will need to be modified to increase the overall height by 1/4".

Since the price quoted for the stock closure seems to be on the expensive side for a polypropylene closure of this (3 oz.) size, we would like to have your suggestions for an alternate development supplier or suppliers.

Attached are drawings of a cap modified to meet our current need. Although the general dimensions and style should remain unchanged, minor modifications may be necessary on the final overcap.

We would appreciate any effort on your part to expedite this matter.

C. K. Varner

jb

Attachment

It was estimated that approximately 1,500,000 units would be required during the product market-testing stage, and the development supplier would be required to produce this number of caps.

The Buyer sent inquiries to a number of molders (Exhibit 4) to solicit their quotations for market-test cap requirements, including the preliminary development effort. Ten proposals were received and are summarized in Exhibit 5. An investigation by the Buyer indicated that all ten molders probably were qualified to make the cap.

The Buyer considered three key points of *cost* comparison:

1. The cost of the test mold, which was small.
2. The cost of the production mold, which was substantial.
3. The price of the caps, with two alternative delivery points. The price of the caps varied according to order quantity—from 50,000 to 1,000,000 units.

Because of the development schedule and the plans for the market test, the time required for development would be an important factor. The number of cavities in the production mold and the consequent production capacity per week would be a significant consideration.

In view of the apparent availability of sufficient capacity within rea-

**EXHIBIT 3**

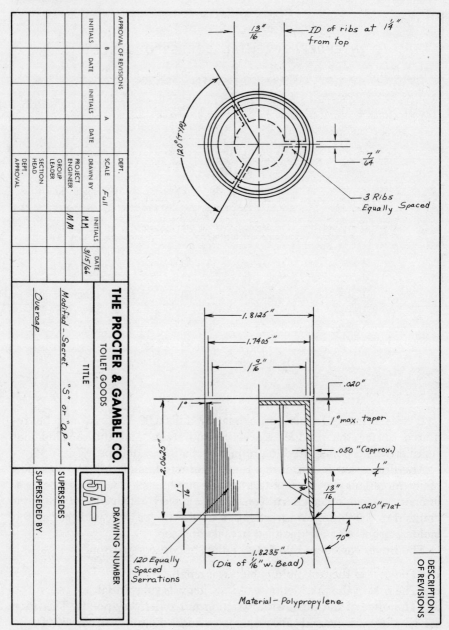

## EXHIBIT 4

REPLY TO: **THE PROCTER & GAMBLE CO.**

Buying Department, P.O. Box 599
ATTN: (Buyer's name shown below)
CINCINNATI, OHIO 45201

| **INQUIRY DATE** | PLEASE QUOTE BY | **THIS IS NOT AN ORDER** | REQUIRED DELIVERY DATE | **INQUIRY NO.** |
|---|---|---|---|---|
| 3/21/66 | 4/6/66 | | | 108 |

For Delivery To
**THE PROCTER & GAMBLE CO.**
(See under ITEMS if for delivery to more than one point)

⌐                                              ¬


L                                              ⌐

Please quote your lowest price on the items listed below; we reserve the right to accept all or any part of this bid.
Please price each item separately, although quotations on combinations of items are invited when savings will result therefrom.

BUYING DEPARTMENT____T. S. Grey____

| REQ. NO. | QUANTITY | ITEMS                     For Delivery To (If more than one) | PRICE & TRADE DISCOUNT |
|---|---|---|---|
| | | Polypropylene Overcap Inquiry | |

We are enclosing a copy of P&G Dwg. 5A and ask that you
quote on this new item:

Your proposal should include:

1. Price per thousand overcaps, molded in white polypropylene, for quantities of 50,000 up to potentially
   1,000,000 per month, delivered to Cincinnati, Ohio
   or Iowa City, Iowa.

2. Unit mold costs and sampling charges.

3. Production mold costs – please state number of
   cavities, estimated production rate, and whether
   or not frame cost is included.

4. Lead time each for unit mold and production tooling.

5. Price differential for standard polypropylene vs.
   polypropylenes having anti-stat properties. Please
   indicate specific resin(s) you propose using.

6. Weight per thousand overcaps.

7. Cash terms, F.O.B. point and manufacturing point.

8. Any suggestions that would be helpful in considering
   your proposal per this item.
   PLEASE BE SURE TO FURNISH THE INFORMATION REQUESTED BELOW        (continued pg. 2)

G-8019-C       We agree to furnish any or all of the above items in accordance with prices and items herein quoted.
We warrant that the prices set forth in this Agreement are valid under the provisions of the Robinson-Patman
(Price Discrimination) Act and all other pertinent laws, orders and regulations.

F.O.B. POINT _____ SHIPPING POINT _____

TERMS OF PAYMENT _____ SHIPPING DATE _____

EST. SHIPPING WT. _____ LBS.   SIGNED _____ DATE _____

9. An expression of your experience and knowledge in the
   overcap product line.

Your proposal will be considered along with others in our
selection of a development supplier(s) for this item. However, all quotations and information will be kept confidential.

Due to our need to choose a development source(s) for this
item we must have your proposal in our hands no later than
April 6, 1966.

## EXHIBIT 5.   Development proposals received

| | Order Qty. | $/M Del'd To Cinti. | $/M Del'd To Iowa City | Mold Costs & Constru'n Time Test Mold | Prod'n Mold | Ideal Prod'n Per Wk. | No. of Cavit's | Est. Lbs./M Caps | | | Comments | |
|---|---|---|---|---|---|---|---|---|---|---|---|---|
| Supplier "A" | 50M | 17.30 | 17.35 | $ 1,500 | $11,900 | 300M | 6 | 26 | | | | |
| | 150M | 17.21 | 17.30 | 12 wks. | 20 wks. | | | | | | | |
| | 1MM | 17.16 | 17.19 | | | | | | | | | |
| Supplier "B" | 50M | 10.32 | 10.32 | $ 1,000 | $20,000 | 525M | 24 | 22 | | Only P&G experience was | cake-mix bowl | |
| | 1MM | 9.40 | 9.40 | 5 wks. | 14 wks. | | | | | premium. | | |
| Supplier "C" | 250M | 17.60 | 17.65 | $   400 | $ 9,350 | – | 16 | 28.2 | External gate. | | | |
| | 1MM | 17.15 | 17.20 | 5 wks. | 14 wks. | | | | | | | |
| Supplier "D" | 50M | 22.97 | 23.65 | $ 2,500 | $13,975 | 250M | 16 | 25 | External gate. | | | |
| | 1MM | 15.19 | 15.50 | 7 wks. | 15 wks. | | | | | | | |
| Supplier "E" | 50M | 19.90 | 19.49 | $ 1,100 | $ 8,944 | – | N.A. | 28.4 | | | | |
| | 1MM | 16.64 | 16.49 | 8 wks. | 12 wks. | | | | | | | |
| Supplier "F" | 500M | 15.17 | 15.17 | $ 1,100 | $ 7,000 | 185M | 8 | 32.6 | Glass development source. | | | |
| | | | | 7 wks. | 13 wks. | | | | | | | |
| Supplier "G" | 50M | 16.71 | 17.42 | $   740 | $11,310 | 325M | 16 | 28.5 | | | | |
| | 1MM | 16.21 | 16.39 | 6 wks. | 16 wks. | | | | | | | |
| Supplier "H" | 500M | 15.65 | 15.70 | $   900 | $18,500 | 290M | 16 | – | Make Secret aerosol cap. | | | |
| | 1MM | 15.25 | 15.30 | 6 wks. | 14 wks. | | | | | | | |
| Supplier "I" | 50M | 12.81 | 13.11 | $   525 | $14,000 | 500M | 32 | 29.1 | | | | |
| | 1MM | 12.42 | 12.57 | | | | | | | | | |

M=Thousand

G-8063 11-59
11-60 SFW

| | Order Qty. | $/M Del'd To Cinti. | $/M Del'd To Iowa City | Mold Costs & Constru'n Time Test Mold | Prod'n Mold | Ideal Prod'n Per Wk. | No. of Cavit's | Est. Lbs./M Caps | | | Comments | |
|---|---|---|---|---|---|---|---|---|---|---|---|---|
| Supplier "J" | 50M | 15.23 | 14.54 | $ 1,100 | $22,900 | 435M | 32 | 28.5 | | | | |
| | 1MM | 14.54 | 14.37 | 6 wks. | 14 wks. | | | | | | | |
| | | | | | | | | | T. S. Grey | | | |

sonable time limits, the Buyer decided that the choice of a development supplier should rest principally on two factors—cost and ability to produce.

Molders C and D quoted on an "external gate"; so C and D were ruled out. Packaging preferred to use an inside gate, at least initially, for appearance reasons.[2]

Of the remaining molders, B looked most promising to the Buyer and showed a clear advantage in price per thousand caps.

Molder B had previous experience in developing a cake-mix bowl, which had been used in a promotion campaign for another P&G brand. The caps offered by Molder B had a much lower weight per thousand caps than that of any other molder, and his capacity was well above that of any other.

In order to more thoroughly investigate the capabilities of Molder B, the Buyer and the Packaging Engineer visited his plant for an evaluation. Both were well impressed with what they learned, and Exhibit 6 shows their report.

Following this visit, it was decided to award the development project to Molder B, even though B's experience with P&G has been limited to making a cake-mix bowl, which was not nearly so demanding in quality and performance as the aerosol overcap. B was authorized to construct a test mold for the overcap.

When the test mold was completed, test mold samples were run, which yielded significant information about mold performance and characteristics of the molded cap. This information indicated the need for several design changes, which the Packaging Engineer requested in order to facilitate production and to improve the function of the cap.

The production mold was authorized and constructed, following which orders for caps were entered and the market-test phase initiated. The market test lasted between a year and a year and a half, and throughout this period B delivered approximately 1½ million units of good quality, and adequately fulfilled his obligation as a development supplier. Performance had been technically satisfactory throughout the market-test period.

During the market-test production period, B requested that the Buyer consider price adjustments on three separate occasions:

1. In the first instance, the changes in the cap design, mentioned above, caused B to request a price increase on caps from $9.40/M to $12.30/M, as well as an increase in the mold charge from $20,000 to $24,000. This increase was approved.

---

[2] The term "gate" refers to the opening in the mold through which the molten plastic is injected. When the plastic has cured and the finished item ejected from the mold, a slight "birthmark" is left on the item where the gate was located. In the case of an inside gate this birthmark is hidden.

**EXHIBIT 6**

```
┌──────────────────────────────────────────────────────────────────────┐
│              INTERDEPARTMENTAL  CORRESPONDENCE                          │
│                                                                        │
│ FROM Mr. T. S. Grey                      DATE 4-22-66                   │
│                                                                        │
│   TO Mr. J. F. Miller                    ATTENTION                     │
│                                          IN REPLY TO                    │
│ SUBJECT SUPPLIER "B" VISIT, APRIL, 1966  LETTER OF                      │
│                                                                        │
│                                                                        │
│     Purpose:      To evaluate "B's" capabilities as development source  │
│                   for polypropylene overcap.                           │
│                                                                        │
│     Conclusion:   Toilet Goods Packaging Development and Buying believe │
│                   that "B" has the know-how and facilities to do the   │
│                   job.                                                  │
│                                                                        │
│     Background:   "B" quoted prices @ 30% below market level for overcap│
│                   per P&G tentative drawing. They have been competitive │
│                   when quoting on other P&G cap business, but never     │
│                   offered enough incentive to warrant a contract award. │
│                                                                        │
│     Personnel:    Supplier "B" - Pres. & Treas.                        │
│                                  Sales Mgr.                             │
│                                  Supt.                                  │
│                                  Engr.                                  │
│                                                                        │
│                   P&G -         Mr. C. K. Varner, TG Pkg. Development   │
│                                 Mr. T. S. Grey, Buying                  │
│                                                                        │
│     History:      Individual proprietorship; 15 years in business.     │
│                   Present sales level exceeds $1.0 million; profitable. │
│                                                                        │
│     Facilities    13 presses of reciprocating screw type (4 to 40 oz.),│
│                   of which 3 are new Huskies. One-story block building  │
│                   8,000 sq. ft. Own property for possible expansion of  │
│                   present building. Were leasing nearby warehouse space │
│                   for storage. Premises clean and neat, but somewhat    │
│                   crowded. Limited area for machine repair and quality  │
│                   control. Disposing of one blow molding machine.       │
│                                                                        │
│     Employment:   30                                                   │
│                                                                        │
│     Items Produced: About 30% for packaging - overcaps, spice can tops,│
│                   two-piece snap-on talc caps, non-threaded, non-lined  │
│                   items. Some toys, plastic handles, fasteners.        │
│                   Produced mixing bowl for cake-mix premium.            │
│                                                                        │
│     Accounts:     About 75 customers, including food, drug, military,   │
│                   industrial. Well diversified for small company.      │
│                                                                        │
│     Management:   Experienced team approach to new projects, evidence  │
│                   of innovation, some patents on multipack carriers.    │
│                   Know-how to design good, efficient molds.            │
│                                                                        │
└──────────────────────────────────────────────────────────────────────┘
```

**EXHIBIT 6** (*Continued*)

---

## INTERDEPARTMENTAL CORRESPONDENCE

FROM                                                    DATE

TO Mr. J. F. Miller                           ATTENTION
April 22, 1966                         IN REPLY TO
Page 2                                 LETTER OF


Quality Control:   Simple, hourly checks by foremen, recorded on data sheets,
                   shipping containers are coded to show shift, operator
                   and date.  Will need our guidance in setting up quality
                   control procedures.  Suggest statistical sampling plan
                   with Acceptable Quality Level at outset.

General:           1.  Producing to about 75% of capacity.
                   2.  Eager to work with P&G, and presently do not have a
                       backlog of new items.
                   3.  Use a wide variety of resin types from different
                       recognized suppliers.
                   4.  Can mix own color or anti-stat additive or buy pre-
                       mixed, but pre-mixed more expensive.
                   5.  Design own molds; experienced in designing good cooling
                       characteristics, for simple or complex parts.
                   6.  In discussing the development project, they seemed to
                       understand reasonably well what dimensions would be
                       critical in molding the item, and foresaw no insur-
                       mountable problems.


                                   T. S. Grey


TSG:mm

2. In the second case, B requested a price differential for smaller order quantities. It became apparent during the market-test period that demand was sporadic, limited in quantity, and somewhat uncertain. As a result, production runs of the cap were intermittent and short. Understandably, the impact of such circumstances on costs was difficult for a supplier to predict, so the Buyer agreed to the increase in the form of a small-quantity price differential.

3. In the third instance, B requested that the Buyer allow him to convert his quoted price to an *f.o.b. shipping point* from *f.o.b. delivered* basis. The implications were that P&G would pay the freight costs, which had previously been included in the unit cost of the cap. Given the quantity being shipped, such an adjustment would result in a significant upward adjustment in the price of the cap.[3] Since this change was not related to development costs, P&G protested it. B subsequently rescinded the increase.

## SELECTING EXPANSION SUPPLIERS FOR THE *SECRET* CAP

Test marketing of the aerosol antiperspirant spray deodorant appeared to be a success, and it was decided to expand the new product into national distribution. From a buying standpoint, this meant moving from the smaller-order quantity levels of the development and market-test phase into mass production. The time had come for the Buyer to assure a high-volume supply of quality overcaps on a continuing basis.

The Buyer had been advised to anticipate an annual requirement of 30 million units. Experience during the development stage indicated B's one production mold could provide an annual capacity of approximately 16 million units. Clearly, additional mold capacity would be required, irrespective of any other considerations.

The Buyer drew up a selected list of possible suppliers and prepared an inquiry to solicit proposals for national distribution quantities of aerosol caps on a contract basis (see Exhibit 7). A total of 19 molders responded with proposals, and the Buyer summarized the pertinent aspects of their bids (see Exhibit 8). This exhibit revealed that unit prices ranged from $10.59 to $16.96 per thousand caps and from $9,800 to $25,740 for the mold.

The summary showed that no one molder, even with maximum efficiency, could satisfy the total annual requirement of 30 million units with just one mold. B was chosen as an expansion supplier within the limits of the capacity of the one existing production mold since B's prices were acceptable, and P&G representatives had satisfactory development

---

[3] This type of closure was larger than a standard overcap. For example, only 400,000 of these caps could be shipped in a truckload, whereas one million units of the standard closure made up a truckload shipment.

**EXHIBIT 7**

# THE PROCTER & GAMBLE COMPANY

BUYING DEPARTMENT                                         P. O. BOX 599     CINCINNATI, OHIO 45201

July 16, 1968

Gentlemen:

You are invited to quote on all or any portion of our potential requirements
for snap-on aerosol overcaps based on the enclosed sample, drawing, and
specifications.

Potential requirements for an overcap based on specification 58.8892 are
estimated to be between 15MM to 30MM annually. Please quote on this
item two ways: a) tooling to produce 15MM-20MM annually; b) tooling to produce up to 35MM annually. Quote prices for spot purchase, a six-month contract, or a one-year contract. If any other contract period would enable
you to offer more attractive prices, please so indicate.

We will assume that your quotation applies to any quantity allocated to you
unless you specify otherwise.

Any suggestions enabling you to provide better value are most welcome. These
should be in addition to your quotes on the enclosed specifications.

Please include all information requested on the attached page, and have your
quotation in our hands by August 5, 1968.

If you have any questions, please call the writer.

                                     Sincerely,


                                     T. S. Grey
                                     Buying Department

TSG:mm

Enc.:   SPEC. NOS. CL 58.8892-5
                      100.451-6
        A.S.P. NO. 59.106-3
        DRWG. NO. 2A-33089-2
        Sample Overcap

**EXHIBIT 7** (*Continued*)

```
Snap-on Aerosol Overcap Inquiry
Page 2
7/16/68



Please include all of the following in your proposal:

1.  Quote delivered prices per thousand for truckload and less than truckload
    for Chicago, Illinois, and Danville, Illinois.  Show separately freight
    rates per thousand reflected in delivered costs.  If optimum freight
    differs, please specify.  Also, indicate normal transit time.

2.  Manufacturing point(s).

3.  Labor unions, and contract expiration dates.  Note any reopener clauses.

4.  Weight per thousand caps; number of caps per truckload.

5.  Resin:  Supplier   -
            Type       -
            Price/Lb.  -
               Indicate whether bulk, bagged, or gaylord.

6.  Effect in $/M caps of a $.01 change in resin price.

7.  Unit tooling costs and lead time.  What part of cost is applicable to
    production tooling?

8.  Production tooling costs and lead time.

9.  Number of molds and number of cavities per mold.

10. Daily production rates, normal number of workdays/week, and normal number
    of work shifts.

11. Cash terms.
```

**EXHIBIT 8. Prices $/M net (delivered truckload unless otherwise indicated)**

| | | Price/M | | Unit Tooling | | Production Tooling | | | Annual | Est. Lbs./M |
|---|---|---|---|---|---|---|---|---|---|---|
| | Terms | Danville | Chicago | Cost | Lead (wks) | Cost | Lead (wks) | Cavities | Capacity | Caps |
| Supplier "K" | N/30 | 10.90 | (1)10.90 | N.A. | 6 | 22,900 | 14-16 | 24 | 28.0 | N.A. |
| Supplier "B" | N/30 | 12.30 | 12.10 | Pd | Pd | 24,500 (3)18-19 | | 24 | 16.0 | 24.0 |
| Supplier "L" | 1/10/30 | 15.11 | 15.11 | 600 | 6-8 | 9,800 | 16-18 | 24 | 20.0 | 27.0 |
| Supplier "M" | N/30 | 13.00 | (1)13.00 | N.A. | N.A. | 12,500 | 14-16 | 12 | 23-27 | 27.0 |
| Supplier "N" | N/30 | 12.25 | (1)12.25 | N.A. | N.A. | 22,625 | 16 | 24 | 17.8 | N.A. |
| Supplier "O" | 1/10/30 | 12.35 | 12.46 | N.A. | N.A. | 12,000 | 8-12 | 16 | 22.6 | 36.0 |
| Supplier "P" | 1/10/30 | 12.37 | 12.10 | 950 | 2 | 15,850 | 9-12 | 16 | 17.5 | 27.0 |
| Supplier "Q" | N/30 | 11.57 | 11.57 | N.A. | N.A. | 12,000 | 12 | 8 | 24.0 | 25.3 |
| Supplier "R" | ½/10/30 | 13.25 | (1)13.25 | 1600 | N.A. | 24,500 | 20 | N.A. | 16.3 | 24.0 |
| Supplier "S" | N/30 | 11.95 | (2)11.95 | N.A. | N.A. | 18,500 | 14-16 | 16 | 22.0 | 25.0 |
| Supplier "G" | 1/10/30 | 13.34 | 13.36 | N.A. | N.A. | 25,740 | 18-19 | 24 | 21.3 | 24.2 |
| Supplier "H" | N/30 | 12.91 | 12.64 | 891 | 6-8 | 17,500 | 16-18 | 32 | 27.5 | 24.3 |
| Supplier "T" | N/30 | 10.92 | (2)10.92 | N.A. | N.A. | 17,955 | 16-18 | 8 | 18.0 | 23.0 |
| Supplier "U" | ½/10/30 | 15.90 | 15.83 | 1250 | 8 | 17,500 | 16 | 16 | 15.0 | 24.0 |
| Supplier "V" | 1/10/30 | 14.77 | 14.77 | 1200 | 7 | 21,000 | 22-26 | 24 | 27.0 | 26.4 |
| Supplier "W" | N/15 | 12.58 | 12.66 | 1500 | 5-6 | 18,800 | 15 | 16 | 20.0 | 27.0 |
| Supplier "X" | ½/10/30 | 12.70 | 12.70 | N.A. | N.A. | 24,000 | 15-17 | 24 | 20.0 | N.A. |
| Supplier "Y" | ½/10/30 | 16.96 | 16.96 | 1600 | 5-7 | 20,750 | 14-16 | 16 | 16.1 | 28.2 |
| Supplier "Z" | N/30 | 10.59 | 10.59 | 2300 | 3 | 16,000 | 14 | 8 | 22.0 | 24.0 |

(1) Prices shown are F.O.B., Shipping Point (2) Prices are F.O.B. delivered with estimated truckload freight cost.
(3) Quotation for additional (second set) tooling.
Comments: Supplier "B" Shipments: 1967-755M; Jan.-March 1968-333M; Apr.-June-580M.
Manufacturer states additional tooling is necessary in order to balance with bottle production capacity at 30MM Units

T. S. Grey
8/21/68

M=Thousand    (4) In Millions

experience with him. The question then became one of where the second production mold should be constructed, and suppliers B and Z seemed the most promising prospects; B because of his experience and Z by virtue of his price.

The unit price per thousand caps offered by B was average or above. B had considerable experience in molding caps, and, at least in the development period, had proved that he could maintain satisfactory production. B's quoted mold cost was high but could be considered realistic in that it was based on known construction costs of the existing production mold, which had proved satisfactory. B's tooling lead time was 19 weeks. B was a proprietorship. There were, however, certain elements of uncertainty in B's position relating to capacity since he had produced only 1½ million caps in a series of short runs, and this could hardly be considered a sustained large-scale production run. Furthermore, B was so short on plant space that he could carry no stock of finished caps but would have to ship caps as soon as they were made.

Z's unit price per thousand was the lowest among those bidding, and Z's mold cost was average or below. Z appeared to have a capacity which was above the average, and Z's tooling lead time was one of the shortest mentioned. Z's current performance as a supplier of another major closure requirement had been entirely satisfactory. The Buyer considered the fact that Z was incorporated and well financed. Awarding the authorization for a second mold to Z would give the added security of supply afforded by two suppliers.

A summary of salient factors in the issue relative to Supplier B and Supplier Z looked something like the following:

| Factor | Supplier B | Supplier Z |
|---|---|---|
| Mold cost | $24,500 | $16,000 |
| Annual capacity | 16,000,000 | 22,000,000 |
| Lead time (unit and production mold) | 19 weeks | 14 weeks |
| Delivered price | $12.10/M | $10.59/M |
| Cost 16,000,000 caps | $193,600 | $169,440 |
| Risk of interruption | Less | Greater |
| Risk of failure to make mold | Less | More |
| Stock-carrying ability | None | Normal |

The Buyer considered contracting with Z for a second mold for several reasons. It would produce savings below B's bid of $8,500 in mold costs and $24,160 per year in cap prices based on an annual production of 16 million caps. Z quoted a production mold construction time of 14 weeks against B's estimate of 19 weeks. Risks of shortages would be reduced. A continuing competitive effort would more likely result with two suppliers.

Others in the Company preferred that the second mold be awarded to B, making B the exclusive expansion supplier, principally for reasons of assuring capacity. They felt that B's chances of being able to duplicate its existing mold within the allowed time were much greater than those of any other molder. Injection molding is an art, as well as a science, and requires a great deal more technical finesse than other types of molding. It could not be determined with certainty whether Z or any other molder could produce overcaps of the required specifications in the quantities and within the time schedule required on the basis of a written proposal. P&G could be reasonably assured of Z's ability to deliver only after subjecting samples of production to extensive examination and thoroughly inspecting the manufacturing facilities. Yet a risk would remain, since demonstrated performance in a full-scale production run would constitute the only proof. It was estimated that within seven months P&G would require 30 million caps annually. Failure to be prepared with adequate capacity would mean a severe setback to the marketing plans for the new product. There was a feeling that B's satisfactory production record during the development phase meant that there was less likelihood of delay in achieving the larger production capacity needed for expansion on a tight time schedule than might be the case with Z. However, as mentioned above, B's good production record during the development period was on a series of short runs; and this was not necessarily indicative of B's ability to maintain satisfactory large-scale production.

P&G was very strongly committed to the policy of having more than one supplier in order to insure against risks of interruption of supply and to get the benefits of improvements in product quality, service, price, and other factors that were apt to result from competition among two or more suppliers. Nevertheless, there was a very real concern over the uncertainties involved with a "new" source. So the issue became whether to pick Supplier B or Supplier Z as a source for the additional requirements . . . or was there another alternative?

# THE PULLMAN-STANDARD DIVISION

Several years ago the Pullman-Standard Division of Pullman, Inc., modified its organization structure by introducing a new profit center system with a staff of product supervisors. The new system seemed to work very well, but as is true of all innovations, it required constant reexamination to check the possible need for modification.

## Organizational background

The Pullman Company was originally organized to manufacture Pullman cars. Through the years it expanded into the making and marketing of all kinds of railroad cars. This business was highly dependent on the cyclical fluctuations of the railroad industry. So the company diversified by the addition of a series of semiautonomous divisions. At the time of this case the Pullman Company operated the following divisions:

1. *Pullman-Standard,* which handled the railroad-car business and was the leading manufacturer in this industry.
2. *Trailmobile,* which manufactured and sold truck trailers and bulk-transport containers for use on trucks, railroad cars, and ships.
3. *Transport Leasing,* which owned several thousand railroad cars of various types and leased them to users.
4. *Swindell-Dressler Company,* which was a leading designer and

builder of steel-producing plants and furnaces for steel producers.

5. *The M. W. Kellogg Division,* which designed and built plants mainly for the chemical industry. Its business also included power piping and chimney construction for various types of industries, particularly the electric power business.

With this highly diversified scope of operations the principle of decentralization of management was well established in company thinking and practice. Before the recent change, however, the Pullman-Standard Division had a fairly centralized system of internal operation. Exhibit 1 shows its organization structure.

Pullman-Standard operated five plants, which were to some extent specialized in the products they made.

A. Butler plant
   Covered hopper cars
   Piggyback flatcars
   Miscellaneous freight cars and parts

B. Michigan City plant
   Insulated boxcars
   Refrigerator boxcars
   Standard boxcars
   Miscellaneous freight cars and parts

C. Bessemer plant
   Serving southeastern railroads
   Boxcars
   Open-top cars
   Miscellaneous freight cars and parts

D. Hammond plant
   Miscellaneous freight cars and parts
   Repair programs
   Specialty products

E. Pullman car works
   All passenger-car business

When the Pullman-Standard Division was originally established, the demand for freight cars had been mainly for a standard boxcar or open-top car. During recent years the situation had changed, and a demand had grown up for special-purpose cars suited to the transport of specific kinds of products. It was not unusual to receive orders for cars to be built to specifications supplied by the buyer or worked out in cooperation with the engineers of the Division and the customer to serve the latter's peculiar transport needs. This tended to channel divisional thinking along the lines of the product and its precise suitability to the needs of the customer, instead of in the direction of purely production considerations.

As a result of some very serious top-management thinking, a plan was worked out that it was hoped would fit the needs of the new situation more exactly than the old form of organization. The new plan was based on the idea of setting up each of the plants as a profit center with a product supervisor as a coordinating agent.

## The new organizational plan

The product supervisor was chairman of a management committee for his plant, composed of the plant controller, the plant engineer, the plant purchasing officer, the plant personnel manager, and the plant manager. This group met once a month. Every three months it was joined by representatives of the headquarters industrial relations, public relations, marketing, and finance departments. It was the job of each of these committees to make suggestions for improving the operations and profit results of the plant profit center.

The plants were used as profit centers primarily because return on investment was a prime objective of the Pullman Company and the chief investment of the Division was in the Plants. The overall annual operational planning of the system worked somewhat as follows. The Vice President for Marketing forecast annual sales by product line. This forecast and the estimated year-end order backlog were assigned to the profit centers by the Vice President for Manufacturing. The President then set annual return-on-investment objectives for each profit center and for the entire Division. Each headquarters department head prepared an annual departmental budget. On the basis of these estimates the controller prepared for the Division and for each profit center an estimate of total dollar sales, costs, and net profit. The way to achieve these goals was up to the product supervisors and their management committees, and to plant management.

The product supervisor had no line authority. He was expected to obtain results by admonition and persuasion. The headquarters Vice President for Manufacturing still had control over production; each plant manager had the authority to run his plant; advertising was done under the direction of the headquarters Public Relations department, and the job of personal selling and sales promotion was managed by the Vice President for Marketing through a force of field sales representatives. The product supervisors reported to the Sales Manager, Administration, who reported to the Vice President for Marketing.

The organization structure of the marketing department is shown in Exhibit 2. Assignments of authority and responsibility may be summarized as follows:

**EXHIBIT 1**

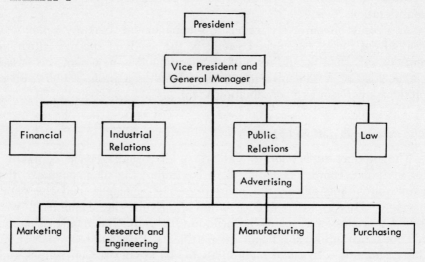

*Manager, Marketing Research and Sales Forecasting*—The functions of this unit are just about what the title indicates.

*Director, International Sales*—The same thing is true here. Most foreign sales are made through native agents.

*Sales Manager, Administration*—Includes pricing and the preparation of estimates and proposals; servicing of orders; coordinating of sales with advertising efforts, which are under Public Relations; personnel administration and office management for the marketing department; and the administration of the product supervisors for the profit centers.

*Manager, Industrial Marketing*—Handles sales to industrial firms wishing to buy cars, oversees the use of demonstrator cars, arranges displays at shipper conventions and association meetings, and seeks and explores customer needs for new products or modifications of existing products.

*Manager, Field Sales*—Handles the sale of cars and parts. This group performs the sales function for all plants of the Division. It is charged with maintaining communications with the product supervisors to keep them thoroughly conversant with the customers' requirements and to enable them to maintain proper customer relationships.

*Manager, Sales, Service and Parts*—Responsible for conveying product information to selected levels of customer organizations, for being informed about customer developments that may affect future business, and for reporting customer interests in Division products to Field Sales. This group is also responsible for selling parts and engineering services to customers, for inspecting, while in use, products built by the Division as well as by competitors and reporting their performance to appropriate units of the Division. In addition, personnel of this group must provide assistance to customers in making repairs on Division products or com-

**EXHIBIT 2**

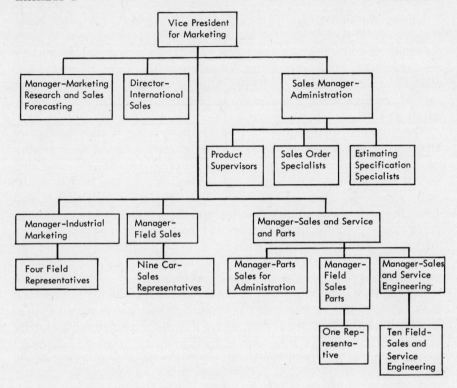

ponents; they must assemble Division package cars and install Division devices; and they must investigate claims and complaints.

*Product Supervisor*—Acts as chairman of the management committee of his plant profit center. He is expected to assume an entrepreneurial attitude. He maintains communication with each operating department of the Division and makes himself the focal point for information concerning the need for new products in his plant's product line. He also explores the potential market for identifiable new products, presents new-product proposals to the new-product committee, and coordinates new-product activities through the developmental, prototype, and testing stages. He oversees the promotion of his products, new and old, and participates in guiding them through the order, production, and delivery stages. In addition, the supervisor serves as liaison between the customer (through salesmen) and sales and service engineering. He must be informed about the legal obligations involved in the manufacture and marketing of his products and must periodically review their market position. He must take the lead in developing a marketing plan for each of his products and must periodically review with the Finance Department the profitability of his profit center as well as his products.

## Some troublesome issues

During the first couple of years after its adoption, the plant profit center–product supervisor plan worked very well. But in the course of its operation, certain questions arose that provoked much discussion among the executives. Is the Marketing Department the right place for the product supervisors to be in the organization structure? Are the product supervisors high enough up in the organization hierarchy to be really effective?

The product supervisors were originally placed in the Marketing Department because, more than any other, that department must be concerned with the customer from whom profit is desired. This sounded logical; but as the product supervisor worked into his job, he found that he must influence, persuade, and work with people from other functional areas. In seeking such cooperation, he sometimes found resistance arising, partly from departmental jealousy and partly from suspicion of conflicting functional interest. For example, some production men did not like the idea of a marketing man making suggestions about manufacturing. Engineers felt the same way about specifications.

The product supervisors were placed two echelons down in the Marketing Department, which meant that much of the time they had to deal with men who were a step or two above them in the executive hierarchy of the Division. Thus they did not always have the organizational stature to meet on equal terms the men they must convince and influence.

Several suggestions for change were possible. They might be moved up to higher positions in the Marketing Department. This would help to remedy the second difficulty but not the first. They might be moved from Marketing to some other department, such as Production or Engineering. This would simply change the locus of the first problem and might not affect the second. They could be set up as a special unit under the Vice President and General Manager or under a Director of Product Supervisors reporting to the President. This would improve their organizational stature and remove their functional stigma. On the other hand it might tempt them to try to speak with the voice of authority instead of persuasion, since they would be operating out of the office of the President or of the Vice President and General Manager. This would tend to antagonize the functional executives and lead to conflicts of authority.

# Indexes

# INDEX OF CASES

Acme Chemical Company, 447–52

Agex Oil Company (A), 452–54

Agex Oil Company (B), 455–57

Agex Oil Company (C), 458–66

Asphalt Corporation of America, 466–74

Atlantic Pulley Lagging Company, 474–83

Beechcraft Hawker Corporation, 484–501

Caterpillar Tractor Company, 502–17

Collis Company, 517–24

Cummins Engine Company, 525–32

Cundy-Betts Corporation, 533–42

Delta Distributing Company, 543–57

Franklin Electric Company, 557–68

Hancock Company (A), 569–72

Hancock Company (B), 573–80

Hays-Hilliard Corporation, 581–96

Heflin Chemical Supply Company (A), 597–601

Heflin Chemical Supply Company (B), 601–7

Hooker Chemical Company, 608–32

Margeann Chemical Company, 633–36

Olin Mathieson, 636–43

Owens-Corning Fiberglas Corporation (A), 644–62

Owens-Corning Fiberglas Corporation (B), 663–70

Procter & Gamble, 670–89

Pullman-Standard Division, 687

# INDEX

## A

Accessory equipment, 40–41
Advertising; *see also* Promotion
  agencies, 7, 359–61
  budget appropriation for, 355
  distributor cooperation, 270–71
  distributor motivation, 348
  information dissemination, 343
  measuring effectiveness, 195–96, 356–58
  media selection, 353–55
  message, 27, 350–53
    trademarks, 352–53
  new customer identification, 344
  product recognition, 344–46
  publicity, 358–59
  salesmen support, 346–48
Agents, 6
  channels of distribution, 8–9
  manufacturers', 6, 246–49
  raw material, marketing, 45–46
  sales, 6, 246–49
Automatic reorder, 80, 89–90

## B

BASIC (Beginners All-purpose Symbolic
  Instruction Code), 120
Basic buying motives, 349–50
Bid, competitive, 60, 81, 83
Bill of materials, 79–80
Bonus, 377–78
Branch house, 5, 7, 250–54
  drawbacks to, 254
  nonstock-carrying, 250, 252–54
  operating characteristics, 251–52
  size and concentration, 252–53
  stock-carrying, 250–54
Branch office, 5, 7
Break-even analysis, 315–19
Broker, 6, 249–50
  raw material marketing, 45–46
Budget; *see* Marketing budget

Bureau of Federal Supply, 74
Buyer, industrial; *see* Industrial buyer
Buyer motives, 54–61
  basic, 349–50
  patronage, 349–50
  price, 57
  product quality, 55
  psychological factors, 59–60
  savings, 57–58
  supply, assurance of, 58–59
Buyer-seller relationship, 9–12
  confidence, 11–12
  franchise agreement, 10
  loyalty, 11
  reciprocity, 12
  sales contract, 9
Byproducts, marketing of, 143–44

## C

Catalogs, 388–91
  distributors, 244–45
Channels of distribution, 7–9, 263–73
  bulk of product, 261–62
  communication, 282–83
  direct, 7, 256–57, 265
  distributor; *see* Industrial distributor
  financial position of marketer, 262
  geographical concentration, 258
  gross profit margin, 259–60
  house accounts, 265–66
  horizontal or vertical market, 257
  indirect, 7, 256
  installation, 260
  intensive distribution, 263–65
  inventory control, 284–88
  location of facilities, 281–82
  maintenance service required, 262
  market potential, 257
  marketing objectives of seller, 262–63
  materials handling, 288–90
  mixed structure, 256
  participants in channels, 3–7
  price, 260

Channels of distribution—*Cont.*
  purchasing policies of user, 258–59
  quality specifications, 260–61
  relationship between participants, 9–
    12, 263
  scheduling, 283–84
  selective distribution, 263–65
  storage and transfer, 277–78
  technical service required, 260
  traffic management, 290–92
  transportation, 278–82
Churchman, C. West, 117
Clayton Act, 334, 351
COBOL (Common Business Oriented
    Language), 119–20
Commercial finance house, 229–30
Commission, 376–77
Commission merchant, 6
Competition
  analysis of, 180–82
  price, 297–300, 319–25
  product life cycle, 297–300
  product mix, 210
  product quality, 298
Competitive bid, 60, 81, 83
Component parts, 41–43
Computer
  hardware, 118–19
  personnel, training of, 120–21
  programs, 120
  software, 119–20
    BASIC, 120
    COBOL, 119–20
    FORTRAN, 119
Confidence in buyer-seller relationship,
    11–12
Consulting firm, 6
Control; *see* Marketing control
Controllable and uncontrollable costs,
    304–5
Corporate mission; *see* Market mission
Corporate planning; *see* Marketing
    strategy
Correlation techniques, 431–32
Cost
  analysis, 176–80
  break-even analysis, 315–19
  elimination of unnecessary costs, 98
  fixed, 318
  historical, 318
  improvement; *see* Value analysis
  marginal business, 318–19
  pricing decisions, 302–7
  variable, 318
Cost analysis, 176–80
  expense category, 176–79
  functional analysis, 179–80
  marketing information system, 127, 129
Cost factor in pricing, 302–7
  controllable and uncontrollable, 304–5

Cost factor in pricing—*Cont.*
  direct, 303–4
  incremental, 305
  indirect (overhead), 303–4
  joint, 306–7
  opportunity, 305–6
  separable, 306–7
Cost improvement; *see* Value analysis
Coverage ratio, 137
Credit terms, 223–25
  distributor, 245
Customer
  buying attitudes and practices, 175–76
  classification by operating systems, 20–
    26
  distributor service, 243–45
  as end user, 16–17
  industrial; *see* Industrial buyer
  marketing organization structure, 31–33
  sales performance, 175
  satisfaction, 15–17

D

Data bank, 125–27
  collection, 126
  presentation, 127
  processing, 126
  storage, 127
Demand, 37–53
  advertising, 348–49
  derived; *see* Derived demand
  inelastic, 314
  input-output system, 157–65
  market levels, 37–46
  measuring market potential, 149–65
  product types, 37–46
  statistical measurements, 150–57
Derived demand, 46–53
  business conditions, 47
  financial considerations, 47
  price, 50–53, 308–10
  ultimate buyer, 47
Direct costs, 303–4
Discounts, 330–36
  cash, 334
  legal considerations, 334–36
  quantity, 332–34
  trade, 331–32
Distribution channels; *see* Channels of
    distribution
Distributor; *see* Industrial distributor
Drop shipping, 8
Drucker, Peter, 15

E

Entertainment, 395–96
Evaluated price, 57
Exclusive franchise, 10
Expense account, 378–80
  automatic allowance, 378–79

Expense account—*Cont.*
  per diem allowance, 379
  reimbursement, 379–80
Expense category analysis, 176–79, 430–31
Expense budget, 435
Extractive industries, 3

**F**

Fabricating parts, 41–43
Facilitating agencies, 7
Factor
  accounts receivable, 227
  inventory holdings, 228–29
Factory pricing, 336–37
Federal Occupational Safety and Health Act, 58
Federal Trade Commission Act, Wheeler-Lea amendment, 351
Field warehousing, 226–27
Financial service, 222–33
  credit terms, 223–25
  commercial financing company, 229–30
  distributors, 242–43
  factor, use of, 227–29
  field warehousing, 226–27
  installment sales, 230–32
    lease-installment, 231–32
  stock-carrying service, 223
  warehouse receipts, 225–26
Food and Drug Administration, testing new products, 207–9
Ford, Henry, 129–30
Forrester, Jay, 123
FORTRAN (FORmula TRANslator), 119–20
Franchise, 10–11
Freight allowance pricing, 337–39
Freight forwarder, 280
Freight pool, 280–81
Functional analysis, 179–80

**G–H**

General house, 5
General line distributor, 238
General Services Administration, 74
Goals, marketing; *see* Strategic goals
Gompertz curve, 419–23
Government agencies and departments
  geographic concentration, 64
  purchasing, 60–61, 63, 74–76
  stockpiling of materials, 212–13
High-price strategy, 313–15
  new markets, 319–20
House accounts, 265–66

**I**

Incremental costs, 305
Indirect (overhead) costs, 303–4

Industrial buyer, 4–5
  advertising, 344–45
  business classification, 62
  geographical concentration, 64–66
  government agencies, 74–76
  motives; *see* Buyer motives
  size distribution, 64–66
  types of, 61
Industrial distributor, 5, 237–45
  advertising, 270–71
  compensation, 268–69
  distribution channels; *see* Channels of distribution
  general house, 5
  geographical concentration, 239–41
  information feedback, 272
  intensive distribution, 263–65
  inventory management, 266
  marketing assistance, 270
  missionary salesmen, 271–72
  pricing policies, 269–70
  protection of, 267–68
  selling, 241–42
  service, 243–45
  training, 272
  warehousing, 242
*Industrial Marketing*, annual survey, 353, 355–56
Industry classification
  interpretation of, 134–39
  major activity basis, 132–33, 135–36
  product classification system, 139
  Standard Industrial Classification System, 131 ff.
Information, marketing; *see* Marketing intelligence system
Input-output system, 157–65
  business concept, 14–15
Inspection, 92–93
Installment sales, 230–32
  lease-installment, 231–32
Institutional buyers, 66–68
Integrated firms, 45
  raw materials, control of, 45
Intensive distribution, 263–65
Inventory control, 284–88
  distributors, 266
  information feedback system, 286–88
  keeping stock low, 276–77
  perpetual system, 286–87
  stock count, 287
  stock-out, 286
  visual systems, 287–88
Invoice handling, 91–92

**J–L**

Joint costs, 306
Lease-installment financing, 231–32

Low-price strategy, 315
  new markets, 319–20
Loyalty in buyer-seller relationship, 11

## M

Machines
  demand affected by price, 52–53
  multipurpose or standard, 39
  single-purpose, 39
McLuhan, Marshall, 353
Major equipment, 37–40
  price, 52–53
Make or buy decisions, 85–87
Management
  information needs; see Marketing intelligence system
  interest and ability, 214
  logistical planning, 274–75
  market manager, 27–28, 30–31
  status of top management, 30–31
Manufacturer's agent, 6, 246–49
Manufacturer's branch; see Branch house and Branch office
Manufacturing establishment, 62
Manufacturing industries, 3–5
Marginal analysis, 195–96
Market area survey, 155–57
  of buyers, 155–56
  of facilities, 156–57
Market evaluation, 147–66
  demand potential measurement, 149–65
    aggregate methods, 157
    input-output system, 157–65
  problem profile, 165–66
    field testing, 165
  profile of market, 147–49
Market identification, 20–26, 131–45, 194
  existing markets, 140–41
  opportunity, 403–4
  untapped markets, 141–45
Market levels, 37–46
Market mission, 17–20
  alternative, 19
  definition of, 18
  strategy to achieve, 185–87
Market opportunity, identification of, 403–4
Market profile, 147–49
Market research, 205–6
  studies, 167–73
Market survey, 155–57
Marketing, industrial, 3
  budget; see Marketing budget
  channels; see Channels of distribution
  control; see Marketing control
  identification; see Market identification
  information; see Marketing intelligence system

Marketing—Cont.
  mission; see Market mission
  organizational structure, 26–33
  performance; see Marketing performance, measurement of
  philosophy of, 14–17
  strategy; see Marketing strategy
  surveys, 155–57
  value analysis; see Value analysis
  vendor analysis; see Vendor analysis
Marketing budget, 432–38
  advertising, 355
  control of, 436–38
  expense, 435–36
  purchasing department, 80–81
  sales, 432–35
Marketing channels; see Channels of distribution
Marketing concept, 14, 16
Marketing control, 401, 438–42
  comparison of standards to performance, 440–42
  correcting performance, 440–42
  reporting system, 438–40
Marketing forecast, 414–26
Marketing information; see Marketing intelligence system
Marketing intelligence group, 27
Marketing intelligence system, 27–30
  computer-based, 117–21, 129
  cost-benefit tradeoff, 127
  design of system, 121–27
    data bank, 125
  distributors' catalogs, 244–45
  external information, 121–22
  information needs of management, 113–17
  internal information, 122–23
  new market development, 141–45
Marketing performance, measurement of, 167–82, 429–42
  competition, 180–82
  cost analysis, 176–80
    expense category, 176–79
    functional, 179
  customer attitudes, 175–76
  data collecting and analysis, 168–72
    interviewing, 170–72
    sampling, 168–70
  sales analysis, 173–76
Marketing policies, 190–91
  enforcement, 191
  procedure, 191
    methods, 191
Marketing services manager, 27–28, 30–31
Marketing strategy, 17, 183–97
  choosing strategy components, 195–96
  control; see Marketing control
  corporate mission, 185–87

Marketing strategy—*Cont.*
  distribution; *see* Channels of distribution
  goals; *see* Strategic goals
  logistical plans, 191
  marginal analysis, 195–96
  measurement of results, 195–96
  operating plans, 189
  organizational plans, 191–92
  price, 188, 297–339
  product definition, 187
  product mix, 187
  promotion, 188
  service definition, 188
  situation analysis, 193–94
  target market analysis, 194
Marketing study, 167–73
Materials handling, 288–89
Media, 353–55
  public relations, 398–99
Merchant wholesaler; *see* Industrial distributor
Middleman; *see* Industrial distributor
Mill supply house, 238
Minor equipment, 40–41
  price, 52–53
Mission; *see* Market mission
Missionary salesman, 271–72
Mogenson, Allan, 96
MRO (maintenance, repair, operating) items, 44
Multipurpose machine, 39
Multiunit company, 71–74

N

National Association of Purchasing Management, 103
Negotiated purchasing, 83–85
New-product development, 198–214; *see also* Product definition, product development
  advertising, 344–45
  commercialization, 209
  evaluation, 202–5
  generating ideas, 199–202
  market research, 205–6
  price strategy, 312–19
  prototype testing, 206–9

O

OEM; *see* Original equipment manufacturer (OEM)
Operating plans, 189–91
  policies, 190–91
    enforcement, 191
    procedures, 191
  programs, 191
    projects, 191
  tactics, 189–90
Operating supplies, 44

Operating systems, 17
  classification of customers by, 20–26
  marketing activities, 185
  production system, 21–26
Original equipment manufacturer (OEM), 5
  channels of distribution, 7
  identification of product, 47

P

Parts
  component, 41–43
  customer service, 55–57
  distribution, 216–19
  pirate, 218–19
  standardized, 216–17
  unstandardized, 217–18
Patents, 315
Patronage buying motive, 349–50
Performance standards, 429–42
  corrections of, 440–42
Perpetual inventory system, 286–87
PERT (Program Evaluation and Review Technique), 383–88
Pirate parts, 218–19
Planning, corporate; *see* Marketing strategy
Price
  analogy and hunch in pricing, 324–25
  competition, 297–300, 319–25
  cost factor; *see* Cost factor in pricing
  demand, influence on, 50–53, 307–10
  distributors, 269–70
  evaluated, 57
  initiating change, 325–29
  leadership; see *Price* leadership
  market strategy, 188, 297–339
  new-product introduction, 312–19
    break-even analysis, 315–19
    high-price strategy, 313
    low-price strategy, 313, 315
  policies; *see* Pricing policies
Price leadership, 301–2
  small versus large firms, 323–24
Price war, 321
Pricing policies, 330
  discounts; *see* Discounts
  geographic considerations, 336–39
    basing point, 338–39
    factory, 336–37
    freight allowance, 337–38
  legal considerations, 334–36
  net, 330
Private labeling agreement, 33
Problem profile, 165–66
Process materials, 43–44
Product classification system, 139
Product definition, 187, 198–215
  company attributes, 213–14

Product definition—*Cont.*
  product development, 198–214; *see also* New-product development
  product mix; *see* Product mix
Product information, 244–45
  competitor, 201–2
  salesmen, 201
  trade literature, 202
Product manager, 32
Product-market levels, 37–46
Product mix, 187–88, 209–13
  competition, 210
  demand shifts, 211–12
  government controls, 212–13
  operating capacity, 210–11
  technology, 209
Product quality, 55
Product types, 37–46
  component parts, 41–43
  major equipment, 37–40
  minor or accessory equipment, 40–41
  operating supplies, 44
  process materials, 43–44
  raw materials, 44–46
Production process, 41
Production system, 21–26
Program Evaluation and Review Technique (PERT), 383–88
Promotion, 188, 341; *see also* Advertising
  catalogs, 388
  entertainment, 395–96
  letters, 392–94
  novelties, 394
  trade shows and exhibits, 381–88
Prototype testing, 206–9
Public relations, 396–99
  media, 398–99
  program planning, 397–98
Publicity, 358–59
Purchasing
  department; *see* Purchasing department
  public institutions, 60–61, 74–76
  systems; *see* Purchasing systems
  types of organization, 66–76
Purchasing department, 66–74; *see also* Purchasing systems
  government buyers, 66, 74–76
  internal organization, 67–74
  manager, 59–60
  policies of, 73–74
    centralized buying, 73–74
    reciprocity, 73
  position in company organization, 68–73
  specialized buyers, 67
  state and local organizations, 76
  vendor-rating systems, 108

Purchasing officer, 68
  psychological motivation, 59–60
Purchasing systems, 78–94
  competitive bids, 81–83
  department; *see* Purchasing department
  expediting orders, 89–91
  follow-up procedure, 89–90
  information sources, 88
  invoice handling, 91
  make or buy decisions, 85–87
  needs, documentation of, 78–81
    automatic reorder, 80, 89–90
    bill of materials, 79
    requisition, 79
  negotiation, 83–85
  order placement, 88
    form, 88–89
  policies, 73–74
  receipt and inspection, 92–93
  supplier, choice of, 87–88
  types of organization, 66–76
  value analysis; *see* Value analysis
  vendor analysis; *see* Vendor analysis

## Q–R

Quality specifications, 260–61
Raw materials, 44–46
Receipt of goods, 92–93
Reciprocity, 12
  purchasing policies, 73
  trading agreements, 33
Replacement parts; *see* Parts, replacement
Reports, 437–40
Requisition, 79
Research and development (R&D)
  company strength, 213–14
  new-product ideas, 200
Robinson-Patman amendment, 334–35

## S

Sales
  budget, 432–35
  forecasts, 414–26
  statistical projections of, 404–28
Sales agent, 6, 246–49
Sales appeals, 349–50
Sales contract, 9–10
Sales promotion; *see* Promotion
Sales training, 368–72
Salesmen
  advertising support, 346–48
  compensation, 376–78
    bonus, 377–78
    commission, 376–77
  distributor, 241–42
  expense account, 378–80
  as information source, 88
  as interviewer, 170–71
  new product ideas, 200

Salesmen—*Cont.*
  performance measurement, 175–76
  selection of, 363–68
    application, 366
    interviewing, 367–68
    personnel profile, 363–65
    references, 367
    sources of candidates, 365–66
    tests, 366–67
  specialization, 31–33
Samples, 391–92
Savings as buyer motivation, 57–58
Selective distribution, 263–65
Selective franchise, 10–11
Separable costs, 306
Service definition, 188, 216–33
  financial aid, 222–33
    commercial finance company, 229–30
    credit terms, 223–25
    factor, use of, 227–29
    field warehousing, 226–27
    installment sales, 230–32
    stock-carrying, 223
    warehouse receipts, 225–26
S.I.C.; see Standard Industrial Classification System
Single-purpose machine, 39
Situation audit, 18–19
  environmental audit, 18
  position audit, 18–19
  self-audit, 18
Sorensen, Charles E., 129–30
Specialization ratio, 136
Specialized buyer, 67–68
Specialty house, 5–6
Standard Industrial Classification System (S.I.C.), 131–46
  manual, 132
  revisions of system, 145
Statistical analysis
  Gompertz curve, 419–23
  marketing control, 401
  Standard Industrial Classification System, 131
  trend projections of sales, 404–12
Stock count inventory system, 287
Stock-out, 223, 286
Strategic goals, 403–28
  correlation-determined, 431–32
  definition, 426–28
  expense-based, 430–31

Strategic goals—*Cont.*
  long-range, 404
  market share, 404–28
    predictions, 412
    statistical projections, 404
  performance standards, 429
  sales forecasts, 414–28
  short-range, 404, 429–32
Sunk costs, 305
Supplier, 58–59; *see also* Vendor analysis
Supply flow, 58–59

**T**

Target market, 194
  resource allocation to, 404
Technical assistance, 219–22
  distributor, 245
Terms of sale; *see* Credit terms
Trade journals, 345
Trademark, 345, 349, 352–53
Trade shows and exhibits, 381–88
  exhibitors' objectives, 381–83
  scheduling and planning, 383–88
  PERT, application of, 383–88
Traffic management
  analysis, 291–92
  planning, 290–91
Transportation network, 278–81

**V**

Value analysis, 96–100
  cost analysis, 98
  operation of system, 99–100
  product specification review, 97–98
Value engineering; *see* Value analysis
Vendor analysis, 100–108
  financial record, 101–2
  management ability, 102
  performance rating, 102–8
    cost ratio plan, 103
    delivery, 105–6
    quality, 104–5
    service, 106–7
  product capability, 101
Visual inventory system, 287–88

**W**

Warehouse, 278
  distributors, 242–43
  field, 226–27
  layout, 289–90
  materials handling, 288–90
Warehouse receipt, 225–26

*This book is set in 10 and 9 point Caledonia,
leaded two points. Part numbers and titles are
24 point Scotch Roman. Chapter numbers and
titles are 30 point and 18 point Scotch Roman.
Case titles are 14 point Scotch Roman. The
size of the type page is 27 x 46½ picas.*